Kurt Aland and Barbara Aland

THE TEXT
OF
THE NEW TESTAMENT

An Introduction to the Critical Editions
and to the Theory and Practice of Modern
Textual Criticism

TRANSLATED BY ERROLL F. RHODES
Second Edition, Revised and Enlarged

WILLIAM B. EERDMANS
GRAND RAPIDS
1989
LEIDEN
E. J. BRILL

Translated from *Der Text des Neuen Testaments,* 2nd edition,
© 1981 Deutsche Biblegesellschaft Stuttgart.
This edition published jointly 1989 by Eerdmans and E. J. Brill,
Postbus 9000, 2300 PA Leiden, The Netherlands.

Library of Congress Cataloging-in-Publication Data

Aland, Kurt
[Text des Neuen Testaments. English]

The text of the New Testament : an introduction to the critical editions
and to the theory and practice of
modern textual criticism / Kurt Aland and Barbara Aland :
translated by Erroll F. Rhodes. —
2nd ed., rev. and enl.
p.   cm.
Translation of: Der Text des Neuen Testaments. 2nd ed.
Includes bibliographical references.
1. Bible. N.T. Greek—Versions. 2. Bible. N.T.— Criticism.
Textual. 3. Bible. N.T.—Versions. I. Aland, Barbara.
II. Title.
BS1937.5A42   1989
225.4'8—dc20   89-27534
                                                          CIP

Eerdmans ISBN 0-8028-3662-3

Brill ISBN 90 04 08367/7

FROM THE PREFACE
TO THE FIRST EDITION

This book is designed as a college text or home study manual for students using the modern text of the Greek New Testament in any of its various editions (the Nestle-Aland *Novum Testamentum Graece* in its twenty-sixth edition, the United Bible Societies' *Greek New Testament* in its third or a later edition, the *Synopsis Quattuor Evangeliorum* in its thirteenth edition, or the Greek-English *Synopsis of the Four Gospels* in its sixth edition), enabling them to make full use of it and to form independent judgments on the text of the New Testament. Its model is the companion volume by Ernst Würthwein from the same publisher, *Der Text des Alten Testaments* (fourth ed., 1973; English translation by Erroll F. Rhodes, *The Text of the Old Testament* [Grand Rapids: Wm. B. Eerdmans, 1979]), but with the difference that here the reader's practical needs can receive more attention. The present book gives the basic information necessary for using the Greek New Testament and for forming an independent judgment on the many kinds of variant readings characteristic of the New Testament textual tradition. Matters primarily of antiquarian interest (e.g., the early printed editions of the New Testament, which have often been discussed in detail elsewhere) have generally been restricted here to their bare essentials, while more concern has been given (within the compass permitted by this book) to forming an overall perspective (cf. the numerous plates and charts), to practical experience in dealing with complex problems, and to developing sound independent judgment.

The purpose of this book is to introduce readers (including beginners with no previous experience) step by step to the difficulties of the material, if they will read it straight through from the beginning. But readers wishing to begin immediately using a particular edition of the Greek New Testament, mastering its arrangement and structure first before proceeding to other matters, should begin with chapter V. Anything not immediately clear or requiring further explanation (e.g., symbols for manuscripts) may be clarified easily by consulting the detailed table of contents or the index for references to relevant passages in other chapters, each of which has been written as a fully self-contained unit, at the cost of occasional repetition.

Münster, Westphalia
March 28, 1983

KURT ALAND
BARBARA ALAND

PREFACE TO THE SECOND EDITION

The first printing of the German edition was sufficiently large, we believed, to allow us ample time to prepare a second edition. But it sold out so rapidly that there was less time than we had expected. Thus there was very little we could do other than bring the text up to date, supplementing it in some places and expanding it in others. Extensive additions (except for the discussion of Synopses in chapter V) have been appended to the text in order to avoid the expense of completely resetting the plates. Where possible the earlier material has simply been replaced with information as of May 1988, e.g., charts 2, 3, and 4, and the charts of the papyri and uncials, to mention only a few instances.

It was the same with the English edition. The first edition of 1987 was so popular that within only a few months a reprint was necessary. The second printing was so rapidly exhausted that another edition became necessary. Confronted inevitably with similar circumstances, the German and English editions are proceding in parallel.

Scholars interested in more specialized bibliographical information than we have given should remember this book's purpose as described in the preface of the first edition. A book three times this size would probably still prove inadequate, because what is sauce for the goose is sauce for the gander. Special studies by the authors themselves are usually not mentioned. While modern textual criticism has made considerable advances in comparison to the state of events in the first half of the twentieth century, its goals are still far from being achieved. An awesome amount of intensive research and thorough discussion remains before the many (and sometimes too) specialized studies now under way can make their contribution to an integrated perspective. The present book is an attempt to promote this. Meanwhile specialized bibliographies can be of critical significance, such as the volume by J. K. Elliot which has just appeared (cf. p. 47), which offers a conspectus of publications and studies dealing with Greek manuscripts of the New Testament.

We are deeply indebted to Michael Welte of the Institute for New Testament Textual Research for general technical oversight of the German edition including the preparation of its indexes, and to Erroll F. Rhodes for the English edition, who has done much more than is expected of a translator.

Münster/Westfalen
March 28, 1988

KURT ALAND
BARBARA ALAND

TRANSLATOR'S PREFACE

Der Text des Neuen Testaments was written in 1979-1980 and published in 1982. Although the English translation was completed in March 1983, certain difficulties prevented its immediate publication. By mid-1985 when these difficulties were resolved, further advances at the Institute for New Testament Textual Research in Münster necessitated a considerable revision of the text, especially in the descriptive list of minuscule manuscripts in chapter 3. The present translation, then, represents a revision of the original German edition of 1982.

Other changes from the original German edition include some adaptation of bibliographical references for English readers. German illustrative examples cited in the original text have generally been retained and supplemented with English parallels. And of course the indexes have had to be compiled afresh.

It is a pleasure to express special gratitude to Eugene A. Nida and Harold P. Scanlin of the American Bible Society for their support and encouragement of this translation from the beginning; to Kurt Aland for generously reviewing the English translation and for providing extensive corrections and supplementary information in May 1985 to bring it up to date; to Wm. B. Eerdmans Publishing Company for meticulous editorial oversight, and in particular for the improved legibility of charts 5 and 6 which identify the textual contents of New Testament papyri and uncial manuscripts; and finally to Harriet Rhodes for invaluable assistance in preparing accurate typescript.

ERROLL F. RHODES

September 29, 1986

TRANSLATOR'S PREFACE
TO THE SECOND EDITION

The reception of the first edition has been most gratifying. We are particularly indebted to the many scholars who reviewed it with valuable criticisms and suggestions.

The present revised edition differs slightly from the second German edition. Chapter VIII consists of two essays on methodology. The materials supplementary to earlier chapters in the German edition have been integrated in the earlier chapters, necessitating some minor adaptations. The indexes have been thoroughly revised.

Special gratitude is due to Kurt and Barbara Aland for their patient assistance with many details, and also to Wm. B. Eerdmans Publishing Company for generous and careful cooperation, especially resetting the plates for this edition to increase its usefulness.

September 13, 1989   ERROLL F. RHODES

CONTENTS

Preface to First Edition   v
Preface to Second Edition   vi
Translator's Preface   vii
Plates   xv
Tables   xvii
Charts   xvii
Abbreviations   xviii

1. THE EDITIONS OF THE NEW TESTAMENT   3

1. *From Erasmus to Griesbach*   3
     Desiderius Erasmus
     The Complutensian Polyglot
     Theodore Beza
     Textus Receptus
     Colinaeus (Simon de Colines)
     Stephanus (Robert Estienne)
     Elzevir
     The Polyglots
     John Fell
     Johann Saubert
     John Mill, Richard Bentley, Edward Wells, Daniel Mace
     Johann Albrecht Bengel
     Johann Jakob Wettstein
     Johann Jakob Griesbach

2. *From Lachmann to Nestle*   11
     Karl Lachmann
     Constantin von Tischendorf
     Brooke Foss Westcott and Fenton John Anthony Hort
     Samuel Prideaux Tregelles
     Eberhard Nestle

3. From the "Old Nestle" to the "New Nestle"   20
   Erwin Nestle
   Kurt Aland
   Hermann Freiherr von Soden
   S. C. E. Legg
   The International Greek New Testament Apparatus Project
   Vinton A. Dearing
   Novi Testamenti Editio Critica Maior
   Alexander Souter
   R. V. G. Tasker, George Dunbar Kilpatrick, Heinrich Greeven,
      J. B. Orchard, M.-E. Boismard
   Heinrich Joseph Vogels, G. Nolli, A. L. Farstad-Z. C. Hodges
   Augustin Merk
   José Maria Bover
   José O'Callaghan Martínez
   The textual scene of the past century
   Agreements between editions of this period
   Differences among editions of this period
   Beginnings of the new text
   An appreciation of the new text

4. A comparison of the major editions   36
   Westcott-Hort
   Tischendorf
   Von Soden
   Nestle-Aland[26] and *GNT*[3]

II. *THE TRANSMISSION OF THE GREEK NEW TESTAMENT*   48

   1. *The collection of the New Testament books*   48

   2. *The canon, church history, and the history of the text*   49

   3. *The origin of text types*   50

   4. *Latin, Syriac, and Coptic versions: the demand for Greek
       manuscripts limited after A.D. 200*   52

   5. *Centers of Greek manuscript production*   53

   6. *Did the West develop its own text type?*   54

   7. *The spread of New Testament manuscripts and their text types* 55

   8. *The text of the early period*   56

   9. *The Age of Constantine*   64

   10. *Summary*   67

III. *THE MANUSCRIPTS OF THE GREEK
NEW TESTAMENT*   72

   1. *The number of manuscripts and their symbols before Gregory*   72

2. *Gregory's system and the increasing number of manuscripts*   73

3. *Writing materials*   75

4. *Distribution by age*   78
   Text manuscripts
   Lectionaries

5. *Distribution by content*   78

6. *The major collections*   79

7. *The papyri*   83
   Descriptive list of papyri

8. *The uncials*   103
   Descriptive list of uncials
   Synopsis of Sigla for correctors in manuscripts   108

9. *The minuscules*   128
   Descriptive list of minuscules

10. *A review of text manuscripts by category*   159

11. *The lectionaries*   163

12. *Patristic citations*   171
   Descriptive list of Greek Church Fathers

IV. *THE EARLY VERSIONS OF THE NEW TESTAMENT*   185

1. *Introduction*   185

2. *The Latin versions*   186
   The Old Latin (Itala)
   The Vulgate

3. *The Syriac versions*   192
   The Diatessaron
   The Old Syriac
   The Peshitta
   The Philoxeniana
   The Harklensis
   The Palestinian Syriac version

4. *The Coptic versions*   200

5. *The Armenian, Georgian, and Ethiopic versions*   204
   The Armenian version
   The Georgian version
   The Ethiopic version

6. *The Gothic, Old Church Slavonic, and other versions*   210
   The Gothic version
   The Old Church Slavonic version
   Versions in other languages

7. *Patristic citations*   214
    Descriptive list of Latin and Eastern Church Fathers

V. *INTRODUCTION TO THE USE OF THE MODERN EDITIONS*   222

1. *"Modern editions"*   222

2. *The Greek New Testament*[3] *(GNT*[3]*)*   224
    The structure of *GNT*[3]
    Selection of passages for the critical apparatus
    An example: Mark 8:15-18
    Citation of witnesses
    Evidence in the critical apparatus
    Differences in the abbreviations used in the apparatuses
        of *GNT*[3] and Nestle-Aland[26]
    Citation of lectionaries
    Treatment of the Byzantine Majority text
    The punctuation apparatus
    The reference apparatus
    The use of [ ] and ⟦ ⟧
    Differences in the critical apparatuses of the two editions

3. *Novum Testamentum Graece*[26] *(Nestle-Aland*[26]*)*   232
    The nature of the apparatus and its critical symbols
    The Parable of the Two Sons (Matt. 21:28-32) as a model
    Multiple occurrences of a critical sign in a verse
    The attestation for the text
    The order of citation of the witnesses
    Summary symbols in the critical apparatus
    Additional symbols
    Signs for Greek witnesses to the text
    "Constant witnesses"
    The second class of "constant witnesses"
    The symbol 𝔐 (the Majority text)
    Frequently cited minuscules
    The early versions and their symbols
    Patristic citations of the New Testament
    Notes in the inner margin
    Notes in the outer margin
    Abbreviations for the books of the Bible
    The Parable of the Two Sons (Matt. 21:28-32) as a model
    Nestle Appendix I: Lists of the Greek and Latin manuscripts
        referred to in the apparatus
    Nestle Appendix II: Survey of variants in modern editions
    Nestle Appendix III: Old Testament quotations and allusions

Nestle Appendix IV: Signs, symbols, and abbreviations
Supplementary keys

4. *The synopses*   260
    A comparison of *Synopsis Quattuor Evangeliorum*
        with other synopses: Greeven, Orchard, Boismard-
        Lamouille, Swanson
    The arrangement of the critical apparatus
    How to find a particular pericope
    The *Synopsis of the Four Gospels*

VI. RESOURCES   268

1. *Concordances*   268

2. *Dictionaries*   271

3. *Grammars*   274

4. *Synopses*   274

5. *Special literature*   274

6. *Commentaries*   277

VII. INTRODUCTION TO THE PRAXIS OF NEW TESTAMENT
TEXTUAL CRITICISM (SELECTED PASSAGES)   280

1. *Twelve basic rules for textual criticism*   280

2. *Selected passages: causes of variants and their evaluation* 282
    Scriptio continua: Mark 10:40; Matt. 9:18
    Confusion of letters: Rom. 6:5; Jude 12; Heb. 4:11;
        1 Cor. 5:8; Acts 1:3
    Dittography and haplography: 1 Thess. 2:7
    Signs of fatigue
    Homoioteleuton and homoioarcton: Matt. 5:19-21; 18:18
    Itacisms: 1 Cor. 15:54-55; Rom. 5:1; 1 Cor. 15:49
    Punctuation: Mark 2:15-16; Matt. 25:15; 11:7-8; John 1:3-4
    Variants of a single letter: Luke 2:14; 1 Cor. 13:3
    Explanatory supplements
    Stylistic improvements: Mark 1:37; 1:2; Matt. 27:9
    Harmonization
    Synonyms
    The tenacity of the textual tradition: the ending of Mark
    Mixed readings: Matt. 13:57; Mark 1:16
    Disturbed texts: the ending of Romans
    The limits of textual criticism: the ending of John

3. *Verses relegated to the apparatus of Nestle-Aland*[26] *and GNT*[3] 297
    The texts with apparatus
    Rom. 16:24
    Matt. 17:21; 18:11; 23:14

Mark 7:16; 9:44, 46; 11:26; 15:28
Luke 17:36; 23:17
John 5:3b-4
Acts 8:37; 15:34; 24:6b-8a; 28:29
Concluding summary

4. *Smaller omissions in the new text* 305
Matt. 5:44; 6:13; 16:2b-3; 20:16; 20:22, 23; 25:13; 27:35
Mark 9:49; 10:7; 10:21, 24; 14:68
Luke 4:4; 8:43; 9:54-56; 11:2-4; 11:11; 22:43-44; 24:42
John
Acts 28:16
Rom. 16:24, 25-27
1 Cor. 11:24; Luke 22:19b-20
1 John 5:7-8

5. *The Parable of the Two Sons (Matt. 21:28-32)* 312

VIII. *CATEGORIES AND TEXT TYPES, AND THE*
TEXTUAL ANALYSIS OF MANUSCRIPTS 317

1. *The evaluation of manuscript texts: a new methodological tool*
for analyzing the New Testament manuscript tradition 317
2. *Categories and text types (cf. pp. 106f., 159)* 332

Index of Biblical Citations 338
Index of Manuscripts 345
Index of Names and Subjects 353

PLATES

(Compiled from the resources of the Institute for New Testament Textual Research, Münster/Westphalia, by H. Bachmann and A. Strauss)

1. First edition of the Greek New Testament by Erasmus
   of Rotterdam, Basel, 1516   2
2. A manuscript used by Erasmus, minuscule 2^e 5
3. Codex Alexandrinus (A, 02)   7
4. New Testament edited by Johann Albrecht Bengel, 1734   8
5. New Testament edited by Johann Jakob Wettstein, 1751-1752   10
6. Codex Ephraemi Syri Rescriptus (C, 04)   12
7. Codex Sinaiticus (ℵ, 01)   13
8. Codex Vaticanus (B, 03)   15
9. Codex Bezae Cantabrigiensis (D^{ea}, 05)   16
10. Codex Claromontanus (D^p, 06)   17
11. First edition of *Novum Testamentum Graece*
    edited by Eberhard Nestle, 1898   21
12. Luke 24 in the editions of Tischendorf, von Soden, Nestle-Aland[26],
    Greek New Testament[3], Westcott-Hort   46
    (foldout)
13. Fragment of a Greek Gospel harmony found at Dura Europus (0212)   58
14. Uncial 0220   60
15. Uncial 057   61
16. p^{48} 62
17. Uncial 0171   63
18. Codex Guelferbytanus (P^e, 024)   80
19. p^{52} 84
20. p^{74} 86
21. p^{46} 88
22. p^{66} 89
23. p^{47} 90
24. p^{75} 91

25. $\mathfrak{p}^{72}$ 92
26. $\mathfrak{p}^{45}$ 94
27. Uncial 0189   105
28. Codex Boernerianus (G^p, 012)   111
29. Codex Regius (L^e, 019)   112
30. Codex Freerianus (W, 032)   114
31. Codex Koridethianus (Θ, 038)   115
32. Codex Rossanensis (Σ, 042)   116
33. Gospels manuscript 047   117
34. Minuscule 1   130
35. Minuscule 13   131
36. Minuscule 33   143
37. Minuscule 36   144
38. Minuscules 322 and 323   145
39. Minuscule 424   146
40. Minuscule 461   147
41. Minuscule 565   148
42. Minuscule 614   149
43. Minuscule 892   150
44. Minuscule 1175   151
45. Minuscule 1241   152
46. Minuscule 1582   153
47. Minuscule 1739   154
48. Minuscule 1881   155
49. Minuscule 2053   156
50. Minuscule 2344   157
51. Minuscule 2427   158
52. Uncial lectionary ℓ 1575   164
53. Minuscule lectionary ℓ 974   165
54. Codex Bobiensis (k)   188
55. Codex Fuldensis (F)   191
56. Palimpsest containing Sinaitic Syriac (sy^s)   195
57. Curetonian Syriac (sy^c)   196
58. Harklensis   198
59. Coptic Codex P. Palau Rib. 182   202
60. Greek-Coptic lectionary ℓ 1602   203
61. Armenian manuscript Matenadaran 2374 (Etchmiadzin 229)   206
62. Georgian Codex A   207
63. An Ethiopic Gospel manuscript   208
64. Gothic Codex Argenteus   211
65. Old Church Slavonic Evangelium Dobromiri   213

TABLES

1. Variant-free verses in the New Testament   29
2. Frequency of variants in the New Testament   30
3. Distribution of early Greek manuscripts by century   57
4. Distribution of Greek manuscripts by century   81
5. Distribution of papyri by New Testament books   85
6. Byzantine type minuscules by number   138
7. Distribution of Byzantine type minuscules by century   140
8. Distribution of Greek manuscripts by century and category   159
9. Test passage no. 2, James 1:12   319
10. Relational statistics for 614 as control manuscript   322
11. Relational statistics for 618 as control manuscript   323
12. Relational statistics for ℵ, A, B, C   324
13. Agreements with control manuscript 614   326
14. Manuscript statistics: reading by category   334

CHARTS

1. Textual relationships in critical editions of the past century   27
2. Distribution of New Testament text manuscripts by century   82
3. Distribution of New Testament lectionaries by century   82
4. Distribution of New Testament text manuscripts by content   83
5. The textual contents of New Testament papyri   Endpaper
6. The textual contents of New Testament uncial manuscripts   Endpaper

ABBREVIATIONS

ANTF	Arbeiten zur neutestamentlichen Textforschung
AP	Archiv für Papyrusforschung
Bibl	Biblica
CSCO	Corpus Scriptorum Christianorum Orientalium
CSEL	Corpus Scriptorum Ecclesiasticorum Latinorum
ETL	Ephemerides Theologicae Lovanensis
GCS	Griechische Christliche Schriftsteller
HTR	Harvard Theological Review
LThK	Lexikon für Theologie und Kirche
MBE	Monumenta Biblica et Ecclesiastica
MPNW	Mitteilungen aus der Papyrussammlung der Nationalbibliothek in Wien
NTS	New Testament Studies
OC	Oriens Christianus
PGLSI	Papiri greci e latini della Società Italiana
PO	Patrologia Orientalis
RB	Revue Biblique
RStR	Rivista di Studi Religiosi
SPP	Studien für Paläographie und Papyruskunde
TU	Texte und Untersuchungen
VBP	Veröffentlichungen aus den Badischen Papyrussammlungen
WS	Wiener Studien
ZNW	Zeitschrift für die neutestamentliche Wissenschaft
ZPE	Zeitschrift für Papyrologie und Epigraphik

THE TEXT
OF
THE NEW TESTAMENT

Plate 1. The first edition of the Greek New Testament (with Latin translation) by Erasmus of Rotterdam, Basel, 1516: p. 192, the beginning of the gospel of John.

I
THE EDITIONS OF
THE NEW TESTAMENT

1. *FROM ERASMUS TO GRIESBACH*

The story of the printed Bible begins with a Latin Bible. Somewhere between 1452 and 1456 — the year cannot be determined more precisely — the book known as Johann Gutenberg's forty-two-line Bible was marketed in Mainz. Only a few dozen copies survive today, each valued in the millions of dollars. The **invention of printing** inaugurated a new age — but not for the Greek New Testament. Before it was printed at the beginning of the sixteenth century, more than one hundred editions of the Latin Bible were published, at least three editions of the Hebrew Old Testament, several of the Greek Psalter, and many editions of the entire Bible in German, French, Italian, and other languages. The theologians of the period were evidently quite satisfied with the Latin text of the New Testament, and anyone interested in the Greek text had to make use of a manuscript.

Then at the beginning of the sixteenth century two editions appeared: printing was completed for the New Testament part of the Complutensian Polyglot on January 10, 1514, and the *Novum Instrumentum Omne* of **Desiderius Erasmus,** the great humanist of Rotterdam, was published and marketed by Johann Froben in Basel on March 1, 1516. Although Erasmus' edition was produced later, it is famous as the first edition (editio princeps) of the Greek New Testament, fulfilling the goal of its editor and of its publisher. Both men were well aware that Francisco Ximénes de Cisneros (1437-1517), cardinal and archbishop of Toledo, had received a license to publish a multivolume polyglot Bible.[1] The scholars of the Spanish university of Alcalá de Henares (Roman Complutum, whence the names Complutensis and **Complutensian Polyglot**), whose efforts the cardinal had enlisted, devoted many years to the task. The

---

1. The Hebrew and Greek texts of the Old Testament, each with a Latin translation, are given in parallel columns on either side of the Latin Vulgate text, along with the Targum text and its Latin translation. For the New Testament only the Vulgate parallels the Greek text, with corresponding words identified by superscript letters.

final volume of the polyglot was completed on July 10, 1517, shortly before the death of Ximénes, but publication of the whole work was delayed until March 22, 1520, when papal authorization for its issuance was finally granted (after the manuscripts loaned from the Vatican library had been returned to Rome).

The identity of these manuscripts (at least for the New Testament) has still not been established with any certainty, but the sources used by Erasmus for his edition are known. He took manuscripts most readily available to him in Basel for each part of the New Testament (the Gospels, the Apostolos [Acts and the Catholic letters], the Pauline letters, and Revelation), entered corrections in them where he felt it necessary, and sent them directly to the printer, who treated these manuscripts like any ordinary typesetter's copy. In two manuscripts preserved at the university library the evidence of this incredible process can still be examined in all its detail (cf. plate 2). Erasmus was unable to find in Basel any manuscript of the Revelation of John, so he borrowed one from his friend Johann Reuchlin. Because its ending was mutilated, Erasmus simply translated Rev. 22:16-21 from Latin back into Greek (introducing several errors). He modified the text elsewhere as well, correcting it to the common Latin version. Work on the magnificent folio volume (with Erasmus' Latin version paralleling the Greek text; cf. plate 1) began in August 1515, and since it was completed in only a few months' time, the rate of its progress can be imagined (*praecipitatum verius quam editum* "thrown together rather than edited" was how Erasmus described it later). But it gained for Erasmus and Froben the fame (and financial profit) of publishing the first edition of the Greek New Testament.

The most serious defect of the first edition of the Greek New Testament was not so much its innumerable errors[2] as the type of text it represented. Erasmus relied on manuscripts of the twelfth/thirteenth century which represented the Byzantine Imperial text, the Koine text, or the Majority text — however it may be known[3]—the most recent and the poorest of the various New Testament text types, and his successors have done the same. This was the dominant form of the text in the fourteenth/fifteenth century manuscript tradition, and even where earlier uncial manuscripts were available they were not consulted. Although the eighth-century uncial E or Basiliensis (which would have given him only a slightly earlier form of the same Byzantine text) was available to Erasmus in Basel, and **Theodore Beza**'s personal library contained both Codex Bezae Cantabrigiensis (D[e a]) and Codex Claromontanus (D[p]),[4] both scholars ignored these resources. This was fortunate in the case of Beza (the friend and successor of John Calvin as leader of the church in Geneva, who was responsible for no fewer than nine editions of the Greek New Testament between 1565 and 1604), for if the text of Codex Bezae Cantabrigiensis had prevailed in the early period it would have proved far more difficult than the **Textus Receptus** for scholarship to overcome, and even this took a full three hundred years. Textus Receptus is

2. Many of these were pointed out to Erasmus by his contemporaries; a nineteenth-century critic in England called it the least carefully printed book ever published.
3. For these terms, cf. p. 66, etc.
4. For the explanation of manuscript symbols, cf. pp. 72ff.

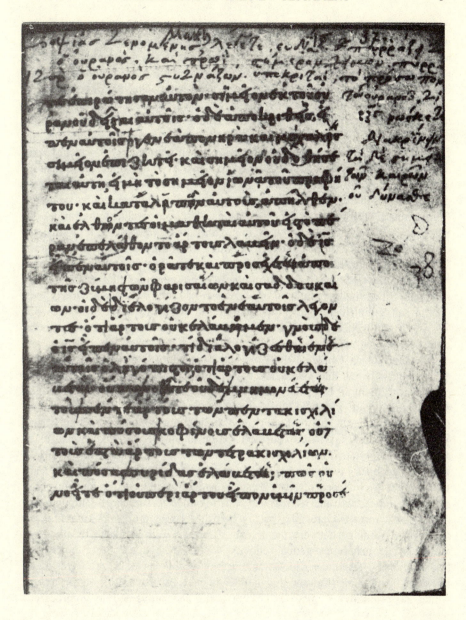

Plate 2. A manuscript used by Erasmus, minuscule 2ᵉ (University Library, Basel, twelfth century; cf. p. 4): Matt. 16:1-11, showing Erasmus' additions and compositor's marks.

the name by which the text of Erasmus has been known ever since an enterprising publisher, Elzevir, characterized it in 1633 in the following words: "Textum ergo habes, nunc ab omnibus receptum: in quo nihil immutatum aut corruptum damus [What you have here, then, is the text which is now universally recognized: we offer it free of alterations and corruptions]." Actually the editions published since Erasmus can in no sense be characterized as having a uniform text: the text published by **Colinaeus (Simon de Colines)** in 1534, the first edition to follow Erasmus' five (constantly revised) editions, shows numerous differences from them, partly derived from the Complutensian text (cf. pp. 3f. above) and partly due to the use of additional manuscripts. After Erasmus, the greatest influence during the sixteenth century was exercised by **Robert Estienne (Stephanus**; 1503-1559) in France, and during the seventeenth century by the publishing house of **Elzevir** in the Netherlands. The most influential editions of Stephanus were the *Editio Regia* of 1550[5] and the edition of 1551 (a smaller edition — the 1550 was in folio). In the latter edition the chapters of the New Testament were divided for the first time into verses. The success of the Leiden publishing house of Elzevir, which produced seven editions in all (1624-1678), may be ascribed to a combination of competent printing, a pleasing format, and skillful marketing (see above). They reproduced essentially the text of Beza.[6]

These were the characteristic editions of the sixteenth and seventeenth centuries. But we should also notice the **polyglots** of the period, i.e., the editions of the Bible which emulated the Complutensian pattern[7] by printing not only the original Hebrew and Greek texts with Latin glosses but by presenting in parallel with them all the other ancient versions then available. These were the Antwerp Polyglot (1569-1572; eight folio volumes), the Paris Polyglot (1629-1645; ten large folio volumes), and the London Polyglot edited by Brian Walton (1655-1657; six folio volumes), parts of which, e.g., the Syriac text, are still of importance today. These polyglots[8] attest how much effort was devoted to establishing the text of the New Testament, although with no real success. Yet no real progress was possible as long as the Textus Receptus remained the basic text and its authority was regarded as canonical. The days of the fifteenth century were long past, when the text of the Latin Vulgate was accepted as sufficient.[9] Every theologian of the sixteenth and seventeenth centuries (and not just the exegetical scholars) worked from an edition of the Greek text of the New Testament which was regarded as the "revealed text." This idea of verbal inspiration (i.e., of the literal and inerrant inspiration of the text), which the orthodoxy of both Protestant traditions maintained so vigorously,

5. This was the normative text in England until 1880. The Greek letter stigma (ς) still used as a symbol for the Textus Receptus in critical editions originally meant the text of Stephanus.

6. Cf. p. 4.

7. Cf. pp. 3f.

8. E.g., in the London Polyglot the Greek and Vulgate texts were accompanied by the Syriac, Ethiopic, and Arabic, while for the Gospels there was also a Persian version, each with its own Latin gloss.

9. Except for the Catholic church and its theology, which maintained this position considerably longer.

was applied to the Textus Receptus with all of its errors, including textual modifications of an obviously secondary character (as we recognize them today).[10]

Yet great progress had been made since the day when Erasmus could base an edition of the text on five or fewer manuscripts. The London Polyglot made use of one of the important uncials, Codex Alexandrinus (A).[11] **John Fell**, then dean of Christ Church and later bishop of Oxford, used more than one hundred manuscripts and also all the versions of the London Polyglot for his 1675 edition of the Greek New Testament, further supplementing them with the

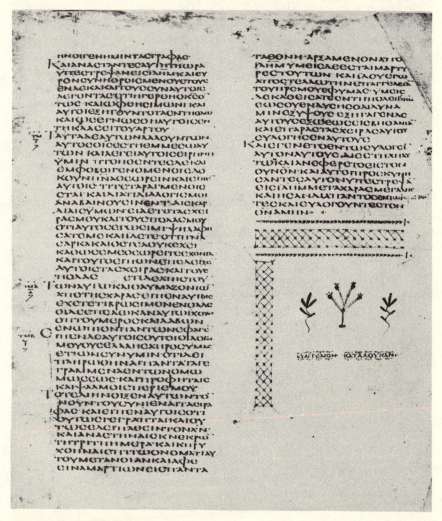

Plate 3. Codex Alexandrinus (A, 02, fifth century; cf. pp. 50, 107): conclusion of the gospel of Luke.

10. Cf. pp. 297ff.
11. Cf. p. 107.

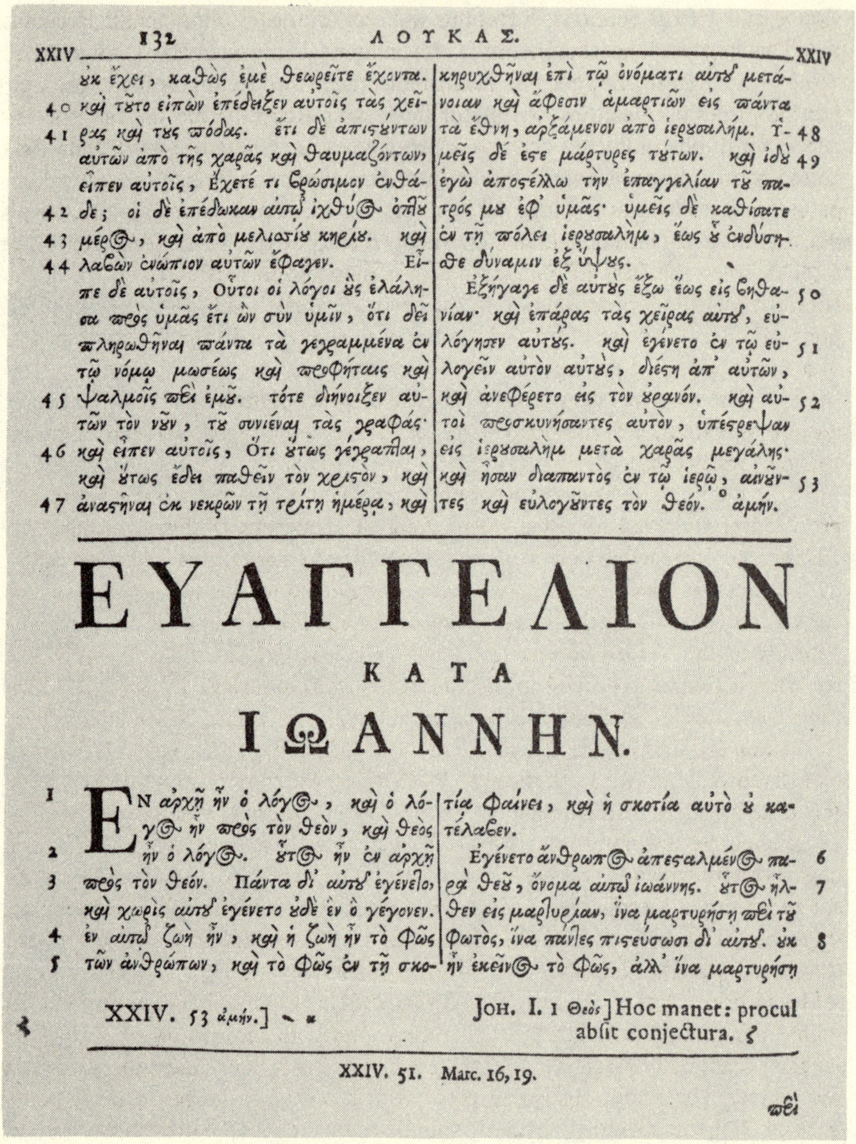

XXIV 132 ΛΟΥΚΑΣ. XXIV

οὐκ ἔχει, καθὼς ἐμὲ θεωρεῖτε ἔχοντα.
40 καὶ τοῦτο εἰπὼν ἐπέδειξεν αὐτοῖς τὰς χεῖ-
41 ρας καὶ τοὺς πόδας. ἔτι δὲ ἀπιστούντων
αὐτῶν ἀπὸ τῆς χαρᾶς καὶ θαυμαζόντων,
εἶπεν αὐτοῖς, Ἔχετέ τι βρώσιμον ἐνθά-
42 δε; οἱ δὲ ἐπέδωκαν αὐτῷ ἰχθύος ὀπτοῦ
43 μέρος, καὶ ἀπὸ μελισσίου κηρίου. καὶ
44 λαβὼν ἐνώπιον αὐτῶν ἔφαγεν. Εἶ-
πε δὲ αὐτοῖς, Οὗτοι οἱ λόγοι οὓς ἐλάλη-
σα πρὸς ὑμᾶς ἔτι ὢν σὺν ὑμῖν, ὅτι δεῖ
πληρωθῆναι πάντα τὰ γεγραμμένα ἐν
τῷ νόμῳ μωσέως καὶ προφήταις καὶ
45 ψαλμοῖς περὶ ἐμοῦ. τότε διήνοιξεν αὐτῶν τὸν νοῦν, τοῦ συνιέναι τὰς γραφάς·
46 καὶ εἶπεν αὐτοῖς, Ὅτι οὕτως γέγραπται,
καὶ οὕτως ἔδει παθεῖν τὸν χριστὸν, καὶ
47 ἀναστῆναι ἐκ νεκρῶν τῇ τρίτῃ ἡμέρᾳ, καὶ
κηρυχθῆναι ἐπὶ τῷ ὀνόματι αὐτοῦ μετάνοιαν καὶ ἄφεσιν ἁμαρτιῶν εἰς πάντα
τὰ ἔθνη, ἀρξάμενον ἀπὸ ἱερουσαλήμ. Ὑ- 48
μεῖς δέ ἐστε μάρτυρες τούτων. καὶ ἰδοὺ 49
ἐγὼ ἀποστέλλω τὴν ἐπαγγελίαν τοῦ πατρός μου ἐφ' ὑμᾶς· ὑμεῖς δὲ καθίσατε
ἐν τῇ πόλει ἱερουσαλὴμ, ἕως οὗ ἐνδύσησθε δύναμιν ἐξ ὕψους.
Ἐξήγαγε δὲ αὐτοὺς ἔξω ἕως εἰς βηθα- 50
νίαν· καὶ ἐπάρας τὰς χεῖρας αὐτοῦ, εὐλόγησεν αὐτούς. καὶ ἐγένετο ἐν τῷ εὐ- 51
λογεῖν αὐτὸν αὐτοὺς, διέστη ἀπ' αὐτῶν,
καὶ ἀνεφέρετο εἰς τὸν οὐρανόν. καὶ αὐ- 52
τοὶ προσκυνήσαντες αὐτὸν, ὑπέστρεψαν
εἰς ἱερουσαλὴμ μετὰ χαρᾶς μεγάλης·
καὶ ἦσαν διαπαντὸς ἐν τῷ ἱερῷ, αἰνοῦν- 53
τες καὶ εὐλογοῦντες τὸν θεόν. ° ἀμήν.

ΕΥΑΓΓΕΛΙΟΝ

ΚΑΤΑ

ΙΩΑΝΝΗΝ.

1 ΕΝ ἀρχῇ ἦν ὁ λόγος, καὶ ὁ λόγος ἦν πρὸς τὸν θεὸν, καὶ θεὸς
2 ἦν ὁ λόγος. οὗτος ἦν ἐν ἀρχῇ
3 πρὸς τὸν θεόν. Πάντα δι' αὐτοῦ ἐγένετο,
καὶ χωρὶς αὐτοῦ ἐγένετο οὐδὲ ἓν ὃ γέγονεν.
4 ἐν αὐτῷ ζωὴ ἦν, καὶ ἡ ζωὴ ἦν τὸ φῶς
5 τῶν ἀνθρώπων, καὶ τὸ φῶς ἐν τῇ σκοτίᾳ φαίνει, καὶ ἡ σκοτία αὐτὸ οὐ κατέλαβεν.
Ἐγένετο ἄνθρωπος ἀπεσταλμένος πα- 6
ρὰ θεοῦ, ὄνομα αὐτῷ ἰωάννης. οὗτος ἦλ- 7
θεν εἰς μαρτυρίαν, ἵνα μαρτυρήσῃ περὶ τοῦ
φωτὸς, ἵνα πάντες πιστεύσωσι δι' αὐτοῦ. οὐκ 8
ἦν ἐκεῖνος τὸ φῶς, ἀλλ' ἵνα μαρτυρήσῃ

XXIV. 53 ἀμήν.] ~ «

JOH. I. 1 Θεός] Hoc manet: procul absit conjectura. ς

XXIV. 51. Marc. 16, 19.

περὶ

Plate 4. The New Testament edited by Johann Albrecht Bengel, 1734: ending of the gospel of Luke and beginning of John.

Coptic and Gothic versions.[12] But this indirect criticism of the Textus Receptus failed to produce any changes in it. Its authority only increased. As early as 1672 Prof. **Johann Saubert** of Helmstedt[13] began collecting variant readings, but the direct implications of this for the Textus Receptus did not become apparent until the eighteenth century. Then the readings found in the manuscripts and versions were not only compiled in increasingly comprehensive critical apparatuses but at times a particular reading was identified as superior to that of the text or even introduced into the text to correct the Textus Receptus. The English were the first to explore this direction: **John Mill**'s edition of 1707, **Richard Bentley**'s proposals of 1720, **Edward Wells'** and **Daniel Mace**'s editions of 1709-1719 and 1729 (which made substitutions in the Textus Receptus in a whole group of passages).

The lead was then taken by the German scholars Bengel and Griesbach, and by Wettstein, a Swiss scholar living in the Netherlands. **Johann Albrecht Bengel** (1687-1752) admittedly reprinted the Textus Receptus in his edition of 1734 (he did not base his work solely on a single edition as did most scholars who preceded or followed him, but rather drew on numerous editions, selecting the readings he considered superior). But he classified each reading in the apparatus by a system in which the first two classes amounted to a virtual revision of the Textus Receptus (α = the original reading, with full certainty; β = a reading superior to the Textus Receptus, though with less than absolute certainty). In Revelation Bengel proceded to edit the text afresh and quite in advance of his time, with special attention to Codex Alexandrinus (A) and the commentary on Revelation by Andreas of Caesarea. **Johann Jakob Wettstein** (1693-1754) then overshadowed the work of Bengel by his two-volume edition of 1751-1752 (cf. plate 5), more than doubling the number of manuscripts ever before cited and assembling an apparatus of parallels to the New Testament from Jewish and pagan writers which is still useful today. He also introduced a system of symbols for manuscripts, designating uncials by capital letters and minuscules by arabic numerals. This system held the field until 1908, when Caspar René Gregory developed it further into the form now in common use (though without changing its basic principles).[14] **Johann Jakob Griesbach** (1745-1812) then brought the eighteenth-century editions to their ultimate form in his edition of 1775-1777 (second edition, 1796-1806). While the range of his influence was extraordinary (as a model for many subsequent editors), it is today in danger of being exaggerated. It is true that he pioneered synoptic criticism, yet the theory he advanced has been proved inadequate. It is true that he spoke of three forms of text (the Occidental or Western, the Alexandrian, and the Byzantine) as we still do today, yet for this he was dependent on Johann Salomo Semler, who in turn followed Bengel. It is true that Griesbach altered the Textus Receptus, but hardly enough

12. It was this edition, the most "advanced" of the time with its thirty-two-page preface on the methods and aims of New Testament research, which August Hermann Francke accepted and recommended as valuable for pietism in 1702.

13. The first German to engage in discussion of specific problems of textual criticism with Dutch and English scholars.

14. Cf. pp. 73ff.

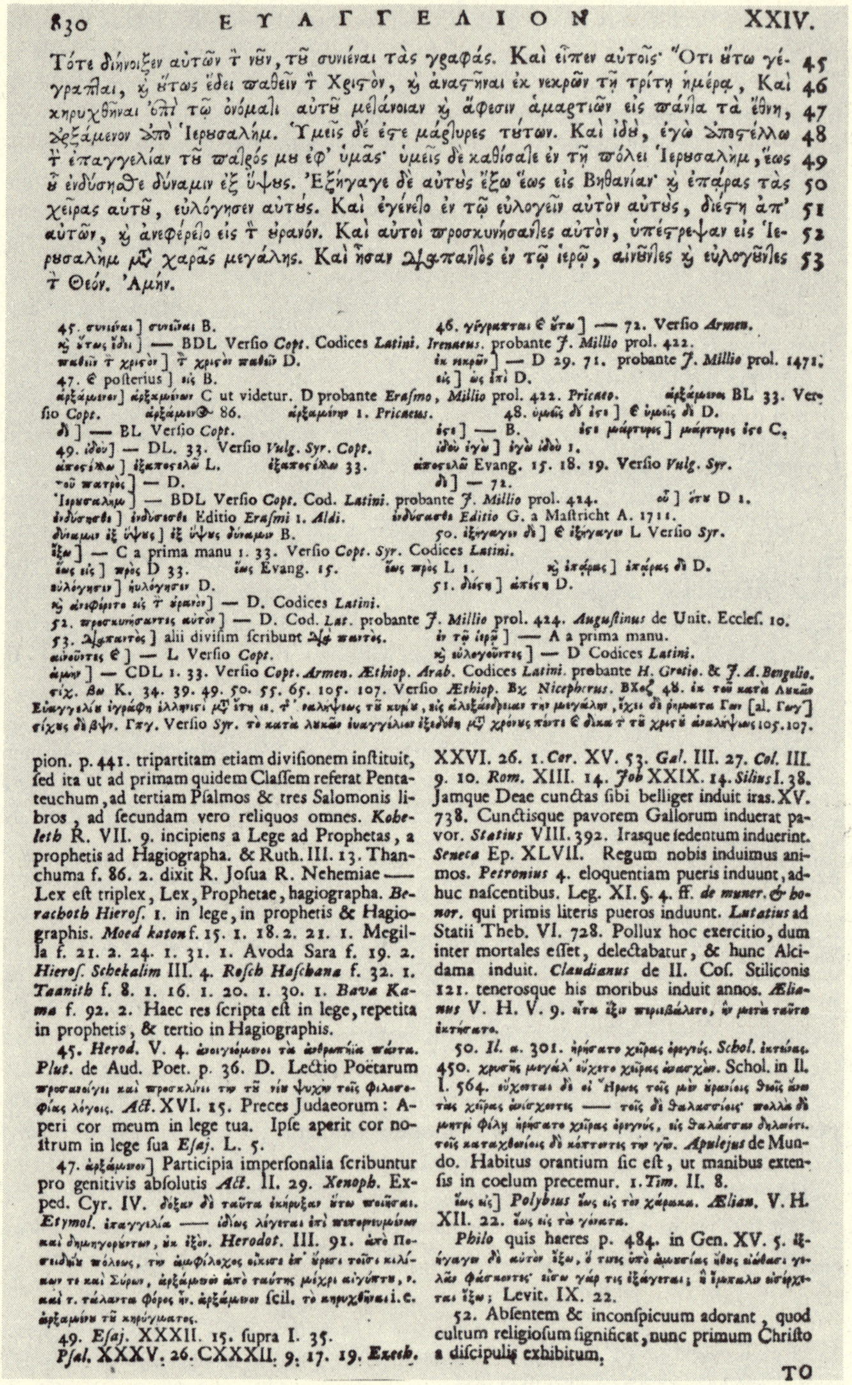

830 ΕΥΑΓΓΕΛΙΟΝ XXIV.

Τότε διήνοιξεν αὐτῶν τὸν νοῦν, τοῦ συνιέναι τὰς γραφάς. Καὶ εἶπεν αὐτοῖς· Ὅτι οὕτω γέ- 45
γραπται, καὶ οὕτως ἔδει παθεῖν τὸν Χριστὸν, καὶ ἀναστῆναι ἐκ νεκρῶν τῇ τρίτῃ ἡμέρᾳ, Καὶ 46
κηρυχθῆναι ἐπὶ τῷ ὀνόματι αὐτοῦ μετάνοιαν καὶ ἄφεσιν ἁμαρτιῶν εἰς πάντα τὰ ἔθνη, 47
ἀρξάμενον ἀπὸ Ἱερουσαλήμ. Ὑμεῖς δέ ἐστε μάρτυρες τούτων. Καὶ ἰδοὺ, ἐγὼ ἀποστέλλω 48
τὴν ἐπαγγελίαν τοῦ πατρός μου ἐφ' ὑμᾶς· ὑμεῖς δὲ καθίσατε ἐν τῇ πόλει Ἱερουσαλὴμ, ἕως 49
οὗ ἐνδύσησθε δύναμιν ἐξ ὕψους. Ἐξήγαγε δὲ αὐτοὺς ἔξω ἕως εἰς Βηθανίαν· καὶ ἐπάρας τὰς 50
χεῖρας αὐτοῦ, εὐλόγησεν αὐτούς. Καὶ ἐγένετο ἐν τῷ εὐλογεῖν αὐτὸν αὐτοὺς, διέστη ἀπ' 51
αὐτῶν, καὶ ἀνεφέρετο εἰς τὸν οὐρανόν. Καὶ αὐτοὶ προσκυνήσαντες αὐτὸν, ὑπέστρεψαν εἰς Ἱε- 52
ρουσαλὴμ μετὰ χαρᾶς μεγάλης. Καὶ ἦσαν διαπαντὸς ἐν τῷ ἱερῷ, αἰνοῦντες καὶ εὐλογοῦντες 53
τὸν Θεόν. Ἀμήν.

45. συνιέναι] συνιεῖναι B. 46. γέγραπται καὶ οὕτω] — 72. Versio *Armen.*
καὶ οὕτως ἔδει] — BDL Versio *Copt.* Codices *Latini. Irenaeus.* probante *J. Millio* prol. 422.
παθεῖν τὸν χριστὸν] τὸν χριστὸν παθεῖν D. ἐκ νεκρῶν] — D 29. 71. probante *J. Millio* prol. 1471.
47. καὶ posterius] εἰς B. εἰς] ὡς ἐπὶ D.
ἀρξάμενον] ἀρξαμένων C ut videtur. D probante *Erasmo, Millio* prol. 422. *Priceo.* ἀρξάμενοι BL 33. Versio *Copt.* ἀρξάμενος 86. ἀρξαμένω 1. *Pricaeus.* 48. ὑμεῖς δέ ἐστε] καὶ ὑμεῖς δὲ D.
δὲ] — BL Versio *Copt.* ἐστε] — B. ἐστε μάρτυρες] μάρτυρές ἐστε C.
49. ἰδοὺ] — DL. 33. Versio *Vulg. Syr. Copt.* ἰδοὺ ἐγὼ] ἐγὼ ἰδοὺ 1.
ἀποστέλλω] ἐξαποστελῶ L. ἐξαποστέλλω 33. ἀποστελῶ Evang. 15. 18. 19. Versio *Vulg. Syr.*
τοῦ πατρὸς] — D. δὲ] — 72.
Ἱερουσαλὴμ] — BDL Versio *Copt.* Cod. *Latini.* probante *J. Millio* prol. 424. οὗ] ὅτου D 1.
ἐνδύσησθε] ἐνδύσεσθε Editio *Erasmi* 1. *Aldi.* ἐνδύσασθε *Editio* G. a Mastricht A. 1711.
δύναμιν ἐξ ὕψους] ἐξ ὕψους δύναμιν B. 50. ἐξήγαγεν δὲ] καὶ ἐξήγαγεν L Versio *Syr.*
ἔξω] — C a prima manu 1. 33. Versio *Copt. Syr.* Codices *Latini.*
ἕως εἰς] πρὸς D 33. ἕως Evang. 15. ἕως πρὸς L 1. καὶ ἐπάρας] ἐπάρας δὲ D.
εὐλόγησεν] ηὐλόγησεν D. 51. διέστη] ἀπέστη D.
καὶ ἀνεφέρετο εἰς τὸν οὐρανὸν] — D. Codices *Latini.*
52. προσκυνήσαντες αὐτὸν] — D. Cod. *Lat.* probante *J. Millio* prol. 424. *Augustinus* de Unit. Eccles. 10.
53. διαπαντὸς] alii divisim scribunt διὰ παντός. ἐν τῷ ἱερῷ] — A a prima manu.
αἰνοῦντες καὶ] — L Versio *Copt.* καὶ εὐλογοῦντες] — D Codices *Latini.*
ἀμὴν] — CDL 1. 33. Versio *Copt. Armen. Æthiop. Arab.* Codices *Latini.* probante *H. Grotio.* & *J. A. Bengelio.* στίχ. Βω K. 34. 39. 49. 50. 55. 65. 105. 107. Versio *Æthiop.* Βχ *Nicephorus.* ΒΧος 48. ἐκ τοῦ κατὰ Λουκᾶν Εὐαγγελίου ἐγράφη ἑλληνιστὶ μετὰ ἔτη ιε. τῆς ἀναλήψεως τοῦ κυρίου, εἰς ἀλεξάνδρειαν τὴν μεγάλην, ἔχει δὲ ῥήματα Γων [al. Γωγ] στίχους δὲ βψν. Γπγ. Versio *Syr.* τὸ κατὰ λουκᾶν εὐαγγέλιον ἐξεδόθη μετὰ χρόνους πέντε καὶ δέκα τῆς τοῦ χριστοῦ ἀναλήψεως 105. 107.

pion. p. 441. tripartitam etiam divisionem instituit, sed ita ut ad primam quidem Classem referat Pentateuchum, ad tertiam Psalmos & tres Salomonis libros, ad secundam vero reliquos omnes. *Koheleth* R. VII. 9. incipiens a Lege ad Prophetas, a prophetis ad Hagiographa. & Ruth. III. 13. Thanchuma f. 86. 2. dixit R. Josua R. Nehemiae —— Lex est triplex, Lex, Prophetae, hagiographa. *Beracboth Hieros.* 1. in lege, in prophetis & Hagiographis. *Moed katon* f. 15. 1. 18. 2. 21. 1. Megilla f. 21. 2. 24. 1. 31. 1. Avoda Sara f. 19. 2. *Hieros. Schekalim* III. 4. *Rosch Haschana* f. 32. 1. *Taanith* f. 8. 1. 16. 1. 20. 1. 30. 1. *Bava Kama* f. 92. 2. Haec res scripta est in lege, repetita in prophetis, & tertio in Hagiographis.

45. *Herod.* V. 4. ἀνοιγνύμενοι τὰ ἀνθρωπήια πάντα. *Plut.* de Aud. Poet. p. 36. D. Lectio Poëtarum προανοίγει καὶ προσκλίνει τὴν τοῦ νέου ψυχὴν τοῖς φιλοσόφοις λόγοις. *Act.* XVI. 15. Preces Judaeorum: Aperi cor meum in lege tua. Ipse aperit cor nostrum in lege sua *Esaj.* L. 5.

47. ἀρξάμενον] Participia impersonalia scribuntur pro genitivis absolutis *Act.* II. 29. *Xenoph.* Exped. Cyr. IV. δόξαν δὲ ταῦτα ἐκήρυξαν οὕτω ποιῆσαι. *Etymol.* ἐπαγγελία —— ἰδίως λέγεται ἐπὶ πεπορισμένων καὶ δημηγορούντων, οὐκ ἔξω. *Herodot.* III. 91. ἀπὸ Ποσειδηΐου πόλιος, τὴν Ἀμφίλοχος οἴκισε ἐπ' οὔροισι τοῖσι Κιλίκων τε καὶ Σύρων, ἀρξάμενοι ἀπὸ ταύτης μέχρι Αἰγύπτου, τ. καὶ ν. τάλαντα φόρος ἦν. ἀρξάμενον scil. τὸ κηρυχθῆναι i. e. ἀρξαμένου τοῦ κηρύγματος.

49. *Esaj.* XXXII. 15. supra I. 35. *Psal.* XXXV. 26. CXXXII. 9. 17. 19. *Ezech.* XXVI. 26. 1. *Cor.* XV. 53. *Gal.* III. 27. *Col.* III. 9. 10. *Rom.* XIII. 14. *Job* XXIX. 14. *Silius* I. 38. Jamque Deae cunctas sibi belliger induit iras. XV. 738. Cunctisque pavorem Gallorum induerat pavor. *Statius* VIII. 392. Irasque sedentum induerint. *Seneca* Ep. XLVII. Regum nobis induimus animos. *Petronius* 4. eloquentiam pueris induunt, adhuc nascentibus. Leg. XI. §. 4. ff. *de muner. & honor.* qui primis literis pueros induunt. *Lutatius* ad Statii Theb. VI. 728. Pollux hoc exercitio, dum inter mortales esset, delectabatur, & hunc Alcidama induit. *Claudianus* de II. Cos. Stiliconis 121. tenerosque his moribus induit annos. *Ælianus* V. H. V. 9. αὐτὰ ἔξω περιεβάλετο, ἃ μετὰ ταῦτα ἐκτήσατο.

50. *Il.* α. 301. ἠρήσατο χεῖρας ὀρεγνύς. *Schol.* ἐκτείνας. 450. χρυσῆς μεγάλ' εὔχετο χεῖρας ἀνασχών. Schol. in Il. I. 564. εὔχονται δὲ οἱ Ἥρωες τοῖς μὲν οὐρανίοις θεοῖς ἄνω τὰς χεῖρας ἀνίσχοντες —— τοῖς δὲ θαλασσίοις· πολλὰ δὲ μητρὶ φίλῃ ἠρήσατο χεῖρας ὀρεγνύς, εἰς θάλασσαν δηλονότι. τοῖς καταχθονίοις δὲ κόπτοντες τὴν γῆν. *Apulejus* de Mundo. Habitus orantium sic est, ut manibus extensis in coelum precemur. 1. *Tim.* II. 8.

ἕως εἰς] *Polybius* ἕως εἰς τὸν χάρακα. *Ælian.* V. H. XII. 22. ἕως εἰς τὰ γόνατα.

Philo quis haeres p. 484. in Gen. XV. 5. ἐξήγαγεν δὲ αὐτὸν ἔξω, ὅ τινες ὑπὸ ἀμουσίας οὐδὲν εἰώθασι γελᾶν φάσκοντες· εἴσω γάρ τις ἐξάγεται; ἢ ἔμπαλιν αὐτὸ ἐξέρχεται ἔξω; Levit. IX. 22.

52. Absentem & inconspicuum adorant, quod cultum religiosum significat, nunc primum Christo a discipulis exhibitum,

TO

Plate 5. The New Testament edited by Johann Jakob Wettstein, 1751-1752: ending of the gospel of Luke.

to challenge seriously the record of Bengel's proposed changes in his first two classes of readings (even Wettstein, who placed his preferred readings between the Textus Receptus which he printed and its apparatus, proposed fewer changes than Bengel). The essential principles of textual criticism which have retained their validity to the present were already formulated by Bengel.[15] To him is due the laurel for the eighteenth century.[16]

2. *FROM LACHMANN TO NESTLE*

We can appreciate better the struggle for freedom from the dominance of the Textus Receptus when we remember that in this period it was regarded as preserving even to the last detail the inspired and infallible word of God himself (and yet Johann Albrecht Bengel was one of the fathers of Württemberg pietism!). The initial campaign in the battle against the Textus Receptus and for a return to an earlier form of the text was launched in the nineteenth century by a professor of classical philology at Berlin, **Karl Lachmann** (1793-1851). His program was first announced in 1830:[17] "Down with the late text of the Textus Receptus, and back to the text of the early fourth-century church!" This slogan set the goal for the generations following. What Lachmann conceived as a program was achieved by **Constantin von Tischendorf** (1815-1874). His first major accomplishment was to decipher Codex Ephraemi Syri Rescriptus (C),[18] a Greek New Testament manuscript written in the fifth century but later washed clean (i.e., a palimpsest)[19] and its text replaced with treatises by the Syrian Church Father Ephraem. His most spectacular discovery was Codex Sinaiticus (א)[20] in the monastery of St. Catherine on Mt. Sinai, but he also discovered on his travels in the Orient sponsored by Czar Nicholas I numerous other uncial manuscripts (twenty-one, to be precise), although they were less extensive and less significant, and he further made careful examinations on a number (twenty-three?) of other neglected uncials. Tischendorf's editions of the New Testament culminated in the *Editio octava critica maior* of 1869-1872. The recent (1965) reprint of this edition is clear proof that even a century later it is still of value for scholarly research.

Tischendorf offers the evidence known in his time, citing it completely and accurately (a rare virtue deserving special notice!).[21] The achievement

15. Although in elaboration of views proposed by Gerhard von Maestricht in 1711.
16. Just as to Brooke Foss Westcott and Fenton John Anthony Hort for the nineteenth century, although they were surpassed by Constantin von Tischendorf in the use of manuscripts, just as Bengel was by Wettstein.
17. The attempt to realize this goal in the editions of 1831 and 1842-1850 was grossly inadequate.
18. Cf. pp. 12 (plate 6), 109.
19. Cf. pp. 12 (plate 6), 80 (plate 18), 109, 113. By applying a chemical reagent (Gioberti tincture) to this and to many other manuscripts Tischendorf was able to bring out the original text. But this process resulted in further damage to the manuscript and in its increasing illegibility today. Plate 6 was made by ultraviolet photography.
20. Cf. pp. 13 (plate 7), 107.
21. Cf. the many inaccuracies in twentieth-century manual editions (among which the Nestle edition has always been a notable exception), as well as in larger editions, especially that of Hermann von Soden.

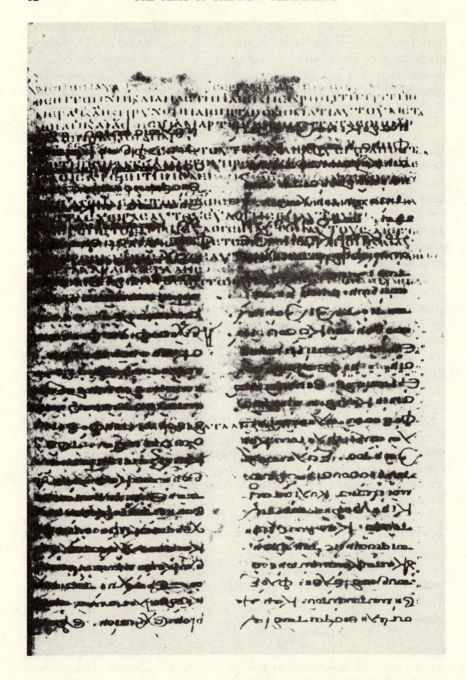

Plate 6. Codex Ephraemi Syri Rescriptus (C, 04, fifth-century lower writing; cf. pp. 11, 109), deciphered by Constantin von Tischendorf: ending of the gospel of Luke.

Plate 7. Codex Sinaiticus (ℵ, 01, fourth century; cf. pp. 11, 107), discovered by Tischendorf: ending of the gospel of Luke.

this represents may be measured by the failure of all later attempts to replace Tischendorf's edition with a comparable collation of all known textual evidence, including Greek manuscripts, early versions, and patristic citations; even the most recent attempts are still far from completion.[22] It is true that Tischendorf made use of only some 64 uncials where today we know of 299,[23] only a single papyrus manuscript (and that a fragment) where we have 96 today, and that he was aware of only a small fraction of the 2,812 minuscules now catalogued. Yet, as we have remarked, his citations are complete and reliable. The importance Tischendorf ascribed to the Codex Sinaiticus he discovered is implicit in the

22. Cf. pp. 23f.
23. Cf. p. 104.

symbol ℵ he assigned to it. Many New Testament scholars have criticized him for this, and have substituted for it the symbol S (which did nothing but create confusion, because S has for generations indicated the uncial Gospels manuscript written in A.D. 949 and preserved at Rome). For Tischendorf ℵ also served as the critical standard for establishing the text. Pride of discovery was not the only factor here — other factors were also partly responsible. At the beginning of his work Tischendorf had practically no access to Codex Vaticanus (B): Angelo Cardinal Mai was planning to publish an edition of it himself and did all he could to discourage Tischendorf's use of it. When Mai's edition then appeared in 1857 (revised and corrected in 1859), and later a full reproduction of the text was published in 1868-1872, it was too late for Tischendorf to alter the basic structure of his edition,[24] quite apart from the fact that by then Tischendorf's basic critical principles had already been formed.

The situation was quite different for the Englishmen **Brooke Foss Westcott** (1825-1901; professor at Cambridge, later bishop of Durham) and **Fenton John Anthony Hort** (1828-1892; professor at Cambridge), whose edition of *The New Testament in the Original Greek* appeared in 1881. Codex Vaticanus was their touchstone. They believed that they had discovered in it a representative of the "Neutral text" which came far closer to the original text than the three forms recognized as Alexandrian, Byzantine, and Western, especially when it stood in agreement with ℵ. Actually there is no such thing as a "neutral" text of the New Testament. Even $\mathfrak{p}^{75}$, which is textually so close to Codex Vaticanus that it could almost be regarded as its exemplar in those portions of Luke and John preserved in it,[25] cannot be called "neutral," although it is more than a hundred and fifty years older. Every manuscript of the New Testament contains a "living text."[26] Furthermore, the textual quality of Codex Vaticanus is inferior in the Pauline corpus: in the Gospels and elsewhere it is far superior to Codex Sinaiticus (and the other uncials), but not in the letters of Paul. Again, the fact that Codex Vaticanus (like Codex Sinaiticus) is from the second half of the fourth century raises the question how Westcott and Hort could describe their edition so confidently as the New Testament "in the original Greek." For in contrast to our own generation, which possesses a wealth of early witnesses dating back to the beginning of the second century, Westcott and Hort had no direct witness to the New Testament text earlier than the fourth century.

Their only access to the earlier period was by inference from agreements of the Old Latin version (whose beginnings were in the late second century) and the Old Syriac version (represented by manuscripts known as the Sinaitic Syriac and the Curetonian Syriac)[27] with the "Western" text[28] (represented by Codex

---

24. Despite all the various changes made in his text through the *Editio octava critica maior*, which could be held up to Tischendorf by theoreticians with no comparable experience of editing a critical edition, the above evaluation stands.
25. Cf. pp. 87, 93.
26. Cf. p. 69.
27. Cf. p. 193f.
28. Cf. p. 54.

Plate. 8. Codex Vaticanus (B, 03, fourth century; cf. 14, 109): ending of the gospel of Luke, beginning of John.

Bezae Cantabrigiensis [D^ea]),[29] which Westcott and Hort ascribed to the second century.[30] This text is characterized by additions, so that where it reads a shorter text (as in the "Western non-interpolations")[31] it was presumed to preserve the original reading. Quite apart from their arbitrariness in applying this rule,[32] its underlying assumptions are also faulty. Codex D^ea can hardly represent a "Western" text of the second century; rather, it must have been copied from an ex-

29. Cf. pp. 16 (plate 9), 109f.
30. ". . . It is, to the best of our belief, substantially a Western text of Cent. II, with occasional readings probably due to Cent. IV" (*The New Testament in the Original Greek* [Cambridge and London, 1881 (1896²; vol. 2 repr. 1987)], 2:138).
31. Cf. p. 37.
32. There are numerous other passages where the conditions are similar, with D standing in agreement with the Old Latin and the Old Syriac in support of a shorter reading against the normal Greek tradition, and which are not classified among the "Western non-interpolations."

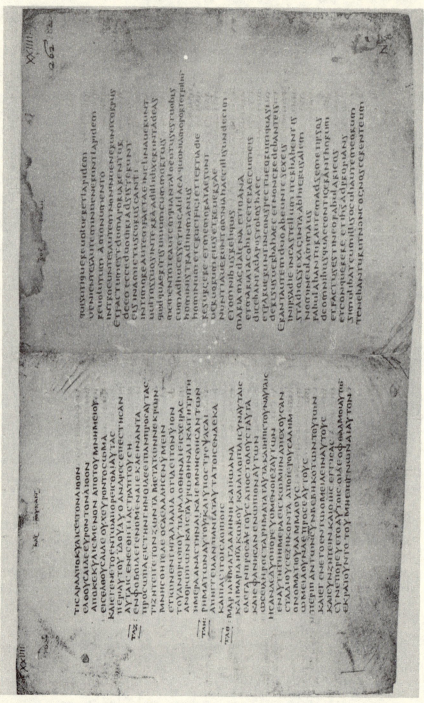

Plate 9. Codex Bezae Cantabrigiensis (D^ea, 05, fifth century; cf. pp. 18, 65, 109f.): Luke 24:1-16.

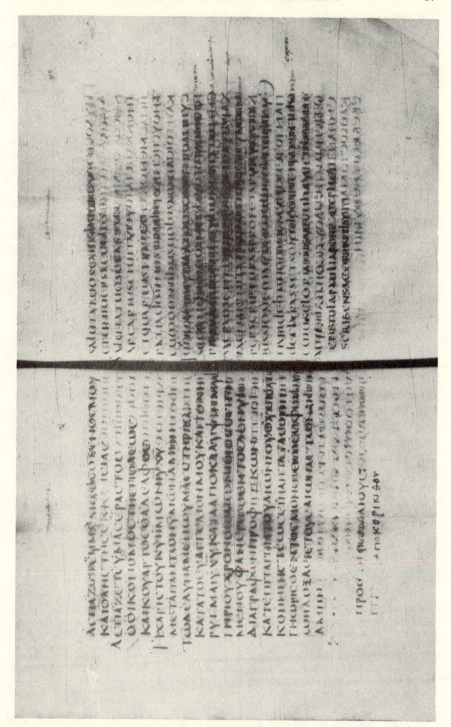

Plate 10. Codex Claromontanus (D^p, 06, sixth century; cf. p. 110): ending of Romans.

emplar which reflected conditions of the period before A.D. 300.[33] Similarly
the text of the Sinaitic Syriac and the Curetonian Syriac can only represent a
fourth-century revision,[34] and can scarcely be traced to the second century, for
only Tatian's Diatessaron,[35] the dominant text of the early Syriac church, goes
back to this early period. Finally, the fact should be noted (on which there is
general agreement) that neither Westcott nor Hort ever actually collated a single
manuscript but worked completely from published material, i.e., critical editions
(viz., Tischendorf). This makes the claim in the first sentence of their appendix
a trifle puzzling, that "the text of this edition of the New Testament has been
formed exclusively on documentary evidence, no account being taken of any
printed edition."[36] The text printed by Westcott and Hort[37] does offer alternative
readings in the outer margin, but there is nothing of a critical apparatus other
than an appendix of "Notes on Select Readings" extending to about 140 pages.
Yet both here and more extensively in the introduction (by Hort) the editors
develop such a penetrating analysis of the material that it is easy to understand
the deep impression made by the work when it first appeared and the continuing
influence of its theories even today, especially in the English-speaking world.[38]
Two excerpts will suffice to show the character of the edition.

    1. With reference to a Bℵ text:

Accordingly, with the exceptions mentioned above, it is our belief (1) that
readings of ℵB should be accepted as the true readings until strong internal
evidence is found to the contrary, and (2) that no readings of ℵB can be
safely rejected absolutely, though it is sometimes right to place them only
on an alternative footing, especially where they receive no support from the
Versions or the Fathers.[39]

    2. Yet the text of Codex Bezae Cantabrigiensis (D[ea]) is ascribed the
highest quality:

The text of D presents a truer image of the form in which the Gospels and
Acts were most widely read in the third and probably a great part of the
second century than any other extant Greek MS.[40]

    The editions of Tischendorf (numerous smaller editions followed the

33. Cf. pp. 107f.
34. Cf. pp. 189f.
35. Cf. p. 189.
36. Westcott and Hort, *New Testament*. 1:541.
37. Cf. p. 47 (plate 12).
38. Cf. Bruce Manning Metzger, *The Text of the New Testament: Its Transmission, Corruption, and Restoration* (New York: 1964; cf. below, p. 275), p. 137: "Though the discovery of
additional manuscripts has required the realignment of certain groups of witnesses, the general
validity of their critical principles and procedures is widely acknowledged by textual scholars today."
In another passage Metzger expresses himself with greater reserve: "By way of retrospect and
evaluation it may be said that scholars today generally agree that one of the chief contributions made
by Westcott and Hort was their clear demonstration that the Syrian (or Byzantine) text is later than
the other types of text" (p. 135). But this had become common knowledge since Griesbach's time
(at the latest)! The statement remains unchanged in the 1968 edition.
39. Westcott and Hort, *New Testament*, 2:225.
40. *Ibid.*, p. 149.

printing of his *Editio octava critica maior*) and of Westcott and Hort were sufficient to make the Textus Receptus obsolete for the scholarly world. Besides these two there was a whole series of other editions, among which we should note in particular the 1857-1872 edition of **Samuel Prideaux Tregelles** (1813-1875), which has been practically eclipsed by Tischendorf's in popular appreciation although its text was remarkably similar. Despite their clamorous rhetoric, the champions of the Textus Receptus (led primarily by Dean John William Burgon) were defending deserted ramparts. But their battle was not conclusively lost until the *Novum Testamentum Graece* of **Eberhard Nestle** (1851-1913) was published in 1898 by the Württemberg Bible Society (Württembergische Bibelanstalt) in Stuttgart. This signaled the retreat of the Textus Receptus from both church and school.

How firmly the Textus Receptus was entrenched in these areas is shown by the fact that the British and Foreign Bible Society, then the largest and most influential of all the Bible societies, continued to distribute it officially for fully twenty years after the publication of Westcott and Hort's edition. It was not until 1904 that it adopted the Nestle text, which was then in its fifth edition.[41] This marked the final defeat of the Textus Receptus, nearly four hundred years after it was first printed.

Voices have been raised recently in the United States claiming superiority for the Textus Receptus over modern editions of the text,[42] but they are finding little favorable response outside some limited circles. The wheels of history will not be reversed (cf. ch. VII, § § 3, 4).

What Eberhard Nestle did was actually quite simple (a radical breakthrough is always simple in retrospect): he compared the texts of Tischendorf (Gebhardt's stereotype edition of 1895) and of Westcott-Hort. When the two differed he consulted a third edition for a deciding vote (at first Richard Francis Weymouth's second edition of 1892, and after 1901 Bernhard Weiss' 1894-1900 edition).[43] This made a majority decision possible: the agreement of two editions determined the text, while the reading of the third was placed in the apparatus, and a series of symbols enabled the reader to reconstruct with accuracy the texts of the editions used (indicating even the marginal readings in Westcott-Hort's edition together with their evaluations). This apparatus is of interest, although it pays relatively little attention to manuscripts:[44] Nestle devoted one or two lines to showing the readings of Codex Bezae Cantabrigiensis (prompted by the views of Westcott and Hort). This may seem rather elementary (characteristically the preface of the first edition occupies only a single page); but it was a breakthrough.

41. The text adopted by the British and Foreign Bible Society in 1904 was that of Nestle's fourth edition (1903), but with an apparatus of the readings of the Textus Receptus and of the reconstructed Greek text underlying the English Revised Version of 1881. [Trans.]

42. E.g., Arthur L. Farstad and Zane C. Hodges eds., *The Greek New Testament According to the Majority Text* (Nashville: 1982), pp. ix, xi.

43. According to the preface in the first edition of 1898, with modifications noted in the prefaces of subsequent editions, p. 1 and elsewhere.

44. Cf. p. 21 (plate 11).

In effect, this purely mechanical system of a majority text summarized the results of nineteenth-century textual scholarship. It eliminated the extremes of Tischendorf (due to his partiality to ℵ) and of Westcott and Hort (with their partiality to B), especially after Weiss' edition was adopted. It produced a text that not only lasted seventy years, but on the whole[45] truly represented the state of knowledge of the time. It is significant that in its 657 printed pages the early Nestle differs from the new text in merely seven hundred passages.

3. FROM THE "OLD NESTLE" TO THE "NEW NESTLE"

To begin an account of New Testament editions in the twentieth century with the statement that the Nestle text achieved a position of absolute preeminence comparable only to that of the Textus Receptus in earlier centuries would be to ignore its own stages of development, especially the contribution of **Erwin Nestle** as he followed the footsteps of his father. The thirteenth edition of the Nestle text in 1927 marked the beginning of a new period in the edition's history.

In this edition Erwin Nestle (1883-1972) did not merely review the text once more. He finally made it conform in fact to the majority principle, for in 1901 the Württemberg Bible Society, with typically Swabian thriftiness, had permitted his father to make only the most important alterations required by the use of Bernhard Weiss' edition.[46] Further, the edition was now finally supplemented with an apparatus of critical textual notes worthy of the name. The readings of the three underlying editions continued to be noted (and those of Hermann Freiherr von Soden's edition were also added), but now all the significant variants cited were supplied with their supporting evidence among the Greek manuscripts, the early versions, and the Church Fathers. Erwin Nestle now satisfied the recommendations repeatedly urged by German New Testament scholars in their annual sessions, and "Nestle" sloughed its primitive format of 1898 to become a scholarly manual outpacing all its competition. Its circulation increased correspondingly, especially in diglot editions with Latin and German.[47]

The critical apparatus of this Greek edition now gave the reader a distinct impression that the text had been established on the basis of manuscripts, whether Greek or versional, and on editions of patristic writings. This was **Kurt Aland**'s impression when about 1950 he first became associated with the work (he was first mentioned as an associate in the 21st edition of 1952, and in the 22nd edition his name first appeared on the title page). He was all the more surprised (despite the disclaimer in the preface) to learn that Erwin Nestle had compiled the critical apparatus with such accuracy solely from evidence meticulously

---

45. Except in passages where it follows the special theories of Westcott and Hort.

46. Characteristically the old plates of the 1898 edition remained in use for the Nestle text even through the twenty-fifth edition, after producing hundreds of thousands of impressions.

47. The Latin text was the Sixto-Clementine Vulgate, and the German was the 1912 Luther revision. Each was provided with a critical apparatus which was somewhat limited, but quite adequate for a beginning.

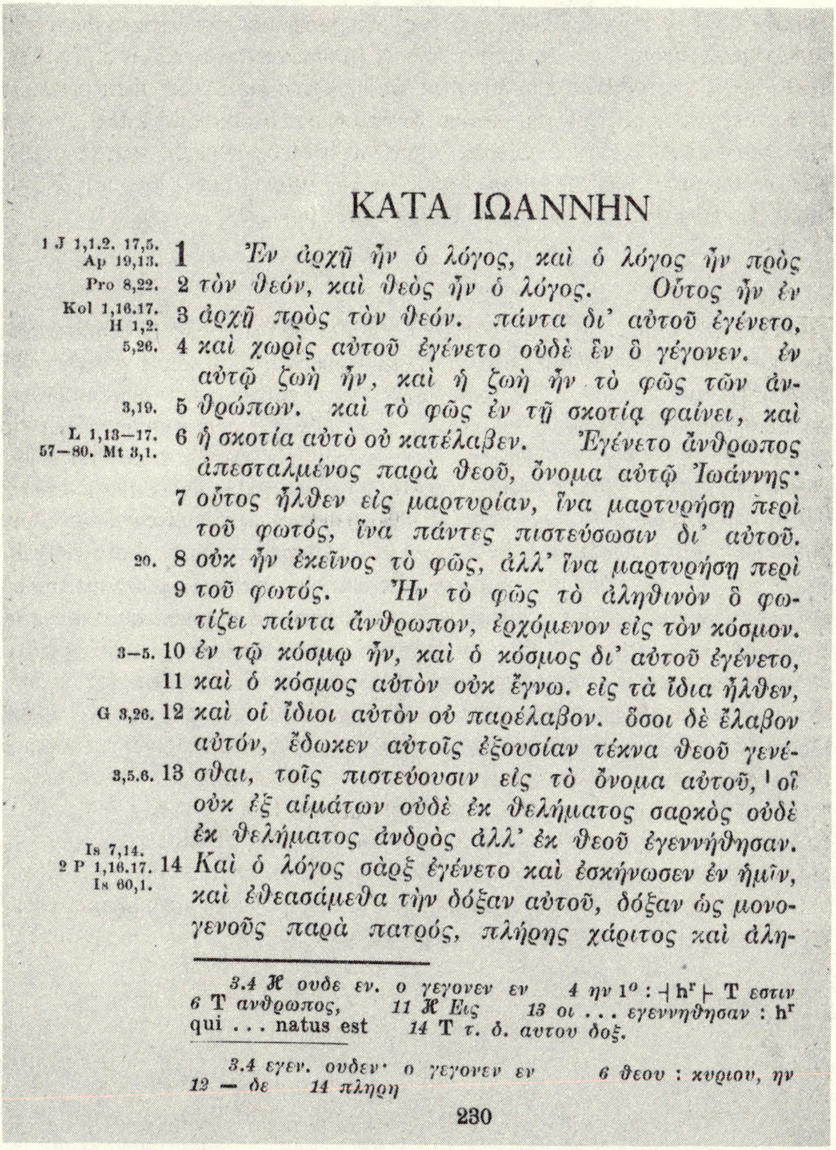

ΚΑΤΑ ΙΩΑΝΝΗΝ

1 J 1,1.2. 17,5.
Ap 19,13.   1   Ἐν ἀρχῇ ἦν ὁ λόγος, καὶ ὁ λόγος ἦν πρὸς
Pro 8,22.   2 τὸν θεόν, καὶ θεὸς ἦν ὁ λόγος.   Οὗτος ἦν ἐν
Kol 1,16.17.
H 1,2.   3 ἀρχῇ πρὸς τὸν θεόν. πάντα δι' αὐτοῦ ἐγένετο,
5,26.   4 καὶ χωρὶς αὐτοῦ ἐγένετο οὐδὲ ἓν ὃ γέγονεν. ἐν
        αὐτῷ ζωὴ ἦν, καὶ ἡ ζωὴ ἦν τὸ φῶς τῶν ἀν-
3,19.   5 θρώπων. καὶ τὸ φῶς ἐν τῇ σκοτίᾳ φαίνει, καὶ
L 1,13—17.
57—80. Mt 3,1.   6 ἡ σκοτία αὐτὸ οὐ κατέλαβεν.   Ἐγένετο ἄνθρωπος
        ἀπεσταλμένος παρὰ θεοῦ, ὄνομα αὐτῷ Ἰωάννης·
    7 οὗτος ἦλθεν εἰς μαρτυρίαν, ἵνα μαρτυρήσῃ περὶ
        τοῦ φωτός, ἵνα πάντες πιστεύσωσιν δι' αὐτοῦ.
29.   8 οὐκ ἦν ἐκεῖνος τὸ φῶς, ἀλλ' ἵνα μαρτυρήσῃ περὶ
    9 τοῦ φωτός.   Ἦν τὸ φῶς τὸ ἀληθινὸν ὃ φω-
        τίζει πάντα ἄνθρωπον, ἐρχόμενον εἰς τὸν κόσμον.
3—5. 10 ἐν τῷ κόσμῳ ἦν, καὶ ὁ κόσμος δι' αὐτοῦ ἐγένετο,
    11 καὶ ὁ κόσμος αὐτὸν οὐκ ἔγνω. εἰς τὰ ἴδια ἦλθεν,
G 3,26. 12 καὶ οἱ ἴδιοι αὐτὸν οὐ παρέλαβον. ὅσοι δὲ ἔλαβον
        αὐτόν, ἔδωκεν αὐτοῖς ἐξουσίαν τέκνα θεοῦ γενέ-
3,5.6. 13 σθαι, τοῖς πιστεύουσιν εἰς τὸ ὄνομα αὐτοῦ, | οἳ
        οὐκ ἐξ αἱμάτων οὐδὲ ἐκ θελήματος σαρκὸς οὐδὲ
        ἐκ θελήματος ἀνδρὸς ἀλλ' ἐκ θεοῦ ἐγεννήθησαν.
Is 7,14.
2 P 1,16.17. 14 Καὶ ὁ λόγος σὰρξ ἐγένετο καὶ ἐσκήνωσεν ἐν ἡμῖν,
Is 60,1.   καὶ ἐθεασάμεθα τὴν δόξαν αὐτοῦ, δόξαν ὡς μονο-
        γενοῦς παρὰ πατρός, πλήρης χάριτος καὶ ἀλη-

3.4 𝕳 ουδε εν. ο γεγονεν εν   4 ην 1⁰ : ┤hʳ├ T εστιν
6 T ανθρωπος,   11 𝕳 Εις   13 οι . . . εγεννηθησαν : hʳ
qui . . . natus est   14 T τ. δ. αυτου δοξ.

3.4 εγεν. ουδεν· ο γεγονεν εν   6 θεου : κυριου, ην
12 — δε   14 πληρη

230

Plate 11. The first edition of *Novum Testamentum Graece* edited by Eberhard Nestle,
1898: beginning of the gospel of John.

combed from citations in published editions of the text since Tischendorf. Aland
was assigned by Erwin Nestle to take the long lists he had compiled of discrep-
ancies in the editions since Tischendorf and to verify the correct readings by
consulting manuscripts and editions of patristic writings — a task which Erwin
Nestle himself had never undertaken (nor was he in a position to do so because

shortly after his father's death his library had been sold to Cambridge). We do not mention this to diminish the memory of Erwin Nestle — quite the opposite! It is almost incredible that by his methods he could have produced the degree of accuracy achieved in his apparatus. In fact, an intensive comparison with the evidence demonstrated (to our utter amazement under the circumstances) that the accuracy of Nestle in instances of disputed readings exceeded 80 percent, while that of von Soden and other modern editors is closer to 20 percent! From Nestle[21] to Nestle[23] the control base was progressively expanded (and with the same results), never relying on secondary sources for the additional evidence — using only originals (by microfilm or by photocopy). This applies especially to the papyri, which began then to be more extensively cited in the critical apparatus.

But this anticipates a later stage. The fact that Erwin Nestle was able to develop the apparatus of his father's edition in such a way was due in large part to the work of a Berlin pastor, **Hermann Freiherr von Soden** (1852-1914), whose readings he transcribed in his critical apparatus with the same meticulous care that characterized his father's work. With the support of Elise König, a wealthy patron who provided him with the necessary funds (and who deserves special recognition — may her tribe increase!), von Soden was able to enlist the efforts of about forty colleagues in all for the task of collating manuscripts in the libraries of Europe and other lands. Under such favorable circumstances the four-volume work appeared in 1902-1913 under the title *Die Schriften des Neuen Testaments in ihrer ältesten erreichbaren Textgestalt hergestellt auf Grund ihrer Textgeschichte*.[48]

But this attempt must be adjudged "a failure, though a splendid one," to borrow the words of the outstanding American textual critic Kirsopp Lake with regard to Westcott-Hort's edition in 1904. There were several reasons for this.

1. Its theoretical presuppositions were false. Von Soden assumed that there were three major text types: the *K* (Koine) text, the *H* (Hesychian, Egyptian) text, and the *I* (Jerusalem) text. According to von Soden these three recensions were derived from the archetype, the original text, which was still available to Origen. Therefore wherever all three text types, or at least two of them, were in agreement, von Soden believed they preserved the original text of the New Testament,[49] provided it had not been distorted by the influence of Tatian (in the Gospels) or of Marcion (in the Pauline corpus). Apart from the fact that von Soden grossly exaggerates the influence of Tatian (for whose text his information was quite inadequate), the *I* text he described never existed, at least not as he describes it. Von Soden ascribed to *I* nearly all the manuscripts and traditions which did not conform to the *K* text or to the *H* text. Further, by placing the *K* text on a par with the other groups he ascribed to it a value it

---

48. I.e., "The Writings of the New Testament, restored to their earliest attainable form on the basis of their textual history."

49. Cf. the brief summary of principles for reconstructing the text, 2:xxviii.

does not deserve.[50] If the *K* text is given a full vote in determining the original text, and if the agreement of two groups is decisive, the result must inevitably be a text that could never be called "original" (imagine the combination of *K* + *I* — a secondary and a fictitious text type!). It would necessarily be weighted in the direction of the Koine text — as actually happens in von Soden's text.

2. The system of symbols designed by von Soden for New Testament manuscripts[51] makes his edition almost impossible to use. It could possibly have worked had he cited manuscripts individually instead of citing them usually by the various subgroups he established (or posited — nearly thirty for the *K* and *I* text types), first identifying the subgroup and then listing individually only the members of the subgroup which do *not* support the reading! It is demanding enough to keep the varieties of subgroups clearly in mind, but it would tax all the powers of a mnemonics expert to remember the members of all the various groups. Consequently the reader always needs to refer to supplementary manuals, and these are usually either incomplete or awkward to use.[52]

3. The information in von Soden's apparatus is so unreliable[53] that the reader soon comes to regard this remarkably full apparatus as little more than a collection of variant readings whose attestation needs verification elsewhere.

Von Soden's edition was distinctly a failure. It was unsuccessful in its original goal of replacing Tischendorf's edition. Nor was it any more successful as a publishing venture. Only recently, after more than fifty years, was the original printing exhausted. But nonetheless, von Soden's edition is a necessary tool for textual critics. Part I is a vast quarry of information that is unavailable elsewhere. Von Soden's studies in the Koine text constitute pioneering research: the groups he distinguished, including even the congeries of groups he assembled under the label of the *I* text, provide extensive evidence for the establishment of manuscript groups and families. Many of the spectacular discoveries made in recent decades may be found anticipated in von Soden's work, sometimes in a well-developed form. The text volume with its wealth of variant readings is also a useful source of information (despite its distribution into two, and frequently three, apparatuses).

The two volumes of the *Novum Testamentum Graece secundum Textum Westcotto-Hortianum* by the Englishman **S. C. E. Legg** (vol. 1, *Mark:* 1935; vol. 2, *Matthew:* 1940) have a certain usefulness in providing information subsequent to Tischendorf in a more accessible way than von Soden. The gospel of Luke in this series was complete in manuscript form when the Oxford Clarendon

---

50. There is undoubtedly an early (although admittedly different) tradition underlying the *K* text (it may even claim one or more papyri of the early period among its ancestors), yet nevertheless it must have received its final form in a revision made about 300 or shortly before, and this gave it a distinctly secondary character.

51. Cf. pp. 40ff.

52. This sounds rather hypercritical, but the reader may examine the sample page from von Soden's edition in plate 12, together with the comments on pp. 41f., to find whether the above description is not actually rather generous.

53. Notwithstanding the reassurances offered in 2:xxii, n. 1.

Press decided not to publish it — due to widespread criticism of not only its restricted manuscript base, but also of its omissions and errors in citing evidence for variant readings.

Legg's venture was succeeded by a project initiated by the outstanding American New Testament textual critic Ernest Cadman Colwell. In 1942 he founded an American committee which was soon joined by a British committee in the **International Greek New Testament Apparatus Project** to continue Legg's edition on a new basis. First the complete evidence of the textual tradition of the gospel of Luke was to be published as an apparatus to the Textus Receptus, and then within two years a critical edition of the text was to be produced on the basis of this evidence. The volumes for the rest of the New Testament books were to appear successively in due sequence. After forty years of labor the edition of Luke has been published (1984-1987), printing the Textus Receptus as originally planned. Although is is useful in many ways (e.g., the patristic citations), its selection of Greek manuscripts is unfortunately limited, some of its data is defective, and the choice of the Textus Receptus as the collation base for the apparatus promises to make the work useful only by a kind of inversion: significant readings will be found exclusively in the apparatus, and that sometimes with difficulty, considering the mass of the data.

Meanwhile **Vinton A. Dearing** is preparing an edition of the readings of manuscripts through the tenth century, i.e., of all the papyri and uncials (and some few minuscules), using a computer program to classify the variant readings by their individual characteristics. When the gospel of John appears as the first volume of this edition it will be possible to tell more about it (there has been no recent word of it). While it lacks any reference to the later manuscripts, the versions, and patristic evidence, the degree of its analytical detail in citing the papyri and the uncials may well compensate for this lack.

In any case, the goal of preparing a critical edition has been abandoned — by Legg, by the International Project, and by Dearing. It is being pursued now only by the *Novi Testamenti editio critica maior* being prepared under the auspices of the **Institute for New Testament Textual Research** at Münster. The first volume to appear will be an edition of the Catholic letters. The preliminary studies have been completed and published (*ANTF* 6-7, 9-11). The methods developed will now be further tested in the Pauline corpus, and then (financial support permitting) the full project will begin.

It is evident, then, that all things considered, the twentieth century has thus far not been able to produce anything comparable to Tischendorf's achievement for the nineteenth century: a comprehensive and reliable survey of the known evidence for the history of the New Testament text. This has been due in large measure to the veritable flood of new materials which have appeared since his time, and to the problems they have raised (Tischendorf knew of only 1 papyrus to our 96, and 64 uncials to our 299. And yet this still represents a serious need, even when we consider that the new text comes closer to the original text of the New Testament than did Tischendorf or Westcott and Hort, not to mention von Soden.

It is in manual editions that development has been achieved. Manual editions of the Greek New Testament have always been plentiful, produced to satisfy the needs of the church for scholarly research and for theological education. Even at the beginning of this century a wide variety of editions was available, although few of them have lasted or enjoyed wide distribution. Besides Nestle, the twentieth century has seen the editions of Vogels, Merk, and Bover. **Alexander Souter**'s edition should also be mentioned. His *Novum Testamentum Graece* appeared first in 1910, and in a second edition in 1947, each edition enjoying several printings. But the text of this edition was merely an adaptation of the Textus Receptus to a reconstruction of the original text that presumably underlay the English Revised Version of 1881, so that its significance has been primarily in its much esteemed apparatus. Another reconstruction of a Greek text from an English version is the 1964 edition of *The Greek New Testament* by **R. V. G. Tasker**. This was based on the New English Bible and represents simply its literal equivalent in Greek. The *Greek-English Diglot for the Use of Translators* prepared by **George Dunbar Kilpatrick** enjoyed only a private and limited circulation, and was abandoned by the British and Foreign Bible Society before its completion. Had it been published it would have offered a radical text based on an eclectic methodology. In 1981 the Greek *Synopsis of the First Three Gospels* by **Heinrich Greeven** appeared, followed by **John Bernard Orchard's** in 1983 and **M.-E. Boismard's** in 1986, each professing an independent text. These will be discussed later (cf. pp. 261ff.). Thus except for the three editions of Vogels, Merk, and Bover mentioned above, the last fifty years have produced nothing of note apart from the new text. **G. Nolli**, *Novum Testamentum Graece et Latine,* although published by the Libreria Editrice Vaticana (1981), is defective throughout both in text and apparatus, while one should beware of *The Greek New Testament According to the Majority Text* by **Arthur L. Farstad** and **Zane C. Hodges** (1982) as an anachronism in every respect (cf. pp. 297, 306).

What is the relationship, then, of the editions of Vogels, Merk, and Bover — the only editions of the New Testament text deserving serious consideration — to the editions of the nineteenth century, and to Nestle and the new text? **Heinrich Joseph Vogels'** *Novum Testamentum Graece et Latine* first appeared at Düsseldorf in 1922 (fourth edition, Freiburg: 1955); **Augustin Merk's** *Novum Testamentum Graece et Latine* first appeared at Rome in 1933 (tenth edition, 1984); **José Maria Bover's** *Novi Testamenti Biblia Graeca et Latina* first appeared at Madrid in 1943 (fifth edition, 1968). As their titles indicate, all three are diglot editions, but the Latin part needs no further comment here because it is simply a reproduction of the Sixto-Clementine Vulgate text. This was dictated by the ecclesiastical rules of the period, all three editors being Roman Catholics (Vogels is known to have preferred a different Latin parallel text, but he was denied the option). These restrictions continued until the trilingual Madrid edition of 1977, *Nuevo Testamento Trilingüe* (^{2}1988), which offers the Neo-Vulgate Latin text and a Spanish version in parallel to the Greek text of Bover (revised by **José O'Callaghan Martínez**). It is hardly a coincidence that these editions were all prepared by Roman Catholic scholars — they were

intended to meet the overwhelming "competition" of the popular Nestle edition which was circulating widely even in Roman Catholic circles. The fact that the Nestle text was produced by the Bible Societies, which were still under official Catholic proscription, only aggravated the situation. But these three editions also stood in substantive contrast to Nestle by the strikingly high number of Koine readings in their texts, due to the influence of von Soden. The dependence on von Soden is most obvious in Merk, who employs von Soden's system of manuscript groupings, but it is hardly less obvious in both the other edtions.

The textual scene of the past century may be most conveniently represented by chart 1. This chart is based on the text of Nestle-Aland[25] because the Nestle text has been the dominant text for eighty of these one hundred years, and during these eighty years it has remained the same (apart from a few minor changes adopted by Erwin Nestle — no more than a dozen at most).

An examination of chart 1 shows first of all that the **greatest number of differences from the Nestle text** is found in von Soden (shown in the column to the far right, which represents von Soden exclusively): 1180 instances in the Gospels, 273 in Acts, 355 in Paul's letters, 115 in the Catholic letters, and 124 in Revelation, a total of 2047 instances. Closely in second place comes Vogels' edition, differing from Nestle 1996 times (1398 in the Gospels, 192 in Acts, 261 in Paul's letters, 67 in the Catholic letters, 78 in Revelation). In comparison Bover's edition differs 1161 times and Merk's only 770 times in all (these are the totals for each of the editions in all five groups of writings).

To pursue further the **relationship of Nestle's editions** (through the twenty-fifth) **to those of Tischendorf and Westcott-Hort,** the totals in their respective columns[54] show for Nestle a closer affinity to Westcott-Hort, with only 558 differences as compared with 1262 differences from Tischendorf. Tischendorf relies too frequently on Codex Sinaiticus for establishing his text; since Weiss, Nestle's third source, shares with Westcott-Hort a tendency to rely on Codex Vaticanus, a relatively close relationship between Nestle and Westcott-Hort is the result (although 558 differences is by no means a negligible amount).

Still more can be gleaned from chart 1: **von Soden's edition** stands much closer to Tischendorf than to Westcott-Hort. It agrees with Tischendorf in differences from the Nestle text in a total of 602 instances (Gospels, 387; Acts, 76; Paul's letters, 71; Catholic letters, 36; Revelation, 32), as compared to 160 instances with Westcott-Hort (Gospels, 87; Acts, 17; Paul's letters, 43; Catholic letters, 3; Revelation, 10).

And finally, to restate the first point, **von Soden's edition has been the strongest influence among the manual editions of the twentieth century** (cf. the shaded portion of the columns). Its influence is seen most extensively in Merk, which agrees with von Soden 657 times in differences from Nestle, disagreeing only 113 times — a ratio of 6:1. Bover stands in second place (with 867 common agreements against 290 disagreements, a ratio of 3:1), and Vogels'

54. Cf. above, pp. 19f.

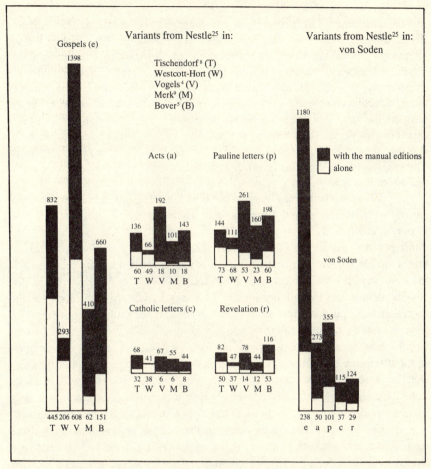

Chart 1. Textual relationships in critical editions of the past century.

comes last (with 1297 agreements and 699 differences, a ratio of 1.8:1). Von Soden was not, of course, always persuasive (cf. the column to the far right, in which the dark part shows where his edition differs from Nestle[25] together with the manual editions, and the white where it stands alone), but this brief survey shows quite clearly the controlling influence it wielded over a generation of manual editions. This is true even for Vogels, which stands last in the list: a glance at the Gospels section of the tables shows a very small white part and an overwhelmingly large dark part. Only in the Gospels does Vogels go its own way independently: here its numerous differences from von Soden (608 instances, approximately 50 percent of the passages concerned) give a false impression of Vogels' independence of von Soden. Further inferences which may be gleaned from this chart will be left to the reader.

Only one further comment may be necessary to avoid a methodological

misunderstanding. **The number of instances where these various editions differ among themselves** and from Nestle seems quite high. In reality their significance is minor. Consider that the text of Nestle-Aland[25] comprises 657 pages. When von Soden and Vogels show 2047 and 1996 differences from it respectively, this amounts to no more than three differences a page. This changes the perspective completely. Admittedly averages can be misleading; e.g., in the Gospels the ratio is higher: for Nestle's 296 pages von Soden shows 1180 differences and Vogels 1398, raising the ratios to 4 and 4.5 to a page, respectively. But then the ratio is correspondingly lower for other parts of the New Testament. The other editions show far fewer differences: Bover has less than 2 to a page, and Merk less than 1.2 to a page of Nestle.

These statistics may suggest the objection that differences between the various editions have simply been counted, and not weighed. But this objection is purely theoretical. From practical experience we find that "important" and "unimportant" variants are about equally distributed in the various editions, so that a simple numerical count actually provides a fairly accurate picture. It is the only way an observer can gain an overall impression. When we begin discussing details the overall perspective becomes hopelessly lost, even for the specialist. The purpose here is to gain a bird's-eye view of the entire field of New Testament textual criticism, letting only the broadest outlines stand out. Ground-level views undoubtedly reveal more lively detail, but any appreciation of the discipline based on a particular perspective will lack a broader balance. Detailed studies should certainly not be disregarded, and we will examine Luke 24 later as an extreme example.[55] But such studies are significant only when a broader frame of reference and basic principles have first been established.

On the whole it must be admitted that statements about the text of the New Testament, whether by amateurs or by specialists, have far too rarely reflected an overall perspective. All too frequently the focus has been on variants found in particular manuscripts or editions. This is true for even the most fundamental aspects of textual criticism; when identifying the text type of a manuscript it is all too easy to overlook the fact that the Byzantine Imperial text and the Alexandrian Egyptian text, to take two examples that in theory are diametrically opposed to each other, actually exhibit a remarkable degree of agreement, perhaps as much as 80 percent! Textual critics themselves, and New Testament specialists even more so, not to mention laypersons, tend to be fascinated by differences and to forget how many of them may be due to chance or to normal scribal tendencies, and how rarely significant variants occur — yielding to the common danger of failing to see the forest for the trees.

It is quite easy to demonstrate that **the amount of agreement among the editions** of the New Testament we have been discussing is greater — far greater — than has generally been recognized. Table 1 gives a count of the verses in which there is complete agreement among the six editions of Tischen-

55. Cf. pp. 37ff.

dorf, Westcott-Hort, von Soden, Vogels, Merk, and Bover with the text of Nestle-Aland[25] (apart from orthographical differences).

Table 1.   Variant-free verses in the New Testament

Book	Total Number of Verses	Variant-Free Verses Total	Percentage
Matthew	1071	642	59.9
Mark	678	306	45.1
Luke	1151	658	57.2
John	869	450	51.8
Acts	1006	677	67.3
Romans	433	327	75.5
1 Corinthians	437	331	75.7
2 Corinthians	256	200	78.1
Galatians	149	114	76.5
Ephesians	155	118	76.1
Philippians	104	73	70.2
Colossians	95	69	72.6
1 Thessalonians	89	61	68.5
2 Thessalonians	47	34	72.3
1 Timothy	113	92	81.4
2 Timothy	83	66	79.5
Titus	46	33	71.7
Philemon	25	19	76.0
Hebrews	303	234	77.2
James	108	66	61.1
1 Peter	105	70	66.6
2 Peter	61	32	52.5
1 John	105	76	72.4
2 John	13	8	61.5
3 John	15	11	73.3
Jude	25	18	72.0
Revelation	405	214	52.8
Total	**7947**	**4999**	**62.9**

Thus in nearly two-thirds of the New Testament text the seven editions of the Greek New Testament which we have reviewed are in complete accord, with no differences other than in orthographical details (e.g., the spelling of names, etc.). Verses in which any one of the seven editions differs by a single word are not counted. This result is quite amazing, demonstrating a far greater agreement among the Greek texts of the New Testament during the past century than textual scholars would have suspected.

A further general inference may be drawn from the above list with regard to the amount of agreement among the seven editions by individual writings. In the Gospels, Acts, and Revelation the agreement is less, while in the letters it is much greater. For another perspective on the data, table 2, which shows the incidence of **disagreements**, may be instructive. It compares the actual number of variants from the Nestle-Aland[25] text in the six editions reviewed (first column) with their relative frequency per printed page of the Nestle edition (second column). In the first column it is particularly noticeable that the

Table 2. Frequency of variants in the New Testament

Book	Total Variants	Variants Per Page	Book	Total Variants	Variants Per Page
Matthew	567	6.8	1 Timothy	25	2.9
Mark	556	10.3	2 Timothy	17	2.8
Luke	637	6.9	Titus	9	2.3
John	567	8.5	Philemon	9	5.1
Acts	395	4.2	Hebrews	71	2.9
Romans	102	2.9	James	50	5.6
1 Corinthians	111	3.5	1 Peter	51	5.7
2 Corinthians	61	2.8	2 Peter	39	6.5
Galatians	35	3.3	1 John	27	2.8
Ephesians	33	2.9	2 John	6	4.5
Philippians	19	2.5	3 John	4	3.2
Colossians	26	3.4	Jude	10	4.2
1 Thessalonians	29	4.1	Revelation	229	5.1
2 Thessalonians	13	3.1			

Gospels, Acts, and Revelation stand apart from the rest of the New Testament with regard to the number of variants in the editions. This is due to the nature of the manuscript tradition: in the Gospels it reflects largely though not exclusively the great number of witnesses, in Acts the considerable differences between two text types, and in Revelation the uncertainty of a relatively late tradition. Yet this impression is deceptive: the differences in the number of variants is not due solely to these factors, but also quite simply to the different lengths of the writings themselves. Therefore the second column has been added to relate the number of variants to the lengths of the individual New Testament writings. The figures are still averages (i.e., not every page has the precise number of variants indicated — some have more, and some have fewer), but the picture now appears quite differently: the Gospels still lead, but the Catholic letters (some of which show more variants to a page than Revelation, or even than Acts) and even the Pauline letters show a greater degree of variation than the numbers alone would suggest. The instances of variation are counted here individually, resulting in relatively higher numbers.

So much for the editions and texts of the past. What of the present scene where the reader of the Greek New Testament now meets the new text of Nestle-Aland[26] and the text of *GNT*[3] which is identical with it? By this we mean the text officially recognized by both the United Bible Societies and the Catholic church (a significantly new factor in the present scene; cf. the *Guiding Principles* and *Guidelines* agreed upon in 1968 and 1987 between the Vatican and the United Bible Societies). Whether the student uses *The Greek New Testament (GNT)* in the third revised edition or the Nestle-Aland in its twenty-sixth edition (the Greek edition, the Greek-English edition, the Greek-German edition, or the Greek-Latin edition, or in the *Synopsis Quattuor Evangeliorum* or the Greek-English *Synopsis of the Four Gospels* edited by Aland), the text is the same, however

much the format and the critical apparatus may differ.[56] How was the **new text** formed?

The beginnings of this text go back to the late 1940s. This was when Aland began his association with the Nestle edition (the twenty-first edition of 1952 was the first to have his name in the preface). His first assignment was to verify the data in the apparatus,[57] and at the same time to reexamine the text itself and prepare for a revision of it — this with the explicit approval of Erwin Nestle, who had consistently affirmed the necessity of the task but with equal consistency shrank from it in respect for his father. Considerable progress had already been made when in 1955, on the initiative of Translations Secretary Eugene A. Nida of the American Bible Society, an international committee was established to prepare an edition of the Greek New Testament designed especially to meet the needs of several hundred Bible translation committees. At that time (as also today) there were programs under way in modern national languages throughout the world to make translations of the New Testament more easily understood, whether by revising earlier versions or by making completely fresh translations from the original texts. In younger churches the existing translations were usually the work of pioneer missionaries, and frequently enough they were also the first printed books in the language. Inevitably the traces of these origins in the translations became a source of embarrassment in time, when cultural and linguistic growth of the peoples or tribes produced radical changes. Consequently in most languages at least revisions of Bible translations were (and are) long overdue, if only to satisfy a sense of pride in a text prepared by national Christian translators. These translation committees had little concern for textual criticism in the academic sense. They were interested in a reliable Greek text, with variants noted only where the text is uncertain or where they are of special importance for translators and interpreters. They also wanted to know clearly and precisely the claims to originality these variants might have, and the degree of doubt or confidence they deserve in comparison to the printed text. To adapt the form and function of the critical apparatus most effectively to the purposes of this intended group of users, a new and special apparatus was added showing the punctuation found not only in the various Greek editions (cf. plate 12), but also in the more important of the modern translations. From the beginning a commentary was planned to explain for the readers not only the decisions of the editorial committee, but also the reasoning which led to them.

The scholars invited to participate in the editorial committee for this Greek New Testament were Matthew Black of St. Andrews, Scotland, Bruce Manning Metzger of Princeton, Allen Paul Wikgren of Chicago, and Kurt Aland of Münster in Westphalia. With the full understanding of his colleagues, Aland continued to work on the new Nestle, thus participating simultaneously in both

---

56. These aspects are discussed on pp. 44ff.
57. Cf. p. 20.

the editorial responsibilities and the practical management of two different (and at least partly competitive) editions. The committee met annually in working sessions extending from four to six weeks for a critical review of materials prepared by themselves and their colleagues in New York, Münster, and elsewhere, and to decide on necessary textual changes. It was several years before the sponsoring Bible Societies (American, Scottish, and Württemberg [now German]) were joined in the undertaking by the Netherlands and British Bible Societies. Both of the latter societies made significant contributions, and the undertaking received broader recognition. The support of the British and Foreign Bible Society was particularly significant under the circumstances; it had been preparing its own edition with the same goals as *GNT*, and had already published several fascicles of a *Greek-English Diglot for the Use of Translators* (edited by Kilpatrick of Oxford). Giving its support to this undertaking simply expressed a basic recognition that the text of the *GNT*, as far as it had been completed, was superior to that of the diglot edition. The publication of the fascicles was accordingly discontinued.

What, then, was the text of *The Greek New Testament* like?

Comparative data from the period 1962-1963 for the Gospels in *GNT* and the new Nestle show the following number of differences from the old Nestle (i.e., the twenty-fifth edition):

	New Nestle	GNT
Matthew	142	150
Mark	110	137
Luke	109	136
John	133	172
Total	**494**	**595**

The incidence of agreement in differences from the old Nestle is quite high, but so is also the incidence of disagreements.

	Agreements	Disagreements
Matthew	103	86
Mark	85	77
Luke	82	81
John	93	119
Total	363	363

Naturally these figures reflect only an early stage. When the first edition of *The Greek New Testament* appeared in 1966 the situation was again quite changed.

In the interim the editorial committee developed a much greater degree of consensus than when they first assembled — an almost inevitable result of their spending about 180 hours a year together in thoroughgoing discussions of textual matters (not to mention the hours spent in preparation before and in review afterward). But this made Aland's position increasingly awkward, because to the extent that the proposals based on his revision of the Nestle text were adopted, the differences between the two editions were reduced. And further,

in the committee discussions Aland received as much as he gave, frequently reconsidering his own proposals for revising Nestle-Aland[25] and adopting the suggestions of others. A critical step toward the convergence of the two editions occurred in the deliberations on the second edition of *GNT* which was published in 1968 (Arthur Vööbus had meanwhile withdrawn from the editorial committee before the publication of the first edition and Carlo Maria Martini, then rector of the Pontifical Biblical Institute and later archbishop of Milan and cardinal, was added). Only a few changes were introduced, but their importance was fundamental: the editorial committee (or more precisely its majority) decided to abandon the theories of Westcott-Hort and the "Western non-interpolations."[58] as Kurt Aland had urged consistently in personal discussion and also in numerous essays. This finally cleared the way for coordinating the two editions. The result of the deliberations may be cited from the preface to the third edition of *GNT*:

> In a series of meetings the Committee . . . undertook a thorough review of the text of the First Edition by carefully considering not only a number of suggestions made by specialists in the field of New Testament studies, but also numerous recommendations resulting from the experience of the members of the Committee as they worked with the text of the First Edition. The greater part of these suggestions for further modification came from Kurt Aland, who had been making a detailed analysis of changes proposed for the 26th edition of the Nestle-Aland text. A number of these were textual alterations which had not been previously discussed by the Committee in their work on the First Edition. As a result of the Committee's discussions, more than five hundred changes have been introduced into this Third Edition. [p. viii]

In this way *The Greek New Testament* and Nestle-Aland[26], originally two quite independent editions, approached a close degree of unity with regard to their text — or more precisely, their wording.[59] There remained, nevertheless, considerable differences between their texts in orthography, punctuation,[60] paragraphing, and so forth, to say nothing of their general format, which will be discussed later.

The unification became complete when the Württemberg Bible Society abandoned plans for an independent edition, deciding that *GNT* and Nestle-Aland[26] should not only offer a common text, but that it should be the responsibility of the same editorial committee: Kurt Aland, Black, Martini, Metzger, and Wikgren. These five names should actually be expanded to seven: Nida should certainly be added, for he not only initiated the undertaking but took an active part in all the editorial committee sessions (making substantial contributions), and Barbara Aland also deserves mention for her significant participa-

---

58. Cf. p. 37.

59. It is occasionally stated that Nestle-Aland[26] adopted the text already at hand in the *GNT,* but this misconstrues the facts: the late publication of Nestle-Aland[26] was due to the amount of time required for preparing its critical apparatus.

60. These differences are eliminated in the revised *GNT*[3], which adopted the punctuation and orthography of Nestle-Aland[26] except in the introduction of direct discourse.

tion in Kurt Aland's contributions. Further, Barbara Aland and Johannes Karavidopoulos of Salonika have now become members of the editorial committee to prepare the fourth edition of *GNT*.

A "committee text" of this kind is occasionally regarded as problematical, and at times it may be so. In a number of instances it represents a compromise, for none of the editors can claim a perfect acceptance record of all recommendations offered.[61]

On the whole each of the editors is probably satisfied that the new text represents the best that can be achieved in the present state of knowledge. In **evaluating the new text** from a philological view the objection can admittedly be raised that the procedure followed (of textual decisions based on shifting majorities) is anomalous; one of the basic principles of philology is that a critical text should be edited by a single responsible editor following consistent principles. This objection is quite reasonable, but it is not relevant to the present situation. Editorial methodology for a classical Greek (or Latin) text proceeds essentially by constructing a stemma to demonstrate the mutual relationships of its extant manuscripts, and then reconstructing the original text on the basis of insights gained from a complete view of the history of the text (distinguishing daughter manuscripts from their parent exemplars, and eliminating them from further consideration). But the construction of such a stemma for the New Testament text is inconceivable either now or in the foreseeable future, not only because the number of witnesses to the New Testament text is incomparably greater than for any profane Greek text (in addition to more than fifty-four hundred Greek manuscripts there are also early versions and quotations by Church Fathers), but also because of basic factors characteristic of the transmission of the New Testament text. Due to the constant change of relationships among manuscripts, each New Testament text requires its own individual treatment with a fresh consideration of not only the external but of the internal factors as well.

The label of "eclecticism" which has frequently been applied to this method is not strictly appropriate, and suggests false associations. Perhaps the modern method of New Testament textual criticism may be more aptly described as a local-genealogical method (i.e., applying to each passage individually the approach used by classical philology for a whole tradition). When editorial responsibility is not borne by a single scholar working alone but shared by several scholars (assuming that each is duly qualified with the necessary knowledge and skills, and is at home with the history of New Testament textual transmission), the deliberations of such a committee promise to issue in a far

---

61. This may be inferred (at least to a degree, because not all the committee members were equally quick to write) from the dissenting notes included in *A Textual Commentary on the Greek New Testament*, a volume compiled by Metzger at the request of the editorial committee, utilizing the minutes of the committee sessions (London and New York: 1971; 2nd ed., 1975). Of the total of thirty dissenting votes, seventeen represent Metzger alone; eight, Metzger and Wikgren; two, Wikgren alone; one, Metzger and Martini; one, Metzger and Kurt Aland; and one, Aland alone. While a certain tendency may be detected here in the distribution of majorities and minorities, the variety of combinations also witnesses to the lack of any consistent lines of division.

more thorough evaluation of viewpoints and possibilities even if, or rather precisely because, each of the editors represents a different background and perspective.

Furthermore, a peculiar kind of responsibility is involved in preparing an edition of the Greek New Testament. It is not just any random text, but the very foundation for New Testament exegesis by theologians of all confessions and denominations throughout the world. Further, this Greek text serves as the base for new translations as well as for revisions of earlier translations in modern languages, i.e., it is in effect the foundation to which the whole contemporary Church looks in formulating expressions of faith. The full awesome weight of this responsibility is better shared by a committee: a single scholar simply could not bear it.

In any event, the new text is a reality, and as the text distributed by the United Bible Societies *and* by the corresponding offices of the Roman Catholic Church (an inconceivable situation until quite recently), it has rapidly become the commonly accepted text for research and study in universities and churches. This holds also for translation projects in modern national languages (cf. the *Guiding Principles* formulated in 1968 by the Vatican and the United Bible Societies and reaffirmed as *Guidelines* in 1987, which prescribe its exclusive use). Naturally many scholars responsible for theological education (in all the church traditions) will be hesitant to relinquish the editions of the text they have grown accustomed to through years of use (whether Nestle-Aland[25] or any other edition). But this process can no more be halted here than for the synopses, where the Huck-Lietzmann edition may be attractive for its low price and simplicity of format, but the questions raised in scholarly circles about the text of this old familiar edition (Opitz edited it with a distinct bias) presage its disuse in the forseeable future. It remains to be seen how popular among users the new edition of Huck's *Synopsis* by Greeven and the editions by Orchard and Boismard will be, but the textual questions will undoubtedly remain.

Of course the new text itself is not a static entity. The members of the editorial committee as well as all others responsible for the edition agree on the tentative nature of the publication. Every change in it is open to challenge — requiring only that arguments for proposed changes be convincing. The publication of Nestle-Aland[26] has made the evidence needed for proposing changes openly available. Despite the limitations of space, its critical apparatus offers a range of material surpassing all previous editions, including Tischendorf and von Soden (because it provides a complete review of the manuscript discoveries of recent generations). It also provides surprising insights about earlier editors. It lists in an appendix all the differences between the text and the significant editions since Tischendorf (including the manual editions of the twentieth century) in such a way that the manuscript evidence for each may be conveniently reviewed. Consequently, any further development of the text must begin from Nestle-Aland.[26] It remains to be seen what the next developments will be. Rash decisions should always be avoided. Many will undoubtedly feel strongly inclined to improve it here and there. This temptation should be resisted despite the in-

sinuation that the new text (despite the competition of other editions) is merely
another new Textus Receptus, comparable to the text of our ancestors from the
sixteenth to the eighteenth centuries. This was practically the situation with the
"old Nestle," which dominated the scene despite rival editions. Its basic difference from the text of the 16th to the 18th centuries is that the new text is
not based on a small group of manuscripts (selected by chance, mostly of late
date and poor quality), but on a review of all the evidence that is in any way
relevant to establishing the original text, whether Greek manuscripts as early as
the second century, or versions, or writings of early Church Fathers in various
languages — always examining the original texts while constantly reviewing
the external factors which affect the value of their testimony.

One of the distinct weaknesses in the earlier twentieth-century editions
was their dependence on secondary (and often even tertiary) sources for the data
in their critical apparatuses. This is why a thoroughgoing revision of GNT[3] is
now under way. In this Fourth Edition all the data in the apparatus will be verified against primary sources, and the number of passages to be provided with a
critical apparatus will also be reviewed (resulting in some considerable changes).
One of the reasons why Nestle-Aland[26] took until 1979 to be published (a fact
regretted by none so much as its editors) was that it accomplished in a single
step a goal not yet achieved by GNT in three editions and fourteen years (and
it will be yet several more years before GNT[4] appears), namely adapting the
apparatus to the new text and verifying it in detail against primary sources. But
even here results are only tentative. Despite all precautions, human error cannot
be entirely eliminated in the long sequence of steps leading from the collation of
individual manuscripts to the correlation of groups of witnesses and their arrangement in an apparatus as concisely as possible, and then on through the various
stages of printing, proofreading, and corrections (e.g., the seventh printing of
Nestle-Aland[26] in 1987 corrected the printing errors and oversights noted in earlier
printings). Before the next revised edition appears a series of further studies
will be made. Attention is now concentrating on the data of patristic citations
and of the papyri, but planning and preparations are under way for the addition
of new minuscules among the "constant witnesses" and a more extensive consideration of the lectionaries, together with omitting the witness of uncials with a
purely Byzantine text. The selection of variants should also be reviewed — but such revisions can only come gradually, considering the enormous amount of work involved.

4. A COMPARISON OF THE MAJOR EDITIONS

This section may at first appear irrelevant and tiresome to the reader of this book
who has a copy of Nestle-Aland[26] or GNT[3] and relies on either or both for New
Testament studies (since they are mutually complementary and not exclusive).
But these are not enough. The editions of Constantin von Tischendorf and Hermann Freiherr von Soden should be more than mere technical terms; they should
be useful reference tools as occasion demands. They are indispensable for spe-

cialized studies on the transmission of particular texts and passages because (unfortunately) they still represent the most detailed collection of variants (von Soden) and the most accurate presentation of the evidence for them (Tischendorf) available today. While a comparison of the critical apparatuses of Tischendorf and Nestle-Aland[26] shows that the latter offers all the variants cited in Tischendorf (and even more), yet with all its advances Nestle-Aland[26] is only a pocket edition (cf. pp. 38f.).

Besides being familiar with the editions of Tischendorf and von Soden, the student should also meet and use the work of Brooke Foss Westcott and Fenton John Anthony Hort. Sample pages of these editions are shown in plate 12, together with corresponding pages from *GNT*[3] and Nestle-Aland[26] to illustrate the special characteristics of their respective formats.

The display of sample pages of these different editions (plate 12) is not intended simply to highlight their parallel features; Nestle-Aland[26] and *GNT*, not to mention Westcott-Hort, have a relatively large proportion of text to the page, while Tischendorf's copious apparatus leaves space for only a few lines of text, and von Soden stands roughly in between. The page number of the sample for each of the editions is indicative: in Tischendorf it is 729, in Westcott-Hort 185, in von Soden 387, while in *GNT* it is 316, and in Nestle-Aland[26] it is 244 (the difference between the last two is due partly to the large size of the type in *GNT*). After several tests it appeared that the pages selected would be the most appropriate, because Luke 24 is useful today as a test for determining where an edition or a textual critic stands.

The **Westcott-Hort** edition (plate 12) requires only the briefest comment. Note that in the text itself a part of verse 36 is placed in brackets, as is also the whole of verse 40. These are two instances of the "Western non-interpolations" that have already been mentioned several times, i.e., later additions to the text in the view of Westcott-Hort. According to the Nestle-Aland[26] apparatus the evidence for this in verse 36 is its omission by D it, i.e., by Codex Bezae Cantabrigiensis and the Old Latins; the omission in verse 40 is further supported by the Sinaitic and Curetonian Syriac — and by nothing more. The entire Greek tradition (beginning with $\mathfrak{p}^{75}$ in the early third century), together with all the early versions, the Church Fathers, and so forth, attests both texts with no hint of a suspicion against their authenticity. In the outer margin of Westcott-Hort is found a group of "alternative readings," all actually representing secondary readings, with the signs ⌐ ¬ in the text indicating the extent of a substitution (vv. 32, 37), and the sign ⊤ in the text indicating the place of an addition to the text (vv. 32, 42). Where a marginal reading is enclosed by ⊣ ⊢ (vv. 32, 42) Westcott-Hort intended to distinguish it as belonging to an inferior class of readings, somewhat interesting but to be rejected. In verses 39, 42, and 46 the sign *Ap* in the margin indicates that the passage is discussed in the appendix. To evaluate the marginal readings it is necessary to go to the apparatus of Nestle-Aland[26] (and to Tischendorf or von Soden for further information). The reading ἦν ἡμῶν κεκαλυμμένη enclosed by ⊣ ⊢ in verse 32

is attested only by D and a few Sahidic manuscripts, and the similarly marked reading in verse 42 (not shown in the Nestle-Aland²⁶ page, plate 12) by Θ Ψ $f^1 f^{13}$ the Majority text, and a great number of versions and Church Fathers; neither can seriously claim originality. The addition of ἐν ἡμῖν in the margin at verse 32 is a good example of the changes since Westcott-Hort; Nestle-Aland²⁶ and *GNT* place it in the text within brackets, although the evidence for its omission has been substantially strengthened since Westcott-Hort by 𝔓⁷⁵. The evidence for replacing πτοηθέντες by θροηθέντες in verse 37 (cf. Nestle-Aland²⁶ apparatus) has also been strengthened, again by 𝔓⁷⁵, yet the combined attestation of 𝔓⁷⁵ B and 1241 remains inadequate. For more about the marginal apparatus, cf. pp. 563-65 in the Westcott-Hort text volume and the references there to sections in the introduction.

Tischendorf's edition offers a complete contrast. The critical apparatus here is predominant, occupying nearly four-fifths of the page. This is partly due, of course, to Tischendorf's use of the lemma system (repeating the text in full in the apparatus before indicating the variant forms, each one in full). Further, he frequently gives patristic quotations in full and supplements the data with additional comments in Latin. Consequently, the actual number of variants treated is not as large as the length of the apparatus would suggest: the sample page shows a total of seventeen in Tischendorf to twelve in Nestle-Aland²⁶ for the same verses. But the actual difference is even less because Tischendorf treats Nestle-Aland's ⌐ in verse 27 in four separate parts, so that the actual ratio is fourteen to twelve. Besides this, Nestle-Aland offers a further variant that was unknown to Tischendorf: the substitution of εἰς τὴν βασιλείαν for εἰς τὴν δόξαν in the first hand of 𝔓⁷⁵.

The variants cited in Tischendorf beyond those in Nestle-Aland may all be classed as irrelevant to a pocket edition: the spelling of Μώσεως for Μωυσέως in verse 27, and the omission of τά from the phrase τὰ περὶ ἑαυτοῦ in the same verse by the uncial L and several minuscules collated by Frederick Henry Ambrose Scrivener (Yˢᶜʳ, "sunt codd. a F. H. Scrivener conlati"; cf. p. xxii of the edition), as well as the fluctuation among manuscripts between ἑαυτοῦ and αὐτοῦ (assuming that αυτου may always be read as αὐτοῦ). Verses 26 and 28 have nothing similar, but in verse 29 there is a change in the tense of παραβιάζομαι found in M P (two less significant uncials of the Koine text type) and a change from the imperative μεῖνον to the infinitive μεῖναι found in the minuscule 69. Neither of these variants has sufficient attestation to be of significance for the text.

The meaning of the symbols and abbreviations used by Tischendorf is not always immediately apparent, and may require reference to volume 1, pp. ix-xvi; especially pp. xxi-xxii; and volume 2, pp. iii-iv. But even this will often be inadequate because the symbols for the manuscripts have since changed. This is true not only for the uncials, but even more so for the minuscules identified by arabic numerals.

For the Gospels the same numbers have always been used for the same manuscripts from the beginning, but Tischendorf's numbers for the minuscules

beginning with Acts are different now because Caspar René Gregory introduced a completely new system (marking a new historic development).[62] As a consequence it is necessary to refer to a comparative table of symbols, such as the index of sigla in Kurt Aland, *Kurzgefasste Liste der griechischen Handschriften des Neuen Testaments*.[63] Otherwise, confusions may easily arise, as it has even in scholarly publications where the authors have overlooked this basic rule in citing Tischendorf. For the uncials, too, care is needed, even in the Gospels. Although the symbols for the "alphabet uncials" (i.e., uncials represented by uppercase roman letter symbols: A B C D etc.) remain unchanged, the generations since Johann Jakob Wettstein saw an accretion of qualifying details which Gregory finally cleared away. Tischendorf's use of capitals with multiple superscripts (especially I, O, T, and W, but also Θ) should be carefully noted, and whenever his information is cited it should be confirmed (especially for the Hebrew symbols) with the concordant sigla lists mentioned above.

Much in Tischendorf's apparatus may simply be ignored. For example, he regularly cites printed editions in support of variants, e.g., in verse 27 (third from last line) for the reading αὐτοῦ: ς^e Gb Sz Ln Ti. This means that the Textus Receptus in Elzevir's edition (ς^e), Johann Jakob Griesbach's edition of 1827 (Gb), Johannes Martin Augustinus Scholz in his edition of 1830-1836 (Sz), Karl Lachmann's edition of 1842-1850 (Ln), and Tischendorf in his edition of 1859 (Ti) read αὐτοῦ; such information is quite dated today and of no value. Tischendorf's data on the readings of the Latin versions are in general still valuable today (although the editions which he used have mostly been superseded), but for the Eastern versions it is practically useless, antiquated by new discoveries, new editions, and new insights. For the Church Fathers one should always first ascertain whether new critical editions have appeared since Tischendorf, and use them to monitor the texts.

As this may sound rather negative, especially to the beginning scholar, we should recall once more what a tremendous achievement this edition represents, remembering that it should be judged by the standards of a century ago and not by those of today. In their time Tischendorf's announcements were the latest discoveries. The fact that his edition is still counted among the indispensable tools of New Testament scholarship a century later is the best possible witness to the stature of his achievement. And further, this work in its entirety was not only characterized by unexcelled standards of accuracy — it was the work of a single man whose death in his fifty-ninth year (his first stroke came when he was fifty-eight and was rapidly followed by others) was brought on by his strenuous labors in New Testament textual research. His discovery of Codex Sinaiticus made him world famous, but this was only one of the many important manuscripts he found. At the age of twenty-five he was the first to decipher Codex Ephraemi Syri Rescriptus,[64] a palimpsest[65] which had defied the efforts

62. Cf. pp. 73ff.
63. *ANTF* 1 (1963): 321-333.
64. Cf. p. 109.
65. Cf. pp. 12 (plate 6), 80 (plate 18), 109, 113.

of many scholars before him. While it is true that he damaged not only this manuscript but other palimpsests as well by using chemical reagents, this was the most advanced technology at the time. The use of ultraviolet photography, which had not yet been invented, now enables us to identify the text despite the damage resulting from the chemical reagent, only increasing our admiration for what Tischendorf was able to accomplish with the primitive equipment at his disposal.

Von Soden's edition, its significance, and its limitations, has already been discussed.[66] Anyone meeting it for the first time in the sample page (plate 12) will be somewhat surprised, first by the division of the apparatus into three parts, and (despite being forewarned) by its symbols and its system of designating manuscripts. The triple division of the apparatus has both advantages and disadvantages. The variant readings for every verse have to be looked for in three different places (and then reassembled in their proper sequence), although it is usually adequate to examine only the first two apparatuses — but it is this "usually" that raises the problem. When a pericope or a particular passage is under examination, *all* the variant readings in the tradition are of interest.

Von Soden's system can be explained only by its origins and its basic structural pattern, but for practical purposes even a regular user will always need some supplementary reference works (von Soden's notes on his format and apparatus in the preface to the text in volume 2 are quite inadequate, although anyone using the edition should certainly read them; they illustrate its limitations quite clearly). To make things easier, Friedrich Krüger published in 1927 a *Schlüssel zu von Sodens Schriften des Neuen Testaments*. Benedikt Kraft, *Die Zeichen für die wichtigeren Handschriften des griechischen Neuen Testaments*, had already appeared a year earlier.[67] Both books are unfortunately now out of print. Both of these aids arrange the manuscripts according to von Soden's groupings and show the corresponding Gregory numbers, but both are incomplete and require the supplementary use of Sigla Index II (correlating von Soden and Gregory) in the above-mentioned *Kurzgefasste Liste*.[68] This index gives the symbols in numerical order (and also in von Soden's original order) to facilitate rapid reference. The intricacy of von Soden's system of symbols is due to his Germanic idealism in attempting to combine in each manuscript's symbol a description of its contents, its date, and its textual character.

Von Soden indicated the contents of a manuscript by prefixing a Greek letter to its number: δ (διαθήκη) for a manuscript containing the whole New Testament, ε (εὐαγγέλιον) for a Four Gospels manuscript, and α (ἀπόστολος) for one containing other parts of the New Testament. Thus there are three series in which von Soden arranged his known manuscripts. Unfortunately Revelation was often lacking in the manuscripts von Soden classed as δ (complete New

---

66. Cf. pp. 22f.
67. (Freiburg/B., 1927; 3rd ed., 1955).
68. *ANTF* 1 (1963): 334-349.

Testaments), and the manuscripts of the second part of the New Testament (α) were quite varied in their content, mostly representing either just the Apostolos (Acts and the Catholic letters) or the Pauline letters.

Von Soden also wished to include the date of a manuscript in its symbol: the third numeral from the end was assigned this function; e.g., δ150 for a manuscript of the eleventh century, δ250 for a manuscript of the twelfth century, δ350 for a manuscript of the thirteenth century, and δ50 (to δ99) for a manuscript of the tenth century. The plan was ingenious, but it had certain weaknesses and blind spots: the period before the tenth century was not accommodated (von Soden assigned to it the numbers δ1 to δ49), but even more awkward was the lack of a firm date for most of the minuscules. What would happen if a manuscript were assigned a new date? To preserve the system, it would have to be assigned a new symbol (which is precisely what von Soden did on occasion). Further, the system as observed for the δ-manuscripts could not be applied without adaptation to ε-manuscripts. There were too many ε-manuscripts from before the tenth century to be accommodated by the numbers from 1 to 99, so that after ε1 to ε99 von Soden continued with ε01 to ε099. Manuscripts of the tenth century began with ε1000, going on to ε1099, after which the eleventh-century manuscripts returned to the pattern beginning with ε100.

Finally, it should also be mentioned that von Soden treated commentary manuscripts as a special group, indicating their authors by capital letters: A for Antiochene commentaries (Chrysostom on Matthew, Victor of Antioch on Mark, Titus of Bostra on Luke), $A^{πϱ}$ for Andreas the Presbyter's commentary on the Apostolos, Av for Andreas of Caesarea's commentary on Revelation, Aϱ for Arethas' commentary on Revelation. When the number of commentary manuscripts was sufficiently large, these were further distinguished by their century on the pattern of the δ, ε, and α manuscripts, and if an author such as Theophylact commented on several books, these were also distinguished, e.g., $Θ^ε$ for Theophylact's commentary on the Gospels, $Θ^π$ for his commentary on the Pauline letters, and then there is also Θδ for Theodoret's commentary on Paul. In addition to all the complexities already posed by the δ, ε, α system — quite frequently with four figure numbers — the alphabetical prefixes require constant vigilance. The slightest slip could lead to utter confusion.

But now let us transpose von Soden's first apparatus on the sample page into modern symbols.

In Luke 24:27 there is first the attestation for τί ἦν. K means the Koine text, H the Egyptian (Hesychian) text. Ta is Tatian. The Koine text and Tatian omit τί ἦν, which is found in the H manuscripts cited. These are $H^{δ2}$, which designates ℵ; δ48f, or 33 and L (019); bo (Bohairic). Along with these witnesses of the H group are found witnesses of the Jerusalem text, including a member of the subgroup $I^{α050}$, or Θ; the entire subgroup $I^{ηa}$, or 1, 1582, 2193; and one member of the subgroup $I^{ηb288}$, or 22. It should be noted that the data are inaccurate for 1582 and 2193, in both of which only the first hand attests τί ἦν and

a second hand has deleted or erased it. Pa is the Palestinian lectionary 342.[69] Thus the total attestation reported for the insertion of τί ἦν is ℵ L Θ 1, 22, 33, 1582, 2193 bo. Nestle-Aland's apparatus has here ℵ L Θ f^1 33, 892 pc bo, which expands the number of minuscules cited by the use of f^1 to represent a group. At first glance it is obvious that the overwhelming majority of witnesses does not support the insertion. And yet in contrast to the other editions represented in the sample pages, which omit τί ἦν, von Soden prints the insertion in his text, albeit in brackets. Further, why he placed [τί ἦν] before τὰ περὶ ἑαυτοῦ is inexplicable, for none of the manuscripts cited by von Soden reads it here — all of them have it before ἐν πάσαις ταῖς γραφαῖς. Is this purely arbitrary, or is it merely an example of a simple error?

The second variant in the first apparatus is another example of how von Soden's judgment differs from other editions: the omission of ἤδη in verse 29 (by the witnesses not listed) versus its insertion by the witnesses listed. The other editions include ἤδη in the text without a challenge. Von Soden places it in brackets — again revealing a characteristic arbitrariness in determining his text. For the details of the data: in the *H* group, δ1 is B; δ2 is ℵ; δ6 is Ψ; δ48f is 33 + L (019); δ1002 is 0139; in the *I* group, α286[70] is 21; η^a again is 1, 1582, 2193; η^{b288} is 22; ι^{b1211} is 124; β^{a121} is 348; β^{b1349} is 1579 (the apparatus has ^{c} for ^{b}, a typographical error); pa and bo as in the previous variant; lat^{exc} c l indicates the Latin witnesses apart from (exc, or exceptus) c and l; sy^p is the Syriac Peshitta. The Greek attestation cited in von Soden may accordingly be transcribed in modern symbols as ℵ B L Ψ 0139, 1, 21, 22, 33, 124, 348, 1579, 1582, 2193. Comparing this again with the Nestle apparatus we find the omission of ἤδω (not recorded in von Soden) attested by A D W f^{13} 𝔐 c l sy$^{s.c.h}$, and its insertion in the text attested by 𝔭^{75} ℵ B L Ψ 0139 f^1 33 pc lat sy^p bo. The pocket Nestle is superior to the larger edition of von Soden here in both explicitness and clarity.

We have dealt with only two variants in the first apparatus from the sample page of von Soden's edition. There is no need for a similar treatment of the eighteen variants in the second apparatus, not to mention the fifty-four variants in the third apparatus, because these two examples should suffice as representative for the readers of this book. The reader who wishes further examples may undertake transcribing the attestation of other variants from von Soden's symbols into modern terms, using the aids mentioned above. The difficulties involved will be only too apparent, and even if they are successfully surmounted (although the amount of skill and experience required would make this improbable) there is still no assurance that the results will be reliable because of the varieties of inaccuracies found in von Soden's apparatus, as we have seen. Furthermore, the minuscules cited by von Soden are by no means all of real

---

69. Cf. von Soden, 2:xvii; also 1:2178.
70. The complete form is *I* ^{α286}; in this group the symbol α occurs with another meaning independent of the classification system for manuscripts by content (where α indicates Apostolos). There should be no real confusion here (minuscules in the apparatus to the Gospels must belong either to the δ or the ε classification: the manuscript here is ε286); yet vigilance is eternally necessary!

significance for the history of the text because so many of them are of secondary value.

Much of the above discussion has been rather complicated — perhaps too complicated for the beginning reader of this book — because many of the things mentioned and many of the terms used are new and unfamiliar. But this has been inevitable in describing the three editions under review; we will refer to them only rarely as we proceed. The reader should not be unduly concerned for the moment with the details and the difficulties — at least a first impression and a general appreciation have been gained. Later, after completing this book and gaining familiarity with the Greek New Testament, the reader may return to these pages and reread them. Even those who use the Nestle-Aland editions or the *GNT* exclusively should have some knowledge of the great editions of the past and of their characteristics. It will reassure them as they use the *GNT* or Nestle-Aland (whatever their perspective or purpose) that these tools fully satisfy the high standards generally required for the academic and exegetical disciplines (although not for specialized research).

While **Nestle-Aland**[26] **and GNT**[3] will be of primary concern through the rest of this book, the sample pages (plate 12) permit a preliminary comparative impression of them that is possible only at this stage. When seen side by side the contrast in character and the difference in format of these two pages are immediately obvious. Nestle-Aland[26] offers thirty-two variants on the selected page, and *GNT* only one (a coincidence, because the average number is nearer two to a page).[71] Both editions have references to parallel passages: in *GNT*[3] they are in the lower margin and are restricted to a simple listing of the most important examples, while in Nestle-Aland[26] they are in the outer margin of the page and far more extensive in scope, arranged according to rules which must be understood to use them to full advantage.[72] Nestle-Aland[26] also shows the Eusebian canon numbers and chapter divisions traditional in Greek New Testament manuscripts in the inner margin of the page (although these do not appear in the sample page).[73] *GNT*[3] lacks both, but provides an apparatus of differences in punctuation found not only in editions of the Greek text but also in the principal modern language translations. This punctuation apparatus does not reproduce the actual signs found in the various editions (e.g., periods, semi-colons, commas, etc.), but indicates degrees of disjunction as "major – minor – none," so that translators in the various national languages of the younger churches (where syntactical structures are often radically different from those of European languages) can interpret the data directly. This punctuation apparatus may at times impress speakers of major international languages as almost cryptic,[74] but it should not be forgotten that frequently the information in this

---

71. It may be noted here in passing that Nestle-Aland[26] lists all the textual differences between the editions from Tischendorf to Nestle-Aland[25] in an appendix, providing a survey of the New Testament text for the past century; for further discussion, cf. pp. 256ff. The special purposes of *GNT*[3] make the inclusion of such information neither expected nor desirable.

72. Cf. pp. 253f.

73. Cf. pp. 252.

74. Cf. pp. 230f.

apparatus about the punctuation of the New Testament text is of critical importance for exegesis (the system will be revised in the fourth edition).

The most striking and also the most important difference between the
two editions is found in their critical apparatuses.

In verse 32 both place ἐν ἡμῖν in brackets (since they share the same
text). The apparatus of Nestle-Aland[26] indicates with maximum brevity that p[75]
B D c e sy[s.c] omit these two words (⌐ is the sign indicating an omission of
more than one word, the last of which is followed by the sign ⟍ , which is not
repeated in the apparatus), i.e., that the Papyrus Bodmer XIV-XV (p[75]) from
the beginning of the third century, Codex Vaticanus (B) from the fourth century,
Codex Bezae Cantabrigiensis (D) from the fifth century, the Old Latin manuscripts c and e, and also the Sinaitic and Curetonian Syriac manuscripts omit
the words ἐν ἡμῖν. This information is quite sufficient for a decision: all the
other important manuscripts not explicitly mentioned support the text. Despite
the importance of the witnesses supporting the omission, their authority is inadequate to remove ἐν ἡμῖν from the text. The words are accordingly placed in
single brackets, which is the philologists' traditional way of indicating that the
authenticity of the words is doubtful, but that the doubt is insufficient to warrant
their removal. GNT[3] first lists explicitly the witnesses which read ἐν ἡμῖν as it
stands in the text, then those which read it in other constructions, and finally
the alternatives offered by e c sy[s.c] which omit not only the words ἐν ἡμῖν but
their context as well (ἐν ἡμῖν ὡς ἐλάλει ἡμῖν) — a matter of considerable
importance in evaluating the Old Latin and Old Syriac witnesses here (dimin-
ishing their weight).

In summary, where GNT[3] has a critical apparatus it is more explicit
than Nestle-Aland[26]. But then, GNT[3] notes only one of the thirty-two variants
in Nestle-Aland[26], while the latter surveys the whole of the textual tradition
more concisely, but quite adequately for making evaluations.

One of the primary characteristics of GNT[3] is a graded evaluation given
for every passage where variants are cited (this and the punctuation apparatus
were insisted upon by Eugene A. Nida against the whole editorial committee,
if I may speak out of school, and in retrospect I believe he was right.) Each set
of variants is classified on a scale from A to D. The official definition for these
classifications is given in GNT:

> By means of the letters A, B, C, and D, enclosed within "braces" { } at the
> beginning of each set of textual variants, the Committee has sought to
> indicate the relative degree of certainty, arrived at on the basis of internal
> considerations as well as of external evidence, for the reading adopted as
> the text. The letter A signifies that the text is virtually certain, while B
> indicates that there is some degree of doubt. The letter C means that there
> is a considerable degree of doubt whether the text or the apparatus contains
> the superior reading, while D shows that there is a very high degree of
> doubt concerning the reading selected for the text.[75]

75. Pp. xii-xiii.

If a set of variants in *GNT*[3] is marked with the letter A, this means that the editors were certain that the reading printed above in the text represents the original form of the text, and that none of the variants cited in the apparatus offers it any real competition. The letter B at the beginning reflects a lesser degree of certainty on the part of the editors, but yet their consensus that the reading printed in the text has a better claim to originality than any of the variants. The letter C (as in the variant in the sample page) means that the editors found the arguments fairly equally balanced for and against the reading, and it is therefore printed in the text in single brackets. But when a set of variants is marked with the letter D, this means that only after considerable discussion did the editors decide which reading to adopt for the text. Many may believe (as the editors of *GNT* did at first) that such a classification of readings in the apparatus goes too far, prejudicing the reader's decision or influencing it unduly. But for translation committees in the younger churches and elsewhere who are the intended users of *GNT*[3] (and for many theological students as well) it cannot be seriously denied that this system answers a real need. The only question is whether the editors have not been too cautious in applying the classifications, so that a B should often be replaced by an A, a C by a B, and a D by a C (a thorough reexamination has led to a revision of these for the fourth edition of *GNT*).

So much for the differences between Nestle-Aland[26] and the *GNT*[3]. They are not limited to these major aspects, however, but extend to minor details as well. In the two sample pages it may be noted that *GNT*[3] shows only one paragraph break (at v. 28), while Nestle-Aland[26] has three (at vv. 28, 33, 36). A more adequate impression may be gained, however, from a comparison of paragraph divisions in the whole chapter (the verse numbers show where the new paragraphs begin):

GNT[3]	Nestle-Aland[26]		*GNT*[3]	Nestle-Aland[26]
23:56b	24:1		24:36	24:36
—	24:9		24:44	24:44
24:13	24:13		24:50	24:50
24:28	24:28		—	24:52
—	24:33			

This illustrates quite clearly that Nestle-Aland[26] tends far more than *GNT*[3] to replace the usual pericope divisions of the text with the original structural divisions of the text — a tendency which may be observed in greater detail elsewhere.

There were also differences in punctuation until *GNT*[3cor]. In the sample pages these are limited to the representation of direct speech. Three times (vv. 25, 29, 32) *GNT*[3] marks the beginning of direct speech with a comma followed by a capital letter (as in English usage, e.g., verse 25 εἶπεν πρὸς αὐτούς, ῏Ω ἀνόητοι etc.), where Nestle-Aland[26] has a colon and continues with a normal lowercase letter (εἶπεν πρὸς αὐτούς· ὦ ἀνόητοι etc.). It is purely coincidental that in the sample pages there are no further instances of

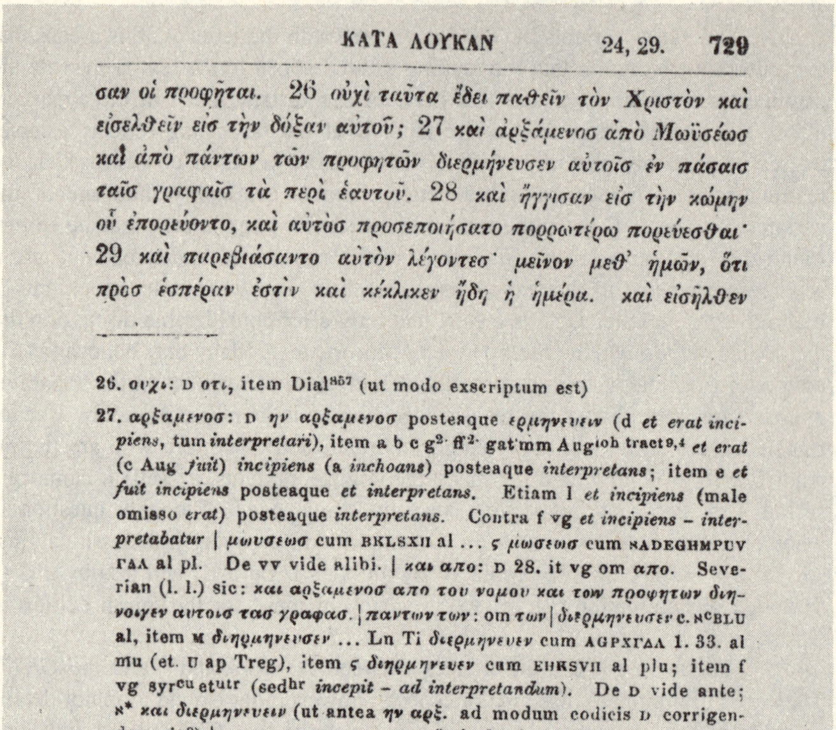

ΚΑΤΑ ΛΟΥΚΑΝ 24, 29. **729**

σαν οἱ προφῆται. 26 οὐχὶ ταῦτα ἔδει παθεῖν τὸν Χριστὸν καὶ
εἰσελθεῖν εἰσ τὴν δόξαν αὐτοῦ; 27 καὶ ἀρξάμενοσ ἀπὸ Μωϋσέωσ
καὶ ἀπὸ πάντων τῶν προφητῶν διερμήνευσεν αὐτοῖσ ἐν πάσαισ
ταῖσ γραφαῖσ τὰ περὶ ἑαυτοῦ. 28 καὶ ἤγγισαν εἰσ τὴν κώμην
οὗ ἐπορεύοντο, καὶ αὐτὸσ προσεποιήσατο πορρωτέρω πορεύεσθαι·
29 καὶ παρεβιάσαντο αὐτὸν λέγοντεσ· μεῖνον μεθ' ἡμῶν, ὅτι
πρὸσ ἑσπέραν ἐστὶν καὶ κέκλικεν ἤδη ἡ ἡμέρα. καὶ εἰσῆλθεν

26. ουχι: D οτι, item Dial^{857} (ut modo exscriptum est)

27. αρξαμενοσ: D ην αρξαμενοσ posteaque ερμηνευειν (d *et erat incipiens*, tum *interpretari*), item a b c g^{2} ff^{2} gat mm Aug$^{ioh\ tract 9,4}$ *et erat* (c Aug *fuit*) *incipiens* (a *inchoans*) posteaque *interpretans*; item e *et fuit incipiens* posteaque *et interpretans*. Etiam l *et incipiens* (male omisso *erat*) posteaque *interpretans*. Contra f vg *et incipiens – interpretabatur* | μωυσεωσ cum BKLSXΠ al ... ς μωσεωσ cum ℵADEGHMPUVΓΔΛ al pl. De vv vide alibi. | και απο: D 28. it vg om απο. Severian (l. l.) sic: και αρξαμενοσ απο του νομου και των προφητων διηνοιγεν αυτοισ τασ γραφασ. | παντων των: om των | διερμηνευσεν c. ℵ^{c}BLU al, item M διηρμηνευσεν ... Ln Ti διερμηνευεν cum AGPXΓΔΛ 1. 33. al mu (et. U ap Treg), item ς διηρμηνευεν cum EHKSVΠ al plu; item f vg syr^{cu} et^{utr} (sed^{hr} *incepit – ad interpretandum*). De D vide ante; ℵ* και διερμηνευειν (ut antea ην αρξ. ad modum codicis D corrigendum sit?) | εν cum ABDPXΓΔΛΠ unc^{8} al pler it vg etc ... ℵL (sed vide post) 1. 33. τι ην εν, item cop *quae sunt* (vel *sint*) *haec quae in* | πασαισ: ℵD g^{1} cop^{petr} om | τα: L y^{scr} om, item a (*interpretans illis in omnib. scripturis de eo*) e (*interpr. eis in omnib. script. de se*) c (*interpr. illis omnes scripturas de semetipso*) arm | εαυτου (et. ς) cum ℵABGHKPSUΓΔΛΠ al plu ... ς^{e} Gb Sz Ln Ti αυτου cum DELMVX al plu. Praeterea b f ff^{2} l vg *de ipso*, a *de se*, g^{1} *de se ipso*, c *de semetipso*; contra d e *de eo*

28. ηγγισαν cum ℵADLPXΓΔΛΠ etc ... B ηγγικαν | προσεποιησατο cum ℵABDL 1. al pauc b c f ff^{2} g^{1} vg (hi omnes *finxit*) e (*simulavit*) l (*dixit*), item syr^{cu} et^{hr} ... ς Ti προσεποιειτο cum PXΓΔΛΠ unc^{8} al pler a (*adfectabat*), item syr^{sch} et^{p} | πορρωτερω cum ℵDLPXΓΔΛΠ unc^{8} al pler (sed P πορροτ.) ... Ln Ti πορρωτερον cum AB 382.

29. παρεβιασαντο (D* παραβι., L -σατο): MP al aliq παρεβιαζοντο | μεινον: 69. μειναι. Libere syr^{cu} pro και παρεβιασαντο etc: *et coeperunt illi rogare eum ut cum eis maneret, quia prope erat ut tenebresceret* | εστιν και: ita f vg (et. am fu san em ing) ... D a b c e ff^{2} l for mm tol syr^{sch} om. Latt enim sic: *quoniam* (*quia*) *ad vesperum* (c *-ram*) *iam* (ff^{2} *iamiam*, c l om) *declinavit dies* | ηδη post κεκλικεν (GHKPΠ al mu κεκληκεν, D κεκλεικεν) cum ℵBL 1. 33. 124. 258. 382. al^{2} a b e f ff^{2} (sed hi it^{5} ante κεκλικ.) vg cop, item transponentes syr^{sch} et (ante προσ εσπερ.) syr^{p} c. ob. (cod^{bars} sine obelo) ... Ln [ηδη], ς Ti

Plate 12. Constantin von Tischendorf, *Editio octava critica maior*, 1869-1872. Hermann Freiherr von Soden, *Die Schriften des Neuen Testaments*, 1913. Nestle-Aland, *Novum Testamentum Graece*, 26th ed., 1979 (7th revised printing, 1983). United Bible Societies, *The Greek New Testament* 3rd ed. (corrected), 1983. B. F. Westcott-F. J. A. Hort, *The New Testament in Greek*, 1881.

difference in punctuation, because they are quite numerous; *GNT* followed the rules of English usage until the revised third edition, and Nestle-Aland[26] attempted (with success, we dare hope) to represent Greek usage, departing from it only when strict consistency might cause difficulties for the modern reader.

These differences have been eliminated in *GNT*[3cor], which adopts the punctuation of Nestle-Aland[26] except for the reservations mentioned. Orthographical differences remain in the use of capital and lowercase letters, not to mention the distinctive ways of identifying Old Testament quotations (boldface in *GNT*, italic in Nestle-Aland[26] — a quite superficial matter, but useful in recognizing the differences). The fact that *GNT* has section headings (in English) while Nestle-Aland[26] does not have them in the Greek edition (although in its diglot editions there are section headings given for the accompanying texts in their respective languages) only accentuates again the different purposes of the two editions, which are intended to supplement each other. Those interested in a scholarly pocket edition will choose Nestle-Aland[26], while translators of the New Testament into modern languages will choose *GNT*, as will others whose interests are primarily practical. The authors of the present book can happily assume a neutral position because the Institute for New Testament Textual Research is responsible for both editions.

In his recent book, *A Survey of Manuscripts Used in Editions of the Greek New Testament* (1987), J. K. Elliott of Leeds has provided a synopsis of particular value for those who would pursue in greater detail what we have outlined in this chapter (cf. also his essays in *Novum Testamentum,* "The Citation of Manuscripts in Recent Printed Editions of the Greek New Testament" [25 (1983): 97-132], and "Old Latin Manuscripts in Printed Editions of the Greek New Testament" [26 (1984): 225-248]. The announcement of another important tool for New Testament textual research came while this book was in press: *A Bibliography of Greek New Testament Manuscripts,* which promises to list all printed or facsimile editions, published collations, and major studies of Greek New Testament manuscripts.

II

THE TRANSMISSION OF
THE GREEK NEW TESTAMENT

1. *THE COLLECTION OF THE NEW TESTAMENT BOOKS*

Each of the twenty-seven books of the New Testament was at first a separate literary unit. The Gospels were each written independently, as were the Acts of the Apostles, each letter of the apostle Paul, the other New Testament letters, and the Revelation of John. Of course the writers of the Gospels knew and relied upon their predecessors, but there was apparently a considerable lapse of time before any one community used more than a single Gospel. Not until A.D. 180 do we hear of the τετραευαγγέλιον, i.e., a collection of four Gospels regarded as equally authoritative accounts of the gospel story, widely known and recognized, e.g., in statements by the Church Father Irenaeus (bishop of Lyons about 180) and in the list known as the Muratorian Canon (a list of canonical books originating in Rome about A.D. 190, named after its discoverer, Lodovico Antonio Muratori). By then it was evidently possible to produce papyrus books which could accommodate the text of all four Gospels (more than three hundred printed pages in Nestle!). $\mathfrak{p}^{45}$, written at the beginning of the third century, originally comprised 55 sheets or double leaves (110 leaves or 220 pages), and contained not only the four Gospels but Acts as well.

The earliest writings to be collected were probably the letters of Paul. Each of the churches having one or more letters from the apostle would not only preserve them carefully, reading them when they assembled for worship, but would also exchange copies of their letters with neighboring churches. This is the only possible explanation for the preservation of the Galatian letter, since the church(es) addressed in it did not survive for long. In Col. 4:16 we read, "And when this letter has been read among you, have it read also in the church of the Laodiceans; and see that you read also the letter from Laodicea." Whether written by Paul or written shortly after his death, this reflects in all probability the practice of the Pauline (or post-Pauline) period.

When the church in Rome sent a formal letter to the church in Corinth about A.D. 95 (known as 1 Clement, the earliest Christian document outside

48

the New Testament), not only did it include references to Paul's letter to the Romans (as might be expected), but also clear citations from 1 Corinthians and Hebrews. This must reflect the existence in Rome at this time of a collection of Paul's letters, although its extent cannot be determined precisely because the quotations and allusions to other letters of Paul cannot be identified conclusively. In Marcion about 140 we find definite quotations from Galatians, both Corinthian letters, Romans, both Thessalonian letters, Ephesians (which he knew as the letter to the Laodiceans), and the letters to the Colossians, Philippians, and Philemon — this was evidently the order of the Pauline letters in the manuscripts used by Marcion. The Muratorian Canon adds to these the Pastoral letters about 190. The letter to the Hebrews does not appear in either (it was rejected by Marcion because of its Old Testament associations, and by the Muratorian Canon because of its denial of a second repentance; cf. Heb. 6:4ff.). The earliest manuscript of the Pauline letters, $\mathfrak{p}^{46}$, dating from about 200, includes it (the early Church assumed Hebrews to be Pauline); unfortunately the text breaks off at 1 Thessalonians, so that it is unknown whether 2 Thessalonians, Philemon, and the Pastoral letters were originally included. Unlike the Gospels, the letters of Paul were apparently preserved from the first as a collection. At first there were small collections in individual churches; these grew by a process of exchange until finally about the mid-second century the Pastoral letters were added and the collection of the fourteen Pauline letters was considered complete. From that time it was increasingly accorded canonical status (with the exception of Hebrews, which the Western church refused recognition until the fourth century because of its rejection of a second repentance).

2. *THE CANON, CHURCH HISTORY, AND THE HISTORY OF THE TEXT*

It is generally understood that Acts and Revelation first circulated as independent writings. But this is also true of all the writings known as the Catholic letters. 1 Peter and 2 Peter, for example, were clearly written by two different authors for completely different occasions and were brought together only by a much later church tradition. A glance at the history of the canon shows that it was not until the fourth century that the seven Catholic letters were recognized as a group. In the third century only 1 Peter and 1 John were generally recognized, with James, 2 and 3 John, 2 Peter, and Jude struggling for acceptance but with unequal success. This is still the situation reflected by Eusebius of Caesarea at the beginning of the fourth century. The evidence is quite clear that in the Eastern churches at this time the book of Revelation was widely rejected.

These insights gained from the history of the canon are fundamental and of vital significance for the history of the text — New Testament textual criticism has traditionally neglected the findings of early Church history, but only to its own injury, because the transmission of the New Testament text is certainly an integral part of that history. If the textual history of Revelation, for example, has been so independent, and if the assessment of its text must be

based on such different criteria (and manuscripts),[1] this is a natural corollary to its history of being contested, or at least not officially accepted, in the Eastern churches. If the Catholic letters received such a varied acceptance well into the fourth century and beyond (considerable parts of the Syriac-speaking church have never accepted the shorter letters as canonical), it can be more easily understood why the different parts of what came to be called the Apostolos (Acts + Catholic letters) exhibit such a varied textual character. The situation with regard to the letter of Jude is typical: even in the earliest manuscript of its text, $\mathfrak{p}^{72}$ from the third/fourth century, the complexity of its textual tradition is apparent. In an Apostolos manuscript not only may the textual character of Acts differ from that of the Catholic letters, but even among the Catholic letters themselves it may differ for each one, depending on the manuscripts from which they were copied. It is probable that by the third century the Gospels were circulating as a single corpus rather than separately, and the Pauline corpus even earlier. Acts, however, was probably at first associated with the Gospels (cf. $\mathfrak{p}^{45}$, and also Codex Bezae Cantabrigiensis). Then in the fourth century, when Acts began to be grouped with the Catholic letters, this meant bringing manuscripts together from different sources; even if the Catholic letters were already in circulation as a single group, they must have been brought together from manuscripts of different origins when the group was first formed.

When the different groups of writings were first gathered into single large manuscripts, or when a complete New Testament was first assembled, it is equally probable that the contributing manuscripts represented textual traditions of varying quality. The best example of this is Codex Vaticanus (B, 03). Earlier textual critics were at a loss to explain why the quality of its text in the Pauline letters is so inferior to its text in the Gospels. It was assumed that in the early period there were several recensions of the text (cf. von Soden), or that at the beginning of the fourth century scholars at Alexandria and elsewhere took as many good manuscripts as were available and applied their philological methods to compile a new uniform text (this was the view of our fathers, and is still that of many textual critics today as well). The question remained unanswered why the editors of such an excellent text in the Gospels could do no better in the Pauline letters. This discrepancy should have disturbed the textual critics. The same question is raised by Codex Alexandrinus (A). Its text in the Gospels is quite poor (differing only slightly from the Majority text). But beginning with Acts its quality changes remarkably: in Acts it is comparable to B and ℵ, while in Revelation it is superior to ℵ and even $\mathfrak{p}^{47}$. If the manuscript were a recensional product, how could these differences be explained?

3. THE ORIGIN OF TEXT TYPES

Modern textual criticism has a clear answer to this question. Major revisions of Greek manuscripts must certainly have occurred toward the end of the third or

---

1. Cf. pp. 246f.

the beginning of the fourth century (probably during the forty years of peace between the end of the Decius-Valerian persecution and 303). It was then, for example, that the Koine text first took form in Antioch, and that elsewhere in the East a manuscript was written which was to become the ancestor of Codex Bezae Cantabrigiensis (D, 05, of the fifth century). In neither of these instances was the primary motivation of the revision philological. It was prompted rather by ecclesiastical or theological interests. The text of the exemplar (or exemplars, probably a different one for each group of New Testament writings) was revised not so much with a concern for establishing or restoring the original text as for determining the "best" text from a particular editorial perspective.

When revisions were made without such tendentious purposes the process was quite different. A manuscript with the current standard text was taken and edited or corrected (but not revised) in a more limited and practical way. This was done in Codex Vaticanus for the Gospels on the basis of a manuscript of the type represented by $\mathfrak{p}^{75}$ (from the early third century). For the Pauline letters nothing comparable was available, so another papyrus with an "early text" of the second/third century (of the type represented by $\mathfrak{p}^{45}$, $\mathfrak{p}^{46}$, $\mathfrak{p}^{66}$) was used as the base and corrected as necessary. This text of the early period of the second/third century was frequently characterized by erratic traits (although there were exceptions; cf. $\mathfrak{p}^{75}$ and several others),[2] such as the free expansions still permitted by the standards of the second century when the New Testament text was not yet regarded as "canonical," much less as sacred in the same sense as Jewish scribes regarded the Hebrew text of the Old Testament (this is discussed below, cf. p. 69). Whatever value Codex Bezae Cantabrigiensis may have as principal representative of the "Western text" is due to the circumstance that its tendentious revision (or more probably that of its ancestor of the third/fourth century) is based on a papyrus with a text of this kind from the early period.[3] It is only the great number of passages where this exemplar escaped revision and stands in agreement with other good uncials that justifies the reputation of D and the authority accordingly attributed to it and the "Western text" — certainly not the readings which constitute its peculiarities (i.e., of the exemplar which it follows), such as innumerable additions, transpositions, omissions, etc. Undoubtedly the achievement of the original editor was significant, but only as a reviser who altered radically the text of his early exemplar in numerous passages. These alterations can make no claim to consideration as original. The reader who wishes to investigate this in detail is referred to Ernst Haenchen's commentary on Acts.[4]

When the term "Western text" is used today, even by its advocates, it is nearly always placed in quotation marks. Palaeography has demonstrated that Codex Bezae Cantabrigiensis was not written in the West (despite its Greek-Latin text),

2. Cf. pp. 59f.

3. Cf. p. 64.

4. Heinrich August Wilhelm Meyer, *Kritisch-exegetischer Kommentar*, vol. 3, 10th-17th ed. (Göttingen: 1956-1977); Engl. trans. by R. McLeish Wilson, *Acts of the Apostles: A Commentary* (Philadelphia: 1971).

but either in North Africa or in Egypt. Of course, the provenance of the exemplar used by the scribe of D (05) is another matter. The evidence of church history, an area largely if not completely ignored by textual critics, is decisive at this point (cf. pp. 49f.; it is utterly amazing how many New Testament scholars fail to observe the historical implications of their theories, changing them as easily as they shift positions at their desks!).

4. *LATIN, SYRIAC, AND COPTIC VERSIONS: THE DEMAND FOR GREEK MANUSCRIPTS LIMITED AFTER A.D. 200*

There is no longer any doubt that Greek was the language in which all the parts of the New Testament were originally written, although Aramaic Christian texts may have circulated in the period before our Gospels (if an Aramaic tradition ever actually existed in a written and not merely an oral form). The quality of this Greek is varied, ranging from the "Jewish Greek" of Revelation to the literary aspirations of the Lucan writings and the relatively polished Greek of Hebrews. Yet when compared with the contemporary literature, none of the New Testament writings stands out for elegance of style, even if it be admitted that the eloquence of Paul created a new literary genre. The New Testament was written in Koine Greek, the Greek of daily conversation. The fact that from the first all the New Testament writings were written in Greek is conclusively demonstrated by their citations from the Old Testament, which are from the Septuagint, the Greek translation of the Old Testament, and not from the original Hebrew text. This is true even of the rabbinic scholar Paul.

Greek was the world language of the time, spoken and understood as well in the West as in the East. When about A.D. 95 the Roman church wrote to the church at Corinth (1 Clement), it was naturally in Greek, and when the author of the Shepherd of Hermas wanted to share his understanding of the delayed Parousia with his fellow Christians in Rome about 150, the language was still Greek. But a change was nearing. All the extant writings of Tertullian in Carthage shortly before 200 were written in Latin, although he was fluent in Greek. And the correspondence between the churches in Rome and Carthage about 250 was in Latin. Hippolytus, the scholarly (counter-) bishop of Rome, died about 235. Although his writings, which were in Greek, represented the most brilliant literary achievement of any Roman bishop of the first four centuries, they fell into immediate oblivion because they evidently found no readership — it remained for modern scholarship to discover them. The magnum opus of Irenaeus, *Adversus haereses,* a work of profound significance in the developing life of the late second-century Church, was written in Greek in Gaul about 180. Except for a few citations in Eastern writers the Greek text has disappeared, and is preserved only in a Latin tradition.

It was about 180, then, that the tide began to turn in the Western church (and not only in the West, but also in the Syriac- and Coptic-speaking areas). Regional languages began to assert themselves, or at least to demand their rights. This was related to the growing number of Christians at this time. Since from

the beginning the spread of the Church was largely among the common people, the number of Christians who could not understand Greek soon became so great that regional languages became the necessary medium for preaching the gospel. In the West, to mention only one area (although it was the same in the other regions), a translation of the whole New Testament was needed. By the middle of the third century a transitional period of bilingual worship (probably with the Greek text read first, followed by a free Latin interpretation or the reading of a newly made Latin version) had given way to the exclusive use of Latin. Consequently if a special form of the Greek text was to develop in the West, the historical opportunity for it was relatively brief. It may be true that Greek settlements and colonies persisted (especially in southern Italy, but also in the north around Ravenna), and that even today worship is observed in Greek in the monastery of Grottaferrata, an eleventh-century foundation at the gates of Rome. But the church in Italy, not to mention Gaul and the other provinces of the West, was a Latin church by the mid-third century if not earlier.

5. CENTERS OF GREEK MANUSCRIPT PRODUCTION

Adolf Harnack's basic study, *Die Mission und Ausbreitung des Christentums in den ersten drei Jahrhunderten* ([4]1924, repr. Leipzig: 1965; Eng. trans. by James Moffatt [London: 1904/5, [2]1908]) is still the best source of information on the development of Christianity in the early period, the number of churches, and their strength. It shows that about 180 the greatest concentration of churches was in Asia Minor and along the Aegean coast of Greece. We know of only a few isolated churches in Cyprus and Crete, although Christianity should have had a strong foothold there. There were large and well-established Christian churches in North Africa (especially in Numidia, but in Cyrenaica as well), in southern Gaul, perhaps also in southern Spain, in the districts around Alexandria in Egypt, around Antioch in Syria, and certainly in Edessa and its environs, as well as in Melitene and its environs. Rome stands out in Italy, but there was probably also a scattering of churches across the country south to Sicily. This is the setting in which the text of the New Testament must have developed and circulated. The overall impression is that the concentration of Christianity was in the East. Churches become fewer in number as we go westward. Large areas of the West were still untouched by Christianity. Even around A.D. 325 the scene was still largely unchanged. Asia Minor continued to be the heartland of the Church. Here as in the coastal region of Thracia opposite, in Cyprus, and in the hinterlands of Edessa, almost half the population was Christian, and the Church expanded with about equal strength from Asia Minor eastward to Armenia. In terms of the numbers of Christians and of churches, the next category includes Syria, the districts along the Nile, the coastlands of Greece and Crete, Numidia and Cyrenaica in North Africa, southern Spain and the western coast north to southern Gaul, and in Italy the environs of Rome and Naples, as well as the coastal lands of the Adriatic Sea.

These are the areas where Christianity was relatively well established

among the people. These were the critical areas for the transmission of New Testament manuscripts and for the development of their textual types.

6. *DID THE WEST DEVELOP ITS OWN TEXT TYPE?*

Our view of the role of the West and of Rome in the early Church has generally been unduly influenced by later history. Rome and Italy played a distinctly subordinate role in the early period of church history with regard to theological and scholarly interests, the area of our present concern. There was certainly a church in Rome when Paul wrote his letter to the Romans. When the ship which brought Paul to Rome as a prisoner moored at Puteoli, he found a church already there as well (Acts 28:13-14). Further, the church in Rome continued to be significantly productive to the end of the second century and on through the first half of the third century, but this was mainly in the area of pastoral matters, particularly in practical theology: expanding the primitive form of the creed, contributing to a definition of the canon (cf. the Muratorian Canon), developing the church practice of penance, and improving the church's administrative structure. In 217, when a new bishop was elected in Rome, it was characteristic that the practical Callistus was chosen over Hippolytus, the most significant theologian Rome had yet seen (we may also observe that not only Callistus' attitude toward theology, but also that of the two bishops who preceded him, was rather negative). The same was true again in 251, when Cornelius was favored over Novatian although the latter had served as interim leader of the church — the theologian deferring once more to the practical leader. Further, Novatian was a Roman while Hippolytus was not. Hippolytus was from Asia Minor, as was most of the theological leadership in second-century Rome. Marcion went to Rome about 140, but he came from the Black Sea area as an adult, presumably bringing with him the New Testament text he had used there. Justin was active in Rome about 150, but he was born in Palestine and had been converted to Christianity in Asia Minor. Others could also be named: all the Apologists, not Justin alone, came from the East, usually from Asia Minor or Greece. The monarchians, who sparked lively theological discussions in Rome toward the end of the second century, were all from Asia Minor. Among the writings of the Apostolic Fathers only 1 Clement and the Shepherd of Hermas were written in the West, possibly also the sermon which circulated under the name 2 Clement — but these were all relatively pedestrian writings, and it is significant that they were so highly esteemed. The only master we find in the West in the latter half of the second century was in Gaul: Irenaeus. And he was from Asia Minor, not only by birth but culturally and theologically as well. The master among the Apostolic Fathers of the first half of the second century was Ignatius — from Antioch.

Wherever we look in the West, nowhere can we find a theological mind capable of developing and editing an independent "Western text" (even if Hebrews was authored in Italy, as suggested occasionally, it does not satisfy the requirements for such a person). In the early period there was no textual tradition in the West that was not shared with the East: there was only a text with individual

characteristics which varied from manuscript to manuscript, for in the second century the New Testament text was not yet firmly established. As late as 150, when the first traces of Gospel quotations are found in the writings of Justin Martyr, the manner of quotation is quite free. Earlier examples are even more allusive or paraphrastic. It is not until 180 (in Irenaeus) that signs of an established text appear. While it is possible that this "Early text" may have had certain characteristics in the West (as a local text), it is impossible to identify any occasion or person associated with its development in the way that B. F. Westcott and F. J. A. Hort and their modern followers suggest. It is quite inconceivable that the text of Codex Bezae Cantabrigiensis could have existed as early as the second century. It is also significant, as we have mentioned, that hardly anyone today refers to this putative Western text without placing the term in quotation marks, i.e., as the "Western text."

7. THE SPREAD OF NEW TESTAMENT MANUSCRIPTS AND THEIR TEXT TYPES

So much for the phantom "Western text." To return to our larger subject: how did a New Testament book first begin circulating, and how were New Testament manuscripts first produced? The circulation of a document began either from the place (or church province) of its origin, where the author wrote it, or from the place to which it was addressed (if it was a genuine letter — formal epistles would be like other New Testament writings). Copies of the original would be made for use in neighboring churches. The circulation of a book would be like the ripples of a stone cast into a pond, spreading out in all directions at once. When a book was shared by repeated copying throughout a whole diocese or metropolitan area, the close ties between dioceses would carry it from one district to another, where the process would be repeated. From the moment the Christian church required the use of sacred books in addition to the Septuagint, i.e., from the time that the worship service incorporated the reading and exposition of lessons taken not only from the Old Testament but also from other writings which were regarded as holy scripture, the number of New Testament manuscripts began to multiply. Thus the letters of Paul would naturally have been read first in the churches he founded, and then become a regular part of the sequence of liturgical lessons. This must have been the situation from the mid-second century, with the founding of each new church requiring the production of another New Testament manuscript.

At this point the history of the New Testament canon is significant. If the founder of a church did not supply a manuscript, a copy would have to be made from his exemplar or from a borrowed one. In the early period copies were made privately: there were no scriptoria (professional copying centers) before A.D. 200 at the earliest. In the course of time the private copying of texts produced a teeming variety of small textual families (mother manuscripts and their children) within larger diocesan groupings (to the extent that such distinctions can be made in the New Testament text). The more loosely organized a

diocese, or the greater the differences between its constituent churches, the more likely different text types would coexist (as in early Egypt).[5] The more uniform its organization, the more likely there would be only a single text type, as exemplified by the Byzantine Imperial text type which expanded its influence rapidly from the fourth century[6] to become increasingly the dominant text of the Byzantine church.

But differences still persisted, and even the Byzantine Imperial text is not a monolithic unit. Rather it developed in a variety of different ways, although these variations did not alter its basic character even when dividing it into two separate groups. Only in churches maintaining their own ancient traditions, or in churches which were either relatively isolated from the Byzantine church or opposed to its practices, could a textual tradition withstand the domination of this Byzantine text type. Yet even in such areas it was impossible in the long run to escape completely the influence of the Imperial text. This is clear from the example of the church in Egypt which led an independent life from at least the fifth century, increasingly in conflict with the Byzantine church in the christo-logical controversies and with a growing resistance to the Greek culture. From the fourth century it had a well-defined text (known as the Alexandrian text type) because the administration of the Alexandrian patriarchs was effectively centralized. But as the years passed even this text showed the corrosive effects of the Koine influence (the later a manuscript's date, the more extensive the influence). Eventually the Alexandrian text produced the Egyptian text. The circulation of this Egyptian text then became increasingly limited by the growing popularity of the Coptic versions. Furthermore, even in the world of the Byzantine Imperial text it should be recognized that individual texts and text types tended to survive stubbornly, because an indomitable stubbornness is one of the basic characteristics of New Testament textual history: once a variant or a new reading enters the tradition it refuses to disappear, persisting (if only in a few manuscripts) and perpetuating itself through the centuries. One of the most striking traits of the New Testament textual tradition is its tenacity.[7]

8. *THE TEXT OF THE EARLY PERIOD*

To understand the textual history of the New Testament it is necessary to begin with the early manuscripts. By this we mean manuscripts no later than the third/fourth century, for in the fourth century a new era begins. Every manuscript of the earlier period, whether on papyrus or on parchment, has an inherent significance for New Testament textual criticism: they witness to a period when the text of the New Testament was still developing freely. These manuscripts are shown in Table 3 on p. 57.

This makes a total of forty-three papyri and five uncials (or more strictly four uncials, because 0212 is a Diatessaron text and should not be counted; cf. p. 104).

5. Cf. pp. 59f.
6. Cf. pp. 64f.
7. Cf. pp. 291ff.

Table 3.   Distribution of early Greek manuscripts by century

Early 2nd century	$\mathfrak{p}^{52}$
2nd century	$\mathfrak{p}^{90}$
About 200	$\mathfrak{p}^{32}$, $\mathfrak{p}^{46}$, $\mathfrak{p}^{64/67}$, $\mathfrak{p}^{66}$
2nd/3rd century	$\mathfrak{p}^{77}$, 0189
3rd century	$\mathfrak{p}^{1}$, $\mathfrak{p}^{4}$, $\mathfrak{p}^{5}$, $\mathfrak{p}^{9}$, $\mathfrak{p}^{12}$, $\mathfrak{p}^{15}$, $\mathfrak{p}^{20}$, $\mathfrak{p}^{22}$, $\mathfrak{p}^{23}$, $\mathfrak{p}^{27}$, $\mathfrak{p}^{28}$, $\mathfrak{p}^{29}$, $\mathfrak{p}^{30}$, $\mathfrak{p}^{39}$, $\mathfrak{p}^{40}$, $\mathfrak{p}^{45}$, $\mathfrak{p}^{47}$, $\mathfrak{p}^{48}$, $\mathfrak{p}^{49}$, $\mathfrak{p}^{53}$, $\mathfrak{p}^{65}$, $\mathfrak{p}^{69}$, $\mathfrak{p}^{70}$, $\mathfrak{p}^{75}$, $\mathfrak{p}^{80}$, $\mathfrak{p}^{87}$, $\mathfrak{p}^{91}$, $\mathfrak{p}^{95}$, 0212, 0220
3rd/4th century	$\mathfrak{p}^{13}$, $\mathfrak{p}^{16}$, $\mathfrak{p}^{18}$, $\mathfrak{p}^{37}$, $\mathfrak{p}^{38}$, $\mathfrak{p}^{72}$, $\mathfrak{p}^{78}$, $\mathfrak{p}^{92}$, 0162, 0171

Among these $\mathfrak{p}^{52}$ holds a special place as the earliest witness to the New Testament text (written *ca.* 125, now in the John Rylands Library, Manchester, and containing John 18:31-33, 37-38). The Chester Beatty papyri and the Bodmer papyri[8] are important not only for their age, but also for the length and character of their text. $\mathfrak{p}^{45}$, $\mathfrak{p}^{46}$, and $\mathfrak{p}^{47}$ (the famous Chester Beatty papyri which were the sensation of the 1930s) contain in $\mathfrak{p}^{45}$ the Gospels and Acts (with considerable lacunae, beginning at Matt. 20:24 and ending at Acts 17:17), in $\mathfrak{p}^{46}$ the letters of Paul (with lacunae, lacking 2 Thessalonians, Philemon, and the Pastorals completely), and in $\mathfrak{p}^{47}$ the book of Revelation (Rev. 9:10–17:2, with small lacunae). The Bodmer papyri, which became known in the 1950s, contain in $\mathfrak{p}^{66}$ the gospel of John (John 1:1–14:30 with almost no lacunae, and the remainder in fragments), in $\mathfrak{p}^{72}$ Jude and 1-2 Peter, and in $\mathfrak{p}^{75}$ the gospels of Luke (from Luke 3:10 with a few lacunae) and of John (John 1:1–15:8 with a few lacunae). $\mathfrak{p}^{66}$ was the first Greek papyrus book to be found with even its sewing almost intact, while $\mathfrak{p}^{75}$ still has its binding, and the other papyri, $\mathfrak{p}^{72}$ in particular, have pages that are quite undamaged. Thus the Bodmer papyri surpass the Chester Beatty papyri in the quality of their preservation, in the length of their texts,[9] and in their textual significance. Until their discovery it was thought on the basis of $\mathfrak{p}^{45}$ and $\mathfrak{p}^{46}$ that the second/third century text was generally characterized by considerable irregularity. $\mathfrak{p}^{66}$ seemed to confirm this. But $\mathfrak{p}^{75}$ proved this to be wrong, because its text was so closely similar to that of Codex Vaticanus that it could even be suspected of being its exemplar. With the discovery of $\mathfrak{p}^{75}$ we have at last found the key to understanding the early history of the text.

These "great" papyri should be introduced to students from the start because they are just as important, and in many ways more important, than the

---

8. Both are named for their owners. The former are now in Dublin and the latter in Cologny (near Geneva), both in private museums built by their owners, except for parts of $\mathfrak{p}^{72}$ containing 1 and 2 Peter, which Dr. Bodmer has donated to the Vatican. For details, cf. pp. 87ff. and plates 20-26.

9. No one had ever thought it possible, for example, that a complete text of the letter of Jude and the two letters of Peter would be found preserved in a papyrus of the third/fourth century.

Plate 13. 0212, a fragment of a Greek Gospel harmony found at Dura Europus (Tatian's Diatessaron; cf. pp. 104, 125): Matt. 27:56 and parallel.

great uncial manuscripts of the New Testament. The other papyri and uncials described below on pp. 96-102 and pp. 107-128 take second place to the papyri described above, and with due reason (because most of them are fragmentary). Nor should we forget that each of these fragments represents a complete manuscript, once containing at least the book represented by the surviving text. If a fragment preserves a passage where there is any variation in the tradition, it is quite sufficient to signal the textual character of the whole manuscript. There is no need to consume a whole jar of jelly to identify the quality of its contents — a spoonful or two is quite adequate!

The methods and terms traditionally used by textual critics to define the textual character of these fragments has tended rather to confuse than to

clarify matters. Typical is the appendix to Bruce M. Metzger's *The Text of the New Testament,* pp. 247-256, with its "Check-list of the Greek Papyri of the New Testament." In describing $\mathfrak{p}^{32}$, for example, it states: "agrees with $\aleph$, also with F and G" (p. 250). What does this mean? About A.D. 200, when $\mathfrak{p}^{32}$ was being written, $\aleph$ of the fourth century did not yet exist, nor yet F or G, both of the ninth century. Of $\mathfrak{p}^{47}$ it states: "agrees with A, C, and $\aleph$" (p. 252). Here as in so many other instances the relationships which do exist are described in reverse (for $\mathfrak{p}^{47}$ they are demonstrably wrong: it is allied to $\aleph$, but not to A or to C, which are of a different text type). Besides, the affinities of early manuscripts should not be described in terms of later manuscripts, but rather the reverse (a father does not inherit his son's traits, but a son his father's). Descriptions in such terms as "mixed text," "partly Alexandrian, partly Western (pre-Caesarean) text," etc., to describe manuscripts of a period when these groups had not yet developed and could hardly be "mixed" contribute nothing to clear thinking.

Such a terminology may sound very scholarly, but it only beclouds the issue. We should not forget that apart from 0212 (found at Dura Europus), all the early witnesses listed above on p. 57 are from Egypt, where the hot, dry sands preserved the papyri through the centuries (similar climatic conditions are found in the Judaean desert where papyri have also been discovered). From other major centers of the early Christian church nothing has survived. This raises the question whether and to what extent we can generalize from the Egyptian situation. Egypt was distinguished from other provinces of the Church, so far as we can judge, by the early dominance of gnosticism; this was not broken until about A.D. 200, when Bishop Demetrius succeeded in reorganizing the diocese and establishing communications with the other churches. Not until then do we have documentary evidence of the church in Egypt, although undoubtedly not only the gnostic but also the broader Church was represented there throughout the whole period. At almost the same time the Catechetical School of Alexandria was instituted as the first "Christian university."

Quite possibly Bishop Demetrius had manuscripts prepared for his newly reorganized diocese (now under the direction of his newly appointed chorepiscopoi) and for its churches in a scriptorium related to the Catechetical School (which probably existed despite the lack of any documentary evidence). Designating particular manuscripts (which probably were imported from other provinces of the broader church) to be master exemplars would have created a special "Alexandrian" text. But this hypothesis, however intrinsically possible, does not square with the evidence of the manuscripts up to the third/fourth century. Thus $\mathfrak{p}^{45}$, $\mathfrak{p}^{46}$, $\mathfrak{p}^{66}$, and a whole group of other manuscripts offer a "free" text, i.e., a text dealing with the original text in a relatively free manner with no suggestion of a program of standardization (or were these manuscripts also imported from elsewhere?). Some have gone so far as to interpret these "free" texts as typical of the early period. But this cannot be correct, as a fresh collation of all the manuscripts of the early period[10] by the Institute for New Testament Textual

10. For definitions, cf. pp. 50f. above.

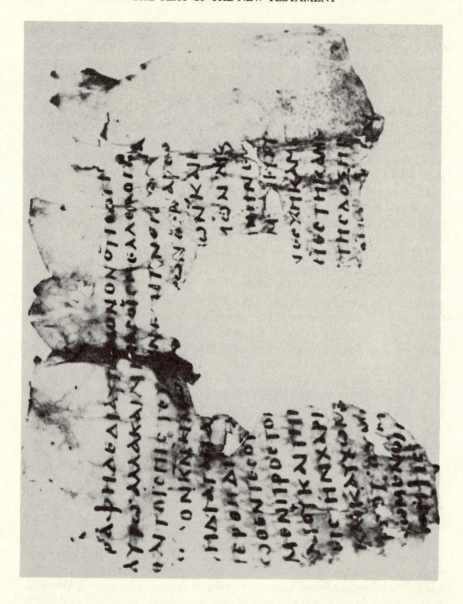

Plates 14/15. 0220 (left; cf. p. 104), a fragment representing Rom. 4:23–53 in the "strict text" of the third century, and 057 (right; cf. p. 119), a fragment representing a category I text of the fourth/fifth century (cf. p. 106), show how carefully the text was still then being preserved.

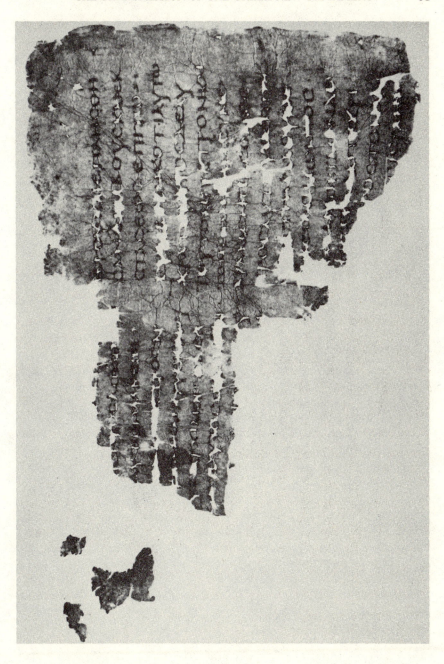

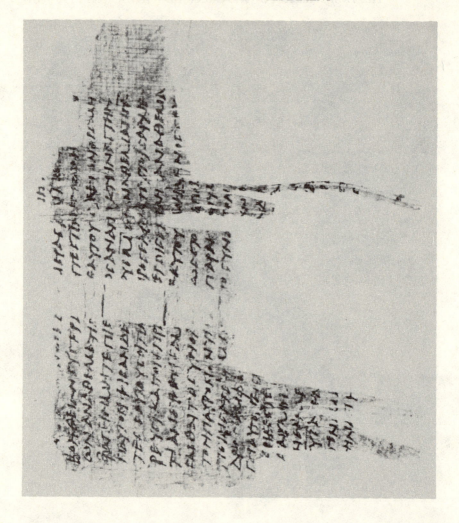

Plates 16/17. An early (or secondary?) form of the D text; p[48] (third century; cf. p. 99), showing Acts 23:11-17, and 0171 (ca. 300; one of the earliest uncials, cf. pp. 104, 123), showing Luke 22:44-50.

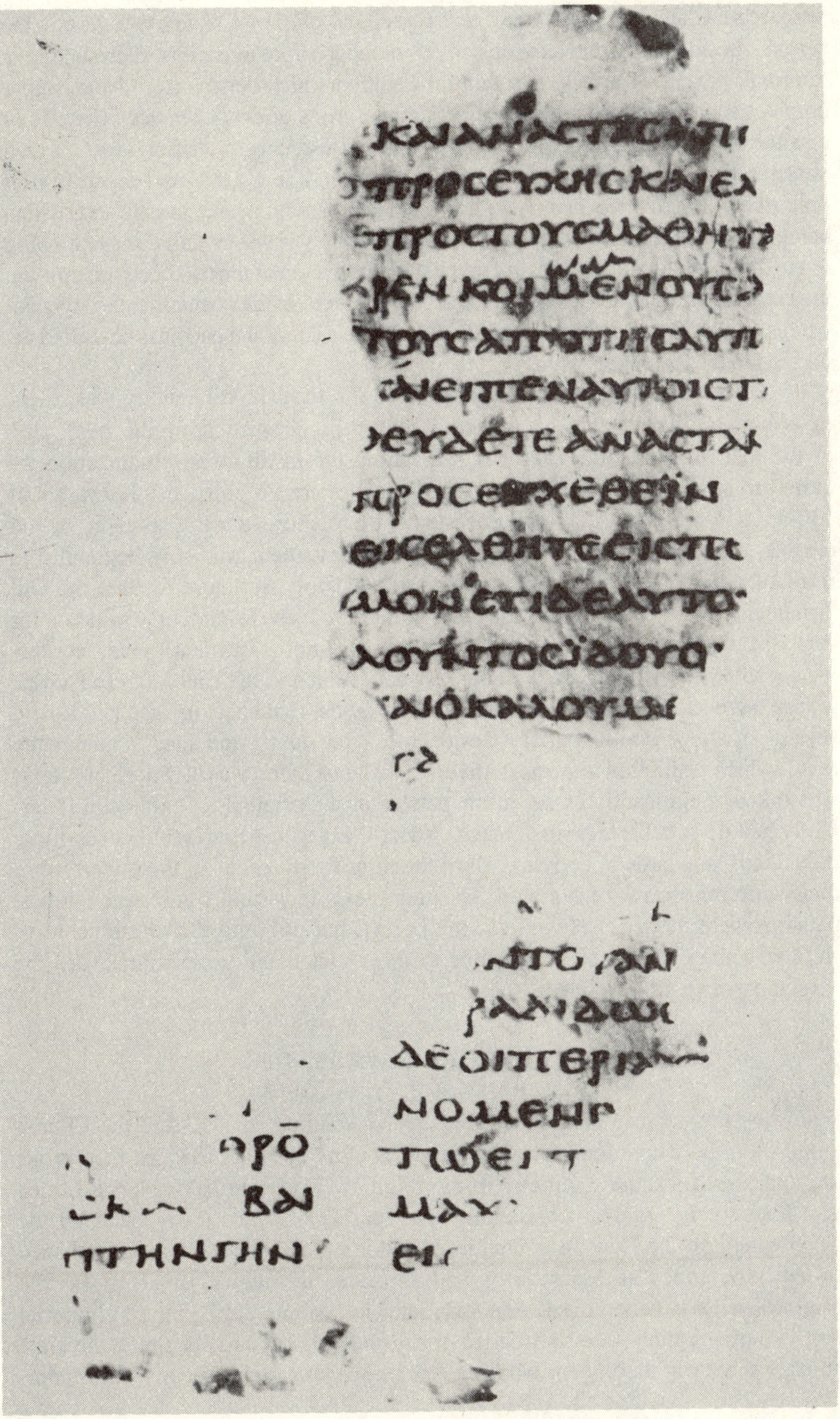

Research has shown. The "free" text represents only one of the varieties of the period. Beside it there is a substantial number of manuscripts representing a "normal" text, i.e., a relatively faithful tradition which departs from its exemplar only occasionally, as do New Testament manuscripts of every century. There is an equally substantial number of manuscripts representing a "strict" text, which transmit the text of an exemplar with meticulous care (e.g., $\mathfrak{p}^{75}$) and depart from it only rarely. Finally, we also find a few manuscripts with a paraphrastic text, which belong in the neighborhood of the D text. Apparently it was not until the beginning of the fourth century even in Egypt that a standardization of the text occurred through the circulation of numerous copies of a "model text" from a central authority. (For details, cf. the list of papyri on pp. 96-102, where each of the papyri is classified according to these categories.)

The text of the early period prior to the third/fourth century was, then, in effect, a text not yet channeled into types, because until the beginning of the fourth century the churches still lacked the institutional organization required to produce one. Its earliest representatives are Polycarp and Justin, about 130-150 (in earlier writings New Testament quotations are too sporadic or too elusive, especially for the Gospels). The Old Testament was only beginning to retreat from its traditionally central position as Holy Scripture (at first the Old Testament held the position in the Church that the New Testament now holds for us). But the text of the New Testament was still not controlled by any ecclesiastical authority. About 180 the Four Gospel canon and the canon of the Pauline letters were closed, but Hebrews and Revelation remained in dispute, as did several of the Catholic letters. Beside the "free text" and the "paraphrastic text" which exhibited the most diverse variants there was a "normal" text, which kept significantly closer to the pattern of the original text although it certainly had its peculiarities also, and a "strict" text which represented even more meticulous standards of copying. Until the third/fourth century, then, there were many different forms of the New Testament text, including some which anticipated or were more closely akin to the D text, but not until the fourth century, following the decades of peace prior to the Diocletianic persecutions, did the formation of text types begin.

9. THE AGE OF CONSTANTINE

Following the persecutions under Decius and Valerian *ca.* 250-260 the Church enjoyed on the whole four decades of peace before 303. Persecution then broke out again with a sudden ferocity in the reign of Diocletian as paganism rallied in a final combat against Christianity. This period of peace was critical for the development of the New Testament text. In Antioch the early form was polished stylistically, edited ecclesiastically, and expanded devotionally.[11] This was the origin of what is called the Koine text, later to become the Byzantine Imperial text. Fourth-century tradition called it the text of Lucian. At the same time another scholarly theologian working from a papyrus with an early text under-

11. Cf. pp. 306f.

took a more thorough revision (probably of only the Gospels and Acts). But in the fourth century the text of Lucian received strong support, while its rival text (a precursor of Codex Bezae Cantabrigiensis) was given no official support and was consequently preserved in only a few manuscripts, no more than Codex Bezae Cantabrigiensis (D^{ea}, 05) and its very few precursors and descendants. This has been called the D text (following a widespread usage) because of its principal representative.

The major text types trace their beginnings to the Diocletianic persecutions and the Age of Constantine which followed. This seems paradoxical. But the period of persecution which lasted almost ten years in the West and much longer in the East was characterized by the systematic destruction of church buildings (and church centers), and any manuscripts that were found in them were publicly burned. Church officials were further required to surrender for public burning all holy books in their possession or custody. Although clergy who submitted to the demands of the state were branded as traitors and defectors from the faith, their number was by no means small. The result was a widespread scarcity of New Testament manuscripts which became all the more acute when the persecution ceased. For when Christianity could again engage freely in missionary activity there was a tremendous growth in both the size of the existing churches and the number of new churches. There also followed a sudden demand for large numbers of New Testament manuscripts in all provinces of the empire. Privately made copies contributed significantly, but they were inadequate to satisfy this growing need, which could be met only by large copying houses. Bishops were no longer prevented from opening their own scriptoria: any text used as the exemplar in such a production center would naturally be widely distributed and wield a dominant influence. The exegetical school of Antioch, where students of Origen's theology and Arians maintained a well-organized center, provided bishops for many dioceses throughout the East (with the support of the court bishop, Eusebius of Nicomedia; here again a knowledge of church history is indispensable for understanding the history of the text). Each of these bishops took with him to his diocese the text he was familiar with, that of Lucian (i.e., the Koine text), and in this way it rapidly became very widely disseminated even in the fourth century. Athanasius, the powerful bishop of Alexandria, whose authority was felt far beyond the borders of Egypt as early as 328, governed his church with a tightly centralized administrative structure. We do not know precisely what manuscript he designated for use as a model, but it must have been of the type represented by Codex Vaticanus or p^{75}. Naturally any errors in the model manuscript, whether real or imagined, would have been corrected. The association of the name of Hesychius with the type of text preferred in Alexandria would seem to imply that it had been completed by him before the outbreak of persecution (tradition has it that both Hesychius and Lucian died as martyrs in the persecution of Diocletian).

The Church Father Jerome, who not only edited the Vulgate but was concerned with the text of the scriptures in many other respects as well, remarked toward the end of the fourth century with regard to the Greek Old Testament that Hesychius was known as the editor of the Septuagint text used in Alexandria

and Egypt, while "in Constantinople and as far as Antioch copies made by the martyr Lucian are regarded as authoritative; the provinces between these two read the Palestinian manuscripts prepared by Origen and widely promoted by Eusebius and Pamphilus."[12] Thus Jerome mentions three major types of text for the Greek Old Testament, and his statement confirms the view expressed above that these types did not originate as our fathers imagined, but that they survived because they were the texts of the great scriptoria (of Alexandria, Caesarea, and the episcopal sees from Antioch to Constantinople, i.e., the Antiochene school), and consequently were circulated almost exclusively. It is interesting that in his dedicatory letter to Damasus before the Gospels Jerome does not mention the text types of Hesychius, Lucian, and Origen (Pamphilus and Eusebius), but only those of Lucian and Hesychius — and with small praise at that.[13]

In any event, these statements attest the existence of two text types: the Alexandrian text (Hesychius) and the Koine, the later Byzantine text (Lucian). When New Testament textual criticism goes beyond these to speak of Caesarean and Jerusalem text types the theoretical possibility of these must be conceded. The Caesarea of Eusebius at the beginning of the fourth century was undoubtedly an important center of manuscript production — significantly, it was here that Emperor Constantine turned for manuscripts to supply the churches in his newly established capital of Constantinople. But the widely acclaimed Caesarean text of the New Testament, we must insist, is thus far purely hypothetical. Jerome would seem to imply that Caesarea offered a distinctive local text (as the result of Origen's studies) only for the Greek Old Testament. If a distinctive text of the New Testament had also been developed in Caesarea (whether by Origen or by Eusebius), it should be possible to identify it in the writings of one of these Fathers, or preferably of both. But research has not yet been able to establish any such identification. In effect, all claims for the Caesarean text, however confidently expressed, need critical verification.

The same may be said of the Jerusalem text type. Von Soden's theories[14] belong completely to the world of whim and fantasy. After the early days of the Church it was not until the fourth century that Jerusalem again assumed any real significance — as textual critics would have known if they had not ignored church history so completely. After the destruction of Jerusalem in the Jewish War, and after the Bar Kokhba rebellion of 132-135, the Christian church there had to make a completely new beginning. In the third century Caesarea was still the cultural and ecclesiastical center of the region. It was no coincidence that in 231 Origen chose to settle there and not in Jerusalem to build his theological school, which was soon to extend its influence throughout the East. In the second half of the third century Jerusalem was already beginning to attract a growing number of pilgrims to its sacred sites, but it was only in the age of Constantine

---

12. Preface to Chronicles in the Roman edition of the Vulgate, vol. 7, p. 4 (Stuttgart edition, p. 546).

13. John Wordsworth-H. J. White, *Novum Testamentum Domini nostri Iesu Christi* 1 (Oxford: 1898): 2, 14 (Stuttgart edition, p. 1515).

14. Cf. pp. 22f.

and later that it became again a cultural and religious center — continuing until its final destruction in 614 by the Persian invasion. Byzantium was able to repulse the Persians in 627, but after the Arab invasion of 638 Palestine became an Arab province, eliminating the possibility for either Jerusalem or Caesarea to exercise any further influence on the text of the Greek New Testament in the Church. The only period in which Jerusalem could have been influential in the textual development of the Greek New Testament was between the fourth and sixth centuries. While there are hints of such an influence, they require far more careful study than they have yet received.

Asia Minor and Greece, the centers of early Christianity, undoubtedly exercised a substantive if not critical influence on the development of the New Testament text, but it is impossible to demonstrate because the climate in these regions has been unfavorable to the preservation of any papyri from the early period.

10. *SUMMARY*

But we are ahead of ourselves again, constantly mentioning things which are unfamiliar to beginning students of the Greek New Testament. It is increasingly important to keep the basic facts in clear focus as we proceed. If it seems too complicated at first, remember that only the Alexandrian text, the Koine text, and the D text are incontestably verified. Whatever else may be proposed, especially with reference to the so-called Western, Caesarean, and Jerusalem text types, is theoretical, based on dubious foundations and often built completely in the clouds. Particular caution is needed with any proposed textual group qualified by the prefix "pre-" (such as the pre-Caesarean text). The origin of the "Western" text lies anywhere but in the direction its name would suggest. Its actual role in the manuscript tradition of the New Testament has been minimal, quite in contrast to the amount of attention it has received in modern critical literature. These comments should suffice for the moment: the supporting evidence will be discussed frequently enough later. For the student interested in general outlines without all the details of the above discussion the following summary is offered not only as a review, but also as an outline for a fresh perspective.

1. New Testament textual criticism must always keep in mind and consider the implications of what has been learned from studies in the history of the canon and from early Church history if its conclusions are to be sound.

2. The latter half of the second century is indicated as particularly important, for it was then that the Gospels, which had previously circulated only as separate documents, were first brought together into Four Gospels manuscripts, and that the Pauline corpus, with its beginnings reaching back into the first century, was brought to completion by the addition of the Pastoral letters. At this time the Western church (at least a considerable part of it) rejected the letter to the Hebrews as part of the Pauline corpus, while the Eastern church continued to include it in the corpus as before. The Four Gospels manuscripts

(which sometimes included Acts; cf. $\mathfrak{p}^{45}$) must have been compiled at this time from single Gospel manuscripts (possibly, or even probably, of different textual characteristics). The process must have been the same as early as the first century for the Pauline corpus, and surely also for the corpus of Catholic letters which was not completed until the fourth century. In view of the variety of ways in which manuscripts were compiled at various times and in different places, the possibility of an inconsistency in their textual character, even from letter to letter, is only to be expected. This is particularly true for those letters which were accepted late (2 Peter, 2 and 3 John, Jude, and also James): the textual tradition of the letter of Jude is a clear example.

3. The year 200 represents an important watershed. Alongside the Greek New Testament manuscript tradition, Latin manuscripts came into use at this time throughout the West, Coptic manuscripts in Egypt, and Syriac manuscripts in Syria (i.e., the exclusively Syriac-speaking region around Edessa, with the Roman province at first taking second place). The number of simple church members whose knowledge of Greek was inadequate at best had become so great that translation into the regional languages was an absolute necessity. By A.D. 250 the church in the West was a Latin church.

4. By this date at the latest the West was no longer a formative factor in the history of the Greek text of the New Testament. There were of course Greek-speaking enclaves which continued to thrive and preserve their texts well into the medieval period, e.g., in Italy (cf. the manuscript groups f^1 and f^{13} which developed in southern Italy). But the main tradition of the Greek text was preserved in the Greek-speaking East, of which Egypt was an integral part. For although as early as the third/fourth century Coptic was the language of Egyptian monasticism, the official Church remained essentially Greek into the fifth century and later (even to the present, e.g., St. Catherine's Monastery on Mt. Sinai).

5. The concentration of the Church in the early centuries was in the East, centering in Asia Minor and adjacent areas. Both in numbers and in strength the churches in the West were far behind. Our view of the Western church's role in the early period has been unduly colored by the developments of later centuries. In the first two centuries all the theologians who achieved fame in the West were themselves from the East (from Marcion and the Apologists through Irenaeus and Hippolytus). Novatian of about A.D. 250 was the first to come from the West, and he was no more welcome in the Roman church than Hippolytus had been a little earlier because the interest at Rome was not so much in theology as in church practice, if we may use this (inadequate) term to summarize the achievements of Rome during the period. In the practical area Rome built soundly, formulating the creed, defining the New Testament canon, and developing the episcopal office — but without exhibiting a trace of scholarly interests in the strict sense. All the significant theologians of any influence in the West in the early period came from Eastern church backgrounds, bringing their New Testament texts with them.

6. Consequently the theory of a special "Western" type of the text is improbable from the outset, and even its most passionate proponents never refer

to it as "Western" without using quotation marks. No important personality can be identified at any time or place in the early Western church who would have been capable of the singular theological achievement represented by the text of the Gospels and Acts in the ancestor of Codex Bezae Cantabrigiensis (D). The Western church in the early period may possibly, or even probably, have had a special local text, but its deviations from the "normal" text were no greater than elsewhere. The text found in Codex Bezae Cantabrigiensis (D) of the fifth century, however, represents (in its exemplar) the achievement of an outstanding early theologian of the third/fourth century. In its day it attracted only a limited following; what the nineteenth/twentieth century has made of it is incredible.

7. Until the beginning of the fourth century the text of the New Testament developed freely. It was a "living text" in the Greek literary tradition, unlike the text of the Hebrew Old Testament, which was subject to strict controls because (in the oriental tradition) the consonantal text was holy. And the New Testament text continued to be a "living text" as long as it remained a manuscript tradition, even when the Byzantine church molded it to the procrustean bed of the standard and officially prescribed text. Even for later scribes, for example, the parallel passages of the Gospels were so familiar that they would adapt the text of one Gospel to that of another. They also felt themselves free to make corrections in the text, improving it by their own standards of correctness, whether grammatically, stylistically, or more substantively. This was all the more true of the early period, when the text had not yet attained canonical status, especially in the earliest period when Christians considered themselves filled with the Spirit. As a consequence the text of the early period was many-faceted, and each manuscript had its own peculiar character. This can be observed in such papyri as $\mathfrak{p}^{45}$, $\mathfrak{p}^{46}$, $\mathfrak{p}^{66}$, and so forth. The fact that this was not the normative practice has been proved by $\mathfrak{p}^{75}$, which represents a strict text just as $\mathfrak{p}^{52}$ of the period around A.D. 125 represents a normal text. It preserves the text of the original exemplar in a relatively faithful form (and is not alone in doing so; cf. p. 59).

8. Variant readings in the New Testament text which are not due to simple scribal error (or to the confusion of similar sounds when transcribing from dictation in a scriptorium) may be explained by its character as a "living text." While it is true that from at least the third century the scribes tried to copy their exemplars faithfully to the letter, they also followed the meaning as they transcribed the text (which they knew practically by heart), and this gave rise to variants. And yet balancing this, one of the characteristics of the New Testament textual tradition is tenacity, i.e., the stubborn resistance of readings and text types to change. The practice of concluding the gospel of Mark at 16:8, for example, continued to be observed in some Greek manuscripts as well as in versional manuscripts for centuries, although the "longer ending" of Mark 16:9-20 was recognized as canonical and its contents must have made it extremely attractive. Other examples are quite numerous (the ending of Romans, the pericope of the Woman Taken in Adultery, etc.; cf. pp. 297ff.). In fact, the very plurality of New Testament text types can be explained only by the tenacity of the New

Testament textual tradition. Some 10 to 20 percent of the Greek manuscripts have preserved faithfully the different text types of their various exemplars, even in the latest period when the dominance of the Byzantine Imperial text became so thoroughly pervasive. This is what makes it possible to retrace the original text of the New Testament through a broad range of witnesses.

9. The circulation of all the New Testament writings began where they were first written — the genuine letters were the only exceptions (their circulation began from their earliest destinations). As copies multiplied their circulation became steadily wider, like the ripples from a pebble cast into a pond. This means that from the writing of a document to its use in all the churches of a single diocese or throughout the whole Church, a certain amount of time must have elapsed. Meanwhile every copy made from another copy repeated the same pattern of expansion, like another pebble cast into the pond making a new series of ripples. These rippling circles would intersect. Two manuscripts in a single place (each with its own range of textual peculiarities, depending on its distance from the original text) would influence each other, producing a textual mixture and starting a new pattern of ripples — a process which would be repeated continually. Finally, to continue the metaphor, the pool becomes so filled with overlapping circles that it is practically impossible to distinguish their sources and their mutual relationships. This is precisely the situation the textual critic finds when attempting to analyze the history of the New Testament text.

10. All manuscripts must have been copied privately by individuals in the early period. A scriptorium with professional scribes producing manuscripts (a large number at a time, usually following dictation from a single exemplar) would have been an impossibility at the time, especially when Christians were threatened or suffering persecution. Of course it is possible that among the scribes in the scriptoria there were Christians who made copies of the scriptures at home. The earliest Christian scriptorium may have been in Alexandria about 200, but this would have served only the church in Egypt. Until then in Alexandria and until much later elsewhere (including the hinterlands of Egypt), in fact generally to the beginning of the fourth century, the production of manuscripts was quite limited, with only one copy of a manuscript being made at a time. Each copy would in turn be copied only singly, so that families of manuscripts were never very large.

11. The persecution by Diocletian left a deep scar not only in church history but also in the history of the New Testament text. Innumerable manuscripts were destroyed during the persecutions and had to be replaced. Even more were needed to supply the flood of new churches which sprang up in the Age of Constantine. This produced the conditions necessary for establishing church scriptoria in all the diocesan centers, or at least in all the provinces of the Church. The form of text or the particular manuscripts which were used as exemplars and undoubtedly mass produced in these scriptoria now became a determinative influence. And so Egypt, where the most varied texts had been in circulation, saw the development of what we know as the Alexandrian text, which was to develop further (under the influence of the Koine text) and in the

course of centuries become the Egyptian text. And in the different parts of the empire what is called the Koine text (later to become the Byzantine Imperial text) spread rapidly as students from the exegetical school at Antioch, who occupied many of the important sees of the time, either adopted the text of Antioch for their newly established diocesan scriptoria, or used it to replace the earlier standard exemplar where a scriptorium already existed. Quite understandably, true to the tenacity of the New Testament textual tradition, any local traditions would continue to be preserved alongside the text promoted by a church center. Readings representing other forms of the text familiar to particular church groups would continue to be transcribed and preserved, although now copied only singly and less frequently. Identifying the original form of the text is a decision which must be weighed afresh passage by passage, for the judgments made in Alexandria or in Antioch at the end of the third century or the beginning of the fourth century may appear less cogent today. This is particularly true for Antioch.

III

THE MANUSCRIPTS OF THE GREEK NEW TESTAMENT

1. THE NUMBER OF MANUSCRIPTS AND THEIR SYMBOLS BEFORE GREGORY

The first printed edition of the Greek New Testament produced by Erasmus[1] was based on four (or five) manuscripts. The number of manuscripts used increased rapidly in the period following. Although the details cannot be pursued here, we should at least note Johann Jakob Wettstein's edition of 1751-1752, which inaugurated the modern period. Wettstein knew and identified more than two hundred manuscripts, classifying them as uncials, minuscules, and lectionaries.[2] He used capital letters to identify the uncials, as we still do today: A = Codex Alexandrinus, B = Codex Vaticanus, C = Codex Ephraemi Syri Rescriptus, D = Codex Bezae Cantabrigiensis, etc. He used arabic numbers for the minuscules as well as for the lectionaries, beginning a new number series in each of the four groups of New Testament writings, because most manuscripts are found in only one of these groups. In the Gospel manuscripts he recorded uncials to the letter O, minuscules to 112, and lectionaries to 24; in the Pauline letters uncials to H, minuscules to 60, and lectionaries to 3;[3] in the Apostolos (i.e., Acts and the Catholic letters) uncials to H, minuscules to 58, and lectionaries to 4; in Revelation uncials to C, and minuscules to 28.

From even this brief description it is clear that in Wettstein's system the same letters and the same numbers were used for different manuscripts. We have replaced this practice today for the minuscules and lectionaries (except for the minuscules 1, 2, 4, and 7, where each number has a double reference), but not for the uncials. The use of a single letter for more than one manuscript was free of problems only for A and C, because these manuscripts actually contain the whole of the New Testament (though with lacunae). Even for B there was an awkward ambiguity: in the first three parts of the New Testament the symbol B

1. Cf. pp. 3f.
2. Cf. p. 9.
3. Wettstein's New Testament follows the order of Gospels (vol. 1), Paul's letters (ending with Hebrews), Acts, Catholic letters, Revelation (vol. 2).

represented the invaluable fourth-century manuscript Codex Vaticanus (which breaks off at Heb. 9:14), whereas in Revelation it represented a late uncial which is quite worthless (now 046, tenth century). Today as a heritage from Wettstein the letters through L and also P have a double reference, while for H it is triple. Depending on the part of the New Testament, each symbol has a different meaning — a source of constant confusion that can be dealt with only by adding superscript letters, e.g., D^{ea} = Codex Bezae Cantabrigiensis, D^p = Codex Claromontanus, etc., or by using the Gregory numbers (cf. below).

Succeeding generations followed Wettstein's pattern. Newly discovered manuscripts were duly registered in his fourfold system. One amusing complication arose when Constantin von Tischendorf discovered Codex Sinaiticus: he wished to give it a special position in the alphabetical order worthy of the importance he attributed to it, so he assigned it the symbol א. A greater difficulty was soon posed when the number of manuscripts grew so large that the number of letters in the Latin alphabet was no longer adequate. The Greek alphabet was then drawn upon, but it was also soon exhausted, and finally recourse was made to the use of Greek and Hebrew letters with additional superscripts.

By 1900 there were such symbols as Θ^h and $\daleth^{14}$, and the Latin capitals I, O, T, and W had 9, 11, 9, and 14 subdivisions respectively. Among the minuscules the confusion was even greater. Not only would a single number be used for four different manuscripts, each in a different part of the New Testament (and occasionally for a fifth manuscript as well — a lectionary), but the expansion of the Wettstein list was not controlled, so that a single number could be assigned to as many as six or seven different manuscripts. And on the other hand, a minuscule containing the whole of the New Testament would be identified with four different numbers. Thus the manuscript we know as minuscule 69 was identified by the number 69 in the Gospels, but it was called 429 in Acts, 421 in the Pauline letters, and 628 in Revelation.

2. GREGORY'S SYSTEM AND THE INCREASING NUMBER OF MANUSCRIPTS

Hermann Freiherr von Soden's ill-fated system for classifying manuscripts has been discussed above.[4] Caspar René Gregory (1846-1917), an American by birth but German by naturalization,[5] brought an American pragmatism to bear on the chaotic scene with his new manuscript list of 1908 *(Die griechischen Handschriften des Neuen Testaments),* establishing a system that has lasted to the present. Since Gregory the papyri have been indicated by an initial $\mathfrak{p}$ ($\mathfrak{p}^1$, $\mathfrak{p}^2$, etc.), and the uncials by numerals with an initial 0 (while retaining Wettstein's use of capital letters for the uncials through 045, e.g., א = 01, A = 02, B = 03, C = 04, D^{ea} = 05, D^p = 06, etc.), the minuscules with simple arabic numerals (1, 2, 3, etc.), and the lectionaries similarly but with a prefixed ℓ (ℓ1, ℓ2, ℓ3, etc.).

---

4. Cf. pp. 40f.
5. At the age of sixty-eight Gregory volunteered for active service on the German side in World War I, and he died in action.

No one would claim logical consistency for this system. One of the groups is defined by the nature of the material used (papyrus), two groups by the form of script (uncial, minuscule), and a fourth by the content of the manuscript (lectionaries). The papyri are generally written in the uncial script, as are the lectionaries before A.D. 1000, with minuscules appearing first in the ninth century. Nor did Gregory avoid all the flaws of earlier systems: as we have noticed, the numbers 1, 2, 4, and 7 still retained a double reference (in deference to tradition). The uncials all received new numbers, but they also retained their alphabetical symbols with double references through P, and sometimes with triple references which were distinguished by the use of various superscripts. And yet it was a great relief to be rid of earlier confusions. The new manuscript list of 1908 had none of the gratuitous tensions of an overly perfectionist system (such as von Soden's, or Alfred Rahlfs' list of Septuagint manuscripts). As a result the data in the critical apparatuses of all editions prior to 1908 must now be read with the aid of conversion tables (as a glance at Tischendorf's edition[6] will show).

Gregory's success was not due solely to the utility of his system (although he tested it repeatedly by circulating questionnaires among his colleagues), but also to the remarkable increase in the number of known New Testament manuscripts which he achieved by dint of his untiring efforts. Before Constantin von Tischendorf the number of known Greek New Testament manuscripts amounted to a mere 1,000. In contrast, Gregory's Prolegomena to Tischendorf's eighth edition (Leipzig: 1892) describes a total of 3,060! Then in 1908, when he published his *Die griechischen Handschriften des Neuen Testaments*, the number of known papyri had advanced to $\mathfrak{p}^{14}$, uncials to 0161, minuscules to 2304, and lectionaries to ℓ 1547. By 1915 Gregory had raised the numbers further to $\mathfrak{p}^{19}$, 0169, 2326, and ℓ 1565. From 1923 to 1933 his successor Ernst von Dobschütz further expanded the numbers to $\mathfrak{p}^{48}$, 0208, 2401 (but with some extensive lacunae), and ℓ 1609, although solely by recording discoveries reported to him by others — quite unlike Gregory who had augmented the list with his own discoveries. This tradition was revived by Kurt Aland, through whose efforts (first reporting in 1953) the number of New Testament manuscripts has risen among the papyri to $\mathfrak{p}^{96}$, the uncials to 0299, the minuscules to 2812, and the lectionaries to ℓ 2281. Of these newly reported manuscripts about 1,000 were discovered on research trips organized by the Institute for New Testament Textual Research in Münster. The total number of manuscripts now stands at 5,487 according to the official registry of manuscripts maintained by Aland in the Institute for New Testament Textual Research. This is only a nominal figure, however, and the actual number of New Testament manuscripts in existence today is probably more than 5,000. As a heritage of the past certain items have been counted which should not be included; several uncial fragments now identified as parts of single manuscripts have been counted separately; and, furthermore, a great many manuscripts have been irretrievably

6. Cf. pp. 38f.

lost in the nineteenth and twentieth centuries through wars and their consequences and through natural disasters. After the impressive growth in the number of manuscripts recorded in the nineteenth century by Gregory and in the twentieth century by the Institute for New Testament Textual Research, it is unlikely that the future will bring any comparable increases. Of course, such events as the recent discovery of a long forgotten room at St. Catherine's Monastery on Mt. Sinai could change the situation.

3. *WRITING MATERIALS*

In the early period New Testament texts were written on papyrus, as was all the literature of the time. This writing material was produced primarily (though not exclusively) in Egypt, manufactured from the papyrus plant which grew luxuriantly in the Nile delta. The papyrus plant grew to a height of six meters (the ornamental plant we know as papyrus gives a completely inadequate impression of it). Its thick stem was divided into sections and sharp tools were used to cut it lengthwise into wafer-thin strips. These strips were laid side by side to form a single layer with the fibers of the pith running in parallel, and on top of it a second layer was placed with the fibers running at right angles to the first. The two layers were then moistened, pressed together, and smoothed down. Finally, any projecting fibers were trimmed off and the papyrus sheet was cut to a desired size. The product did not have the brown to dark brown color we are familiar with from the samples of papyrus in museum showcases, but ranged from a light gray to a light yellow (the darker color results from centuries under the Egyptian sands). Nor was it at all as fragile as surviving samples appear, but sufficiently flexible for sheets to be pasted together in rolls of up to ten meters in length, to be written on and have a useful library life of several decades. The sheets were arranged in scrolls with the fibers of the inner (written) side running horizontally, and those of the outer (usually blank) side running vertically.

All the literature of the period was written on scrolls (including Jewish literature, with the sole qualification that leather was used for the Holy Scriptures); yet apparently from the very beginning Christians did not use the scroll format for their writings, but rather the codex.[7] They would buy a supply of papyrus sheets and fold them down the center. This had several disadvantages. Each sheet was now written on both sides, front and back — i.e., not only on the side with the fibers running horizontally, where writing was easy, but also on the side with the fibers running vertically, which made writing more difficult. Further, the total number of sheets required had to be estimated closely before reaching the midpoint of the text being composed or copied. Probably at first the sheets were placed together in simple sequence and folded once, producing a single quire, such as we have in $\mathfrak{p}^{46}$ ca. A.D. 200 or in $\mathfrak{p}^{75}$ at the beginning of the third century. Then multiple quires very soon came into use, with a regular number of sheets to a quire. For $\mathfrak{p}^{66}$ at the beginning of the third century the

---

7. Cf. p. 102.

number is irregular, with quires consisting variously of four or five double folios. Finally, the four-sheet quire with sixteen pages became standard; even today the most popular format is a sixteen-page quire (one sheet). These quires were then (as also now) gathered together and finally bound ($\mathfrak{p}^{66}$ shows traces of sewing, and $\mathfrak{p}^{75}$ preserves even its leather binding).

But the codex form was not the only distinctive characteristic of Christian literature (the earliest known New Testament papyrus, $\mathfrak{p}^{52}$ of about A.D. 125, was written as a codex). The Christians also introduced the abbreviations for what are known as nomina sacra, e.g., κύριος written as $\overline{\text{KC}}$, θεός as $\overline{\Theta\text{C}}$, etc. Manuscripts of the Septuagint, the Greek version of the Old Testament, can be assigned with confidence to a Christian or Jewish origin on the basis of their use or nonuse of these nomina sacra forms; when sifting through unclassified Greek materials in the manuscript sections of libraries or museums this is a useful key for identifying Christian texts. Although there has been much debate as to why the early Christians introduced the codex and the use of abbreviated nomina sacra, no clear consensus has emerged (the codex form may possibly be explained by economic factors).

New Testament papyri are known from as late as the eighth century (see chart 2, p. 82), but beginning in the fourth century the use of parchment for writing material became increasingly popular. One parchment manuscript is known from the second/third century (0189), two from the third century (0212, 0220), and two from the third/fourth century (0162, 0171); but then from the fourth century the picture changes, with a ratio of fourteen New Testament manuscripts on papyrus to fourteen on parchment (or fifteen, if we include ℓ 1604). From the fifth century there are only two papyri to thirty-six parchment manuscripts (or thirty-seven, if we include ℓ 1043; cf. chart 3, p. 82). Christians were following the trend of the times in changing to parchment. Although papyrus manuscripts were more durable than we imagine them today, yet they could not match the durability of parchment. The story is recounted by Pliny the Elder (first century) that King Eumenes of Pergamum wished to build a rival to the famous library at Alexandria, but was hindered by an Egyptian embargo on the export of papyrus. Thereupon he chose parchment as the material for manuscripts in his library. This story is mentioned here only because it has been widely repeated in texts and manuals, although there is very little likelihood of its authenticity. Parchment was in use well before Eumenes, and it did not become popular as a writing material until centuries later (the legend is probably based on the fact that Pergamum in Asia Minor was known for the production of a particularly good quality of parchment).

Parchment is made from animal hide. The hide (theoretically of any animal, but usually of a sheep or goat) first had the hair and flesh removed by a solution of lime mordant, and was then trimmed to size, polished, and smoothed with chalk and pumice stone to prepare the surface for use. The fibers of a papyrus sheet helped the scribe to write in straight lines, but with parchment the lines had to be drawn. This was done with a metal stylus. The impression it made can often still be seen in manuscripts. The line was drawn on the hair

side, so that it still appears there as a depression and on the flesh side as a slight ridge (guide lines for the columns in manuscripts were marked in the same way). The difference between the hair side and the flesh side posed a difficulty with parchment manuscripts, because the one side was darker in color and the other lighter. A convenient solution was found by arranging the four-sheet quire (which became standard) so that hair side faced hair side and flesh side faced flesh side.

Another problem posed by the change to parchment was a limitation on the size of a page. One sheep or goat could provide only two double folios, i.e., only four folios of the finished manuscript, the size of which would be determined by the size of the animal. A manuscript containing a group of New Testament writings in the average format (about 200-250 folios of approximately 25 × 19 cm.) required the hides of at least fifty to sixty sheep or goats. This would mean quite a good size flock. Manuscripts would often need to be larger to accommodate more than a single group of writings,[8] and this would require a greater number of hides. Only by considering this aspect can we gain some idea of what a manuscript of the New Testament would have cost in past centuries. For a larger manuscript (Codex Sinaiticus was originally at least 43 × 38 cm. in size) or one of a particularly fine quality of parchment, the expense would have multiplied. In fact, a manuscript of the New Testament represented a small fortune because the preparation of the parchment was only the first step. Once it had been prepared there was still the writing of the text to be done, as well as the illumination of the initials, and frequently also the addition of miniatures by an artist. When the parchment was stained with purple and inscribed with silver and gold lettering (and several such manuscripts have survived from the sixth century), clearly the manuscript must have been commissioned by persons of the upper classes who could afford to ignore the expense. The fact that the text of these manuscripts is without exception of the Byzantine type simply demonstrates the textual preference of the persons who commissioned them.

Parchment continued to be used for writing until recent centuries. But from the twelfth century paper began to gain in popularity (the earliest manuscript of the New Testament on paper dates from the ninth century). It is well known (cf. any encyclopedia) that paper was invented by the Chinese in the first century A.D., and that its use spread throughout the Arab world from the eighth century. But in the West it did not assume a significant role until the twelfth century. Of the 5,400 known manuscripts of the New Testament, about 1,300 are written on paper (2 uncials, 698 minuscules, and 587 lectionaries; in 11 minuscules and 5 lectionaries parchment and paper sheets are found together). In the tradition of technical progress it is only natural that this early paper (known as bombycine paper) should have imitated parchment models, just as it is no accident that the spoked wheels of early automobiles resembled those of the horse-drawn carriages they replaced.

8. Cf. pp. 78f.

4. *DISTRIBUTION BY AGE*

Table 4 (p. 81) shows the distribution of manuscripts by century (as of May 1988). For those who prefer visual representation, chart 2 is a graphic transcription of the same data illustrating the distribution of **text manuscripts**.[9]

This highlights the increased number of (surviving) New Testament text manuscripts from the eleventh to the fourteenth centuries. An estimate of the number of manuscripts actually produced in each century is of course possible only within limits because of varying rates of attrition; i.e., losses would be greater during the Diocletianic persecution than before, and in the fifteenth century the Islamic invasion of the Christian Greek world produced a similar situation. Yet the chart gives a general impression. The differences between the table and the chart are due to the listing of cross-century dates (e.g., second/third) separately in the table, while in the chart they are included in the later century. The distribution of **lectionary manuscripts** by century is shown in chart 3. Here again the number is highest from the eleventh to the fourteenth centuries.

5. *DISTRIBUTION BY CONTENT*

The contents of New Testament manuscripts can only be sketched here in outline. Only 3 uncials (ℵ 01, A 02, C 04) and 56 minuscules (or 57, if 205[abs] is counted separately) contain the whole of the New Testament. In 2 uncials and 147 minuscules only Revelation is lacking because of its canonical history. Otherwise the groups of New Testament writings are generally found in a variety of combinations. One uncial and 75 minuscules contain the New Testament without the Gospels; 11 minuscules have the Gospels together with Revelation; 2 papyri, 1 uncial, and 8 minuscules have the Gospels with Acts and the Catholic letters, while 2 more minuscules include Revelation as well. The Pauline letters are found with Revelation in 6 minuscules; Acts and the Catholic letters are with Revelation in 3 more minuscules. The Gospels are found with the Pauline letters in 5 minuscules. A particularly large group of manuscripts contains Acts together with the Catholic and Pauline letters: 8 uncials and 265 minuscules — this is more than any group containing a single group of writings; e.g., the Apostolos (i.e., Acts and the Catholic letters) is found alone in 18 papyri (12 fragmentary), 29 uncials (27 fragmentary), and 40 minuscules (5 fragmentary), For the Pauline letters the numbers are somewhat higher: 26 papyri (18 fragmentary), 58 uncials (46 fragmentary), 138 minuscules (6 fragmentary). For Revelation the numbers are understandably lower: 5 papyri (4 fragmentary), 7 uncials (3 fragmentary), and 118 minuscules (1 fragmentary). All of these groups, however, are far outnumbered by the Four Gospels manuscripts: 43 papyri (31 fragmentary), 184 uncials (110 fragmentary), 1,896 minuscules (57 fragmentary). These figures produce the following totals for each group of writings: the Gospels are preserved

---

9. Cf. p. 82.

in 2,361 manuscripts, the Apostolos in 662, the Pauline letters in 792, and Revelation in 287 Greek manuscripts. This is illustrated in chart 4, p. 83.

The sequence of the New Testament writings varies in the manuscripts, not only in the order of the four groups of writings themselves but also in the order of the writings within each group. The only characteristic common to the whole manuscript tradition (extending also to canon lists, patristic references, and other sources which allude to the sequence of the writings) is that the Gospels stand at the beginning and Revelation at the end. Otherwise all variations of sequence occur, e.g., Acts-Paulines-Catholics, Acts-Catholics-Paulines (as in A B C and the majority of the manuscripts), Paulines-Acts-Catholics (as in ℵ and a group of minuscules), Paulines-Catholics-Acts — possibly reflecting theological evaluations or historical hypotheses. A glimpse of the developing New Testament canon may be caught in the varied and sometimes arbitrary sequences of the Gospels and the letters of Paul in the manuscripts. The Gospels circulated separately at first, and their association in a single corpus developed under varied circumstances. The Pauline corpus represents a cumulative development from smaller collections, raising additional problems with its expansion to include the deutero-Pauline letters. The present sequence of the Gospels is found in the great majority of manuscripts and versions, but there is also the "Western" sequence of Matthew-John-Luke-Mark, and one beginning with John (followed by as varied orders as when beginning with Matthew). In the Pauline corpus the range of variation is greater than hitherto suspected. Our three known witnesses from the second century (Marcion, the Muratorian Canon, and $\mathfrak{p}^{46}$) differ completely among themselves, with $\mathfrak{p}^{46}$ exhibiting the present order (to the extent of its preservation, with the exception that Hebrews comes between Romans and 1 Corinthians, and Ephesians before Galatians).

6. *THE MAJOR COLLECTIONS*

Collections of New Testament manuscripts are found throughout the world. For the most part they represent the efforts of collectors rather than natural accumulations. The principal examples of natural development are the monasteries of Mt. Athos (where the Great Treasury alone has more than 254 manuscripts) and St. Catherine's Monastery on Mt. Sinai (where until recently 230 manuscripts were known, though with new discoveries this number has been increased to 301). At present the most extensive collections of New Testament manuscripts are found in the following places.

50-100 manuscripts	Cambridge	66	Grottaferrata	69
	Florence	79	Patmos	81
	Moscow	96		
100-200 manuscripts	Jerusalem	146	Oxford	158
200-500 manuscripts	Leningrad	233	London	271
	Sinai	301	Rome	367
	Paris	373	Athens	419
Over 500 manuscripts	Mt. Athos	900		

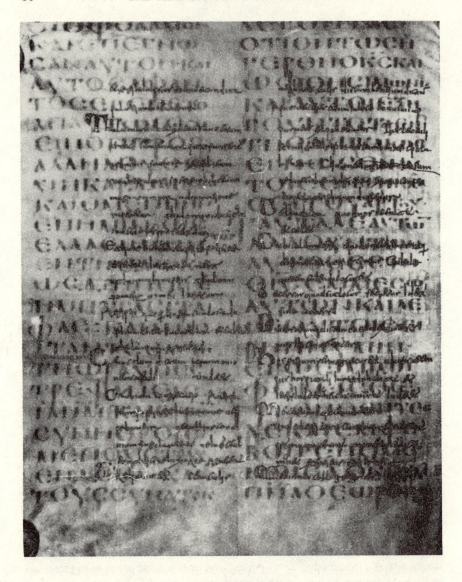

Plate 18. Codex Guelferbytanus (P^e, 024; cf. p. 113; a palimpsest like Codex Ephraemi Syri Rescriptus, C, 04; cf. p. 109), a Gospels manuscript written in the sixth century: Luke 24:31-37, erased and written over with a Latin text from Isidore of Seville.

Table 4.   Distribution of Greek manuscripts by century

Century	NEW TESTAMENT MANUSCRIPTS			LECTIONARIES	
	Papyri	Uncials	Minuscules	Uncials	Minuscules
2nd	2	—	—	—	—
ca. 200	4	—	—	—	—
2nd/3rd	1	1	—	—	—
3rd	28	2	—	—	—
3rd/4th	8	2	—	—	—
4th	14	14	—	1	—
4th/5th	8	8	—	—	—
5th	2	36	—	1	—
5th/6th	4	10	—	—	—
6th	7	51	—	3	—
6th/7th	5	5	—	1	—
7th	8	28	—	4	—
7th/8th	3	4	—	—	—
8th	2	29	—	22	—
8th/9th	—	4	—	5	—
9th	—	53	13	113	5
9th/10th	—	1	4	—	1
10th	—	17	124	108	38
10th/11th	—	3	8	3	4
11th	—	1	429	15	227
11th/12th	—	—	33	—	13
12th	—	—	555	6	486
12th/13th	—	—	26	—	17
13th	—	—	547	4	394
13th/14th	—	—	28	—	17
14th	—	—	511	—	308
14th/15th	—	—	8	—	2
15th	—	—	241	—	171
15th/16th	—	—	4	—	2
16th	—	—	136	—	194

We can see reflected here an aspect of cultural history, and incidentally an example of colonialism in its broadest sense. Observe how the collections in France and England grew — partly from the enterprise of their world-traveling citizens. Manuscript donations were attracted as if by magic to Moscow, the "Third Rome," seat of the Patriarch and center of the only surviving Orthodox kingdom after 1453, and also to Leningrad, residence of the Tsars and the cultural capital of their nation, just as they were to Rome, the center of Western Christianity. Political skills also contributed to concentrations of holdings both in the East and in the West. In Moscow, for example, there was the archimandrite Suchanov in the seventeenth century who arranged the transfer of at least twenty-five New Testament manuscripts from Athos, while Rome "acquired" the Heidelberg Palatinate Library. In neither instance was piety or patriotism the sole motivating factor. Even a cursory review of the various foundations of the Vatican Library or of the notes on the derivation of the Leningrad New Testament manuscripts can be vividly suggestive. But even in Athens, where a collection could well be expected to have developed naturally from local sources, the evidence is otherwise. The Greek National Library, which possesses the greatest number

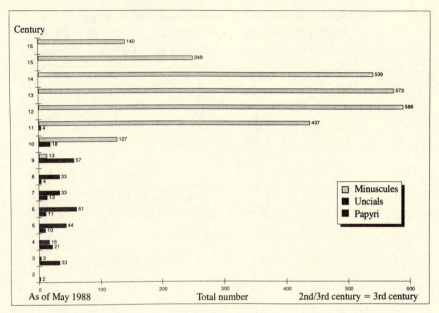

Chart 2. Distribution of New Testament text manuscripts by century.

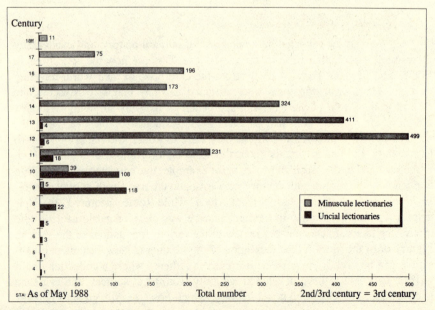

Chart 3. Distribution of New Testament lectionaries by century.

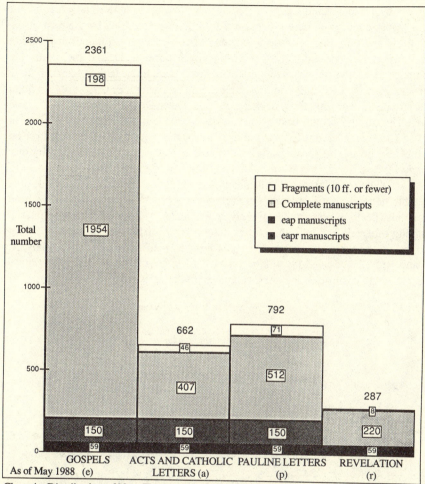

Chart 4. Distribution of New Testament manuscripts by content.

of manuscripts, was founded only in the nineteenth century, and the other manuscripts are all in public or private collections whose origins are no earlier. Although neither the Federal Republic of Germany (including West Berlin — with a total of 100 manuscripts, 21 of which are in the Institute for New Testament Textual Research), nor even the United States (although showing a growth from 45 New Testament manuscripts in 1912 to 291 in 1964), is represented among the major collections, this is due in the United States to its relative youth as a nation and the distribution of the manuscripts in so many collections, and in the Federal Republic of Germany to a short-sighted cultural policy. Apart from the Institute in Münster, the museums and libraries of Germany have not acquired a single manuscript of the Greek New Testament for decades.

7. *THE PAPYRI*

Not until the twentieth century did the New Testament papyri achieve the special prestige they enjoy so widely now. Classified almost accidentally as a separate

group by Caspar René Gregory,[10] they played only a subordinate role in the nineteenth century — only nine papyri were known or edited by the turn of the century, and only one of these was cited in the critical apparatus of any edition ($\mathfrak{p}^{11}$, cited only partially by Constantin von Tischendorf). By the 1930s the number of known papyri had grown to more than forty without any of them arousing any special attention, despite the fact that many of them were of a quite early date. Then came the discovery of the Chester Beatty papyri: $\mathfrak{p}^{45}$, $\mathfrak{p}^{46}$, and $\mathfrak{p}^{47}$. The excitement aroused by these manuscripts had not yet subsided when in 1935 Colin Henderson Roberts published $\mathfrak{p}^{52}$ dating from about A.D. 125. The problems raised by these papyri were still being debated when the Bodmer papyri $\mathfrak{p}^{66}$, $\mathfrak{p}^{72}$, and $\mathfrak{p}^{74}$ were published between 1956 and 1961.

The term "papyrus" has since held an almost magical charm, not only for the general public but for New Testament scholars as well, though with no real justification. Papyrus is merely a particular variety of writing material among others,[11] and only the papyri before the third/fourth century (i.e., prior to the period when the major text types were formed) have any inherent significance (for the reasons mentioned on pp. 56f.). From then on the only critical factor is the quality of the text, whatever material it may be written on. The

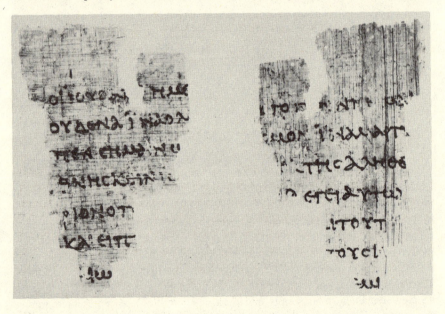

Plate 19. The earliest manuscript of the New Testament, $\mathfrak{p}^{52}$ (ca. 125; cf. p. 99): John 18:31-33 (obverse), 18:37-38 (reverse).

10. Cf. pp. 73f.
11. Cf. p. 75.

significance of $\mathfrak{p}^{74}$, a seventh-century manuscript of Acts and the Catholic letters (cf. plate 20), is not due to its being written on papyrus but to the excellent text it preserves. Among the ninety-six items which now comprise the official list of New Testament papyri there are several which by a strict definition do not belong there, such as talismans ($\mathfrak{p}^{50}$, $\mathfrak{p}^{78}$), lectionaries ($\mathfrak{p}^{2}$, $\mathfrak{p}^{3}$, $\mathfrak{p}^{44}$), various selections ($\mathfrak{p}^{43}$, $\mathfrak{p}^{62}$), songs ($\mathfrak{p}^{42}$), texts with commentary ($\mathfrak{p}^{55}$, $\mathfrak{p}^{59}$, $\mathfrak{p}^{60}$, $\mathfrak{p}^{63}$, $\mathfrak{p}^{80}$), and even writing exercises ($\mathfrak{p}^{10}$) and occasional notes ($\mathfrak{p}^{12}$). The presence of lectionaries may be explained as due to a structural flaw in the overall system, the inclusion of commented texts to the lack of an adequate definition for this genre (probably akin to the popular religious tracts of today which feature selected scripture verses with oracular notes), and the other examples are due to the occasionally uncritical attitude of earlier editors of the list. But these peculiarities are on the whole negligible. Table 5 shows the distribution of the papyri among the books of the New Testament.

Table 5.   Distribution of papyri by New Testament books

Matthew	18	(7 early) papyri	1 Timothy	—	(— early) papyri
Mark	3	(1 early) papyri	2 Timothy	—	(— early) papyri
Luke	8	(4 early) papyri	Titus	2	(1 early) papyri
John	22	(11 early) papyri	Philemon	2	(1 early) papyri
Acts	13	(6 early) papyri	Hebrews	6	(3 early) papyri
Romans	8	(3 early) papyri	James	4	(2 early) papyri
1 Corinthians	7	(2 early) papyri	1 Peter	3	(1 early) papyri
2 Corinthians	2	(1 early) papyri	2 Peter	2	(1 early) papyri
Galatians	2	(1 early) papyri	1 John	2	(1 early) papyri
Ephesians	3	(3 early) papyri	2 John	1	(— early) papyrus
Philippians	3	(2 early) papyri	3 John	1	(— early) papyrus
Colossians	2	(1 early) papyri	Jude	3	(2 early) papyri
1 Thessalonians	4	(3 early) papyri	Revelation	5	(2 early) papyri
2 Thessalonians	2	(2 early) papyri			

Of course the figures in table 5 cannot be taken cumulatively, but only in terms of individual New Testament books. Adding them together would give a distorted picture, because papyri containing more than a single book are repeated here for each of the books ($\mathfrak{p}^{30}$, $\mathfrak{p}^{34}$, $\mathfrak{p}^{44}$, $\mathfrak{p}^{45}$, $\mathfrak{p}^{46}$, $\mathfrak{p}^{53}$, $\mathfrak{p}^{61}$, $\mathfrak{p}^{72}$, $\mathfrak{p}^{74}$, $\mathfrak{p}^{75}$, $\mathfrak{p}^{84}$; cf. chart 5). This applies to the early papyri as well, i.e., those dating from the third/fourth century and earlier. And yet these come to about forty-three in all, i.e., nearly half the known number of papyri. Parchment did not come into use as a writing material for the New Testament until the fourth century — in the meanwhile papyrus was the rule (with five exceptions, cf. table 4).

We cannot conclude this survey of the papyri without some further comments on the truly amazing discoveries of the past generation. The critical significance of $\mathfrak{p}^{52}$, which preserves only a fragment of John 18, lies in the date of "about 125" assigned to it by the leading papyrologists. Although "about 125" allows for a leeway of about twenty-five years on either side, the consensus has come in recent years to regard 125 as representing the later limit, so that $\mathfrak{p}^{52}$ must have been copied very soon after the Gospel of John was itself written in the early 90s A.D. (with the recent discovery of $\mathfrak{p}^{90}$ another second century frag-

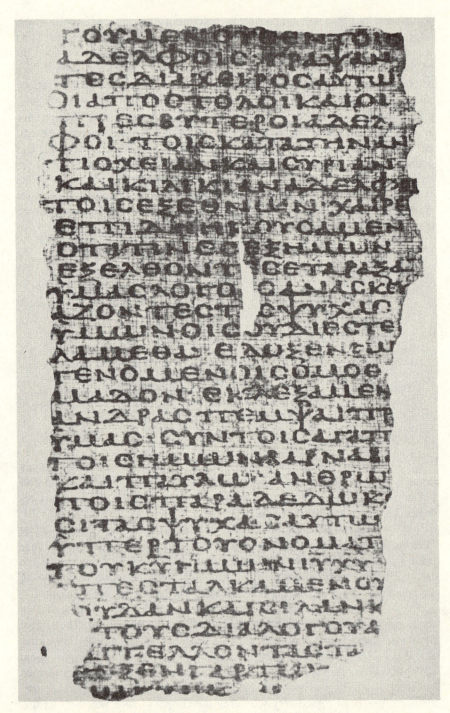

Plate 20. p⁷⁴ (Bodmer XVII, seventh century; cf. p. 101): Acts 15:23-28 (f. 51ʳ).

ment of the Gospel of John is now known). It provides a critical witness to the quality of the New Testament textual tradition, further confirming it by exhibiting a "normal text", i.e., attesting the text of today (that of Nestle-Aland[26] and *GNT*[3]). While it is true that papyri from the third century were known before the discovery of the Chester Beatty papyri, none of them was as early as $\mathfrak{p}^{46}$, which contains the Pauline letters and has been dated "about 200" (with some leeway on either side). But more significantly, all the early papyri known previously contain no more than a few verses of the New Testament text, with the exception of $\mathfrak{p}^{15}$ from the third century which preserves almost a whole leaf. Now for the first time entire New Testament writings became available from the early period. The character of their text was posing serious problems for scholarship when the Bodmer papyri $\mathfrak{p}^{66}$, $\mathfrak{p}^{72}$, and $\mathfrak{p}^{75}$ were discovered.

Even in its physical aspects the first published Bodmer papyrus $\mathfrak{p}^{66}$ presented a completely new phenomenon, something which had been considered impossible. Here was a gospel of John preserved in the form of a book, except for some minor damage around the edges: from the first folio with the superscription of the book there were 52 leaves (26 double leaves to ch. 14) preserved in their entirety, with the remainder of the book more or less fragmentary (cf. plate 22). Even the original sewing of the quires could be recognized, with traces of the papyrus strips used, etc. No one had ever thought it possible that a papyrus manuscript could survive over 1750 years (it was dated about A.D. 200) in such good condition. Among the Chester Beatty papyri $\mathfrak{p}^{45}$ preserved only fragments of leaves (cf. plate 26), and although the leaves of $\mathfrak{p}^{46}$ were better preserved, they had suffered considerable damage, usually with the last two to seven lines of each page missing (cf. plate 21), while $\mathfrak{p}^{47}$, the best preserved, lacked from one to four lines at the top of its pages, and its upper inner and lower outer corners were damaged with a loss of text (cf. plate 23). But if the physical aspects of $\mathfrak{p}^{66}$ (Papyrus Bodmer II) were unparalleled, so was its text. Properly understood, it finally provided the key to a full appreciation of the Chester Beatty papyri and of the New Testament text in the late second century.

The implications of Papyrus Bodmer XIV/XV ($\mathfrak{p}^{75}$) of the gospels of Luke and John went even further. Written somewhat later, at the beginning of the third century, it comprised twenty-seven almost perfectly preserved sheets (cf. plate 24) together with a part of their binding. This papyrus marked another revolution in our understanding of how the New Testament text developed: its text proved to be so close to that of Codex Vaticanus (B) that the theory of recensions, i.e., of thoroughgoing revisions of the New Testament text made in the fourth century, was no longer defensible.[12] One of the main pillars supporting the dominant theory of New Testament textual history was now demolished.

Then a third Bodmer papyrus (Bibliotheca Bodmeriana ms. VII/VIII) made the deepest of impressions. This is $\mathfrak{p}^{72}$ (cf. plate 25), which dates from the third/fourth century and contains the letters of Peter and Jude as a single collection of writings. This fact alone is startling enough, but when we consider

12. Cf. pp. 49f.

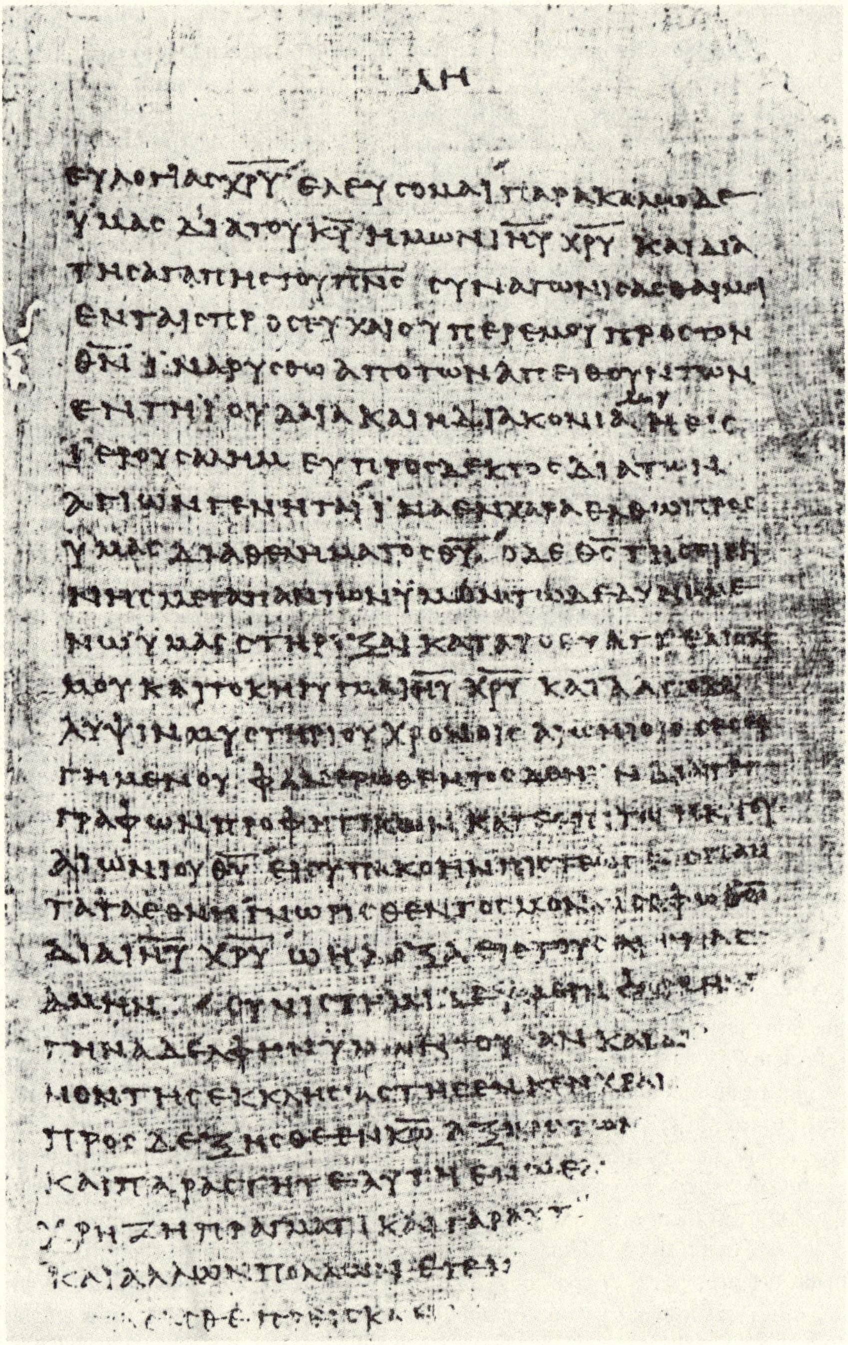

Plate 21. p⁴⁶ (Chester Beatty II, ca. 200; cf. p. 99): Rom. 15:29-33; 16:25-27, 1-3 (f. 20ʳ).

Plate 22. 𝔭⁶⁶ (Bodmer II, ca. 200; cf. p. 100): the beginning of the gospel of John.

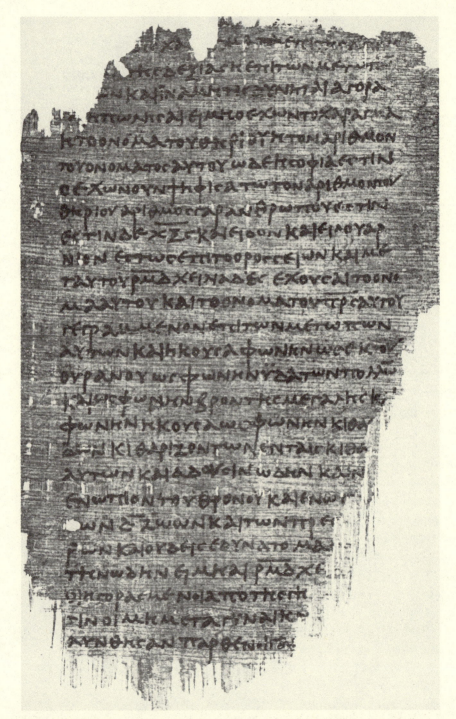

Plate 23. p⁴⁷ (Chester Beatty III, second century; cf. p. 99): Rev. 13:16–14:4 (f. 7ʳ).

Plate 24. p⁷⁵ (Bodmer XIV, XV, early second century; cf. p. 101): the ending of the gospel of Luke and the beginning of John (f. 44ʳ).

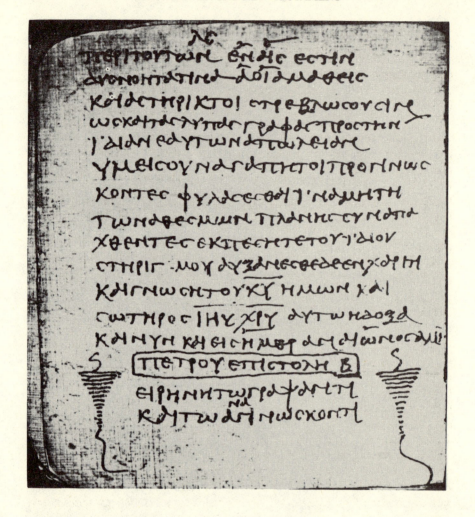

Plate 25. 𝔭⁷² (Bodmer VII, VIII, third/fourth century; cf. p. 100): the ending of 2 Peter, with the scribe's concluding prayer for himself and the reader (f. 36).

it in the context of the history of the canon and of the period when Jude and 2 Peter were originally written,[13] this early papyrus becomes extraordinarily significant. The text it offers corresponds to the expectations aroused by its outward characteristics. For the Catholic letters $\mathfrak{p}^{72}$ is one of the most important textual witnesses, if not itself the most important. And further, it is clearly not the work of a professional scribe (cf. the awkward hand).

The view of the text of the early period which emerged after $\mathfrak{p}^{66}$ joined the Chester Beatty papyri was basically along the following lines. There was a "normal" text which transmitted the original text with the limited amount of variation characteristic of the New Testament textual tradition down to the latest period (in contrast to the Hebrew Old Testament and other oriental traditions such as the Koran, where an almost letter-perfect transcription was the rule). Beside this there was a "free" text (e.g., $\mathfrak{p}^{45}$, $\mathfrak{p}^{46}$, $\mathfrak{p}^{66}$), characterized by a greater degree of variation than the "normal" text, and also a "strict" text (e.g., $\mathfrak{p}^{75}$), which reproduced the text of its exemplar with greater fidelity (although still with certain characteristic liberties), exhibiting far less variation than the "normal" text. There was also a group of transitional forms, including such examples as $\mathfrak{p}^{38}$, $\mathfrak{p}^{48}$, $\mathfrak{p}^{69}$, which may be regarded as precursors or branches of the D text. Below is a complete list of the papyri indicating in a somewhat condensed form the contents of those containing more than one biblical book (cf. endsheet for a summarizing chart, and for further details cf. Kurt Aland, *Kurzgefasste Liste der griechischen Handschriften des Neuen Testaments*, and especially *Repertorium der griechischen christliches Papyri* 1: *Biblische Papyri* [Berlin: 1976]). We have taken particular care to indicate the editions which must be relied on (although they are not all easily available) pending the publication of *Das Neue Testament auf Papyrus* (volume I, with the Catholic letters, appeared in 1986, and volume II, with Romans–2 Corinthians, is at press).

At least as important as the bibliography for each papyrus is information about its textual character, which we have added in the descriptive list (with explicit evaluations of the text for those of the third/fourth century and earlier, and classifications by category for later texts; cf. pp. 129ff.). Of special importance are the early papyri, i.e., of the period up to the third/fourth century. As we have said, these have an inherent significance for New Testament textual studies because they witness to a situation before the text was channeled into major text types in the fourth century. Our research on the early papyri has yielded unexpected results that require a change in the traditional views of the early text. We have inherited from the past generation the view that the early text was a "free" text, and the discovery of the Chester Beatty papyri seemed to confirm this view. When $\mathfrak{p}^{45}$ and $\mathfrak{p}^{46}$ were joined by $\mathfrak{p}^{66}$ sharing the same characteristics, this position seemed to be definitely established. $\mathfrak{p}^{75}$ appeared in contrast to be a loner with its "strict" text anticipating Codex Vaticanus. Meanwhile the other witnesses of the early period had been ignored. It is their collations which have changed the picture so completely. The "free" text of $\mathfrak{p}^{45}$,

13. Cf. pp. 49f., 64.

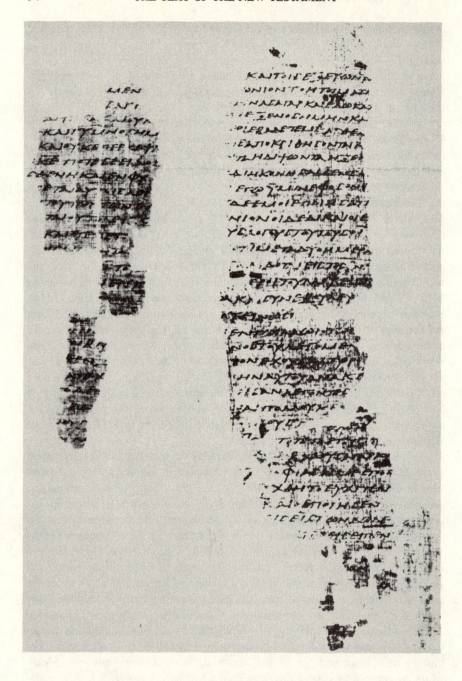

Plate 26. 𝔭⁴⁵ (early third century; cf. p. 98): Matt. 25:41–26:18 (f. 2ʳ), the only fragment preserved in Vienna (right) is aligned with its page in the Chester Beatty Library.

$\mathfrak{p}^{46}$, $\mathfrak{p}^{66}$, is further represented only in $\mathfrak{p}^9$(?), $\mathfrak{p}^{13}$(?), $\mathfrak{p}^{29}$, $\mathfrak{p}^{37}$, $\mathfrak{p}^{40}$, $\mathfrak{p}^{69}$, $\mathfrak{p}^{72}$ (Jude), $\mathfrak{p}^{78}$. In contrast to the "free" text of these eleven papyri (some of which are questionable), there is a group of nine papyri with a "strict" text, including $\mathfrak{p}^{75}$ together with $\mathfrak{p}^1$, $\mathfrak{p}^{23}$, $\mathfrak{p}^{27}$, $\mathfrak{p}^{35}$, $\mathfrak{p}^{39}$, $\mathfrak{p}^{64+67}$, $\mathfrak{p}^{65}$(?), $\mathfrak{p}^{70}$, The "normal" text is found in eleven papyri: $\mathfrak{p}^4$, $\mathfrak{p}^5$, $\mathfrak{p}^{12}$(?), $\mathfrak{p}^{16}$, $\mathfrak{p}^{18}$, $\mathfrak{p}^{20}$, $\mathfrak{p}^{28}$, $\mathfrak{p}^{47}$, $\mathfrak{p}^{52}$, $\mathfrak{p}^{72}$ (1,2 Peter), $\mathfrak{p}^{87}$, and between the "normal and the "strict" texts there are seven more papyri ("at least normal text" indicates a more or less distinct tendency toward the "strict" text). The three papyri with affinities to the D text have already been mentioned: $\mathfrak{p}^{38}$, $\mathfrak{p}^{48}$, $\mathfrak{p}^{69}$. A classification cannot be assigned to $\mathfrak{p}^{80}$ because of its brevity. To these papyri with an early text the further witness of four uncials should be added here (0212 is omitted as a Diatessaron text): 0162, 0171, 0189, 0220. Among these 0220 has a "strict" text, and the others stand between it and the "normal" text, except for 0171, which has a "paraphrastic" text.[14]

Although many details are obviously still debatable, there can be no doubt that the earlier view of the textual situation before the rise of the major text types is now due for a radical and thorough review (for an explanation of the terms "category I, II," and so forth, cf. pp. 106, 159, and 232ff. All the papyri before the third/fourth century are placed in the highest category because of their age, even when their "free" text sets them at a distance from the original text. Even in such instances their witness should always be considered. $\mathfrak{p}^{38}$, $\mathfrak{p}^{48}$, and $\mathfrak{p}^{69}$ are placed in category IV because of their affinity to the D text.[15] But then $\mathfrak{p}^{74}$, is placed in category I in the review below in spite of its seventh-century date because of its textual quality. According to the system described in detail on pp. 106 and 159, the relationships of its readings in Acts are $3^1\ 25^{1/2}\ 60^2\ 8^s$, i.e., in the test passages in Acts for determining textual relationships is has 3 agreements with the Byzantine text, 8 singular or distinctive readings, and 85 agreements with the original text (25 of which are of limited significance because they represent instances where the original text and the Majority reading coincide). In the Catholic letters the relationships for $\mathfrak{p}^{74}$, are $0^1\ 1^{1/2}\ 7^2\ 2^s$. This system of classification by categories and the program of selective collations underlying it are discussed below in the treatment of the uncial manuscripts (pp. 106f., etc.) rather than here with the papyri because the comparison of complete manuscripts is essential to both. It is nonetheless interesting to note the statistics for the longer papyri: for Luke in $\mathfrak{p}^{75}$, $2^1\ 1^{1/2}\ 26^2\ 5^s$; for Paul's letters in $\mathfrak{p}^{46}$, $16^1\ 22^{1/2}\ 105^2\ 43^s$; for the Catholic letters in $\mathfrak{p}^{72}$, $3^1\ 2^{1/2}\ 24^2\ 9^s$.

In the list of papyri below the following special bibliographical abbreviations are used.

Casson Lionel Casson and Ernest Leopold Hettich, *Excavations at Nessana* II (Princeton: 1950)

14. For details, cf. Kurt Aland, "Der neue 'Standard-Text' in seinem Verhältnis zu den frühen Papyri und Majuskeln," pp. 257-275 in *New Testament Textual Criticism, Its Significance for Exegesis: Essays in Honour of Bruce M. Metzger,* ed. Eldon Jay Epp and Gordon D. Fee (Oxford: 1981).

15. Cf. pp. 109f.

Grenfell-Hunt Bernard Pyne Grenfell and Arthur Surridge Hunt, *The Oxy-rhynchus Papyri* I-XV (London: 1898-1922)

Sanz Peter Sanz, *Griechische literarische Papyri christlichen Inhalts.* MPNW (Baden: 1946)

Schofield Ellwood M. Schofield, *The Papyrus Fragments of the Greek New Testament* (diss., Southern Baptist Theological Seminary, Louisville, 1936)

Wessely Karl Wessely, "Les plus anciens monuments du christianisme," *PO* 4/2 (1907)

Descriptive List of Papyri

$\mathfrak{p}^1$ Matt. 1:1-9,12,14-20; third century. Philadelphia: University Museum, University of Pennsylvania E 2746. Grenfell-Hunt, I (1898):4-7; Wessely, 142-44; Schofield, 86-91. *(Strict text, category I)*

$\mathfrak{p}^2$ John 12:12-15 (Greek), Luke 7:22-26,50 (Coptic); sixth. Florence: Museo Archaeologico Inv. no. 7134. E. Pistelli, "Papiri evangelici," *RStR* 6/2 (1906):129-140; Schofield, 92-95. *(Category III)*

$\mathfrak{p}^3$ Luke 7:36-45; 10:38-42; sixth/seventh. Vienna: Österreichische Nationalbibliothek, P. Vindob. G 2323. Wessely, "Evangelien-Fragmente auf Papyrus," *WS* 4 (1882):198-214; "Neue Evangelien-Fragmente auf Papyrus," *WS* 7 (1885):69-70; Schofield, 96-99. *(Category III)*

$\mathfrak{p}^4$ Luke 1:58-59; 1:62–2:1,6-7; 3:8–4:2,29-32, 34-35; 5:3-8; 5:30–6:16; third. Paris: Bibliothèque Nationale, Suppl. Gr. 1120. Vincent Scheil, "Archéologie, Varia," *RB* 1 (1892):113-15; *Mémoires publiés par les membres de la Mission archéologique française au Caire* 9/2 (Paris: 1893):215; Schofield, 100-106; J. Merell, "Nouveaux fragments du papyrus IV," *RB* 47 (1938):5-22. *(Normal text, category I)*

$\mathfrak{p}^5$ John 1:23-31,33-40; 16:14-30; 20:11-17,19-20,22-25; third. London: British Library, Inv. nos. 782, 2484. Grenfell-Hunt, II (1899):1-8 (P. Oxy. 208); XV (1922):8-12; Wessely, 145-48; Schofield, 107-117. *(Normal text, category I)*

$\mathfrak{p}^6$ John 10:1-2,4-7,9-10; 11:1-8,45-52 (Greek), John 10:1-12,20; 13:1-2,11-12; Jas. 1:13–5:20 (Coptic); fourth. Strasbourg: Bibliothèque Nationale et Universitaire, P. Copt. 379, 381, 382, 384. Friedrich Rösch, ed., *Bruchstücke des ersten Clemens-brief nach dem achmimischen Papyrus der Strassburger Universitäts- und Landes-bibliothek* (Strasbourg: 1910), pp. 119-122, 131-34, 143-48 (Greek); Schofield, 118-125. *(Category II)*

$\mathfrak{p}^7$ Luke 4:1-2 (patristic fragment?); fourth/sixth(?). Kiev: Ukrainian National Library, Petrov 553 (lost). Kurt Aland, "Neue neutestamentliche Papyri," *NTS* 3 (1957):261-65.

$\mathfrak{p}^8$ Acts 4:31-37; 5:2-9; 6:1-6,8-15; fourth. Berlin: Staatliche Museen, Inv. no. 8683. Caspar René Gregory, *Textkritik des Neuen Testaments* III (Leipzig: 1909):1087-1090; A. H. Salonius, "Die griechischen Handschriftenfragmente des Neuen Testaments in den Staatlichen Museen zu Berlin," *ZNW* 26 (1927):97-119; Schofield, 128-133. *(Category II)*

$\mathfrak{p}^9$ 1 John 4:11-12,14-17; third. Cambridge: Harvard University, Semitic Museum, no. 3736. Grenfell-Hunt, III (1903):2-3 (P. Oxy. 402); Schofield, 134-36. *(Text too brief for certainty, somewhat carelessly written; a free text? Category I)*

$\mathfrak{p}^{10}$ Rom. 1:1-7; fourth. Cambridge: Harvard University, Semitic Museum, no. 2218. Grenfell-Hunt, II (1899):8-9 (P. Oxy. 209); Wessely, 148-150; Schofield, 137-140. *(Category I)*

$\mathfrak{p}^{11}$ 1 Cor. 1:17-22; 2:9-12,14; 3:1-3,5-6; 4:3–5:5,7-8; 6:5-9,11-18; 7:3-6,10-14; seventh. Leningrad: Public Library, Gr. 258A. Kurt Aland, "Neutestamentliche Papyri," *NTS* 3 (1957):267-278, 286; Schofield, 141-151. *(Category II)*

p¹² Heb. 1:1; third. New York: Pierpont Morgan Library, no. G. 3. Bernard Pyne Grenfell and Arthur Surridge Hunt, *Amherst Papyri* I (London: 1900):28-31 (P. Amherst 3b); Schofield, 152-54. *(Text too brief for certainty; normal text? Category I)*

p¹³ Heb. 2:14–5:5; 10:8-22; 10:29–11:13; 11:28–12:17; third/fourth. London: British Library, Inv. no. 1532v; Florence: Biblioteca Laurenziana; Grenfell-Hunt, IV (1904):36-48 (P. Oxy. 657); Schofield, 155-167; Vittorio Bartoletti and M. Norsi, *PGLSI* XII (1951):209-210 (PSI 1292). *(A number of distinctive readings, often with* p⁴⁶; *free text? Category I)*

p¹⁴ 1 Cor. 1:25-27; 2:6-8; 3:8-10,20; fifth. Sinai: St. Catharine's Monastery, Harris 14. James Rendel Harris, *Biblical Fragments from Mount Sinai* (London: 1890): 54-56; Schofield, 168-170. *(Category II)*

p¹⁵ 1 Cor. 7:18–8:4; third. Cairo: Egyptian Museum, JE 47423. Grenfell-Hunt, VII (1910):4-8 (P. Oxy. 1008); Schofield, 171-74. *(At least normal text, category I)*

p¹⁶ Phil. 3:10-17; 4:2-8; third/fourth. Cairo: Egyptian Museum, JE 47424. Grenfell-Hunt, VII (1910):8-11 (P. Oxy. 1009); Schofield, 175-78. *(Normal text, category I)*

p¹⁷ Heb. 9:12-19; fourth. Cambridge: University Library, Add. 5893. Grenfell-Hunt, VIII (1911):11-13 (P. Oxy. 1078); Schofield, 179-181. *(Category II)*

p¹⁸ Rev. 1:4-7; third/fourth. London: British Library, Inv. no. 2053v. Grenfell-Hunt, VIII (1911):13-14 (P. Oxy. 1079); Schofield, 182-85. *(Normal text, category I)*

p¹⁹ Matt. 10:32–11:5; fourth/fifth. Oxford: Bodleian Library, Gr. bibl. d. 6. (P). Grenfell-Hunt, IX (1912):7-9 (P. Oxy. 1170); Schofield, 186-89. *(Category II)*

p²⁰ Jas. 2:19–3:9; third. Princeton: University Library, AM 4117. Grenfell-Hunt, IX (1912):9-11 (P. Oxy. 1171); Schofield, 190-93. *(Normal text, category I)*

p²¹ Matt. 12:24-26,32-33; third. Allentown: Muhlenberg College, Theol. Pap. 3. Grenfell-Hunt, X (1914):12-14 (P. Oxy. 1227); Schofield, 194-95. *(Category III)*

p²² John 15:25–16:2,21-32; third. Glasgow: University Library, Ms. Gen 1026. Grenfell-Hunt, X (1914):14-16 (P. Oxy. 1228); Schofield, 196-99. *(At least normal text, category I)*

p²³ Jas. 1:10-12,15-18; third. Urbana: University of Illinois, G. P. 1229. Grenfell-Hunt, X (1914):16-18 (P. Oxy. 1229); Schofield, 200-202. *(Strict text, category I)*

p²⁴ Rev. 5:5-8; 6:5-8; fourth. Newton Centre: Andover Newton Theological School, Franklin Trask Library, O.P. 1230. Grenfell-Hunt, X (1914):18-19 (P. Oxy. 1230); Schofield, 203-205. *(Category I)*

p²⁵ Matt. 18:32-34; 19:1-3,5-7,9-10; fourth. Berlin: Staatliche Museen, Inv. no. 16388. Otto Stegmüller, "Ein Bruchstück aus dem griechischen Diatessaron," *ZNW* 37 (1938):223-29. *(Unclassifiable because of Diatessaric character of text)*

p²⁶ Rom. 1:1-16; *ca.* 600. Dallas: Southern Methodist University, Perkins School of Theology, Bridwell Library. Grenfell-Hunt, XI (1915):6-9 (P. Oxy. 1354); Schofield, 215-18). *(Category I)*

p²⁷ Rom. 8:12-22,24-27; 8:33–9:3,5-9; third. Cambridge: University Library, Add. 7211. Grenfell-Hunt, XI (1915):9-12 (P. Oxy. 1355); Schofield, 219-222. *(Strict text, category I)*

p²⁸ John 6:8-12,17-22; third. Berkeley: Pacific School of Religion, Palestine Institute Museum, Pap. 2. Grenfell-Hunt, XIII (1919):8-10 (P. Oxy. 1596); Schofield, 223-25. *(Normal text, category I)*

p²⁹ Acts 26:7-8,20; third. Oxford: Bodleian Library, Gr. bibl. g. 4 (P). Grenfell-Hunt, XIII (1919):10-12 (P. Oxy. 1597); Schofield, 226-228; B. Aland, *ETL* 62 (1986): 42f. *(Free text, category I)*

p³⁰ 1 Thess. 4:12–5:18, 25-28; 2 Thess. 1:1-2; third. Ghent: Rijksuniversiteit, Bibliotheek, Inv. 61. Grenfell-Hunt, XIII (1919):12-14 (P. Oxy. 1598); Schofield, 229-233. *(At least normal text, category I)*

p³¹ Rom. 12:3-8 (reverse blank, talisman?); seventh. Manchester: John Rylands Library, Gr. P. 4. Arthur Surridge Hunt, *Catalogue of the Greek Papyri in the John Rylands Library* I: *Literary Texts* (Manchester: 1911):9 (P. Ryl. 4); Schofield, 234-37. *(Category I)*

𝔓[32] Tit. 1:11-15; 2:3-8; *ca.* 200. Manchester: John Rylands Library, Gr. P. 5. Hunt, *Catalogue of the Greek Papyri in the John Rylands Library* I (Manchester: 1911):10-11 (P. Ryl. 5); Schofield, 238-241. *(At least normal text, category I)*

𝔓[33]
[+58] Acts 7:6-10,13-18; 15:21-24,26-32; sixth. Vienna: Österreichische National-bibliothek, P. Vindob. G. 17973, 26133, 35831, 39783. Karl Wessely, *SPP* XII (1912):245; Sanz, 67-68; Schofield, 242-45. *(Category II)*

𝔓[34] 1 Cor. 16:4-7,10; 2 Cor. 5:18-21; 10:13-14; 11:2,4,6-7; seventh. Vienna: Öster-reichische Nationalbibliothek, P. Vindob. G. 39784. Karl Wessely, *SPP* XII (1912):246; Schofield, 246-252. *(Category II)*

𝔓[35] Matt. 25:12-15,20-23; fourth(?). Florence: Biblioteca Laurenziana. E. Pistelli, *PGLSI* I (1912):1-2 (PSI); Schofield, 253-55. *(Strict text, category I)*

𝔓[36] John 3:14-18,31-32,34-35; sixth. Florence: Biblioteca Laurenziana. E. Pistelli, *PGLSI* I (1912):5-6 (PSI); Schofield, 256-258; A. Carlini, "Riesame di due fram-menti fiorentini del vangelo di Giovanni," *AP* 22/23 (1974):219-222; *Papiri letterari greci* (Pisa: 1978):193-99. *(Category III)*

𝔓[37] Matt. 26:19-52; third/fourth. Ann Arbor: University of Michigan, Inv. no. 1570. Henry A. Sanders, "An Early Papyrus Fragment of the Gospel of Matthew in the Michigan Collection," *HTR* 19 (1926):215-226; J. G. Winter *et al.*, *Michigan Papyri* III: *Miscellaneous Papyri* (Ann Arbor: 1936), 9-14 (P. Mich. 137); Schofield, 259-265. *(Free text, frequently with* 𝔓[45], *category I)*

𝔓[38] Acts 18:27-19:6,12-16; *ca.* 300. Ann Arbor: University of Michigan, Inv. no. 1571. Henry A. Sanders, "A Papyrus Fragment of Acts in the Michigan Collection," *HTR* 20 (1927):1-19; S. New, "The Michigan Papyrus Fragment 1571," *Beginnings of Christianity* V (London: 1933):262-68; J. G. Winter *et al.*, *Michigan Papyri* III: *Miscellaneous Papyri* (Ann Arbor: 1936), 14-19 (P. Mich. 138); Schofield, 266-272; B. Aland, *ETL* 62 (1986): 12-32. *(Free text, related to D, category IV)*

𝔓[39] John 8:14-22; third. Rochester: Ambrose Swabey Library, Inv. no. 8864. Grenfell-Hunt, XV (1922):7-8 (P. Oxy. 1780); Schofield, 273-77. *(Strict text, category I)*

𝔓[40] Rom. 1:24-27; 1:31-2:3; 3:21-4:8; 6:4-5,16; 9:16-17,27; third. Heidelberg: Papy-russammlung der Universität, Inv. no. 45. Friedrich Bilabel, "Römerbrieffrag-mente," *VBP* IV (Heidelberg: 1924):28-31, 124-127 (P. Baden 57); Schofield, 278-284. *(Free text, carelessly written, category I because of date)*

𝔓[41] Acts 17:28-18:2,17-18,22-25,27; 19:1-4,6-8,13-16,18-19; 20:9-13,15-16,22-24,26-38; 21:3,4,26-27; 22:11-14,16-17 (Greek); Acts 17:30-18:2,25,27-28; 19:2-8,15,17-19; 20:11-16,24-28; 20:36-21:3; 22:12-14,16-17 (Coptic); eighth. Vienna: Öster-reichische Nationalbibliothek, P. Vindob. K. 7377, 7384, 7396, 7426, 7541-48, 7731, 7912, 7914. Wessely, *SPP* XV (Leipzig: 1914):107-118; Schofield, 285-291; F.-J. Schmitz, "Neue Fragmente zum 𝔓[41]," *Bericht der Hermann Kunst-Stiftung zur Förderung der neutestamentlichen Textforschung für die Jahre 1985-1987*, 78-97. *(Category III)*

𝔓[42] Luke 1:54-55; 2:29-32 (Greek); Luke 1:46-51 (Coptic); seventh/eighth. Vienna: Ös-terreichische Nationalbibliothek, P. Vindob. K. 8706. Sanz-Till, "Eine griechisch-koptische Odenhandschrift," *MBE* 5 (1939):9-112. *(Category II)*

𝔓[43] Rev. 2:12-13; 15:8-16:2; sixth/seventh. London: British Library, Inv. no. 2241. Walter Ewing Crum and Harold Idris Bell, *Wadi Sarga: Coptic and Greek Texts* (Copenhagen: 1922), 43-45; Schofield, 292-95. *(Category II)*

𝔓[44] Matt. 17:1-3,6-7; 18:15-17,19; 25:8-10; John 9:3-4; 10:8-14; 12:16-18; sixth/seventh. New York: Metropolitan Museum of Art, Inv. no. 14.1.527. Walter Ewing Crum and H. G. Evelyn White, *The Monastery of Epiphanius at Thebes* II. *Metropolitan Museum of Art Egyptian Expedition* (New York: 1926):120-21, 301; Schofield, 296-301. *(Category II)*

𝔓[45] Matt. 20:24-32; 21:13-19; 25:41-26:39; Mark 4:36-9:31†; 11:27-12:28†; Luke 6:31-7:7†; 9:26-14:33†; John 10:7-25; 10:30-11:10,18-36,42-57; Acts 4:27-17:17†; third. Dublin: P. Chester Beatty I; Vienna: Österreichische Nationalbibliothek,

P. Vindob. G. 31974. Frederic G. Kenyon, *Chester Beatty Biblical Papyri* II/1: *The Gospels and Acts, Text* (London: 1933); II/2: *The Gospels and Acts, Plates* (London: 1934); Hans Gerstinger, "Ein Fragment des Chester Beatty-Evangelienkodex in der Papyrussammlung der Nationalbibliothek in Wien," *Aegyptus* 13 (1933):67-72; Augustin Merk, "Codex Evangeliorum et Actuum ex collectione P Chester Beatty," *Miscellanea Biblica* II (Rome: 1934):375-406; Günther Zuntz, "Reconstruction of one Leaf of the Chester Beatty Papyrus of the Gospels and Acts (Mt 25:41-26:39)," *Chronique d'Égypte* 26 (1951):191-211. *(Free text, category I)* Plate 26

p⁴⁶ Rom. 5:17-6:14†; 8:15-15:9†; 15:11-16:27; 1 Cor. 1:1-16:22†; 2 Cor. 1:1-13:13†; Gal. 1:1-6:18†; Eph. 1:1-6:24†; Phil. 1:1-4:23†; Col. 1:1-4:18†; 1 Thess. 1:1; 1:9-2:3; 5:5-9,23-28; Heb. 1:1-13:25†; *ca.* 200. Dublin: P. Chester Beatty II; Ann Arbor: University of Michigan, Inv. no. 6238. George Milligan, *The New Testament and its Transmission* (London: 1932):191ff.; Frederic G. Kenyon, *Chester Beatty Biblical Papyri* III/1: *Pauline Epistles and Revelation, Text* (London: 1934); III/3 (Supplement): *Pauline Epistles, Text* (London: 1936); III/4: *Pauline Epistles, Plates* (London: 1937); Henry A. Sanders, *A Third Century Papyrus Codex of the Epistles of Paul* (Ann Arbor: 1935). *(Free Text, category I)* Plate 21

p⁴⁷ Rev. 9:10-17:2†; third. Dublin: P. Chester Beatty III. Frederic G. Kenyon, *Chester Beatty Biblical Papyri* III/1: *Pauline Epistles and Revelation, Text* (London: 1934); III/2: *Revelation, Plates* (London: 1936). *(Normal text, category I)* Plate 23

p⁴⁸ Acts 23:11-17,23-29; third. Florence: Biblioteca Laurenziana. G. Vitelli and S. G. Mercati, *PGLSI* X (1932):112-18 (PSI 1165); Schofield, 326-329; B. Aland, *ETL* 62 (1986): 34-40. *(Free text, related to D, category IV)* Plate 16

p⁴⁹ Eph. 4:16-29; 4:31-5:13; third. New Haven: Yale University Library, P. Yale 415 + 531. W. H. P. Hatch and C. Bradford Welles, "A Hitherto Unpublished Fragment of the Epistle to the Ephesians," *HTR* 51 (1958):33-37. *(At least normal text, category I)*

p⁵⁰ Acts 8:26-32; 10:26-31; fourth/fifth. New Haven: Yale University Library, P. Yale 1543. Carl H. Kraeling, "p⁵⁰: Two Selections from Acts," 163-172 in *Quantulacumque: Studies Presented to Kirsopp Lake*, ed. Robert P. Casey, Silva Lake, and Agnes Kirsopp Lake (London: 1937). *(Orthographical peculiarities and corrections, category III)*

p⁵¹ Gal. 1:2-10,13,16-20; *ca.* 400. Oxford: Ashmolean Museum. Edgar Lobel, Colin H. Roberts, and E. P. Wegener, *Oxyrhynchus Papyri* XVIII (London: 1941):1-3 (P. Oxy. 2157). *(Category II)*

p⁵² John 18:31-33,37-38; *ca.* 125. Manchester: John Rylands Library, Gr. P. 457. Colin Henderson Roberts, *An Unpublished Fragment of the Fourth Gospel in the John Rylands Library* (Manchester: 1935); Schofield, 330-34. *(Normal text, category I because of age)* Plate 19

p⁵³ Matt. 26:29-40; Acts 9:33-10:1; third. Ann Arbor: University of Michigan, Inv. no. 6652. Henry A. Sanders, "A Third Century Papyrus of Matthew and Acts," 151-161 in *Quantulacumque: Studies Presented to Kirsopp Lake* (London: 1937). *(At least normal text, category I)*

p⁵⁴ Jas. 2:16-18,22-26; 3:2-4; fifth/sixth. Princeton: University Library, P. Princeton 15 (earlier Garrett Deposit 7742). Edward Harris Kase, *Papyri in the Princeton University Collections* II (Princeton: 1936):1-3; Schofield, 206-214. *(Category III, possibly II)*

p⁵⁵ John 1:31-33,35-38; sixth/seventh. Vienna: Österreichische Nationalbibliothek, P. Vindob. G. 26214. Sanz, 58-59. *(Category II)*

p⁵⁶ Acts 1:1,4-5,7,10-11; fifth/sixth. Vienna: Österreichische Nationalbibliothek, P. Vindob. G. 19918. Sanz, 65-66. *(Category II)*

p⁵⁷ Acts 4:36-5:2,8-10; fourth/fifth. Vienna: Österreichische Nationalbibliothek, P. Vindob. G. 26020. Sanz, 66-67. *(Category II)*

p⁵⁸ Cf. p³³.

p⁵⁹ John 1:26,28,48,51; 2:15-16; 11:40-52; 12:25,29,31,35; 17:24-26; 18:1-2,16-17,22;

21:7,12-13,15,17-20,23; seventh. New York: Pierpont Morgan Library. Casson, 79-93 (P. Colt 3). *(Category III)*

p⁶⁰ John 16:29–19:26†; *ca.* 700. New York: Pierpont Morgan Library. Casson, 94-111 (P. Colt 4). *(Category III)*

p⁶¹ Rom. 16:23-27; 1 Cor. 1:1-2,4-6; 5:1-3,5-6,9-13; Phil. 3:5-9,12-16; Col. 1:3-7,9-13; 4:15; 1 Thess. 1:2-3; Tit. 3:1-5,8-11,14-15; Philem. 4-7; *ca.* 700. New York: Pierpont Morgan Library. Casson, 112-122 (P. Colt 5). *(Category II)*

p⁶² Matt. 11:25-30; fourth. Oslo: University Library, P. Osloensis 1661. Leiv Amundsen, "Christian Papyri from the Oslo Collection," *Symbolae Osloenses* 24 (1945):121-147. *(Category II)*

p⁶³ John 3:14-18; 4:9-10; *ca.* 500. Berlin: Staatliche Museen, Inv. no. 11914. Otto Stegmüller, "Zu den Bibelorakeln im Codex Bezae," *Bibl* 34 (1953):13-22. *(Category II, influenced by V)*

p⁶⁴
⁺⁶⁷ Matt. 3:9,15; 5:20-22,25-28; 26:7-8,10,14-15,22-23,31-33; *ca.* 200. Barcelona: Fundació Sant Lluc Evangelista, Inv. no. 1; Oxford: Magdalen College, Gr. 18. R. Roca-Puig, "P. Barc. Inv. Nr. 1," *Studi in onore di Aristide Calderini e Roberto Paribeni* II (Milan-Varese: 1957):87-96; "Nueva publicación del papiro número uno de Barcelona," *Helmantica* 37 (1961):5-20; Colin Henderson Roberts, "An Early Papyrus of the First Gospel," *HTR* 46 (1953):233-37. *(Strict text, category I)*

p⁶⁵ 1 Thess. 1:3–2:1,6-13; third. Florence: Instituto Papirologico G. Vitelli. Vittorio Bartoletti, *PGLSI* XIV (1957):5-7 (PSI 1373). *(Strict text (?), too brief for certainty; category I)*

p⁶⁶ John 1:1–6:11; 6:35–14:26,29-30; 15:2-26; 16:2-4,6-7; 16:10–20:20,22-23; 20:25–21:9; *ca.* 200. Cologny: Bibliotheca Bodmeriana, P. Bodmer II; Dublin: P. Chester Beatty; Cologne: Institut für Altertumskunde, Inv. no. 4274/4298. Victor Martin, *Papyrus Bodmer II: Evangile de Jean, 1–14* (Cologny/Geneva: 1956); *Papyrus Bodmer II: Supplément, Evangile de Jean, 14–21* (Cologny/Geneva: 1958); Victor Martin and J. W. B. Barns, *Papyrus Bodmer II: Supplément, Evangile de Jean, 14–21* (Cologny/Geneva: ²1962); Kurt Aland, "Neue neutestamentliche Papyri III," *NTS* 20 (1974):357-381 (previously unidentified fragments). *(Free text, category I)* Plate 22

p⁶⁷ Cf. p⁶⁴.

p⁶⁸ 1 Cor. 4:12-17; 4:19–5:3; seventh(?). Leningrad: Public Library, Gr. 258B. Kurt Aland, "Neue neutestamentliche Papyri," *NTS* 3 (1957):265-67. *(Category III)*

p⁶⁹ Luke 22:41,45-48,58-61; third. Oxford: Ashmolean Museum. Edgar Lobel, Colin H. Roberts, E. G. Turner, and J. W. B. Barns, *Oxyrhynchus Papyri* XXIV (London: 1957):1-4 (P. Oxy. 2383); K. Aland, *Festschrift R. Roca-Puig* (Barcelona:1987): 57-60. *(Very free text, characteristic of precursors of the D-text; therefore category IV)*

p⁷⁰ Matt. 2:13-16; 2:22–3:1; 11:26-27; 12:4-5; 24:3-6,12-15; third. Oxford: Ashmolean Museum; Florence: Instituto Papirologico G. Vitelli, CNR 419, 420. Edgar Lobel, Colin H. Roberts, E. G. Turner, and J. W. B. Barns, *Oxyrhynchus Papyri* XXIV (London: 1957):4-5 (P. Oxy. 2384); M. Naldini, "Nuovi frammenti del vangelo di Matteo," *Prometheus* 1 (1975):195-200. *(Strict text, somewhat carelessly written; category I)*

p⁷¹ Matt. 19:10-11,17-18; fourth. Oxford: Ashmolean Museum. Lobel- Roberts- Turner- Barns, *Oxyrhynchus Papyri* XXIV (London: 1957):5-6 (P. Oxy. 2385). *(Category II)*

p⁷² 1 Pet. 1:1–5:14; 2 Pet. 1:1–3:18; Jude 1–25; third/fourth. Cologny: Bibliotheca Bodmeriana, P. Bodmer VII-VIII (1–2 Peter now in Biblioteca Vaticana). Michael Testuz, *Papyrus Bodmer VII-IX: L'Epître de Jude, Les deux Epîtres de Pierre, Les Psaumes 33 et 34* (Cologny/Geneva: 1959); Carlo M. Martini, *Beati Petri Apostoli Epistulae, Ex Papyro Bodmeriano VIII* (Milan: 1968). *(1, 2 Peter normal text, Jude free text, both with certain peculiarities, category I)* Plate 25

p^{73} Matt. 25:43; 26:2-3; seventh. Cologny: Bibliotheca Bodmeriana. Still unpublished. *(Text too brief for certainty, category V)*

p^{74} Acts 1:2–28:31†; Jas. 1:1–5:20†; 1 Pet. 1:1-2,7-8,13,19-20,25; 2:6-7,11-12,18,24; 3:4-5; 2 Pet. 2:21; 3:4,11,16; 1 John 1:1,6; 2:1-2,7,13-14,18-19,25-26; 3:1-2,8,14,19-20; 4:1,6-7,12,18-19; 5:3-4,9-10,17; 2 John 1,6-7,13; 3 John 6,12; Jude 3,7,11-12,16,24; seventh. Cologny: Bibliotheca Bodmeriana, P. Bodmer XVII. Rudolf Kasser, *Papyrus Bodmer XVII: Actes des Apôtres, Epîtres de Jacques, Pierre, Jean et Jude* (Cologny/Geneva: 1961). *(Egyptian text, category I because of quality)* Plate 20

p^{75} Luke 3:18–4:2†; 4:34–5:10; 5:37–18:18†; 22:4–24:53; John 1:1–11:45,48-57; 12:3–13:1,8-9; 14:8-30; 15:7-8; third. Cologny: Bibliotheca Bodmeriana, P. Bodmer XIV-XV. Rudolf Kasser and Victor Martin, *Papyrus Bodmer XIV-XV*, I: *XIV: Luc chap. 3–24;* II: *XV: Jean chap. 1–15* (Cologny/Geneva: 1961); Kurt Aland, "Neue neutestamentliche Papyri III," *NTS* 22 (1976):375-396 (previously unidentified fragments). *(Strict text, category I)* Plate 24

p^{76} John 4:9,12; sixth. Vienna: Österreichische Nationalbibliothek, P. Vindob. G. 36102. Herbert Hunger, "Zwei unbekannte neutestamentliche Papyrusfragmente der Österreichischen Nationalbibliothek," *Biblos* 8 (1959):7-12; "Ergänzungen zu zwei neutestamentlichen Papyrusfragmenten der Österr. Nationalbibliothek," *Biblos* 19/2 (1970):71-75. *(Category III)*

p^{77} Matt. 23:30-39; second/third. Oxford: Ashmolean Museum. L. Ingrams, P. Kingston, Peter Parsons, and John Rea, *Oxyrhynchus Papyri* XXXIV (London: 1968):1-3 (P. Oxy. 2683). *(At least normal text, by a careless scribe; category I)*

p^{78} Jud. 4-5,7-8; third/fourth. Oxford: Ashmolean Museum. L. Ingrams, P. Kingston, Peter Parsons, and John Rea, *Oxyrhynchus Papyri* XXXIV (London: 1968):4-6 (P. Oxy. 2684). *(Free text, category I)*

p^{79} Heb. 10:10-12,28-30; seventh. Berlin: Staatliche Museen, Inv. no. 6774. K. Treu, "Neue neutestamentliche Fragmente der Berliner Papyrussammlung," *AP* 18 (1966):37-48. *(Category II)*

p^{80} John 3:34; third. Barcelona: Fundació Sant Lluc Evangelista, Inv. no. 83. R. Roca-Puig, "Papiro del evangelio de San Juan con 'Hermeneia,' " 225-236 in *Atti dell' XI Congresso Internazionale di Papirologia* (Milan: 1966). *(Text too brief for certainty, category I because of date)*

p^{81} 1 Pet. 2:20–3:1,4-12; fourth. Trieste: Property S. Daris, no. 20. S. Daris "Un nuovo frammento della prima lettera di Pietro," *Papyrologica Castroctaviana. Studia et Textus* 2 (Barcelona: 1967):11-37. *(Category II)*

p^{82} Luke 7:32-34,37-38; fourth/fifth. Strasbourg: Bibliothèque Nationale et Universitaire, P. Gr. 2677. J. Schwartz, "Fragment d'évangile sur papyrus," *ZPE* 3 (1968):157-58. *(Category II)*

p^{83} Matt. 20:23-25,30-31; 23:39–24:1,6; sixth. Louvain: Bibliothèque de l'Université, P. A. M. Khirbet Mird, 16, 29. Still unpublished. *(Category III)*

p^{84} Mark 2:2-5,8-9; 6:30-31,33-34,36-37,39-41; John 5:5; 17:3,7-8; sixth. Louvain: Bibliothèque de l'Université, P. A. M. Khirbet Mird, 4, 11, 26, 27. Still unpublished. *(Category III, influenced by V)*

p^{85} Rev. 9:19–10:2,5-9; fourth/fifth. Strasbourg: Bibliothèque Nationale et Universitaire, P. Gr. 1028. J. Schwartz, "Papyrus et tradition manuscrite," *ZPE* 4 (1969):178-182. *(Category II)*

p^{86} Matt. 5:13-16,22-25; fourth. Cologne: Institut für Altertumskunde, P. Col. theol. 5516. Charalambakis-Hagedorn-Kaimakis-Thüngen, "Vier literarische Papyri der Kölner Sammlung," *ZPE* 14 (1974):37-40. *(Category II)*

p^{87} Philem. 13-15,24-25; third. Cologne: Institut für Altertumskunde, P. Col. theol. 12. C. Römer, "Kölner Papyri 4," *Papyrologica Colonensia* 7 (1982):28-31. *(Normal text, category I)*

𝔭⁸⁸ Mark 2:1-26; fourth. Milan: Università Cattolica, P. Med. Inv. no. 69.24. S. Daris, "Papiri letterari dell' Università Cattolica di Milano," *Aegyptus* 52 (1972):80-88. *(Category III)*

𝔭⁸⁹ Heb. 6:7-9, 15-17; fourth. Florence: Biblioteca Medicea Laurenziana, PL III/292. Rosario Pintaudi, "N.T. Ad Hebraeos VI, 7-9; 15-17," *ZPE* 42 (1981):42-44.

𝔭⁹⁰ John 18:36-19:7; second. Oxford: Ashmolean Museum. T. C. Skeat, *Oxyrhynchus Papyri* L (London: 1983):3-8 (P. Oxy. 3523).

𝔭⁹¹ Acts 2:30-37; 2:46-3:2; third. North Ryde, Australia: Macquarie University, Inv. 360 a,b; Milan: Istituto di Papirologia, P. Mil. Vogl. Inv. 1224. Claudio Gallazzi "P. Mil. Vogl. Inv. 1224 NT, Act. 2,30-37 e 2,46-3,2," *Bulletin of the American Society of Papyrologists* 19 (1982):39-45; S. R. Pickering, *ZPE* 65 (1986):76-79.

𝔭⁹² Eph. 1:11-13, 19-21; 2 Thess. 1:4-5, 11-12; third/fourth. Cairo: Egyptian Museum, P. Narmuthis, Inv. 69,39a + 69,229a. Claudio Gallazzi, "Frammenti di un codice con le Epistole de Paolo," *ZPE* 46 (1982):117-122.

𝔭⁹³ John 13:15-17; fifth. Florence: Istituto Papirologico "G. Vitelli," PSI Inv. 108. Guido Bastianini, *Trenta testi greci* 4 (1983):10f.

𝔭⁹⁴ Rom. 6:10-13, 19-22; fifth/sixth. Cairo: Egyptian Museum, P. Cair. 10730. Jean Bingen, 76-78 in *Miscellània Papirològica Ramon Roca-Puig* (Barcelona: 1987): 76-78.

𝔭⁹⁵ John 5:26-29, 36-38; third, Florence: Biblioteca Medicea Laurenziana, PL II/31. Jean Lenaerts, "Un papyrus de l'Évangile de Jean: PL II/31," *Chronique d' Egypte* 60 (1985):117-120.

𝔭⁹⁶ Matt. 3:10-12 (Coptic; Greek lost), 3:13-15 (Greek; Coptic lost); sixth. Vienna: Österreichische Nationalbibliothek, K. 7244.

All the papyri listed above are from codices, not from scrolls, with the exception of only 𝔭¹², 𝔭¹³, 𝔭¹⁸, and 𝔭²² (see below). In contrast to pagan and also to Jewish literature (which were written on scrolls, the former on papyrus and the latter on leather), from all appearances the codex form was used by Christian writers from the very beginning. It is amazing how long it took for this fact to be recognized, since all the New Testament papyri, from the first one to be discovered, were from codices. Only four of the ninety-six known papyri (𝔭¹², 𝔭¹³, 𝔭¹⁸, 𝔭²²) are from scrolls, and all of these are either opisthographs or written on reused material. It is not clear what reasons (economic?) led the Christians to make this change, especially as it was evidently accompanied by the introduction of the nomina sacra (i.e., abbreviations of certain words, at first a fluid practice but very early stabilized; cf. pp. 75f.).

In studying any New Testament text it is important to know in which papyri (and uncials; cf. chart 6, foldout in endpaper pocket) it is found. But a great amount of effort is required to find this information in the literature (for the uncials it is almost impossible). Chart 5 (foldout in endpaper pocket) should assist these efforts or make them minimal (for the uncials, cf. chart 6). It shows at a glance which papyri are extant in any given chapter. To emphasize their importance, the papyri of the third/fourth century and earlier, which have an inherent significance,[16] are indicated by an exclamation point (e.g. P⁴⁵!).

16. Cf. pp. 56f.

8. *THE UNCIALS*

The uncials have played a dominant role well into the twentieth century, with three manuscripts in particular enjoying the limelight: ℵ 01, Codex Sinaiticus; B 03, Codex Vaticanus; D^ea 05, Codex Bezae Cantabrigiensis. ℵ was the lodestar for Constantin von Tischendorf's editions, as was B for Brooke Foss Westcott and F. J. A. Hort in determining their text.[17] This Bℵ text of the nineteenth century gained universal currency in Eberhard Nestle's *Novum Testamentum Graece*, as it was based upon the editions of Tischendorf and Westcott-Hort together with that of Bernhard Weiss (which also gave preference to B).[18] A rival position was taken by scholars who regarded D, the chief "Western" representative, as the most important manuscript of a text traceable to the second century. In the twentieth century the papyri have eroded the dominance of the uncials, and a group of minuscules presently under study promises to diminish it further. A great number of uncials (especially those of the later centuries) actually preserve little more than a purely or predominantly Byzantine Majority text (e.g., E^e 07, F^e 09, G^e 011, H^e 013, H^a 014, K^e 017, K^ap 018, L^ap 020, M 021, N 022, O 023, etc.; cf. the descriptive list of uncials, pp. 106f., and category V of chart 5). These should properly be classified with the mass of minuscule manuscripts.

A further qualification should also be mentioned: of the 299 uncial manuscripts registered at present, only 104 comprise more than two folios, and of the uncials after 046 only 59 have more than two folios, with only 18 having more than thirty folios.

Ms.	Date	Content	Number of Folios	Ms.	Date	Content	Number of Folios
047	8th	Gospels†	152	0142	10th	Apostolos, Paul (comm.)	381
049	9th	Apostolos, Paul†	149	0150	9th	Paul (comm.)	150
051	10th	Revelation (comm.)	92	0151	9th	Paul (comm.)	192
055	11th	Gospels (comm.)	303	0211	7th	Gospels	258
056	10th	Apostolos, Paul (comm.)	381	0233	8th	Gospels*	93
070	6th	Gospels†	44	0248	9th	Matthew†	70
075	10th	Paul (comm.)	333	0250	8th	Gospels†	33
0141	10th	John (comm.)	349	0257	9th	Gospels†	47
				0278	9th	Paul†	120
				0281	7/8th	Matthew	48

This demonstrates that most of the major manuscripts (in terms of length) have been well known since the beginning of modern research. Here again it was Tischendorf who reaped the greatest harvest. His successors have found many manuscripts, but only rarely have they been of any length.

The scope of an uncial's text, however, is no key to its importance. A fragment with a valuable text is far more significant than a newly found complete uncial manuscript with a Byzantine text. When we remember that of the 218

17. Cf. p. 14.
18. Cf. pp. 19f.

uncials following 046, no fewer than 99 are from the sixth century or earlier (as compared with 20 before 056 from this period), the perspective becomes clearer. The period from the fourth to the sixth century is represented by the following uncials.

4th	01, 03, 058, 0169, 0185, 0188, 0206, 0207, 0221, 0228, 0230, 0231, 0242, 0258
4th/5th	057, 059, 0160, 0176, 0181, 0214, 0219, 0270
5th	02, 04, 05, 016, 026, 029, 032, 048, 061, 062, 068, 069, 077, 0163, 0165, 0166, 0172, 0173, 0174, 0175, 0182, 0201, 0216, 0217, 0218, 0226, 0227, 0236, 0240, 0244, 0252, 0254, 0261, 0264, 0267, 0274.
5th/6th	071, 072, 076, 088, 0158, 0170, 0186, 0213, 0232, 0247
6th	06, 08, 015, 022, 023, 024, 027, 035, 040, 042, 043, 060, 064, 065, 066, 067, 070, 073, 078, 079, 080, 081, 082, 085, 086, 087, 089, 091, 093, 094, 0143, 0147, 0159, 0184, 0187, 0198, 0208, 0222, 0223, 0225, 0237, 0241, 0245, 0246, 0251, 0253, 0260, 0263, 0265, 0266, 0296

But it should also be remembered that the date of a manuscript is no more a clue to its significance than is its length. Thus from the sixth century there have been preserved several manuscripts of consummate artistry (parchment stained purple, inscribed with silver letters, and illuminated with gold), and yet since they offer nothing more than a Byzantine text — even in the renowned Codex Rossanensis (cf. plate 32) — they are in consequence quite irrelevant for textual criticism. In terms of age, only uncial manuscripts which derive from the third/fourth century or earlier have an inherent significance, i.e., those of the period *before* the development of the great text types.[19] Unfortunately, these amount to no more than five:

0189 from the third/fourth century (formerly assigned to the fourth century), containing Acts 5:3-21. 1 f., 1 col., 32 ll., 18 × 11 cm., Berlin: Staatliche Museen, P. 11765. Cf. plate 27.

0212 from the third century, the famous Diatessaron fragment from Dura. 1 f., 1 col., 15 ll., 10.5 × 9.5 cm., New Haven: Yale University, P. Dura 10. Cf. plate 13.

0220 from the third century, with Rom. 4:23–5:3,8-13. Fragment, 1 col., *ca.* 24 ll., *ca.* 15 × 13 cm., formerly Boston: Leland C. Wyman; in 1988 London: Quaritch. Cf. plate 14.

0162 from the third/fourth century (formerly assigned to the fourth century), with John 2:11-22. 1 f., 1 col., 19 ll., 16 × 15 cm., New York: Metropolitan Museum of Art, 09.182.43 (P. Oxy. 847).

0171 from about 300 (formerly assigned to the fourth century), with Matt. 10:17-23, 25-32; Luke 22:44-56,61-64. 2 ff., 2 cols., 24 ll., *ca.* 15 × 11 cm., Florence: Biblioteca Laurenziana, PSI 2.124; Berlin: Staatliche Museen. P. 11863, 1f.; K. Aland, *Festschrift R. Roca-Puig* (Barcelona:1987): 45-56.

Although 299 uncials have now been recognized (strictly 301, because both 092 and 0121 have a double reference), this is only a nominal figure. The actual figure should be much lower as a result of the Institute for New Testament Textual Research's success in identifying fragments separated from their manuscripts. At present no fewer than thirty manuscripts hitherto regarded as independent have been demonstrably associated with others (usually among the lower numbers of the list; cf. below, pp. 107ff.), e.g., 074, 084, 090, 092a, 092b, 0110, 0112, 0113, 0117,

19. Cf. pp. 56f.

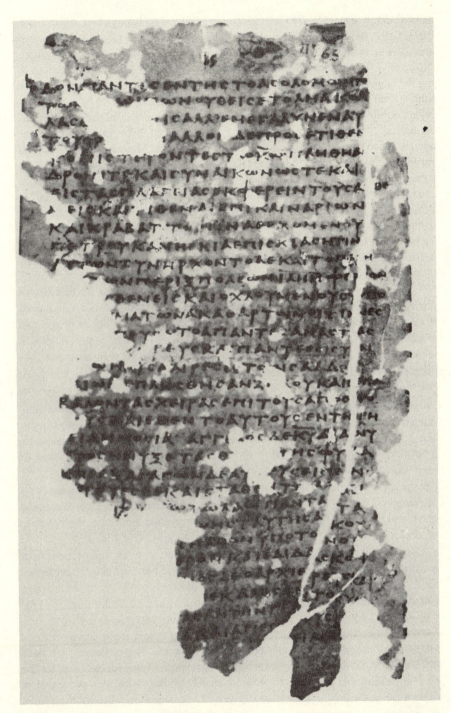

Plate 27. 0189, the earliest parchment manuscript of the New Testament (second/third century; cf. p. 104): Acts 5:12-21 (reverse).

0119, 0123, 0124, 0125, 0137, 0138, 0139, 0149, 0178, 0179, 0180, 0190, 0191, 0193, 0194, 0195, 0202, 0215, 0224, 0235, 0285, 0293. Another eight numbers should be deleted (for reasons given in the list below): 055, 0100, 0129, 0152, 0153, 0192, 0203. This reduces the total number of uncials now recognized to 263 (including the manuscripts which have been examined from the recent discoveries at Mt. Sinai). With some hesitation we have decided to enumerate them all (however briefly) in the following list. It was tempting to limit the list to uncials of particular interest for textual criticism, omitting not only a large number of fragments but also the uncials which have a purely or predominantly Byzantine Majority text — groups of very little importance for the student. But there was also the counterargument that a complete list would be useful for identifying references to uncials in critical editions and in scholarly literature, especially as Kurt Aland's *Kurzgefasste Liste* goes only to 0250 (because it appeared in 1963), and the supplements extending it to 0299 are scattered in various publications. Furthermore, the present book is intended not only for beginners but also for advanced students who would find such a list useful, especially considering the fact that relatively complete lists of New Testament manuscripts are not available elsewhere.

In any event, we considered it necessary not to restrict this list of uncials to such minimal information as contents, date (material is not indicated because it is consistently parchment), number of folios, etc., but to provide an assessment of the text wherever possible. This will give the manuscripts an identity for the student — and frequently for the advanced scholar as well — because many of the uncials have never yet been examined for their text type. For this assessment it seemed best to use five categories:

Category I: Manuscripts of a very special quality which should always be considered in establishing the original text (e.g., the Alexandrian text belongs here). The papyri and uncials through the third/fourth century also belong here automatically, one may say, because they represent the text of the early period (if they offer no significant evidence they are bracketed.

Category II: Manuscripts of a special quality, but distinguished from manuscripts of category I by the presence of alien influences (particularly of the Byzantine text), and yet of importance for establishing the original text (e.g., the Egyptian text belongs here).

Category III: Manuscripts of a distinctive character with an independent text, usually important for establishing the original text, but particularly important for the history of the text (e.g., f^1, f^{13}).

Category IV: Manuscripts of the D text.

Category V: Manuscripts with a purely or predominantly Byzantine text.

Every student should be familiar with the manuscripts in categories I and II, and also if possible with those in category III. The beginner who finds the statistical data for the categories somewhat puzzling may ignore them for the present. These are intended for the advanced scholar, who will recognize in them a rationale for the assessments given. They summarize briefly the results

of a systematic test collation,[20] indicating for each manuscript its incidence of:

1:    agreements with the Byzantine text

1/2: agreements with the Byzantine text where it has the same reading as the original text

2:    agreements with the original text

S: independent or distinctive readings (i.e., special readings, "Sonderlesarten")

It should also be noted that "Evv" refers only to the Synoptic Gospels because test collations for John were dealt with separately (with the further attempt made to determine on the basis of the distinctive readings of the major manuscripts whether and where there might be special dependency relationships among them). "Paul" (the Pauline letters) always includes Hebrews. "Acts" and "Cath" (the Catholic letters) are indicated separately. No test collations were made of Revelation in view of the magnum opus by Josef Schmid. Naturally this kind of data can be given only where a manuscript is represented in a sufficient number of test passages. The data are accordingly omitted for manuscripts preserved only in fragments. In the present list the assignment of an uncial fragment to a particular category has been made only when complete collation has been made at the Institute for New Testament Textual Research (in six instances the fragments were too meager for an evaluation; only seven fragments have been impossible to examine even in photocopy, five of which are in Damascus and two of which are either unlocated or known to be lost). Any assessment of a text naturally involves a certain element of subjectivity; readings which have been identified as "distinctive" may yet require reclassification in the light of further research. Yet we dare hope that the present classification of manuscripts into categories (done first by each of us independently and then together) will prove useful.

Descriptive List of Uncials

ℵ **01** Codex Sinaiticus, eapr,[21] fourth century, 148 ff., 4 cols., 48 ll., 43 × 38 cm. London: British Library, Add. 43725. Complete Bible (parts of the Old Testament lost, 11ff. of the Pentateuch and 1f. of the Shepherd of Hermas discovered in 1975 in St. Catherine's Monastery), with the letter of Barnabas and the Shepherd of Hermas, the only four-column manuscript of the New Testament. The romance of its discovery was recounted by Constantin von Tischendorf himself (43 Old Testament folios first discovered in 1844, followed in 1853 by an abortive attempt and in 1859 by successful access to the rest of the manuscript, which was eventually "presented" to the Tsar by a complicated arrangement); bought from the Soviet government by England in 1933 for £100,000. Facsimile edition by Kirsopp Lake (Oxford: 1911). The text with numerous singular readings (and careless errors) was highly overrated by Tischendorf, and is distinctly inferior to B, together with which (and $\mathfrak{p}^{75}$) it represents the Alexandrian text. (Evv: 23^1 $80^{1/2}$ 170^2 95^s; Acts 11^1 $24^{1/2}$ 68^2 18^s; Paul: 74^1 $43^{1/2}$ 172^2 53^s; Cath: 23^1 $6^{1/2}$ 63^2 16^s; *category I*) Plate 7.

A **02** Codex Alexandrinus, eapr†, fifth, 144 ff., 2 cols., 49+ ll., 32 × 26 cm. London: British Library, Royal 1 D.VIII. This manuscript, which was in the Patriarchal Library

20. Cf. pp. 128, 317ff.

21. e = Gospels; a = Apostolos (Acts and Catholic letters); p = Pauline letters; r = Revelation; † = defective, with lacunae (e.g., A lacks Matt. 1:1–25:6; John 6:50–8:52; 2 Cor. 4:13–12:6); cf. p. 128.

Synopsis of Sigla for Correctors in Manuscripts

ℵ 01, B 03, C 04, D 05, D 06

The symbols for indicating the correctors in the great uncials have varied considerably (cf. Tischendorf in ℵ). In Nestle-Aland[26] various groups of correctors are sometimes combined, and arranged where possible in chronological sequence. The following survey assists in comparing the usage in editions of particular uncials, in Tischendorf's *Editio Octava Critica Maior* and in Nestle-Aland[26] and *SQE*.

Edition	Ed. oct. crit. maior	NA[26], SQE[13]
	ℵ 01	
Tischendorf, *Novum Testamentum Sinaiticum sive Novum Testamentum cum Epistula Barnabae et fragmentis Pastoris: Ex Codice Sinaitico*, (Leipzig: 1863)	Tischendorf, *Novum Testamentum Graece: Editio Octava Critica Maior* (Leipzig: 1869)	
A B B^a and A^{obliqu}	ℵ^a ℵ^b	ℵ^1 (4th-6th).
C C^a C^b and C*	ℵ^c ℵ^{ca} ℵ^{cb} ℵ^{cc} ℵ^{cc*}	ℵ^2 (*ca.* from 7th)
C^c	ℵ^e	ℵ^c (12th)
	B 03	
Tischendorf, *Novum Testamentum Vaticanum, post Angeli Maii aliorumque imperfectos labores ex ipso Codice* (Leipzig: 1867)	Sigla as in edition of manuscript (see column to left)	
B^2		B^1 (contemporary with B*)
B^2 et B^3 (when B^3 confirms B^2)		B^1
B^3		B^2 (6th/7th)
	C 04	
Tischendorf, *Codex Ephraemi Syri Rescriptus sive fragmenta Novi Testamenti* (Leipzig: 1843)		
A	C**	C^1 (contemporary)
B	C^2	C^2 (*ca.* 6th)
C	C^3	C^3 (*ca.* 9th)
	D 05	
Scrivener, *Bezae Codex Cantabrigiensis* (Cambridge: 1864)		
A B C D	A = D^2; B = D^B; C = D^C	D^1 (6th-7th)
E F G H J K L	D to M = D^2	D^2 (*ca.* 9th)
M		D^c (12th)
NB: E and G are correctors of the Latin column	NB: Only Scrivener's correctors A B C are distinguished; the rest are served by a single symbol	
	D 06	
Tischendorf, *Codex Claromontanus sive Epistulae Pauli Omnes* (Leipzig: 1852)		
D**	D^b	D^1 (*ca.* 7th)
D** et D*** (when D*** confirms D**	D$^{b\ et\ c}$	D^1
D***	D^c	D^2 (*ca.* 9th)
D$^{**}_{**}$ D^{nov}	D^d D^{nov}	D^c (date unknown, but later than the other correctors)

of Alexandria from the eleventh century, was presented by the Patriarch Cyril Lucar of Constantinople to Charles I of England in 1628. A complete Bible, the New Testament lacks the first 26 ff. (to Matt. 25:6), 2 ff. (John 6:50–8:52), and 3 ff. (2 Cor. 4:13–12:6). Contains 1 and 2 Clement (to 12:4), but lacks the Psalms of Solomon. Facsimile edition by Frederic G. Kenyon (London: 1909) (in reduced size), earlier by E. Maunde Thompson (London: 1879-1883). The text is of uneven value (based on exemplars of different types in its different parts), inferior in the Gospels, good in the rest of the New Testament, but best in Revelation, where with C it is superior to $\mathfrak{p}^{47}$ $\aleph$. (Evv: 151^1, $84^{1/2}$, 18^2 15^s; Acts: 10^1 $22^{1/2}$ 64^2 13^s; Paul: 19^1 $32^{1/2}$ 157^2 39^s; Cath: 18^1 $6^{1/2}$ 62^2 13^s; *category: Gospels III* — strictly V, elsewhere I) Plate 3.

B 03 Codex Vaticanus, eap†,[22] fourth, 142 ff., 3 cols., 42 ll., 27 × 27 cm. Rome: Vatican Library, Gr. 1209. Complete Bible with lacunae, lacking 31 ff. (to Gen. 46:28), 20 ff. (Ps. 105:27–137:6), and in the New Testament from Heb. 9:14 on (and texts of the Apostolic Fathers which were probably present here as in $\aleph$ and A; pp. 1519-1536 of the manuscript are a fifteenth-century supplement which is catalogued separately as minuscule 1957). The provenance and early history of B is unknown; it was recorded in the Vatican inventory in 1475. Tischendorf's access to it was too little and too late because Angelo Cardinal Mai was preparing his own edition of it (published 1857, corrected edition 1859); Brooke Foss Westcott and F. J. A. Hort made intensive use of the 1868-1872 facsimile edition. The facsimile edition of 1904 has been superseded by the 1968 reproduction in color with an introduction by Carlo M. Martini, published in Rome. B is by far the most significant of the uncials. (Evv: 9^1 $54^{1/2}$ 196^2 72^s; Acts: 2^1 $22^{1/2}$ 72^2 11^s; Paul: 9^1 $32^{1/2}$ 141^2 28^s; Cath: 1^1 9^1 $^{/2}$ 80^2 10^s, *category I*) Plate 8.

C 04 Codex Ephraemi Syri Rescriptus (so called because the manuscript was erased in the twelfth century to be reused for a Greek translation of thirty-eight tractates by Ephraem), the best known of the New Testament palimpsests (63 of the 263 known uncials are palimpsests), eapr†, fifth, 145 ff., 1 col., 40+ ll., 33 × 27 cm. Paris: Bibliothèque Nationale, Gr. 9. Attempts to read the manuscript were made in 1834 by Ferdinand Florian Fleck, and in 1840-1841 by Tischendorf with the aid of chemical reagents.[23] Tischendorf's 1843 edition needs thorough revision (resources now include ultraviolet photographs in the Institute, and the dissertation by Robert W. Lyon [St. Andrews: 1956]). Originally a complete Bible, today C has considerable lacunae,[24] especially in the Old Testament but also in the New Testament. (Evv: 87^1 $66^{1/2}$ 66^2 50^s; Acts: 13^1 $13^{1/2}$ 38^2 11^s; Paul: 29^1 $26^{1/2}$ 104^2 17^s; Cath: 16^1 $3^{1/2}$ 41^2 14^s; *category II*) Plate 6.

D^{ea} 05 Codex Bezae Cantabrigiensis, ea†,[25] fifth, 415 ff., 1 col., 33 ll., 26 × 21.5 cm. Cambridge: University Library, Nn. II 41. A Greek-Latin diglot (Greek text on verso), written in sense lines (for convenience in liturgical reading), this has been the most controversial of the New Testament uncials, the principal witness of the text called "Western," although it was written in either Egypt or North Africa, probably by a scribe whose mother tongue was Latin. The Latin text is related to the accompanying Greek text, standing independently of the main Latin tradition, and probably representing a secondary product. When and how the Greek exemplar of D originated is unknown ($\mathfrak{p}^{38}$, $\mathfrak{p}^{48}$, $\mathfrak{p}^{69}$, and 0171 of the third/fourth century show earlier or related forms), but the additions, omissions, and alterations of the text (especially in Luke and Acts) betray the touch of a significant theologian. The manuscript he adapted was an outstanding example of the early text, and it contributed to D an element of authority. D of the D-text has

22. In B Hebrews follows 2 Thessalonians, so that it lacks at least the remainder of Hebrews, as well as 1 Timothy-Philemon and Revelation.

23. Cf. p. 11.

24. For lacunae, cf. Nestle-Aland[26], p. 689.

25. For lacunae in D^{ea}, as well as passages supplied by a later hand, cf. Nestle-Aland[26], p. 689.

had little following (e.g., in 614 and its sister manuscript 2412), and only rarely in its additions, omissions, and textual changes. Only manuscripts in full agreement should be identified with the D text, otherwise confusion of terminology will never be overcome. When D supports the early tradition the manuscript has a genuine significance, but it (as well as its precursors and followers) should be examined most carefully when it opposes the early tradition. (Evv: 65¹ 48¹ᐟ² 77² 134ˢ; Acts: 21¹ 7¹ᐟ² 15² 33ˢ; *category IV*) Plate 9.

Dᵖ 06 Codex Claromontanus, p†,²⁶ sixth, 533 ff., 1 col., 21 ll., 24.5 × 19.5 cm. Paris: Bibliothèque Nationale, Gr. 107, 107AB. A Greek-Latin diglot written in sense lines (shorter than in 05), and like 05 once in Theodore Beza's possession, the source of two copies: Dᵃᵇˢ ¹, ninth, in Leningrad; Dᵃᵇˢ ² with Ephesians, tenth, in Mengeringhausen. The attempt to find here or in other diglot manuscripts any similarities to the textual expansions or abbreviations found in 05 must be considered unsuccessful. Dᵖ 06* (51¹ 12¹ᐟ² 111² 74ˢ; *category II*), Dᵖ 06ᶜ (139¹ 30¹ᐟ² 44² 35ˢ; *category III*) Plate 10.

Eᵉ 07 Codex Basilensis, e†,²⁷ eighth, 318 ff., 1 col., 23+ ll., 23 × 16.5 cm. Basel: Universitätsbibliothek, A.N. III 12. Brought to Europe for the Council of Basel in 1431, cited since the eighteenth century. (209¹ 107¹ᐟ² 1² 9ˢ; *Byzantine text, category V*)

Eᵃ 08 Codex Laudianus (once owned by Archbishop William Laud), Acts†, sixth, 227 ff., 2 cols., 24+ ll., 27 × 22 cm. Oxford: Bodleian Library, Laud. Gr. 35. A Latin-Greek diglot, with Latin text on verso, written in very short sense lines. (36¹ 21¹ᐟ² 22² 22ˢ; *category II*)

Fᵉ 09 Codex Boreelianus, e†, ninth, 204 ff., 2 cols., 19+ ll., 28.5 × 22 cm. Utrecht: Rijksuniversiteits Bibliotheek Ms. 1. (156¹ 78¹ᐟ² 0² 11ˢ; *Byzantine text, category V*)

Fᵖ 010 Codex Augiensis, p, ninth, 136 ff., 2 cols., 28 ll., 23 × 19 cm. Cambridge: Trinity College, B.XVII.1. Formerly in the monastery of Reichenau, a Greek-Latin diglot, with Hebrews in Latin (Vulgate) only. (43¹ 11¹ᐟ² 89² 70ˢ; *category II*)

Gᵉ 011 Codex Seidelianus I, e†, ninth, 252 ff. (1 f. in Cambridge), 2 cols., 21+ ll., 25.7 × 21.5 cm. London: British Library, Harley 5684; Cambridge, Trinity College, B.XVII.20. (176¹ 87¹ᐟ² 4² 21ˢ; *Byzantine text, category V*)

Gᵖ 012 Codex Boernerianus, p†, ninth, 99 ff., 1 col., 20+ ll., 25 × 19 cm. Dresden: Sächsische Landesbibliothek, A 145b. A diglot from St. Gallen, with interlinear Latin above Greek text (i.e., for scholarly use); lacking Hebrews, and with superscription for the Laodicean letter following Philemon, although without its text. (44¹ 13¹ᐟ² 88² 66ˢ; *category III*) Plate 28.

Hᵉ 013 Codex Seidelianus II, e†, ninth, 194 ff. (1 f. in Cambridge), 1 col., 23 ll., 22 × 18 cm. Hamburg: Universitätsbibliothek, Cod. 91 in scrin; Cambridge: Trinity College, B.XVII.20,21. (174¹ 82¹ᐟ² 2² 7ˢ; *Byzantine text, category V*)

Hᵃ 014 Codex Mutinensis, Acts†, ninth, 43 ff., 1 col., 30 ll., 33 × 23 cm. Modena: Biblioteca Estense, G.196 (II.G.3), ff. 9-51. (48¹ 22¹ᐟ² 2² 1ˢ; *Byzantine text, category V*)

Hᵖ 015 Codex Coislinianus, pP,²⁸ sixth, 41 ff., 1 col., 16 ll., *ca.* 30 × 25 cm. Scattered: Athos, Great Lavra (8 ff.); Kiev (3 ff.); Leningrad (3 ff.); Moscow (3 ff.); Paris (22 ff.); Turin (2 ff.). Parts of 1-2 Corinthians, Galatians, Colossians, 1 Thessalonians, Hebrews, 1-2 Timothy, Titus. (7¹ 0¹ᐟ² 12² 3ˢ; *category III*)

I 016 Codex Freerianus (Washingtonensis), 1 Corinthians–Hebrews†, fifth, 84 ff., 1 col., 30 ll., *ca.* 25 × 20 cm. Washington D.C.: Freer Gallery of Art, 06.275. (1¹ 5¹ᐟ² 22² 6ˢ; *Egyptian text, category II*)

---

26. In Dᵖ Rom. 1:1-7 is lacking; Rom. 1:27-30 and 1 Cor. 14:13-22 have been supplied by a later hand.

27. For data on lacunae and contents from this point the reader is referred to Nestle-Aland²⁶, pp. 690ff.; contents will be indicated hereafter only for fragments.

28. P = incomplete ("partly").

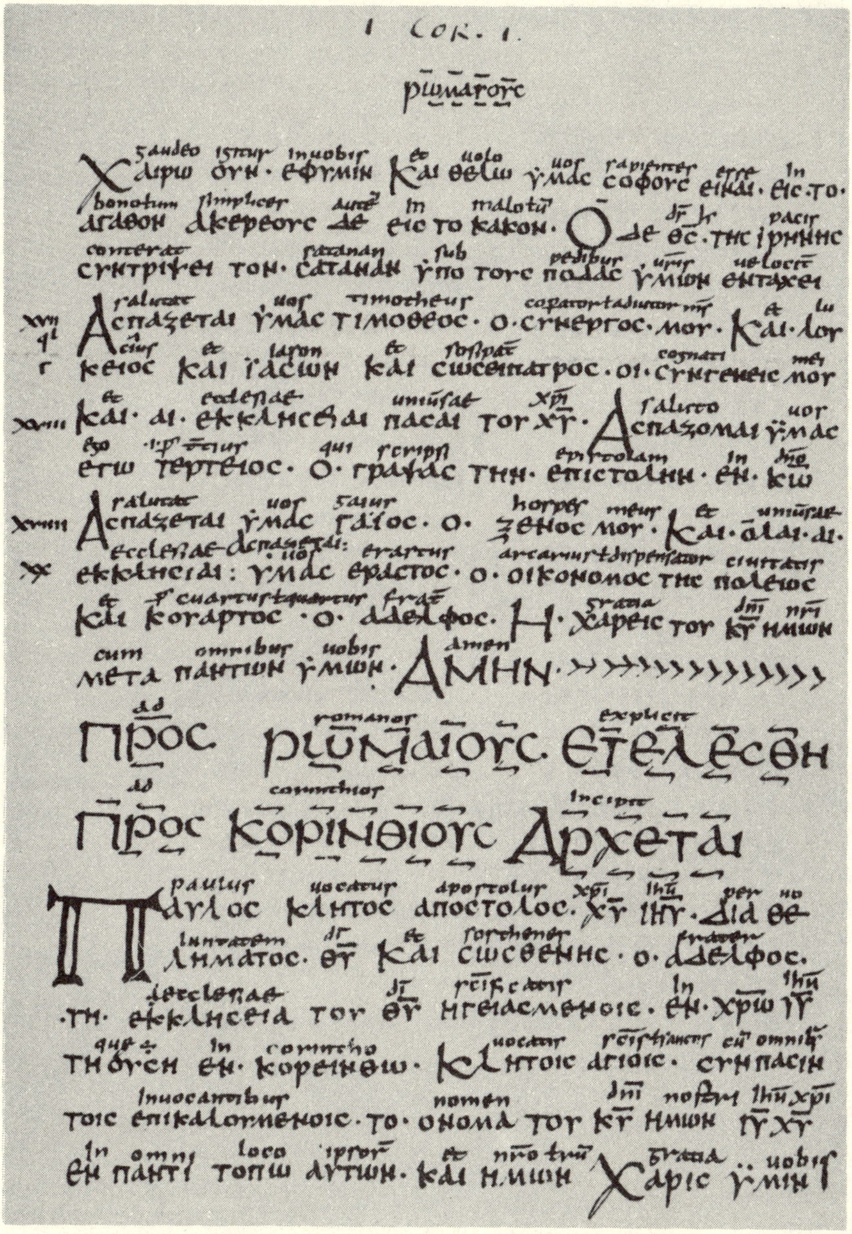

Plate 28. Codex Boernerianus (G^p, 012, ninth century; cf. p. 110), a Greek-Latin diglot: the ending of Romans and the beginning of 1 Corinthians (f. 21^r).

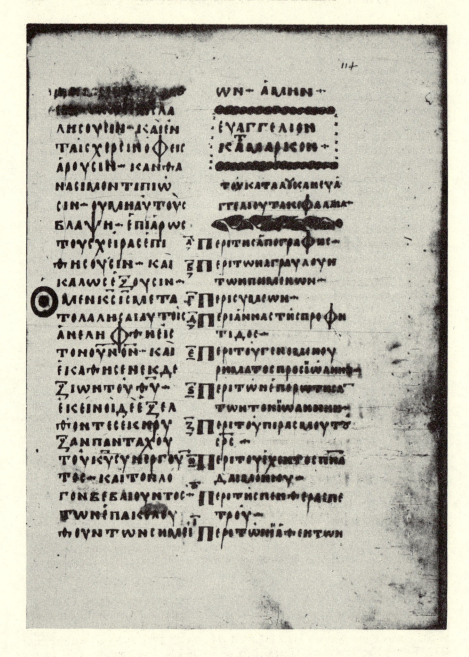

Plate 29. Codex Regius (L^e, 019, eighth century; cf. p. 113): the ending of the gospel of Mark and the beginning of Luke (kephalaia; cf. p. 252) (f. 114^r).

K^e 017 Codex Cyprius, e, ninth, 267 ff., 1 col., 16-31 ll., 26 × 19 cm. Paris: Bibliothèque Nationale, Gr. 63. (197^1 107$^{1/2}$ 8^2 15^s; *Byzantine text, category V*)

K^{ap} 018 Codex Mosquensis, apK^{29}†, ninth, 288 ff., 2 cols., 27 ll., 33.8 × 24.2 cm. Moscow: Historical Museum, V.93, S.97. With commentary. (Paul: 154^1 33$^{1/2}$ 8^2 8^s; Cath: 80^1 11$^{1/2}$ 4^2 4^s; *Byzantine text, category V*)

L^e 019 Codex Regius, e†, eighth, 257 ff., 2 cols., 25 ll., 23.5 × 17 cm. Paris: Bibliothèque Nationale, Gr. 62. (52^1 75$^{1/2}$ 125^2 64^s; *Egyptian text, double Marcan ending, category II*) Plate 29.

L^{ap} 020 Codex Angelicus, ap†, ninth, 189 ff., 2 cols., 26 ll., 27 × 21.5 cm. Rome: Biblioteca Angelica 39. (Acts: 52^1 25$^{1/2}$ 1^2 2^s; Paul: 187^1 45$^{1/2}$ 4^2 5^s; Cath: 81^1 9$^{1/2}$ 5^2 3^s; *Byzantine text, category V*)

M 021 Codex Campianus, e, ninth, 257 ff., 2 cols., 24 ll., 22 × 16.3 cm. Paris: Bibliothèque Nationale, Gr. 48. (202^1 106$^{1/2}$ 7^2 12^s; *Byzantine text, category V*)

N 022 Codex Petropolitanus Purpureus, e†, purple parchment, sixth, 231 ff., 2 cols., 16 ll., *ca.* 32 × 27 cm. Leningrad: Public Library, Gr. 537 (182 ff.); Patmos: Ioannou (33 ff.); single ff. in London, Athens, Lerma, New York, Rome, Vienna. (89^1 48$^{1/2}$ 8^2 15^s; *Byzantine text, category V*)

O 023 Codex Sinopensis, Matthew†, sixth, 44 ff., 1 col., 15+ ll., 30 × 25 cm. Paris: Bibliothèque Nationale, Suppl. Gr. 1286 (43 ff.). Purple parchment with silver writing and gold illumination; cf. N. (9^1 4$^{1/2}$ 0^2 3^s; *Byzantine text, category V*)

P^e 024 Codex Guelferbytanus A, eP, sixth, 44 ff., 2 cols., 24 ll., 26.5 × 21.5 cm. Wolfenbüttel: Herzog August Bibliothek, Weissenburg 64 (loose ff.). Palimpsests: upper text Latin, Isidore of Seville's *Origins* and letters. (24^1 16$^{1/2}$ 3^2 0^s; *Byzantine text, category V*) Plate 18.

P^{apr} 025 Codex Porphyrianus, apr†, ninth, 327 ff., 1 col., 24 ll., 16 × 13 cm. Leningrad: Public Library, Gr. 225. Palimpsest: upper text is the minuscule 1834 (Euthalius), dated 1301. (Acts: 69^1 29$^{1/2}$ 1^2 1^s; Paul: 82^1 36$^{1/2}$ 87^2 31^s; Cath: 48^1 7$^{1/2}$ 26^2 9^s; *category V in Acts and Revelation, elsewhere III*)

Q 026 Codex Guelferbytanus B, Luke-John†, fifth, 13 ff., 2 cols., 28 ll., 26.5 × 21.5 cm. Wolfenbüttel: Herzog August Bibliothek, Weissenburg 64 (loose ff.). Palimpsest: upper text Isidore of Seville, as in 024. (5^1 5$^{1/2}$ 0^2 2^s; *Byzantine text, category V*)

R 027 Codex Nitriensis, Luke†, sixth, 48 ff., 2 cols., 25 ll., 29.5 × 23.5 cm. London: British Library, Add. 17211 (earlier in a monastery of the Nitrian desert). Palimpsest: upper text Syriac, Severus of Antioch against Johannes Grammaticus. (11^1 4$^{1/2}$ 0^2 5^s; *Byzantine text, category V*)

S 028 Codex Vaticanus 354, e, 949, 235 ff., 2 cols., 27 ll., 36 × 24. Rome: Vatican Library, Gr. 354. (206^1 105$^{1/2}$ 4^2 12^s; *Byzantine text, category V*)

T 029 Codex Borgianus, Luke-John†, fifth, 23 ff., 2 cols., 26-33 ll., 26 × 21 cm. Rome: Vatican Library, Borg., Copt. 109 (8 ff.) and T. 109 (13 ff.); New York: Pierpont Morgan Library (2 ff.). Sahidic-Greek diglot (Sahidic verso), belongs to same manuscript as 0113, 0125, 0139 (all Paris: Bibliothèque Nationale, 3 ff., frag. 5 ff.). (*Egyptian text, category II*)

U 030 Codex Nanianus, e, ninth, 291 ff., 2 cols., 21 ll., 22.5 × 16.7 cm. Venice: Biblioteca San Marco 1397 (I, 8). (105^1 38$^{1/2}$ 1^2 11^s; *Byzantine text, category V*)

V 031 Codex Mosquensis, e† ninth, 220 ff., 1 col., 28 ll., 15.7 × 11.5 cm. Moscow: Historical Museum, V, 9. (192^1 101$^{1/2}$ 8^2 17^s; *Byzantine text, category V*)

W 032 Codex Freerianus, e†, fifth, 187 ff., 1 col., 30 ll., 21 × 14.3 cm. Washington, D.C.: Smithsonian Institution, Freer Gallery of Art 06.274. Text irregular, with "Freer logion" at Mark 16:14. (118^1 70$^{1/2}$ 54^2 88^s; *category III*) Plate 30.

X 033 Codex Monacensis, eK†, tenth, 160 ff., 2 cols., 45 ll., 37.5 × 25.5 cm. Munich: Universitätsbibliothek, fol. 30. (118^1 53$^{1/2}$ 6^2 14^s; *Byzantine text, category V*)

29. K = with commentary.

Plate 30. Codex Freerianus (W, 032, fifth century; cf. p. 113): the ending of the gospel of Mark, with the Freer Logion.

Plate 31. Codex Koridethianus (Θ, 038, ninth century; cf. p. 118): the ending of the gospel of Luke and the beginning of John (kephalaia; cf. p. 252).

Plate 32. Codex Rossanensis (Σ, 042, sixth century; cf. p. 118), a purple parchment manuscript famous for its almost full-page illustrations, but typically of the sumptuous manuscripts of the period it has little textual value. Shown are Christ before Pilate (Matt. 27:2) and the repentance and death of Judas (Matt. 27:3-5).

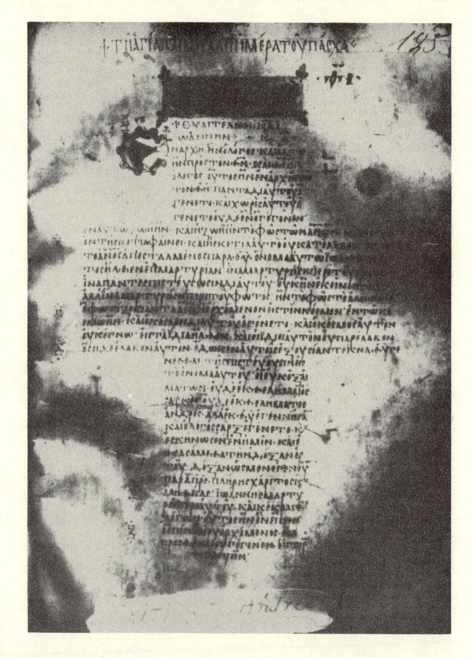

Plate 33. A distinctive format: the Gospels manuscript 047 (eighth century; cf. p. 118) preserves a (Byzantine) text in cruciform: the beginning of the gospel of John.

Y 034 Codex Macedoniensis, e†, ninth. 309 ff., 1 col., 16+ ll., 18 × 13 cm. Cambridge: University Library, Add. 6594. (192^1 $95^{1/2}$ 4^2 6^s; *Byzantine text, category V*)

Z 035 Codex Dublinensis, Matthew†, sixth, 32 ff., 1 col., 21+ ll., *ca.* 27 × 20 cm. Dublin: Trinity College, K 3.4. Palimpsest: upper text patristic. (3^1 $5^{1/2}$ 11^2 2^s; *category III*)

Γ 036 Codex Tischendorfianus, e†, tenth, 257 ff., 1 col., 24+ ll., 30 × 23 cm. Leningrad: Public Library, Gr. 33 (99 ff.); Oxford: Bodleian Library, Auct. T. infr. 2.2 (158 ff.). (182^1 $91^{1/2}$ 1^2 12^s; *Byzantine text, category V*)

Δ 037 Codex Sangallensis, e†, ninth. 198 ff., 1 col., 17+ ll., 23 × 18.5 cm. St. Gallen: Stiftsbibliothek 48. Greek-Latin diglot, with Latin interlinear as in **012**. (120^1 $88^{1/2}$ 69^2 47^s; *category III*)

Θ 038 Codex Coridethianus, e†, ninth, 249 ff., 2 cols., 25+ ll., 29 × 24 cm. Tiflis: Manuscript Institute Gr. 28. Discovered in Caucasia, of uneven textual quality, written in an awkward hand by a scribe evidently unfamiliar with Greek; regarded by many as the chief representative of the "Caesarean text" associated also with 565, 700, etc. (89^1 $59^{1/2}$ 75^2 95^s; *category II*) Plate 31.

Λ 039 Codex Tischendorfianus III, Luke-John, ninth, 157 ff., 2 cols., 23 ll., 21 × 16.5 cm. Oxford: Bodleian Library, Auct. T. infr. 1.1. (41^1 $10^{1/2}$ 0^2 2^s; *Byzantine text, category V*)

Ξ 040 Codex Zacynthius, Luke 1–11†, sixth, 89 ff., 36 × 29 cm. London: British and Foreign Bible Society 24. Text surrounded by commentary. Palimpsest: upper text *l* 299. Edited by J. Harold Greenlee (1957). (2^1 $2^{1/2}$ 8^2 3^s; *category III*)

Π 041 Codex Petropolitanus, e†, ninth, 350 ff., 1 col., 21 ll., 14.5 × 10.5 cm. Leningrad: Public Library, Gr. 34. (190^1 $104^{1/2}$ 11^2 18^s; *Byzantine text, category V*)

Σ 042 Codex Rossanensis, Matthew-Mark, sixth, purple parchment magnificently illuminated, 188 ff., 2 cols., 20 ll., 31 × 26 cm. Rossano: Archbishopric. (140^1 $83^{1/2}$ 15^2 25^s; *Byzantine text, category V*) Plate 32.

Φ 043 Codex Beratinus, Matthew-Mark, sixth, purple parchment, 190 ff., 2 cols., 17 ll., 31 × 27 cm. Tiranë: National Archives 1. (131^1 $83^{1/2}$ 11^2 18^s; *Byzantine text, category V*)

Ψ 044 Codex Athous Lavrensis, eap†, eighth/ninth, 261 ff., 1 col., 31 ll., 21 × 15.3 cm. Athos: Lavra B' 52. (Evv: 40^1 $21^{1/2}$ 52^2 19^s; Acts 42^1 $25^{1/2}$ 23^2 15^s; Paul: 127^1 $45^{1/2}$ 40^2 34^s; Cath: 21^1 $8^{1/2}$ 54^2 14^s; *category II in Cath, III elsewhere*)

Ω 045 e, ninth, 259 ff., 2 cols., 19+ ll., 22 × 16 cm. Athos: Dionysiou (10) 55. (208^1 $104^{1/2}$ 3^2 10^s; *Byzantine text, category V*)

046 r, tenth, 20 ff., 1 col., 35 ll., 27.5 × 19 cm. Rome: Vatican Library, Gr. 2066. *(Category V)*

047 e†, eighth, 152 ff., cruciform text, 37 ll., 20.5 × 15.2 cm. Princeton, N.J.: University Library, Med. and Ren. Mss., Garrett 1. (175^1 $96^{1/2}$ 6^2 21^s; *Byzantine text, category V*) Plate 33.

048 apP, fifth, 21 ff., 3 cols. 40+ ll., 30 × 27 cm. Rome: Vatican Library, Gr. 2061, double palimpsest. (Paul: 3^1 $7^{1/2}$ 30^2 4^s; *category II*)

049 ap†, ninth, 149 ff., 1 col., 30 ll., 27.5 × 18.5 cm. Athos: Lavra A' 88. (Acts: 70^1 $29^{1/2}$ 3^2 3^s; Paul: 109^1 $37^{1/2}$ 0^2 3^s; Cath: 86^1 $9^{1/2}$ 1^2 3^s; *Byzantine text, category V*)

050 John†, ninth, 19 ff., *ca.* 32.5 × 24 cm. Athens (2 ff.); Athos: Dionysiou (7 ff.); Moscow (7 ff.); Oxford (3 ff.). With commentary in margin. *(Category III)*

051 Rev. 11–22†, tenth, 92 ff., 1 col., 22 ll., 23 × 18 cm. Athos: Pantokratoros 44. Commentary manuscript. *(Category III)*

052 Rev. 7:16–8:12, tenth, 4 ff., 2 cols., 27 ll., 29.5 × 23 cm. Athos: Panteleimonos 99,2. Commentary manuscript. *(Byzantine text, category V)*

053 Luke 1:1–2:40, ninth, 14 ff., 3 cols., 42 ll., 27.5 × 23 cm. Munich: Bayerische Staatsbibliothek, Gr. 208, fol. 235-248. Commentary manuscript, text and scholia alternating. *(Category V?)*

054 John 16:3–19:41, eighth, 6 ff., 1 col., 36 ll., 29 × 18.5 cm. Rome: Vatican Library, Barb. Gr. 521. *(Category V?)*

055 eK, eleventh, 303 ff., 1 col., 37 ll., 26 × 19.5 cm. Paris: Bibliothèque Nationale, Gr. 201. Commentary with incomplete text, does not strictly belong in uncial list.

056 apK. tenth, 381 ff., 1 col., 40 ll., 29.8 × 23.3 cm. Paris: Bibliothèque Nationale, Coislin Gr. 26. (Acts: 75^1 $27^{1/2}$ 0^2 3^s; Paul: 189^1 $46^{1/2}$ 5^2 8^s; Cath: 80^1 $6^{1/2}$ 3^2 8^s; *Byzantine text, category V*)

057 Acts 3:5-6,10-12, fourth/fifth, 2 cols., *ca.* 27 ll., (9 × 13 cm.). Berlin: Staatliche Museen, P. 9808. *(Category I)* Plate 15.

058 Matt. 18:18-29, fourth, 2 cols., *ca.* 26 ll., *ca.* 19 × 13 cm. Vienna: Österreichische Nationalbibliothek, Pap. G. 39782. *(Category III?)*

059 Mark 15:29-38, fourth/fifth, 1 col., *ca.* 19 ll., *ca.* 15 × 11 cm. Vienna: Österreichische Nationalbibliothek, Pap. G. 39779. From the same manuscript as **0215** (Mark 15:20-21,26-27; Vienna: Pap. G. 36112). *(Category III)*

060 John 14†, sixth, 2 cols., *ca.* 24 ll., *ca.* 14 × 12 cm. Berlin: Staatliche Museen, P 5877. *(Category III)*

061 1 Tim. 3:15-16; 4:1-3; 6:2-8, fifth, 2 ff., 1 col., *ca.* 19 ll., *ca.* 14 × 12 cm. Paris: Louvre Ms. E 7332. *(Category V, singular readings)*

062 Gal. 4:15–5:14, fifth, 1 f., 2 cols., 33 ll., 22 × 18.5 cm. Formerly Damascus: Kubbet el Chazne. Palimpsest: upper text Arabic. *(Category III)*

063 Luke 16–John 6†, ninth, 20 ff., 2 cols., 29 ll., *ca.* 26 × 19 cm. Athos: Vatopediou 1219 (14 ff.); Moscow: Historical Museum, V. 137,181 (6 ff.); belongs with **0117** (Luke 20†, 2 ff.; Paris: Bibliothèque Nationale, Suppl. Gr. 1155, II). (**063**: 15^1 $3^{1/2}$ 0^2 0^s; *Byzantine text, category V*)

064 Matt. 27:7-30, sixth, 2 ff., 2 cols., 25 ll., *ca.* 28 × 21 cm. Kiev: Ukrainian National Library, Petrov 17; from same manuscript as **074** (Matt. 25, 26, 28†, Mark 1, 2, 5†; Sinai Harris 10; 10 ff.) and **090** (Matt. 26:59-70; 27:44-56; Mark 1:34–2:12; Leningrad: Public Library, Gr. 276; 4 ff.). Palimpsest: upper text Syriac liturgica in **064, 074**; blank in **090**. *(Byzantine text, category V)*

065 John 11–12, 15–16, 19†, sixth, 3 ff., 2 cols., 29 ll., *ca.* 29 × 23 cm. Leningrad: Public Library Gr. 6 I. Palimpsest: upper text Georgian calendar. *(Category V)*

066 Acts 28:8-17, sixth, 1 f., 2 cols., 25 ll., *ca.* 25 × 20 cm. Leningrad: Public Library, Gr. 6 II, fol. 4. Palimpsest: upper text Georgian calendar. *(Category III)*

067 Matt. 14, 24–26†, Mark 9, 14†, sixth, 6 ff., 2 cols., 22+ ll., (20 × 15.5 cm.). Leningrad: Public Library, Gr. 6 III. Palimpsest: upper text Georgian, tenth century. *(Category III, influenced by V)*

068 John 13:16-27; 16:7-19, fifth, 2 ff., 2 cols., *ca.* 18+ ll., 26 × 24 cm. London: British Library, Add. 17136. Double palimpsest: upper texts Syriac. *(Category III)*

069 Mark 10:50-51; 11:11-12, fifth, 1 col., *ca.* 25 ll., (8 × 4.5 cm.). Chicago: University of Chicago, Oriental Institute, 2057. *(Category III)*

070 Luke-John†, sixth, 44 ff., 2 cols., 35 ll., 37 × 28 cm., Greek-Coptic diglot. Luke 9:9-17; 10:40–11:6; 12:15–13:32; John 5:31-42; 8:33-42; 12:27-36. Oxford: Clarendon Press b.2; Paris: Bibliothèque Nationale, Copt. 132,2, fol. 75, 133,1, fol. 120; Louvre MSE 10014, 10092k, 13 ff.; from the same manuscript as **0110** (John 8:13-22, London: British Library, Add. 34274, 1f.), **0124** (Luke 3:19-30; 10:21-30; 11:24-42; 22:54-65; 23:4-24,26; John 5:22-31; 8:42–9:39; 11:48-56; 12:46-13:4; Paris: Bibliothèque Nationale, Copt. 129,7, fol. 14, 72, 87, 89-90, 119-124, 139, 147-154, 156, 22 ff.), **0178** (Luke 16:4-12; Vienna: Österreichische Nationalbibliothek, 1 f.), **0179** (Luke 21:30-22:2; *ibid.*, 1 f.), **0180** (John 7:3-12; *ibid.*, 1 f.), **0190** (Luke 10:30-39; *ibid.*: 1f.), **0191** (Luke 12:5-14; *ibid.*, 1 f.), **0193** (John 3:23-32; Paris: Bibliothèque Nationale, Copt. 132,2, fol. 92, 1 f.), **0194** = **0124**, and **0202** (Luke 8:13-19; 8:55–9:9; London: British Library, Or. 3579 B [29], fol. 46, 47, 2 ff.). The Coptic texts are not completely identical with the Greek. *(Category III)*

071 Matt. 1:21-24,25–2:2, fifth/sixth, (1 col.), (13 ll.), (7 × 9.5 cm.). Cambridge: Harvard University, Semitic Museum 3735. *(Category II)*

072 Mark 2:23–3:5, fifth/sixth, 1 f., 1 cols., 22 ll., 20 × 15 cm. Formerly Damascus: Kubbet el Chazne. Palimpsest: upper text Arabic. *(Category III)*

073 Matt. 14:28-31, sixth, 2 cols., *ca*. 34 ll., *ca*. 28 × 23 cm. Sinai Harris 7; from the same manuscript as **084** (Matt. 14:19–15:8; Leningrad: Public Library, Gr. 277, 1 f.). *(Category II)*

074 Cf. **064**.

075 pK†, tenth, 1 col., 31 ll., 27 × 19 cm. Athens: National Library, Gr. 100. (85^1 19$^{1/2}$ 17^2 16^s; *category III*)

076 Acts 2:11-22, fifth/sixth, 1 f., 2 cols., 23 ll., 17 × 15 cm. New York: Pierpont Morgan Library, Pap. G. 8. *(Category II)*

077 Acts 13:18-29, fifth, Sinai Harris App. 5. *(Category II)*

078 Matt. 17–18, 19†; Luke 18:14-25; John 4:52–5:8; 20:17-26, sixth, 6 ff., 2 cols., 22 ll., 27 × 20 cm. Leningrad: Public Library, Gr. 13, fol. 1-7. Palimpsest: upper text Georgian, tenth century. *(Category III, influenced by V)*

079 Luke 7:39-49; 24:10-19, sixth, 2 ff., 2 cols., 23 ll., *ca*. 31 × 25 cm. Leningrad: Public Library, Gr. 13, fol. 8-10. Palimpsest: upper text Georgian. *(Category III)*

080 Mark 9–10†, sixth, purple parchment, 2 ff., 2 cols., *ca*. 18 ll. Leningrad: Public Library, Gr. 275 (3). Alexandria: Patriarchate 496. *(Text too brief to classify)*

081 2 Cor. 1:20–2:12, sixth, 2 ff., 2 cols., 18 ll., *ca*. 28 × 23 cm. Leningrad: Public Library, Gr. 9. *(Category II)*

082 Eph. 4:2-18, sixth. 1 f., 2 cols., *ca*. 25 ll. Moscow: Historical Museum, V, 108. Cut into strips to reinforce a binding. *(Category III)*

083 John 1:25-41; 2:9–4:14,34-49, sixth/seventh, 6 ff., 2 cols., 25 ll., *ca*. 28 × 26 cm. Leningrad: Public Library, Gr. 10; from the same manuscript as **0112** (Mark 14:29-45; 15:27–16:8; shorter Marcan ending; 16:9-10; Sinai Harris 12, 4 ff.) and **0235** (Mark 13†, Leningrad: Public Library, frag.). *(Category II)*

084 Cf. **073**.

085 Matt. 20:3-32: 22:3-16, sixth, 3 ff., 2 cols. 27+ ll., 24 × 21 cm. Leningrad: Public Library, Gr. 714. *(Category II)*

086 John 1†, 3, 4†, sixth, 13 ff., 2 cols., 20+ ll., *ca*. 27 × 23 cm. London: British Library, Or. 5707. Greek-Coptic diglot. Palimpsest: upper text Coptic tables and formulae. *(Category III)*

087 Matt. 1:23–2:2; 19:3-8; 21:19-24; John 18:29-35, sixth, 3 ff., 1 col., 18 ll., 34 × 26 cm. Leningrad: Public Library, Gr. 12,278; Sinai Gr. 218; from the same manuscript as **092b** (Mark 12:32-37; Sinai Harris 11, 1 f.). *(Category II)*

088 1 Cor. 15:53–16:9; Tit. 1:1-13, fifth/sixth, 2ff., 2 cols., 24 ll., 23.5 × 20 cm. Leningrad: Public Library, Gr. 6, II, fol. 5-6. Palimpsest: upper text Georgian, tenth century. *(Category II)*

089 Matt. 26:2-4,7-9, sixth, 1 f., 1 col., *ca*. 17 ll., *ca*. 36 × 28 cm. Leningrad: Public Library, Gr. 280; from the same manuscript as **092a** (Matt. 26:4-7,10-12; Sinai Harris 11, 1 f.) and **0293** (Sinai: St. Catherine's Monastery). *(Category II)*

090 Cf. **064**.

091 John 6:13-14,22-24, sixth, 2 cols., *ca*. 23 ll., *ca*. 32 × 28 cm. Leningrad: Public Library, Gr. 279. *(Category II)*

092a Cf. **089**.

092b Cf. **087**.

093 Acts 24:22-25:5; 1 Pet. 2:22–3:7, sixth, 2 ff., 2 cols., 24 ll., 25 × 18 cm. Cambridge: University Library, Taylor-Schechter Coll. 12,189; 12,208. Palimpsest: upper text Hebrew(!). *(Category V in Acts, II in 1 Peter?)*

094 Matt. 24:9-21, sixth, 1 f., 2 cols., 20 ll., 30 × 24 cm. Athens: National Library, Gr. 2106. Palimpsest: upper text Greek menaeon. *(Category II)*

095 Acts 2:45–3:8, eighth, 1 f., 1 col., 21 ll., *ca*. 28 × 19 cm. Leningrad: Public

Library, Gr. 17; from the same manuscript as **0123** (Acts 2:22,26-28,45–3:2†; Leningrad: Public Library, Gr. 49, 1-2, frag.). *(Category III)*

096 Acts 2:6-17; 26:7-18, seventh, 2 ff., 1 col., 26 ll., *ca.* 29 × 22 cm. Leningrad: Public Library, Gr. 19. Palimpsest: upper text Georgian, tenth century. *(Category III)*

097 Acts 13:39-46, seventh, 1 f., 2 cols., 18 ll., *ca.* 26 × 21 cm. Leningrad: Public Library, Gr. 18. Palimpsest: upper text Georgian, tenth century. *(Category III, influenced by V)*

098 2 Cor. 11:9-19, seventh, 1 f., 1 col., 24 ll., 22.2 × 16 cm. Grottaferrata: Biblioteca della Badia, Z' a' 24. Palimpsest: upper text *Iliad*(!). *(Category I)*

099 Mark 16:6-8, short ending, 9-18, seventh, 1 f., 2 cols., 32 ll., 32 × 26 cm. Paris: Bibliothèque Nationale, Copt. 129,8. *(Category III)*

0100 John 20:26-27,30-31, seventh, 2 cols., *ca.* 33 ll., *ca.* 37 × 38 cm. Paris: Bibliothèque Nationale, Copt. 129,10. Greek-Coptic diglot, identical with **0195**, represents a part of *l* 963, and accordingly classified more properly among the lectionaries than among the uncials.

0101 John 1:29-32, eighth, 1 col., *ca.* 14 ll., *ca.* 11 × 9 cm. Vienna: Österreichische Nationalbibliothek, Pap. G. 39780. *(Category II)*

0102 Luke 3:23–4:2 (Athos: Vatopediou 1219); 4:3-29 (Paris: Bibliothèque Nationale, Suppl. Gr. 1155, I); 4:30-43; 21:4-18 (Athos: *idem*), seventh, 5 ff., 2 cols., 24 ll., *ca.* 30 × 23 cm. Probably from the same manuscript as **0138** (Matt. 21:24–24:15, Athos: Protatou 56, 8 ff.). *(Category II)*

0103 Mark 13:34–14:25, seventh, 2 ff., 2 cols., 30 ll., 22.5 × 16.5 cm. Paris: Bibliothèque Nationale, Suppl. Gr. 726, ff. 6-7. Palimpsest: upper text homily on Hebrews. *(Category V)*

0104 Matt. 23†, Mark 1†, 13–14†, sixth, 4 ff., 2 cols., 36 ll., 32 × 22 cm. Paris: Bibliothèque Nationale, Suppl. Gr. 726, ff. 1-5, 8-10. Palimpsest: upper text homily on Hebrews. *(Category V)*

0105 John 6:71–7:46, tenth, 4 ff., 2 cols., 24 ll., 32 × 24 cm. Vienna: Österreichische Nationalbibliothek, Suppl. Gr. 121. *(Category III, influenced by V)*

0106 Matt. 12–15†, seventh, 5 ff., 1 col., 20 ll., *ca.* 30 × 22 cm. Leningrad: Public Library, Gr. 16, 1 f.; Leipzig: Universitätsbibliothek, Cod. Gr. 7, 4 ff.; Birmingham: Selly Oak College, Mingana Chr. Arab. 93, fragment. From same manuscript as **0119** (Matt. 13–15†, 4 ff., Sinai Harris 8). *(Category III)*

0107 Matt. 22–23†, Mark 4–5†, seventh, 6 ff., 2 cols., 23 ll., *ca.* 27 × 21 cm. Leningrad: Public Library, Gr. 11. *(Category III)*

0108 Luke 11:37-45, seventh, 2 cols., 23-24 ll., *ca.* 30 × 24 cm. Leningrad: Public Library, Gr. 22. *(Category II)*

0109 John 16:30–17:9; 18:31-40, seventh, 2 ff., 1 col., 22 ll., 17 × 15 cm. Berlin: Staatliche Museen, P. 5010. *(Category III)*

0110 Cf. **070**.

0111 2 Thess. 1:1–2:2, seventh, 1 f., 2 cols., 24 ll., *ca.* 16 × 14 cm. Berlin: Staatliche Museen, P. 5013. *(Category II)*

0112 Cf. **083**.

0113 Cf. **029**.

0114 John 20:4-10, eighth, 2 cols., 32 ll., *ca.* 39 × 30 cm. Paris: Bibliothèque Nationale, Copt. 129,10, f. 198. Greek-Coptic diglot. *(Category II)*

0115 Luke 9:35-47; 10:12-22, ninth/tenth, 2 ff., 2 cols., 23 ll., 25 × 18 cm. Paris: Bibliothèque Nationale, Gr. 314, ff. 179, 180. *(Category III)*

0116 Matt. 19–21†; 26:52–27:1; Mark 13:21–14:67; Luke 3:1–4:20, eighth, 14 ff., 2 cols., 25 ll., 26 × 20 cm. Naples: Biblioteca Nazionale, II C 15. Palimpsest: upper text typicon. *(Category V)*

0117 Cf. **063**.

0118 Matt. 11:27-28, eighth, frag. (11 × 10 cm.). Sinai Harris 6. *(Text too brief to classify)*

0119 Cf. **0106.**

0120 Acts 16:30–17:17,27-29,31-34; 18:8-26, ninth, 6 ff., 1 col., 21 ll., 27 × 19 cm. Rome: Vatican Library, Gr. 2302. Palimpsest: upper text menaeon. *(Category III)*

0121a 1 Cor. 15:52–2 Cor. 1:15; 10:13–12:5, tenth, 2 ff., 2 cols., 38 ll., 26 × 21 cm. London: British Library, Harley 5613. *(Category III)*

0121b Heb. 1:1–4:3; 12:20–13:25, tenth, 2 ff., 2 cols., 45 ll., 26 × 21 cm. Hamburg: Universitätsbibliothek, Cod. 50 in scrin. *(Category III)*

0122 Gal. 5:12–6:4; Heb. 5:8–6:10, ninth, 2 ff., 2 cols., 28 ll., *ca.* 25 × 20 cm. Leningrad: Public Library, Gr. 32. *(Category III)*

0123 Cf. **095.**

0124 Cf. **070.**

0125 Cf. **029.**

0126 Mark 5:34–6:2, eighth, 1 f., 2 cols., 24 ll., *ca.* 30 × 22 cm. Formerly Damascus: Kubbet el Chazne. *(Category III)*

0127 John 2:2-11, eighth, 1 f., 2 cols., 22 ll., 26.5 × 21.2 cm. Paris: Bibliothèque Nationale. Copt. 129,10, f. 207. *(Category III)*

0128 Matt. 25:32-45, ninth. 1 f., 2 cols., *ca.* 33 ll., *ca.* 35 × 25.5 cm. Paris: Bibliothèque Nationale, Copt. 129,10, f. 208. *(Category III)*

0129 Paris: Bibliothèque Nationale, Copt. 129,11. Greek-Coptic diglot, from the same manuscript as **0203** (London: British Library) and *ℓ 1575* (Vienna: Österreichische Nationalbibliothek), and accordingly classified more properly among the lectionaries than among the uncials. The textual character of **0129** suggests that *ℓ 1575* deserves more careful study. Plate 52.

0130 Mark 1:31–2:16; Luke 1:20-31,64-79; 2:24-48, ninth, 7 ff., 2 cols., 22 ll., 29.5 × 21.3 cm. St. Gallen: Stiftsbibliothek, 18, fol. 143-46; 45, fol. 1-2; Zürich: Zentralbibliothek, C 57, fol. 5, 74, 93, 135. Palimpsest: upper text Latin Vulgate. *(Category III, influenced by V)*

0131 Mark 7:3,6-8,30–8:16; 9:2,7-9, ninth, 4 ff., 1 col., 24 ll., 24.5 × 18.5 cm. Cambridge: Trinity College, B VIII, 5. *(Category III)*

0132 Mark 5:16-40, ninth, 1 f., 2 cols., *ca.* 33 ll., *ca.* 25 × 17 cm. Oxford: Christ Church College, Wake 37, f. 237. Palimpsest: upper text minuscule 639. *(Category III, influenced by V)*

0133 Matt. 1, 5, 23–27†; Mark 1–6†, 10–11†, ninth, 29 ff., 2 cols., 20 ll., 33 × 26 cm. London: British Library, Add. 31919. Palimpsest: upper text menaeon. *(Category V)*

0134 Mark 3:15-32; 5:16-31, eighth, 2 ff., 1 col., 26 ll., 17 × 14 cm. Oxford: Bodleian Library, Seld. sup. 2, ff. 177-78. *(Category V)*

0135 Matt. 25–27†; Mark 1–3†; Luke 1–2, 4, 6, 8, 9, 17, 18, 22–24 +, ninth, 16 ff., 1 col., 22+ ll., *ca.* 14.3 × 12.5 cm. Milan: Biblioteca Ambrosiana. Q. 6, sup. Palimpsest: upper text *Erotemata* by Manuel Moschopoulos. *(Category V)*

0136 Matt. 14:6-13; 25:9-16,41–26:1, ninth, 3 ff., 2 cols., 16+ ll., 33 × 27 cm. Leningrad: Public Library, Gr. 281, from the same manuscript as:

0137 (Matt. 13:46-52, 1 f., Sinai Harris 9). Greek-Arabic diglot. *(Category V?)*

0138 Cf. **0102.**

0139 Cf. **029.**

0140 Acts 5:34-38, tenth. 1 col., 18+ ll., 14.5 × 12 cm. Sinai Harris App. 41. *(Category III)*

0141 John†, tenth, 349 ff., 1 col., 31 ll., 28 × 20 cm. Paris: Bibliothèque Nationale, Gr. 209. With commentary. *(Category III)*

0142 apK, tenth, 381 ff., 1 col., 40 ll., 32 × 24.5 cm. Munich: Bayerische Staatsbibliothek, Gr. 375. (Acts: 74[1] 27[1/2] 0[2] 4[s]; Paul: 192[1] 44[1/2] 4[2] 7[s]; Cath: 77[1] 6[1/2] 3[2] 8[s]; *Byzantine text, category V)*

0143 Mark 8:17-18,27-28, sixth, 2 cols., *ca.* 24 ll., (14.5 × 6 cm.). Oxford: Bodleian Library, Gr. bibl. e, 5 (P). *(Category III)*

0144 Mark 6:47-14, seventh, 2 ff., 2 cols., 28 ll., *ca.* 29 × 21 cm. Formerly Damascus: Kubbet el Chazne; now National Museum? (Not accessible)

0145 John 6:26-31, seventh, 1 f., 1 col., 18 ll., 24 × 19 cm. Formerly Damascus: Kubbet el Chazne. With commentary. *(Category III)*

0146 Mark 10:37-45, eighth, 1 f., 2 cols., 20 ll., *ca.* 27 × 21 cm. Formerly Damascus: Kubbet el Chazne. *(Category III)*

0147 Luke 6:23-35, sixth, 2 cols., *ca.* 24 ll., *ca.* 32× 24 cm. Formerly Damascus: Kubbet el Chazne. *(Category III)*

0148 Matt. 28:5-19, eighth, 1 f., 2 cols., 24 ll., 21.5 × 16.5 cm. Vienna: Österreichische Nationalbibliothek suppl. Gr. 106. *(Category III)*

0149 = 0187.

0150 pK†, ninth, 150 ff., 1 col., 34 ll., 26 × 17.5 cm. Patmos: Ioannou 61. (101[1] 34[1/2] 65[2] 23[s]; *category III)*

0151 pK†, ninth, 192 ff., 2 cols., 33 ll., 34 × 25 cm. Patmos: Ioannou 62. (174[1] 44[1/2] 9[2] 7[s]; *Byzantine text, category V)*

0152 = Talisman. (Delete from list)

0153 = Ostracon. (Delete from list)

0154 Mark 10:35-46; 11:17-28, ninth, 2 ff., 2 cols., 22 ll., 27 × 21 cm. Formerly Damascus: Kubbet el Chazne. (Not accessible)

0155 Luke 3:1-2,5,7-11; 6:24-31, ninth, 2 ff., 2 cols., *ca.* 22 ll., *ca.* 27 × 20 cm. Formerly Damascus: Kubbet el Chazne. *(Category II)*

0156 2 Pet. 3:2-10, eighth, 1 f., 1 col., 21 ll., 12 × 8 cm. Formerly Damascus: Kubbet el Chazne. *(Category II)*

0157 1 John 2:7-13, seventh/eighth, 1 f., 2 cols., 21 ll., (21.5) × 28.4 cm. Formerly Damascus: Kubbet el Chazne. (Not accessible)

0158 Gal. 1:1-13, fifth/sixth, 2 cols., *ca.* 25 ll., *ca.* 30 × 22 cm. Formerly Damascus: Kubbet el Chazne. Palimpsest: upper text Arabic. (Not accessible)

0159 Eph. 4:21-24; 5:1-3, sixth, 1 f., 2 cols., 25 ll., 24 × 17 cm. Formerly Damascus: Kubbet el Chazne. Palimpsest: upper text Luke in Arabic. *(Category III)*

0160 Matt. 26:25-26,34-36, fourth/fifth, 2 cols., 24 ll., (9.1 × 6.5 cm.). Berlin: Staatliche Museen, P. 9961. *(Category III)*

0161 Matt. 22:7-46, eighth, 1 f., 2 cols., 37 ll., 22 × 16 cm. Athens: National Library, 139, ff. 245-46. Palimpsest: upper text Greek notes, bound with minuscule *1419*. *(Category III, influenced by V)*

0162 Cf. p. 104. *(At least normal text,*[30] *category I because of date)*

0163 Rev. 16:17-20, fifth, 1 col., *ca.* 17 ll., 12 × 8.5 cm. Chicago: University of Chicago, Oriental Institute, 9351 (P. Oxy. 848). *(Category III)*

0164 Matt. 13:20-21, sixth/seventh. 2 cols., (8 ll.), (8 × 13 cm.). Berlin: Staatliche Museen, P. 9108. Greek-Coptic diglot. *(Category III?)*

0165 Acts 3:24–4:13,17-20, fifth, 1 f., 2 cols., 32 ll., 19 × 16.5 cm. Berlin: Staatliche Museen, P. 13271. *(Occasional agreement with D, but without its distinctive readings, category III)*

0166 Acts 28:30-31; Jas. 1:11, fifth, 2 cols., *ca.* 28 ll., (5 × 7.4 cm.). Heidelberg: Universitäts Bibliothek, Pap. 1357. *(Category III)*

0167 Mark 4:24-29,37-41; 6:9-11,13-14,37-39,41,45, seventh, 6 ff., 2 cols., *ca.* 12 ll., 28 × 25 cm. Athos: Lavra Δ' 61; Louvain: Bibliothèque de l'Université, Sect. des mss., frag. Omont no. 8. *(Category III)*

0168 e portions (?), eighth, palimpsest, further details unavailable, lost (last in Verria: Melissa Brothers).

0169 Rev. 3:19–4:3, fourth, 1 f., 1 col., 14 ll., 9.3 × 7.7 cm. Princeton: Theological Seminary, Speer Library, Pap. 5 (P. Oxy. 1080). *(Category III)*

0170 Matt. 6:5-6,8-10,13-15,17, fifth/sixth, 2 cols., *ca.* 27 ll., *ca.* 25 × 20 cm. Princeton: Theological Seminary, Pap. 11 (P. Oxy. 1169). *(Category III)*

0171 Cf. p. 104, *ca.* 300 *(Paraphrastic text, category IV)* Plate 17.

30. Cf. p. 104.

0172 Rom. 1:27-30,32–2:2, fifth, 1 col., *ca.* 19 ll., *ca.* 14 × 11 cm. Florence: Biblioteca Laurenziana, PSI 4. *(Category II)*

0173 Jas. 1:25-27, fifth, 1 f., 1 col., 9 ll., *ca.* 8 × 6.5 cm. Florence: Biblioteca Laurenziana, PSI 5. *(Category II)*

0174 Gal. 2:5-6, fifth, 1 col., 6 ll., (6 × 2.3 cm.). Formerly Florence: Biblioteca Laurenziana, PSI 118. Verso of fragment is blank. *(Text too brief to classify)*

0175 Acts 6:7-15, fifth, 1 f., 1 col., 20 ll., 17 × 12 cm. Florence: Biblioteca Laurenziana, PSI 125. *(Category II)*

0176 Gal. 3:16-25, fourth/fifth, 1 f., 1 col., 22 ll., *ca.* 12 × 7 cm. Florence: Biblioteca Laurenziana, PSI 251. *(Category III)*

0177 Luke 1:73–2:7, tenth, 1 f., 2 cols., 36 ll., 36 × 27.5 cm. Vienna: Österreichische Nationalbibliothek, Pap. K. 2698. Greek-Coptic diglot. *(Relatively many scribal peculiarities; category II)*

0178 Cf. **070**.

0179 Cf. **070**.

0180 Cf. **070**.

0181 Luke 9:59–10:14, fourth/fifth, 1 f., 1 col., 26 ll., 15 × 14 cm. Vienna: Österreichische Nationalbibliothek, Pap. G. 39778. *(Category II)*

0182 Luke 19:18-20,22-24, fifth, 1 col., *ca.* 21 ll., *ca.* 15 × 9 cm. Vienna: Österreichische Nationalbibliothek, Pap. G. 39781. *(Category III)*

0183 1 Thess. 3:6-9; 4:1-5, seventh, 1 col., *ca.* 28 ll., *ca.* 26 × 16 cm. Vienna: Österreichische Nationalbibliothek, Pap. G. 39785. *(Normal text with many singular omissions; category III)*

0184 Mark 15:36-37,40-41, sixth, 2 cols., *ca.* 23 ll., *ca.* 29 × 23 cm. Vienna: Österreichische Nationalbibliothek, Pap. K. 8662. Greek-Coptic diglot. *(Category II)*

0185 1 Cor. 2:5-6,9,13; 3:2-3, fourth, 2 cols. *ca.* 24 ll., *ca.* 19 × 15 cm. Vienna: Österreichische Nationalbibliothek, Pap. G. 39787. *(Category II)*

0186 2 Cor. 4:5-8,10,13, fifth/sixth. 2 cols., *ca.* 17 ll., *ca.* 18 × 15 cm. Vienna: Österreichische Nationalbibliothek, Pap. G. 39788; from the same manuscript as **0224** (2 Cor. 4:5,12-13, fragment, *ibid.*, Pap. G. 3075). *(Category III)*

0187 Mark 6:30-41, sixth, 2 cols., 26 ll., *ca.* 24 × 18 cm. Heidelberg: Universitäts Bibliothek, Pap. 1354. *(Category III)*

0188 Mark 11:11-17, fourth, 1 f., 2 cols., 21 ll., 13 × 11 cm. Berlin: Staatliche Museen, P. 13416. *(Many singular readings; category III)*

0189 Cf. p. 104. *(At least normal text: category I because of date)* Plate 27.

0190 Cf. **070**.

0191 Cf. **070**.

0192 = *l* 1604. (delete from list).

0193 Cf. **070**.

0194 Cf. **070**.

0195 = **0100**.

0196 Matt. 5:1-11; Luke 24:26-33, ninth, 2 ff., 1 col., 19 ll., 18.5 × 14 cm. Damascus: National Museum. Palimpsest; lower text Syriac. (Not accessible)

0197 Matt. 20:22-23,25-27; 22:30-32,34-37, ninth, 2 ff., 1 col., 12 ll., *ca.* 27 × 24.5 cm. Beuron: Benedictine Abbey. Palimpsest: upper text typicon. *(Byzantine text, category V)*

0198 Col. 3:15-16,20-21, sixth. 1 col., (7 ll.), (11 × 7.5 cm.). London: British Library, Pap. 459. *(Category III)*

0199 1 Cor. 11:17-19,22-24, sixth/seventh, 1 col., (13 ll.), (8.5 × 5 cm.). London: British Library, Pap. 2077 B. *(Category III)*

0200 Matt. 11:20-21, seventh. (2 cols.), (17 ll.), (16.5 × 7 cm.). London: British Library, Pap. 2077 C. Greek-Coptic diglot. *(Category III)*

0201 1 Cor. 12:2-3,6-13; 14:20-29, fifth, 2 ff., 2 cols., *ca.* 19 ll., *ca.* 15 × 15 cm. London: British Library, Pap. 2240. *(Category II)*

0202 Cf. **070**.

0203 Cf. **0129**; London: British Library, Or. 3579B (59), Greek-Coptic diglot lectionary belonging with **0129** to *ℓ 1575*, and therefore to be removed from this list.

0204 Matt. 24:39-42,44-48, seventh, 2 cols., *ca.* 26 ll., *ca.* 25 × 21 cm. London: British Library, Gr. 4923 (2). Greek-Coptic diglot. *(Category II)*

0205 Tit. 2:15–3:7, eighth, 2 ff., 2 cols., *ca.* 35 ll. Cambridge: University Library, Or. 1699. Greek-Coptic diglot. *(Category II)*

0206 1 Pet. 5:5-13, fourth, 1 f., 1 col., 8 ll., 14 × 10 cm. Dayton, Ohio: United Theological Seminary (P. Oxy. 1353). *(Category III)*

0207 Rev. 9:2-15, fourth, 1 f., 2 cols., 29 ll., 19 × 15 cm. Florence: Biblioteca Laurenziana, PSI 1166. *(Category III)*

0208 Col. 1:29–2:10,13-14; 1 Thess. 2:4-7,12-17, sixth, 2 ff., 2 cols., 31 ll., (23 × 16 cm.). Munich: Bayerische Staatsbibliothek, 29022 e. Palimpsest: upper text Prosper of Aquitaine, *Chronicon. (Category III)*

0209 Rom. 14:9-23; 16:25-27; 15:1-2; 2 Cor. 1:1-15; 4:4-13; 6:11–7:2; 9:2–10:17; 2 Pet. 1:1–2:3, seventh, 8 ff., 2 cols., 32 ll., (27 × 19 cm.). Ann Arbor: University of Michigan, Ms. 8, ff. 96, 106-112. Palimpsest: upper text Greek liturgica. *(Category III, influenced strongly by V)*

0210 John 5:44; 6:1-2,41-42, seventh, 2 ff., 1 col., 8+ ll., *ca.* 10 × 7 cm. Berlin: Staatliche Museen, P. 3607, 3623. *(Category III)*

0211 e, seventh, 258 ff., 2 cols., 24+ ll., 27 × 19.5 cm. Tiflis: Institute for Manuscripts, Gr. 27. (189^1 101$^{1/2}$ 10^2 23^s; *Byzantine text, category V)*

0212 Cf. p. 104. *(Unclassifiable because of Diatessaric text, category III)* Plate 13.

0213 Mark 3:2-3,5, fifth/sixth, 2 cols., *ca.* 23 ll., *ca.* 33 = 23 cm. Vienna: Österreichische Nationalbibliothek, Pap. G. 1384. *(Category III)*

0214 Mark 8:33-37, fourth/fifth, 2 cols., *ca.* 24 ll., *ca.* 20 × 18 cm. Vienna: Österreichische Nationalbibliothek, Pap. G. 29300. *(Category III)*

0215 Cf. **059**.

0216 John 8:51-53; 9:5-8, fifth, 1f., 2 cols., *ca.* 27 ll., *ca.* 19 × 12 cm. Vienna: Österreichische Nationalbibliothek, Pap. G. 3081. *(Category III)*

0217 John 11:57–12:7, fifth, 1 col., 19 ll., 13 × 9 cm. Vienna: Österreichische Nationalbibliothek, Pap. G. 39212. *(Category III)*

0218 John 12:2-6,9-11,14-16, fifth, 2 cols., *ca.* 27 ll., *ca.* 18 × 16 cm. Vienna: Österreichische Nationalbibliothek, Pap. G. 19892 B. *(Category III)*

0219 Rom. 2:21-23; 3:8-9,23-25,27-30, fourth/fifth, 2 ff., 2 cols., *ca.* 26 ll., *ca.* 20 × 14 cm. Vienna: Österreichische Nationalbibliothek, Pap. G. 36113, 26083. *(Category III)*

0220 Cf. p. 105. *(Strict text, category I)* Plate 14.

0221 Rom. 5:16-17,19,21–6:3, fourth, 2 cols., *ca.* 20 ll., *ca.* 18 × 16 cm. Vienna: Österreichische Nationalbibliothek, Pap. G. 19890. *(Category III)*

0222 1 Cor. 9:5-7,10,12-13, sixth, 2 cols., 20 ll., 15 × 12 cm. Vienna: Österreichische Nationalbibliothek, Pap. G. 29299. *(Category III)*

0223 2 Cor. 1:17–2:2, sixth, 1 f., 2 cols., 17 ll., *ca.* 12 × 8.5 cm. Vienna: Österreichische Nationalbibliothek, Pap. G. 3073. *(Category II)*

0224 Cf. **0186**.

0225 2 Cor. 5:1-2,8-9,14-16,19–6:1,3-5; 8:16-24, sixth, 3 ff., 1 col., 21-27 ll., *ca.* 25 × 18 cm. Vienna: Österreichische Nationalbibliothek, Pap. G. 19802. Palimpsest: the leaves were added (without erasing text) to a scroll for a Pehlevi text. *(Category II)*.

0226 1 Thess. 4:16–5:5, fifth, 2 cols., *ca.* 25 ll., *ca.* 17 × 12 cm. Vienna: Österreichische Nationalbibliothek, Pap. G. 31489. *(Category III)*

0227 Heb. 11:18-19,29, fifth, 2 cols., *ca.* 23 ll., *ca.* 21 × 17 cm. Vienna: Österreichische Nationalbibliothek, Pap. G. 26055. *(Category III)*

0228 Heb. 12:19-21,23-25, fourth, 1 col., *ca.* 17 ll., *ca.* 15 × 12 cm. Vienna: Österreichische Nationalbibliothek, Pap. G. 19888. *(Category III)*

0229 Rev. 18:16-17; 19:4-6, eighth, 2 ff., 1 col., (16 ll.), (11 × 23 cm.). Formerly

Florence: Biblioteca Laurenziana, PSI 1296b. Palimpsest: lower text Coptic. *(Category III)*
0230 Eph. 6:11-12, fourth, 2 cols., (4 ll.), *ca.* 34 × 27 cm. Formerly Florence: Biblioteca Laurenziana, PSI 1306. Greek-Latin diglot. *(Text too brief to classify)*
0231 Matt. 26:75–27:1,3-4, fourth, 2 cols., 15 ll., *ca.* 15 × 11.5 cm. Oxford: Bodleian Library, P. Ant. 11. *(Category III)*
0232 John 1-9, fifth/sixth, 1 f., 1 col., 20 ll., 10 × 9 cm. Oxford: Bodleian Library, P. Ant. 12. *(Category II)*
0233 e†, eighth, 93 ff., 2 cols., 23-27 ll., 27 × 21 cm. Münster/Westf. Ms. 1. Palimpsest: upper text *ℓ* 1684. (47^1 $23^{1/2}$ 3^2 5^s; *category III*)
0234 Matt. 28:11-15; John 1:4-8, 20-24 (John follows Matthew immediately), eighth, 2 ff., 2 cols., *ca.* 30 ll., 24 × 21 cm. Formerly Damascus: Kubbet el Chazne. *(Category II)*
0235 Cf. 083.
0236 Acts 3:12-13,15-16, fifth, 2 cols., *ca.* 26 ll., *ca.* 22 × 18 cm. Moscow: Pushkin Museum, Golenischev Copt. 55. Greek-Coptic diglot. *(Category III)*
0237 Matt. 15:12-15,17-19, sixth, 2 cols., *ca.* 23 ll., *ca.* 23 × 18 cm. Vienna: Österreichische Nationalbibliothek, Pap. K. 8023 bis. Greek-Coptic diglot. *(Category III)*
0238 John 7:10-12, eighth, 1 col., (10 ll.), (9.5 × 7 cm.). Vienna: Österreichische Nationalbibliothek, Pap. K. 8668. Greek-Coptic diglot. *(Category III)*
0239 Luke 2:27-30,34, seventh, 2 cols., *ca.* 25 ll., *ca.* 26 × 21 cm. London: British Library, Or. 4717 (16). Greek-Coptic diglot. *(Category III)*
0240 Tit. 1:4-8, fifth, 1 f., 2(?) cols., *ca.* 23 ll., *ca.* 26 × 22 cm. Tiflis: Institute for Manuscripts, 2123, ff. 191, 198. Palimpsest: upper text Georgian menologion. *(Category II)*
0241 1 Tim. 3:16–4:3,8-11, sixth, 1(?) col., (12 ll.). Cologny: Bodmer Library. *(Category III)*
0242 Matt. 8:25–9:2; 13:32-38,40-46, fourth, 2 ff., 2 cols., *ca.* 25 ll., *ca.* 23 × 20 cm. Cairo: Egyptian Museum, no. 71942. *(Category III)*
0243 1 Cor. 13:4–2 Cor. 13:13, tenth, 7 ff., 2 cols., 48 ll., 32.5 × 24 cm. Venice: Biblioteca San Marco, 983 (II, 181). (7^1 $8^{1/2}$ 21^2 5^s; *category II?*)
0244 Acts 11:29–12:5, fifth, 1 f., 1 col., 18+ ll., 18 × 14 cm. Louvain: Bibliothèque de l'Université, P. A. M. Khirbet Mird 8. *(Category II)*
0245 I John 3:23–4:1,3-6, sixth, 1 col., *ca.* 23 ll., *ca.* 27 × 20 cm. Birmingham: Selly Oak College, Mingana Georg. 7. Palimpsest: upper text Georgian. *(Category II)*
0246 Jas. 1:12-14,19-21, sixth, 1 col., *ca.* 27 ll., *ca.* 29 × 20 cm. Cambridge: Westminster College. Palimpsest: no upper text. *(Category V)*
0247 1 Pet. 5:13-14; 2 Pet. 1:5-8,14-16; 2:1, fifth/sixth, 2 cols., *ca.* 36 ll., *ca.* 29 × 23 cm. Manchester: John Rylands Library, P. Copt. 20. Palimpsest: upper text Coptic prayer. *(Category II)*
0248 Matthew†, ninth, *ca.* 70 ff., 2 cols., 24+ ll., 21 × 15.5 cm. Oxford: Bodleian Library, Auct. T 4.21, ff. 47-57, 91-145, 328-331. Palimpsest: twice rewritten. *(Byzantine text, category V)*
0249 Matt. 25:1-9, tenth, 2 ff., 2(?) cols., 15+ ll., 21 × 15 cm. Oxford: Bodleian Library, Auct. T 4.21, ff. 326, 327. Palimpsest: upper text Psalm commentary. *(Category III, influenced by V)*
0250 Codex Climaci rescriptus, eP, eighth, 33 ff., 2 cols., 31+ ll., 23 × 15.5 cm. Cambridge: Westminster College. Palimpsest: upper text Johannes Climacus (Syriac). *(Category III)*
0251 3 John 12-15; Jude 3-5, sixth, 1 col., *ca.* 22 ll., *ca.* 24 × 20 cm. Paris: Louvre, S.N. 121. *(Category III)*
0252 Heb. 6:2-4,6-7, fifth, 2(?) cols., *ca.* 25 ll., *ca.* 20 × 17 cm. Barcelona: Fundació Sant Lluc Evangelista, P. Barc. 6. *(Category III)*
0253 Luke 10:19-22, sixth, 1 f., 1 col., 14 ll., *ca.* 31 × 25 cm. Formerly Damascus: Kubbet el Chazne. *(Byzantine text, category V)*

0254 Gal. 5:13-17, fifth, 2 ff., 1 col., 20 ll., *ca.* 18 × 12 cm. Formerly Damascus: Kubbet el Chazne. Palimpsest: upper text Arabic. *(Category I)*

0255 Matt. 26:2-9; 27:9-16, ninth, 2 ff., 1 col., *ca.* 24 ll., *ca.* 15 × 10 cm. Formerly Damascus: Kubbet el Chazne. *(Byzantine text, category V)*

0256 John 6:32-33,35-37, eighth, 1 col., (4, 6 ll.), (4 × 4 cm.). Vienna: Österreichische Nationalbibliothek, Pap. G. 26084. With commentary. *(Category III)*

0257 Matt. 5–26†, Mark 6–16†, ninth, 47 ff., 2 cols., 23 ll., 29.5 × 22 cm. Zavorda: Nikanoros, 2, ff. 1-16, 289-319. Palimpsest: upper text *ℓ 2094*. *(Category V)*

0258 John 10:25-26, IV, 1(?) col., 5 ll., (4.7 x 4 cm.). Location unknown. (Not accessible)

0259 1 Tim. 1:4-7, seventh, 2 ff. (f. 2 blank), 1 col., *ca.* 11 11., *ca.* 12 × 10 cm. Berlin: Staatliche Museen, P. 3605. *(Category III)*

0260 John 1:30-32, sixth, 2(?) cols., 16 ll., *ca.* 21 × 17 cm. Berlin: Staatliche Museen, P. 5542. Greek-Fayyumic diglot. *(Category III)*

0261 Gal. 1:9-12,19-22; 4:25-31, fifth, 2 ff., 2 cols., *ca.* 25 ll., *ca.* 20 × 15 cm. Berlin: Staatliche Museen, P. 6791, 6792, 14043. *(Category III)*

0262 1 Tim. 1:15-16, seventh, 1 f., 2(?) cols., *ca.* 6 ll., *ca.* 9.5 × 13(?) cm. Berlin: Staatliche Museen, P. 13977. *(Category III)*

0263 Mark 5:26-27,31, sixth, 1 col., *ca.* 17 ll., *ca.* 28 × 22 cm. Berlin: Staatliche Museen, P. 14045. *(Text too brief to classify)*

0264 John 8:19-20,23-24, fifth, 1 col., *ca.* 18 ll., *ca.* 15 × 12 cm. Berlin: Staatliche Museen, P. 14049. *(Text too brief to classify)*

0265 Luke 7:20-21,34-35, sixth, 2(?) cols., *ca.* 25 ll., *ca.* 27 × 22 cm. Berlin: Staatliche Museen, P. 16994. *(Category V?)*

0266 Luke 20:19-25,30-39, sixth, 1 f., 1 col., *ca.* 33 ll., *ca.* 28 × 22 cm. Berlin: Staatliche Museen, P. 17034. *(Category III)*

0267 Luke 8:25-27, fifth, (1 col.), (10 ll.), 7.v × 9.5 cm.). Barcelona: Fundació Sant Lluc Evangelista, P. Barc. 16. *(Text too brief to classify)*

0268 John 1:30-33, seventh, 1 f., 1 col., *ca.* 10 ll., *ca.* 11 × 8 cm. Berlin: Staatliche Museen, P. 6790. *(Text too brief to classify)*

0269 Mark 6:14-20, ninth, 1 f., 2(?) cols., 25 ll., *ca.* 33 × 25 cm. London: British Library, Add. 31919, f. 23. Palimpsest. *(Category III, influenced by V)*

0270 I Cor. 15:10-15,19-25, fourth/fifth, 1 col., *ca.* 26 ll., *ca.* 15.5 × 10.5 cm. Amsterdam: Universiteits Bibliothek, GX 200. *(Category II)*

0271 Matt. 12:27-39, ninth, 1 f., 2 cols., 26 ll., 33 × 26 cm. London: British Library, Add. 31919, f. 22. Palimpsest: upper text Greek menaeon (formerly included in **0133**). *(Category II)*

0272 Luke 16–17†, 19†, ninth, 3 ff., 2 cols., 28 ll., 33 × 26 cm. London: British Library, Add. 31919, ff. 21, 98, 101 (formerly included in **0133**). *(Category V)*

0273 John 2:17–3:5; 4:23-37; 5:35–6:2, ninth, 3 ff., 2 cols., 25 ll., 33 × 26 cm. London: British Library, Add. 31919, ff. 29, 99, 100 (formerly included in **0133**). *(Category V?)*

0274 Mark 6–10†, fifth, 4 ff., 2 cols., 30 ll., 28 × 33 cm. At present London: Egyptian Exploration Society. (0[1] 6[1/2] 19[2] 2[s]; *category II*)

0275 Matt. 5:25-26, 29-30, seventh, 2 cols., 12+ ll., *ca.* 28 × 25 cm. Dublin: Trinity College, TCD PAP F 138. Greek-Coptic diglot.

0276 Mark 14:65-67, 68-71; 14:72–15:2, 4-7, eighth, 2 cols., 20+ ll., *ca.* 16 × 13.5 cm. Paris: Louvre, 10039b. Greek-Coptic diglot.

0277 Matt. 14:22, 28-29, seventh/eighth, 1 col., 7 ll., 7.7 = 6.7 cm. Florence: Istituto Papirologico "G. Vitelli," PSI Inv. CNR 32 C.

0278-0296 Newly discovered manuscripts at St. Catherine's Monastery, Sinai

0297 Matt. 1:1-14; 5:3-19, ninth, 2 ff., 2 cols., 25 ll., 33 × 25.8 cm. London: British Library, Add. 31919, fol. 105, 108. Palimpsest.

0298 Matt. 26:24-29 (Greek); 26:17-21 (Coptic), eighth/ninth, 1 col., 19 ll., 17 × 8.8

cm. Barcelona: Fundació Sant Lluc Evangelista, P. Barc. 4. Palimpsest, Greek-Coptic diglot.
0299 John 20:1-7 (Greek); 21:23-25 (Coptic), tenth/eleventh (?), 2 cols., 36-41 ll., 30.2 ×
23.4 cm. Paris: Bibliothèque Nationale, Copt. 129,10, fol. 199. Greek-Coptic diglot.

As indicated on p. 102, chart 6 (endpaper pocket insert) exhibits the
textual contents of the uncials by book and chapter. Without such a tool it would
be impossible to make as full use of the uncials.

9. *THE MINUSCULES*

New Testament minuscule manuscripts begin to appear in the ninth century.[31]
The earliest dated minuscule manuscript is the Gospels minuscule 461 from the
year 835 (Leningrad Public Library, Gr. 219; cf. plate 4). Minuscules have always played a role in textual studies — in the early editions it was even an
exclusive role (Desiderius Erasmus evidently avoided using E 07 although it was
available to him in Basel; Theodore Beza's editions show no use of his own
manuscripts D[ea] 05 and D[p] 06).[32] There is admittedly a whole group of minuscules that have long been recognized for the importance of their texts (e.g.,
33 has long been called "Queen of the minuscules"; cf. plate 36). But most of
the minuscules have not yet been examined for their textual value (at least half
of them are certainly underrated) simply because of the examination of 2,812
manuscripts is beyond the capacity of any one scholar, or even a team of scholars,
unless equipped with a method to produce reliable results without having to
compare them in every sentence. After Kurt Aland devised a program of test
passages for gauging the textual character of a manuscript, it took years of
collating before the research on the Catholic letters could be published (cf.
p. 317). The Pauline letters, Acts, and the Synoptic Gospels have now been
studied, demonstrating that more than 80 percent of the manuscripts contain
exclusively the Majority text (i.e., essentially the Byzantine, Imperial, or Koine
text, however it may be called in its various shadings and gradings). But
approximately 10 percent of them offer a valuable early text which can compete
with even the best of the uncials. The "Queen" now has many rivals, a number
of which are of superior value.

The most important minuscules are listed in the following pages. This
represents our present knowledge. The descriptions are as concise as possible:
the manuscript number is followed by a statement of content (e = Gospels;
a = Apostolos, i.e., Acts and the Catholic letters; p = the Pauline letters, including Hebrews; r = Revelation; K = with commentary; P = incomplete
["partly"]; † = defective, with lacunae), date, and material (pch = parchment,
pa = paper), then the present location and library of the manuscript, and finally
in parentheses a classification of its readings in the same way as for the
uncials,[33] and its characterization by category. The differences noted often
reveal how complex the situation is, and how much our traditional views are

---

31. Cf. p. 81, table 4.
32. Cf. p. 4.
33. Cf. pp. 106f.

in need of revision. The nineteenth century was impressed by the uncials, and the first three quarters of the twentieth century by the papyri. In the last quarter of this century a whole group of minuscules is advancing claims for equal recognition, and with equal justification. This process has already begun in Nestle-Aland[26] and *GNT*[3] — and this is only a beginning.

Descriptive List of Minuscules

1 eap, twelfth century, pch. Basel: Universitätsbibliothek, A. N. IV. 2. Comprises with 118, 131, 209, 1582, etc. the well-known Family 1 (*f*[1]). (Evv: 119[1] 80[1/2] 60[2] 69[s]; Acts: 74[1] 29[1/2] 2[2] 0[s]; Cath: 83[1] 11[1/2] 2[2] 0[s]; Paul: 194[1] 47[1/2] 2[2] 4[s]; *category III in Gospels, V elsewhere*) Plate 34.

5 eap, fourteenth, pch. Paris: Bibliothèque Nationale, Gr. 106, (Evv: 201[1] 103[1/2] 7[2] 12[s]; Acts: 56[1] 26[1/2] 14[2] 9[s]; Cath: 47[1] 7[1/2] 31[2] 13[s]; Paul: 165[1] 45[1/2] 24[2] 12[s]; *category III in Acts, Catholic letters and Paul, V in Gospels?*)

6 eap†, thirteenth, pch. Paris: Bibliothèque Nationale, Gr. 112. (Evv: 209[1] 99[1/2] 4[2] 11[s]; Acts: 62[1] 26[1/2] 6[2] 11[s]; Cath: 57[1] 7[1/2] 25[2] 9[s]; Paul: 110[1] 44[1/2] 60[2] 25[s]; *category III in Catholic letters and Paul, V in Gospels and Acts*)

13 e†, thirteenth, pch. Paris: Bibliothèque Nationale, Gr. 50. Comprises with 69, 124, 174, 230, 346, 543, 788, 826, 828, 983, 1689, 1709 the Ferrar Group, Family 13 (*f*[13]). (150[1] 71[1/2] 31[2] 54[s]; *category III*) Plate 35.

28 e†, eleventh, pch. Paris: Bibliothèque Nationale, Gr. 379. (154[1] 70[1/2] 31[2] 58[s]; *category III in Mark only; V elsewhere due to ratio of type 1 to type 2 readings*)

33 eap†, ninth, pch. Paris: Bibliothèque Nationale, Gr. 14 (Evv: 93[1] 72[1/2] 57[2] 39[s]; Acts: 21[1] 20[1/2] 34[2] 12[s]; Cath: 20[1] 4[1/2] 44[2] 15[s]; Paul: 50[1] 56[1/2] 113[2] 54[s]; *category II in Gospels, I elsewhere*) Plate 36.

36 aK, twelfth, pch. Oxford: New College, 58. (Acts: 34[1] 21[1/2] 32[2] 19[s]; Cath: 61[1] 8[1/2] 16[2] 13[s]; *category II in Acts, III in Catholic letters*) Plate 37.

61 eapr, sixteenth, pa. Dublin: Trinity College, A 4,21. (Evv: 192[1] 98[1/2] 10[2] 29[s]; Acts: 62[1] 26[1/2] 8[2] 6[s]; Cath: 60[1] 7[1/2] 17[2] 13[s]; Paul: 165[1] 41[1/2] 35[2] 27[s]; *category III, but V in Gospels and Acts*)

69 eapr†, fifteenth, pch/pa. Leicester: Town Museum, Cod. 6D 32/1. (Evv: 134[1] 63[1/2] 22[2] 50[s]; Acts: 63[1] 19[1/2] 5[2] 8[s]; Cath: 64[1] 11[1/2] 9[2] 5[s]; Paul: 154[1] 42[1/2] 35[2] 17[s]; *category III in Paul, but V elsewhere*)

81 ap†, 1044, pch. London: British Library, Add. 20003 (57 ff.); Alexandria: Greek Patriarchate 59 (255 ff.). (Acts: 7[1] 20[1/2] 40[2] 5[s]; Cath: 31[1] 6[1/2] 44[2] 17[s]; Paul: 44[1] 32[1/2] 131[2] 39[s]; *at least category II*)

88 apr, twelfth, pch. Naples: Bibliotheca Nazionale, II, A, 7. (Acts: 51[1] 25[1/2] 15[2] 14[s]; Cath: 64[1] 7[1/2] 17[2] 10[s]; Paul: 157[1] 43[1/2] 28[2] 23[s]; *category III*)

94 aprK, twelfth (r), thirteenth (ap), pch. Paris: Bibliothèque Nationale, Coislin Gr. 202 bis. (Acts: 45[1] 21[1/2] 23[2] 16[s]; Cath: 67[1] 7[1/2] 12[2] 12[s]; Paul: 172[1] 47[1/2] 12[2] 14[s]; *category III, but clearly lower for Paul and Revelation*)

103 apK, eleventh, pch. Moscow: Historical Museum V. 96, S. 347. (Acts: 65[1] 25[1/2] 6[2] 9[s]; Cath: 82[1] 7[1/2] 2[2] 7[s]; Paul: 172[1] 43[1/2] 11[2] 19[s]; *category V*)

104 apr, 1087, pch. London: British Library, Harley 5537. (Acts: 61[1] 26[1/2] 9[2] 8[s]; Cath: 61[1] 5[1/2] 15[2] 13[s]; Paul: 124[1] 41[1/2] 56[2] 31[s]; *category III, Acts and Revelation V*)

157 e, twelfth, pch. Rome: Vatican Library, Urbin. Gr. 2. With the "Jerusalem colophon" found also in 20, 164, 215, 262, 300, 376, 428, 565, 686, 718, 1071, etc., and in Λ 039. 180[1] 94[1/2] 21[2] 23[s]; *category III*)

180 eapr, twelfth (e), 1273 (apr), pch. Rome: Vatican Library, Borg. Gr. 18. (Evv: 204[1] 102[1/2] 4[2] 12[s]; Acts: 44[1] 21[1/2] 24[2] 19[s]; Cath: 82[1] 9[1/2] 2[2] 9[s]; Paul: 192[1] 47[1/2] 2[2] 5[s]; *category III in Acts, V elsewhere*)

181 apr†, eleventh (ap), fifteenth (r), pch. Rome: Vatican Library, Reg. Gr. 179. (Acts:

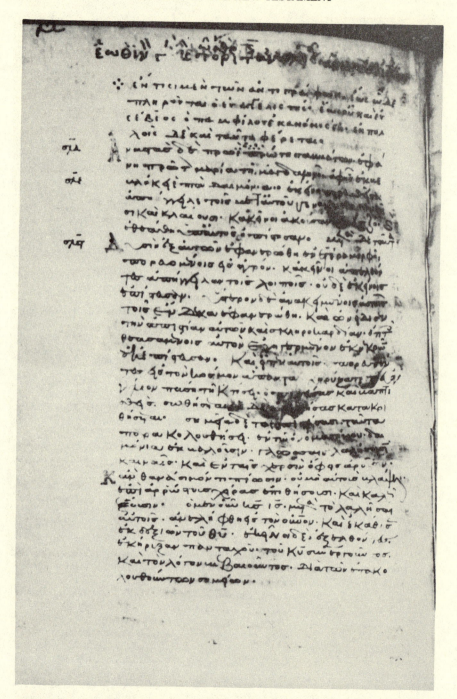

Plates 34/35. The minuscules 1 (left, twelfth century; cf. p. 129) and 13 (right, thirteenth century; cf. p. 129) are both leading members of well-known textual families: f^1 (the Lake group), and f^{13} (the Ferrar group): the ending of the gospel of Mark is shown for each.

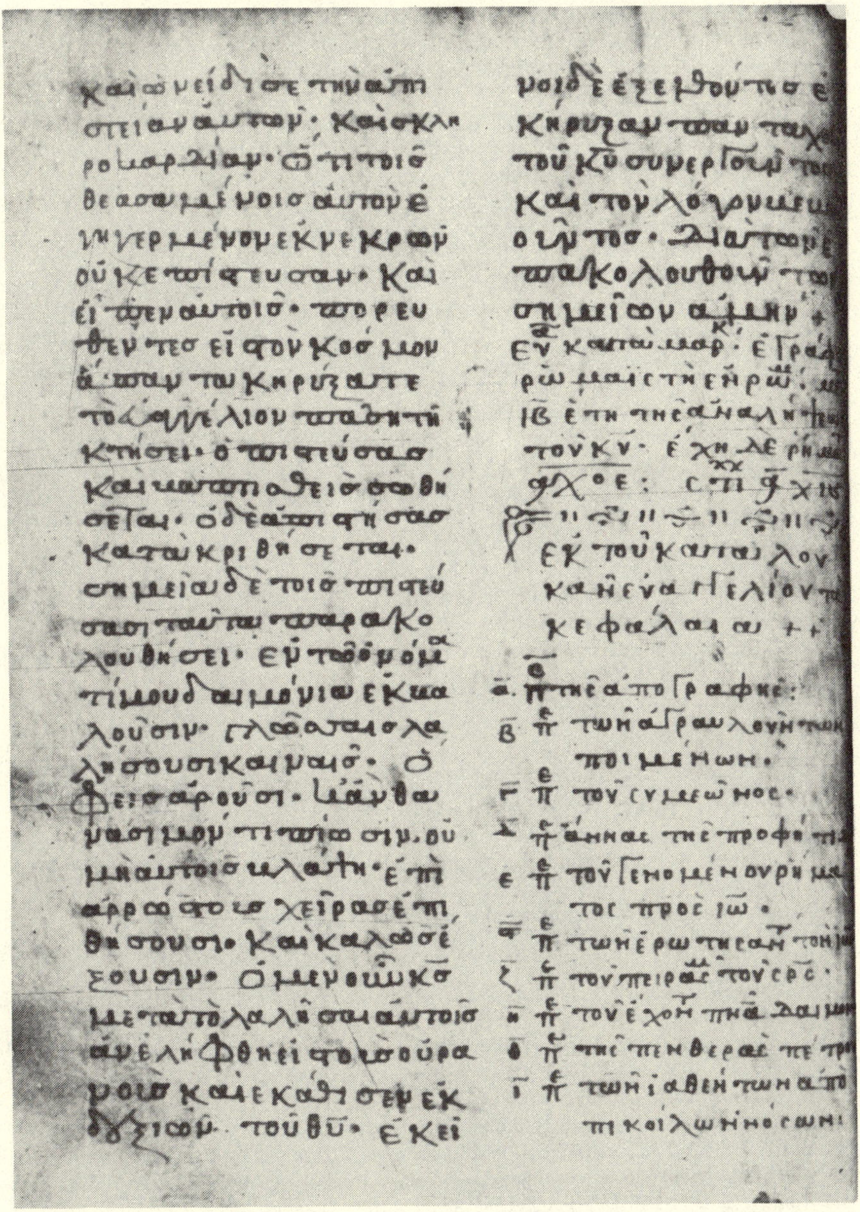

34[1] 22[1/2] 33[2] 17[s]; Cath: 70[1] 14[1/2] 13[2] 4[s]; Paul: 160[1] 46[1/2] 31[2] 13[s]; *category III, Revelation V*)
189 eap†, fourteenth (e), twelfth (ap), pch. Florence: Biblioteca Laurenziana, VI, 27. (Evv: 202[1] 101[1/2] 2[2] 9[s]; Acts: 70[1] 24[1/2] 1[2] 10[s]; Cath: 84[1] 8[1/2] 3[2] 3[s]; Paul: 192[1] 48[1/2] 2[2] 4[s]; *category V*)
205 (OT and) eapr, fifteenth, pch. Venice: Biblioteca San Marco, 420 (Fondo ant. 5; NT = ff. 362-441). (Evv: 134[1] 79[1/2] 47[2] 62[s]; Acts: 72[1] 26[1/2] 2[2] 5[s]; Cath: 83[1] 10[1/2] 2[2] 3[s]; Paul: 191[1] 47[1/2] 2[2] 7[s]; *category III in Gospels and Revelation, V elsewhere*)
206 ap†, thirteenth, pa. London: Lambeth, 1182. (Acts: 61[1] 25[1/2] 7[2] 11[s]; Cath: 60[1] 7[1/2] 20[2] 12[s]; Paul: 183[1] 46[1/2] 9[2] 9[s]; *category III in Catholic letters, V elsewhere*)
209 eapr, fourteenth (eap), fifteenth (r), pch. Venice: Biblioteca San Marco, 394 (Fondo ant. 10). (Evv: 136[1] 80[1/2] 46[2] 60[s]; Acts: 72[1] 27[1/2] 3[2] 8[s]; Cath: 83[1] 10[1/2] 3[2] 5[s]; Paul: 193[1] 47[1/2] 5[2] 7[s]; *category III in Gospels and Revelation, V elsewhere*)
218 (OT and) eapr†, thirteenth, pch. Vienna: Österreichische Nationalbibliothek, Theol. Gr. 23 (NT = fol. 486-623). (Evv: 207[1] 101[1/2] 5[2] 7[s]; Acts: 65[1] 29[1/2] 10[2] 1[s]; Cath: 62[1] 10[1/2] 18[2] 7[s]; Paul: 144[1] 43[1/2] 35[2] 16[s]; *category III in Catholic and Pauline letters, V elsewhere, a short form of the Andreas commentary in Revelation*)
254 aprK, fourteenth, pa. Athens: National Library, 490. (Acts: 73[1] 28[1/2] 1[2] 2[s]; Cath: 64[1] 5[1/2] 18[2] 12[s]; Paul: 182[1] 44[1/2] 9[2] 17[s]; *category III in Catholic letters, V elsewhere*)
256 apr†, eleventh/twelfth, pch. Paris: Bibliothèque Nationale, Armen. 9. Greek-Armenian diglot. (Acts: 54[1] 24[1/2] 1[2] 2[s]; Cath: 84[1] 9[1/2] 1[2] 5[s]; Paul: 101[1] 38[1/2] 76[2] 34[s]; *category II in Pauline letters, V elsewhere*)
263 eap, thirteenth, pch. Paris: Bibliothèque Nationale, Gr. 61. (Evv: 213[1] 100[1/2] 1[2] 9[s]; Acts: 73[1] 28[1/2] 2[2] 2[s]; Cath: 86[1] 8[1/2] 1[2] 4[s]; Paul: 114[1] 39[1/2] 58[2] 36[s]; *category III in Pauline letters, V elsewhere*)
307 aK, tenth, pch. Paris: Bibliothèque Nationale, Coislin Gr. 25. (Acts: 35[1] 20[1/2] 32[2] 19[s]; Cath: 62[1] 8[1/2] 17[2] 15[s]; *category III*)
322 ap, fifteen, pa London: British Library, Harley 5620. (Acts: 51[1] 23[1/2] 20[2] 11[s]; Cath: 27[1] 7[1/2] 49[2] 15[s]; Paul: 184[1] 47[1/2] 9[2] 6[s]; *category II in Catholic letters, III elsewhere*) Plate 38.
323 ap†, eleventh, pch. Geneva: Bibliothèque Publique et Universitaire, Gr. 20. (Acts: 51[1] 23[1/2] 20[2] 11[s]; Cath: 27[1] 7[1/2] 49[2] 15[s]; Paul: 185[1] 47[1/2] 8[2] 6[s]; *category same as for 322, apparently a sister manuscript*) Plate 38.
326 ap†, twelfth, pch. Oxford: Lincoln College, Gr. 82. (Acts: 63[1] 27[1/2] 8[2] 7[s]; Cath: 61[1] 10[1/2] 18[2] 6[s]; Paul: 155[1] 39[1/2] 30[2] 22[s]; *category III*)
330 eap†, twelfth, pch. Leningrad: Public Library, Gr. 101. (Evv: 206[1] 101[1/2] 6[2] 10[s]; Acts: 74[1] 29[1/2] 2[2] 0[s]; Cath: 81[1] 9[1/2] 2[2] 6[s]; Paul: 152[1] 42[1/2] 32[2] 23[s]; *category III in Pauline letters, V elsewhere*)
346 3†, twelfth, pch. Milan: Biblioteca Ambrosiana, S. 23 sup. (172[1] 82[1/2] 24[2] 53[s]; *category III*)
365 eap, thirteenth, pch. Florence: Biblioteca Laurenziana, VI, 36. (Evv: 208[1] 101[1/2] 4[2] 11[s]; Acts: 48[1] 21[1/2] 1[2] 4[s]; Cath: 60[1] 6[1/2] 3[2] 6[s]; Paul: 108[1] 38[1/2] 63[2] 31[s]; *category III in Pauline letters, V elsewhere*)
378 ap, twelfth, pch. Oxford: Bodleian Library, E. D. Clarke 4. (Acts: 71[1] 25[1/2] 4[2] 1[s]; Cath: 61[1] 7[1/2] 17[2] 17[s]; Paul: 194[1] 48[1/2] 2[2] 3[s]; *category III in Catholic letters, V elsewhere*)
398 ap†, eleventh, pch. Cambridge: University Library, Kk. VI, 4. (Acts: 75[1] 28[1/2] 0[2] 1[s]; Cath: 62[1] 7[1/2] 16[2] 13[s]; Paul: 158[1] 48[1/2] 3[2] 0[s]; *category III in Catholic letters, V elsewhere*)
424 apr, eleventh, pch. Vienna: Österreichische Nationalbibliothek, Theol. Gr. 302. Plate 39.
424 * (Acts: 72[1] 29[1/2] 3[2] 0[s]; Cath: 86[1] 10[1/2] 0[2] 1[s]; Paul: 193[1] 46[1/2] 5[2] 3[s])
424 [c] (Acts: 71[1] 26[1/2] 4[2] 4[s]; Cath: 62[1] 8[1/2] 21[2] 9[s]; Paul: 117[1] 41[1/2] 65[2] 24[s]; *category III, strictly a category V manuscript corrected against an early text, cf. especially the increase of type 2 readings in the Catholic and Pauline letters*)
429 apr, fourteenth (ap), fifteenth (r), pa. Wolfenbüttel: Herzog August Bibliothek, 16.7

Aug. 4^0. (Acts: 51^1 $23^{1/2}$ 13^2 18^s; Cath: 60^1 $6^{1/2}$ 22^2 14^s; Paul: 183^1 $45^{1/2}$ 9^2 10^s; *category III, but V in Pauline letters and Revelation)*

431 eap, eleventh, pch. Strasbourg: Seminary, 1. (Evv: 211^1 $99^{1/2}$ 2^2 9^s; Acts: 42^1 $24^{1/2}$ 25^2 13^s; Cath: 70^1 $8^{1/2}$ 11^2 9^s; Paul: 193^1 $48^{1/2}$ 3^2 4^s; *category III in Acts and Catholic letters, V elsewhere)*

436 ap, eleventh, pch. Rome: Vatican Library, Gr. 367. (Acts: 60^1 $24^{1/2}$ 14^2 8^s; Cath: 42^1 $7^{1/2}$ 41^2 9^s; Paul: 131^1 $37^{1/2}$ 50^2 29^s; *category III)*

441 apPK, thirteenth, pch. Uppsala: Universitetsbiblioteket, Gr. 1, pp. 3-182. (Acts: 34^1 $23^{1/2}$ 14^2 8^s; Paul: 47^1 $23^{1/2}$ 20^2 11^s; *category III)*

442 apPK, thirteenth, pch. Uppsala: Universitetsbiblioteket, Gr. 1, pp. 183-440. (Cath: 42^1 $7^{1/2}$ 35^2 15^s; Paul: 68^1 $22^{1/2}$ 45^2 21^s; *category II)*

451 ap, eleventh, pch. Rome: Vatican Library, Urbin. Gr. 3. (Acts: 75^1 $27^{1/2}$ 2^2 1^s; Cath: 81^1 $9^{1/2}$ 2^2 6^s; Paul: 142^1 $40^{1/2}$ 39^2 27^s; *category III in Pauline letters, elsewhere V)*

453 aK, fourteenth, pch. Rome: Vatican Library, Barb. Gr. 582. (Acts: 36^1 $20^{1/2}$ 34^2 15^s; Cath: 61^1 $7^{1/2}$ 15^2 15^s; *category III)*

459 apr. 1092, pch. Florence: Biblioteca Laurenziana, IV, 32. (Acts: 63^1 $27^{1/2}$ 8^2 6^s; Cath: 71^1 $7^{1/2}$ 9^2 11^s; Paul: 126^1 $40^{1/2}$ 53^2 27^s; *category III in Pauline letters, V elsewhere)*

461 e, 835, pch. Leningrad: Public Library, Gr. 219. 213^1 $101^{1/2}$ 3^2 5^s; *category V, included only because it is the oldest dated minuscule)* Plate 40.

467 apr, fifteenth, pa. Paris: Bibliothèque Nationale, Gr. 59. (Acts: 56^1 $23^{1/2}$ 14^2 12^s; Cath: 73^1 $7^{1/2}$ 13^2 9^s; Paul: 134^1 $41^{1/2}$ 44^2 31^s; *category III in Pauline letters, lower elsewhere)*

522 eapr, 1515, pa. Oxford: Bodleian Library, Canon. Gr. 34. (Evv: 206^1 $100^{1/2}$ 4^2 10^s; Acts: 52^1 $23^{1/2}$ 10^2 18^s; Cath: 52^1 $6^{1/2}$ 24^2 15^s; Paul: 191^1 $48^{1/2}$ 4^2 4^s; *category III in Acts and Catholic letters, V elsewhere)*

543 e†, twelfth, pch. Ann Arbor: University of Michigan, Ms. 15. (151^1 $72^{1/2}$ 31^2 57^s; *category III)*

565 e†, ninth, purple pch. Leningrad: Public Library, Gr. 53. (135^1 $67^{1/2}$ 48^2 75^s; *category III; the average is raised by Mark, with Matthew, and Luke far lower)* Plate 41.

579 e†, thirteenth, pch. Paris: Bibliothèque Nationale, Gr. 97. 117^1 $85^{1/2}$ 68^2 45^s; *category II in Mark and Luke)*

597 e, thirteenth, pch. Venice: Biblioteca San Marco, 1277 (I, 59). 208^1 $103^{1/2}$ 5^2 7^s; *category V)*

610 aKP†, twelfth, pch. Paris: Bibliothèque Nationale, Gr. 221. (Acts: 31^1 $20^{1/2}$ 28^2 18^s; Cath: 51^1 $6^{1/2}$ 2^2 2^s; *category III in Acts, V in Catholic letters)*

614 ap, thirteenth, pch. Milan: Biblioteca Ambrosiana, E 97 sup. (Acts: 60^1 $19^{1/2}$ 9^2 18^s; Cath: 44^1 $4^{1/2}$ 26^2 15^s; Paul: 192^1 $48^{1/2}$ 2^2 5^s; *category III because of its special textual character [related to the D text?]; a sister manuscript to 2412)* Plate 42.

621 apP(K), fourteenth, pch. Rome: Vatican Library, Gr. 1270. (Acts: 53^1 $26^{1/2}$ 17^2 9^s; Cath: 45^1 $7^{1/2}$ 29^2 15^s; Paul: 51^1 $22^{1/2}$ 21^2 9^s; *category III)*

623 apK†, 1037, pch. Rome: Vatican Library, Gr. 1650. (Acts: 45^1 $24^{1/2}$ 18^2 10^s; Cath: 47^1 $7^{1/2}$ 52^2 14^s; Paul: 171^1 $44^{1/2}$ 28^2 10^s; *category III)*

629 ap, fourteenth, pch. Rome: Vatican Library, Ottob. Gr. 298. Greek-Latin diglot. (Acts: 47^1 $22^{1/2}$ 26^2 16^s; Cath: 54^1 $7^{1/2}$ 22^2 21^s; Paul: 142^1 $36^{1/2}$ 39^2 32^s; *category III)*

630 ap, fourteenth, pa. Rome: Vatican Library, Ottob. Gr. 325. (Acts: 40^1 $24^{1/2}$ 25^2 13^s; Cath: 46^1 $6^{1/2}$ 33^2 13^s; Paul: 136^1 $42^{1/2}$ 49^2 17^s; *category III)*

642 ap†, fifteenth, pa. London: Lambeth Palace, 1185. (Acts: 60^1 $23^{1/2}$ 4^2 1^s; Cath: 63^1 $9^{1/2}$ 19^2 7^s; Paul: 163^1 $43^{1/2}$ 5^2 5^s; *category III in Catholic letters, V elsewhere)*

700 e, eleventh, pch. London: British Library, Egerton, 2610. (153^1 $81^{1/2}$ 35^2 58^s; *category III)*

720 eapPK†, thirteenth, pa. Vienna: Österreichische Nationalbibliothek, Theol. Gr. 79, 80. (Evv: 208^1 $101^{1/2}$ 5^2 13^s; Cath: 72^1 $10^{1/2}$ 14^2 9^s; Paul: 182^1 $48^{1/2}$ 7^2 15^s; *category strictly below III)*

788 e, eleventh, pch. Athens: National Library, 74. (144^1 $78^{1/2}$ 38^2 63^s; *category III)*

826 e, twelfth, pch. Grottaferrata: Biblioteca della Badia, A' α' 3. (157^1 $77^{1/2}$ 27^2 60^s; *category III*)

828 e, twelfth, pch. Grottaferrata: Biblioteca della Badia, A' α' 5. (148^1 $77^{1/2}$ 27^2 64^s; *category III*)

849 ePK: John seventeenth, pa, Rome: Vatican Library, Barb. Gr. 495. *(Category III)*

886 eaprPK, 1454, pa. Rome: Vatican Library, Reg. Gr. 6. (Evv: 209^1 $99^{1/2}$ 2^2 14^s; Acts: 15^1 $3^{1/2}$ 3^2 4^s; Paul: 171^1 $43^{1/2}$ 9^2 23^s; *category V*)

892 e†, ninth, pch. London: British Library, Add. 33277. 94^1 $80^{1/2}$ 111^2 53^s; *category II*) Plate 43.

911 aprPK†, twelfth, pch. London: British Library, Add. 39599, 39601. (Acts: 73^1 $29^{1/2}$ 2^2 1^s; Cath: 45^1 $5^{1/2}$ 1^2 1^s; Paul: 196^1 $48^{1/2}$ 3^2 0^s; *category V*)

915 ap†, thirteenth, pch. Escorial: Biblioteca T III 12. (Acts: 56^1 $25^{1/2}$ 11^2 13^s; Cath: 62^1 $8^{1/2}$ 18^2 10^s; Paul: 152^1 $41^{1/2}$ 37^2 20^s; *category III*)

917 ap, twelfth, pch. Escorial: Biblioteca, X III 10. (Acts: 69^1 $28^{1/2}$ 6^2 2^s; Cath: 80^1 $9^{1/2}$ 3^2 6^s; Paul: 161^1 $47^{1/2}$ 27^2 11^s; *category III in Pauline letters, elsewhere V*)

918 apP†, sixteenth, pa. Escorial: Biblioteca, Σ I 5. (Cath: 63^1 $7^{1/2}$ 15^2 15^s; Paul: 165^1 $44^{1/2}$ 1^2 6^s; *category low III in Catholic letters, V in Pauline letters*)

945 eap, eleventh, pch. Athos: Dionysiou, 124 (37). (Evv: 212^1 $98^{1/2}$ 5^2 9^s; Acts: 37^1 $22^{1/2}$ 27^2 20^s; Cath: 41^1 $6^{1/2}$ 41^2 10^s; Paul: 195^1 $45^{1/2}$ 4^2 4^s; *category III in Acts and Catholic letters, V elsewhere; member of f^{1424}?*)

983 e†, twelfth, pch. Athos: Esphigmenou, 29. (157^1 $76^{1/2}$ 29^2 62^s; *category III*)

1006 er, eleventh, pch. Athos: Iviron, (56) 728. (202^1 $97^{1/2}$ 7^2 18^s; *category V, but II in Revelation*)

1010 e†, twelfth, pch. Athos: Iviron, (66) 738. (211^1 $100^{1/2}$ 2^2 10^s; *category V; a member of f^{1424}?*)

1067 apP, fourteenth, pch. Athos: Koutloumousiou, 57. (Acts: 3^1 $0^{1/2}$ 0^2 0^s; Cath: 40^1 $7^{1/2}$ 40^2 11^s; Paul: 31^1 $15^{1/2}$ 2^2 1^s; *category II in Catholic letters, V elsewhere*)

1071 e, twelfth, pch. Athos: Lavra, A' 104. (180^1 $90^{1/2}$ 21^2 33^s; *category III*)

1175 ap†, eleventh, pch. Patmos: Ioannou, 16. (Acts: 18^1 $22^{1/2}$ 51^2 14^s; Cath: 49^1 $8^{1/2}$ 28^2 14^s; Paul: 84^1 $40^{1/2}$ 91^2 20^s; *category I*) Plate 44.

1241 eap†, twelfth, pch. Sinai: St. Catherine's Monastery, Gr. 260. (Evv: 139^1 $80^{1/2}$ 46^2 41^s; Acts: 74^1 $29^{1/2}$ 0^2 1^s; Cath: 17^1 $4^{1/2}$ 51^2 19^s; Paul 144^1 $42^{1/2}$ 42^2 19^s; *category I in Catholic letters, V in Acts, III elsewhere*) Plate 45.

1243 eap, eleventh, pch. Sinai: St. Catherine's Monastery, Gr. 262. (Evv: 192^1 $101^{1/2}$ 12^2 18^s; Acts: 66^1 $27^{1/2}$ 7^2 5^s; Cath: 22^1 $6^{1/2}$ 53^2 17^s; Paul: 166^1 $44^{1/2}$ 12^2 16^s; *category I in Catholic letters, III elsewhere*)

1251 eap†, thirteenth, pa. Sinai: St. Catherine's Monastery, Gr. 270. (Evv: 211^1 $105^{1/2}$ 4^2 4^s; Acts: 69^1 $26^{1/2}$ 4^2 6^s; Cath: 82^1 $9^{1/2}$ 2^2 4^s; Paul: 184^1 $42^{1/2}$ 10^2 10^s; *category V?*)

1292 eap, thirteenth, pch. Paris: Bibliothèque Nationale, Suppl. Gr. 1224. (Evv: 202^1 $102^{1/2}$ 4^2 6^s; Acts: 61^1 $22^{1/2}$ 7^2 15^s; Cath: 46^1 $6^{1/2}$ 29^2 17^s; Paul: 193^1 $47^{1/2}$ 3^2 5^s; *category II in Catholic letters, V elsewhere*)

1319 eap†, twelfth, pch. Jerusalem: Taphou, 47. (Evv: 199^1 $101^{1/2}$ 7^2 17^s; Acts: 62^1 $27^{1/2}$ 8^2 9^s; Cath: 81^1 $8^{1/2}$ 2^2 6^s; Paul: 119^1 $41^{1/2}$ 53^2 32^s; *category III in Pauline letters, V elsewhere*)

1342 e†, thirteenth/fourteenth, pch. Jerusalem: Saba, 411. (122^1 $76^{1/2}$ 71^2 43^s; *category II in Mark*)

1359 eap, twelfth, pch. Paris: Bibliothèque Nationale, Suppl. Gr. 1335. (Evv: 212^1 $101^{1/2}$ 3^2 7^s; Acts: 66^1 $28^{1/2}$ 9^2 2^s; Cath: 60^1 $10^{1/2}$ 21^2 6^s; Paul: 181^1 $46^{1/2}$ 11^2 8^s; *category III in Catholic letters, V elsewhere*)

1398 eap†, thirteenth, pch. Athos: Pantocratoros, 56. (Evv: 188^1 $92^{1/2}$ 3^2 14^s; Acts: 74^1 $29^{1/2}$ 1^2 1^s; Cath: 81^1 $10^{1/2}$ 3^2 3^s; Paul: 144^1 $44^{1/2}$ 41^2 23^s; *category III in Pauline letters, V elsewhere*)

1409 eap†, fourteenth, pa. Athos: Xiropotamou, 244. (Evv: 207^1 $100^{1/2}$ 3^2 8^s; Acts 37^1 $24^{1/2}$ 23^2 17^s; Cath: 45^1 $7^{1/2}$ 36^2 10^s; Paul: 194^1 $47^{1/2}$ 3^2 4^s; *category II in Acts and Catholic letters, V in Gospels and Pauline letters*)

1424 eKapr, ninth/tenth, pch. Chicago, Ill.: Jesuit-Krauss-McCormick Library, Gruber Ms. 152. Probably a member of the family including M **021** and a large number of other minuscules, e.g., 7, 27, 71, 115, 160, 179, 185, 267, 349, 517, 659, 692, 827, 945, 954, 990, 1010, 1082, 1188, 1194, 1207, 1223, 1293, 1391, 1402, 1606, 1675, 2191, etc. (Evv: 152^1 $85^{1/2}$ 33^2 51^s; Acts: 75^1 $29^{1/2}$ 0^2 1^s; Cath: 85^1 $9^{1/2}$ 1^2 4^s; Paul: 192^1 $46^{1/2}$ 5^2 5^s; *category III in Mark with* 88^1 $63^{1/2}$ 23^2 35^s, *while Matthew and Luke have only 9 and 2 type 2 readings respectively; V elsewhere —* the whole of Family 1424 *deserves a more thorough textual study than it has yet received)*

1448 eap, eleventh, pch. Athos: Lavra: A' 13. (Evv: 209^1 $102^{1/2}$ 5^2 8^s; Acts: 71^1 $27^{1/2}$ 2^2 6^s; Cath: 68^1 $7^{1/2}$ 23^s 9^2; Paul: 192^1 $49^{1/2}$ 6^2 1^s; *category III in Catholic letters, V elsewhere)*

1505 eap, 1084, pch. Athos: Lavra, B' 26. (Evv: 211^1 $99^{1/2}$ 3^2 9^s; Acts: 55^1 $26^{1/2}$ 15^2 9^s; Cath: 35^1 $4^{1/2}$ 41^2 18^s; Paul: 147^1 $46^{1/2}$ 25^2 29^s; *category III, but V in the Gospels)*

1506 e(pP)K, 1320, pch. Athos: Lavra, B' 89. (Evv: 188^1 $92^{1/2}$ 5^2 29^s; Paul: 12^1 $12^{1/2}$ 16^2 5^s; *category II in Pauline letters: V in Gospels)*

1523 apPK(1 John–Romans, 2 Corinthians–Galatians), fourteenth, pch. Vienna: Österreichische Nationalbibliothek, Theol. Gr. 141. (Cath: 24^1 $4^{1/2}$ 13^2 4^s; Paul: 80^1 $26^{1/2}$ 2^2 10^s; *category III, but V in the Pauline letters)*

1524 apK, fourteenth, pa. Vienna: Österreichische Nationalbibliothek, Theol. Gr. 150. (Acts: 73^1 $27^{1/2}$ 2^2 3^s; Cath: 62^1 $6^{1/2}$ 18^2 12^s; Paul: 175^1 $44^{1/2}$ 8^2 21^s; *category III in Catholic letters, V? elsewhere)*

1542b eP(Mark Luke†), twelfth, pch. Athos: Vatopediou, 897, ff. 75, 76, 100-120. (Mark 38^1 $12^{1/2}$ 8^2 15^s; *probably category III in Mark, V in Luke)*

1563 eapP†, thirteenth, pch. Athos: Vatopediou, 929. (Evv: 203^1 $96^{1/2}$ 6^2 19^s; Acts: 67^1 $28^{1/2}$ 6^2 4^s; Cath: 61^1 $10^{1/2}$ 19^2 7^s; Paul: 117^1 $40^{1/2}$ 11^2 6^s; *category below III?)*

1573 eap, twelfth/thirteenth, pch. Athos: Vatopediou, 939. (Evv: 199^1 $94^{1/2}$ 9^2 19^s; Acts: 72^1 $28^{1/2}$ 2^2 3^s; Cath: 85^1 $9^{1/2}$ 1^2 3^s; Paul: 118^1 $39^{1/2}$ 62^2 31^s; *category III only in Pauline letters, elsewhere probably V)*

1582 e, 949, pch. Athos: Vatopediou, 949. (138^1 $81^{1/2}$ 62^2 71^s; *category III, although further study of the unusually numerous distinctive readings may indicate II)* Plate 46.

1611 aprt, twelfth, pch. Athens: National Library, 94. (Acts: 57^1 $24^{1/2}$ 9^2 15^s; Cath: 44^1 $5^{1/2}$ 34^2 17^s; Paul: 153^1 $44^{1/2}$ 27^2 27^s; *category III, but II in Revelation)*

1642 eap, 1278, pa. Athos: Lavra, Λ' 128. (Evv: 213^1 $102^{1/2}$ 3^2 5^s; Acts: 46^1 $21^{1/2}$ 24^2 20^s; Cath: 83^1 $10^{1/2}$ 1^2 5^s; Paul: 184^1 $48^{1/2}$ 5^2 10^s; *category III in Acts, V elsewhere)*

1678 eaprK, fourteenth, pa. Athos: Panteleimonos, 770. (Evv: 206^1 $99^{1/2}$ 6^2 15^s; Acts: 37^1 $19^{1/2}$ 31^1 18^s; Cath: 58^1 $7^{1/2}$ 16^2 14^s; Paul: 181^1 $45^{1/2}$ 14^2 15^s; *category III?)*

1704 eapr, 1541, pa. Athos: Koutloumousiou, 356. (Evv: 201^1 $98^{1/2}$ 10^2 16^s; Acts: 41^1 $22^{1/2}$ 27^2 18^s; Cath: 81^1 $11^{1/2}$ 1^2 1^s; Paul: 186^1 $47^{1/2}$ 2^2 3^s; *category III in Acts, V elsewhere)*

1718 ap, twelfth, pch. Athos: Vatopediou, 851. (Acts: 62^1 $29^{1/2}$ 11^2 3^s; Cath: 59^1 $10^{1/2}$ 21^2 7^s; Paul: 178^1 $43^{1/2}$ 15^2 10^s; *category III, though with reservation)*

1735 ap†, eleventh/twelfth, pch. Athos: Lavra, B' 42. (Acts: 59^1 $26^{1/2}$ 10^2 8^s; Cath: 35^1 $7^{1/2}$ 43^2 13^s; Paul: 173^1 $43^{1/2}$ 14^2 16^s; *category II in Catholic letters, III elsewhere)*

1739 ap, tenth, pch. Athos: Lavra, B' 64. (Acts: 32^1 $22^{1/2}$ 35^2 16^s; Cath: 15^1 $7^{1/2}$ 67^2 14^s; Paul: 40^1 $38^{1/2}$ 146^2 38^s; *category I in Catholic and Pauline letters, II in Acts)* Plate 47.

1751 ap, 1479, pa. Athos: Lavra, K' 190. (Acts: 46^1 $23^{1/2}$ 20^2 14^s; Cath: 70^1 $11^{1/2}$ 8^2 9^s; Paul: 166^1 $44^{1/2}$ 17^2 20^s; *category III, but only in Acts without reservation)*

1836 apP(1 John–2 Timothy, Hebrews), tenth, pch. Grottaferrata: Biblioteca della Badia, A, β' 1. (Cath: 21^1 $4^{1/2}$ 9^2 0^s; Paul: 152^1 $44^{1/2}$ 29^2 13^s; *category III)*

1838 apP†, eleventh, pch. Grottaferrata: Biblioteca della Badia, A' β' 6. (Acts: 55^1 $24^{1/2}$ 8^2 12^s; Cath: 60^1 $5^{1/2}$ 12^2 17^s; Paul: 109^1 $32^{1/2}$ 30^2 23^s; *category III, but only in Pauline letters without reservation)*

1841 aprt, ninth/tenth, pch. Lesbos: Limonos, 55. (Acts: 69^1 $29^{1/2}$ 2^2 2^s; Cath: 85^1 $10^{1/2}$ 1^2 2^s; Paul: 197^1 $48^{1/2}$ 0^2 0^s; *category II in Revelation, V elsewhere)*

1842 aK, fourteenth, pa. Rome: Vatican Library, Gr. 652. (Acts: 59^1 $26^{1/2}$ 16^2 14^s; Cath: 68^1 $9^{1/2}$ 11^2 10^s; *category III with reservation*)

1844 aPK(1 John–Jude), fifteenth, pa. Rome: Vatican Library, Gr. 1227. (Cath: 26^1 $3^{1/2}$ 13^2 4^s; *category III*)

1845 ap, tenth, pch. Rome: Vatican Library, Gr. 1971. (Acts: 73^1 $27^{1/2}$ 2^2 4^s; Cath: 60^1 $10^{1/2}$ 23^2 9^s; Paul: 184^1 $48^{1/2}$ 10^2 7^s; *category III, with reservation*)

1846 apP†, eleventh, pch. Rome: Vatican Library, 2099. (Acts: 15^1 $7^{1/2}$ 1^2 2^s; Cath: 9^1 $4^{1/2}$ 16^2 7^s; Paul: 131^1 $41^{1/2}$ 5^2 6^s; *category V in Acts, III elsewhere, but with reservation in the Pauline letters*)

1852 apr†, thirteenth, pch. Uppsala: Universitetsbiblioteket, Ms. Gr. 11. (Acts: 39^1 $22^{1/2}$ 9^2 4^s; Cath: 18^1 $6^{1/2}$ 56^2 16^s; Paul: 159^1 $45^{1/2}$ 27^2 13^s; *category II in Catholic letters, V in Revelation, III elsewhere*)

1854 apr, eleventh, pch. Athos: Iviron, (25) 231. (Acts: 74^1 $28^{1/2}$ 2^2 3^s; Cath: 85^1 $9^{1/2}$ 1^2 3^s; Paul: 193^1 $48^{1/2}$ 3^2 3^s; *category V, but II in Revelation*)

1874 ap, tenth, pch. Sinai: St. Catherine's Monastery, Gr. 273. (Acts: 67^1 $29^{1/2}$ 6^2 3^s; Cath: 79^1 $9^{1/2}$ 4^2 6^s; Paul: 161^1 $47^{1/2}$ 34^2 22^s; *category III in Pauline letters, V elsewhere*)

1875 apP†, tenth, pch. Athens: National Library, 149. (Acts: 34^1 $20^{1/2}$ 23^2 14^s; Cath: 66^1 $11^{1/2}$ 12^2 3^s; Paul: 151^1 $45^{1/2}$ 28^2 15^s; *category III*)

1877 ap, fourteenth, pa. Sinai: St. Catherine's Monastery, Gr. 280. (Acts: 68^1 $28^{1/2}$ 5^2 7^s; Cath: 82^1 $10^{1/2}$ 2^2 6^s; Paul: 149^1 $43^{1/2}$ 32^2 23^s; *category III in Pauline letters, V elsewhere*)

1881 apP(1 Peter–Hebrews), fourteenth, pa. Sinai: St. Catherine's Monastery, Gr. 300. (Cath: 16^1 $3^{1/2}$ 42^2 12^s; Paul: 74^1 $41^{1/2}$ 102^2 32^s; *category II*) Plate 48.

1884 P† (Acts), sixteenth, pa. Gotha: Landesbibliothek, Chart B, 1767. (35^1 $20^{1/2}$ 22^2 22^s; *category III*)

1891 ap, tenth, pch. Jerusalem: Saba, 107 (233 ff.), Leningrad: Public Library, Gr. 317 (2 ff.). (Acts: 34^1 $22^{1/2}$ 34^2 16^s; Cath: 85^1 $7^{1/2}$ 0^2 5^s; Paul: 193^1 $44^{1/2}$ 4^2 4^s; *category II in Acts, V elsewhere*)

1908 pK, eleventh, pch. Oxford: Bodleian Library, Roe 16. (149^1 $48^{1/2}$ 37^2 20^s; *category III*)

1910 pPK(Galatians–Hebrews), eleventh/twelfth, pch. Paris: Bibliothèque Nationale, Coislin Gr. 204. (57^1 $12^{1/2}$ 26^2 15^s; *category III*)

1912 pP†, tenth, pch. Naples: Biblioteca Nazionale, Cod. Vien. 8. (125^1 $40^{1/2}$ 49^2 27^s; *category III*)

1942 pPK†, twelfth, pch. Milan: Biblioteca Ambrosiana, A 51b sup. (89^1 $34^{1/2}$ 37^2 19^s; *category III*)

1959 p, fifteenth, pa. Leiden: Rijksuniversiteits Bibliotheek, B. P. Gr. 66. (131^1 $42^{1/2}$ 45^2 31^s; *category III*)

1962 pPK†, eleventh, pch. Vienna: Österreichische Nationalbibliothek, Theol. Gr. 157. (99^1 $38^{1/2}$ 72^2 31^s; *category II*)

2005 apP†, (Acts, 2 Corinthians–Hebrews), fourteenth, pa. Escorial: Ψ III, 2, (Paul: 73^1 $18^{1/2}$ 21^2 21^s; *category III*)

2030 r†, twelfth, pch. Moscow: University, 2. (*Category III*)

[2040] = part of 911.

2050 r†, 1107, pch. Escorial: X,III, 6. (*Category II*)

2053 rK, thirteenth, pch. Messina: Biblioteca Universitarià, 99. (*Category I; textual value comparable to A* 02 *and C* 04 *in Revelation*) Plate 49.

2062 rK†, thirteenth, pch. Rome: Vatican Library, Gr. 1426. (*Category I; textual value comparable to 2053*)

2110 pK, tenth, pch. Paris: Bibliothèque Nationale, Gr. 702. (143^1 $44^{1/2}$ 43^2 18^s; *category III*)

2127 eapP, twelfth, pch. Palermo: Biblioteca Nazionale, Dep. Mus. 4; Philadelphia: Free Library, Lewis Collection. (Evv. 201^1 $94^{1/2}$ 7^2 14^s; Acts: 68^1 $28^{1/2}$ 3^2 6^s; Cath: 79^1 $8^{1/2}$ 2^2 7^s; Paul: 95^1 $41^{1/2}$ 72^2 33^s; *category II in Pauline letters, elsewhere V*)

2138 apr†, 1072, pch. Moscow: University, 2. (Acts: 49^1 $25^{1/2}$ 12^2 15^s; Cath: 36^1 $3^{1/2}$ 35^2 16^s; Paul: 163^1 $45^{1/2}$ 15^2 17^s; *category III, but V in revelation*)

2147 eap†, eleventh, pch. Leningrad: Public Library, Gr. 224. (Evv: 184^1 $84^{1/2}$ 4^2 13^s; Acts: 68^1 $19^{1/2}$ 4^2 14^s; Cath: 56^1 $6^{1/2}$ 18^2 18^s; Paul: 186^1 $44^{1/2}$ 3^2 5^s; *category V, but III in Catholic letters*)

2193 e, tenth, pch. Athos: Iviron, 247. (192^1 $98^{1/2}$ 36^2 67^s; *category III*)

2197 apPK, fourteenth, pch. Athos: Vatopediou, 245. (Cath: 61^1 $8^{1/2}$ 17^2 14^s; Paul: 170^1 $43^{1/2}$ 10^2 22^s; *category somewhat below III*)

2200 eapr, fourteenth, pa. Elasson: Olympiotisses, 79. (Evv: 163^1 $83^{1/2}$ 8^2 20^s; Acts: 39^1 $22^{1/2}$ 25^2 14^s; Cath: 46^1 $6^{1/2}$ 32^2 14^s; Paul: 134^1 $44^{1/2}$ 49^2 16^s; *category III, but V in the Gospels and Revelation*)

2298 ap, eleventh, pch. Paris: Bibliothèque Nationale, Gr. 102. (Acts: 49^1 $21^{1/2}$ 17^2 18^s; Cath: 35^1 $8^{1/2}$ 43^2 12^s; Paul: 192^1 $46^{1/2}$ 3^2 7^s; *category III, II in Catholic letters, V in Pauline letters*)

2329 r, tenth, pch. Meteora: Metamorphosis, 573, ff. 210-245r. (*Category II*)

2344 apr†, eleventh, pch. Paris: Bibliothèque Nationale, Cioslin Gr. 18. (Acts: 34^1 $25^{1/2}$ 32^2 13^s; Cath: 27^1 $5^{1/2}$ 50^2 13^s; Paul: 164^1 $43^{1/2}$ 18^2 14^s; *category I in Catholic letters, III elsewhere, but I in Revelation where of textual value comparable to A* **02** *and C* **04**) Plate 50.

2351 rK†, tenth, pch. Meteora: Metamorphosis, 573, ff. 245v-290. (*Category III*)

2374 eap, thirteenth, pch. Baltimore: Walters Art Gallery, Ms. 525. (Evv: 211^1 $101^{1/2}$ 1^2 10^s; Acts: 58^1 $27^{1/2}$ 13^2 7^s; Cath: 56^1 $8^{1/2}$ 25^2 8^s; Paul: 190^1 $48^{1/2}$ 5^2 3^s; *category III in Catholic letters, elsewhere below*)

2377 r†, fourteenth, pa. Athens: Byzantine Museum, 117. (*Category III*)

2400 eap†, thirteenth, pch. Chicago: University of Chicago Library, Ms. 965. (Evv: 198^1 $101^{1/2}$ 5^2 14^s; Acts: 66^1 $26^{1/2}$ 3^2 1^s; Cath: 84^1 $10^{1/2}$ 2^2 1^s; Paul: 149^1 $41^{1/2}$ 37^2 27^s; *obviously category V*)

2412 ap†, twelfth, pch. Chicago: University of Chicago Library, Ms. 922. (Acts: 60^1 $19^{1/2}$ 8^2 18^s; Cath: 46^1 $4^{1/2}$ 29^2 19^s; Paul: 194^1 $47^{1/2}$ 3^2 3^s; *category III, sister manuscript to 614*)

2427 eP(Mark), fourteenth, pch. Chicago: University of Chicago Library, Ms. 972. (12^1 $44^{1/2}$ 102^2 44^s; *category I*) Plate 51.

2464 apP†, ninth, pch. Patmos: Ioannou. 742. (Acts: 10^1 $7^{1/2}$ 14^2 5^s; Cath: 30^1 $6^{1/2}$ 34^2 12^s; Paul: 80^1 $28^{1/2}$ 56^2 20^s; *category II*)

2492 eap, thirteenth, pa. Sinai: St. Catherine's Monastery, Gr. 1342 (Evv: 201^1 $99^{1/2}$ 2^2 19^s; Acts: 71^1 $29^{1/2}$ 1^2 4^s; Cath: 58^1 $8^{1/2}$ 17^2 10^s; Paul: 137^1 $41^{1/2}$ 44^2 25^s; *category III clearly in Pauline letters and with reservation in Catholic letters, V? elsewhere*)

2495 eapr†, fourteenth/fifteenth, pa. Sinai: St. Catherine's Monastery, Gr. 1992. (Evv: 191^1 $92^{1/2}$ 3^2 8^s; Acts: 55^1 $24^{1/2}$ 14^2 12^s; Cath: 37^1 $4^{1/2}$ 38^2 18^s; Paul: 160^1 $46^{1/2}$ 18^2 22^s; *category III with reservation, but higher in Catholic letters*)

2516 eap†, thirteenth, pch. Dimitsane: Municipal Library, 27. (Evv: 198^1 $102^{1/2}$ 10^2 7^s; Acts: 69^1 $27^{1/2}$ 4^2 4^s; Cath: 87^1 $8^{1/2}$ 0^2 3^s; Paul: 125^1 $40^{1/2}$ 26^2 17^s; *category III certainly in Pauline letters, V elsewhere*)

2523 eap, 1453, pch/pa. Athens: National Library, 2720. (Evv: 208^1 $101^{1/2}$ 2^2 13^s; Acts: 75^1 $27^{1/2}$ 0^2 4^s; Cath: 78^1 $9^{1/2}$ 5^2 6^s; Paul: 153^1 $45^{1/2}$ 32^2 19^s; *category III in Pauline letters, V elsewhere*)

2541 ap, twelfth, pch. Leningrad: Public Library, Gr. 693. (Acts: 71^1 $27^{1/2}$ 4^2 3^s; Cath: 51^1 $7^{1/2}$ 31^2 8^s; Paul: 194^1 $48^{1/2}$ 2^2 3^s; *category III in Catholic letters, V elsewhere*)

2542 eP(Matthew Mark Luke†), thirteenth, pch. Leningrad: Public Library, Gr. 694. (129^1 $66^{1/2}$ 33^2 59^s; *category III*)

2544 ap, sixteenth/seventeenth, pa. Leningrad: Public Library, Kir. Belozersk 120/125. (Acts: 68^1 $26^{1/2}$ 2^2 11^s; Cath: 73^1 $10^{1/2}$ 10^2 11^s; Paul: 163^1 $43^{1/2}$ 24^2 26^s; *category III in Pauline letters, V elsewhere*)

2596 pPK†, eleventh, pch. Venice: Biblioteca San Marco, 1051 (II 178). (9^1 $2^{1/2}$ 3^2 1^s; *category III?*)

2652 ap, fifteenth, pa. Athens: National Library, 103. (Acts: 61¹ 17¹ᐟ² 5² 12ˢ; Cath: 56¹ 5¹ᐟ² 18² 18ˢ; Paul: 194¹ 49¹ᐟ² 1² 3ˢ; *category III in Catholic letters, elsewhere V?*)

2718 eap, thirteenth, pch. Lindos, Rhodes: Panagias, 4. (Evv: 201¹ 95¹ᐟ² 7² 18ˢ; Acts: 37¹ 22¹ᐟ² 16² 3ˢ; Cath: 67¹ 8¹ᐟ² 14² 9ˢ; Paul: 185¹ 47¹ᐟ² 8² 7ˢ; *category III*)

2744 eP(Mark), twelfth, pch. Goslar: C. W. Adam, Inv. Nr. 2550. (*Category III*)

2786 e, fourteenth, pch. Thira: Proph. Iliou 28.

2787 e†, eleventh, pch. Eptakomi, Cyprus: Naos s.n.

2788 e†, thirteenth, pch. Kyrinia, Cyprus: Mitropolis s.n.

2789 eP (John), tenth, pch. Kyrinia, Cyprus: Mitropolis s.n.

2790 e†, tenth, pch. Leukosia, Cyprus: Mrs. S. M. Logidou.

2791 e†, twelfth, pch. Cyprus: Moni Neophytou s.n.

2792 eP (Matt.-Luke), twelfth, pch. Leukosia, Cyprus: Kentron Epistim. Erevnon s.n. (8 ff.); Paphos, Cyprus: Mitropolis s.n. (8 ff.).

2793 eP (Matt), thirteenth/fourteenth, pch. Münster/Westf., Ms. 11.

2794 er†, twelfth, pch. Vienna: Mechitarist House, cod, gr. s.n.

2795 = *ℓ* 2198.

2796 eP (Luke), thirteenth, pch. Oldenburg: Landesbibliothek, Cim I, 7.

2797-2801 Newly discovered manuscripts at St. Catherine's Monastery, Sinai.

2802 eP (Luke), eleventh, pch. Athos: Grigoriou 158.

2803 eap†, fourteenth, pa. Athos: Dimitriou 53.

2804 e, thirteenth, pch. Patras: Chrysopodaritissis 1.

2805 ap, twelfth/thirteenth, pch. Athens: Studitou 1.

2806 e, 1518, pa. Trikala: Dousikou 5.

2807 (a)p (Heb), thirteenth, pch. Belgrade: National Library, RS 657.

2808 e†, thirteenth/fourteenth, pch. Kalymnos: National Library, 1.

2809 e†, fourteenth, pch. Kalymnos: National Library, 2.

2810 e†, 1514, pa. Tripotamon: Moni Tatarnis 2.

2811 e†, ninth/tenth, pch. Boston: Boston University, School of Theology Library, 1.

2812 eK, tenth, pch. Madrid: Biblioteca Nacional, Res. 235.

The above list contains a little more than 175 minuscules (including all manuscripts of both primary and secondary ranks cited regularly as "constant witnesses" as well as minuscules which are "cited frequently" in Nestle-Aland[26]). In comparison with the list of uncials fewer manuscripts of category V have been included here. This is because those with a developed Byzantine text have been omitted (except where their age or some other factor demands their notice), and this group accounts for more than 1,175 minuscules (as of May 1988; cf. table 6).

Table 6. Byzantine type minuscules by number

2e, 2ap, 3, 7p, 8, 9, 11, 12, 14, 15, 18, 20, 21, 23, 24, 25, 27, 29, 30, 32, 34, 36e, 37, 39, 40, 44, 45, 46, 47, 49, 50, 52, 53, 54, 55, 57, 58, 60, 63, 65, 66, 68, 70, 73, 74, 75, 76, 77, 78, 80, 82, 83, 84, 89, 90, 92, 95, 97, 98, 99, 100, 105, 107, 108, 109, 110, 111, 112, 116, 119, 120, 121, 122, 123, 125, 126, 127, 128, 129, 132, 133, 134, 135, 136, 137, 138, 139, 140, 141, 142, 143, 144, 146, 147, 148, 149, 150, 151, 155, 156, 159, 162, 167, 169, 170, 171, 177, 182, 183, 185, 186, 187, 190, 192, 193, 194, 195, 196, 197, 198, 199, 200, 201, 202, 203, 204, 207, 208, 210, 212, 214, 215, 217, 219, 220, 221, 223, 224, 226, 227, 231, 232, 235, 236, 237, 240, 243, 244, 245, 246, 247, 248, 250, 259, 260, 261, 262, 264, 266, 267, 268, 269, 270, 272, 275, 276, 277, 278a, 278b, 280, 281, 282, 283, 284, 285, 286, 287, 288, 289, 290, 291, 292, 293, 297, 300, 301, 302, 303, 304, 305, 306, 308, 309, 313, 314, 316, 319, 320, 324, 325, 327, 328, 329, 331, 334, 335, 337, 342, 343, 344, 347, 350, 351, 352, 353, 354, 355, 356, 357, 358, 359, 360, 361, 362, 364, 366, 367, 368, 369,

371, 373, 374, 375, 376, 379, 380, 381, 384, 385, 386, 387, 388, 390, 392, 393, 394, 395, 396, 399, 401, 402, 404, 405, 407, 408, 409, 410, 411, 412, 413, 414, 415, 417, 418, 419, 422, 425, 426, 432, 438, 439, 443, 445, 446, 448, 449, 450, 452, 454, 457, 458, 461, 465, 466, 469, 470, 471, 473, 474, 475, 476, 477, 478, 479, 480, 481, 482, 483, 484, 485, 490, 491, 492, 493, 494, 496, 497, 498, 499, 500, 501, 502, 504, 505, 506, 507, 509, 510, 511, 512, 514, 516, 518, 519, 520, 521, 523, 524, 525, 526, 527, 528, 529, 530, 531, 532, 533, 534, 535, 538, 540, 541, 546, 547, 548, 549, 550, 551, 553, 554, 556, 558, 559, 560, 564, 568, 570, 571, 573, 574, 575, 577, 578, 580, 583, 584, 585, 586, 587, 588, 592, 593, 594, 596, 597, 600, 601, 602, 603, 604, 605, 607, 616, 618, 620, 622, 624, 625, 626, 627, 628, 632, 633, 634, 637, 638, 639, 640, 644, 645, 648, 649, 650, 651, 655, 656, 657, 660, 662, 663, 664, 666, 668, 669, 672, 673, 674, 677, 680, 684, 685, 686, 688, 689, 690, 691, 692, 694, 696, 698, 699, 705, 707, 708, 711, 714, 715, 717, 718, 721, 724, 725, 727, 729, 730, 731, 734, 736, 737, 739, 741, 745, 746, 748, 750, 754, 755, 756, 757, 758, 759, 760, 761, 762, 763, 764, 765, 768, 769, 770, 773, 774, 775, 777, 778, 779, 781, 782, 783, 784, 785, 786, 787, 789, 790, 793, 794, 797, 798, 799, 801, 802, 806, 808, 809, 811, 818, 819, 820, 824, 825, 830, 831, 833, 834, 835, 836, 839, 840, 841, 843, 844, 845, 846, 848, 852, 853, 857, 858, 860, 861, 862, 864, 866a, 867, 868, 870, 877, 880, 884, 887, 889, 890, 893, 894, 896, 897, 898, 900, 901, 902, 904, 905, 906, 910, 911, 912, 914, 916, 919, 920, 921, 922, 924, 928, 936, 937, 938, 942, 943, 944, 950, 951, 952, 953, 955, 956, 957, 958, 959, 960, 961, 962, 963, 964, 965, 966, 967, 969, 970, 971, 973, 975, 977, 978, 980, 981, 987, 988, 991, 993, 994, 995, 997, 998, 999, 1000, 1003, 1004, 1007, 1008, 1011, 1013, 1014, 1015, 1016, 1017, 1018, 1019, 1020, 1023, 1024, 1025, 1026, 1028, 1030, 1031, 1032, 1033, 1036, 1044, 1045, 1046, 1050, 1052, 1053, 1054, 1055, 1056, 1057, 1059, 1060, 1061, 1062, 1063, 1065, 1068, 1069, 1070, 1072, 1073, 1074, 1075, 1076, 1077, 1078, 1080, 1081, 1083, 1085, 1087, 1088, 1089, 1094, 1099, 1100, 1101, 1103, 1104, 1105, 1107, 1110, 1112, 1119, 1121, 1123, 1129, 1148, 1149, 1150, 1161, 1168, 1169, 1171, 1172, 1173, 1174, 1176, 1177, 1185, 1186, 1187, 1188, 1189, 1190, 1191, 1193, 1196, 1197, 1198, 1199, 1200, 1201, 1202, 1203, 1205, 1206, 1207, 1208, 1209, 1211, 1212, 1213, 1214, 1215, 1217, 1218, 1220, 1221, 1222, 1223, 1224, 1225, 1226, 1227, 1231, 1232, 1233, 1234, 1235, 1236, 1238, 1239, 1240, 1242, 1244, 1247, 1248, 1249, 1250, 1252, 1254, 1255, 1260, 1264, 1277, 1283, 1285, 1296, 1297, 1298, 1299, 1300, 1301, 1303, 1305, 1309, 1310, 1312, 1313, 1314, 1315, 1316, 1317, 1318, 1320, 1323, 1324, 1328, 1330, 1331, 1334, 1339, 1340, 1341, 1343, 1345, 1347, 1350a, 1350b, 1351, 1352a, 1354, 1355, 1356, 1357, 1358, 1360, 1362, 1364, 1367, 1370, 1373, 1374, 1375, 1377, 1384, 1385, 1392, 1395, 1400, 1417, 1437, 1438, 1444, 1445, 1447, 1449, 1452, 1470, 1476, 1482, 1483, 1492, 1503, 1504, 1508, 1513, 1514, 1516, 1517, 1520, 1521, 1539, 1540, 1543, 1545, 1547, 1548, 1556, 1566, 1570, 1572, 1577, 1583, 1594, 1597, 1604, 1605, 1607, 1613, 1614, 1617, 1618, 1619, 1622, 1626, 1628, 1636, 1637, 1649, 1656, 1662, 1668, 1672, 1673, 1683, 1693, 1701, 1714, 1717, 1720, 1723, 1725, 1726, 1727, 1728, 1730, 1731, 1732, 1733, 1734, 1736, 1737, 1738, 1740, 1741, 1742, 1743, 1745, 1746, 1747, 1748, 1749, 1750, 1752, 1754, 1755a, 1755b, 1756, 1757, 1759, 1761, 1762, 1763, 1767, 1768, 1770, 1771, 1772, 1800, 1821, 1826, 1828, 1829, 1835, 1847, 1849, 1851, 1855, 1856, 1858, 1859, 1860, 1861, 1862, 1869, 1870, 1872, 1876, 1878, 1879, 1880, 1882, 1883, 1888, 1889, 1897, 1899, 1902, 1905, 1906, 1907, 1911, 1914, 1915, 1916, 1917, 1918, 1919, 1920, 1921, 1922, 1923, 1924, 1925, 1926, 1927, 1928, 1929, 1930, 1931, 1932, 1933, 1934, 1936, 1937, 1938, 1941, 1946, 1948, 1951, 1952, 1954, 1955, 1956, 1957, 1958, 1964, 1970, 1971, 1972, 1974, 1975, 1978, 1979, 1980, 1981, 1982, 1986, 1988, 1992, 1997, 1998, 2001, 2003, 2007, 2009, 2013, 2096, 2098, 2111, 2119, 2125, 2126, 2132, 2133, 2135, 2139, 2140, 2141, 2142, 2144, 2160, 2172, 2173, 2175, 2176, 2177, 2178, 2181, 2183, 2187, 2189, 2191, 2199, 2218, 2221, 2236, 2261, 2266, 2267, 2273, 2275, 2277, 2281, 2289, 2295, 2300, 2303, 2306, 2307, 2309, 2310, 2311, 2352, 2355, 2356, 2373, 2376, 2378, 2381, 2382, 2386, 2389, 2390, 2406, 2407, 2409, 2414, 2415, 2418, 2420, 2322, 2423, 2424, 2425, 2426, 2430, 2431, 2437, 2441, 2442, 2445, 2447, 2450, 2451, 2452, 2454, 2455, 2457, 2458, 2459, 2466, 2468, 2475,

2479, 2483, 2484, 2490, 2491, 2496, 2497, 2499, 2500, 2501, 2502, 2503, 2507, 2532, 2534, 2536, 2539, 2540, 2545, 2547, 2549, 2550, 2552, 2554, 2555, 2558, 2559, 2562, 2563, 2567, 2571, 2572, 2573, 2578, 2579, 2581, 2584, 2587, 2593, 2600, 2619, 2624, 2626, 2627, 2629, 2631, 2633, 2634, 2635, 2636, 2637, 2639, 2645, 2646, 2649, 2650, 2651, 2653, 2656, 2657, 2658, 2660, 2661, 2665, 2666, 2668, 2670, 2671, 2673, 2675, 2679, 2690, 2691, 2696, 2698, 2699, 2700, 2704, 2711, 2712, 2716, 2721, 2722, 2723, 2724, 2725, 2727, 2729, 2746, 2760, 2761, 2765, 2767, 2773, 2774, 2775, 2779, 2780, 2781, 2782, 2783, 2784, 2785, 2787, 2790, 2791, 2794.

The number of these minuscules is steadily increasing as work continues at the Institute for New Testament Textual Research. Since these manuscripts are omitted both from the descriptive list above and from the table by categories below (for the reasons given on p. 142), they are listed separately in table 7 according to their distribution by century with the exception of only 632, 1227, and 2306, which are composites of manuscripts from different centuries.

Table 7. Distribution of Byzantine type minuscules by century

9th

461, 1080, 1862, 2142, 2500

9th/10th

399

10th

14, 27, 29, 34, 36e, 63, 82, 92, 100, 135, 144, 151, 221, 237, 262, 278b, 344, 364, 371, 405, 411, 450, 454, 457, 478, 481, 564, 568, 584, 602, 605, 626, 627, 669, 920, 1055, 1076, 1077, 1078, 1203, 1220, 1223, 1225, 1347, 1351, 1357, 1392, 1417, 1452, 1662, 1720, 1756, 1829, 1851, 1880, 1905, 1920, 1927, 1954, 1997, 1998, 2125, 2373, 2414, 2424, 2545, 2722, 2790

10th/11th

994, 1073, 1701

11th

7p, 8, 12, 20, 23, 24, 25, 37, 39, 40, 50, 65, 68, 75, 77, 83, 89, 98, 108, 112, 123, 125, 126, 127, 133, 137, 142, 143, 148, 150, 177, 186, 194, 195, 197, 200, 207, 208, 210, 212, 215, 236, 250, 259, 272, 276, 277, 278a, 300, 301, 302, 314, 325, 331, 343, 350, 352, 354, 357, 360, 375, 376, 422, 458, 465, 466, 470, 474, 475, 476, 490, 491, 497, 504, 506, 507, 516, 526, 527, 528, 530, 532, 547, 548, 549, 559, 560, 583, 585, 596, 607, 624, 625, 638, 639, 640, 651, 672, 699, 707, 708, 711, 717, 746, 754, 756, 773, 785, 809, 831, 870, 884, 887, 894, 901, 910, 919, 937, 942, 943, 944, 964, 965, 991, 1014, 1028, 1045, 1054, 1056, 1074, 1110, 1123, 1168, 1174, 1187, 1207, 1209, 1211, 1212, 1214, 1221, 1222, 1244, 1277, 1300, 1312, 1313, 1314, 1317, 1320, 1324, 1340, 1343, 1373, 1384, 1438, 1444, 1449, 1470, 1483, 1513, 1514, 1517, 1520, 1521, 1545, 1556, 1570, 1607, 1668, 1672, 1693, 1730, 1734, 1738, 1770, 1828, 1835, 1847, 1849, 1870, 1878, 1879, 1888, 1906, 1907, 1916, 1919, 1921, 1923, 1924, 1925, 1932, 1933, 1934, 1946, 1955, 1980, 1981, 1982, 2001, 2007, 2098, 2132, 2133, 2144, 2172, 2176, 2181, 2183, 2199, 2275, 2277, 2281, 2386, 2295, 2307, 2381, 2386, 2430, 2442, 2447, 2451, 2458, 2468, 2475, 2539, 2547, 2559, 2563, 2567, 2571, 2587, 2637, 2649, 2661, 2723, 2746, 2760, 2782, 2787

2306 (composite of parts from the 11th to the 14th centuries)

11th/12th

655, 657, 660, 1013, 1188, 1191, 1309, 1358, 1540, 1566, 2389, 2415, 2784

12th

2e, 2ap, 3, 9, 11, 15, 21, 32, 44, 46, 49, 57, 73, 76, 78, 80, 84, 95, 97, 105, 110, 111, 116, 119, 120, 122, 129, 132, 134, 138, 139, 140, 146, 156, 159, 162, 183, 187, 193, 196, 199, 202, 203, 217, 224, 226, 231, 240, 244, 245, 247, 261, 264, 267, 268, 269, 270, 275, 280, 281, 282, 297, 304, 306, 319, 320, 329, 334, 337, 347, 351, 353, 355, 356, 366, 374, 387, 392, 395, 396, 401, 407, 408, 419, 438, 439, 443, 452, 471, 485, 499, 502, 505, 509, 510, 514, 518, 520, 524, 529, 531, 535, 538, 550, 551, 556, 570, 571, 580, 587, 618, 620, 622, 637, 650, 662, 673, 674, 688, 692, 721, 736, 748, 750, 760, 765, 768, 770, 774, 777, 778, 779, 782, 787, 793, 799, 808, 843, 857, 860, 862, 877, 893, 896, 902, 911, 916, 922, 924, 936, 950, 967, 971, 973, 975, 980, 987, 993, 998, 1007, 1046, 1081, 1083, 1085, 1112, 1169, 1176, 1186, 1190, 1193, 1197, 1198, 1199, 1200, 1217, 1218, 1224, 1231, 1240, 1301, 1315, 1316, 1318, 1323, 1350a, 1355, 1360, 1364, 1375, 1385, 1437, 1539, 1583, 1673, 1683, 1714, 1737, 1752, 1754, 1755a, 1755b, 1800, 1821, 1826, 1872, 1889, 1914, 1915, 1917, 1926, 1951, 1970, 1971, 1974, 1986, 1988, 2013, 2096, 2126, 2135, 2139, 2173, 2177, 2189, 2191, 2289, 2382, 2426, 2437, 2445, 2459, 2490, 2491, 2507, 2536, 2549, 2550, 2552, 2562, 2639, 2650, 2657, 2671, 2700, 2712, 2725, 2727, 2781, 2785, 2791, 2794
632 and 1227 (composites of parts from the 12th to the 14th centuries)

12th/13th

905, 906, 1310, 1341, 1897, 2311

13th

52, 55, 60, 74, 107, 121, 128, 136, 141, 147, 167, 170, 192, 198, 204, 219, 220, 227, 248, 260, 283, 284, 291, 292, 293, 303, 305, 309, 327, 328, 342, 359, 361, 362, 384, 388, 390, 410, 449, 469, 473, 477, 479, 482, 483, 484, 496, 500, 501, 511, 519, 533, 534, 546, 553, 554, 558, 573, 574, 592, 593, 597, 601, 663, 666, 677, 684, 685, 689, 691, 696, 705, 714, 715, 725, 729, 737, 757, 759, 775, 811, 820, 825, 830, 835, 840, 897, 898, 900, 912, 914, 966, 969, 970, 981, 995, 997, 999, 1000, 1004, 1008, 1011, 1015, 1016, 1031, 1050, 1052, 1053, 1057, 1069, 1070, 1072, 1087, 1089, 1094, 1103, 1107, 1129, 1148, 1149, 1150, 1161, 1177, 1201, 1205, 1206, 1208, 1213, 1215, 1226, 1238, 1255, 1285, 1339, 1352a, 1400, 1594, 1597, 1604, 1622, 1717, 1727, 1728, 1731, 1736, 1740, 1742, 1772, 1855, 1858, 1922, 1938, 1941, 1956, 1972, 1992, 2111, 2119, 2140, 2141, 2236, 2353, 2376, 2380, 2390, 2409, 2420, 2423, 2425, 2457, 2479, 2483, 2502, 2534, 2540, 2558, 2568, 2584, 2600, 2624, 2627, 2631, 2633, 2645, 2646, 2658, 2660, 2665, 2670, 2696, 2699, 2724, 2761

13th/14th

266, 656, 668, 1334, 2499, 2578

14th

18, 45, 53, 54, 66, 109, 155, 171, 182, 185, 190, 201, 214, 223, 232, 235, 243, 246, 290, 308, 316, 324, 358, 367, 369, 381, 386, 393, 394, 402, 404, 409, 412, 413, 414, 415, 417, 425, 426, 480, 492, 494, 498, 512, 521, 523, 540, 577, 578, 586, 588, 594, 600, 603, 604, 628, 633, 634, 644, 645, 648, 649, 680, 686, 690, 698, 718, 727, 730, 731, 734, 741, 758, 761, 762, 763, 764, 769, 781, 783, 784, 786, 789, 790, 794, 797, 798, 802, 806, 818, 819, 824, 833, 834, 836, 839, 845, 846, 848, 858, 864, 866a, 867, 889, 890, 904, 921, 928, 938, 951, 952, 953, 959, 960, 977, 978, 1020, 1023, 1032, 1033, 1036, 1061, 1062, 1075, 1099, 1100, 1119, 1121, 1185, 1189, 1196, 1234, 1235, 1236, 1248, 1249, 1252, 1254, 1283, 1328, 1330, 1331, 1345, 1350b, 1356, 1377, 1395, 1445, 1447, 1476, 1492, 1503, 1504, 1516, 1543, 1547, 1548, 1572, 1577, 1605, 1613, 1614, 1619, 1637, 1723, 1725, 1726, 1732, 1733, 1741, 1746, 1747, 1761, 1762, 1771, 1856, 1859, 1899, 1902, 1918, 1928, 1929, 1952, 1975, 2085, 2160, 2261, 2266, 2273, 2303, 2309, 2310, 2355, 2356, 2406, 2407, 2431, 2441, 2454, 2466, 2484, 2503, 2593, 2626, 2629, 2634, 2651, 2653, 2666, 2668, 2679, 2698, 2716, 2765, 2767, 2773, 2774, 2775, 2780, 2783

15th

30, 47, 58, 70, 149, 285, 286, 287, 288, 313, 368, 373, 379, 380, 385, 418, 432, 446, 448, 493, 525, 541, 575, 616, 664, 694, 739, 801, 841, 844, 853, 880, 955, 958, 961, 962, 1003, 1017, 1018, 1024, 1026, 1059, 1060, 1105, 1202, 1232, 1233, 1247, 1250, 1260, 1264, 1482, 1508, 1617, 1626, 1628, 1636, 1649, 1656, 1745, 1750, 1757, 1763, 1767, 1876, 1882, 1948, 1957, 1958, 1964, 1978, 2003, 2175, 2178, 2221, 2352, 2418, 2452, 2455, 2554, 2673, 2675, 2691, 2704, 2729

15th/16th

99, 1367

16th

90, 335, 445, 724, 745, 755, 867, 957, 1019, 1030, 1065, 1068, 1088, 1239, 1362, 1370, 1374, 1618, 1749, 1768, 1861, 1883, 1911, 1930, 1931, 1936, 1937, 1979, 2009, 2218, 2378, 2422, 2496, 2501, 2532, 2555, 2572, 2573, 2579, 2635, 2636, 2690, 2711, 2721, 2779

16th/17th

1371

17th and later

289, 868, 956, 963, 988, 1044, 1063, 1101, 1104, 1303, 1748, 1869, 2267, 2450, 2497, 2581, 2619, 2656

All of these minuscules exhibit a purely or predominantly Byzantine text. And this is not a peculiarity of the minuscules, but a characteristic they share with a considerable number of uncials.[34] They are all irrelevant for textual criticism, at least for establishing the original form of the text and its development in the early centuries. Admittedly no adequate history has yet been written of the Byzantine text — a text which is in no sense a monolithic mass because its manuscripts share the same range of variation characteristic of all Greek New Testament manuscripts.[35] But this is a task we may well leave to a future generation, or to specialists particularly interested in it today, and consider our own generation fortunate if we can succeed in tracing the history of manuscripts with non-Byzantine texts, and that in its general outlines. Once this has been done the way will be clear for a better appreciation of the Byzantine text, for from the fourth century it began to exercise its influence on the other text types. In fact, the "Majority text" (using the term in a purely pragmatic sense) with its symbol 𝔐 (which is used solely as a space-saving device in Nestle-Aland[26]) may yet prove to hold a multiple significance for the history of the text. But this cannot be tested systematically until the critical apparatus of Nestle-Aland[26] has been recorded on tape (which is now being done) and examined by computer from all the necessary perspectives. Until this has been done we must continue to use the term "Majority Text" and the symbol 𝔐.

34. Cf. list on pp. 107-128.
35. Cf. pp. 69f.

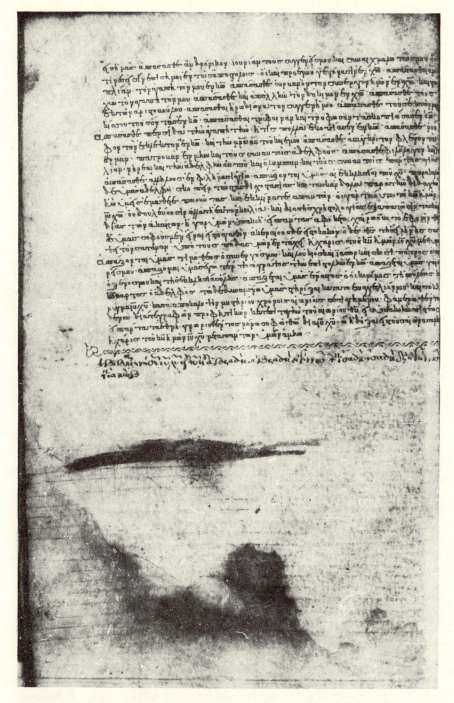

Plate 36. The minuscule 33 (long known as "Queen of the minuscules," ninth century; cf. p. 129): the ending of Romans (f. 100ʳ).

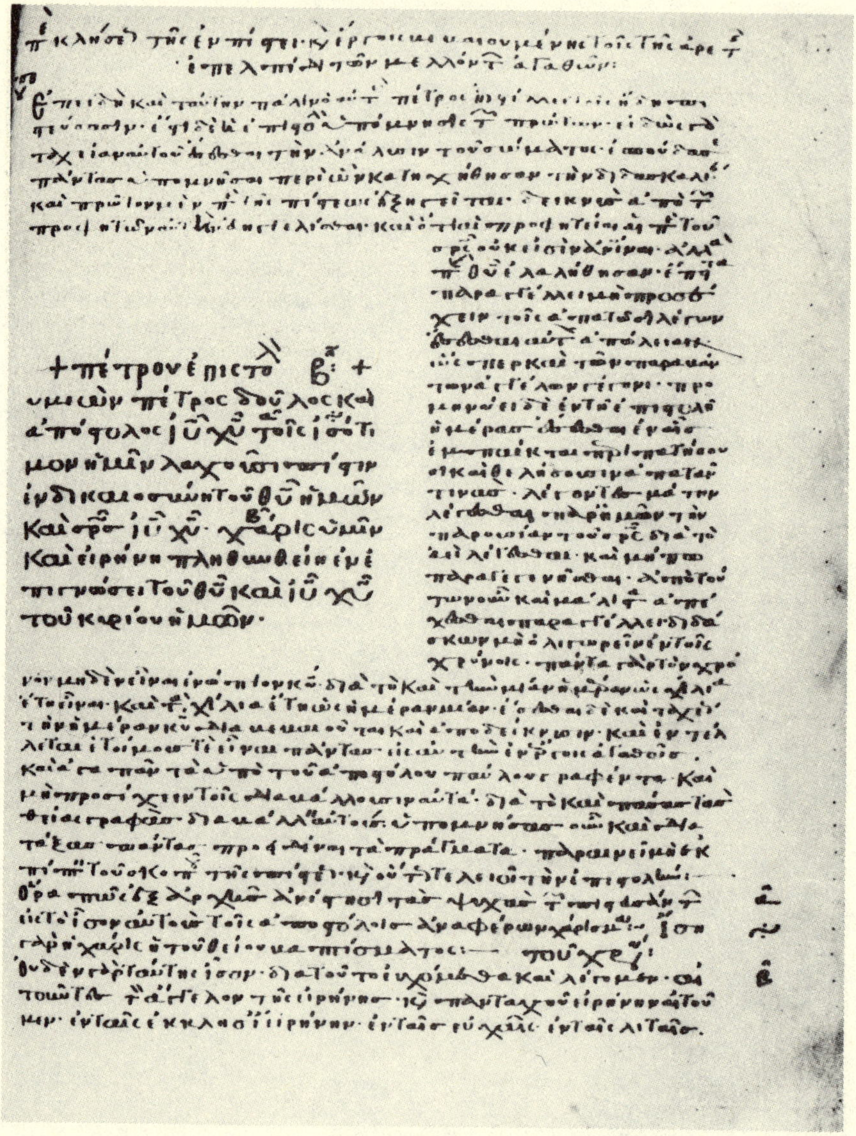

Plate 37. The minuscule 36 (twelfth century; cf. p. 129) is an example of a catena (or chain) manuscript, so called because excerpts from patristic commentaries are arranged in a "chain" beside the text: 2 Pet. 1:1-2 (f. 213[r]) is in the format of a frame or marginal catena, but catenae may also be written in a continuous text format, with the text and commentary distinguished by script, color of ink, or marginal notes.

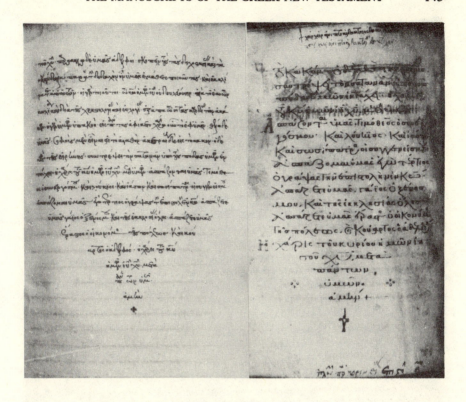

Plate 38. Sister manuscripts 322 (fifteenth century, f. 72ʳ; cf. p. 132) and 323 (eleventh century): the ending of Romans.

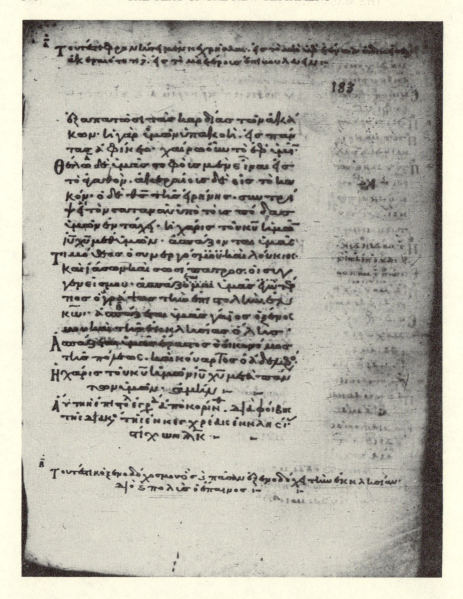

Plate 39. The minuscule 424 (eleventh century; cf. p. 132): the ending of Romans, with corrections that are most revealing (f. 183ʳ).

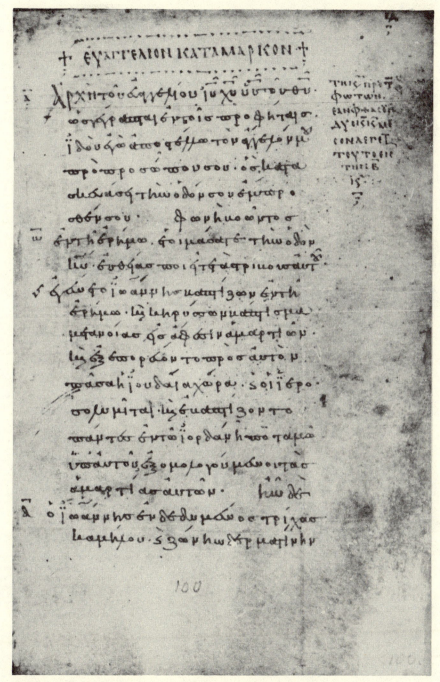

Plate 40. The minuscule 461 (cf. p. 133), written in the year 835 according to its colophon, is not significant for its (Byzantine Majority) text but for its age as the earliest dated minuscule: the beginning of the gospel of Mark (f. 100ʳ).

Plate 41. The purple parchment minuscule 565 (eleventh century; cf. p. 133) is associated with Θ (038) and the minuscule 700 as principal representatives of the "Caesarean text": the beginning of the gospel of John (f. 300ʳ).

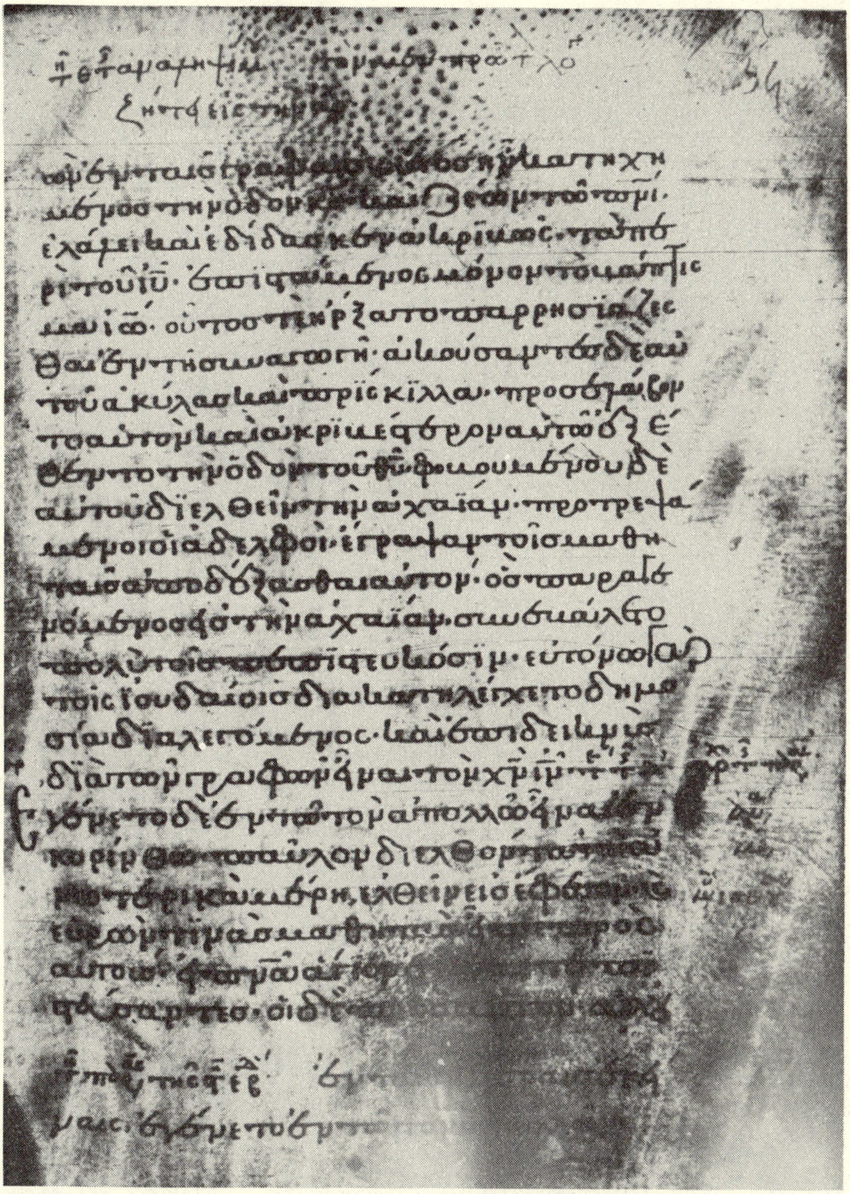

Plate 42. The minuscule 614 (thirteenth century; cf. p. 133) is important in discussing the "Western text" because of its affinities with Codex Bezae Cantabrigiensis: Acts 18:24–19:2 (f. 54ʳ).

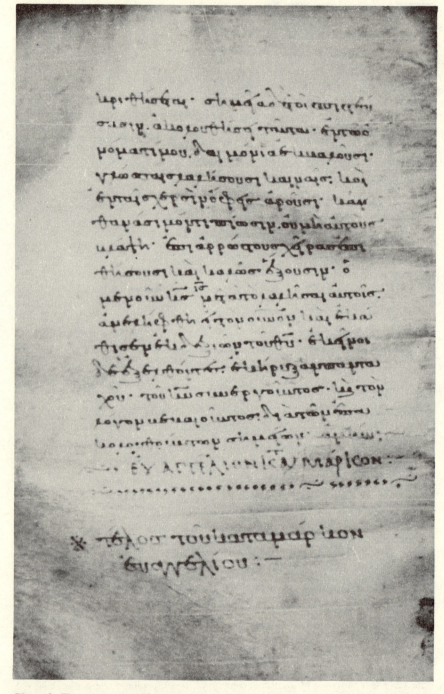

Plate 43. The minuscule 892 (ninth century; cf. p. 134) has a valuable Gospel text: the ending of the gospel of Mark (f. 171ᵛ).

Plate 44. The minuscule 1175 (eleventh century; cf. p. 134) is significant for the history of the text: the ending of Romans (f. 118ʳ).

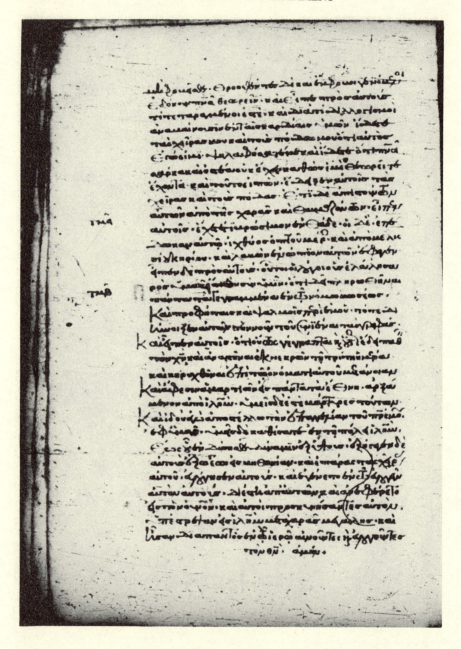

Plate 45. The minuscule 1241 (twelfth century; cf. p. 134) is also important for the history of the text: the ending of the gosple of Luke (f. 90ᵛ).

Plate 46. The minuscule 1582 (949; cf. p. 135): the beginning of the gospel of John (f. 223ʳ).

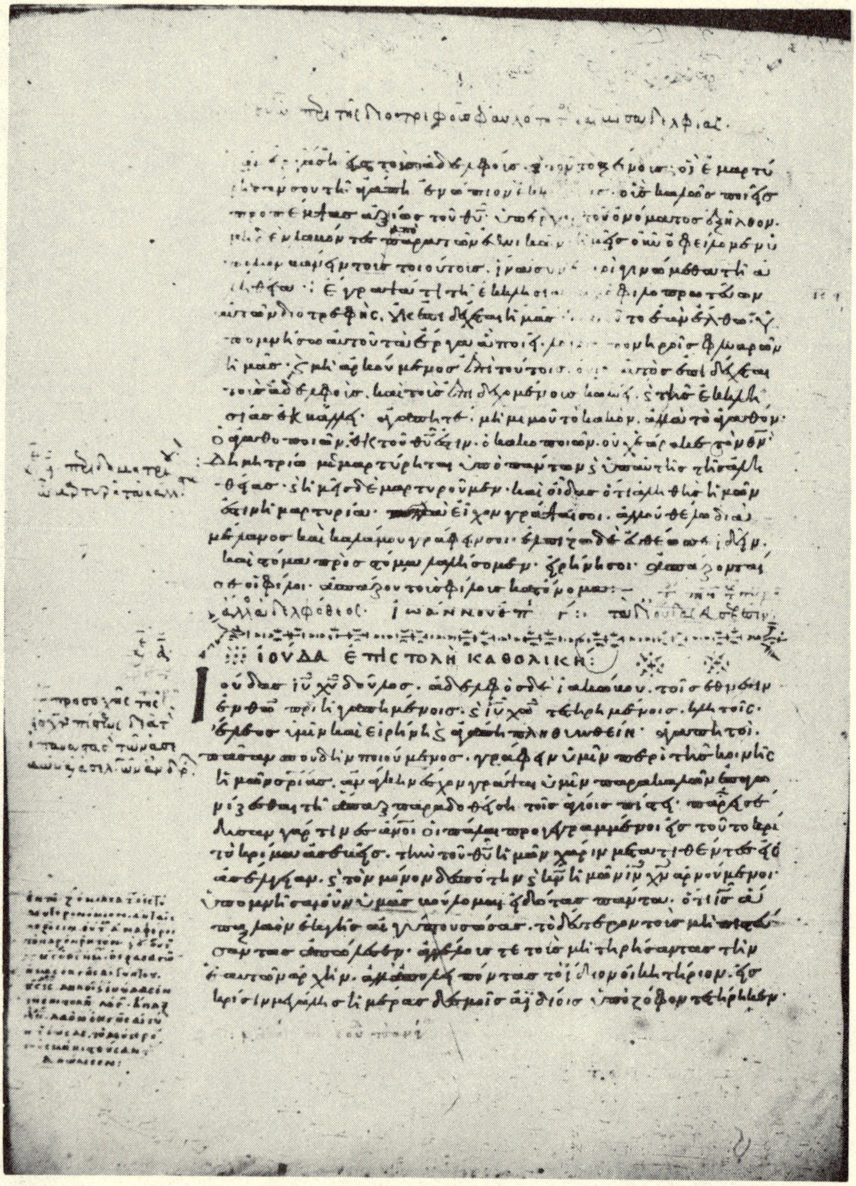

Plate 47. The minuscule 1739 (tenth century; cf. p. 135) has a valuable text: the ending of 3 John and the beginning of Jude (f. 43ᵛ).

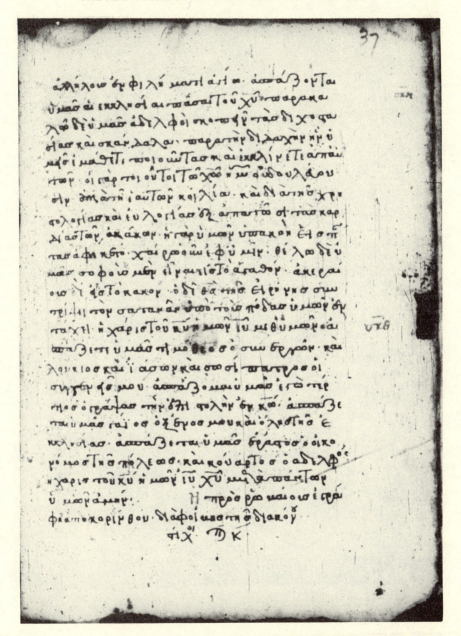

Plate 48. The minuscule 1881 (fourteenth century; cf. p. 136): the ending of Romans (f. 37ʳ).

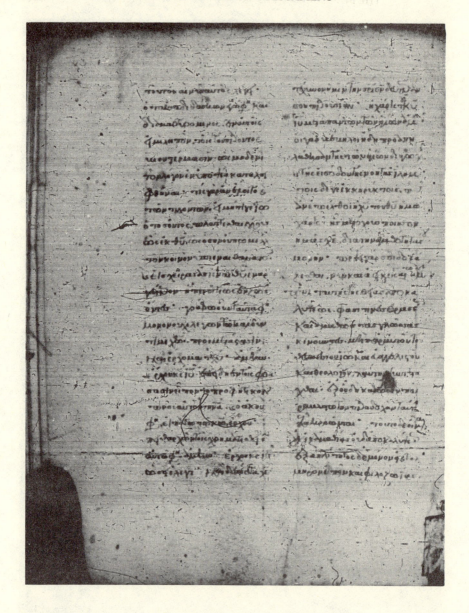

Plate 49. The minuscule 2053 (thirteenth century; cf. p. 136) is one of the most important witnesses for Revelation: the ending of Revelation.

Plate 50. The minuscule 2344 (eleventh century; cf. p. 137) has a valuable text, especially in Revelation: the ending of Romans (f. 200^r).

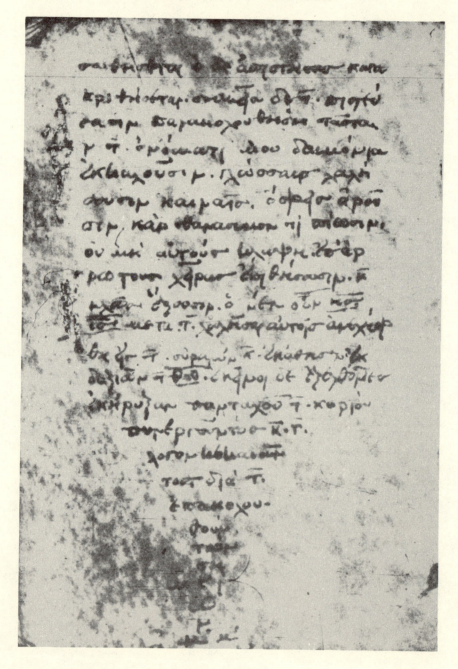

Plate 51. The minuscule 2427 (fourteenth century; cf. p. 137): the ending of the gospel of Mark (f. 43ᵛ).

10. *A REVIEW OF TEXT MANUSCRIPTS BY CATEGORY*
(cf. also pp. 332-37)

In the foregoing descriptive lists of papyri (pp. 96-102), uncials (pp. 107-128), and minuscules (pp. 129-138), more than five hundred manuscripts have been noted individually and usually classified in terms of the five categories defined on pp. 106f. Few readers of this book will have memorized all these data. Accordingly, it may be useful to review them here in tabular form. Further, in order to avoid any necessity for referring back, the definitions of the five categories are repeated here.

Category I: Manuscripts of a very special quality which should always be considered in establishing the original text (e.g., the Alexandrian text belongs here). The papyri and uncials up to the third/fourth century belong here almost automatically because they represent the text of the early period (those whose witness is slight are shown in parentheses).

Category II: Manuscripts of a special quality, but distinguished from manuscripts of category I by the presence of alien influences (particularly of the Byzantine text), and yet of importance for establishing the original text (e.g., the Egyptian text belongs here).

Category III: Manuscripts of a distinctive character with an independent text, usually important for establishing the original text, but particularly important for the history of the text (e.g., f^1, f^{13}).

Category IV: Manuscripts of the D text.

Category V: Manuscripts with a purely or predominantly Byzantine text.

Table 8. Distribution of Greek manuscripts by century and category
[Bold indicates manuscripts of more than ten folios]

	Category I	Category II	Category III	Category IV	Cateory V
2nd	$\mathfrak{p}^{52}, \mathfrak{p}^{90}$				
2nd/ 3rd	$\mathfrak{p}^{32}, \mathbf{P}^{46},$ $\mathbf{P}^{64+67}, \mathbf{P}^{66}, \mathfrak{p}^{77}, 0189$				
3rd	$\mathfrak{p}^1, \mathfrak{p}^4, \mathfrak{p}^5, (\mathfrak{p}^9)$ $(\mathfrak{p}^{12}), \mathfrak{p}^{15}, \mathfrak{p}^{20},$ $\mathfrak{p}^{22}, \mathfrak{p}^{23}, \mathfrak{p}^{27}, \mathfrak{p}^{28}, \mathfrak{p}^{29},$ $\mathfrak{p}^{30}, \mathfrak{p}^{39}, \mathfrak{p}^{40}, \mathbf{P}^{45},$ $\mathbf{P}^{47}, \mathfrak{p}^{49}, \mathfrak{p}^{53}, \mathfrak{p}^{65},$ $\mathfrak{p}^{70}, \mathbf{P}^{75}, (\mathfrak{p}^{80}),$ $\mathfrak{p}^{87}, 0220$		(0212)	$\mathfrak{p}^{48}, \mathfrak{p}^{69}$	
3rd/ 4th	$\mathbf{P}^{13}, \mathfrak{p}^{16}, \mathfrak{p}^{18},$ $\mathfrak{p}^{37}, \mathbf{P}^{72}, \mathfrak{p}^{78}, 0162$			$\mathfrak{p}^{38}, 0171$	
4th	$\mathfrak{p}^{10}, \mathfrak{p}^{24}, \mathfrak{p}^{35},$ $\aleph(01), \mathbf{B}(03)$	$\mathfrak{p}^6, \mathfrak{p}^8, \mathfrak{p}^{17},$ $\mathfrak{p}^{62}, \mathfrak{p}^{71},$ $\mathfrak{p}^{81}, \mathfrak{p}^{86},$ 0185	$\mathfrak{p}^{88}, 058?, 0169,$ $0188, 0206, 0207,$ $0221, 0228, 0231,$ 0242		
4th/ 5th	057	$\mathfrak{p}^{19}, \mathfrak{p}^{51},$ $\mathfrak{p}^{57}, \mathfrak{p}^{82},$ $\mathfrak{p}^{85}, 0181,$ 0270	$\mathfrak{p}^{21}, \mathfrak{p}^{50}, 059,$ $0160, 0176, 0214,$ 0219		

	Category I	Category II	Category III	Category IV	Category V
5th	A (02 exc. Evv), 0254	p^{14}, C (04), I (016), T (029), **048**, 077, 0172, 0173, 0175, 0201, 0240, 0244, 0274	A (02 Evv), W (032), 062, 068, 069, 0163, 0165?, 0166, 0182, 0216, 0217, 0218, 0226, 0227, 0236, 0252, 0261	D^{ea} (05)	Q (026), 061,
5th/ 6th		p^{56}, 071, 076, 088, 0232, 0247	p^{54}, p^{63}, 072, 0170, 0186, 0213		
6th		p^{33+58}, D^{p} (06), E^{a} (08), 073, 081, 085, 087, 089, 091, 093 (exc. Acts), 094, 0184, 0223, 0225, 0245	p^{2}, p^{36}, p^{76}, p^{83}, p^{84}, D^{p} (06^{c}), H^{p} (015), Z (035), Ξ (040), 060, 066, 067, **070**, 078, 079, 082, **086**, 0143, 0147, 0159, 0187, 0198, 0208, 0222, 0237, 0241, 0251, 0260, 0266		N (022), O (023), P^{e} (024), R (027), Σ (042), Φ (043), **064**, 065, 3 (Acts), 0246, 0253, 0265?
6th/ 7th	p^{26}	p^{43}, p^{44}, p^{55}, **083**	p^{3}, 0164, 0199		
7th	P^{74}, 098	P^{11}, p^{31}, p^{34}, p^{79}, **0102**, 0108, 0111, 0204	P^{59}, p^{68}, 096, 097, 099, **0106**, 0107, 0109, 0145, 0167, 0183, 0200, 0209, 0210, 0239, 0259, 0262		0103, 0104, **0211**
7th/8th		p^{42}, p^{61}	P^{60}		
8th		L^{e} (019), 0101, 0114, 0156, 0205, 0234	P^{41}, 095, 0126, 0127, 0146, 0148, 0161, 0229, **0233**, 0238, **0250**, 0256		E^{e} (07), **047**, 054?, **0116**, 0134
8th/ 9th		Ψ (044, Cath)	Ψ (044, exc. Cath)		
9th	33 (Acts-Paul)	F^{p} (010), Θ (038), 0155, 0271, **33** (Evv), 892, 2464	G^{p} (012), P^{apr} (025 exc. Acts, Rev), Δ (037), **050**, 0122, 0128, 0130, 0131, 0132, **0150**, 0269, **565**		F^{e} (09), G^{e} (011), H^{e} (013), H^{a} (014), K^{e} (017), K^{ap} (018), L^{ap} (020), M (021), P^{apr} (025 Acts, Rev), U (030), V (031), Y (034), Λ (039), Π (041), Ω (045), **049**, **053?**,

	Category I	Category II	Category III	Category IV	Category V
					063, 0120, **0133**, **0135**, 0136? **0151**, 0197, **0248**, 0255, **0257**, 0272, 0273?, **461**
9th / 10th		1841 (Rev)	0115, **1424** (Mk)		**1424** (exc. Mk), **1841** (exc. Rev)
10th	1739 (exc. Acts)	0177, 0243?, **1739** (Acts), **1891** (Acts), **2329**	**051, 075**, 0105, 0121a, 0121b, 0140, **0141**, 0249, 307, 1582, **1836**, 1845, **1874** (Paul), **1875, 1912, 2110**, **2193, 2351**		S (028), X (033), Γ (036), **046**, 052, **056, 0142, 1874** (exc. Paul), **1891** (exc. Acts)
11th	1175, 1243 (Cath), 2344 (Cath, Rev)	81, 323 (Cath), **945** (Acts, Cath), **1006** (Rev), **1854** (Rev), **1962, 2298** (Cath)	28, **104** (exc. Acts, Rev), **181** (exc. Rev), **323** (exc. Cath), **398** (Cath), **424, 431** (Acts, Cath), **436, 451** (Paul), **459** (Paul), 623, 700, 788, **1243** (exc. Cath), **1448** (Cath), **1505** (exc. Evv), **1838, 1846** (exc. Acts), **1908**, **2138** (exc. Rev), **2147** (Cath), **2298** (exc. Cath, Paul), **2344** (exc. Cath, Rev), **2596?**		103, 104 (Acts, Rev), 181 (Rev), 398 (exc. Cath), 431 (Evv, Paul), 451 (exc. Paul), 459 (exc. Paul), 945 (Evv, Paul), 1006 (Evv), **1448** (exc. Cath), **1505** (Evv), **1846** (Acts), 1854 (exc. Rev), 2138 (Rev), 2147 (exc. Cath), **2298** (Paul)
11th / 12th		256 (Paul), **1735** (Cath)	**1735** (exc. Cath), **1910**		256 (exc. Paul)
12th	1241 (Cath)	**36** (Acts), **610** (Acts), **1611** (Rev), 2050, **2127** (Paul)	1 (Evv), **36** (Cath), **88, 94?** (Rev), **157**, 326, **330** (Paul), **346, 378** (Cath), **543, 826, 828**, **917** (Paul), **983**, 1071, **1241** (exc. Acts, Cath), **1319** (Paul), **1359** (Cath), **1542b** (Mk), **1611** (exc. Rev), **1718**, **1942, 2030, 2412**, **2541** (Cath), 2744		1 (Acts-Paul), **180** (Evv), **189** (Acts-Paul), **330** (exc. Paul), **378** (exc. Cath), **610** (Cath), **911**, **917** (exc. Paul), **1010, 1241** (Acts), **1319** (exc. Paul), **1359** (exc. Cath), **1542b?** (Lk), **2127** (exc. Paul), **2541** (exc. Cath)
12th / 13th			**1573** (Paul)		**1573** (exc. Paul)

	Category I	Category II	Category III	Category IV	Category V
13th	2053, 2062	442, 579 (Mk, Lk), 1292 (Cath), 1852 (Cath)	6 (Cath, Paul), 13, 94 (exc. Paul, Rev), 180 (Acts), 206 (Cath), 218 (Cath, Paul, 263 (Paul), 365 (Paul), 441, 614, 720 (Cath), 915, 1398 (Paul), 1563, 1642 (Acts), 1852 (exc. Cath, Rev), 2374 (Cath), 2492 (Cath, Paul) 2516 (Paul), 2542, 2718?		6 (Evv, Acts), 94? (Paul), 180 (Cath, Paul, Rev), 206 (Acts, Paul), 218 (Evv, Acts), 263 (exc. Paul), 365 (exc. Paul), 597, 720 (exc. Cath), 1251?, 1292 (exc. Cath), 1398 (exc. Paul), 1642 (exc. Acts), 1852 (Rev), 2374 (exc. Cath), 2400, 2492? (exc. Cath, Paul), 2516 (exc. Paul)
13th/14th			1342 (Mk)		
14th	2427	1067 (Cath), 1409 (Acts, Cath), 1506 (Paul), 1881	5 (Acts-Paul), 209 (Evv), 254 (Cath), 429 (exc. Paul, Rev), 453, 621, 629, 630, 1523 (exc. Paul), 1524 (Cath), 1678?, 1842, 1877 (Paul), 2005, 2197, 2200 (exc. Evv), 2377 Evv), 2377		5? (Evv), 189 (Evv), 209 (exc. Evv, Rev), 254 (exc. Cath), 429 (Paul), 1067 (exc. Cath), 1409 (Evv, Paul), 1506 (Evv), 1523 (Paul), 1524 (exc. Cath), 1877 (exc. Paul), 2200 (Evv, Rev)
14th/15th			2495		
15th		322 (Cath)	69 (Paul), 205 (Evv, Rev), 209 (Rev), 322 (exc. Cath), 467 (Paul), 642 (Cath), 1751, 1844, 1959, 2523 (Paul), 2652 (Cath)		69 (exc. Paul), 181 (Rev), 205 (Acts, Paul), 429 (Rev), 467 (exc. Paul), 642 (Acts, Paul), 886, 2523 (exc. Paul), 2652? (Acts, Paul)
16th			61 (Cath, Paul, Rev), 522 (Acts, Cath), 918 (Cath), 1704 (Acts), 1884		61 (Evv, Acts), 522 (exc. Acts, Cath), 918 (Paul), 1704 (exc. Acts)
16th/17th and later			849, 2544 (Paul)		2544 (exc. Paul)

The above survey calls for a few comments. Manuscripts of more than ten folios are shown in boldface in order to make them more easily distinguishable. Thus every papyrus fragment in category I naturally has in principle a value equal to that of papyri comprising ten or more folios, but their special frequency in the third century, for example, deserves notice. The same is true in category II for uncials of the fifth and sixth centuries. Categories III and V require no

further comment. About sixty uncials appear in the column for category V, with nearly forty of them in boldface. These are all either purely or predominantly of the Majority text and are therefore classified in category V; they are almost all cited in the critical apparatuses of both Nestle-Aland[26] and *GNT*[3] because both editions have hitherto adopted the principle of citing not only the witness of all the papyri but of all the uncials as well. This principle calls for serious reconsideration: it has already been modified in the 13th edition of *Synopsis Quattuor Evangeliorum,* and it is probable that one of the next thorough revisions of Nestle-Aland will follow suit. It is not only misleading for the reader, who may naively assume that all uncials are of equal value, but it also occupies too much space in the critical apparatus where the witness of these uncials is adequately represented by $\mathfrak{M}$ (in Nestle[26]) and *Byz* (in *GNT*). It is only because of this circumstance that the uncials of category V have been included individually in the above survey. The number could have been expanded considerably by adding the nearly twelve hundred minuscules with a Byzantine text listed on pp. 138ff. These were omitted to restrict the list to manuscripts with a significance for textual criticism. In any event, the student of the Greek New Testament should commit to memory at least the papyri, uncials, and minuscules in boldface in categories I and II. If those in category III can be included, so much the better, but if not, then constant reference to table 8 is strongly recommended as a simplifying aid for research.

11. *THE LECTIONARIES*

To this point we have been concerned exclusively with continuous text manuscripts, i.e., with manuscripts containing the uninterrupted text of at least one New Testament book. These include (with only a few exceptions) all the papyri, all the uncials, and all the minuscules. But in addition to these continuous text manuscripts, which number approximately 3,200, there are 2,280 more lectionary manuscripts, i.e., manuscripts in which the text of the New Testament books is divided into separate pericopes, arranged according to their sequence as lessons appointed for the church year. There are many different kinds of lectionaries. There are lectionaries with lessons principally for Saturday and Sunday services, and lectionaries with lessons for services on other days of the week. The latter were probably intended for monasteries where services were said daily, while the former were for parish use. Then there were lectionaries containing only the Gospel lessons, and others with lessons only from the Apostolos (i.e., the rest of the New Testament apart from Revelation, which was not read in the Byzantine lectionary system). There were also lectionaries with texts from both the Gospels and the Apostolos. The lectionaries included in the list of New Testament manuscripts present a most varied assortment of types, even apart from about two hundred entries which actually should not have been included at all because they are only broadly of a liturgical nature, containing only scattered New Testament texts (this heritage from the past will not easily be shed).

Plate 52. The uncial lectionary ℓ 1575 (earlier identified as 0129 and 0203, ninth century, Greek-Coptic): 1 Pet. 2:24–3:4 Coptic, 5:1-5 Greek, 5:1 Coptic. The Greek text is of remarkably good quality.

Plate 53. A curiosity: a slipper carved by a monk from *ℓ* 974, a thirteenth-century minuscule lectionary. The lessons shown are from the gospels of Mark and Luke (during Lent).

A complete lectionary in the Byzantine tradition is made up of two parts, called the synaxarion and the menologion. The text of the synaxarion begins with Easter and proceeds through the "regular" services of the church year (a total of fifty-seven weeks, considering the accommodations necessary for the varying dates of Easter). The menologion begins on September 1 (i.e., the beginning of the civil year) and provides texts for set days celebrating events in the lives of Jesus and Mary, for feasts of the great apostles and church teachers, of the saints and martyrs of the church, and finally (appended) for special needs of the church in both public and private life (i.e., occasional services). Naturally the synaxarion had from the first a more fixed form then the menologion, because the latter varied by region in the particular saints who were celebrated only locally, and any lesson appointed for them would be limited to manuscripts of a local tradition.

The synaxarion provides for reading through the New Testament by a carefully developed system evidently given its final form by a central authority. With regard to Gospel lessons, the Saturday-Sunday lessons for the first part of the church year from Easter to Pentecost are taken from the gospel of John (here the lectionaries also include lessons for weekday services, because in this season daily services are observed for which the lessons are also taken from the gospel of John). From the Monday after Pentecost to mid-September (a period of sixteen weeks) the Gospels for the Saturday-Sunday services are from Matthew; for the weekday services during the first eleven weeks they are also read from Matthew, but from the twelfth week they are from Mark. The Saturday-Sunday lessons from mid-September (Holy Cross Day) to Lent are taken from Luke, as are the weekday lessons usually for the first twelve weeks, and then to the end of the seventeenth week the lessons are from the second half of Mark. For the six Saturday-Sunday services to Palm Sunday ten lessons are from Mark and two from John. Then in Holy Week the Passion Narrative is read from all four Gospels. So much for the Gospel lessons — an account of the distribution of the Apostolos may be omitted here.

There is now the question of the antiquity of this system which has been preserved with such impressive consistency by the Greek lectionaries (apart from a very few important exceptions). The date of its introduction has definite implications for the kind of text found in its original exemplars. If it were anterior to A.D. 300, it would represent the text of the early period. If it were of the fourth century there would be several possibilities, depending on the region in which it was composed. If it were somewhat later, or even considerably later, it would most probably have been based on the Byzantine Imperial text. Caspar René Gregory believed (although he stated it cautiously as a "theory") that the beginnings of the Saturday-Sunday sequence of lessons "probably" go back to the first half of the second century, and the rest to "the late second century." He regarded the completion of the weekday system as impossible before the age of Constantine, and this is the latest date he would propose. We can observe here the fatal consequences incurred when textual critics pay inadequate attention to the history of the church and of the canon (even in 1972 Bruce M. Metzger still

wrote: "Whether these dates are too early, it is not for the present writer to judge"; yet he preferred to believe, in agreement with the majority of lectionary scholars among whom he is himself outstanding, "that the lectionary system current today in the Orthodox Church had its origin sometime during the fourth century").[36]

Now the textual critic is particularly impressed by the fact that the notes ἀρχ(ή) and τέλ(ος) are found in so many manuscripts, either in the text or in the margin, and further by the fact that lists are found at the beginning or at the end of manuscripts of the pericopes which are marked in this way. Then in chart 3 showing the chronological listing of lectionary manuscripts (cf. p. 82) some are dated as early as the fourth century. But it is striking that of all the lectionaries which can actually be dated before the eighth century (and not all have been accurately dated!), there is not one exhibiting a system of pericopes that agrees in the least with that of the normal Greek lectionary. Furthermore, the earliest of the ἀρχή/τέλος notes comes from the eighth century: there is no trace of this pattern from any earlier period.

Obviously Gregory's reconstruction is without any historical foundation. Not until Justin Martyr, about A.D. 150, do quotations from the New Testament become at all recognizable,[37] and it was the end of the second century before the Four Gospels corpus was itself established. The Pauline corpus in its full form was certainly adopted earlier, but the Catholic letters as a whole corpus were not recognized before the fourth century. It is very difficult to imagine a lectionary system based on a full New Testament canon "in the late second century" (even without Revelation, of course, and a few other minor exceptions). Even in the fourth century it would still be problematic. Only then did most of the Catholic letters become commonly accepted in the Church (with more or less hesitation),[38] and it must have taken several more generations before they could be integrated in a system of liturgical pericopes, accepted on a par with the traditional scriptures of the Church. This suggests that even a fourth-century date for the origin of a lectionary system is doubtful.

It may be objected that lectionary manuscripts actually existed in the fourth century, but this is beside the point because these early manuscripts represent something quite different from the Byzantine lectionary system — a system which is understandably although incorrectly assumed to represent the only lectionary system because it is found in more than two thousand manuscripts. As the papyri and the lectionary texts prove, the church in Egypt had another lectionary. Jerusalem had its own form (attested in late Greek manuscripts recently discovered in the Sinai monastery), as did Antioch, despite the fact that Greek manuscripts of their traditions have not survived (in contrast to

---

36. "Greek Lectionaries and a Critical Edition of the Greek New Testament," *Die alten Übersetzungen des Neuen Testaments, die Kirchenväterzitate und Lektionare*, ed. Kurt Aland. ANTF 5 (Berlin: 1972): 483, 495-96.

37. Cf. p. 55.

38. Cf. p. 49.

Egypt). Far too little research has been done on the lectionary text, again because textual critics have ignored the general historical presuppositions of the documents manuscripts they study. Lectionaries are not related simply to the history of the New Testament text: they are essentially far more closely related to the history of the liturgy. They are the product of liturgical needs, and liturgical necessities have constantly influenced their form (cf., for example, the menologion). Research in the lectionaries should have started with an appreciation of liturgical studies. It should have been known that the Byzantine calendar arose in the period between the mid-seventh century and the first half of the eighth century, and that as Albert Ehrhard, the dean of liturgical scholars, stated in 1937 in his fundamental study on the transmission and present state of hagiographic and homiletic literature, "that this innovation . . . also extended to the Old Testament and New Testament lessons appointed for the great feasts and the Sundays of the movable church year."[39]

This arrangement of lessons certainly did not emerge suddenly from nowhere. The Church had long associated certain feasts with certain scripture passages — almost inevitably for Holy Week, Easter, Pentecost, as well as for particular dominical feasts (cf. the early evidence of the papyri) — but when and how a fixed lectionary system was developed for the whole Church is not at all clear. Chrysostom (d. 407), with his great cycles of homilies, does not provide the evidence frequently attributed to him. His exegesis of whole books at a time would seem rather to argue against the existence of a fixed lectionary as early as the fourth century, and for a tradition of expounding the New Testament scriptures continuously by books. Chrysostom's habit of not commenting on every verse, simply skipping over some texts, would seem to show that he was attracted by particularly preachable texts. The fact that the beginnings of his sermon texts often coincide with the Byzantine lectionary system is hardly an argument: a fair amount of coincidental agreement is only to be expected in analyses of the New Testament text, however independent the approaches. Yet it should not be denied that in the Byzantine church — probably even in the fourth century — particular texts for particular services, and even particular sequences of texts, had become more or less established in usage. But the Byzantine lectionary system as it is found in the "normal" New Testament lectionary was evidently not developed until the seventh/eighth century. This date was proposed by Klaus Junack in 1970 at a session of the Institute for New Testament Textual Research,[40] and I believe it deserves preference over other dates suggested in the literature on lectionaries.

The text we find in the lectionaries agrees completely with this dating (Junack's study reviewed a greater number of manuscripts than was used for all the lectionary studies in the Chicago series). Even Metzger concedes that "ba-

---

39. Albert Ehrhard, *Überlieferung und Bestand der hagiographischen und homiletischen Literatur der griechischen Kirche von den Anfängen bis zum Ende des 16. Jahrhunderts 1.* TU, ser. 4, 511 (Leipzig: 1937): 34.

40. Published in "Zu den griechischen Lektionaren und ihrer Überlieferung der Katholischen Briefe," ANTF 5 (1972): 498-591.

sically, the Greek lectionary text presents a Byzantine type of text."[41] Actually, the text we find in the Greek lectionaries is almost identical with the Byzantine Imperial text. The results of lectionary research in America (which has centered primarily in Chicago) were far less conclusive than was imagined because the collations were made against the Textus Receptus (Oxford 1873 edition). When variants from this base were found in the lectionaries they were thought to be traces of an earlier text, whereas only too frequently they merely represented deviations of the printed Textus Receptus from the Byzantine Imperial text. Although the Textus Receptus shows a notable textual consistency, it does occasionally divide into two separate traditions, and furthermore it is also typically a "living text,"[42] with all the possibilities of variation this implies.

The lectionary text is similarly a living tradition. However firmly established the pericope system might be, the scribe would still be reminded of parallel passages, e.g., in copying the Gospels, so that a susceptibility to the same tendencies were operative here as for the scribe of a continuous text manuscript.[43] But the critical factor overriding all other considerations is the fact that for the lectionary scribe the exemplar used was itself a lectionary manuscript. It is most improbable that a scribe preparing a lectionary manuscript would follow a schedule of lesson references to transcribe the texts afresh from one or more continuous text manuscripts. Such a process would have required far too much effort, and is conceivable only at the initial compilation stage of the lectionary system. While with text manuscripts it is possible to assume that a scribe could move from one exemplar to another, thereby changing from one text type to another, with lectionary manuscripts such a possibility is ruled out (apart from absolute exceptions). The very complexity of the lectionary structure made it necessary for the scribe to follow the exemplar with the closest attention (in comparison with the rules generally observed by scribes copying continuous text manuscripts of the New Testament).

Summarizing these considerations we can only conclude that for New Testament textual criticism, so far as the original text and its early history is concerned, nearly all the approximately 2,300 lectionary manuscripts can be of significance only in exceptional instances. And yet they can be important for the later history of the text. For this reason only five lectionary manuscripts are noted after the hundreds of text manuscripts listed in appendix I of Nestle-Aland[26]. But this may change because lectionaries with an independent text have been found not only among the recent discoveries at Sinai, but also in the preparations for *GNT*[4]. Finally, in concluding these remarks on the lectionaries, the fact should not be ignored that even "normal" lectionaries also exercised an influence on continuous text manuscripts because a monastic scribe would be particularly familiar with their readings from constant repetition in worship services. This is particularly true for the beginnings of the pericopes, i.e., of the lessons. A passage read in the worship service would frequently

41. ANTF 5 (1972): 495.
42. Cf. p. 69.
43. *Idem.*

need some adaptation in its introductory phrasing to provide contextual information about who is speaking and to whom, as well as the place and occasion
of the event, etc. The most frequent formulas are: εἶπεν ὁ κύριος, τῷ καιρῷ
ἐκείνῳ, ἐν ταῖς ἡμέραις ἐκείναις, etc. When such phrases occur in text
manuscripts at the beginnings of lessons, their source and secondary nature are
evident. Introductory phrases are often altered for stylistic reasons, and concluding phrases adapted or expanded for greater effect. In this respect the
lectionaries should always be considered when working in textual criticism. A
recognition of their characteristics is useful in evaluating a large number of
variant readings.

List of Recently Discovered Lectionaries

𝓵 2210 𝓵 ᵃ (Greek-Coptic), sixth/seventh century, uncial, pch. Florence: Biblioteca Medicea
    Laurenziana, PL III/550
𝓵 2211 𝓵 (Greek-Arabic), 995/996, uncial, pa. Sinai: St. Catherine's Monastery, Arab. 116
𝓵 2212-𝓵2259 Manuscripts newly discovered at Sinai, St. Catherine's Monastery
𝓵 2260 𝓵 ᵃP, fourteenth, pch. Athos: Grigoriou 158 (X 36) A; fol. 1-23, 25-50
𝓵 2261 𝓵 eP, eleventh, pch. Athos: Grigoriou 182 A; fol. 1
𝓵 2262 𝓵 P, fourteenth, pch. Athos: Grigoriou 182 B; fol. 9
𝓵 2263 𝓵 P, eleventh, pch. Athos: Grigoriou 182 C; fol. 11, 12
𝓵 2264 𝓵 P, fourteenth, pch. Athos: Grigoriou 182 D; fol. 27
𝓵 2265 𝓵 e†, twelfth, pch. Athos: Iviron 28 (X 15)
𝓵 2266 𝓵 e, thirteenth, pch. Athos: Iviron 30 (X 1)
𝓵 2267 𝓵 e, twelfth, pch. Athos: Iviron 46 (X 4)
𝓵 2268 𝓵 e, thirteenth, pch. Athos: Iviron 73 (X 17)
𝓵 2269 𝓵 esk, twelfth, pch. Athos: Iviron 75 (X 14)
𝓵 2270 𝓵 e†, thirteenth, pch. Athos: Iviron 111 (X 18)
𝓵 2271 𝓵 e, fifteenth, pa. Athos: Iviron 193 (X 9)
𝓵 2272 𝓵 esk†, twelfth, pch. Cairo: Coptic Museum 2912
𝓵 2273 𝓵 e, 1672, pa. Seriphos: Taxiarchon 1
𝓵 2274 𝓵 ⁺ᵃ(e)sk†, seventeenth, pa. Seriphos: Taxiarchon 21
𝓵 2275 𝓵 ⁺ᵃsel, fifteenth, pa. Salonica: Vlatadon
𝓵 2276 𝓵 esk†,thirteenth/fourteenth, pch. Münster: Bible Museum Ms. 21
𝓵 2277 𝓵 P: John sk Matthew, thirteenth, pch. Athens: Archbishopric 6
𝓵 2278 𝓵 ⁺ᵃ, sixteenth, pa. Skopelos: Moni Timiou 5
𝓵 2279 𝓵 esk, twelfth, pch. Kapstadt: Suid-Afrikaanse Biblioteek 4 C 1
𝓵 2280 𝓵 e, 1269, pch. Kapstadt: Suid-Afrikaanse Biblioteek 4 C 6
𝓵 2281 𝓵 e, twelfth/thirteenth, pch. Birmingham: Woodbrooke College

Key to sigla for lectionaries:

𝓵   = the text of the Gospel lessons following the Byzantine Church order.
𝓵 ᵃ   = the text of the Apostolos (Acts and letters) following the Byzantine Church order.
𝓵 ⁺ᵃ = the text of the Apostolos and of the Gospels following the Byzantine Church order.
𝓵 e   = weekday Gospel lessons.
𝓵 sk = Saturday/Sunday Gospel lessons only.
𝓵 esk = weekday Gospel lessons from Easter to Pentecost and Saturday/Sunday Gospel lessons for
    the other weeks.
sel   = lessons for selected days only.
P   = fragment (pars). Textual contents indicated after colon.
†   = with lacunae.

12. *PATRISTIC CITATIONS*

It is as true of New Testament quotations in the Church Fathers as it is of the versions that they are often misjudged and consequently misused. The route from a modern edition of a Church Father's works back to the text which he read in his New Testament may be long and tortuous. To begin with, not all patristic works of importance for textual criticism are available in critical editions, and all too frequently a student's only resource is Jacques Paul Migne, ed., *Patrologia,* or something similar. But even when a modern critical edition is available there is no certainty that it preserves the New Testament quotations of a work as they occurred in its original form.

Take the ideal example of a Church Father's commentary on a New Testament book, which promises to yield the greatest number of quotations. Not only are there constant citations from the book commented on in the commentary proper, but there is usually also the complete text (called the lemma) preceding the commentary. The text of the lemma was endangered from the start because its very length offered a constant temptation to the copyist to replace it with a familiar form. Consequently the lemma must be used with caution and under the constant control of quotations in the commentary itself. The lemma text may be accepted as authentic only when there is positive agreement, and even then only if the editor has edited the text correctly, neither following a poor tradition nor simply replacing the manuscript tradition with one personally preferred. It is bad enough when an edition of Cyprian's works (in *Corpus Scriptorum Ecclesiasticorum Latinorum* [*CSEL*], an outstanding series) can evoke the comment, "It is now generally acknowledged that in its treatment of Cyprian's biblical quotations it erred in following the wrong group of witnesses. The kind of Bible used by the African Father cannot be learned from the edited text, but must be gathered from the apparatus." But it is even worse when an editor not only fails to reconstruct the text of the New Testament quotations successfully (either due to ignorance of the problems involved, or to a simple lack of interest in them) but also neglects completely to record the variant readings in the tradition or gives them inadequately at best. Certainly no one today follows the example of the edition of Cyril of Alexandria of a century ago, where the editor did not collate the lemmata in the manuscripts but only noted their first and last words, and then supplied the text between them from a printed New Testament text. And yet there are today more problems connected with the New Testament quotations, even in the works of outstanding editors, than would be imagined.

Further, even when the text of a Father can be accepted as reliably edited, the problems are not yet over. Very frequently there are new problems. Passage by passage it must be established whether the text is a quotation from the New Testament (and if so, from which book — a difficult if not impossible distinction with parallel Gospel passages) or only an allusion. While this may be relatively easy to do in commentaries, these constitute only a small fraction of the patristic literature. If it is a quotation, the next question is whether the Father was intentionally rephrasing or was quoting from memory, or if it can be assumed that he was copying the text from a manuscript—for only then

would it have full value as a witness. But this does not mean that only such quotations should be collated. Rather, from the beginning all the allusions should also be brought together representing as many different occasions of reference as possible, so that they may all make their contribution to a decision. Nor should examination be restricted to the passages editors have noted in the indexes of their editions: the student should read the texts in their context (repeatedly) with a New Testament concordance at hand, even when the New Testament text is familiar. Its careful use may reveal rich sources where none had been suspected. With the use of proper methods the results can be significant. Although past generations have produced a whole range of studies on the text of the New Testament used by various Church Fathers, there is not one of them which would not be worth doing over, beginning with Marcion and continuing with Justin and Irenaeus. For Marcion, Adolf Harnack's collection[44] would still be the basis, but it could be improved and developed throughout; it is amazing how many modern critical apparatuses cite Marcion as witnessing an omission, for example, merely because Harnack does not cite him as including a particular passage. Although the magnum opus of Irenaeus, *Adversus haereses,* is preserved almost exclusively in a Latin version from a later period, it is such a literal translation that the text of Irenaeus' New Testament can practically be reconstructed from it. Especially in Irenaeus we have an example of a control in two respects: first for our great papyri with the text of the early period, and second for the development of a "Western" text in the second century. We should note here in passing that in any case the text of the New Testament in Tertullian and Irenaeus is of critical significance for tracing the early history of the Latin version (for patristic quotations in the languages represented by the early versions. cf. pp. 214f.). There have been many attempts to solve the great riddle of the New Testament text used by Origen, but always on much too narrow a basis and with unrealistic presuppositions. If the question of the existence of a "Caesarean text" and its character is to be answered fully and finally, this must be done from Origen's quotations. But it still remains unexplained why most of the known alternative readings are also usually found attested in Origen's writings. Nor has anyone yet been able to trace the "Caesarean text" in Eusebius of Caesarea, although Eusebius is the most likely creator and promoter of this text type in view of his scriptorium and the influence he enjoyed in official places.

And so we could continue. Establishing the New Testament text of the Church Fathers has a strategic importance for textual history and criticism. It shows us how the text appeared at particular times and in particular places: this is information we can find nowhere else. With a Greek manuscript there is no way of knowing the age of the exemplar it was copied from, nor when we know the provenance of a manuscript (as we do in exceptional instances) is there any way of knowing the provenance of its exemplar, which is even more important. Only the papyri from the period before A.D. 300 may be relied on for such information, but these are relevant only to developments in Egypt when it was

---

44. *Marcion: Das Evangelium vom fremden Gott.* TU 45 (Leipzig: 1921; ²1929).

hardly a leading province of the Church. For an appreciation of the development of the text in the major church centers of the period they are useless.[45] Many important tasks challenge us here. With more adequate information about the Church Fathers' text of the New Testament we would have firmer guidelines for a history of the text. This is a field ripe for innumerable doctoral dissertations and learned investigations. Any volunteers?

Descriptive List of Greek Church Fathers

And now, one more practical tool. In the introductions to *GNT*[3] (pp. xxxvii-x1) and to Nestle-Aland[26] (p. 62*) the names of the Church Fathers cited in their respective critical apparatuses are listed (in Nestle the abbreviations used are also indicated), and the attempt is made to identify them further for the reader by adding their dates. But we suspect that this is inadequate (not without some justification). At times the student may be confused by the Latin form of a name in Nestle-Aland[26] when the English form is more familiar, and frequently enough a relatively unknown Church Father is referred to. Therefore in the following list of the Greek Church Fathers cited in these two editions, besides giving the abbreviations used in Nestle-Aland[26] and the alternative forms not so readily recognized from the forms used in *GNT,* the attempt is made to provide at least enough information to suggest for the reader something of the person behind the name. It should also be noted that the number of Church Fathers cited in *GNT* is far too large (the relation of quantity to quality is disproportionate), and some considerations have been realized in *GNT*[4]. But because their names have been cited it is necessary to include them in this introduction together with some descriptive comment, even at the expense of extending the survey unduly and disproportionately despite all efforts to be concise. For those interested in more information about individual Church Fathers than can be given in these necessarily brief notes, bibliographical references are included citing current manuals and reference works where more can be found. For convenience the following bibliography includes references for the Fathers in the languages of the early versions listed below, pp. 215-221.

Altaner	Berthold Altaner, *Patrologie: Leben, Schriften und Lehre der Kirchenväter*, ed. A. Stuiber (Freiburg and Basel: [9]1980). *Patrology,* Eng. trans. by Hilda C. Graef [based on [2]1961 ed.] (New York: 1961)
Assfalg	Julius Assfalg and Paul Krüger, *Kleines Wörterbuch des christlichen Orients* (Wiesbaden: 1975)
Bardenh.	Otto Bardenhewer, *Geschichte der Altkirchlichen Literatur.* 5 vols. (1913-1932; repr. Darmstadt: 1962)
Baumstark	Anton Baumstark, *Geschichte der syrischen Literatur* (1922; repr. Berlin: 1968)
Beck	Hans-Georg Beck, *Kirche und theologische Literatur im Byzantinischen Reich.* Handbuch der Altertumswissenschaft XII/2.1 (1959; repr. Munich: [2]1977)

45. Cf. p. 53.

BHG	François Halkin, *Bibliotheca hagiographica graeca*. Subsidia hagiographica 8a. 3 vols. (Brussels: 1957)
BHL	*Bibliotheca hagiographica latina et mediae aetatis*. Subsidia hagiographica 6. 2 vols. (Brussels: 1898-1901)
BHO	Paul Peeters, *Bibliotheca hagiographica orientalis*. Subsidia hagiographica 10 (Brussels: 1910)
Cayré	Fulbert Cayré, *Patrology and History of Theology,* Trans. H. Howitt. 2 vols. (Paris: 1936-1940) [Based on *Précis de Patrologie et d'Histoire de la Théologie* (Paris: 1927-1930)]
Cross	Frank Leslie Cross and Elizabeth A. Livingstone, *The Oxford Dictionary of the Christian Church* (Oxford: ²1974)
CPG	Mauritius Geerard, *Clavis Patrum Graecorum*. 5 vols. (Turnhout: 1974-1987) [Cited by number]
CPL	Eligius Dekkers, *Clavis Patrum Latinorum*. Sacris Eruditi III (Steinbrügge: ²1961) [Cited by number]
Ehrhard	Albert Ehrhard, "Theologie," in Krumbacher, *q.v.*
Fischer	Bonafatius Fischer, *Vetus Latina: Die Reste der altlateinischen Bibel*. I/1: *Verzeichnis der Sigel für Kirchenschriftsteller* (Freiburg: 1963)
Hunger	Herbert Hunger, *Die hochsprachliche profane Literatur der Byzantiner.* Handbuch der Altertumswissenschaft XII/5.1. 2 vols. (Munich: 1978)
Jurgens	W. A. Jurgens, *The Faith of the Early Fathers*. 3 vols. (Collegeville: 1970-1979)
Krumbacher	Karl Krumbacher, *Geschichte der byzantinischen Literatur von Justinian bis zum Ende des oströmischen Reiches (527-1453)*. Handbuch der klassischen Altertumswissenschaft IX/1 (Munich: ²1897)
Manitius	Maximilianus Manitius, *Geschichte der lateinischen Literatur des Mittelalters*. Handbuch der Altertumswissenschaft IX/2.1-3. 3 vols. (Munich: 1911-1931)
Ortiz de Urbina	Ignacio Ortiz de Urbina, *Patrologia Syriaca* (Rome: ²1965)
Quasten	Johannes Quasten, *Patrology*. 3 vols. (Utrecht: 1950-1960)
Spicq	Ceslas Spicq, *Esquisse d'une histoire de exégèse latine au moyen-âge* (Paris: 1944)
Stegmüller	Friedrich Stegmüller, *Repertorium Biblicum Medii Aevi*. 7 vols. (Madrid: 1950-1961) [Cited by number]

In Nestle-Aland[26] and (even more freely) in *GNT* the following Greek Church Fathers are cited in the apparatus.

Acacius of Caesarea (Acac[ius Caesariensis]), d. 365/366. Student of Eusebius and his successor as bishop of Caesarea. Altaner, 224 (Eng. trans., 271); Bardenh., III:262; Cayré, 316; Cross, 8f.; *CPG*, 3510-15; Jurgens, I:347.

Adamantius (Ad). The dialogue *De recta in deum fide* with Adamantius as defender of the faith was written in Syria or in Asia Minor and circulated under the name of Origen, although directed against him. Written after 325, it was translated into Latin by Rufinus. Altaner, 216 (Eng. trans., 244); Quasten, II:146-47; Bardenh., III:553-54; Cayré, I:287; Cross, 15; Jurgens, III:245.

Africanus, mid-second to mid-third centuries. Sextus Julius Africanus, born in Jerusalem, friend of Origen, founded the public library in the Pantheon of Rome for Caesar Alexander Severus, and wrote the first Christian world history and an encyclopedia *(Kestoi = Embroideries).* Altaner, 209-210 (Eng. trans. 235-36); Bardenh., II:263-271; Cayré, I:279-280; Cross, 768.

Alexander of Alexandria, 312/313-328. Bishop of Alexandria when the Arian controversy erupted. Only fragments of his writings survive in Greek. Altaner, 269 (Eng. trans., 309-310); Quasten, III:13-19; Bardenh., III:34-41; Cayré, I:327-28; Cross, 33; Jurgens, I:300; *CPG,* 2000-2021.

Ammonius, third century. Bishop of Thmuis in Lower Egypt, noted by Eusebius as an Alexandrian contemporary of Origen, probably to be identified as the editor of a Gospels synopsis (based on Matthew's order) used by Eusebius. Altaner, 210 (Eng. trans., 236-37); Bardenh., II:198-202; Cayré, I:279; Cross, 45.

Ammonius of Alexandria, fifth or sixth century. A presbyter. Fragments of his commentaries on Daniel, John, and Acts are preserved in catenae. Altaner, 516-17 (Eng. trans., 328); Bardenh., IV:83-86; Cayré, II:102; Jurgens, III:305; *CPG,* 5500-5509.

Amphilochius of Iconium, 340/345-after 394. Friend of the three great Cappadocians, student of Libanius, in 373 bishop of Iconium at the instance of Basil the Great. Altaner, 308-309 (Eng. trans., 357-58); Quasten, III:296-300; Bardenh., III:220-28; Cayré, I:430-31; Cross, 46; Jurgens, III:64-65; *CPG,* 3230-3254.

Anastasius I of Antioch, d. 599. From Palestine, first a monk, then Alexandrian patriarchal delegate in Antioch, from 559 Patriarch of Antioch, deposed in 570 and restored in 593 after more than twenty years in exile. His dogmatic writings and sermons survive only partially in Latin translation. Beck, 380-81; Altaner, 512 (Eng. trans., 619); Bardenh., V:146-49; Cayré, II:296; *CPG,* 6944-6969.

Anastasius Abbot (Anast[asius] S[inaita]), d. soon after 700. Monk and abbot at Sinai. In Egypt and Syria for controversies. Writings include exegetical works in the Alexandrian tradition, also *Eroteseis kai Apokriseis.* Beck, 442-46; Altaner, 524-25 (Eng. trans., 633-34); Bardenh., V:41-46; Cayré, II:296-97; Cross, 49; Jurgens, I:81, 277; *CPG,* 7745-7758.

Andreas (Andrew) of Caesarea, sixth/seventh century. Archbishop of Caesarea in Cappadocia, wrote a commentary on Revelation. Beck, 418-19; Altaner, 517 (Eng. trans., 625); Bardenh., V:102-105; *CPG,* 7478-79.

Andrew of Crete (Andr[eas Cretensis]), ca. 670-740. From Damascus, 678 monk in Monastery of the Holy Sepulchre in Jerusalem and cleric, 685 deacon in Constantinople, 692 Metropolitan of Crete. Beck, 500-502; Altaner, 534 (Eng. trans., 645); Bardenh., V:152-57; Cayré, II:292-93; Cross, 51; Jurgens, III:325; *CPG,* 8170-8228.

Anthony (Antonius), eleventh/twelfth century. Called "Melissa" after his work of that name, a collection of ethicoreligious selections drawn from John of Damascus' *Sacred Parallels* and Maximus' *Eclogues* (eighth century). Beck, 643.

Antiochus, seventh century. Born in Ancyra (Ankara), a monk in Sabas monastery, earned the sobriquet "Pandect" ("codifier") for his magnum opus, a compilation of a large number of biblical and patristic quotations (including the Shepherd of Hermas and other Apostolic Fathers) arranged for monastic use in 130 sections. Not to be confused with Antiochus Strategius. Beck, 449; Altaner, 519 (Eng. trans., 627); Bardenh., V:77-79; Cayré, II:324-25; *CPG,* 7842-44.

Apollinaris the Younger, of Laodicea, ca. 310-390. Bishop of Laodicea in Syria from 361. About 374 in Antioch as teacher of Jerome, who attests to his lost commentaries on several Old Testament as well as New Testament books. Altaner, 313-15 (Eng. trans., 363-65); Quasten, III:377-383; Bardenh., III:285-291; Cayré, I:447-452; Cross, 72-73; Jurgens, II:54-55; *CPG,* 3645-3700.

Apostolic Canons, late fourth century. Eighty-five canons appended as the last chapter of the *Apostolic Constitutions,* Book VIII, treating of the selection, consecration, and duties of the clergy; fifty canons were translated into Latin by Dionysius Exiguus in the sixth century for his collection of canons. Beck, 143; Altaner, 256 (Eng. trans., 59-60); Bardenh., IV:266-67; Cayré, I:372-73; Cross, 75; Jurgens, II:130.

Apostolic Constitutions, ca. 380. The largest canonical-liturgical collection of the early period, probably compiled in Syria (Antioch) by a single editor. Beck, 143; Altaner, 255-56 (Eng. trans., 57-59); Quasten, II:183-85; Bardenh., IV:262-275; Cayré, I:373-74; Cross, 75-76; Jurgens, II:127-28.

Archelaus, first half of fourth century. A bishop who disputed successfully with Mani and his disciple Turbo in the fictional debate *Acta Archelai* by Hegemonius *(q.v.).*

Arethas, ca. 850-after 944. Native of Patrai (Peloponnesus), cleric in Constantinople, *ca.* 902 bishop of Caesarea in Cappadocia (to whom the important primary manuscript of the works of the Apologists is traced). His commentary on Revelation is a revision of the commentary by Andrew of Caesarea. Beck, 591-94; Altaner, 517-18 (Eng. trans., 625); Quasten, I:188.

Aristides, second century. From Athens, author of an Apology addressed to Hadrian or to Antoninus Pius, which was first known only through Eusebius but is now recognized in a Greek (two papyri, *Romance of Barlaam and Joasaph* 26-27), a Syriac, and an Armenian recension. Altaner, 64-65 (Eng. trans., 118-19); Quasten, I:191-95; Bardenh., I:187-202; Cayré, I:111; Cross, 84-85; Jurgens, I:48.

Arius, ca. 260-336. From Libya, a presbyter in Alexandria, student of Lucian of Antioch, his *Thaleia* is preserved only in fragments. Altaner, 269-270 (Eng. trans., 310); Quasten, III:7-13; Bardenh., III:41-42; Cayré, I:313-14; Cross, 87; Jurgens, I:275-77; *CPG,* 2025-2042.

Asterius, d. after 341. Rhetor and sophist, converted to Christianity as a student of Lucian of Antioch. Probably author of homilies on texts from the Gospels and Romans preserved among the pseudo-Chrysostomica. Altaner, 270 (Eng. trans., 311-12); Quasten, III:194-97; Bardenh., III:122-23; Cayré, I:315; Cross, 100; *CPG,* 2815-19.

Athanasius of Alexandria (Ath), 295-373. Native of Alexandria, deacon and secretary to his predecessor Alexander at the Council of Nicea, 325. Patriarch of Alexandria from 328 to his death. A prolific author, but represented today only by fragments of his exegetical writings. Altaner, 271-79 (Eng. trans., 312-323); Quasten, III:20-79; Bardenh., III:44-79; Cayré, I:336-354; Cross, 101-102; Jurgens, I:320-21; *CPG,* 2090-2309.

Athanasius, Ps(eudo)-. Writings wrongly attributed to Athanasius, partly from the eighth century, including a synopsis of the Holy Scriptures. Altaner, 274 (Eng. trans., 315-16, 319-326); Quasten, III:29-34, 39, 65-66; Bardenh., III:46-47.

Athenagoras, second century. An apologist from Athens, *ca.* 177 author of a defense of Christians addressed to Caesar Marcus Aurelius and his son Commodus, also of a work on the Resurrection. Altaner, 74-75 (Eng. trans., 130-31); Quasten, I:229-236; Bardenh., I:289-302; Cayré, I:131-33; Cross, 102-103; Jurgens, I:69.

Basil the Great (Bas[ilius Caesariensis]), ca. 330-379. Known as "the Great" during his own lifetime. From a wealthy family, Christian for generations, he studied in Constantinople and in Athens, then retired to a hermitage in Pontus, from *ca.* 364 a presbyter and counselor to Bishop Eusebius of Caesarea (Asia Minor), succeeding him in 370. Brother of Gregory of Nyssa and friend of Gregory of Nazianzus (the three great Cappadocians). Altaner, 290-98 (Eng. trans., 335-425); Quasten, III:204-236; Bardenh., III:130-162; Cayré, I:406-415; Cross, 139-141; Jurgens, II:3-26; *CPG,* 2835-3005.

Caesarius of Nazianzus, fourth century. Brother of Gregory of Nazianzus, and associated with the *Dialogorum libri quattuor (Erotapokriseis),* which are probably of fourth-century origin. Beck, 388-89; Altaner, 301 (Eng. trans., 348); Cross, 218.

Carpocrates, second century. An Alexandrian gnostic. Altaner, 101 (Eng. trans., 141); Quasten, I:266-67; Bardenh., I:358; Cross, 243.

Chronicon Paschale. See *Paschal Chronicle.*

Chrysostom ([Johannes] Chr[ysostomus]), ca. 344-407. John Chrysostom, born of a wealthy family in Antioch, educated by the rhetor Libanius among others, he once evaded episcopal appointment by flight. Finally deaconed and priested in Antioch where he was soon noted for his sermons (called "the golden mouth" from the sixth century). Against his will he was appointed Patriarch of Constantinople. Intrigues at court led to his exile and

consequent death. The most prolific Eastern theological writer, sermons constitute the greater part of his writings. Altaner, 322-331 (Eng. trans., 373-387); Quasten, III:424-482; Bardenh., III:324-361; Cayré, I:460-493; Cross, 285-86; Jurgens, II:84-126; *CPG*, 4305-4495.

Chrysostomus, Ps(eudo)-. The two best-known spurious works circulated under the name of Chrysostom (apart from numerous homilies) are the *Liturgy of Chrysostom* (still the liturgy of the Orthodox Church) and a *Synopsis Veteris et Novi Testamenti*. Beck, 242-43, 245-46; Altaner, 328 (Eng. trans., 381); Quasten, III:472-73; Bardenh., III:350-52; *CPG*, 4500-5197.

Clement of Alexandria (Cl[emens Alexandrinus]), mid-second century-before 215. Titus Flavius Clemens was probably born of pagan parents in Athens, and from *ca*. 180 was active as a Christian teacher in Alexandria. In the persecution of Christians in Alexandria under Septimius Severus he left Alexandria in 202/203, and died in Asia Minor before 215. Altaner, 190-97 (Eng. trans., 215-222); Quasten, II:5-36; Bardenh., II:40-95; Cayré, I:177-191; Cross, 303; Jurgens, I:176-188.

Clement of Alexandria (Cl[lat]*)*. About 540 Clement of Alexandria's *Hypotyposeis* was translated into Latin for Cassiodorus. The original Greek text of this exposition of 1 Peter, Jude, and 1-2 John is lost. Altaner, 194 (Eng. trans., 218); Quasten, II:16-17; Bardenh., II:72-76, V:277.

Clement of Rome (Cl[emens] R[omanus]), ca. 95. Author of a letter in the name of the church at Rome to the church at Corinth. The second letter ascribed to him in the manuscript tradition is spurious, as are also other writings circulated under his name. Altaner, 45-57 (Eng. trans., 99-103); Quasten, I:42-53; Bardenh., I:116-131; Cayré, I:52-61; Cross, 299-300; Jurgens, I:6-13.

Clement, Ps(eudo)- (Cl[hom]*, Ps-Cl, Pseudo-Clementines)*. An apocryphon describing the life of Clement of Rome in the form of a romantic narrative. The *Recognitions* has survived only in a Latin version which is probably from the fourth century. Altaner, 134-35 (Eng. trans., 103-106); Quasten, I:59-63; Bardenh., II:615-626, I:130-31; Cayré, I:54.

Cosmas Indicopleustes, sixth century. From Egypt (Alexandria?). His work, the *Christianike topographia*, can be dated only by internal evidence. This Christian itinerary is basically an exegetical work. Hunger, I:528-530; Altaner, 517 (Eng. trans., 624); Bardenh., V:95-98; Cross, 350; *CPG*, 7468.

Cyril of Alexandria (Cyr), d. 444. Born of a distinguished family in Alexandria, from 412 Patriarch of Alexandria, one of the leading figures in the christological controversy. The major part of his writings is exegetical. Altaner, 283-88 (Eng. trans., 328-334); Quasten, III:116-142; Bardenh., IV:23-74; Cayré, II:19-40; Cross, 369-370; Jurgens, III:205-236; *CPG*, 5200-5438.

Cyril of Jerusalem (Cyr J), ca. 315-386/387. Born in Jerusalem, became a deacon in 335 and presbyter in 345; was bishop of Jerusalem 348-350, exiled three times, best known for his twenty-four *Catechetical Lectures*. Altaner, 312-13 (Eng. trans., 361-63); Quasten, III:362-63; Bardenh., III:273-281; Cayré, I:364-69; Cross, 369; Jurgens, I:347-371; *CPG*, 3585-3618.

Diadochus of Photice, mid-fifth century. Bishop of Photice (Epirus), author of a work on asceticism and a homily on the ascension of Christ. Altaner, 334-35 (Eng. trans., 391); Quasten, III:509-513; Bardenh., IV:186-88; Cayré, II:107-111; Cross, 399; *CPG*, 6106-6111.

Didache, early second century. A church order probably composed in Syria or Palestine, also called *Teaching of the Twelve Apostles*. Altaner, 79-82 (Eng. trans., 50-54); Quasten, I:29-39; Bardenh., I:90-103; Cayré, I:43-51; Cross, 401; Jurgens, I:106.

Didascalia, third century A collection of ethical and legal regulations probably composed in Syria or Palestine for gentile Christians. The original Greek text is almost completely lost, but it is preserved entire in a Syriac version and partially in a Latin version. Altaner, 84-85 (Eng. trans., 56-57); Quasten, II:147-152; Bardenh., II:304-312; Cayré, 287-88; Cross, 401.

Didymus of Alexandria (Did), ca. 313-398. Born in Alexandria, called "the Blind" because he was blind from childhood; served as director of the Catechetical School for decades. His extensive writings include commentaries on biblical books, New Testament as well as Old (cf. the recently discovered Tura papyri). Altaner, 280 (Eng. trans., 237); Quasten, III:85-100; Bardenh., III:104-115; Cayré, I:400-406; Cross, 402; Jurgens, II:60-64; *CPG,* 2544-2572.

Diodore of Tarsus, d. before 394. From a prominent family in Antioch, for years director of a monastery in Antioch, from 378 bishop of Tarsus. His extensive literary activity includes exegesis of most of the New Testament. Altaner, 318-19 (Eng. trans., 369-370); Quasten, III:397-401; Bardenh., III:304-311; Cayré, I:452-54; Cross, 405; *CPG,* 3815-3822.

Diognetus, late second century. Addressee of an apology in epistolary form (numerous identifications have been proposed) preserved in a single Strasbourg manuscript of the thirteenth/fourteenth century which was destroyed in 1870 and now survives only in copies. Altaner, 77-78 (Eng. trans. 135-36); Quasten, I:248-253; Bardenh., I:316-325; Cayré, I:113-14; Cross, 405; Jurgens, I:40-42.

Dionysius the Great of Alexandria (Dion[ysius Alexandrinus]), late second century-264/265. From a propertied pagan family, a prominent official before accepting Christianity. As a student of Origen in 231/232 he assumed the direction of the Catechetical School in Alexandria, became a priest, then in 247/248 bishop of Alexandria. Only fragments of his writings survive. Altaner, 210-11 (Eng. trans., 237); Quasten, II:101-109; Bardenh., II:203-227; Cayré, I:275-78; Cross, 406; Jurgens, I:250.

Dionysius the Areopagite, Ps(eudo)-, fifth century. A corpus of writings transmitted under the name of Dionysius the Areopagite whom Paul converted. Altaner, 501-505 (Eng. trans., 604-609); Bardenh., IV:282-299; Cayré, II:86-101; Cross, 406-407; Jurgens, II:300-302; *CPG,* 6600-6635.

Epiphanius (Epiph[anius Constantiensis]), ca. 315-403. Born in Judea, founder and for thirty years the director of a monastery. From 376 bishop of Salamis (Constantia) on Cyprus. His New Testament text represents an early stage of the Koine text type; his *De mensuris et ponderibus* anticipates the Bible dictionary genre. Altaner, 315-18 (Eng. trans., 365-68); Quasten, III:384-396; Bardenh., III:293-302; Cayré, I:395-400; Cross, 464-65; Jurgens, II:67-76; *CPG,* 3744-3807.

Eulogius, sixth/seventh century. Abbot and presbyter in Antioch, and 580-607 patriarch of Alexandria. Altaner, 512-13 (Eng. trans., 620); Bardenh., V:19-20; Cayré, II:295; *CPG,* 6971-79.

Eusebius of Caesarea (Eus[ebius Caesariensis]), ca. 263-339. Student of the presbyter Pamphilus, *ca.* 313 bishop of Caesarea, and "father of church history," his prolific writings deserve close examination for New Testament quotations. For his canon tables, cf. pp. 247f. Altaner, 217-224 (Eng. trans., 263-271); Quasten, III:309-345; Bardenh., III:240-262; Cayré, I:319-327; Cross, 481; Jurgens, I:290-99; *CPG,* 3465-3507.

Eustathius of Antioch, d. before 337. A native of Side in Pamphylia, *ca.* 323/324 appointed bishop of Antioch after serving as leader of the church in Berrhoea (Aleppo). Exiled by Constantine the Great in 326 or 330 to Thrace, where he died. Altaner, 309-310 (Eng. trans., 385-86); Quasten, III:302-306; Bardenh., III:230-37; Cayré, I:328-330; Cross, 483; *CPG,* 3350-3398.

Euthalius, fourth century. A Christian grammarian, perhaps also deacon and bishop, edited the Apostolos in sense lines following Greek rhetorical principles. Bardenh., II:292, III:283-85; Cross, 483-84; *CPG,* 3640-42; *LThK s.v.* (Kraft).

Eutherius, first half fifth century. Bishop of Tyana (Cappadocia). Engaged in christological controversies, excommunicated in 431 at the Council of Ephesus, and exiled in 434. Altaner, 338 (Eng. trans., 395); Quasten, III:619-621; Bardenh., IV:200-202; *CPG,* 6147-6153.

Euthymius Zigabenus, twelfth century. Monk in Constantinople, compiled an extensive

heresiology, the *Panoplia dogmatike*, and commentaries on the Gospels and Pauline letters. Beck, 614-16; Bardenh., IV:202; Cross, 484.

Gelasius of Cyzicus, fifth century. Son of a presbyter from Cyzicus, later in Bithynia, where he composed a church history (*ca.* 475). Altaner, 227-28 (Eng. trans., 275); Bardenh., IV:145-48; Cayré, II:112; Cross, 552-53; *CPG*, 6034.

Gennadius I of Constantinople, 458-471 patriarch of Constantinople. His extensive writings survive only in fragments, representing among his exegetical works on the New Testament only 1-2 Corinthians, Galatians, Hebrews, and especially Romans. Altaner, 335-36 (Eng. trans., 392); Quasten, III:525-26; Bardenh., IV:208-211; Cayré, II:105; Cross, 556; *CPG*, 5970-5986.

Gregory of Nazianzus, ca. 329-*ca.* 390. From a Christian family (father was bishop of Nazianzus), priest in 362, interim coadjutor of the see of Nazianzus and reluctantly consecrated bishop; bishop of the Nicaean church in Constantinople from 379, renowned as a speaker, and associated with Gregory of Nyssa and Basil the Great as one of the "three great Cappadocians." Altaner, 298-303 (Eng. trans., 345-351); Quasten, III:236-254; Bardenh., III:162-188; Cayré, I:415-423; Cross, 599; Jurgens, II:27-42; *CPG*, 3010-3125.

Gregory of Nyssa (Gr[egorius] Ny[ssenus]), ca. 335-394. Younger brother of Basil of Caesarea, a trained rhetor, appointed bishop of Nyssa by Basil in 371, later metropolitan of Sebaste in Little Armenia, a significant speculative theologian. Altaner, 303-308 (Eng. trans., 351-57); Quasten, III:254-296; Bardenh., III:188-220; Cayré, I:423-430; Cross, 599-600; Jurgens, II:42-59; *CPG*, 3135-3226.

Gregory Thaumaturgus (Gregory the Wonderworker), ca. 213-*ca.* 270. From a pagan family in Neocaesarea on the Pontus, as a student of Origen he became a Christian, and shortly afterward bishop of Neocaesarea. Altaner, 211-12 (Eng. trans., 238-39); Quasten, II:123-28; Bardenh., II:315-332; Cayré, I:283-84; Cross, 600-601; Jurgens, I:251-52.

Hegemonius, fourth century. Probable author of the *Acta Archelai* (preserved complete only in Latin), a polemic against the Manichaeans probably written in Syria. Altaner, 310-11 (Eng. trans., 360); Quasten, III:357-58; Bardenh., III:265-69; Cayré, I:369; *CPG*, 3570-71.

Hegesippus, second century. From the East, recorded his journey to Rome in five volumes of *Hypomnemata.* Altaner, 109-110 (Eng. trans., 148-150); Quasten, I:284-87; Bardenh., I:385-392; Cayré, I:140; Cross, 628; Jurgens, I:79-80.

Heracleon, second century. Student of the gnostic Valentinus, author of a commentary on the gospel of John. Altaner, 101 (Eng. trans., 142); Quasten, I:262; Bardenh., I:360-61; Cross, 637.

Hesychius of Jerusalem (Hes), first half fifth century. A monk, from *ca.* 412 a presbyter in Jerusalem, commented on probably the entire Bible. Altaner, 333-34 (Eng. trans., 389-390); Quasten, III:488-496; Bardenh., IV:257-261; Cayré, II:102; Cross, 644-45; *CPG*, 6550-6596.

Hesychius Salonitan, 405-426 bishop of Salona (Dalmatia). Corresponded with John Chrysostom. *Dictionnaire d' histoire et de géographie ecclésiastiques,* ed. Alfred Baudrillart, XV:1094-96.

Hieracas, ca. 300. Ascetic, and director of an ascetic community in Leontopolis, Egypt. Wrote numerous biblical commentaries, now lost. Bardenh., II:251-53; Cayré, I:279.

Hippolytus (Hipp), d. 235. Probably of Eastern origin (Asia Minor?), presbyter in Rome and counterbishop, died in exile on Sardinia. Altaner, 82-84, 164-69 (Eng. trans., 55-56, 183-190); Quasten, II:163-207; Bardenh., II:550-610; Cayré, I:220-29; Cross, 652-53; Jurgens, I:162-175.

Hippolytus, Ps(eudo)-. Writings wrongly attributed to Hippolytus. Altaner, 77, 168 (Eng. trans., 187-88); Bardenh., I:319-320, II:570, 577, 610-12.

Ignatius, d. *ca.* 110. Bishop of Antioch, wrote seven letters to different churches in Asia Minor and to Rome while going to his martyrdom under Trajan in Rome. Altaner, 47-50 (Eng. trans., 106-109); Quasten, I:63-76; Bardenh., I:131-158; Cayré, I:61-73; Cross 688-89; Jurgens, I:17-26.

Ignatius, Ps(eudo)-, fourth/fifth century. Later revisions and expansions of Ignatius' letters. Altaner, 48, 256 (Eng. trans., 59); Quasten, I:74; Bardenh., I:140-41, 150-55; Jurgens, I:27-28.

Irenaeus (Ir), second century. From Asia Minor, presbyter in Lyons in the time of Marcus Aurelius, bishop from 177/178. Writings survive only in translation except for a few fragments in the original Greek. Altaner, 110-17 (Eng. trans., 150-58); Quasten, I:287-313; Bardenh., I:399-430; Cayré, I:141-153; Cross, 713-14; Jurgens, I:84-106.

Irenaeus (Ir[lat]*)*. Irenaeus' *Adversus haereses,* originally written in Greek, survives only in a Latin version dated variously from 200 to 396. Altaner, 111-12 (Eng. trans., 150-51); Quasten, I:290-91; Bardenh., I:402-408; Fischer, 335.

Irenaeus (Ir[arm]*)*. Irenaeus' *Apostolic Preaching* was discovered at the beginning of the twentieth century in an Armenian version from the fourth/fifth century. Altaner, 112 (Eng. trans., 152); Quasten, I:292-93; Bardenh., I:409-411.

Isidore of Pelusium, ca. 360–*ca.* 435. From Alexandria, a monk and presbyter at Pelusium on the Nile. His voluminous correspondence is mostly exegetical. Altaner, 267-68 (Eng. trans., 308-309); Quasten, III:180-85; Bardenh., IV:100-107; Cayré, I:498-99; Cross, 717; *CPG,* 5557-58.

John of Damascus, ca. 650–mid-eighth century. Born of Christian parents in Damascus, his father was a high treasury officer of the Caliph, whose service John also entered. Before 700 entered Sabas monastery near Jerusalem, where he became a priest. His prolific writings include a commentary on the Pauline letters (compiled from the writings of Chrysostom, Theodoret, and Cyril of Alexandria). Beck, 476-486; Altaner, 526-532 (Eng. trans., 635-642); Bardenh., V:51-65; Cayré, II:326-340; Cross, 748-49; Jurgens, III:330-350; *CPG.,* 8040-8127.

Justin (Ju), d. *ca.* 165. "Philosopher and martyr," the best known of the apologists, from a pagan family in Nablus (Flavia Neapolis) in Palestine, a student of the most varied philosophies until his conversion. An active missionary, he was beheaded in Rome. Altaner, 65-71 (Eng. trans., 120-27); Quasten, I:196-219; Bardenh., I:206-262; Cayré, I:114-129; Cross, 770; Jurgens, I:50-64.

Justin, Ps(eudo)-. Writings wrongly attributed to Justin, mostly of the fourth/fifth century. Altaner, 68 (Eng. trans., 124); Quasten, I:205-207, III:548; Bardenh., I:237-246.

Leontius of Byzantium, sixth century. Probably born in Constantinople, later a monk in Palestine. Analysis of his genuine writings is clarifying his relationship to others of the same name, but some confusion remains. Beck, 373-74; Altaner, 509-510 (Eng. trans., 615-17); Bardenh., V:9-13; Cayré, II:73-78; Cross, 815-16; Jurgens, III:302-304; *CPG,* 6813-6820.

Macarius Magnes, fourth/fifth century. Probably named after the city of Magnesia, where he served as bishop. His *Apocriticos,* a five-volume apology (probably answering the arguments of Porphyry) drew primarily on the Gospels and Pauline letters. Altaner, 332-33 (Eng. trans., 388); Quasten, III:486-88; Bardenh., IV:189-195; Cayré, I:495; Cross, 854; Jurgens, III:254-55; *CPG,* 6115-18.

Marcion (Mcion), second century. Son of a bishop from Sinope on the Black Sea, excommunicated both by his father and by the Roman church in 144, he founded a powerful rival church with a New Testament comprising Luke and ten Pauline letters (both revised and abbreviated). Altaner, 106-107 (Eng. trans., 143-44); Quasten, I:268-272, II:274-75; Bardenh., I:371-74; Cayré, I:104-105; Cross, 870-71.

Marcus Eremita (Marc), d. after 430. At first bishop of a monastery at Ancyra, later a hermit. Author of many writings. Altaner, 334 (Eng. trans., 390-91); Quasten, III:504-509; Bardenh., IV:178-186; Cayré, I:508-509; Cross, 876; *CPG,* 6090-6102.

Maximus Confessor, 580-662. Received his sobriquet (Greek: Homologetes) for his fight against monophysitism and monotheletism. From a prominent family in Constantinople, he renounced the position of secretary to Emperor Heraclius to enter a monastery in Chrysopolis, later in Cyzicus. During the christological controversies in 653 he was arrested in Rome. After a political trial in Constantinople he was exiled to Thrace in

655, later maimed and deported to Lazica, where he died. Beck, 436-442; Altaner, 521-24 (Eng. trans., 629-633); Bardenh., V:28-35; Cayré, II:306-313; Cross, 895; *CPG*, 7688-7721.

Melitius, d. 381. At first bishop of Sebaste, later of Antioch, with several periods of exile. Died during the Council of Constantinople. Altaner, 260 (Eng. trans., 299); Bardenh., III:238; Cayré, I:329; Cross, 900; *CPG*, 3415-3425.

Methodius of Olympus (Meth), late third century. Bishop of Olympus in Lycia, although associated with other sees, e.g., Tyre and Patara. Died a martyr according to Jerome, Theodoret of Cyrrhus, and others. His writings are almost completely lost, and are known partly through Slavonic versions. Altaner, 215-16 (Eng. trans., 242-43); Quasten, II:129-137; Bardenh., II:334-351; Cayré, I:285-86; Cross, 910-11; Jurgens, I:260.

Nestorius, ca. 381-after 451. Of Persian origin, with theological education in Antioch where he achieved a great reputation as priest and monk for his sermons. Called to the patriarchate of Constantinople in 428, deposed at the Council of Ephesus in 431, he died in Egypt in exile. Altaner, 336-38 (Eng. trans., 393-95); Quasten, III:514-19; Bardenh., IV:74-78; Cayré, II:15-19; Cross, 961-63; Jurgens, III:201-204; *CPG*, 5665-5766.

Nilus of Ancyra (Nil[us Ancyranus]), d. *ca.* 430. Director of a monastery at Ancyra (now Ankara; not associated with Sinai, as earlier supposed). Altaner, 334 (Eng. trans., 390); Quasten, III:496-504; Bardenh., IV:161-178; Cayré, I:507-508; Cross, 976-77; *CPG*, 6043-6084.

Nonnus of Panopolis (Non), fifth century. The poet of the epic *Dionysiaca*, composed a metrical paraphrase of the gospel of John. Altaner, 283 (Eng. trans., 327-28); Quasten, III:114-16; Bardenh., IV:122-24; Cross, 980; *CPG*, 5641-42.

Oecumenius, sixth century. Earlier misidentified with a bishop of Tricca. A philosopher and rhetor, he wrote a supportive letter to Severus of Antioch. His major work is a commentary on Revelation. Beck, 417-18; Altaner, 517 (Eng. trans., 625); Bardenh., V:99-102; Cross, 993; *CPG*, 7470.

Oecumenius, Ps(eudo)-. Commentaries on New Testament books (Acts, Pauline letters, Catholic letters) wrongly ascribed to Oecumenius. Beck, 417-18; Altaner, 517 (Eng. trans., 625); Bardenh., V:100-101; *CPG*, 7471-75.

Origen (Or), 185-253/254. Of a Christian family (son of Leonidas, martyr), taught grammar at 17, and soon became director of the Alexandrian Catechetical School. Dismissed and excommunicated in 230/231, moved to Caesarea (Palestine), which became a thriving international center of theological scholarship. Torture suffered during the Decian persecution was probably the cause of his death. The most significant and widely influential Greek theologian of the early Church, he exercised extensive influence on the text of the Greek Old Testament by his Hexapla; a similar influence on the New Testament text has not been demonstrated and is improbable. Altaner, 197-209 (Eng. trans., 223-235); Quasten, II:37-101; Bardenh., II:96-194; Cayré, I:191-220; Cross, 1008-1010; Jurgens, I:189-215.

Origen (Or[lat]*)*. Exegetical writings of Origen translated into Latin, partly anonymously, partly by Rufinus. Altaner, 201-203 (Eng. trans., 227, 229); Quasten, II:45-48; Bardenh., II:124-26; Fischer, 387, 445-49.

Orsisius, d. *ca.* 380 (also spelled Horsiesius and Orsiesius). Student and successor of Pachomius as abbot. His *Doctrina de institutione monachorum*, a devotional manual, was translated by Jerome. Altaner, 263-64 (Eng. trans., 303); Quasten, III:159-160; Bardenh., III:85-87; Cross, 1012; *CPG*, 2363-2371.

Palladius, 363/364-before 431. Student of Evagrius Ponticus, from *ca.* 400 bishop of Hellenopolis, in 406 exiled as a supporter of John Chrysostom, from 412/413 bishop of Aspona. His chief work is the *Historia Lausiaca*. Altaner, 238-240 (Eng. trans., 254-55); Quasten, III:176-180; Bardenh., IV:148-155; Cayré, I:501-502; Cross, 1024; *CPG*, 6036-38.

Pamphilus, d. 309/310. From Berytus (Phoenicia), presbyter and later director of the school in Caesarea founded by Origen; martyred. Wrote an apology for Origen while in

prison. Altaner, 213 (Eng. trans., 240); Quasten, II:144-46; Bardenh., II:287-292; Cayré, I:280; Cross, 1026.

Papias, second century. Bishop of Hierapolis in Phrygia. A disciple of the presbyter John and a friend of Polycarp according to Irenaeus. Compiled accounts of the sayings and deeds of Jesus and his disciples in five books (only a few fragments survive). Altaner, 52-53 (Eng. trans., 113); Quasten, I:82-85; Bardenh., I:445-454; Cayré, I:76-77; Cross, 1028; Jurgens, I:38.

Paschal Chronicle (Chronicon Paschale), seventh century. An anonymous Easter chronicle probably originating in Constantinople. Hunger, I:328-330; Krumbacher, 337-39; Altaner, 235 (Eng. trans., 284); Bardenh., V:122-24; Cayré, II:282; Cross, 284.

Peter of Alexandria, d. 311. Bishop of Alexandria from *ca.* 300, died a martyr. Altaner, 212-13 (Eng. trans., 239-240); Quasten, II:113-17; Bardenh., II:239-247; Cayré, I:279; Cross, 1070-71; Jurgens, I:259-260.

Peter of Laodicea, seventh century. Identified as the compiler of a catena on the gospel of Matthew. Beck, 468-69; Altaner, 518 (Eng. trans., 626); Bardenh., V:107-110; Cross, 1073.

Philo of Carpasia, ca. 400. Bishop of Carpasia on Cyprus, wrote a commentary on the Song of Songs. Quasten, III:394-95; Bardenh., III:303; Cayré, I:495; *CPG,* 3810.

Photius, ca. 820-after 886. Byzantine theologian and church statesman, twice patriarch of Constantinople (858-867 and 877-886). Commissioned the return of Cyril and Methodius as missionaries to Moravia. His role in scholarly biblical exegesis is attested by his *Amphilochia* and *Bibliotheke.* Beck, 520-28; Ehrhard, in Krumbacher, I:73-78; Cayré, II:378-380; Cross, 1087-88.

Pierius, d. after 309. Presbyter in Alexandria, director of the Catechetical School. Exegete and author of twelve *Logoi,* according to Photius. Altaner, 212 (Eng. trans., 239); Quasten, II:111-13; Bardenh., II:234-39; Cayré, I:278.

Pilate, Acts of, early fifth century. Part of the gospel of Nicodemus, preserved in two Greek recensions and in a number of versions. Altaner, 127 (Eng. trans., 70); Quasten, I:115-18; Bardenh., I:543-47; Cross, 1090.

Pistis Sophia (Pist S), third century. Originally a Greek gnostic writing, preserved in a Coptic version in a parchment manuscript of the fifth or sixth century. Altaner, 131-32 (Eng. trans., 144); Bardenh., I:354-58; Cross, 1093-94; Jurgens, II:138-39.

Polycarp, d. 156 as martyr. Bishop of Smyrna. Of the letters mentioned by Irenaeus, only the letter (or two letters) to the Philippians has been preserved. Altaner, 50-52 (Eng. trans., 110-12); Quasten, I:76-82; Bardenh., I:160-170; Cayré, I:73-75; Cross, 1107; Jurgens, I:28-30.

Porphyry, 233-*ca.* 301/304. A neoplatonist from Tyre, attacked Christianity in a polemic which has survived only in fragments. Schmidt-Stählin, II:852-861; Cross, 1110.

Proclus, d. 446. Patriarch of Constantinople 434-446, wrote many homilies (some proven spurious), mainly on dominical feasts. Altaner, 338-39 (Eng. trans., 395-96); Bardenh., IV:202-208; Cayré, II:94; Cross, 1129-1130; *CPG,* 5800-5915.

Procopius of Gaza, ca. 465-528 (475-538?). Director of the Christian school of sophists at Gaza, compiled several Old Testament catenae. Beck, 414-16; Altaner, 516 (Eng. trans., 623-24); Bardenh., V:86-91; Cayré, II:103-104; Cross, 1130; *CPG,* 7430-7448.

Ptolemy (Ptolemaeus), second century. Gnostic, student of Valentinus, wrote a *Letter to Flora* preserved by Epiphanius, and a commentary on the prologue to John which is cited by Irenaeus. Altaner, 101 (Eng. trans., 142); Quasten, I:261-62; Bardenh., I:360-61.

Serapion of Thmuis, d. *ca.* 362. Director of the monastery, then from 339 bishop of Thmuis in Lower Egypt, author of a collection of liturgical prayers *(Euchologion).* Altaner, 257, 280 (Eng. trans., 323-24); Quasten, III:80-85; Bardenh., III:98-102; Cayré, I:370-71; Cross, 1261; Jurgens, I:334, II:131-34; *CPG,* 2485-2504.

Severian of Gabala, d. after 408. Bishop of Gabala in Syria. Parts of his commentary on the Pauline letters have been preserved in catenae. Altaner, 332 (Eng. trans., 387-88), Quasten, III:484-86; Bardenh., III:363-65; Cayré, I:494-95; Cross, 1266; *CPG,* 4185-4292.

Severus of Antioch, d. 538. From Sozopolis in Pisidia, patriarch of Antioch in 512, fled to Egypt as a monophysite in 518, excommunicated by the Council of Constantinople in 536. His writings in Greek are lost except for fragments, but many have been preserved in Syriac versions. Beck, 387-390; Altaner, 505 (Eng. trans., 610-12); Bardenh., V:3-5; Cayré, II:66-69; Cross, 1266-67; *CPG,* 7022-7081.

Socrates, ca. 380-*ca.* 439. Born in Constantinople, a layman; author of a church history considered as a sequel to Eusebius. Altaner, 226-27 (Eng. trans., 274); Quasten, III:532-34; Bardenh., IV:137-141; Cayré, II:111-12; Cross, 1285; Jurgens, III:250-51; *CPG,* 6028.

Sozomen, fifth century. From Gaza, practiced law in Constantinople, wrote a church history of the years 324-425. Altaner, 227 (Eng. trans., 274); Quasten, III:534-36; Bardenh., IV:141-44; Cayré, II:112; Cross, 1296; Jurgens, III:252-53; *CPG,* 6030.

Synesius of Cyrene, ca. 370/375-*ca.* 413/414. From an aristocratic pagan family in Cyrene, *ca.* 410 appointed bishop of Ptolemais and metropolitan of Pentapolis, although married and still cool toward Christianity. Altaner, 282-83 (Eng. trans., 326-27); Quasten, III:106-114; Bardenh., IV:110-122; Cayré, I:486-87; Cross, 1332; *CPG,* 5630-5640.

Tatian, second century. From "Assyria," a student of Justin in Rome, author of an apology. Returned in 172 to the East. For his *Diatessaron,* cf. p. 189. Altaner, 71-74 (Eng. trans., 127-29); Quasten, I:220-28; Bardenh., I:262-284; Cayré, I:130-31, 375; Cross, 1341; Jurgens, I:65-68; Ortiz de Urbina, 35-37.

Theodore of Heraclea, d. 355. *Ca.* 335-355 bishop of Heraclea in Thrace, wrote commentaries on various New Testament books, according to Jerome. Bardenh., III:265; *CPG,* 3561-67.

Theodore of Mopsuestia, ca. 352-428. Born in Antioch, studied rhetoric and literature under Libanius. Bishop of Mopsuestia in 392. Most of his writings (including many commentaries on Old and New Testament books) have not survived because of their condemnation by the Council of Constantinople in 553. Altaner, 319-322 (Eng. trans., 370-73); Quasten, III:401-423; Bardenh., III:312-322; Cayré, I:455-460; Cross, 1358-59; Jurgens, II:77-84; *CPG,* 3827-3873.

Theodore the Studite (Theodorus Studita), 759-826. A Byzantine theologian from Constantinople, cofounder with his uncle Plato of a monastery in Saccudion (Bithynia) which he directed as abbot from 794, transferring in 798 to the Studios monastery in Constantinople. Involvement in ecclesiastical controversies led to his repeated imprisonment and exile. Died on the island of Prinkipo. Beck, 491-95; Krumbacher, 712-15; Ehrhard, in Krumbacher, I:147-151; Cayré, II:294, 340-49; Cross, 1359-1360.

Theodoret of Cyrrhus (Thret), ca. 393-*ca.* 466. Born in Antioch, became first a monk in a monastery near his home, then in 423 reluctantly bishop of the city of Cyrrhus. Deposed and exiled by the Robber Synod of Ephesus in 449, restored by Chalcedon in 451. His prolific writings include commentaries on the fourteen Pauline letters. Altaner, 339-341 (Eng. trans., 396-99); Quasten, III:536-554; Bardenh., IV:219-247; Cayré, II:40-46; Cross, 1360-61; Jurgens, III:238-248; *CPG,* 6200-6288.

Theodotus of Ancyra, early fifth century. Bishop of Ancyra, author of homilies, sermons, and an exposition of the Nicene Creed. Bardenh., IV:197-200; Cross, 1362; *CPG,* 6124-6141.

Theodotus, second century. Gnostic, student of Valentinus. Altaner, 101 (Eng. trans., 132, 142); Quasten, I:265-66; Bardenh., I:362-64; Cross, 1362.

Theodulus, Ps(eudo)-, sixth/seventh century(?). Some writings circulated under the name of a fifth-century presbyter Theodulus, mentioned by Gennadius and Ebedjesu but almost completely lost. Bardenh., IV:262; Cayré, II:103; *CPG,* 6540-44.

Theophilus, second century. Born near the Tigris and Euphrates, the sixth bishop of Antioch according to Eusebius. Apart from three books inscribed *To Autolycus,* his writings are lost. Altaner, 75-77 (Eng. trans., 131-33); Quasten, I:236-242; Bardenh., I:302-315; Cayré, I:133-34; Cross, 1364; Jurgens, I:73-76.

Theophylact, eleventh century. From Euboea, student of Michael Psellos in Constantinople, a deacon and teacher of rhetoric. Archbishop of Bulgaria from *ca.* 1090 with

residence in Ochrida. Of his commentaries on the Old and New Testament, the most important are those on the gospel of Matthew and the Pauline letters. Beck, 649-651; Ehrhard, in Krumbacher, I:133-35; Cross, 1364.

Theotecnus, third century. Bishop of Caesarea, one of six bishops who wrote to Paul of Samosata seeking his support for a creed they had formulated. Of questionable authenticity. Bardenh., II:277-78.

Titus of Bostra (Tit), d. before 378. Bishop of Bostra. His commentary on Luke in the form of homilies survives in fragments; book IV of his work against the Manichaeans, which is preserved completely in a Syriac version though only fragmentarily in Greek, complains of his opponents' corruption of the New Testament text. Altaner, 311 (Eng. trans., 360-61); Bardenh., III:269-273; Cayré, I:370; Cross, 1382; *CPG,* 3575-3581.

Valentinus, second century. A gnostic from Egypt, *ca.* 135-160 in Rome. His writings are mentioned by Clement of Alexandria, Hippolytus, and others. Altaner, 101 (Eng. trans., 142); Quasten, I:260-61; Bardenh., I:358-364; Cayré, I:104; Cross, 1423.

Victor of Antioch, ca. 500. Wrote (compiled?) a commentary on Mark. Beck, 421; Altaner, 515 (Eng. trans., 623); Bardenh., IV:255-57; Cross, 1437; *CPG,* 6529-6534; Stegmüller, 8286.

IV

THE EARLY VERSIONS OF THE NEW TESTAMENT

1. *INTRODUCTION*

The early versions, as mentioned above,[1] start from about A.D. 180. This is true of the Latin, Syriac, and Coptic versions; the other versions, such as the Gothic and Old Church Slavonic, are either associated with the christianizing of nations, or represent the products of a later stage, well after the language of missionaries (usually Greek, but sometimes Syriac) had already exercised a formative influence on the new church, as in the Armenian and Georgian versions. These translations usually formed the first literary monument in the language. Frequently an alphabet had to be developed to accommodate them (e.g., for the Gothic version).

The only versions which can be considered as useful sources or as tools for New Testament textual criticism are the ones which were either derived immediately from a Greek text, or were thoroughly revised from a Greek base (if originally based on another version). Even where a version has been made directly from a Greek base (as were all the following versions except for the Armenian, Georgian, and Ethiopic, and even in these the Greek influence is considerable), the value of a version is further affected by whether it represents an original translation with subsequent modifications or is the coalescence in one or more traditions of several independent versions, each of which was produced to meet a translation need that was felt in a number of different places at the same time. Only in rare instances can a single original translation be demonstrated, as in the Gothic and the Old Church Slavonic. Elsewhere the question is usually debatable. When a single original translation can be identified the value of the version as a witness to the original text is reduced, its whole manuscript tradition and all its variant readings are restricted in their significance to intraversional relationships, and it offers only a reflection of the Greek text(s) on which the first translation was originally based — unless in its later history it was revised from Greek manuscripts.

The situation is different when translations were undertaken at the same

1. Cf. p. 52.

time at different places, in different provinces, quite independently of each other, as is most probable in Latin versions.

It must be emphasized that the value of the early versions for establishing the original Greek text and for the history of the text has frequently been misconceived, i.e., they have been considerably overrated. An inadequate appreciation of how their linguistic structures differ from Greek has all too often permitted the early versions to be cited in critical apparatuses of Greek texts where their evidence is irrelevant. Nestle-Aland[26] advisedly restricts citation of the versions in its apparatus to instances where their witness to a Greek exemplar is unequivocal. Furthermore, far-reaching inferences for the Greek text have often been drawn from purely intraversional developments. If the assumption of a single original translation is accepted, these dependent variants may all be ignored. Overrating the versions can lead to dire consequences. It is understandable that B. F. Westcott and F. J. A. Hort should attempt to reach the text of the second century by means of the Old Latin and the Old Syriac versions when they are supported by Codex Bezae Cantabrigiensis (D[ea]), because the Greek witnesses available to them were no earlier than the fourth century. But there is no excuse for anyone to persist in their theories today when we have the text of the second century available in a large number of Greek witnesses, especially as Westcott and Hort's assumptions can no longer be maintained either for the Old Syriac[2] or for the Old Latin.[3]

And yet the importance of the versions is substantial. They are authoritative in confirming the identity of the regional or provincial text where they were produced (e.g., the Coptic version for the Egyptian text).[4] And of course their witness as local controls should be supplemented by patristic quotations from the New Testament in their respective languages far more rigorously than has yet been done.

Handbooks:
Kurt Aland, ed., *Die alten Übersetzungen des Neuen Testaments, die Kirchenväterzitate und Lektionare.* ANTF 5 (Berlin: 1972). Thirteen studies by specialists on various themes.
Bruce M. Metzger, *The Early Versions of the New Testament: Their Origin, Transmission, and Limitations* (Oxford: 1977). With contributions by specialists on the limitations, as well as comprehensive bibliographies and surveys of the present state of research.

2. *THE LATIN VERSIONS*

a. The Old Latin (Itala). The earliest Latin texts are found in Tertullian's numerous quotations from the New Testament. We do not know precisely when he began writing, but it was probably about 195. These quotations, however, are of little use in tracing the history of the Latin version because Tertullian evidently translated his scripture quotations (apparently even in passages cited from Marcion) directly from Greek, in which he was quite competent, making no

2. Cf. pp. 193f.
3. Cf. pp. 187-190.
4. Cf. pp. 200f.

use of any manuscripts of the Latin New Testament. Not until Cyprian (about A.D. 250) is there any evidence of the use of such manuscripts.

The earliest manuscripts of the Latin New Testament are from the fourth century. But the manuscript k (fourth/fifth century) was copied from an exemplar of the period before Cyprian and presents a text whose Greek base is thought by some to be traceable to the second century. The number of surviving manuscripts, however, is disappointing. Altogether more than fifty manuscripts (or fragments) of the Old Latin New Testament are mentioned in Nestle-Aland[26] (pp. 712-716), but these manifestly constitute only a small fraction of the number that originally existed. Augustine complained, for example, in his *De doctrina christiana* (in a passage apparently written before 396/397) that anyone obtaining a Greek manuscript of the New Testament would translate it into Latin, no matter how little he knew of either language (ii.16). This agrees with Jerome's complaint about the variety of texts found in the Latin manuscripts of his time (*ca.* 347-419/420): "tot sunt (exemplaria) paene quot codices" ("There are almost as many different translations as there are manuscripts"). While this is undoubtedly an exaggeration (as are many of Jerome's statements), still it gives a fair impression of the complexity of the Latin tradition toward the end of the fourth century.

The fact that the latest Old Latin manuscript is from the thirteenth century gives some indication of this early text's sturdy durability. It should, of course, be noted that the influence of Jerome's Vulgate was felt from the moment it appeared (it is especially noticeable in the manuscripts f, c, ff[1], g[1], 1, aur, q), while the manuscripts of the Vulgate were also in turn influenced by Old Latin manuscripts. The result was a profusion of mixtures. The thirteenth-century manuscript is typical in retaining the Old Latin text only in Acts and Revelation while following the Vulgate elsewhere. This late manuscript is also famous for its physical characteristics. Its name "codex gigas" is well earned: the pages measure 49×89.5 cm.! After a checkered career it is now in the Royal Library at Stockholm.

This manuscript appears in the apparatus of critical editions under the symbol gig. Old Latin manuscripts are traditionally represented by lowercase letters.[5] None of them contains the whole New Testament, and the same letter is used in different parts of the New Testament to refer to different manuscripts, quite like the symbols for Greek minuscule manuscripts before Gregory's system.[6] Bonifatius Fischer has accordingly designed a revised system identifying the manuscripts with arabic numerals.[7] These new symbols have been observed only in specialized studies, and accordingly the earlier system has been followed in the critical apparatuses of both *GNT* and Nestle-Aland[26].

In view of the listing of Old Latin manuscripts in Nestle-Aland[26], pp. 712-16 (where the extent of their contents is given in detail), we will notice

---

5. Cf. Nestle-Aland[26], pp. 712-16.

6. Cf. pp. 72f.

7. Cf. the numbers added after the lowercase roman letters in Nestle-Aland[26], Appendix I, pp. 712-16.

Plate 54. Codex Bobiensis (k, fourth/fifth century; cf. p. 187): the ending of Mark (f. 41ʳ). This is the only known example of the "shorter ending" added directly to Mark 16:8.

here only the most important ones. We have already mentioned k (Codex Bob-iensis).[8] In every respect this is a remarkable manuscript; e.g., it is the only witness in the whole of the New Testament tradition to end the gospel of Mark with only the "shorter ending." It is associated with e (Codex Palatinus of the fifth century, a purple parchment manuscript with silver ink, gold illumination, and a text exhibiting European influence in part) as a member of the African type of text known as afra, which is represented by a separate text line in Adolf Jülicher's edition. This "African" form of the text has traditionally been con-trasted with the "European" form (a, b, c, etc.). This is fair enough, but recent scholarship has construed the term afra more broadly than was common earlier, recognizing its style and vocabulary as only primarily and not exclusively char-acteristic of Africa. Among the manuscripts known as "European" the most important are: *Codex Vercellensis* a of the fourth century, containing the Gospels in the Western order of Matthew-John-Luke-Mark; *Codex Veronensis* b of the fifth century, on purple parchment with silver ink and gold illumination, containing the Gospels in the same order as a; *Codex Colbertinus* c of the twelfth/thirteenth century, earlier identified as an African type, and containing the Gospels in the usual order; *Codex Corbeiensis* ff[2] of the fifth century, the earliest Latin manu-script to contain the summaries before each Gospel, i.e., the lists of "chapters" with their titles; and *Codex Vindobonensis* i of the fifth century, containing only fragments of Mark and Luke.

The Latin text of d on the recto pages of Codex Bezae Cantabrigiensis deserves special comment. The description in Bruce Manning Metzger's manual represents a widely held consensus:

. . . though corrected here and there from the Greek side (it) preserves an ancient form of the Old Latin text. Since *d* appears occasionally with the readings of *k* and of *a* when all other authorities differ, it witnesses to a text that was current no later than the first half of the third century and may be earlier still.[9]

Fischer has contested this view with vigor:

Today it is nearly universally recognized that the (Latin) text is almost completely dependent on its parallel Greek text, whether it be described as a Latin version so thoroughly corrected to the Greek text that its character as a Latin witness is valid only when supported by other Latin witnesses, or as itself a slavish translation of the parallel Greek text or its ancestor in a diglot manuscript using a Latin text either as an aid in translating or as a vocabulary source. In any event, the Latin text of d (5) is distinct from that of other Latin Bibles.[10]

Meanwhile Metzger has concurred.[11] It is important to recognize that even in

---

8. Cf. pp. 187.

9. *The Text of the New Testament* (New York: [2]1968), p. 277.

10. "Die Neue Testament in lateinischer Sprache," *Die alten Übersetzungen des Neuen Testaments, die Kirchenväterzitate und Lektionare*, ed. Kurt Aland. ANTF 5 (Berlin: 1972): 42.

11. *The Early Versions of the New Testament* (Oxford: 1977), p. 318.

the Latin pages of Codex D^{ea} there is no trace to be found of the early text postulated by Westcott-Hort and their followers.

Editions:
Gospels: *Itala, Das Neue Testament in altlateinischer Überlieferung. Nach den Handschriften hrsg. von A. Jülicher, durchgesehen und zum Druck besorgt von W. Matzkow† und K. Aland.* I: Matthew (²1972); II: Mark (²1970); III: Luke (²1976); IV: John (1963)
Pauline letters: for Ephesians-Colossians, *Vetus Latina* 24/1-2, ed. Hermann Josef Frede (1962-1971); for 1 Thessalonians-Hebrews, *ibid.* 25, ed. Frede (1975-1989)
Catholic letters: *Vetus Latina* 26/1, ed. Walter Thiele (1956-1969)

Thus only the Gospels, the shorter of the Pauline letters, and the Catholic letters are now available in critical editions. The citation of the Old Latin tradition in the other parts of the New Testament in Nestle-Aland[26] has therefore been based upon direct collations of the manuscripts themselves. Earlier editions of manuscripts are frequently inadequate — Johannes Belsheim's editions in particular should be used with caution. As to terminology, we should note that Jülicher's designation of the Old Latin tradition as Itala follows a tradition that goes back to Augustine. But what Augustine intended by the term Itala is still uncertain and a matter of debate, so that Old Latin (Vetus Latina) is a better term for the early Latin tradition, in parallel to Old Syriac (Vetus Syra) for the earliest Syriac tradition.[12] The use of "it" in Nestle-Aland[26] is continued partly in deference to tradition, but also for practical reasons. For the same reasons the use of lowercase letters has been retained to designate individual manuscripts: vl for vetus latina would be easily confused with v(e)l (for "or") and with v.l. (varia lectio for "variant reading"), just as the adoption of Fischer's excellent system of identifying the manuscripts with arabic numerals would be susceptible to confusion with the similar system used for Greek minuscule manuscripts.

b. The Vulgate. Vulgate is the name given the form of the Latin text which has been widely circulated (vulgata) in the Latin church since the seventh century, enjoying recognition as the officially authoritative text, first in the edition of Pope Sixtus V (Rome, 1590), and then of Pope Clement VIII (Rome, 1592), until the Neo-Vulgate. The Neo-Vulgate, which was undertaken on the initiative of Pope Paul VI (promulgated by Pope John Paul II by Apostolic Constitution on April 25, 1979), represented not only innumerable alterations of the traditional text in purely stylistic matters, but more significantly a correction of it to the Greek text. This was an urgent need, for neither the edition of 1590 nor that of 1592 (which introduced roughly five thousand changes in the text despite the fact that changes in the 1590 text were expressly forbidden on pain of excommunication) succeeded in representing either Jerome's original text (see below) or its Greek base with any accuracy. The latter purpose is now served by the Neo-Vulgate (*Nova Vulgata Bibliorum sacrorum editio* [Rome: 1979; 2nd edition, 1986; pocket edition, Nestle-Aland, *Novum Testamentum Latine*, 1984; also *Novum Testamentum graece et latine*, 3rd printing, 1987]). The recovery of the original text of the Vulgate is concurrently being pursued in three different places. The monks of the Benedictine monastery of San Girolamo

---

12. Cf. pp. 193f.

(St. Jerome) in Rome have been at work since 1907, but although many volumes of this basic work have been published, they have been limited thus far to the Old Testament. The *Novum Testamentum Domini nostri Iesu Christi latine secundum editionem Sancti Hieronymi*, prepared by John Wordsworth, H. J. White, and H. F. D. Sparks in Oxford, has appeared in three volumes, the first published in 1889 and the final volume in 1954. The two-volume *Biblia sacra iuxta Vulgatam versionem*, known as the "Stuttgart Vulgate," appeared in 1969, edited by Robert Weber in cooperation with Bonifatius Fischer, Herman Josef Frede, Jean Gribomont, Sparks, and Walter Thiele (3rd edition, 1984).

The Vulgate is generally regarded as the work of Jerome. But this is not true for the New Testament, where he merely revised the text of the Old Latin Gospels (completing it in 383). His major contribution was in the Old Testament, which he translated afresh from the Hebrew, with the exception of the Psalter (which he revised following the Greek Hexapla of Origen) and the books of Wisdom, Sirach, and Maccabees, which he did not work on. It is not

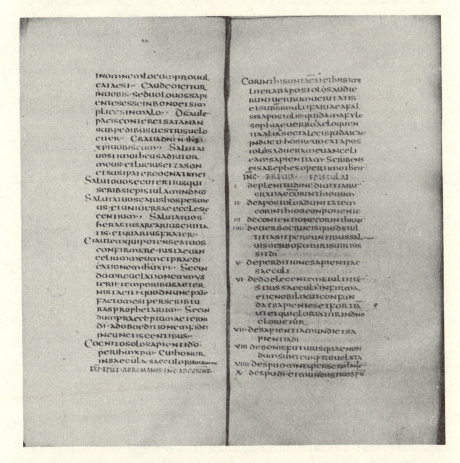

Plate 55. Codex Fuldensis of the Latin Vulgate (F, 547; cf. p. 192): the ending of Romans and the beginning (kephalaia list) of 1 Corinthians.

known with any certainty when the rest of the New Testament was revised, or by whom. The Vulgate text of the New Testament beyond the Gospels is not found until the early fifth century in the writings of Pelagius and his followers. Further, the work of revision here was done more carefully and consistently than in the Gospels by Jerome. The question of what Greek exemplar was used is disputed. Earlier it was considered to be a manuscript of the ℵ B L type, but the consensus today favors the view that Jerome used a contemporary manuscript of the early Koine type.

The number of Vulgate manuscripts surviving today can hardly be gauged, but it must be well over eight thousand. The center from which the Vulgate circulated was naturally at first in Italy, but following the course of medieval church history, in time distinctive text types were developed in Spain, in Gaul, and in Ireland. The age of Charlemagne produced recensions influenced primarily by Alcuin which determined the development of the Vulgate into the high middle ages. It was a thirteenth-century Sorbonne copy of the Paris Bible that provided the exemplar for the first printed Bible, and consequently the textual base for printed editions down to the Sixto-Clementine editions. The most significant manuscripts of the Vulgate (on which the Stuttgart Vulgate is primarily based) are the following.

A   Codex Amiatinus of the early eighth century, the oldest surviving complete Bible in Latin, written in Northumbria, and now in the Biblioteca Medicea Laurenziana, Florence.
F   Codex Fuldensis (New Testament), written in 547 for Bishop Victor of Capua (who also corrected it), and now in the Landesbibliothek of Fulda (cf. plate 55).
G   Codex Sangermanensis (New Testament), written in Paris in the early ninth century, now in the Bibliothèque Nationale, Paris.
M   Codex Mediolanensis (Gospels), written in northern Italy in the second half of the sixth century, now in the Biblioteca Ambrosiana, Milan.
N   (Gospels), written in Italy in the fifth century (palimpsest), now in the Municipal Library of Autun and the Bibliothèque Nationale, Paris.
R   Codex Reginensis (Pauline letters), written near Ravenna in the eighth century, now in the Vatican Library.
S   Codex Sangallensis (Gospels), written in Italy in the early fifth century, now in the Stiftsbibliothek, St. Gallen, and elsewhere in Switzerland (also in Kärnten, Austria).
Z   Codex Harleianus (Gospels), written in Italy in the sixth century, now in the British Library, London.

3. *THE SYRIAC VERSIONS*

Research on the New Testament versions in Syriac labors under a special handicap. Peculiarly among the versions, the first stage of the tradition was not a translation of the four canonical Gospels, but Tatian's Diatessaron. This harmony came into use toward the end of the second century as the "Gospel" of the "orthodox" of Edessa, and succeeded in maintaining its position into the fifth century against increasing opposition. The many historical and critical textual problems of the Syriac version may be traced to it. For not only does the Syriac tradition present translation problems which are formidable, but the ubiquitous heritage of the Diatessaron must also be dealt with properly. In the course of

history a constant process of revision produced a whole series of Syriac New Testament versions with the result that they cannot always be distinguished from each other with precision: besides the Diatessaron there is the Old Syriac (Vetus Syra), the Peshitta, the Philoxeniana and the Harklensis, as well as the Palestinian Syriac version.

a. The Diatessaron. It cannot be determined with certainty from the surviving evidence whether Tatian's Gospel harmony, known as the Diatessaron, was compiled originally in Greek or in Syriac. We can be relatively certain only about the history of its influence, especially from the time of Ephraem (310-373). Ephraem made use of and commented on the Diatessaron, evidently as *the* Gospel text of the orthodox Christians of Edessa. The quotations in the nearly complete Syriac original of his commentary discovered just a few years ago represents the only surviving example of a relatively continuous text of the Diatessaron, but then it should also be remembered that Ephraem was certainly not always precise in his quotations. The Armenian version of his commentary is now useful only as a control. It is, however, quite certain that the Diatessaron was translated into many languages including Latin, Old High German, Old Dutch, Persian, Arabic, and so forth, yet all of these versions with their variants cannot compare in textual value with the witness of Ephraem's commentary.
the witness of Ephraem's commentary.

Editions:

Louis Leloir, *Saint Ephrem: Commentaire de l'Evangile concordant, text syriaque (Manuscrit Chester Beatty 709), édité et traduit.* Chester Beatty Monograph 8 (Dublin: 1963)

_____ , *L'Evangile d'Ephrem d'après les oeuvres éditées.* CSCO 180 (Louvain: 1958)

_____ , *Saint Ephrem: Commentaire de l'Evangile concordant, version arménienne.* CSCO 137 (Louvain: 1953); Latin translation, CSCO 145 (Louvain: 1954)

_____ , "Le commentaire d'Ephrem sur le Diatessaron, Quarante et un folios retrouvés," *RB* 94 (1987):481-518

_____ , in *Studia Ephemeridis "Augustinianum"* 27 (1988):361-391

Pedro Ortiz Valdivieso, "Un nuevo fragmento siríaco del Comentario de S. Efrén al Diatésaron (PPalau-Rib. 2)," *Studia Papyrologica* 5 (1966):7-17

Ignacio Ortiz de Urbina, *Vetus Evangelium Syrorum et exinde excerptum Diatessaron Tatiani.* Biblia Polyglotta Matritensia ser. VI (Madrid: 1967)

b. The Old Syriac. This term is applied to the earliest Syriac translation of the New Testament. It survives in two (incomplete) Four Gospels manuscripts: Curetonianus (sy^c; cf. plate 57), named for its discoverer William Cureton, and Sinaiticus (sy^s; cf. plate 56), discovered by Agnes Smith Lewis and Margaret Dunlop Gibson at Mt. Sinai. Although they do not offer completely identical texts, yet they exhibit so great a similarity in their translation style, in their close relationship to the Diatessaron as a kind of basic text, and in their character (additions, omissions, transpositions, paraphrases) that in contrast to the later versions they may be described as an independent version. This version, however, underwent repeated revision, so that it never became a fixed "received text." Possibly sy^c is a revision of the earlier sy^s. Differences between the stages of this version make it difficult to identify quotations from it in the Syriac literature with any precision. In the early Syriac translation literature from Greek

(Titus of Bostra, Eusebius), New Testament quotations seem not to have been translated ad hoc but taken from a version already current. For practical reasons this could not have been the Diatessaron, because it did not contain all the texts cited by the Greek Fathers. And yet the version used was not identical with sy[s] and sy[c], although it shared the translation style characteristic of these as well as of the tetraevangelium used by Ephraem.

For historical reasons the translation of the Four Gospels into Syriac should not be dated too late (probably around 300, perhaps earlier). A fifth-century *terminus ad quem* for sy[s] and sy[c] is provided by the dates of the manuscripts themselves (sy[s] may be from the late fourth century). The date of the exemplars represented in sy[s] and sy[c] may have been some time in the fourth century after the rise of the great Greek text types (the second-century date commonly accepted formerly has now been generally abandoned). The presence of idiosyncrasies and a strong diatessaric element in the text betray preliminary stages in the background.

The above comments have been restricted to the Gospels. The Old Syriac also included a translation of Acts and the fourteen Pauline letters, but as no manuscripts of these have survived their text can only be reconstructed fragmentarily from the patristic quotations of the period.

Bibliography:

Francis Crawford Burkitt, *Evangelion da-mepharreshe: The Curetonian Version of the Four Gospels, with the readings of the Sinai Palimpsest . . .* I: *Text;* II: *Introduction and Notes* (Cambridge: 1904)

A. Smith Lewis, *The Old Syriac Gospels, or Evangelion da-mepharreshe; being the text of the Sinai or Syro-Antiochene Palimpsest, including the latest additions and emendations, with the variants of the Curetonian Syriac . . .* (London: 1910)

Josef Kerschensteiner, *Der altsyrische Paulustext.* CSCO 315 (Louvain: 1970)

Arthur Vööbus, "Die Entdeckung von Überresten der altsyrischen Apostelgeschichte," *OC* 64 (1980): 32-35

———— , *Studies in the History of the Gospel Text in Syriac* (1951; repr. Louvain : 1987).

c. The Peshitta. The term Peshitta was first used by Moses bar Kepha in 903. It is usually interpreted as meaning "simple" in contrast to the Harklean version with its apparatus. The Peshitta version of the New Testament is the most widely attested and most consistently transmitted of the Syriac New Testament versions. The Syriac church still preserves it and holds it in reverence in this form today.

It contains twenty-two New Testament books, lacking the shorter Catholic letters (2-3 John, 2 Peter, Jude) and Revelation (as well as the Pericope Adulterae [John 7:53–8:11] and Luke 22:17-18). At the beginning of the twentieth century there were already more than three hundred known manuscripts (only a few containing the complete text of the New Testament), and since then the number has steadily grown. A systematic search of the libraries and churches of the East would undoubtedly increase the number further. The earliest known manuscripts are from the fifth and sixth centuries.

The text printed in the London edition prepared by Philip Edward Pusey and George Henry Gwilliam is obviously a late form, i.e., the text which achieved common acceptance. It reveals nothing of the early stages of the Peshitta's development, which is a matter of controversy. No definite conclusions

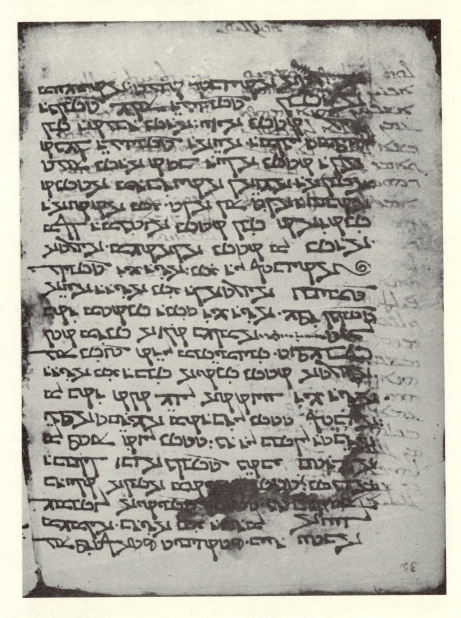

Plate 56. A palimpsest. The lower text is the Sinaitic Syriac (sy^s) of the late fourth or early fifth century: Luke 23:1-8. The upper (inverted) text is from a *Lives of the Saints*.

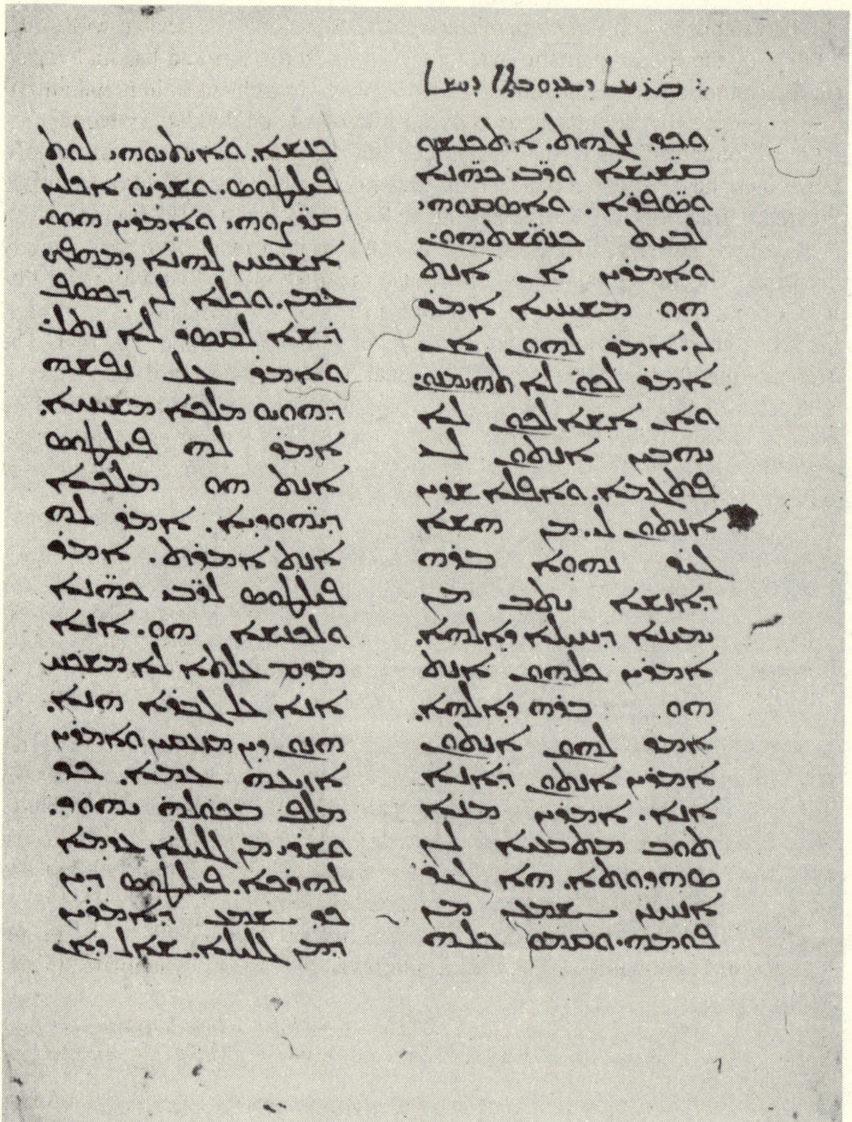

Plate 57. The Curetonian Syriac (sy^c) of the fifth century: Luke 22:66–23:6.

can be established until a comprehensive critical edition is available with a full citation of the Syriac patristic evidence such as Barbara Aland has undertaken for the Catholic letters (the edition of Romans–1 Corinthians is in preparation).

Since the Peshitta is used by both parts of the divided Syriac church, by the Monophysites and the Nestorians, its origin and acceptance as authoritative must have occurred before their division, i.e., by the mid-fifth century at the latest. Tradition ascribes the Peshitta to Rabbula, bishop of Edessa (411-435). It is certain, however, that the text as it stands today cannot have been entirely his work. The very presence of Old Syriac readings in the Peshitta proves that it was not a new version but the result of a revision (or revisions) of a form of the Old Syriac text following an exemplar of a (mainly) Koine type text. The evidence therefore suggests rather a gradual development toward the standardized form of the Peshitta text promoted vigorously in the first half of the fifth century, undoubtedly by Rabbula among others. The textual character of the erstwhile stages of the "pre-Peshitta" naturally differed from that of the final standard version.

Bibliography:

Philip Edward Pusey and George Henry Gwilliam, *Tetraevangelium sanctum iuxta simplicem Syrorum versionem* . . . (Oxford: 1901)

————, *The New Testament in Syriac* (London: British and Foreign Bible Society, 1905-1920). Frequently reprinted.

J. Joseph Overbeck, *S. Ephraemi Syri, Rabbulae*. . . , *Balaei aliorumque opera selecta* (Oxford: 1865)

d. The Philoxeniana.

d. The Philoxeniana. The Philoxeniana, as it is called, is the first of the Syriac versions which we can trace to a single translator, the chorepiscopus Polycarp (commissioned by the famous monophysite bishop Philoxenus of Mabbug, 485-523), and identify with a precise date, 507/508. Furthermore, we also know the writer's intentions. He planned to make a new and precise translation of the Greek text primarily for dogmatic theological reasons.

Unfortunately the Philoxeniana has not survived. Work on its reconstruction has continued over several generations, but without conclusive results.

Bibliography:

John Gwynn, *Remnants of the Later Syriac Versions of the Bible* I: *New Testament: The Four Minor Catholic Epistles in the Original Philoxenian Version* . . . (1909; repr. Amsterdam: 1974)

————, *The Apocalypse of St. John in a Syriac Version hitherto unknown* . . . (Dublin: 1897)

André de Halleux, ed., *Philoxenus de Mabbug: Commentaire du prologue johannique.* CSCO 380 (Louvain: 1977)

e. The Harklensis.

e. The Harklensis. At the Enaton monastery near Alexandria in the year 616 Thomas of Harkel (monk, and sometime bishop of Mabbug) undertook a revision of the Philoxenian version on the basis of collations he made of several Greek manuscripts (three for the Gospels, two for the Pauline letters, and one for Acts and the Catholic letters). After a long controversy over the historicity and extent of this revision of the Philoxenian version, it is now clear that Thomas undertook a thorough revision. His text is characterized by slavish adaptation to the Greek text, reproducing not only Greek word order, but even Greek words

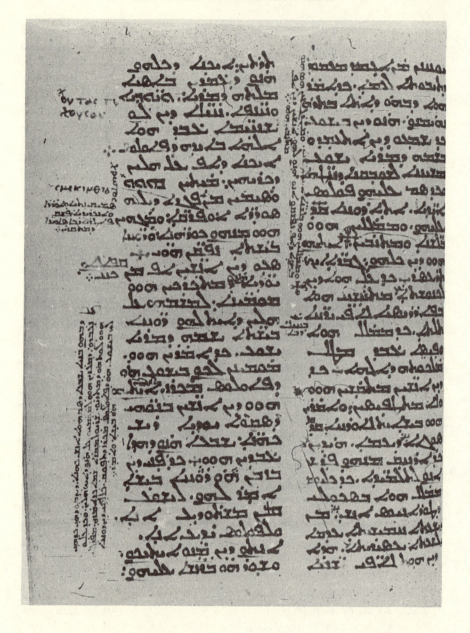

Plate 58. An eleventh-century manuscript of the Harklean version: Acts 19:4-16, with asterisks and obeli in the text, and variant Syriac readings and several Greek words in the margin.

in Syriac transliteration, to such an extent that it not only violates good Syriac style but idiomatic usage as well. For the textual critic this is a stroke of good fortune because here (in contrast to all other Syriac versions) it is possible to reconstruct in detail the Greek exemplar followed by the translator. But unfortunately the result only demonstrates that the Harklean text, except in the Catholic letters, is an almost (though not absolutely) pure Koine type. The textual critic's interest is attracted by the apparatus Thomas provided with his translation, especially in Acts where he made use of the "Western" type (or was he merely indicating where his exemplar differed from the text he considered superior?). The function of the obeli and asterisks used (somewhat unevenly) in his translation still remains uncertain: their transmission has been affected by a degree of confusion, with some manuscripts ignoring their use completely (cf. Barbara Aland, pp. 111ff.

Joseph White, *Sacrorum Evangeliorum versio Syriaca Philoxeniana* (Oxford: 1778)

─────── , *Actuum Apostolorum et Epistolarum tam Catholicarum quam Paulinarum versio Syriaca Philoxeniana* (Oxford: 1799-1803)

Robert Lubbock Bensly, *The Harklean Version of the Epistle to the Hebrews, Chap. XI, 28–XIII, 25* (Cambridge: 1889)

Georg Heinrich Bernstein, *Das heilige Evangelium des Johannes, Syrisch in harklensischer Uebersetzung . . . nach einer vaticanischen Handschrift* (Leipzig: 1853)

Arthur Vööbus, *The Apocalypse in the Harklean Version: A Facsimile Edition of Ms. Mardin Orth. 35, fol. 143r-159v, with an Introduction.* CSCO 400 (Louvain: 1978)

Barbara Aland (with Andreas Juckel), *Das Neue Testament in syrischer Überlieferung.* I: *Die Grossen Katholischen Briefe.* ANTF 7 (Berlin: 1986)

f. The Palestinian Syriac Version. This version is usually discussed with the Syriac versions, although it is related to them only indirectly.

Its language, the Aramaic dialect of Palestine in the first Christian centuries, is closer to Jewish Palestinian Aramaic than to classical Syriac. The principal connection is its use of the Syriac estrangelo script found also in the Palestinian "Syriac" version. This was the language of the group known as the Melchites, a name indicating their "Imperial" loyalty, i.e., support of the Council of Chalcedon. Inscriptional evidence shows that they were found far beyond the borders of Palestine in adjacent areas (Jerash), with substantial settlements also in Egypt.

The date of the Palestinian Syriac version is debated. Possibly an oral tradition in the fourth century preceded the establishment of a written form in the fifth century. The earliest witnesses of the meager manuscript tradition are probably from the sixth century. Its textual character is for the most part a normal Koine type with occasional Alexandrian readings, showing agreements with Codex Vaticanus in particular. An affinity to the "Caesarean" text type, with which this version is occasionally associated, is quite doubtful. It has stronger associations with the Peshitta and the Old Syriac readings of the pre-Peshitta, which suggest that the origins of the version may be traced to the fifth century.

Bibliography:
A. Smith Lewis and M. Dunlop Gibson, *The Palestinian Syriac Lectionary of the Gospels, re-edited from two Sinai Mss. and from P. de Lagarde's Edition of the 'Evangeliarum Hierosolymitanum'* (London: 1899)

Charles Perrot, "Un fragment christo-Palestinien découvert à Khirbet Mird," *RB* 70 (1963): 506-555 (with a comprehensive list of Christian Palestinian texts to 1963)

4. *THE COPTIC VERSIONS*

The difficulties posed by the Coptic versions of the New Testament differ in kind from those of the Syriac versions, but they are no less challenging. The early period of Christianity in Egypt lies in obscurity.

All accounts of the beginnings are legendary, e.g., of Mark founding Christian churches, or the note in Codex Bezae Cantabrigiensis that Apollos received his Christian training before leaving his home in Egypt. Even the Greek-speaking church does not appear there before A.D. 180/190, but then it occurs in a most impressive way, first with Bishop Demetrius of Alexandria, and then with the Alexandrian Catechetical School under Clement, who was soon succeeded by Origen. Evidence of the earlier presence of Christianity is provided by New Testament papyri. If p[52] was written about 125, there must have been Christians in Egypt at that time. The lack of any reference to the church in Egypt before 180 is probably to be explained by the predominantly gnostic character of the churches, which hindered their recognition by official churches elsewhere. While we have no information about the beginnings of the Greek-speaking church, we know even less about the beginnings of the Coptic church. At least as far as its official representations are concerned, the Egyptian church was Greek-speaking well into the sixth century and beyond. Nearly all the writings of its theologians and bishops were in Greek, and the survival of fragments of the Easter Epistles of Athanasius (295-373) in Coptic presents a unique exception. It is significant for the close relationship between Coptic and Greek that the Coptic alphabet is itself largely an adaptation of the Greek alphabet, augmented with a few letters to accommodate its special needs.

And yet by the end of the third century, or the beginning of the fourth century at the latest, there must have existed a definite and rather extensive Coptic tradition of the New Testament text (together with at least the Psalms from the Old Testament, if not more). When Anthony withdrew into the desert (shortly before A.D. 300), he spent the day reciting substantial parts of the scriptures from memory. This must have been in Coptic, because Anthony was poor in Greek. And when Pachomius instituted his monastery about 320, the rules for the monks included a regular reading of the scriptures. This also assumes the availability of Coptic manuscripts, because few of the monks in the monastery were competent in Greek. But this is only one part of the problem. Our grandfathers distinguished only three Coptic dialects: Sahidic, Bohairic, and Fayyumic. Today Akhmimic, Subakhmimic, Middle Egyptian, and Protobohairic are also recognized. Precisely how these seven dialects of the various regions are mutually related and how the Coptic language developed are subjects for the greatest variety of speculation among specialists, with no solution in sight. While this is true of the linguistic scene, it is equally true of the history of Coptic Bible translations.

Further, there are two extensive editions of the Coptic New Testament

(of four and seven volumes respectively) edited by George Horner in the principal dialects of Bohairic and Sahidic.

The Coptic Version of the New Testament in the Northern Dialect, otherwise called Memphitic and Bohairic, 4 vols. (1898-1905; repr. Osnabrück: 1969)
The Coptic Version of the New Testament in the Southern Dialect, otherwise called Sahidic and Thebaic, 7 vols. (1911-1924; repr. Osnabrück: 1969)

But although both editions were significant achievements in their time, they are now antiquated. In the twentieth century our knowledge of Coptic New Testament manuscripts has expanded explosively, not only in terms of their quantity but of their quality as well. Further, the fragments scattered in numerous libraries are now being correlated in their original unities (by F. J. Schmitz and Gerd Mink). Horner pieced together his edition of the Sahidic New Testament from isolated fragments, producing a text with extensive lacunae. But today, in the Pierpont Morgan Library in New York alone, there is a Four Gospels manuscript (M 569), two manuscripts of the Pauline letters (M 570, 571), and a manuscript of the Catholic letters (M 572). These manuscripts are all from the ninth century. There are also the Hamuli H in Cairo (ninth century), the Chester Beatty manuscripts A (*ca.* 600), and B (seventh century), containing the gospel of John (three times), the Paulines, and Acts. Besides the parts of these manuscripts edited by Herbert Thompson, there is also an edition of Papyrus Bodmer XIX containing Matt. 14–28 (and Rom. 1) from the fourth/fifth century edited by Rudolf Kasser. Hans Quecke has edited Mark, Luke, and John from a manuscript of the fifth century in Barcelona. Fritz Hintze and Hans-Martin Schenke have published the Berlin manuscript of Acts from the fourth century. Then there is also the "Mississippi Codex" (probably *ca.* 400) with its gratuitous aura of mystery. Horner's edition of the Bohairic New Testament printed the text of a single manuscript with an apparatus of the readings from other manuscripts he was acquainted with. Today the available material is so extensive that a critical edition of the Bohairic edition based on the many known complete manuscripts (not to mention fragments) of the various parts of the New Testament is not only a possibility, but an inevitability.

Akhmimic:
Friedrich Rösch, ed., *Bruchstücke des ersten Clemensbriefes nach dem achmimischen Papyrus der Strassburger Universitäts- und Landesbibliothek mit biblischen Texten derselben Handschrift* (Strasbourg: 1910) (John, James; fourth century)

Subakhmimic:
Herbert Thompson, ed., *The Gospel of St. John according to the Earliest Coptic Manuscript* (London: 1924) (John; fourth century)

Middle Egyptian:
H.-M. Schenke, *Das Matthäusevangelium im mittelägyptischen Dialekt des Koptischen (Codex Scheide)* (Berlin: 1981) (Matthew; fourth/fifth century?)
Glazier Collection G 67, Pierpont Morgan Library, New York (Acts; fifth century)

Middle Egyptian Fayyumic:
Elinor M. Husselman, ed., *The Gospel of John in Fayumic Coptic (P. Mich. Inv. 3521)* (Ann Arbor: 1962) (John; fourth/fifth century?)

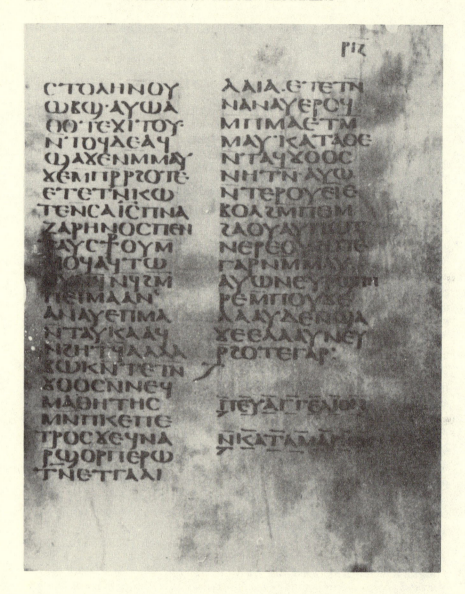

Plate 59. The Coptic Codex P. Palau Rib. 182 (fifth century; cf. pp. 200ff.); the ending of the gospel of Mark.

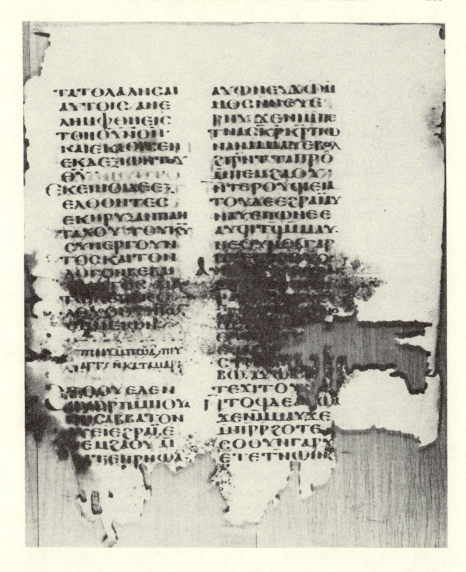

Plate 60. The Greek-Coptic lectionary *ℓ*1602 (eighth century; cf. pp. 200ff.): Mark 16:19-20 Greek, 16:2-6 Sahidic (f. 4ʳ).

Proto-Bohairic:
Rudolf Kasser, ed., *Papyrus Bodmer III: Evangile de Jean et Genèse I–IV, 2 en bohairique.*
CSCO 177 (Louvain: 1958) (John; fourth/fifth century?)

Sahidic:
F. Hintze and H.-M. Schenke, eds., *Die Berliner Handschrift der sahidischen Apostelge-schichte (P. 15926).* TU 109 (Berlin: 1970) (Fourth century)

Rudolf Kasser, ed., *Papyrus Bodmer XIX: Evangile de Matthieu XIV, 28–XXVIII, 20; Epître aux Romains I, 1–II, 3 en sahidique* (Geneva: 1962) (Fourth/fifth century)

Hans Quecke, ed., *Das Markusevangelium saïdisch: Text der Handschrift PPalau Rib. Inv. Nr. 182 mit den Varianten der Handschrift M 569* (Barcelona: 1972) (Fifth century)
———, *Das Lukasevangelium saïdisch: Text der Handschrift PPalau Rib. Inv. Nr. 181 mit den Varianten der Handschrift M 569* (Barcelona: 1977) (Fifth century)

——— , *Das Johannesevangelium saïdisch: Text der Handschrift PPalau Rib. Inv. Nr. 183 mit den Varianten der Handschriften 813 und 814 der Chester Beatty Library und der Handschrift M 569.* Papyrologica Castroctaviana 11 (Rome/Barcelona: 1984) (Fifth century)

H. Thompson, ed., *The Coptic Version of the Acts of the Apostles and the Pauline Epistles* (Cambridge: 1932) (Chester Beatty Codex A/B: Acts and Paul; A *ca.* 600, B seventh century)

K. Schüssler, ed., *Epistularum catholicarum versio Sahidica* (diss., Münster, 1969) (Pierpont Morgan Library 572; ninth century)

A chronological review of the manuscripts edited in the above publications makes it evident that the Coptic New Testament tradition was already broadly established by the fourth/fifth century. And yet these represent only a small part of the Coptic manuscript materials scattered throughout the world and only too inadequately catalogued. When the attempt of the Institute for New Testament Textual Research to assemble these materials has been at least somewhat achieved, and after they have been duly studied and evaluated, and coptologues have come to a consensus on the various dialects, then it will be possible to sketch a history of the Coptic versions of the New Testament more completely. Critical editions will then be possible, and the tradition will be able to make its contribution to New Testament textual criticism. For the Coptic New Testament is among the primary resources for the history of the New Testament text. Important as the Latin and Syriac versions may be, it is of far greater importance to know precisely how the text developed in Egypt. The Alexandrian and Egyptian text types are not only of the greatest importance by far, but the special climatic conditions of Egypt have also preserved for us nearly 100 percent of all the known witnesses to the New Testament text from the period up to the fourth century. A control of these by the tradition in the national language promises significant results.

5. THE ARMENIAN, GEORGIAN, AND ETHIOPIC VERSIONS

The early versions discussed above were all made directly from Greek, and their evidence is consequently of immediate critical and historical significance for the text of the New Testament. In this respect the three versions we are now to consider are different: their translation base is either subject to dispute, or it is known that Greek manuscripts either contributed only partially to their original translation or influenced them only at a later stage in a revision of their text.

a. *The Armenian version*. For the New Testament, and for the Gospels in particular, the first Armenian translation of the New Testament (Arm. 1) was probably based on a Syriac text of the Old Syriac type. This is consonant with the history of the church in the Armenian-speaking world. Christianity had gained an early foothold here: in 301 King Tiridates III (287-332) declared it the state religion. Gregory the Illuminator was the leading missionary. But it was not until the beginning of the fifth century that Mesrop (*ca*. 361-439) invented the Armenian alphabet which made possible under Patriarch Sahak (*ca*. 350-439) the earliest Armenian version. Armenia was in the Syriac cultural sphere when Christianity was first introduced, but it had since lost its independence and was now divided between Rome and Persia. The first version had been made in the Persian area, where Greek literature was forbidden. Accordingly the scriptures used by the church were written in Syriac — which explains why Arm. 1 was based on the Syriac version. Arm. 2, i.e., the Armenian majority text, was produced as a revision of the original version on the basis of Greek manuscripts, and was completed in the twelfth century by Nerses of Lampron, bishop of Tarsus, when he revised the book of Revelation. Meanwhile the early Armenian lectionary was based directly on a Greek model derived from the pre-Byzantine rite of Jerusalem. The manuscripts in Soviet Armenia have now all been collected in the Matenadaran, the national library in Erevan (there are no longer any manuscripts remaining in the ecclesiastical center at Etchmiadzin). But due to the diaspora of the Armenian people, valuable Armenian manuscripts (the earliest date from the ninth century) are to be found throughout the world (e.g., there are particularly important manuscripts at the Patriarchate in Jerusalem and in the Mechitarist House in Venice).

Bibliography:

Yovhannes Zohrapean (Zohrab), *Astuacašunč' matean hin ew nor ktakaranc'* (Venice: 1805)

Frédéric Macler, ed., *L' évangile arménien: Édition phototypique du manuscrit n°. 229 de la Bibliothèque d' Etchmiadzin* (Paris: 1920)

H. S. Anasyan, *Haykakan matenagitut' yun V-XVII dd.* (Erevan: 1976), 308-667 (for an extensive bibliography to 1973, see pp. 545-667)

T. A. Izmailova, "Charberdskij obrazee v zaglavnych listach rukopisi Avag Vanka 1200 g.," *Patmabanasirakan Handes* 3 (1977): 206-220

Erroll F. Rhodes, *An Annotated List of Armenian New Testament Manuscripts* (Tokyo: 1959)

b. *The Georgian version*. A succession of stages may also be distinguished in the Georgian version. The evangelization of Georgia from Armenia in the early fourth century determined the character of the Georgian New Testament. Arm. 1 must have provided the base for the first translation, with its mixture of Syriac and Armenian elements, beside which the lectionary reveals an unmistakably Greek base (as in Armenian). In effect, "the Old Georgian version can therefore at best, as a witness to the Old Syriac heritage, serve indirectly toward the recovery of the original Greek text."[13] This first translation (geo^1) was followed by a revision (geo^2) based on a Greek text which was made after the separation from the Armenian church in the early seventh century and has left extensive

_____

13. Joseph Molitor, "Das Neue Testament in georgischer Sprache," ANTF 5 (1972): 327.

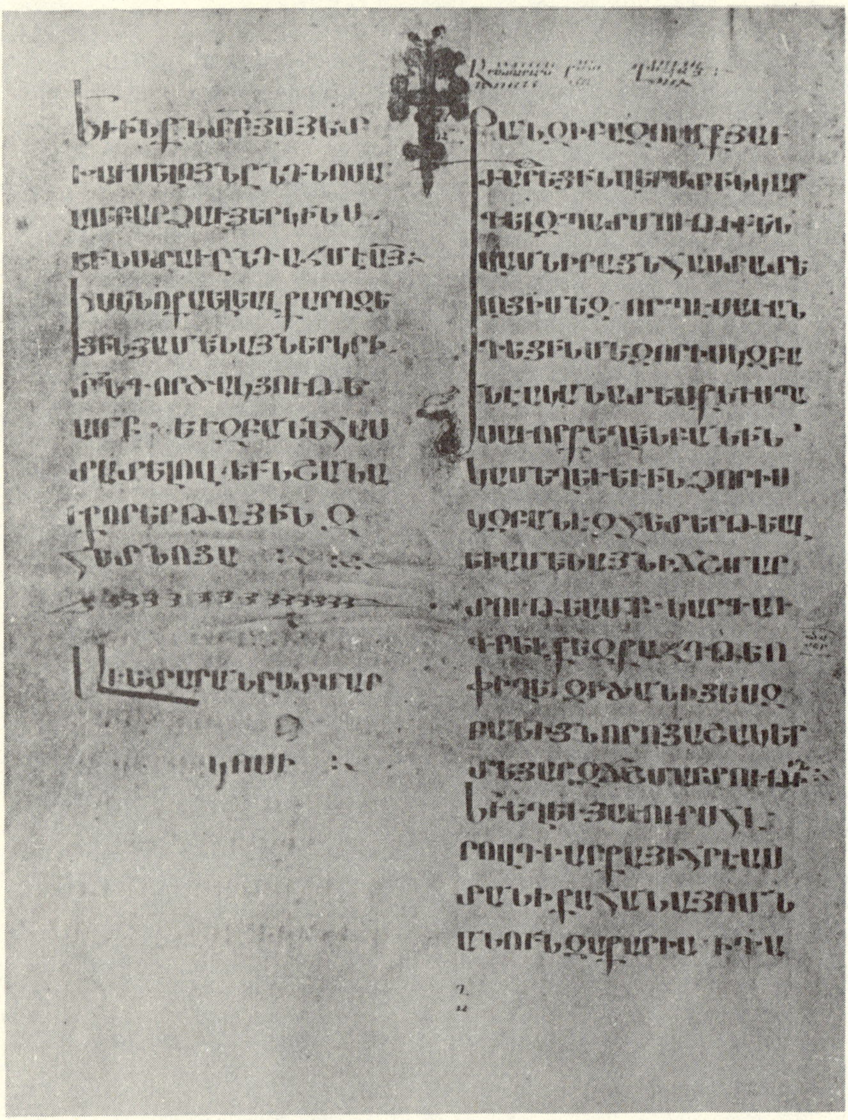

Plate 61. An Armenian manuscript (Matenadaran 2374, earlier Etchmiadzin 229; cf. p. 205), written in 989: the ending of the gospel of Mark and the beginning of Luke (f. 111ᵛ).

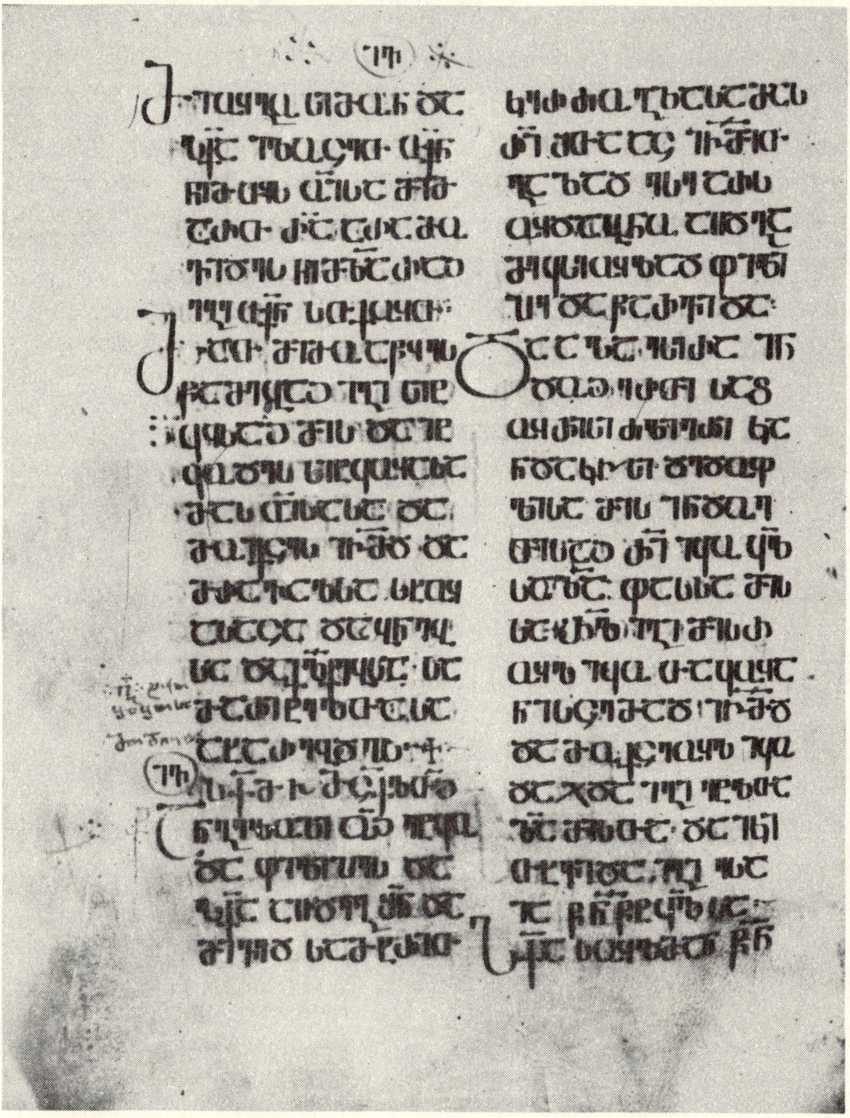

Plate 62. A Georgian manuscript (Codex A; cf. pp. 205f.), written in 897: Acts 8:24-29 (f. 54ᵛ).

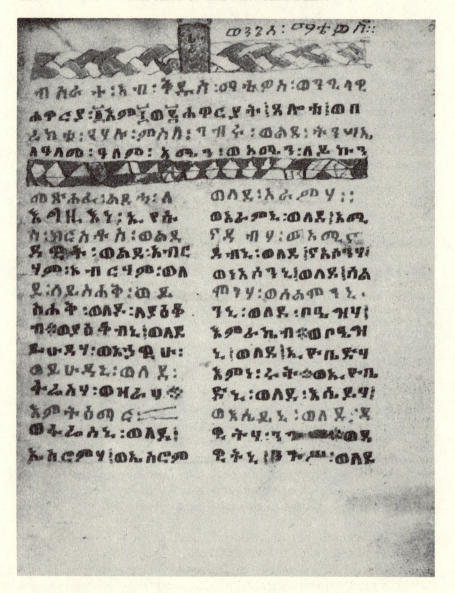

Plate 63. An Ethiopic manuscript (Munich, Bayerische Staatsbibliothek cod. Aeth. 42, seventeenth century; cf. pp. 209f.): the beginning of the gospel of Matthew (f. 5ʳ). Most Ethiopic manuscripts are very late.

traces. Greek influence is unmistakable elsewhere as well: the liturgical text of the Georgian church still in use today was derived from a version of the Greek text made by Euthymius (d. 1028), abbot of the Georgian monastery on Mt. Athos.

Bibliography:

Vladmirus Benešević, *Quattuor evangeliorum versio georgiana vetus* (St. Petersburg: 1909 [Matthew], 1911 [Mark])

Robert Pierpont Blake, *The Old Georgian Version of the Gospel of Mark*. PO 20 (Paris: 1929): 435-574

―――――, *The Old Georgian Version of the Gospel of Matthew*. PO 24 (Paris: 1933): 1-168

―――――, and Maurice Brière, *The Old Georgian Version of the Gospel of John*. PO 26 (Paris: 1950): 454-599

Maurice Brière, *The Old Georgian Version of the Gospel of Luke*. PO 27 (Paris: 1955): 276-448

Gérard Garitte, *L'ancienne version géorgienne des Actes des apôtres d'après deux manuscrits du Sinai*. Bibliothèque du Muséon 38 (Louvain: 1955)

K'. Dzocenidze and K. Daniela, *Pavles epistolet'a k'art'uli versiebi*. Dzveli k'art'uli enis kat'edris sromebi 16 (Tiflis: 1974)

K'et'evan I. Lort'k'ip'anidze, *Kat'olike epistolet'a k'art'uli versiebi X-XIV saukunet'a helnacerebis mihedvit'*. Dzveli k'art'uli enis dzeglebi 9 (Tiflis: 1956)

Ilia V. Imnaišvili, *Iovanes gamoc'hadeba da misi t'argmaneba* (Tiflis: 1961)

Joseph Molitor, *Monumenta iberica antiquiora: Textus chanmeti et haemeti ex inscriptionibus*. CSCO 166 = Subs. 10 (Louvain: 1956)

J. Neville Birdsall, "The Georgian Versions of the Acts of the Apostles," in T. Baarda et al., eds. *Text and Testimony: Essays on New Testament and Apocryphal Literature in Honour of A. F. J. Klijn* (Kampen: 1988); also "The Gregorian Version of the Book of Revelation," *Le Muséon* 91 (1978): 355-366

c. The Ethiopic version. The character of the Ethiopic version is still more controversial. It has not yet been determined whether the Gospels were translated from Greek or from Syriac. The translation of Acts seems to have been made from Greek. The Catholic letters were more certainly translated from Greek, and for Revelation it is possible not only to be certain of the language from which it was translated, but to identify the source even more precisely: it represents the text type of A and C, with subsequent influence from the Coptic and Arabic versions.

This obscure situation corresponds to the variety of theories about the early period of Christianity in Ethiopia. Tracing its beginnings to Philip's conversion of the eunuch of Candace "the Queen of Ethiopia," as recounted in Acts 8:26-39, is purely a matter of legend. The account ascribing the Ethiopic version of the Bible to Frumentius is also legendary. According to an early Church tradition the Christians Frumentius and Aedesius came to Ethiopia as slaves in the fourth century and rose to positions of prominence at the royal court. After receiving his freedom, Frumentius went to Alexandria where he was consecrated by Athanasius as bishop of the Ethiopians. Returning to Ethiopia he undertook a most successful mission which involved his translating the Bible into Ethiopic. This probably reflects a confusion of names (as in the letter of Abgar of Edessa to Jesus). Frumentius is called Abba Salama; there was a famous Ethiopian patriarch of the same name in Ethiopia in the fourteenth century. Coincidentally

the earliest manuscript of the Ethiopic New Testament is of the same period (the tenth/eleventh century date of the "Abba-Garima" manuscripts deserves more thorough examination).

In any event, it is certain that in the second half of the fifth century the church in Ethiopia received a definite stimulus from the activities of Syrian monks. It was in all probability at that time that the translation of the New Testament into Ethiopic received a fresh impetus. According to Ethiopic tradition, the translation of the Bible was finished in 678 with the completion of the book of Sirach.

Bibliography:

Petrus Aethiops, ed., *Testamentum Novum cum epistula Pauli ad Hebraeos* (Rome: 1548)
————, *Epistulae XIII divi Pauli* (Rome: 1549)
Thomas Pell Platt, ed., *Evangelia Sancta Aethiopice* (London: 1826)
————, *Novum Testamentum Domini nostri et Salvatoris Jesu Christi Aethiopice* (London: 1830); revised by Franz Praetorius (Leipzig: 1899)
Josef Hoffmann, ed., *Die äthiopische Übersetzung der Johannes-Apokalypse*. CSCO 281 (Louvain: 1967)

6. *THE GOTHIC, OLD CHURCH SLAVONIC, AND OTHER VERSIONS*

a. The Gothic version. The fact that the Gothic version was made directly from the Greek text is unquestioned. Nevertheless, the Gothic version is not cited along with the Latin, Syriac, and other versions as a primary witness in the critical apparatuses of editions of the Greek New Testament. As a rule it is cited only casually, because the general character of its textual base is rather precisely known: for his translation Wulfilas made use of a manuscript of the early Byzantine text differing little from what we find in the Greek manuscripts.

Naturally it would be of considerable significance for the history of the text to determine precisely the form of the Greek text used by Wulfilas, because this would reveal the stage of development of the Koine text about 350 in a purer form than is available elsewhere. But unfortunately this is impossible because the Germanics specialists who have reconstructed the underlying Greek text have not followed the Gothic text as it stands, but proposed a hypothetical Greek text of their own. The standard edition by Wilhelm Streitberg differs from the Gothic text (under the influence of Hermann Freiherr von Soden's views among others) in hundreds of instances in a way that can only be described as arbitrary. Ernst Bernhardt's reconstruction has other faults because of its assumption that Wulfilas followed an exemplar of the type of Codex Alexandrinus. For the Gothic version to make its full contribution to New Testament textual criticism, what is needed from Germanics scholars is a reconstruction of the Greek exemplar based exclusively on the Gothic materials apart from any theories of its textual history. Wulfilas' version is, after all, quite literal, attempting to render the Greek words consistently whenever possible. While admittedly an element of Latin influence may be detected in it, there is the question whether this was already present with Wulfilas himself (certainly a possibility in Moesia), or whether it is a later element due to textual transmission in a Latin environment

Plate 64. The Gothic Codex Argenteus (Stockholm): the ending of the gospel of Mark, which was discovered in 1970 in Trier as the wrapping for a relic.

(Codex Argenteus is dated in the sixth century). But this should be determined by textual criticism and not by Germanics scholarship — at least not exclusively.

The version was begun soon after 341 (if not earlier), when Wulfilas came to Byzantium as a member of a Gothic delegation and was consecrated "bishop of the Gothlands" by Bishop Eusebius of Nicomedia. Christianity had already spread among the Goths (brought by Roman Christians taken as prisoners of war), but it expanded vigorously in the years following. Although the Christians under Wulfilas were expelled in 348 (crossing the Danube into Moesia, where Wulfilas completed his version), the triumphal advance of Christianity among the Goths and other Germanic tribes could not be checked.

For his translation Wulfilas devised a special alphabet of twenty-seven letters, two thirds of which were derived from Greek, and the rest from Latin and the Old German runes. Apart from the Gospels (in the order of Matthew, John, Luke, Mark) and the Pauline letters (incomplete), which are preserved in a total of nine manuscripts, only about fifty verses from Neh. 5–7 have survived of the Gothic Bible.

Bibliography:

W. Streitberg, *Die gotische Bibel* 1: *Der gotische Text und seine griechische Vorlage mit Einleitung, Lesarten und Quellennachweisen sowie den kleineren Denkmälern als Anhang* (Heidelberg: 1908, corrected ed. ²1919, rev. ed. ⁵1965, ⁶1971)

Ernst Bernhardt, *Vulfila oder Die gotische Bibel mit dem entsprechenden griechischen Text und mit kritischem und erklärendem Commentar* (Halle: 1875)

G. W. S. Friedrichsen, *The Gothic Version of the Gospels* (Oxford: 1926)

————, *The Gothic Version of the Epistles* (Oxford: 1939)

Elfriede Stutz, *Gotische Literaturdenkmäler* (Stuttgart: 1966)

b. The Old Church Slavonic version. The translation into Old Church Slavonic was begun in the ninth century, primarily as the work of the brothers Cyril (Constantine; d. 869) and Methodius (d. 885). Contemporary accounts of their lives (partly legendary) tell of their missionary activities and of their translation of the Bible. Lectionaries came first, three varieties of which have been preserved: the "short lectionary," the "long lectionary," and the Sunday lectionary. The Sunday lectionary, which was the earliest, was expanded into the "short lectionary," while the "long lectionary" was not developed until the twelfth century, probably in Galicia-Wolhynia. The Four Gospels were translated in Bulgaria at the turn of the tenth century, manuscripts of Acts and the Catholic letters appear first in the twelfth century (although they may have been translated much earlier), while Revelation was probably not translated before the twelfth century. The manuscript tradition of the Old Church Slavonic version dates from the tenth/eleventh century.

The base from which the Old Church Slavonic was translated has not been determined (the Russian Orthodox Church claims divine inspiration for it), but most probably it was made from Greek manuscripts of the Byzantine Imperial text type.

Bibliography:

Josef Vajs, *Evangelium sv. Matouse: Text rekonstruovaný* (Prague: 1935)

————, *Evangelium sv. Marka: Text rekonstruovaný* (Prague: 1935)

————, *Evangelium sv. Lukáše: Text rekonstruovaný* (Prague: 1936)

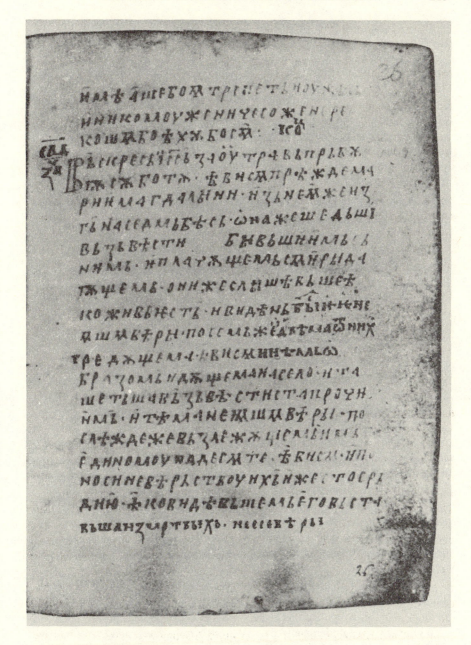

Plate 65. An Old Church Slavonic manuscript (Evangelium Dobromiri, twelfth century): Mark 16:8-14 (f. 26ʳ).

_____, *Evangelium sv. Jana: Text rekonstruovaný* (Prague: 1936)

Vatroslav Jagić, *Quattuor evangeliorum codex glagoliticus olim Zographensis nunc Petro-politanus* (Berlin: 1879)

_____, *Quattuor evangeliorum versionis palaeoslovenicae codex Marianus glagoliticus* Berlin: 1883)

Josef Vajs and Josef Kurz, *Evangeliarum Assemani: Codex vaticanus 3, slavicus glagoliticus* I-II (Prague: 1929-1955)

Viačeslav Nikolaević Ščepkin, *Savvina kniga* (St. Petersburg: 1903)

Aemilianus Kalužniacki, *Actus epistolaeque apostolorum palaeoslovenice ad fidem codicis Christinopolitani* (Vienna: 1896)

Grigorij Andreevich Il'inskij, *Slepčenskij apostol XII veka* (Moscow: 1912)

Arch. Amfilochij, *Apokalipsis XIV veka Rumjancevskago muzeja* (Moscow: 1886)

c. Versions in other languages. The fact that the Old Church Slavonic version as well as the Gothic has rarely been cited in modern critical apparatuses is undoubtedly a weak point. But there are versions in other languages which have never been cited at all, and in all likelihood will not be cited in the foreseeable future, e.g., versions in Arabic, Nubian, Persian, Soghdian, Old English, Old High German, and so forth. This despite the fact that the Arabic version is not based just on the languages of the areas subjugated by Islam since the eighth century, but on Greek sources as well. Its manuscripts (including those from a demonstrable Greek base) date back to the ninth century, making it quite comparable in age to other versions. But unfortunately the arabists of today are hardly concerning themselves with the transmission of the New Testament in Arabic or with its sources, although there are many interesting problems here (even apart from the Greek-based texts), e.g., an Arabic version of the Harklean text, the existence of which has been demonstrated.

In the three Nubian kingdoms of late antiquity there were Christian churches with established traditions even before the sixth century, when the Christian mission became full fledged. It is not known when the New Testament was translated into Nubian, nor yet what its sources may have been (only lectionary fragments have survived).

Christianity was active in Persia from the third century, and it was in all probability then (cf. the witness of Chrysostom), or perhaps somewhat later, that the New Testament was translated into the national language. But no manuscripts have yet been found, and the only Persian texts known are in modern Persian.

From Central Asia there are several fragments of a version in Soghdian, but they are too brief and have been inadequately studied for any definite conclusions. The surviving versions of the New Testament in Old English or in Old High German were undoubtedly derived from Latin sources, so that they have no direct value for the history of the Greek text.

7. PATRISTIC CITATIONS

For quotations by Church Fathers in the languages discussed above the same qualifications apply as for the Greek Church Fathers (cf. above, pp. 171ff.). Yet their value is even greater in at least one of the versions than in Greek,

namely in Syriac. Significantly here the reconstruction of the text of Tatian's Diatessaron is critically dependent on the writings of the Syriac Church Father Ephraem. Further, only from an extensive study of Syriac patristic quotations can we anticipate any progress in our understanding of the history of the extraordinarily important Syriac New Testament version. There is still much to be done. A beginning with this great mass of material is being made at Münster (cf. Barbara Aland, *ANTF* 7, p. 199 above). The quotations that have been most thoroughly investigated are those of the Latin Church Fathers, represented in volumes of the Vetus Latina which have appeared to date, edited by the Archabbey of Beuron.[14]

Quotations from the following Fathers in the languages discussed above are cited in Nestle-Aland[26] and/or *GNT*[3]. For bibliographical abbreviations see pp. 173f.; the remarks there apply especially to the number of Latin Church Fathers listed and the space devoted to them in this manual — they will be considerably modified in *GNT*[4].

Descriptive List of the Latin and Eastern Church Fathers
Latin Church Fathers

Ambrose (Ambr), 333/340-397. Born of a prominent Roman family in Trier *ca.* 370, became Consularis Liguriae et Aemiliae with residence in Milan. Despite his reluctance he was consecrated bishop only days after his baptism (374). Exegetical works include his *Hexaemeron* (in six books), tractates on the Old and New Testaments, and his largest work, a commentary on the gospel of Luke in ten books. Altaner, 378-389 (Eng. trans., 443-457); Bardenh., III:498-547; Cayré, I:520-547; Cross, 42-43; Jurgens, II:145-177; *CPL*, 123-169.

Ambrose, Pseudo- (PsAmbr). Works from later centuries circulating spuriously under the name of Ambrose. Altaner, 385-86 (Eng. trans., 450); Bardenh., IV:542, 546; *CPL*, 170-183; Fischer, 67-72.

Ambrosiaster (Ambst), fourth century. A commentary on thirteen Pauline letters (omitting Hebrews) from the time of Pope Damasus (366-384) circulated under the name of Ambrose; also *Quaestiones Veteris et Novi Testamenti* by the same author. Altaner, 389-390 (Eng. trans., 457-58); Bardenh., III:520-25; Cayré, I:605; Cross, 44; Jurgens, II:177-78; *CPL*, 184-88.

Ansbert, d. 693. A chancellor of Clothar III, metropolitan of Rouen. *CPL*, 2089.

Apringius (Apr), mid-sixth century. Bishop of Pace (Beja in Portugal), wrote a commentary on Revelation shortly after 551. Altaner, 492 (Eng. trans., 591-92); Bardenh., V:395-96; Cayré, II:257; *CPL*, 1093.

Arnobius the Younger (Arn), d. after 455. A monk in Rome, probably fled from the Vandals in Africa. Compiled a loose collection of scholia on various passages from Matthew, Luke, and John. Altaner, 459 (Eng. trans., 546); Bardenh., IV:603-606; Cayré, II:174-75; Cross, 92; *CPL*, 239-243.

Augustine (Aug), 354-430. Born in Tagaste, Numidia, of a pagan official and his Christian wife Monica. After an early catechumenate, alienated from Christianity by the influence of Cicero, Manichaeism, and skepticism. Taught rhetoric in Milan in 384. Converted in 386, baptized by Ambrose in 387, returned to Africa where he lived in monastic seclusion. Became priest under popular pressure, appointed coadjutor in 395, and shortly thereafter sole bishop of Hippo Regius. The most important of the Western Church Fathers for his extensive writings and numerous works on biblical exegesis. Died as the Vandals laid siege to Hippo. Altaner, 412-449 (Eng. trans., 487-534); Bardenh.,

14. Cf. p. 190.

IV:434-511; Cayré, I:612-716; Cross, 108-110; Jurgens, III:1-178; *CPL*, 250-360.

Augustine, Pseudo-. Works circulated spuriously under the name of Augustine. Bardenh., IV:501-502; *CPL*, 361-386; Stegmüller, 1480-1497; Fischer, 131-161.

Beatus of Liébana (Bea), d. 798. Spanish abbot of Liébana near Santander, compiled a commentary on Revelation. Altaner, 373 (Eng. trans., 437-38); Bardenh., V:396; Quasten, II:412; *CPL*, 710, 1752a, 1753; Stegmüller, 1597.

Bede (Beda), 672/673-735. Called "Venerable" since the Synod of Aachen in 836. English Benedictine and church teacher. Compiled the *Historia ecclesiastica gentis anglorum*, and commented on the Gospels, Acts, and Revelation. Cayré, II:272-76; Cross, 149-150; Stegmüller, 1598-1688.

Caelestinus I, fourth/fifth century. Pope of Rome 422-432. Altaner, 356 (Eng. trans., 417); Bardenh., 614-15; Cayré, I:519; Cross, 258; Jurgens, III:183-84; *CPL*, 1650-54.

Caesarius, ca. 470-542. Bishop of Arles. Writings include a commentary on Revelation. Altaner, 475 (Eng. trans., 569-571); Bardenh., V:345-357; Cayré, II:199-209; Cross, 218; Jurgens, III:282-84; *CPL*, 1008-1019a.

Cassian (Cn, Johannes Cassianus), ca. 360-*ca.* 435. Probably born in today's Dobruja (Rumania), first entered a monastery in Bethlehem, was later among the anchorites in Egypt, then after 399 deaconed by John Chrysostom in Constantinople. In Rome in 405; *ca.* 415 founded a monastery and a convent in Marseilles. Altaner, 452-54 (Eng. trans., 537-540); Bardenh., IV:558-564; Cayré, I:594-603; Cross, 246; *CPL*, 512-14.

Cassiodorus (Cass), ca. 485-*ca.* 580. Flavius Magnus Aurelius Cassiodorus, from a prominent official family in Calabria, in 507 quaestor and private secretary to Theodoric the Great. Although of the highest rank and ultimately a patrician, he withdrew *ca.* 540 to a monastery he founded in Vivarium. Along with writings as a statesman he also wrote theological works in the monastery, e.g., *Complexiones in Epistulas et Acta apostolorum et Apocalypsin*. Book I of his *Institutiones* contains an introduction to the study of the Bible. Altaner, 486-88 (Eng. trans., 584-86); Bardenh., V:264-277; Cayré, II:221-25; Cross, 246-47; *CPL*, 896-911.

Chromatius, ca. 387-407 bishop of Aquileia. Besides his homilies, twenty-five tractates on Matthew have been preserved. Altaner, 457-58; Bardenh., III:548-49; Cayré, I:605; Cross, 283; *CPL*, 217-19.

Claudius, d. *ca.* 827. Born in Spain, bishop of Turin in 817/818, author of commentaries on Genesis and Kings which circulated under the name of Eucherius of Lyons. Altaner, 455 (Eng. trans., 541); Manitius, I:390-96; Cross, 299; *CPL*, 498; Stegmüller, 1949-1975.

Cyprian (Cyp), ca. 200/210-258. Thascius Caecilius Cyprianus, probably from Carthage, of a pagan family, baptized *ca.* 246, bishop of Carthage 248/249. Beheaded in 258 in the persecution under Valerian. The most influential writer of the Latin church before Ambrose and Augustine, since Tertullian was officially repudiated. Altaner, 172-181 (Eng. trans., 193-207); Quasten, II:340-383; Bardenh., II:442-517; Cayré, I:254-268; Cross, 367-68; Jurgens, I:216-239; *CPL*, 38-67.

Cyprian, Pseudo- (Ps Cyp, Ps Cyprian). Writings attributed to Cyprian, some contemporary, e.g., *De Rebaptismate*. Altaner, 177-78 (Eng. trans., 199-201); Quasten, II:367-373; Bardenh., II:490-506; *CPL*, 57-67; Fischer, 234-37.

De Promissionibus, fifth century. The treatise *De promissionibus et praedictionibus dei* deals with biblical prophecies about Christ and the Church. Attributed by Cassiodorus to Prosper of Aquitaine, and by recent scholars to Quodvultdeus. Altaner, 449 (Eng. trans., 534); Bardenh., IV:522-25; *CPL*, 413; Stegmüller, 7018.

De Rebaptismate. A polemic against Cyprian, formerly included among Cyprian's works (cf. Pseudo-Cyprian). Altaner, 177 (Eng. trans., 200); Bardenh., II:499-502; *CPL*, 59.

Druthmarus, d. after 880. Known as Druthmar of Corvey (Corbie) since Trithemius, identical with Christian of Stablo. Monk, author of Gospel commentaries. Spicq, 49-50; Stegmüller, 1926ff.

Eugippius, d. after 533. Student of Severin, whose biography he wrote *ca.* 511. Altaner, 479-480 (Eng. trans., 574); Bardenh., V:220-24; Cayré, II:227; Cross, 480; *CPL*, 676-79; Stegmüller, 2266.

Facundus, mid-sixth century. Bishop of Hermiane in Africa. Altaner, 490-91 (Eng. trans., 589-590); Bardenh., V:320-24; Cayré, II:153; Cross, 498-99; *CPL,* 866-68.

Fastidius, first half fifth century. Mentioned by Gennadius as a bishop in Britain. Altaner, 377 (Eng. trans., 442); Bardenh., IV:518-520; Cross, 503; *CPL,* 736, 763.

Faustinus, fourth century. Roman presbyter of the Luciferian schismatics, addressed to Theodosius I a creed in 380, and a petition in 383/384. Altaner, 367 (Eng. trans., 430); Bardenh., III:475; Cayré, I:333; *CPL,* 119-120, 1571.

Faustus of Mileve, fourth century. From Mileve (Africa) by birth, sometime bishop of the Manichaeans in Rome. At Carthage in 383 met Augustine, who wrote *Contra Faustum ca.* 400 to confute him. Altaner, 427 (Eng. trans., 489); Bardenh., IV:512; Cayré, I:623-24; Cross, 504; *CPL,* 726.

Faustus of Riez, d. 490/500. A Briton by birth, monk, and *ca.* 433 abbot of Lerinum. *Ca.* 458 bishop of Reji (Riez) in Provence, exiled 477-485. Altaner, 473-74 (Eng. trans., 566-67); Bardenh., IV:582-89; Cayré, II:171-74; Cross, 504-505; *CPL,* 961-65.

Ferrandus, sixth century. Deacon in Carthage, student and biographer of Fulgentius. Altaner, 489 (Eng. trans., 588); Bardenh., V:316-19; Cayré, II:227; Cross, 508; *CPL,* 847-48.

Firmicus Maternus (Firm), first half fourth century. Julius Firmicus Maternus, a Sicilian rhetor converted to Christianity, addressed an indictment of paganism to the emperor. Altaner, 360-61 (Eng. trans., 422-23); Bardenh., III:456-460; Cross, 514; *CPL,* 101-103.

Fulgentius of Ruspe (Fulg), 467-533. Born in Telepte (Africa) of a senatorial family, first a procurator, then a monastic monk. Bishop of Ruspe *ca.* 507, in exile 508-515 and 517-523. Altaner, 489 (Eng. trans., 587-590); Bardenh., V:303-316; Cayré, II:191-99; Cross, 541; Jurgens, III:285-300; *CPL,* 814-846.

Gaudentius, d. after 406. Bishop of Brescia. Altaner, 369 (Eng. trans., 432); Bardenh., III:485-86; Cayré, I:605; Cross, 550-51; *CPL,* 215-19.

Gennadius of Marseilles, fifth century. Presbyter in Marseilles, authored a history of Christian literature as sequel to Jerome's *De viris illustribus,* also *Adversus omnes haereses* in eight books. Altaner, 474 (Eng. trans., 567-68); Bardenh., IV:595-98; Cayré, II:225-26; Cross, 556; *CPL,* 957-960.

Gildas, ca. 500-*ca.* 570. A Briton by birth, his magnum opus *De excidio et conquestu Britanniae* is full of biblical quotations. Bardenh., V:399-401; Cayré, II:272; Cross, 566-67; *CPL,* 1319-1324; Manitius, I:208-210.

Gregory of Elvira, d. after 392. Bishop of Eliberis in Granada, a leading Luciferian. Altaner, 370 (Eng. trans., 434-35); Bardenh., III:396-401; Cayré, I:333; Cross, 598; Jurgens, I:392-94; *CPL,* 546-557.

Haymo of Auxerre, mid-ninth century. Benedictine monk at St. Germain of Auxerre, author of commentaries on the Pauline letters and Revelation. Bardenh., V:334; Stegmüller, 3064-3072, 3088-3099.

Jerome (Hier), ca. 347-419/420. Sophronius Eusebius Hieronymus, born of a Christian family in Dalmatia. For a while a hermit, then ordained presbyter, later secretary to Pope Damasus. Settled in Bethlehem in 386. Worked on biblical text (Vulgate; cf. pp. 187f.), also wrote New Testament commentaries, homilies, and sermons. Altaner, 394-404 (Eng. trans., 462-476); Bardenh., III:605-654; Cayré, I:569-593; Cross, 731-32; Jurgens, II:182-214; *CPL,* 580-642.

Jerome, Pseudo-. Spurious writings ascribed to Jerome. *CPL,* 623a-642; Fischer, 307-316.

Hilary of Poitiers (Hil, Hilarius), ca. 315-367. Of a pagan family, bishop of his home city of Poitiers in 350. After exile to Asia Minor combatted Arianism in Gaul. A commentary on Matthew is preserved from the period before his exile. Altaner, 361-66 (Eng. trans., 423-28); Bardenh., III:365-393; Cayré, I:354-364; Cross, 649; Jurgens, I:372-389; *CPL,* 427-472.

Julian of Eclanum (Julianus of Aeclanum), d. *ca.* 454. Bishop of Eclanum near Beneventum, defender of Pelagianism, author of many commentaries. Altaner, 377 (Eng. trans., 442-43); Bardenh., IV:516-18; Cayré, I:394; Cross, 766; Jurgens, II:217-18; *CPL,* 773-77.

Julius I, fourth century. Pope of Rome 337-352. Altaner, 353 (Eng. trans., 413); Bardenh., III:583-85; Cross, 767; Jurgens, I:346; *CPL,* 1627.

Juvencus, fourth century. Gaius Vettius Aquilinus Juvencus, a Spanish presbyter of prominent descent, author of a Gospel harmony in hexameters *ca.* 330. Altaner, 405 (Eng. trans., 477); Bardenh., III:429-432; Cayré, I:554; Cross, 771; *CPL,* 1385.

Lactantius (Lact), third/fourth century. Lucian Caecilius Firmianus Lactantius, from a pagan family probably in Africa, student of Arnobius. Teacher of Latin rhetoric in Nicomedia under Diocletian, resigned his position in the persecution, called to Trier as tutor to Constantine the Great's son *ca.* 317. Altaner, 185-88 (Eng. trans., 208-212); Quasten, II:392-410; Bardenh., II:525-549; Cayré, I:271-74; Cross, 791-92; Jurgens, I:264-272; *CPL,* 89-92.

Leo I, the Great, fifth century. Pope of Rome 440-461. Surviving literary works include letters and homilies. Altaner, 357-360 (Eng. trans., 417-422); Bardenh., IV:617-623; Cayré, II:122-141; Cross, 811-12; Jurgens, III:268-280; *CPL,* 1656-1661.

Liberatus, sixth century. Deacon in Carthage, wrote a history of heresies to 553. Altaner, 491 (Eng. trans., 590); Bardenh., V:328-29; Cayré, II:154, 228; *CPL,* 865.

Lucifer of Calaris (Lcf), d. 370/371. Bishop of Cagliari (Sardinia). Exiled after the Synod of Milan (355). From this period are his polemical writings of particular importance for their citations of the biblical text from the period before Jerome. Altaner, 367 (Eng. trans., 429-430); Bardenh., III:469-475; Cayré, I:332-33; Cross, 841-42; *CPL,* 112-18.

Macrobius, fourth century. Presbyter in Africa, and bishop of the Donatists in Rome. Bardenh., III:490; *CPL,* 721.

Marius Mercator, fourth/fifth century. Probably African by birth, later in the eastern part of the Roman Empire, probably in Constantinople. Translated many writings from Greek. Altaner, 449-450 (Eng. trans., 534-35); Bardenh., IV:525-29; Cayré, II:178-79; Cross, 874; Jurgens, III:184-85; *CPL,* 780-81.

(Gaius) Marius Victorinus (M Vict, Victorinus Rome, Marius), d. *ca.* 363. From Africa, a renowned teacher of rhetoric in Rome. Became Christian late in life, giving up teaching in 362 (Edict of Emperor Julian). Wrote important commentaries on the Pauline letters. Altaner, 368-69 (Eng. trans., 430-32); Bardenh., III:460-68; Cayré, I:331-32; Cross, 1438; Jurgens, I:394-96; *CPL,* 94-100.

Maximus, fourth/fifth century. Arian bishop of the Goths, author of a polemic against Ambrose. Altaner, 372-73 (Eng. trans., 335); Bardenh., III:595-96; *CPL,* 692-702.

Maximus of Turin, fourth/fifth century. Bishop of Turin. Died between 408 and 423 according to Gennadius. Not to be confused with the bishop Maximus of Turin who attended the Synods of Milan in 451 and of Rome in 465. Nearly one hundred sermons have been preserved. Altaner, 458-59 (Eng. trans., 545-46); Bardenh., IV:610-13; Cross, 894-95; *CPL,* 220-26b.

Nicetas of Remesiana (Nic), d. after 414. Bishop of Remesiana (now in Serbia), and friend of Paulinus of Nola, who is the best source on the life of Nicetas. Altaner, 391 (Eng. trans., 458-59); Bardenh., III:598-605; Cayré, I:603-604; Cross, 969; *CPL,* 646-652.

Novatian (Nov), mid-third century. *Ca.* 250 presbyter in Rome, in 251 ordained counterbishop in opposition to Cornelius, beginning the Novatian schism and founding a counterchurch. Altaner, 170-72 (Eng. trans., 191-93); Quasten, II:212-233; Bardenh., II:626-635; Cayré, I:250-54; Cross, 984; Jurgens, I:246-48; *CPL,* 68-76.

Optatus of Mileve, fourth century. Bishop of Mileve, mentioned by Augustine about 400 as dead, his writings against Donatism are a valuable historical source. Altaner, 371-72 (Eng. trans., 435-36); Bardenh., III:491-94; Cayré, I:608-610; Cross, 1001; Jurgens, II:139-141; *CPL,* 244-49.

Orosius (Oros), d. after 418. Paulus Orosius, born in Braga (Portugal), priest, 414 with Augustine in Hippo, 415 in Palestine with Jerome at Bethlehem, returned to Africa where he wrote *Historiarum adversus paganos libri septem,* an historical work extending to 417. Altaner, 213-14 (Eng. trans., 280-81); Bardenh., IV:529-533; Cayré, I:560-61, 607-608; Cross, 1012; Jurgens, III:185-86; *CPL,* 571-74.

Pacian, d. between 379 and 392. Bishop of Barcelona, esteemed by Jerome for his classical education. Altaner, 369-370 (Eng. trans., 433-34); Bardenh., III:401-403; Cayré, I:606; Cross, 1021; Jurgens, II:141-44; *CPL,* 561-63.

Paulinus of Nola, 353-431. Born in Bordeaux of a wealthy senatorial family. Student of Ausonius, 379 governor of Campania, *ca.* 409 bishop of Nola. Altaner, 409-410 (Eng. trans., 482-83); Bardenh., III:569-582; Cayré, I:551-54; Cross, 1054; *CPL,* 202-206.

Pelagius (Pel), mid-fourth century–*ca.* 423/429. From Britain, an ascetic in Rome until 410, then in Carthage and Palestine. Of the writings ascribed to him a commentary on the Pauline letters is among those recognized as genuine. On his part in the Vulgate, cf. p. 188. Altaner, 374-76 (Eng. trans., 439-441); Bardenh., IV:513-15; Cayré, I:392; Cross, 1058-59; Jurgens, II:214-16; *CPL,* 728-766; Stegmüller, 6355-6371.

Petilian, fourth/fifth century. First a lawyer, then bishop of Cirta (Constantina in Numidia), a leading Donatist. Bardenh., IV:512-13; *CPL,* 714.

Phoebadius, fourth century. Also Foebadius. Bishop of Agennum (Agen in Guyenne) in southern France until at least 392. Altaner, 367 (Eng. trans., 430); Bardenh., III:395-96; Cross, 1087; Jurgens, I:391; *CPL,* 473.

Possidius of Calama, fifth century. Student and biographer of Augustine. Altaner, 419 (Eng. trans., 488); Cayré, I:611; Cross, 1113; *CPL,* 358-59; *BHL,* 786.

Primasius (Prim), d. after 552. Bishop of Hadrumetum (Africa), author of a commentary on Revelation. Altaner, 491 (Eng. trans., 590); Bardenh., V:332-34; Cayré, II:153; Cross, 1124; *CPL,* 873; Stegmüller, 6988.

Priscillian (Prisc), d. 385. From a wealthy Spanish family, 380 bishop of Avila, 385 executed for magic. His *Canones in epistulas Paulinas* represents a collection of theses from the fourteen Pauline letters. Altaner, 374 (Eng. trans., 438-39); Bardenh., III:403-412; Cayré, I:606-608; Cross, 1126-27; *CPL,* 785-796b.

Prosper (Prosp), d. after 455. Prosper Tiro of Aquitaine, lay theologian and monk near Marseilles, from 440 in the service of the papal court under Pope Leo I. Corresponded with Augustine, an advocate of his doctrine of justification. Altaner, 450-52 (Eng. trans., 535-37); Bardenh., IV:533-542; Cayré, II:184-190; Cross, 1134; Jurgens, III:188-196; *CPL,* 516-535; Stegmüller, 7010-11, 1.

Quodvultdeus (Qu), d. *ca.* 453. Deacon, from *ca.* 437 bishop of Carthage, in 439 banished by Geiserich. Probable author of some sermons traditionally attributed to Augustine; the authorship of *De promissionibus* remains in question. Altaner, 449 (Eng. trans., 534); Bardenh., IV:522-24; *CPL,* 401-417.

Rufinus, ca. 345-410. Tyrannius Rufinus, born of Christian parents at Aquileia, where he also lived as a monastic monk, spent six years in Egypt, going then to Jerusalem. Returned in 397 to Italy and died in Messina. Important for translations from Greek. Altaner, 392-94 (Eng. trans., 459-462); Bardenh., III:549-558; Cayré, I:562-67; Cross, 1207-1208; Jurgens, II:179-182; *CPL,* 195-200.

Rupert of Deutz, ca. 1075/1080-1129/1130. Abbot of the monastery at Deutz. His writings include a commentary on the Benedictine Rule and on the New Testament books of Matthew, John, and Revelation. Bardenh., V:234; Cayré, II:695; Stegmüller, 7549-7582; Spicq, 114-17.

Salvian, ca. 400-*ca.* 480. Priest, born of an influential family near Cologne, first married, then a monk in Lerinum, later moved to Marseilles. His major work *De gubernatione dei* is a trenchant social critique of a period of radical cultural upheaval. Altaner, 456-57 (Eng. trans., 486); Bardenh., IV:573-78; Cayré, II:159-161; Cross, 1231; *CLP,* 485-87.

Sedulius Scotus, ninth century. Priest, scholar, and poet from Ireland, author of commentaries on Matthew and the Pauline letters. Cross, 1256; Stegmüller, 7595; Manitius, I:315-323, II:802.

Speculum, Pseudo-Augustine (Spec), ca. 427. A collection of moral precepts from the Old and New Testaments, ascribed to Augustine for reasons unknown. Altaner, 432 (Eng. trans., 513); Bardenh., IV:491; Stegmüller, 1479; *CPL,* 272.

Sulpicius Severus, ca. 363-*ca.* 420. From a prominent family in Aquitaine. A lawyer who became a monk. His principal work is a world chronicle extending to A.D. 400. Altaner,

231 (Eng. trans., 278-79); Bardenh., III:421-27; Cayré, I:558-560; Cross, 1321; *CPL,* 474-79.

Tertullian (Tert), ca. 160-after 220. Quintus Septimus Florens Tertullianus, son of a pagan centurion in Carthage, active as a lawyer in Rome. Returned *ca.* 195 as a Christian to Carthage where he engaged in extensive writing, becoming a Montanist *ca.* 207. Altaner, 148-163 (Eng. trans., 166-182); Quasten, II:246-340; Bardenh., II:377-442; Cayré, I:229-249; Cross, 1352-53; Jurgens, I:111-161; *CPL,* 1-36.

Titus, Pseudo-, probably fifth century. A letter on virginity *(De dispositione sanctimonii).* Altaner, 140-41 (Eng. trans., 83).

Tyconius (Tyc), fourth century. From Africa, a Donatist, author of a commentary on Revelation preserved in fragments (mainly by Beatus). Altaner, 373 (Eng. trans., 437-38); Bardenh., III:495-98; Cayré, I:391; Cross, 1400; *CPL,* 709-710.

Valerian, d. *ca.* 460. Bishop of Cemenelum (Cimiez near Nice) in southern Gaul; surviving works include twenty homilies. Bardenh., IV:572-73; Cross, 1424; *CPL,* 1002-1004.

Varimadum, 445-480. The influential compendium of anti-Arian statements entitled *Contra Varimadum arianum* compiled *ca.* 445-480 has been variously ascribed to Vigilius of Thapsus and Idacius Clarus, bishop of Ossonuba. Altaner, 232-33, 489; Bardenh., III:413-14; *CPL,* 364.

Victor of Tunnuna (Victor-Tunis), sixth century. Bishop in Africa, died after 566 in exile in a monastery in Constantinople; author of a world chronicle. Altaner, 233 (Eng. trans., 281); Bardenh., V:329-331; Cayré, II:228; *CPL,* 2260.

Victor of Vita, fifth century. Bishop of Vita (Africa), author of *Historia persecutionis Africanae provinciae.* Altaner, 488 (Eng. trans., 587); Bardenh., IV:550-52; Cayré, II:228; Cross, 1438; Jurgens, III:281-82; *CPL,* 798-802.

Victorinus of Pettau (Vic), d. 304 a martyr. Probably Greek by birth, author of commentaries in Latin on books of the Old and New Testaments, of which only one on Revelation has survived. Altaner, 182-83 (Eng. trans., 205); Quasten, II:411-13; Bardenh., II:657-663; Cayré, I:274-75; Cross, 1438; *CPL,* 79-83.

Vigilius of Thapsus (Vig), fifth century. Bishop of Thapsus in Africa, wrote against various heretical doctrines, probably died after 484. Altaner, 489 (Eng. trans., 587); Bardenh., III:414, IV:553-57; Cayré, II:192; Cross, 1441; *CPL,* 806-812.

Vigilius, Pseudo-. Besides *Contra Varimadum,* works ascribed to Vigilius include *De trinitate* in twelve books. Altaner, 489 (Eng. trans., 287); Bardenh., IV:556-57; *CPL,* 809-811; Fischer, 483-84.

Zeno of Verona, fourth century. From Mauretania, bishop of Verona 362-371/372. Altaner, 369 (Eng. trans., 432); Bardenh., III:477-481; Cayré, I:332; Cross, 1511; *CPL,* 208-209.

Eastern Church Fathers

Addai, fifth century. An apocryphal work entitled *The Teaching of Addai* written in Syriac, expanding the earlier legendary correspondence between Jesus and Abgar V, king of Edessa (cf. Eusebius *H.E.* i.13). A typical mission church product, long highly esteemed in the Syriac churches. Baumstark, 27-28; Ortiz de Urbina, 44; Altaner, 139 (Eng. trans., 78); Bardenh., I:590-96, IV:326; Cayré, I:164; Cross, 16.

Aphraates (Syr. Afrahat), ca. 260/275-after 345. The "Persian Sage," an early witness to Christianity in Persia under the Zoroastrian Sassanids. His *Demonstrationes* (336/337 and 343-345) show him in conflict with the Jews living in Persia and with their faith, but without any further trace of questions then affecting the church in the Roman Empire. Baumstark, 30-31; Ortiz de Urbina, 46-51; Assfalg-Krüger, 2; Altaner, 342 (Eng. trans., 400); Bardenh., IV:327-340; Cayré, I:376-78; Cross, 68-69; Jurgens, I:302-306.

Barsalibi (Dionysios bar Salibi), d. 1171. Bishop in Mabbug and later in Amida, a Jacobite known especially for his scholarly commentaries on the Bible, especially his popular commentary on the Gospels (Peshitta text), along with prolific prose works on speculative and polemic theology. Baumstark, 295-98; Ortiz de Urbina, 220-21; Cayré, II:71 (Jacob bar Salibi).

Ephraem (Afrem) Syrus (Ephr), 306-373. Born in Nisibis, where he became a deacon and teacher, fleeing after the capture of Nisibis by the Persians (363) to Edessa where with other "Persian" refugees he revived the earlier catechetical school which now became known as the "Persian school." His extensive works, including many biblical commentaries, are preserved mainly in Armenian versions. Important historically and for textual criticism is his commentary on the Diatessaron (cf. p. 189). Baumstark, 31-52; Ortiz de Urbina, 56-83; Altaner, 343-46 (Eng. trans., 401-405); Bardenh., IV:342-373; *CPG,* 3905-4175; Assfalg-Krüger, 109; Cayré, I:378-384; Cross, 462-63; Jurgens, I:309-314.

Jacob of Nisibis, d. 338. Bishop (?) of Nisibis, mentioned as teacher of Ephraem. Baumstark, 34; Cross, 721; Jurgens, I:309 (James of Nisibis).

Liber Graduum, fourth/fifth century. Anonymous collection of ascetic tractates, probably from the fifth century, witnessing to early forms of Syrian (Mesopotamian) monasticism. Related to the Messalians? Important in textual criticism for its use of the Diatessaron. Ortiz de Urbina, 89-91; Assfalg-Krüger, 218.

Mani (Manes), 216-*ca.* 276/277. Born in Babylon, raised in an Elkesaite Baptist community, founder of Manichaeism which pervaded the world of antiquity. Altaner, 123 (Eng. trans., 360); Bardenh., I:516; Cayré, I:170-71; Cross, 864-65.

Shenute of Atripe, d. 466. Monk and organizer of Egyptian monasticism, with hellenistic education and familiar with Greek, created the Coptic literary language (Sahidic) as a unifying force for the Egyptian church. Wrote numerous sermons and catechetical material, still partly unedited. Altaner, 268-69 (Eng. trans., 309); Bardenh., IV:98-100; Assfalg-Krüger, 316-18; Cayré, I:505; Cross, 1269-1270.

Thomas, Acts of, third century. An apocryphal apostolic romance narrating the miracles of the Syrian apostle Thomas in India. Originally written in Syriac in the third century incorporating earlier elements (e.g., Hymn of the Pearl), but soon translated into Greek and then into other Eastern languages. Baumstark, 14-15; Ortiz de Urbina, 37-51; Altaner, 138-39 (Eng. trans., 77); Bardenh., I:579-584; Assfalg-Krüger, 352; Cayré, I:164; Cross, 1369-1370.

V

INTRODUCTION TO THE USE OF THE MODERN EDITIONS (*GNT*[3], NESTLE-ALAND[26], *SQE*[13], ETC.)

1. *"MODERN EDITIONS"*

The editions of the Greek New Testament selected and the sequence of their consideration here follows their popularity in distribution throughout the world. *The Greek New Testament* (third edition, corrected, 1983), comes first, followed by the twenty-sixth edition of the *Novum Testamentum Graece* of Nestle-Aland, (with preference for the seventh or a later printing), and finally the *Synopsis Quattuor Evangeliorum* of Kurt Aland, with the thirteenth edition preferred for its new apparatus. The corrected third edition of *GNT* differs from earlier editions by offering a new text. This text is identical with that of Nestle-Aland[26]. The successive printings of Nestle-Aland[26] since it first appeared in 1979 have eliminated typographical errors as they were discovered, so that the seventh revised and later printings are preferable. An international and interconfessional committee of five editors was responsible for the Greek text of the New Testament found in both editions. The New Testament text of these editions was formally approved as the basis for translations in the *Guiding Principles* of 1968, and further confirmed in the *Guidelines* for translators promulgated by the Vatican and the United Bible Societies in 1987.

Beside these there are other editions of the Greek New Testament designed for particular purposes or representing textual theories other than those defined by the five editors of *GNT*[3] and Nestle-Aland[26]. They enjoy a more limited distribution, but they deserve mention here. The latest Greek-Latin edition by José Maria Bover (first edition, 1943) was published in 1968. It was issued again in 1977 ([2]1988) in a new edition by J. O'Callaghan as *Nuevo Testamento Trilingüe* (obviously intended for the Hispanic world, with a Spanish text accompanying the Greek and Latin — now the Neo-Vulgate). Also worthy of mention is the edition by Augustin Merk, which was widely used among Catholic theologians before the work of the five editors. Its apparatus is strongly influenced by Hermann von Soden's controversial but very valuable

work (1913). After being unavailable for years, a reprint of Merk was issued in 1984. New editions have also appeared, such as G. Nolli's *Novum Testamentum Graece et Latine* (Rome: 1981), with the Greek text accompanied by the Nova Vulgata, that is, the new Latin version initiated by Pope Paul VI and issued in 1979. This new version was based on the text of *GNT* and Nestle-Aland, and consequently presents the anomaly of a Latin text based on the new Greek text but accompanied by a Greek text which differs from it. The apparatus of the edition leaves much to be desired. Finally, mention should be made of the edition by Arthur L. Farstad and Zane C. Hodges, *The Greek New Testament According to the Majority Text* (Nashville: 1982). The title clearly reveals the intention of the edition: it offers the Textus Receptus, and is hardly a critical edition in the strict sense.

The Synopsis Quattuor Evangeliorum (SQE) mentioned above has offered the text of *GNT* and Nestle-Aland since the ninth edition of 1976, but the thirteenth edition is recommended not only because of its correction of earlier errors and oversights, but also for its thoroughly revised apparatus. The thirteenth edition now has by far the greatest amount of evidence for the text of the Gospels, and all of it is based on a fresh collation of the manuscripts— we hope that the number of errors in it has at least been reduced. As for Greek-English editions, the *Synopsis of the Four Gospels (SFG)* has printed the new text since the second edition of 1975 ([8]1987). Persons interested especially in the English apparatus should use *SFG*[3] (1979) or a later edition ([7]1984), where the English text has been accommodated to the Revised Standard Version second edition of 1971.[1] These two synopses are certainly not the only ones on the market, but the widely circulated Albert Huck-Hans Lietzmann *Synopsis* was seven-eighths adapted to the text of Nestle[15] (1932),[2] and the rest is dubious — quite apart from the fact that it has now been superseded by Heinrich Greeven's new edition, which he reports as differing from the text of Nestle-Aland[26] and *GNT*[3] by an average of nine instances to a chapter.[3] The synopses of John Bernard Orchard and M.-E. Boismard also offer their own texts. In each there is a very limited critical apparatus which does not provide a constant control. Greeven's apparatus is fuller, but it is generally difficult to use; further, a close study of this synopsis makes the suspicion inescapable that at least in part it is not based on an examination of manuscripts (for details, cf. pp. 261ff.).

The synopses of Kurt Aland employ the same symbols, signs, and abbreviations as Nestle-Aland. These do not, therefore, require special attention here and can be discussed together at the end of this section. The only difference is in the arrangement of the critical apparatus to the Greek text in *SQE*, which was compiled independently although with no differences in the use of the Nestle system. Anyone familiar with this system can proceed directly to the editions, and will only find their information supplementary.

---

1. A corrected edition of the English text with apparatus appeared separately in 1982.
2. According to Heinrich Greeven, "The Gospel Synopsis from 1776 to the Present Day," pp. 22-49 in *Synoptic and Text-Critical Studies 1776-1976*, ed. John Bernard Orchard and T. R. W. Longstaff (Cambridge: 1978), esp. p. 40.
3. I.e., 2.5 variants per page. Cf. p. 262.

2. *THE GREEK NEW TESTAMENT* [3] *(GNT* [3]*)*

Let us first examine *GNT* [3] and Nestle-Aland [26]. We have already noted the characteristics of these two editions on pp. 43ff. in a comparison of the major editions, discussing them together with the editors of Tischendorf and Westcott-Hort. The sample pages show not only the individual character of each edition, but their specific structural differences as well. Nothing new actually needs to be noted which would not become obvious with some experience in using the editions. Nothing can be said about their structure, in particular, which the reader would not infer from their stated differences of purpose: the *GNT* edition is intended for translators, while the Nestle-Aland edition is for students, professors, and expositors of the New Testament, and a wide variety of other specialists. But then, this distinction is by no means precise. The *GNT* edition is appropriate for the use of students and others who are content to read the new text without taking an interest in the details of its transmission and its textual history as found in the apparatus of Nestle-Aland. *GNT* is frequently considered the more convenient edition for those who find the system in Nestle-Aland somewhat complicated — not just its apparatus, but the parallel references in its outer margin as well. The decision must depend on the interests of the individual. This handbook can be quite objective about the respective virtues of each edition because the authors and their associates in the Institute for New Testament Textual Research in Münster bear editorial responsibility equally for both editions.

The **structure of GNT** is best appreciated as adapted to the interests of New Testament translators. In nearly eight hundred places throughout the world (including no less than thirty in Europe alone) traditional versions of the Bible in national languages are undergoing revision or new translations are being made in them for the first time. This explains why the Greek text is divided by (English) section headings, and in the Gospels these section headings are followed by parallel references. The Greek text of Nestle-Aland is not interrupted by section headings, and parallel references are indicated in a special size type in the outer margin. The structure and composition of the *GNT* apparatus is also translator-oriented: words and phrases are marked by superscript numbers for notes in the critical apparatus, while the apparatus for parallel references shows the first and last words of the text to which a parallel passage in the Old Testhe first and last words of the text to which a parallel passage in the Old or New Testament applies. Most striking, however, ie the use of the capital letters A, B, C, and D within braces at the beginning of each of the paragraphs in the critical apparatus. These letters designate the relative degrees of certainty ascribed to their decisions by the editors. We have already discussed the meaning of these letters. [4]

The needs of translators have naturally determined the **selection of passages for the critical apparatus.** Accordingly, a review of the passages has

---

4. Cf. pp. 44f.

been made for an improved fourth edition of *GNT*. This review was based on a survey of the passages where the major modern versions have textual notes, i.e., where translators have themselves recognized the readings of value either for their own or for their readers' information. For example, let us take a page at random from *GNT*[3] and examine the apparatus structure apart from the question whether the specific passages selected are the most "meaningful" in terms of the stated purpose of the edition, or whether others might have been better. One of the pages in *GNT*[3] with the most variants is p. 154, with no fewer than five instances of variation for **Mark 8:15-18**. The composition and structure of the critical apparatus here is particularly instructive beside the example given above on p. 44. For convenience this page is reproduced in full on p. 226.

In both verses 15 and 16 of Mark 8 there are two instances of variation shown, and one in verse 17. The consistent repetition in the apparatus of the verse numbers together with the superscript numbers for the pertinent words in the text (from 4 to 8) makes them readily identifiable. The structure of the apparatus is equally clear. The first reading is always the reading chosen by the editors for the text; it is followed by the alternative readings, each given in its full, unabbreviated form, and separated by double diagonal lines. Before considering the attestation (the way it is presented is discussed on pp. 227f.), we observe that the readings given are the following.

[4]15	ὁρᾶτε, βλέπετε	[7]16	ἔχουσιν
	ὁρᾶτε καὶ βλέπετε		ἔχομεν
	βλέπετε		εἶχον
	ὁρᾶτε		ἐλάβομεν
	videte	[8]17	πεπωρωμένην ἔχετε τὴν καρδίαν ὑμῶν
	cavete		πεπωρωμένη ἐστὶν ἡ καρδία ὑμῶν
[5]15	Ἡρῴδου		πεπωρωμένη ὑμῶν ἐστὶν ἡ καρδία
	τῶν Ἡρῳδιανῶν		ἔτι πεπωρωμένην ἔχετε τὴν καρδίαν ὑμῶν
[6]16	πρὸς ἀλλήλους		ὅτι πεπωρωμένην ἔχετε τὴν καρδίαν ὑμῶν
	πρὸς ἀλλήλους λέγοντες		omit completely
	ἐν ἑαυτοῖς λέγοντες		

This number of variant readings could be still further increased by noting the following:

[7]16 ἔχωμεν
[8]17 πεπηρωμένη ἐστὶν ἡ καρδία ὑμῶν
       ἔτι πεπωρωμένην τὴν καρδίαν ὑμῶν ἔχετε
       ὅτι πεπωρωμένην ἔχετε τὴν καρδίαν

In *GNT*[3] itself these subvariants are considered worthy of being indicated parenthetically within the major variants.

To demonstrate the differences in format it may be useful to insert here without comment the section of Nestle-Aland[26] which parallels p. 154 of *GNT*[3], deferring further discussion for the moment to focus here on the characteristics of *GNT*[3].

αὐτοῖς λέγων, Ὁρᾶτε, βλέπετε[4] ἀπὸ τῆς ζύμης τῶν
Φαρισαίων καὶ τῆς ζύμης Ἡρῴδου[5]. 16 καὶ διελογίζοντο
πρὸς ἀλλήλους[6] ὅτι[a] ἄρτους οὐκ ἔχουσιν[7]. 17 καὶ γνοὺς
λέγει αὐτοῖς, Τί διαλογίζεσθε ὅτι ἄρτους οὐκ ἔχετε; οὔπω
νοεῖτε οὐδὲ συνίετε; πεπωρωμένην ἔχετε τὴν καρδίαν
ὑμῶν[8]; 18 ὀφθαλμοὺς ἔχοντες οὐ βλέπετε καὶ ὦτα ἔχοντες
οὐκ ἀκούετε;[b] καὶ οὐ μνημονεύετε,[b] 19 ὅτε τοὺς πέντε

---

[4] **15** {C} ὁρᾶτε, βλέπετε ℵ A B K L W X Π 33 892 1009 1010 1071 1079 1195 1241 1242 1344 1365 1546 1646 2148 *Byz Lect* vg^{ww} syr$^{(p),h}$ cop$^{bo mss}$ Diatessaron^{a} // ὁρᾶτε καὶ βλέπετε $\mathfrak{p}^{45}$ C 0131 f^{13} 28 1216 1230 1253 2174 it^{aur,c,f,l} vg^{cl} cop^{sa,bo} goth Diatessaron // βλέπετε D^{gr} Θ f^{1} 565 syr^{s} arm geo Diatessaron^{p} // ὁρᾶτε Δ 700 // *videte* it^{b,d,ff2,i,q,r1} // *cavete* it^{a,k}

[5] **15** {A} Ἡρῴδου ℵ A B C D K L X Δ Π 0131 33 700 892 1009 1010 1071 1079 1195 1216 1230 1241 1242 1253 1344 1546 1646 2148 2174 *Byz Lect* it^{a,aur,b,c,d,f,ff2,l,q,r1} vg syr^{s,p,h} cop^{bo} goth eth Diatessaron^{a,p} // τῶν Ἡρῳδιανῶν (*see* 3.6) $\mathfrak{p}^{45}$ W Θ f^{1} f^{13} 28 565 1365 it^{i,k} cop^{sa} arm geo

[6] **16** {C} πρὸς ἀλλήλους $\mathfrak{p}^{45}$ ℵ B D W f^{1} 28 565 700 it$^{a,b,(c),d,ff2,i,k,q}$ cop^{sa} geo // πρὸς ἀλλήλους λέγοντες (*see* Mt 16.7) A C K L X Δ Θ Π 0131 f^{13} 33 892 1009 1010 1079 1195 1216 1230 1241 1242 1253 1344 1365 1546 1646 2148 2174 *Byz Lect* it^{aur,f,l} vg syr$^{(s,p),h}$ cop^{bo} goth arm eth // ἐν ἑαυτοῖς λέγοντες (*see* Mt 16.7) 1071

[7] **16** {C} ἔχουσιν $\mathfrak{p}^{45}$ B W f^{1} 28 565 700 it^{k} syr$^{s?}$ cop^{sa,bo} // ἔχομεν ℵ A C L X Δ Θ Π (K 1009 1344 2174 ἔχωμεν) f^{13} 33 892 1010 1071 1079 1195 1216 1230 1241 1242 1253 1365 1546 1646 2148 *Byz Lect* it^{aur,f,l} vg syr$^{s?p,h}$ cop$^{bo mss}$ goth arm eth geo Diatessaron^{p,t} // εἶχον D it^{a,b,c,d,ff2,i,q,r1} // ἐλάβομεν (*see* Mt 16.7) 579 1396 1424

[8] **17** {B} πεπωρωμένην ἔχετε τὴν καρδίαν ὑμῶν $\mathfrak{p}^{45 vid}$ ℵ B C L W Δ f^{1} f^{13} (28 ἔχοντες) 33 892* 1009 1195 1241 arm eth geo^{2} // πεπωρωμένη ἐστὶν ἡ καρδία ὑμῶν (D* πεπηρωμένη) D^{c} 0143^{vid} it$^{a,(b,c,d,ff2,i)}$ cop^{sa,bo} geo^{1} // πεπωρωμένη ὑμῶν ἐστὶν ἡ καρδία Θ 565 // ἔτι πεπωρωμένην ἔχετε τὴν καρδίαν ὑμῶν A K X Π 700 892^{c} 1010 1071 1079 1216 (1242 τὴν καρδίαν ὑμῶν ἔχετε) 1344 1365 1546 (1646 *omit* ὑμῶν) 2148 2174 *Byz Lect* ($l^{70,1579}$ *omit* ὑμῶν) it$^{(aur),f,l,(q)}$ vg syr$^{(s,p),h}$ // ὅτι πεπωρωμένην ἔχετε τὴν καρδίαν ὑμῶν 047 1230 1253 goth // *omit* 245

---

[a] **16** *a* indirect: Jer // *a* causal: RV^{mg} ASV^{mg} Seg // different text: TR AV RV ASV RSV NEB Zür Luth Seg^{mg}

[b b] **18** *b* question, *b* minor: (WH) Bov BF^{2} Zür Luth Jer Seg // *b* minor, *b* question: TR // *b* question, *b* question: AV RV ASV RSV NEB

---

15 βλέπετε...Φαρισαίων Lk 12.1 **17** Τί διαλογίζεσθε...ὑμῶν Mk 6.52 **18** ὀφθαλμοὺς ...ἀκούετε Jr 5.21; Eze 12.2; Mk 4.12; Ac 28.26 **19** Mt 14.15–21; Mk 6.35–44; Lk 9.12–17; Jn 6.5–13

λετο αὐτοῖς λέγων· ⸂ὁρᾶτε, βλέπετε⸃ ἀπὸ τῆς ζύμης τῶν
⁸⁰_{VI} Φαρισαίων καὶ τῆς ζύμης ⸀Ἡρῴδου. 16 ⸆καὶ διελογίζοντο
πρὸς ἀλλήλους ⸆ ὅτι ἄρτους οὐκ ⸀ἔχουσιν. 17 καὶ γνοὺς
⸆ λέγει αὐτοῖς· τί διαλογίζεσθε ⸆ ὅτι ἄρτους οὐκ ἔχετε;
οὔπω νοεῖτε οὐδὲ συνίετε⸃; πεπωρωμένην ἔχετε τὴν καρδίαν ὑμῶν⸃;

    18 *ὀφθαλμοὺς ἔχοντες οὐ βλέπετε*
    καὶ ὦτα ἔχοντες οὐκ ἀκούετε;
καὶ οὐ μνημονεύετε, **19** ὅτε τοὺς πέντε ἄρτους ἔκλασα

Mt 16,6!

J 4,33
3,5!

Jr 5,21 Ez 12,2
Mt 13,13

6,41-44

15 ⸀(2 D Θ f¹ 565 ¦ 1 Δ 700 ¦ ορατε και βλεπετε 𝔓⁴⁵ C 0131 f¹³ 28. 1424 *pc* c vg^{cl} ¦ *txt*
ℵ A B L W 𝔐 vgst sy^{p.h} | Γτων Ηρωδιανων 𝔓⁴⁵ W Θ f¹.¹³ 28. 565 *pc* i k sa^{mss} ● **16** Γοι
δε 𝔓⁴⁵ W 565 | Τ*p*) λεγοντες A C L Θ 0131 f¹³ 𝔐 vg sy bo ¦ *txt* 𝔓⁴⁵ ℵ B D W f¹ 28.
565. 700 *pc* it sa | Γεχομεν ℵ A C L Θ f¹³ 𝔐 vg sy^{p.h} bo^{mss} ¦ ειχαν D it ¦ *p*) ελαβομεν
1424 *pc* ¦ *txt* 𝔓⁴⁵ B W f¹ 28. 565. 700 *pc* k co   ● **17** Τ*p*) ο Ιησους ℵ* A C D (ƒ L) W
Θ f¹.¹³ 𝔐 lat sy sa^{mss} ¦ *txt* ℵ¹ B Δ 892* aur i sa^{mss} bo ¦ Τ*p*) εν εαυτοις, ολιγοπιστοι, 𝔓⁴⁵
W f¹³ *pc* (sa^{mss}) ¦ εν ταις καρδιαις υμων, ολιγοπιστοι (D) Θ 28. 565. 700 *pc* (it) sy^{h**} ¦
⸆ετι (οτι 047. 1424 *pc*) πεπωρωμενην εχετε την καρδιαν υμων A 𝔐 vg sy^{(s.p).h} ¦ πεπω-
ρωμενη υμων εστιν η καρδια (D) Θ (0143^{vid}). 565 (it) co ¦ *txt* 𝔓⁴⁵vid ℵ B C L N W Δ
f¹.¹³ (28). 33. 892*. 1241 *pc*

The greater explicitness of *GNT*³ is apparent not only in the general
arrangement of the apparatus but also in the **citation of witnesses**, because of
the special interests of its intended users. The names of the Church Fathers are
written out in full (not abbreviated as in Nestle-Aland²⁶), and the Diatessaron
is also cited with superscript letters to indicate precisely which of its various
traditions is intended, e.g.:

Diatessaron^a (cf. ⁴15) for the Arabic tradition
Diatessaron^p (cf. ⁴15) for the Persian tradition

The information is sometimes even more detailed, e.g.,

Diatessaron^f for the Latin tradition (= Fulda)
Diatessaron^s for the Old High German tradition (= Stuttgart)
Diatessaron^t (= Tuscan)
Diatessaron^v (= Venetian)
Diatessaronⁱ (= Italian, the agreement of ^t and ^v)
Diatessaron^l for the Old Dutch tradition (= Liege)

    Whether it is useful to identify the textual traditions of the Diates-
saron in such detail (especially for translators) is questionable, and it has been decided negatively for the fourth edition of *GNT*. The secondary traditions will be
eliminated, and the apparatus will cite only the most important witnesses, e.g.,

Diatessaron^{e arm} = citations in the Armenian version of Ephraem's commentary on the
               Diatessaron.
Diatessaron^{e-syr} = citations in the Syriac original of this commentary, whose witness
               is superior to all other sources. Nowhere else do we come so close
               to Tatian's Diatessaron.

    *GNT*³ is equally explicit for other textual traditions as well. In citing
the Old Latin, for example, all the witnesses included in the group symbol "it"
are named for or against a variant, as in the example at ⁵15:

it^{a,aur,b,c,d,f,ff2,1,q,r1} supporting the reading Ἡρῴδου
it^{i,k} supporting the reading τῶν Ἡρῳδιανῶν

Here again explicitness is the dominant principle. Nestle-Aland[26] summarizes the situation by citing only "i k" in support of τῶν Ἡρῳδιανῶν (cf. p. 227), clearly implying that all the rest of the Latin tradition supports the reading Ἡρῴδου in the text (the obvious superiority of which eliminates the need for any explicit citation of support). It should be remarked in passing that the data given hitherto in *GNT* for the Old Latin tradition apart from the Gospels (where the Adolf Jülicher-Walter Matzkow-Kurt Aland edition is available) and the Catholic and shorter Pauline letters (to the extent they have appeared in the Vetus Latina edition) must be accepted with caution because they are derived from printed editions which are not always reliable (especially Johannes Belsheim), and not directly from themanuscripts. In *GNT*[4] this is changed.

In other respects also the **evidence in the critical apparatus of GNT** is more fully spelled out than in other editions (for the convenience of its users). The Sinaitic Syriac is represented by syr^s instead of sy^s, the Curetonian Syriac by syr^c instead of sy^c, and similarly syr^p, syr^{pal}, and so forth (cf. pp. xxxiv-xxxv of the introduction), as well as cop^{sa}. cop^{bo}, and so forth where Nestle has sa, bo, and so forth. This is all immediately obvious to anyone using these editions, and when there are differences in the citation of the Coptic evidence it should be remembered that *GNT* is based on George W. Horner's editions, while Nestle-Aland[26] is based on a fresh review of the manuscripts themselves.[5]

It is important to notice the differences between the **abbreviations used in the critical apparatuses** of the two editions. Nestle-Aland[26] not only uses *vid v* vid (= videtur), as does *GNT*[3] (although in italics), but also v (= vide). The *v.r. v.l.* use of v.r. (= variant reading) in *GNT*[3] and of v.l. (= varia lectio) in Nestle-Aland[26] reflects the use of English and Latin respectively as editorial languages, and requires no further explanation. Similarly supp in *GNT*[3] and ^{s} or suppl in Nestle-Aland[26] are easily recognized as abbreviating "supplement(um)," and indicating a later addition to a manuscript, inferior in value and not to be confused with its original hand. Both editions make identical use of the superscripts ^{txt} and ^{comm} with the names of Church Fathers: in citing patristic commentaries there can be a considerable difference between a reading found in the text preceding the comments (where the connecting passages could easily have been replaced from a different manuscript by a later scribe) and a reading in the commentary as it quotes phrases from the text (in the commentary itself alterations by a later scribe are less probable, and here we may be more confident of finding the original text of the Church Father). But note: this is true only of the superscript use of "txt" and "comm" in the citation of patristic evidence in the critical *txt comm* apparatus, e.g., Or^{txt} and Or^{comm}. In the critical apparatus of Nestle-Aland "txt" regularly stands in normal type size to introduce the symbols for the witnesses supporting the text as printed above, and "comm" (e.g., with variants of punctuation and with conjectures) to refer to modern commentators. The question *cj cjj* mark is also used with different meanings. In *GNT*[3] it indicates uncertainty as *?* to whether the manuscript or the version concerned actually supports the reading

5. Cf. p. 251.

for which it is cited; in Nestle-Aland it means simply that the data cited could not be verified against the original Greek source, or that the text underlying a version cannot be determined unequivocally.

More important, both theoretically and practically, are two systems in which *GNT*[3] and Nestle-Aland[26] differ. One concerns the **citation of lectionaries**. It is distinctly a weakness in Nestle-Aland[26] that in the comprehensive list of manuscripts on which the edition is based (pp. 684-711) only five lectionaries are mentioned. This is due to a conviction that the Greek lectionaries represent the Byzantine tradition, and that therefore they provide less information about the original text of the New Testament and its history than has generally been thought.[6] Certainly more references to the lectionary text should be included in future editions of Nestle-Aland. Meanwhile *GNT*[3] offers the evidence of the lectionaries in a wide variety of categories.[7]

Lect	The reading of the majority of lectionaries in the Synaxarion (the so-called "movable year" beginning with Easter) and in the Menologion (the "fixed year" beginning September 1), when these agree
Lect[m]	The reading of the majority of lectionaries in the Menologion when it differs from that of the Synaxarion or occurs only in the Menologion
ℓ [12,etc.]	An individual lectionary cited by number, following the Gregory-Aland list, when it differs from the majority reading in the Synaxarion passages
ℓ [135m,etc.]	An individual lectionary in its Menologion which differs from the majority of other lectionaries
ℓ [76s,m,etc.]	An individual lectionary in which both the Synaxarion and the Menologion passages are in agreement
ℓ [135pt,etc.]	An individual lectionary which contains a passage two or more times, with readings differing from each other, hence listed as supporting a reading "in part"

The number of lectionaries cited in *GNT*[3] on the basis of original collations (cf. Introduction, pp. xxviii-xxix) is substantially less than those cited from printed editions. Nevertheless, *GNT*[3] has a definite advantage here which is easily understood in view of its historical beginnings, just as Nestle-Aland[26] may claim that its own practice stands in the tradition of the earlier (and major) editions.

Also of importance is the difference between the two editions in their **treatment of the Byzantine Majority text**, the Koine text type, or the Byzantine Imperial text, however it may be called. *GNT*[3] uses the following symbols:

Byz	The reading of the majority of Byzantine manuscripts
Byz [pt]	A part of the Byzantine manuscript tradition

Nestle-Aland[26] uses the symbol:

𝔐	The Majority text

The symbol 𝔐, which is fully discussed on pp. 248f., has a more extensive meaning than the term *Byz* as used in *GNT*[3]. The manuscripts of the Koine or Byzantine text are naturally always in the majority, but they do not stand

---

6. Cf. pp. 166f.
7. Cf. *GNT*[3], Introduction, p. xxxi.

alone. In most instances they are accompanied by others, frequently by representatives of the Egyptian text—the Greek text of the New Testament is characterized by a far greater degree of textual unity than the number of variants discussed by textual critics would suggest; cf. p. 29 for statistics on verses where modern editions show no textual variants. The relationship between *Byz* in *GNT*[3] and 𝔐 in Nestle-Aland[26] may be expressed in the following formula:

Byz	𝔐 (or included in 𝔐)
𝔐	*Byz* + manuscripts of other groups which vary from book to book (cf. pp. 247f.)

The **punctuation apparatus of GNT**[3], like the evaluation of the variants, is a feature designed especially for the convenience of translators and is not included in editions for scholars and textual specialists. Here are recorded the variations of punctuation found not only in several editions of the Greek New Testament (the Textus Receptus, Westcott-Hort, José Maria Bover, etc.), but also of a number of modern versions which are useful as references for translation committees, e.g., the Revised Standard Version (RSV) with its predecessors, the English Revised Version (ERV), the American Standard Edition of the English Revised Version (ASV), and the Authorized (King James) Version (AV), as well as the New English Bible (NEB), and also the French Jerusalem Bible (Jer) and Segond version of the New Testament (Seg), including even the revised (1956) Luther version (Luth), and the Zürich Bible (Zür). The use of the punctuation apparatus represents a degree of syntactical abstraction. It does not simply transcribe the commas, semicolons, and so forth, found in the editions cited. Rather, it presents a carefully weighed functional analysis of their punctuation; this is useful to translators in the younger churches whose languages are often structured so differently from European languages that no direct comparison is possible.

The **punctuation apparatus** makes use of the following classifications.

paragraph, major — A paragraph break in contrast with a full sentence break.

major, minor, none — A major break (often equivalent to a period or full stop, a colon, or a semicolon) in contrast with a minor break (usually indicated by a comma), and in further contrast with no punctuation.

question, statement, command — The contrast between question and non-question is usually clearly indicated in Greek texts, but in certain contexts the additional contrast between statement and command may be made explicit only in translation.

exclamation — A category not marked in Greek but often used in translations to render rhetorical questions (which may be marked in Greek as questions) or emphatic statements (which are marked in Greek only by a period or full stop.

dash, parens — Dashes and parenthesis marks indicate breaks in structure. A dash is generally employed to indicate a break in the syntax of a sentence, while parenthesis marks are used to enclose explanatory or supplementary material.

ellipsis — Words in an incomplete sentence which need to be supplied, indicated by three dots.

direct (or recitative), *indirect, causal, interrogative* — Different uses of ὅτι, though in some instances it is difficult to interpret the function of ὅτι, since an editor may have preferred to leave it ambiguous.

different text — The underlying text is so different that no correspondence can be indicated.

In addition the following abbreviations and symbols in the punctuation apparatus should be noted.

?	Indicates that citation of a particular edition or translation is doubtful, since the evidence does not clearly support one or another alternative
()	Parenthesis marks show minor differences of detail in punctuation, while indicating that the authority supports in general the punctuation for which it is cited
ed	A different edition of a Greek text or a translation which does not agree with other editions at a given point
mg	A marginal reading in one of the translations
mg^1,mg^2	Successive alternatives in the margin of a translation

The above information should suffice at present for the reader to interpret the punctuation apparatus on *GNT*^{3}, p. 154 (reproduced on p. 221), or the sample in plate 12.

This may best be done by taking one or two of the editions cited and comparing them with the apparatus, observing how faithfully the periods, commas, semicolons, and so forth have been evaluated and represented. Here again there will be changes in *GNT*^{4}.

The **reference apparatus** in *GNT*^{3} is not only far less comprehensive than that of Nestle-Aland^{26}, but with its repetitive references to parallels in other books of the New Testament it serves a quite different function. References are given here to ten passages at most and usually far fewer, while the outer margin of Nestle-Aland^{26} lists far more. In *GNT*^{3} (corrected) the index of Old Testament quotations (with an important reverse index, pp. 897ff.) is separated from the index of allusions and verbal parallels; Nestle-Aland^{26} combines the two (cf. the useful key for citations from the Septuagint at the beginning of each book, pp. 739ff.).

As we have stated repeatedly, the texts of *GNT* (from the third edition) and Nestle-Aland^{26} are identical. Their differences in paragraphing, punctuation, and orthography have been discussed above.[8] The departure of Nestle-Aland^{26} from the practice of earlier editions to insert verse numbers in the continuous text marks another point of similarity, but a noticeable difference remains in the representation of Old Testament quotations: *GNT*^{3} (like the earlier Nestle) prints Old Testament quotations in bold type, while Nestle-Aland^{26} prints them in italics (quite understandably in view of its different purpose), and differs with respect to their extent and their number.

Nestle-Aland^{26} has placed the verse numbers within the body of the text in the interests of greater clarity and convenience (the use of a special marker ' was required in earlier editions because verse divisions and the sentence structure of the text do not always coincide). The earlier usage was derived from the model of the manuscript tradition where verse divisions were unknown (verses were not introduced until the sixteenth century, and as a convenience they leave much to be desired). But the manuscript tradition also lacked our

---

8. Cf. pp. 33, 45f.

modern chapter divisions and numbers (which are a thirteenth-century heritage); and besides, clarity and convenience should take precedence over tradition.

      The two editions now agree in their **use of single and double brackets.**
[ ] Words enclosed in single brackets [ ] have only a dubious claim to authenticity as part of the original text of the New Testament writings. A text enclosed in
[[ ]] double brackets [[ ]] is clearly not a part of the original text; e.g., however early the tradition of the pericope of the Woman Taken in Adultery (in John 7:53– 8:11) may be, it is certain that these verses did not form a part of the original text of the gospel of John when it was first circulated in the Church. At least the shorter ending of Mark (as well as the longer ending of Mark 16:9-20) was not a part of the gospel in its original form, although both may well be from the beginning of the second century. Accordingly both are placed in double brackets. These examples are both discussed below, together with verses which have been removed completely from the text, in the chapter on "Introduction to the Praxis of New Testament Textual Criticism (Selected Passages)" (pp. 280-316), and are mentioned here only for comparing GNT^3 with Nestle-Aland[26]. Certainly many of the symbols used are different because the two editions are based on different assumptions and are intended for groups with different purposes, but the discussion in the above paragraphs has offered a comprehensive survey of these differences. If the reader of GNT^3 has any questions still unanswered, the key included with the edition and the "Master List of Symbols and Abbreviations" on pp. xlvii-liii of GNT^3 should prove useful.

      After comparing the Nestle-Aland[26] and GNT^3 editions there remain certain **differences between their critical apparatuses** which have not been discussed. But these differences are only apparent. It must be stressed that not every difference implies an actual contradiction. For example, Nestle-Aland[26] cites the early versions sparingly, only where their witness is unequivocal, while GNT^3 cites them more freely. The systems of citation are also different. The Old Latin witnesses are cited by GNT^3 individually for each reading, whereas Nestle-Aland[26] uses the group symbol "it," and notes individually only the manuscripts which support a different reading. For the Coptic the data of GNT^3 are based on Horner's editions[9] while Nestle-Aland[26] is based on the manuscripts. Finally and fundamentally, the treatment of variants differs between GNT^3 and Nestle-Aland[26] in a way that may be recognized at first glance. GNT always gives the variant in its full form, however insignificant it may be. Nestle-Aland[26] does not report every variant, including, e.g., the obviously singular readings of individual manuscripts. It also divides longer passages into multiple variants in order to report them in as concise a way as possible.

3. NOVUM TESTAMENTUM GRAECE [26] (NESTLE-ALAND [26])

As we proceed to the Nestle-Aland *Novum Testamentum Graece*, twenty-sixth edition, we have already taken account of the symbols and abbreviations whose use in GNT^3 differs in any way, however slightly. The basic distinction, as we

9. Cf. p. 228.

have noted above, is found in the structure of **its apparatus and the critical signs** it uses. Although these signs have been in use for decades (and are identical with those used in earlier editions of Nestle-Aland except for one addition), they can appear formidably complex at first encounter. The signs which need to be learned are only seven in number.

○ The word following is omitted in a part of the tradition.   ○

⌐ The word following is replaced by one or more different words in a part of ⌐
the tradition.

⊤ At this point there is an insertion, usually of a single word but sometimes of ⊤
more, in a part of the tradition.

□ ＼ The words enclosed between these two signs are omitted in a part of the □ ＼
tradition.

⌐ ˥ The words enclosed between these two signs are replaced by other words ⌐ ˥
in a part of the tradition.

ſ ι The words enclosed between these two signs are preserved in a different ſ ι
order in a part of the tradition.

ſ The order of the words as transposed in the different variants is indicated by ſ *3214*
the numerals.

ſ Indicates usually the transposition of the word following to a place designated ſ
in the apparatus.

These are easily remembered, especially because their forms suggest their functions: ○ and □ for omissions, ⊤ for insertions, ſ for transpositions, and so forth. Their presence in the text is not distracting, and yet they alert the reader interested in the state of the textual tradition to the presence and character of any variations. For example, in Matt. 21:33-35 there are no critical signs. This means that these verses have been transmitted without any significant variation. But in the immediately preceding verses (vv. 28-32) the signs are rather numerous, and in the verses following (vv. 36-44) there are relatively few. The reader can therefore tell at a glance some important facts about the character of the textual tradition. A knowledge of the seven signs given above and their meanings shows the nature of the variants without even a glance at the apparatus. To show precisely how the critical signs are used, let us take the example of the **Parable of the Two Sons in Matt. 21:28-32**, where all but two of them are found.

The sign ○ appears in the first line (v. 28), and once more in line 4 (v. 29):

(verse 28) ○καὶ προσελθὼν τῷ πρώτῳ εἶπεν
(verse 29) ὕστερον ○δὲ μεταμεληθεὶς ἀπῆλθεν

In verse 28 καὶ is omitted, and a glance at the apparatus shows that it is omitted by ℵ* (the first hand, as indicated by the asterisk, of Codex Sinaiticus), by the uncials L and Z, by the Old Latins e and ff¹, by both sy^s and sy^c, i.e., the Old Syriac (though with some negligible contextual adaptation), and by the Coptic tradition. The reading in these manuscripts is therefore προσελθὼν τῷ πρώτῳ εἶπεν. The presence of † before the list of witnesses indicates that καί is also omitted in Nestle-Aland²⁵. In verse 29 the δέ is omitted, namely by ℵ*(again

L 15,11　　**28** Τί δὲ ὑμῖν δοκεῖ; ἄνθρωπος ᵀ εἶχεν ⌐τέκνα δύο⌐. ᵒκαὶ ⁴⁹₂₁₈
προσελθὼν τῷ πρώτῳ εἶπεν· τέκνον, ὕπαγε σήμερον ἐρ- ˣ
γάζου ⌐ἐν τῷ ἀμπελῶνι⌐ᵀ. **29** ὁ δὲ ἀποκριθεὶς εἶπεν·⌐οὐ
7,21!　　θέλω, ὕστερον ᵒδὲ μεταμεληθεὶς ἀπῆλθεν⌐. **30** ⌐προσελθὼν
δὲ⌐ τῷ ⌐ἑτέρῳ εἶπεν ὡσαύτως. ὁ δὲ ἀποκριθεὶς εἶπεν·⌐ἐγώ,
κύριε, καὶ οὐκ ἀπῆλθεν⌐. **31** τίς ἐκ τῶν δύο ἐποίησεν τὸ
θέλημα τοῦ πατρός; λέγουσινᵀ·⌐ὁ πρῶτος⌐. λέγει αὐτοῖς
L 3,12; 7,29;　　ὁ Ἰησοῦς· ἀμὴν λέγω ὑμῖν ὅτι οἱ τελῶναι καὶ αἱ πόρναι
18,14; 19,1-10 ·
L 7,36-50　　προάγουσιν ὑμᾶς εἰς τὴν βασιλείαν τοῦ θεοῦ. **32** ἦλθεν
2P 2,21 Prv 8,20;　　γὰρ ⌐Ἰωάννης πρὸς ὑμᾶς⌐ ἐν ὁδῷ δικαιοσύνης, καὶ οὐκ
12,28; 21,21 ⊕
25 J 7,48 L 7,29s　　ἐπιστεύσατε αὐτῷ, οἱ δὲ τελῶναι καὶ αἱ πόρναι ἐπίστευ-
σαν αὐτῷ· ὑμεῖς δὲ ἰδόντες ⌐οὐδὲ μετεμελήθητε ὕστερον
τοῦ πιστεῦσαι αὐτῷ.

● **28** Τtις C Δ Θ

f¹·¹³ 33. 892ᶜ. 1241. 1424 *pm* it vg^cl sy | ⌐ B 1424 *pc* lat | Oᵀ ℵ* L Z e ff¹ (sy^s·c) co ¦ *txt*
ℵ² B C D W Θ 0138 f¹·¹³ 𝔐 lat sy^p·h | ⌐εις τον αμπελωνα D 1424 | ᵀμου B C² W Z
0138. 28. 1010. 1241. 1424 *pm* lat sa mae bo^pt ¦ *txt* ℵ C* D K L Δ Θ f¹·¹³ 33. 565. 700. 892
pm it sy bo^pt ● **29-31** ⌐┼ εγω (υπαγω Θ f¹³ 700 *pc*), κυριε (- Θ)· και ουκ απηλθεν *et*
⌐┼ ου θελω, υστερον (+ δε Θ f¹³ 700 *pc*) μεταμεληθεις απηλθεν *et* ⌐┼ ο υστερον (εσχατος Θ f¹³ 700 *pc*) B Θ f¹³ 700 *al* sa^mss bo; Hier^mss ¦ *txt* (ℵ) C (L) W (Z) 0138 (f¹) 𝔐 f q
vg^ww sy^p·h sa^mss mae; Hier^mss ¦ *txt, sed* + εις τον αμπελωνα *p*. απηλθεν¹ *et* εσχατος *loco*
πρωτος D it sy^s·(c) | O ℵ* (B) 1010 *pc* it sa^mss | ⌐και προσελθων C W 0138 𝔐 h q sy^p·h
(- sy^s·c) ¦ *txt* ℵ B D L Z Θ f¹·¹³ 33. 700. 892 *pc* lat mae bo | ᵀ┼δευτερω ℵ² B C² L Z f¹ 28.
33. 700. 892. 1424 *pm* mae bo | ᵀαυτω C W 0138 f¹ 𝔐 it vg^cl sy sa mae bo^ms ¦ *txt* ℵ B D
L Θ f¹³ 33. 892 *pc* lat bo ● **32** ⌐ D W Θ 0138 f¹·¹³ 𝔐 lat ¦ *txt* ℵ B C L 33. 892. 1010 *pc* c
r¹; Or | ⌐ου ℵ C L W 𝔐 ¦ - D (c) e ff¹* sy^s ¦ *txt* B Θ 0138 f¹·¹³ 33. 700. 892 *al* lat sy^c·p·h

the first hand of Sinaiticus), by B (Vaticanus, with slight contextual adaptations),
by the minuscule 1010 and a few other Greek manuscripts, by the Old Latins,
and by a part of the Sahidic tradition. In these the reading is ὕστερον μεταμεληθεὶς ἀπῆλθεν.

The sign ⌐ is found in line 5 (v. 30), and again in the next to last line
(v. 32):

verse 30　τῷ ⌐ἑτέρῳ εἶπεν ὡσαύτως
verse 32　ὑμεῖς δὲ ἰδόντες ⌐οὐδὲ μετεμελήθητε

This indicates that there are substitutes for the words marked in this way. As the
apparatus shows, in place of ἑτέρῳ in verse 30 δευτέρῳ is read by the uncials
ℵ² (the second hand of Sinaiticus), B (Vaticanus), C² (the second hand of Codex
Ephraemi Syri Rescriptus), L and Z, as well as by the minuscule family f¹ (cf.
p. 244), and the minuscules 28, 33, 700, 892, 1424, and a large number of
others *(pm)*, together with the Middle Egyptian and Bohairic traditions. The
presence of the † again indicates that this is also the reading of the earlier Nestle-
Aland²⁵. In verse 32 οὐδέ is replaced by οὐ in ℵ (Sinaiticus), C (Codex Ephraemi
Syri Rescriptus), L and W, and manuscripts of the Majority text (𝔐; cf. pp. 247f.),
to read ὑμεῖς δὲ ἰδόντες οὐ μετεμελήθητε. The negative is omitted by D
(Codex Bezae Cantabrigiensis), by Old Latin c (with a slight contextual adaptation), e, ff¹* (i.e., the first hand; the second hand adds the negative), and by
sy^s (Sinaitic Syriac) to read ὑμεῖς δὲ ἰδόντες μετεμελήθητε. The text with
οὐδέ is read by B (Vaticanus), Θ (Codex Koridethianus), and the uncial 0138,
by the minuscule families f¹ and f¹³, and the minuscules 33, 700, 892, and

others, by the whole Latin tradition (i.e., by Itala and the Vulgate) with the
exception of the Old Latin c e ff¹* cited for the preceding variant, and by the
Curetonian Syriac (sy^c), the Peshitta (sy^p), and the Harklean Syriac (sy^h; when
more than one Syriac witness is cited the symbol sy is not repeated for each but
given only once, with the identification of the various witnesses added to it as
superscripts).

The sign ^{T} for insertions appears in the first line (v. 28), and also in
verse 31.

verse 28   ἄνθρωπος ^{T} εἶχεν
verse 31   λέγουσιν ^{T}

Anyone familiar with scribal habits would know what is added without looking
at the apparatus — in verse 28 τὶς:

ἄνθρωπός τις εἶχεν

and in verse 31 αὐτῷ:

λέγουσιν αὐτῷ

Both are typical examples of common scribal expansions to the New Testament
text. In verse 28 τὶς is added by the uncial C (Codex Ephraemi Syri Rescriptus),
Δ, Θ (Codex Koridethianus), by the minuscule families f^1 and f^{13} (here again,
as with the Syriac versions, the symbol is not repeated for the superscripts, so
that $f^{1.13} = f^1$ and f^{13}), and the minuscules 33, 892^c (i.e., the later corrector has
added τὶ where the first hand lacked it), 1241, 1424, and a great number of
others, by the Old Latins together with the Clementine Vulgate (vg^{cl}), and by
the entire Syriac tradition (sy).

In verse 31 αὐτῷ is added after λέγουσιν by the uncials C (Codex
Ephraemi Syri Rescriptus — the names of the great uncials are always repeated
here for the reader as a memory aid), W (Codex Freerianus), and 0138, by the
minuscule family 1 (f^1, named for the leading manuscript of the group), by the
manuscripts of the Majority text $\mathfrak{M}$,[10] by several Old Latin manuscripts (it,
opposed by lat which supports the text!), and the Clementine Vulgate (vg^{cl},
named for Pope Clement VIII who authorized it), by all the Syriac versions (sy),
and by the whole of the Sahidic (sa) and Middle Egyptian (mae) traditions and
one manuscript of the Bohairic tradition (bo^{ms}). For the preceding variants,
as for all the instances we have discussed so far, only the attestation for the
variant reading and not for the text has been given. This is because we believe
that the attestation for the variant reading in each of these instances is too weak
to require listing the evidence for the text. For the omission of αὐτῷ here and
also at verse 32 the apparatus gives the evidence for the text, although actually
even here it should not be necessary because the combined weight of C W and
0138, even together with the support of an impressive list of the versions including the Old Latin (though only partially, counterbalanced by lat), Syriac, and
Coptic all reading αὐτῷ, does not constitute adequate attestation for it. The

10. Cf. p. 248.

rationale: it is only superficially convincing to argue that the texts underlying the early versions all read αὐτῷ and that is was therefore the universal reading in the Greek tradition of the period, because nothing would be more natural than for a translator to make explicit the implied object of λέγουσιν, which in this context would be αὐτῷ. The witness of the versions is consequently of no value for the text of their exemplars. The attestation for the omission is consequently all the stronger because it goes against natural scribal tendencies. When such a reading is supported by ℵ (Codex Sinaiticus), B (Codex Vaticanus), D (Codex Bezae Cantabrigiensis), L, Θ (Codex Koridethianus), the minuscule family f^{13}, the minuscules 33 and 892 (together with a few others, all of which become the more important by running counter to the prevailing scribal tendency of completing implicit constructions, as in the addition of αὐτῷ), as well as by the Vulgate and the Old Latins and the majority of the Bohairic tradition, it represents the coincidence of internal evidence with external evidence that is decisive (for the details of this rationale, cf. chapter VII, "Introduction to the praxis of New Testament textual criticism [selected passages]," pp. 280ff.).

The sign for a longer omission ⌐ , with its conclusion marked by ⌐ , is not found in the present pericope. The closest example is at the end of the paragraph mentioned above, i.e., Matt. 21:44, where the whole verse is enclosed between ⌐ and ⌐ . The verse is omitted by D (Codex Bezae Cantabrigiensis), by the minuscule 33, by some of the Old Latins (it, cf. lat found among the witnesses for the text; the situation is similar with αὐτῷ in v. 31 where the Old Latin tradition is divided), by the Sinaitic Syriac, and by Eusebius. Editors have differed in their treatment of this verse according to the strength they ascribe to this grouping of witnesses. In Nestle-Aland[26] it is placed within single brackets. When it is placed in double brackets it is due to the influence of B. F. Westcott and F. J. A. Hort's theories,[11] according to which the combination of D with the Old Latin and the Old Syriac represents the original form of the New Testament text, especially when it is shorter than other forms of the tradition. According to Westcott-Hort, the combination of D it sy derives from the second century, a period fully two hundred years earlier than the earliest Greek manuscripts available at the time (Codex Vaticanus [B] is from the fourth century). Considering the general tendency of this text toward expansion, they assumed that any major omissions must represent the original form (and Westcott-Hort accordingly called them "Western non-interpolations").[12] Whole generations of textual critics (especially in the English literature) were trained in this perspective, which can only be regarded today as a relic of the past. Today the Greek text of the second century is extensively available in the major papyri, and its evidence does not support the view of Westcott-Hort. Let us first review the external evidence for verse 44. It is found in the uncials ℵ (Codex Sinaiticus), B (Codex Vaticanus), C (Codex Ephraemi Syri Rescriptus), L, W (Codex Freerianus), Z, Θ (Codex Koridethianus, with some minor variations), 0138, the minuscule families f^1 and f^{13}, the manuscripts of the Majority text, and (note

11. Cf. pp. 14ff.
12. Cf. p. 15.

especially) in the Old Latins (though not in all; cf. above), the Vulgate (lat), the
Curetonian Syriac, the Peshitta, and the Harklean Syriac (sy[c.p.h]; for this summary symbol, cf. pp. 250f.), and the Coptic witnesses. The external evidence is
particularly strong, and it would be conclusive if it were supported by one of
the great early papyri, but unfortunately none has been preserved for this passage. Only one further consideration should be mentioned, which takes us into
the realm of internal criteria to engage in the praxis of textual criticism as we
did in the paragraph above, where we proceeded from external criteria but
without ignoring internal criteria (cf. basic rules 2-4, p. 280). In the New Testament there are certain phrases or verses which copyists found particularly
impressive, and which they tended to insert occasionally where they did not find
them in their exemplars, e.g., "If anyone has ears to hear, let him hear," "the
last shall be first and the first last." The first sentence was even printed in editions
of the Greek text of Mark 7:16 and consequently repeated in modern translations
until scholarship succeeded in removing the intrusion (cf. p. 302). Is it possible
that verse 44 could be a sentence of this kind? It is found also in Luke 20:18.
But note, in the first place, that the wording there is not the same; and further,
if verse 44 were a later insertion, surely it would have been placed immediately
after verse 42 with its reference to the stone which the builders rejected and
which becomes the cornerstone. And yet there remains a slight doubt, sufficient
to justify single brackets but inadequate to warrant the use of double brackets
to indicate certainty that the sentence was not a part of the original text. The
explanation that verse 44 dropped from the text by homoioteleuton is moot.[13]
Verse 43 ends with αὐτῆς and verse 44 with αὐτόν, so that a copyist coming
to αὐτῆς could possibly have imagined it to be the end of the next phrase and
continued from there. While this hypothesis is possible, it would be more plausible if verse 44 ended with αὐτῆς, for such leaps from one word to a similar
word over shorter or longer units of text (sometimes involving several verses)
are not at all rare in manuscript transmission, and when an omission occurs one
of the first questions to be raised by textual criticism is whether homoioteleuton
is involved.

Although, as we have said, there are no extensive omissions in our
pericope, there are several instances where clauses or phrases have been transmitted in various forms. The frequency of these variations is due to certain
unusual complications in the tradition which we will discuss later.[14] In these
instances the words in the text which correspond to the variant reading given in
the apparatus are marked with the sign ⌐ at their beginning and ⌐ at their end.

There is an example in the text at the very beginning of our pericope
in verse 28: ⌐ ἐν τῷ ἀμπελῶνι⌐. In the apparatus the sign ⌐ is repeated (there
is obviously no necessity for repeating the final ⌐ as well): εἰς τὸν ἀμπελῶνα
D 1424. D (Codex Bezae Cantabrigiensis) and the minuscule 1424 accordingly
have changed the construction (in a way that occurs frequently in the New
Testament). Then in verse 31 the text reads ⌐ ὁ πρῶτος⌐, and in the apparatus

13. Cf. p. 285.
14. Cf. pp. 312ff.

there is: ⸂ † ὁ ὕστερος (ἔσχατος Θ f^{13} 700 pc) B Θ f^{13} 700 al sa^{mss} bo. This is not simply a rephrasing of the text, but a direct reversal of it: it was not the first son but the second who did the will of the father (this is consistent within the dual tradition of the pericope, which also transposes the sequence at the beginning, making the two contrary statements actually produce the same meaning). Further, there are two different expressions used in the manuscripts: ὁ ὕστερος in B (Codex Vaticanus) and other Greek manuscripts as well as in some Sahidic manuscripts and the whole Bohairic tradition, ὁ ἔσχατος in Θ (Codex Koridethianus), the minuscule family f^{13}, the minuscule 700, and a few others. This special tradition with its supporting witnesses is shown in parentheses because it represents only a (synonymous) subvariant to ὁ ὕστερος and consequently the witnesses Θ f^{13} 700 are repeated after the variant ὁ ὕστερος (ἔσχατος), where the complete attestation for the variant is given. The use of al(ii) for "others" here in contrast to the earlier pc (pauci) for "a few" within the parentheses indicates a whole group of minuscules in support of B and its associates, making the total number significantly higher.

The sign for transpositions in the text (⸃ at the beginning, ⸂ at the end) is easily associated with its form. In the very first line of the text in verse 28 is found ⸂τέκνα δύο⸃. In the apparatus only the first sign is repeated (as with ⸂ the second sign is not required for clarity): ⸂ B 1424 pc lat. Without any further details it is sufficiently clear that B (Codex Vaticanus), the minuscule 1424, and a few others together with the Old Latins and the Vulgate read δύο τέκνα. The same is true where there are three words, if it is impossible to misconstrue how the words are transposed. For verse 32 ⸂ Ἰωάννης πρὸς ὑμᾶς the apparatus reads ⸂ D W Θ 0138 $f^{1.13}$ 𝔐 lat, because there is no possibility that the transposition can be anything other than πρὸς ὑμᾶς Ἰωάννης.

When an alternative word order in a transposition is possible, the new sequence of words is indicated by numbers. There is no example in our pericope, but shortly after at Matt. 21:39 the text reads: ⸂ αὐτὸν ἐξέβαλον ἔξω τοῦ ἀμπελῶνος καὶ ἀπέκτειναν ⸃. There are seven words here in all. The apparatus reads: ⸂ 1 7 6 2-5 D it; Lcf ¦ 7 1 6 2-5 Θ. This means that D (Codex Bezae Cantabrigiensis), the Old Latin, and the Church Father Lucifer read αὐτὸν ἀπέκτειναν καὶ ἐξέβαλον ἔξω τοῦ ἀμπελῶνος, and that Θ (Codex Koridethianus) has ἀπέκτειναν αὐτὸν καὶ ἐξέβαλον ἔξω τοῦ ἀμπελῶνος. Both variant forms, although they begin with different word orders, agree in altering the sequence of events to make the account more logical and vivid. It is relatively uncommon for transpositions to involve as many as seven words. Usually the number is much less, so that the altered word order is simpler to reconstruct. This way of representing a transposition obviously saves more space than the usual practice of repeating the words in full, not to mention making it simpler for the reader to identify where the differences between the multiple forms occur without having to compare the forms in the apparatus with the text word by word.

The device of representing words by numbers is also used in other contexts when appropriate. E.g., in Matt. 21:11 the text reads ⸂ ὁ προφήτης

'Ιησοῦς ꟷ and the apparatus has ⸆ *3 1 2* C L W *f*[1] 𝔐 lat sy mae bo[ms] ¦ *1 2 f*[13] 1241 *pc* a aur. Thus C (Codex Ephraemi Syri rescriptus) L W and so forth read 'Ιησοῦς ὁ προφήτης, and the minuscule family *f*[13] with 1241 and so forth read ὁ προφήτης.

Here again the apparatus achieves conciseness with greater clarity. The sign ⸋ is equally useful. It applies (almost) always to the word it precedes, and the apparatus indicates the word in the sentence before which (*a*[nte]) or after which (*p*[ost]) the listed witnesses transpose it. Since such transpositions in the manuscripts usually occur over considerable intervals, the use of this sign simplifies the apparatus substantially. It occurs fairly infrequently, with no example in Matt. 21, and the first examples appearing in Matt. 25 and 26. In Matt. 25:33 the text reads: καὶ στήσει τὰ μὲν πρόβατα ἐκ δεξιῶν ⸋ αὐτοῦ, τὰ δὲ ἐρίφια ἐξ εὐωνύμων. The apparatus has simply: ⸋ *p.* ευων. א ¦ – A *pc.* Thus, א (Codex Sinaiticus) reads τὰ δὲ ἐρίφια ἐξ εὐωνύμων αὐτοῦ, while A and a few other witnesses omit αὐτοῦ. Or in Matt. 26:53 the text reads: ἢ δοκεῖς ὅτι οὐ δύναμαι παρακαλέσαι τὸν πατέρα μου, καὶ παραστήσει μοι ⸋ ἄρτι πλείω δώδεκα λεγιῶνας ἀλλέλων, and the apparatus has ⸋ *p.* δυναμαι A C D W Θ 0133 *f*[1.13] 𝔐 it (sy[h] mae). In these witnesses, then, ἄρτι is found after δύναμαι, resulting in the reading ἢ δοκεῖς ὅτι οὐ δύναμαι ἄρτι παρακαλέσαι τὸν πατέρα μου, καὶ παραστήσει μοι πλείω δώδεκα λεγιῶνας ἀγγέλων. The simplification achieved in the apparatus by this device is especially clear in this example. Since there are seven words between δύναμαι and ἄρτι the text would otherwise have required the sign ⸋ before δύναμαι followed by the sign ⸌ after ἄρτι, and the apparatus would have read: *1 9 2-8.*

Multiple occurrences of a critical sign in a single verse are rare. The critical signs normally occur no more than once in a single verse, but in the event of exceptions, e.g., if a single word is omitted more than once in a verse, the first instance is marked by the sign ⸉ as indicated above, and the subsequent instances are marked by ⸉1, ⸉2, etc. Repetitions of the other critical signs are ⸉1 ⸉2 marked in the following ways.

⸆	⸆1 ⸆2 etc.	⸆ ⸆1 ⸆2
⸇	⸇1 ⸇2 etc.	⸇ ⸇1 ⸇2
⸉1	⸉2 ⸉3 etc.	⸉1 ⸉2 ⸉3
⸋	⸋1 ⸋2 etc.	⸋ ⸋1 ⸋2
⸋1	⸋2 ⸋3 etc.	⸋1 ⸋2 ⸋3

The reasons for indicating the first repetition of some signs with a dot (⸆ , ⸇ , ⸋) and of other signs with a number (⸉1, ⸉1, ⸋1) are purely technical: with ⸉ or ⸌ a dot can be easily overlooked, and ⸋ has been preempted for another use.

So much for the critical signs in the text and apparatus of Nestle-Aland[26]. Their treatment has been somewhat detailed, as it should be for a first experience in using the apparatus (and incidentally for an initial glimpse of textual criticism in practice), but more so because a clear understanding of the meaning and use of these critical signs is the first significant step for a beginner.

It should now be obvious, at least, that the structure of the Nestle-Aland apparatus differs from that of *GNT*. In the latter the **attestation for the text** stands at the beginning in the apparatus, while in Nestle-Aland the variants and their attestation come first, followed by the **attestation for the text** shown above. Nor does the wording of the text need to be replaced, because it is always assumed: *txt* *txt* (= text). In contrast to earlier editions, the number of instances where the attestation for the text is now given is far greater. But it is still not always given. In these instances the reader may assume that the editors considered the readings so weakly supported that citing any witnesses for the text, which is read by nearly all the rest, would be superfluous. The reader of the edition will ¦ soon recognize that the sign ¦ is used to separate different readings within a | single instance of variation, the sign | to separate the different instances of • variation within a verse, and that the sign • separates verses in the apparatus on a page. From the very first, in order to use the apparatus efficiently and effectively, the reader should recognize that the **witnesses always appear in the same order:** first the Greek witnesses, then the Latin, followed by the Syriac and Coptic, and finally the other witnesses. Then follow the Church ; Fathers (separated by a semicolon). Among the Greek witnesses the order observed is papyri, uncials, minuscules, and lectionaries. The uncials are given with the letter uncials (ℵ A B etc.) in alphabetical order, followed by the rest in numerical order. The minuscules begin with the groups f^1 and f^{13} followed by the individual minuscules in numerical order (with a period between numbers to avoid confusion), and concluding with the Majority text.

The sign 𝔐 is a group symbol.[15] But there are also other **group symbols used in the apparatus** representing manuscripts quite unrelated to 𝔐, because otherwise the individual enumeration of manuscripts would expand the apparatus unreasonably. Only the most important witnesses are cited, and no minuscule manuscript is cited individually if it is not of some substantial significance for the text or for its history. Less important witnesses are cited summarily according *pc al pm* to their number by the following signs: *pc* pauci (a few); *al* alii (others); *pm* *cet rell* permulti (a great many); *cet* ceteri (some others); *rell* reliqui (the rest). The quantities represented by these terms, which are intended to give the reader a general impression of the extent of support for a reading, are obvious. It should, however, be observed that while *al*(ii) and *cet*(eri) are not terms of numerical precision, *al* is somewhere between *pc* (pauci) and *pm* (permulti), but much closer to *pc* than to *pm*; *cet*(eri) does not imply very many; *pm* refers to a large group of the Majority text. When the Majority text is itself divided, *pm* may appear in support of both of its forms.

These are the most important principles, rules, and signs for the reader of Nestle-Aland[26]. There is also a whole group of **additional signs** listed below which are used sometimes to modify and expand their application. These latter signs are all distinctly secondary, and should be learned only after the above signs are quite familiar. It is equally true of both groups of signs that they appear

15. Cf. pp. 248f.

far more formidable at first than they are in practice. Familiarity developed in actual use of the edition is the best teacher.

Especially with the uncials, but elsewhere as well, there are signs to indicate the **scribe** of a manuscript: * for the first hand, i.e., the original scribe, and [1], [2], and [3] for the hand of the first, second, and third correctors of a manuscript when such distinctions are possible; otherwise it is simply noted with [c] when an alteration of the text is due to a **corrector.** The first corrector, at least, may be contemporary with the original scribe (a manuscript completed in a scriptorium was examined immediately for accuracy).

It is not unusual in a manuscript to find a marginal reading, i.e., a reading added beside a column of text. If intended as an alternative reading, the reading is designated as v.l. (varia lectio, a variant reading); if the intention is uncertain, the reading is described simply by a superscript [mg] (in margine, or marginal). Hands that are separated by centuries are easily recognized, but early correctors can be very difficult to distinguish. When the sign for a manuscript is qualified by a superscript [s] (**supplement**), this gives full warning that the reading in question derives from a later addition, and should in no way be associated with the authority of the original manuscript itself.

Single words are frequently **abbreviated** in the apparatus to save space, but a glance at the text above will always show quite clearly what has been abbreviated. Thus at Matt. 1:10 the apparatus reads M-σσην Δ *pc* and M-σση ℵ[1] B, indicating that the manuscripts cited here read variants of the forms Μανασσῆν and Μανασσῆ respectively. At Matt. 2:23 the apparatus reads only -ρεθ, obviously meaning that the form Ναζαρέτ in the text is spelled differently in C K and so forth (and similarly in 4:13 and elsewhere). Longer variants may have a whole series of words represented by their initial letters alone, but these can also be readily identified from the text. When a reading in the apparatus has three periods (. . .) between two words, it means that the intervening text between these two words shows no variation from the text printed above.

If a variant has several **subvariants**, i.e., minor differences within essentially the same reading, this is indicated by parentheses and the signs + (for insertion) and − (for omission), as in the following example. At Matt. 5:44 the apparatus reads:

⌐p) ευλογειτε τους καταρωμενους υμας (υμιν D* *pc*; − ε. τ. κ. υ. 1230. 1242* *pc* lat), καλως ποιειτε τοις μισουσιν υμας (− κ. π. τ. μ. υ. 1071 *pc*; Cl Eus) και (− W) προσευχεσθε υπερ των επηρεαζοντων υμας (− D *pc*) και D L W Θ *f*[13] 𝔐 lat sy(p).h; Cl Eus ¦ *txt* ℵ B *f*[1] *pc* k sys.c sa bopt; Cyp.

First it is clear that the text καὶ προσεύχεσθε ὑπὲρ τῶν, attested by ℵ B and so forth through Cyprian, is superior to the variant supported by D L W and so forth through Eusebius. The *p)* at the beginning signals that this reading is dependent upon a parallel tradition (i.e., in Luke 6:28), and arose from efforts to enrich the text of Matthew and make it consistent with parallel texts. Considering the brevity of Matt. 5:44 it is quite understandable that the expanded text would attract a following. But these followers are characteristically divided, as the parenthetical elements show: e.g., ὑμᾶς is replaced by

ὑμῖν in D*; 1230, 1242* (i.e., the original scribe), and a few others with the majority of the Latin tradition omit (note the sign −) ε. τ. κ. υ. The **abbreviations** correspond to the words immediately preceding: εὐλογεῖτε τοὺς καταρωμένους ὑμᾶς, just as − κ. π. τ. μ. υ. in the next parentheses indicates the omission of the immediately preceding words καλῶς ποιεῖτε τοῖς μισοῦσιν ὑμᾶς by 1071, and so forth. After καὶ comes (− W), i.e., W omits καὶ, just as D and a few other manuscripts omit the following ὑμᾶς. This arrangement of the evidence may appear confusing at first sight to the beginner, but the confusion here is minimal in comparison with the complexity of working through the whole variety of different readings if they were to be exhibited independently and at length (which would incidentally require far more space), and of examining them individually for their similarities and differences. The reader has been spared here (and in innumerable other instances) this greater confusion and no small amount of labor as well: the different traditions are presented in an arrangement that reveals the common textual elements of each. Consequently the character of the subvariants in relation to the principal variants is made clear. The format thus defines both the extent of the subvariants and the origins of the principal variants — all within the space of four lines.

    The apparatus attempts to do without **explanatory notes** altogether, but this has not always been possible. When notes are necessary Latin has provided a neutral solution, and abbreviations have been chosen which are readily understood in modern languages. When the meaning of an abbreviation is not immediately apparent to the reader, it will be found in the alphabetical list in Nestle-Aland[26], Appendix IV, pp. 778-79, where all the **abbreviations** are explained. It would be as well, however, for the reader to commit to memory a

add., om. few which occur most frequently, such as *add.* = addit/addunt = insert(s), *om.*

+ − = omittit/omittunt = omit(s). These abbreviations are used when + and − are

a., p. not practicable. Also important are *a.* = ante = before, and *p.* = post = after,

pon. which usually occur with *pon.* = ponit/ponunt = place(s), to describe the trans-

ˢ position of a word or verse (marked by ˢ in the text) as briefly and precisely

ᵛⁱᵈ as possible. Another important sign is the superscript ᵛⁱᵈ = ut videtur = apparently. Especially in papyri it is not always possible to determine with absolute certainty the reading of a particular passage. In such instances the qualifying sign ᵛⁱᵈ is added in the apparatus (indicating merely a qualified certainty). If

? there is any doubt of its essential reliability a question mark ? is added (to Greek witnesses, when they cannot be verified by film; to a version, when it cannot be determined that their attestation is unequivocal). When a reading seems

(!) not to make sense, it is confirmed by an exclamation point *(!)* = *sic!*. A note is

ex err., occasionally added to explain the origin of a reading, e.g., *ex err*(ore) = by

ex itac., error, *ex itac*(ismo) = explicable as an itacism, *ex lect*(ionariis) = derived
ex lect. from the custom of lectionaries of adapting the text at the beginning or the

ex lat? end of a lesson to make the context clear, *ex lat?* = possibly derived from the

h. t. Latin. The insertion of *h. t.* = homoioteleuton notes that a reading arose from scribal inadvertence, when the scribe's eye skipped from one to another of two similar verses or words in a sequence (cf. p. 285).

The above paragraphs show how Nestle-Aland[26] uses signs to supply each variant with as much information as possible. If a reading is derived from a parallel passage (especially in the Gospels), the sign *p)* is added (cf. Matt.   *p)* 3:10), or the particular source is given in parentheses (e.g., Matt. 1:25, the reference to Luke 2:7 for the variants of υἱόν; Matt. 1:23 to Isa. 7:14 for (Lc 2,7) καλέσουσιν). Parallels within the same book and their variants are also noted: etc. e.g., at Matt. 2:13 the insertion of εἰς τὴν χώραν in Codex Vaticanus (B) is derived from verse 12; the transposition κατ' ὄναρ φαίνεται in C K 33. 700. (12) 892 *pc* parallels the variant reading *(v.l.)* in C L W 0233 𝔐 at verse 19. At times (*v. l.*), the reference is even more precise, e.g., at Matt. 2:18 it is noted that the (19 *v. l.*) insertion of θρῆνος καί in C D L W 0233 *f*[13] 𝔐 sy[s.c.h] may be traced to the Septuagint text of Jer. 38:15.   (Jr38,15ⓖ)

The parenthetical citation of witnesses in the apparatus, whether of Greek manuscripts (cf. the minuscule 700 at Matt. 1:24 ○), the versions, or Church Fathers (Clement of Alexandria at Matt. 4:4 ⸆), indicates that these ( ) witnesses attest the readings in question, but that they also exhibit certain neg-ligible variations which do not need to be described in detail.[16]

Square brackets [] in the apparatus enclose information derived not [ ] from the basic textual witnesses, but from modern editors, whether the conjec-tures of modern commentators (comm = *commentatores*; e.g., Matt. 5:6 Julius comm Wellhausen proposes omitting the entire verse), or punctuation variants (e.g., Matt. 2:4) which are signaled in the text by :, :[1], and so forth. The apparatus : :[1] also tells where the new text differs from the earlier Nestle-Aland[25] by marking with a dagger † the readings which formerly stood in the text but are now in the † apparatus.

The **signs for the Greek witnesses** to the text are given in chapter III on "The manuscripts of the Greek New Testament," where they are identified and described. For manuscripts not described there, reference may be made to Nestle-Aland[26], Appendix I (pp. 684-711, Codices graeci), where all the manu-scripts cited in Nestle-Aland[26] are identified; a similar list is found in the Intro-duction of *GNT*[3], pp. xiii-xxxi. The sequence in citing Greek witnesses in the apparatus of Nestle-Aland[26] is discussed on p. 240. There are two further terms which may be unfamiliar to the reader and require definition: "constant wit-nesses" and the Majority text.

"Constant witnesses" are manuscripts which are cited regularly in the recording of variants (when witnesses are cited). Two groups among these witnesses may be distinguished: those which are always cited explicitly for each variant, and those cited only when they differ from 𝔐, and are otherwise subsumed in 𝔐. Setting the latter group aside for the moment (they are dis-cussed in due course on p. 247), we turn our attention to the "constant wit-nesses" in the full sense of the term, i.e., the Greek manuscripts which are always cited explicitly for each variant. When one of these manuscripts is lack-ing from the attestation of a variant the reader may infer that there is a lacuna

16. Witnesses within parentheses are separated by a comma when they show minor differences.

in the manuscript at this point, or that the manuscript does not contain the passage or text concerned: the last column in Appendix I of Nestle-Aland[26], which describes the precise textual content of each manuscript, is useful for such information.

In the Gospels the "constant witnesses" include:

a) all the available papyri, i.e.:

for Matthew: $\mathfrak{p}^1$(!), $\mathfrak{p}^{19}$, $\mathfrak{p}^{21}$, $\mathfrak{p}^{25}$, $\mathfrak{p}^{35}$(!), $\mathfrak{p}^{37}$, $\mathfrak{p}^{44}$, $\mathfrak{p}^{45}$(!), $\mathfrak{p}^{53}$(!), $\mathfrak{p}^{62}$, $\mathfrak{p}^{64(+\ 67)}$(!), $\mathfrak{p}^{70}$(!), $\mathfrak{p}^{71}$, $\mathfrak{p}^{77}$(!), $\mathfrak{p}^{86}$, $\mathfrak{p}^{96}$
Mark: $\mathfrak{p}^{45}$(!), $\mathfrak{p}^{88}$
Luke: $\mathfrak{p}^3$, $\mathfrak{p}^4$(!), $\mathfrak{p}^{42}$, $\mathfrak{p}^{45}$(!), $\mathfrak{p}^{69}$(!), $\mathfrak{p}^{75}$(!), $\mathfrak{p}^{82}$
John: $\mathfrak{p}^2$, $\mathfrak{p}^5$(!), $\mathfrak{p}^6$, $\mathfrak{p}^{22}$(!), $\mathfrak{p}^{28}$(!), $\mathfrak{p}^{36}$, $\mathfrak{p}^{39}$(!), $\mathfrak{p}^{44}$, $\mathfrak{p}^{45}$(!), $\mathfrak{p}^{52}$(!), $\mathfrak{p}^{55}$, $\mathfrak{p}^{59}$, $\mathfrak{p}^{60}$, $\mathfrak{p}^{63}$, $\mathfrak{p}^{66}$(!), $\mathfrak{p}^{75}$(!), $\mathfrak{p}^{76}$, $\mathfrak{p}^{80}$(!), $\mathfrak{p}^{90}$(!), $\mathfrak{p}^{93}$, $\mathfrak{p}^{95}$(!)

b) all the following uncials:

Matthew: ℵ (01), A (02), B (03), C (04), D (05), L (019), W (032), Z (035), Θ (038), 058, 064, 067, 071, 073 , 074, 078, 084, 085, 087, 089, 090, 092a, 094, 0104, 0106, 0107, 0118, 0119, 0128, 0135, 0136, 0137, 0138, 0148, 0160, 0161, 0164, 0170, 0171(!), 0197, 0200, 0204, 0231, 0234, 0237, 0242, 0249, 0255, 0271, 0275
Mark: ℵ (01), A (02), B (03), C (04), D (05), L (019), W (032), Θ (038), Ψ (044), 059, 067, 069, 072, 074, 090, 092b, 099, 0103, 0104, 0107, 0112, 0126, 0130, 0131, 0132, 0134, 0135, 0143, 0146, 0167, 0184, 0187, 0188, 0213, 0214, 0215, 0235, 0263, 0269, 0274, 0276
Luke: ℵ (01), A (02), B (03), C (04), D (05), L (019), R (027), T (029), W (032), Θ (038), Ξ (040), Ψ (044), 053, 063, 070, 078, 079, 0102, 0108, 0113, 0115, 0117, 0124, 0130, 0135, 0139, 0147, 0171(!), 0177, 0178, 0179, 0181, 0182, 0202, 0239, 0253, 0265, 0266, 0267, 0272
John: ℵ (01), A (02), B (03), C (04), D (05), L (019), T (029), W (032), Θ (038), Ξ (044), 050, 054, 060, 063, 065, 068, 070, 078, 083, 086, 087, 091, 0100, 0101, 0105, 0109, 0110, 0113, 0114, 0124, 0125, 0127, 0145, 0162(!), 0180, 0190, 0191, 0193, 0210, 0216, 0217, 0218, 0234, 0238, 0256, 0260, 0264, 0268, 0273.

All of the above papyri and uncials are cited *in each instance for each variant* when they are extant for a passage. Among them $\mathfrak{p}^{75}$ is the most significant. $\mathfrak{p}^{45}$ and $\mathfrak{p}^{66}$ come close behind in value. But the readings of the other $\mathfrak{p}^1$! papyri (and also of the uncials 0189, 0220, 0162, 0171) which have (!) beside them also have an inherent significance because they were written before the third/fourth century and belong to the period before the rise of the major text types. Among the uncials B has a position of undisputed precedence in the Gospels, while W and Θ are frequently characterized by independent readings. The evidence of D carries special weight *when it is in agreement with other important witnesses*. When D goes its own way in opposition to them, the motives involved should always be given very careful consideration.

Together with these papyri and uncials which are cited explicitly for each variant, the following minuscules are also always cited, beginning with the groups f^1 and f^{13}:

f^1 = 1, 118, 131, 209, 1582 (Kirsopp Lake, *Codex 1 of the Gospels and its Allies*, Cambridge: 1902; repr. 1967)
f^{13} = 13, 69, 124, 174, 230, 346, 543, 788, 826, 828, 983, 1689, 1709 (Thomas Kingsmill Abbott, *A Collation of Four Important Manuscripts of the Gospels*

[Dublin and London: 1887]; Kirsopp and Silva Lake, and Jacob Geerlings, *et al.*, *Family 13 (The Ferrar Group)*. Studies and Documents 11 [1941; repr. Salt Lake City, 1965], 19-21 [1961-1962])

The manuscripts comprising f^1 and f^{13} are usually cited only by their group sign; only in exceptional instances are they cited individually.

In the Acts of the Apostles the "constant witnesses" cited explicitly for each variant where they are extant for a passage include:

a) all the available papyri, i.e.:

$\mathfrak{p}^8$, $\mathfrak{p}^{29}$(!), $\mathfrak{p}^{33(+58)}$, $\mathfrak{p}^{38}$(!), $\mathfrak{p}^{41}$, $\mathfrak{p}^{45}$(!), $\mathfrak{p}^{48}$(!), $\mathfrak{p}^{50}$, $\mathfrak{p}^{53}$(!), $\mathfrak{p}^{56}$, $\mathfrak{p}^{57}$, $\mathfrak{p}^{74}$, $\mathfrak{p}^{91}$(!)

b) all the following uncials:

א (01), A (02), B (03), C (04), D (05), E (08), Ψ (044), 048, 057, 066, 076, 077, 093, 095, 096, 097, 0120, 0123, 0140, 0165, 0166, 0175, 0189(!), 0236, 0244.

The situation with regard to the character of the manuscripts in Acts remains essentially the same as in the Gospels. It should be noted only that $\mathfrak{p}^{74}$ is particularly significant despite its seventh-century date, and that the textual value of A (02) changes here abruptly.

In the Pauline letters the "constant witnesses" cited explicitly for each variant where they are extant include all the available papyri as well as all the uncials mentioned in each of the paragraphs below (where they are listed together to avoid separating the related evidence for each of the fourteen letters — in the manuscript tradition Hebrews is a part of the Pauline corpus):

Romans: $\mathfrak{p}^{10}$, $\mathfrak{p}^{26}$, $\mathfrak{p}^{27}$(!), $\mathfrak{p}^{31}$, $\mathfrak{p}^{40}$(!), $\mathfrak{p}^{46}$(!), $\mathfrak{p}^{61}$, $\mathfrak{p}^{94}$
א (01), A (02), B (03), C (04), D (06), F (010), G (012), Ψ (044), 048, 0172, 0209, 0219, 0220(!), 0221

1 Corinthians: $\mathfrak{p}^{11}$, $\mathfrak{p}^{14}$, $\mathfrak{p}^{15}$(!), $\mathfrak{p}^{34}$, $\mathfrak{p}^{46}$(!), $\mathfrak{p}^{61}$, $\mathfrak{p}^{68}$
א (01), A (02), B (03), C (04), D (06), F (010), G (012), H (015), I (016), Ψ (044), 048, 088, 0121a, 0185, 0199, 0201, 0222, 0243, 0270

2 Corinthians: $\mathfrak{p}^{34}$, $\mathfrak{p}^{46}$(!)
א (01), A (02), B (03), C (04), D (06), F (010), G (012), H (015), I (016), Ψ (044), 048, 081, 098, 0121a, 0186, 0209, 0223, 0224, 0225, 0243

Galatians: $\mathfrak{p}^{46}$(!), $\mathfrak{p}^{51}$
א (01), A (02), B (03), C (04), D (06), F (010), G (012), H (015), I (016), Ψ (044), 062, 0122, 0174, 0176, 0254, 0261

Ephesians: $\mathfrak{p}^{46}$(!), $\mathfrak{p}^{49}$(!), $\mathfrak{p}^{92}$(!)
א (01), A (02), B (03), C (04), D (06), F (010), G (012), I (016), Ψ (044), 048, 082, 0230

Philippians: $\mathfrak{p}^{16}$(!), $\mathfrak{p}^{46}$(!), $\mathfrak{p}^{61}$
א (01), A (02), B (03), C (04), D (06), F (010), G (012), I (016), Ψ (044), 048

Colossians: $\mathfrak{p}^{46}$(!), $\mathfrak{p}^{61}$
א (01), A (02), B (03), C (04), D (06), F (010), G (012), H (015), I (016), Ψ (044), 048, 0198, 0208

1 Thessalonians: $\mathfrak{p}^{30}$(!), $\mathfrak{p}^{46}$(!), $\mathfrak{p}^{61}$, $\mathfrak{p}^{65}$(!)
א (01), A (02), B (03), C (04), D (06), F (010), G (012), H (015), I (016), Ψ (044), 048, 0183, 0208, 0226

2 Thessalonians: $\mathfrak{p}^{30}$(!), $\mathfrak{p}^{92}$(!)

ℵ (01), A (02), B (03), D (06), F (010), G (012), I (016), Ψ (044), 0111

1 Timothy: $\mathfrak{p}$ −

ℵ (01), A (02), C (04), D (06), F (010), G (012), H (015), I (016), Ψ (044), 048, 061, 0241, 0259, 0262

2 Timothy: $\mathfrak{p}$ −

ℵ (01), A (02), C (04), D (06), F (010), G (012), H (015), I (016), Ψ (044), 048

Titus: $\mathfrak{p}^{32}$(!), $\mathfrak{p}^{61}$

ℵ (01), A (02), C (04), D (06), F (010), G (012), H (015), I (016), Ψ (044), 048, 088, 0240

Philemon: $\mathfrak{p}^{61}$, $\mathfrak{p}^{87}$

ℵ (01), A (02), C (04), D (06), F (010), G (012), I (016), Ψ (044), 048

Hebrews: $\mathfrak{p}^{12}$(!), $\mathfrak{p}^{13}$(!), $\mathfrak{p}^{17}$, $\mathfrak{p}^{46}$(!), $\mathfrak{p}^{79}$, $\mathfrak{p}^{89}$

ℵ (01), A (02), B (03), C (04), D (06), H (015), I (016), Ψ (044), 048, 0121b, 0122, 0227, 0228, 0252

It must be observed that in the Pauline letters the textual quality of B shifts, and Codex Vaticanus no longer commands the authority it possesses in the Gospels, while in contrast the authority of Codex Alexandrinus (A) becomes enhanced (cf. p. 50). It should further be noted that beginning with D the capital letters used as symbols for the uncials no longer represent the same manuscripts as in the Gospels (except for Ψ). Thus D in the Pauline letters (Codex Claromontanus) is quite unrelated to D in the Gospels (Codex Bezae Cantabrigiensis). For details, cf. Nestle-Aland[26], Appendix I.

In the Catholic letters the "constant witnesses" cited for each variant where they are extant include all the available papyri together with the uncials mentioned in the paragraphs below:

James: $\mathfrak{p}^{20}$(!), $\mathfrak{p}^{23}$(!), $\mathfrak{p}^{54}$, $\mathfrak{p}^{74}$

ℵ (01), A (02), B (03), C (04), P (025), Ψ (044), 048, 0166, 0173, 0246

1 Peter: $\mathfrak{p}^{72}$(!), $\mathfrak{p}^{74}$, $\mathfrak{p}^{81}$

ℵ (01), A (02), B (03), C (04), P (025), Ψ (044), 048, 093, 0206, 0247

2 Peter: $\mathfrak{p}^{72}$(!), $\mathfrak{p}^{74}$

ℵ (01), A (02), B (03), C (04), P (025), Ψ (044), 048, 0156, 0209, 0247

1 John: $\mathfrak{p}^{9}$(!), $\mathfrak{p}^{74}$

ℵ (01), A (02), B (03), C (04), P (025), Ψ (044), 048, 0245

2 John: $\mathfrak{p}^{74}$

ℵ (01), A (02), B (03), P (025), Ψ (044), 048, 0232

3 John: $\mathfrak{p}^{74}$

ℵ (01), A (02), B (03), C (04), P (025), Ψ (044), 048, 0251

Jude: $\mathfrak{p}^{72}$(!), $\mathfrak{p}^{74}$, $\mathfrak{p}^{78}$(!)

ℵ (01), A (02), B (03), C (04), P (025), Ψ (044), 0251

In the book of Revelation the textual scene and its history differs greatly from the rest of the New Testament. Correspondingly the list of "constant witnesses" cited for each variant is quite different. Not only are all available papyri included in this category (as elsewhere), but also all available uncials (which are

represented elsewhere by only a selection) and a whole group of minuscules. Specifically the following manuscripts are included:

$\mathfrak{p}^{18}$(!), $\mathfrak{p}^{24}$, $\mathfrak{p}^{43}$, $\mathfrak{p}^{47}$(!), $\mathfrak{p}^{85}$

ℵ (01), A (02), C (04), P (025), 046, 051, 052, 0163, 0169, 0207, 0229, 1006 (eleventh century), 1611 (twelfth), 1841 (ninth/tenth), 1854 (eleventh), 2030 (twelfth), 2050 (1107), 2053 (thirteenth), 2062 (thirteenth), 2329 (tenth), 2344 (eleventh), 2351 (tenth/eleventh), 2377 (fourteenth)

   This selection of "constant witnesses" reflects the textual tradition of Revelation. $\mathfrak{p}^{47}$ is the earliest witness, followed in age by ℵ (01), but A (02) and C (04) — both usually considered as uncials of secondary value elsewhere — are superior to them here in textual value. Even $\mathfrak{M}$ is divided into $\mathfrak{M}^A$ (the mass of manuscripts which follow the text of Andreas of Caesarea's commentary on Revelation) and $\mathfrak{M}^K$ (the equally numerous manuscripts of a strictly Koine type). P (025) goes with $\mathfrak{M}^A$ and 046 with $\mathfrak{M}^K$; these two groups together comprise $\mathfrak{M}$. A reading attested by A (02) and C (04) together with their important supporting minuscules 2053, 2062, and 2344 possesses a textual value far superior to $\mathfrak{p}^{47}$ and ℵ. In brief, the scene in Revelation is considerably (if not completely) different from elsewhere.[17] Unfortunately it has not always been possible to cite the readings of minuscules 2344 (whose poor state of preservation makes it difficult and frequently impossible to decipher) and 2377, so that their witness cannot always be inferred when they are not included in the attestation for either the text or a variant reading.

   The usefulness of reviewing these "constant witnesses" in several groups rather than in a single list needs no real defense. Manuscripts usually contain only a single group of writings (e, a, p, or r), or some irregular combination of groups (cf. pp. 78f.: "Distribution by content"). This fourfold grouping is then further modified by distinguishing Acts from the Catholic letters. This is done not simply for convenience, but because the history of the text and its transmission in the early centuries is quite different for Acts and the Catholic letters.

   In addition to the "constant witnesses" which are always explicitly cited where they are extant, there is a **second class of "constant witnesses"** which are cited only where they differ from $\mathfrak{M}$, and are otherwise subsumed in $\mathfrak{M}$. To this class belong the following manuscripts:

Gospels: K (017), N (022), P (024), Q (026), Γ (036), Δ (037), 28 (eleventh century), 33 (ninth), 565 (ninth), 700 (eleventh), 892 (ninth), 1010 (twelfth), 1241 (twelfth), 1424 (ninth/tenth)

Acts: L (020), 33 (ninth), 81 (1044), 323 (eleventh), 614 (thirteenth), 945 (eleventh), 1175 (eleventh), 1241 (twelfth), 1739 (tenth), 2495 (fourteenth/fifteenth)

Pauline letters: K (018), L (020), P (025), 33 (ninth), 81 (1044), 104 (1087), 365 (thirteenth), 630 (fourteenth), 1175 (eleventh), 1241 (twelfth), 1506 (1320), 1739 (tenth), 1881 (fourteenth), 2464 (tenth), 2495 (fourteenth/fifteenth)

---

   17. Cf. Josef Schmid, *Studien zur Geschichte des griechischen Apokalypse-Textes*, 3 vols. (Munich: 1955-1956).

Catholic letters: K (018), L (020), 33 (ninth), 81 (1044), 323 (eleventh), 614 (thirteenth), 630 (fourteenth), 1241 (twelfth), 1739 (tenth), 2495 (fourteenth/fifteenth)

In Revelation this second class of "constant witnesses" does not occur, because here all the manuscripts of importance are always cited explicitly.

But the readings of these manuscripts (when subsumed in 𝔐) can usually be determined for each variant recorded with attestation — although it requires close attention: if a manuscript of this second class of "constant witnesses" is absent from the witnesses cited for a variant with attestation, it may be inferred that it reads with the Majority text unless it has a lacuna (which needs to be ascertained).

The **meaning of the sign** 𝔐 has already been discussed briefly (cf. p. 230). It may be appropriate to deal with it in greater detail here, especially as it is the only group sign other than f^1 and f^{13} used in Nestle-Aland[26].

Following the precedent of Hermann Freiherr von Soden, Erwin Nestle had earlier introduced the signs 𝔥 (for the Hesychian or Egyptian text) and 𝔎 (for the Koine or Byzantine text). The sign 𝔥 was too vague to be retained. While the Alexandrian Egyptian text does represent (beside the Koine and the D text types) the only great text type of the early period which can be identified with confidence, still the later their date, the more the manuscripts of this text type show the influence of the Imperial Byzantine text type which dominated the Greek-speaking world. In the older Nestle editions, then, 𝔥 often represented only a few manuscripts and gave the reader a false impression. This sign therefore had to be replaced by individual manuscript symbols, which is the only way to describe the situation accurately. The sign 𝔎 for the Koine text type, on the other hand, was far more defensible, for the Imperial Byzantine text type is a well-defined entity. Even with its frequent divisions its character remains consistent. Therefore the sign could well have been kept. Actually, however, the Imperial Byzantine text type does not normally stand alone, but is usually found in company with a relatively large number of manuscripts which do not necessarily belong to the Byzantine Imperial text type. The sign 𝔎 (or *Byz.* in *GNT*) cannot, therefore, be said to reflect the situation accurately. The sign 𝔐 (for "Majority" text) was therefore adopted.

This means, of course, that the Koine or Byzantine Imperial text, however we may call it, is only lightly veiled here, and the equation of 𝔎 with 𝔐 is always valid. In fact, this definition could very well stand, because among Greek manuscripts the Koine type always constitutes the majority. But actually in Nestle-Aland[26] the sign 𝔐 means something more. As stated above (p. 243), there is a class of "constant witnesses" which have been collated for each variant but are cited individually only when they are *not* in agreement with 𝔐. Therefore the sign 𝔐 indicates:

in the Gospels: Manuscripts of the Byzantine Imperial text, plus K, N, P, Q, Γ, Δ, 28, 33, 565, 700, 892, 1010, 1241, 1424, minus any of these manuscripts cited explicitly for an alternative reading.

in Acts: Manuscripts of the Byzantine Imperial text, plus L, 33, 81, 323, 614, 945, 1175, 1241, 1739, 2495, minus any of these manuscripts cited explicitly for an alternative reading.

in the Pauline letters: Manuscripts of the Byzantine Imperial text, plus K, L, P, 33, 81, 104, 365, 630, 1175, 1241, 1506, 1739, 1881, 2464, 2495, minus any of these manuscripts cited explicitly for an alternative reading.

in the Catholic letters: Manuscripts of the Byzantine Imperial text, plus K, L, 33, 81, 323, 614, 630, 1241, 1739, 2495, minus any of these manuscripts cited explicitly for an alternative reading.

The manuscript attestation for each variant, therefore, can be found (for those that are extant in the passage) by a process of elimination. When the reading of any of these manuscripts (none of which is unimportant) is in question, it needs only to be seen whether it is cited among the witnesses for any of the alternative readings. If it is not found explicitly elsewhere, then it is in agreement with 𝔐.[18]

Besides the "constant witnesses" we have just described, whose readings can always be determined, there is another class of **minuscules which are cited quite frequently**, although not regularly. Manuscripts whose quality merits their inclusion in this group are:

Acts: 6 (thirteenth century), 36 (twelfth), 104 (1087), 189 (twelfth), 326 (twelfth), 424 (eleventh), 453 (fourteenth), 1704 (1541), 1884 (sixteenth), 1891 (tenth), 2464 (tenth).

Pauline letters: 6 (thirteenth), 323 (eleventh), 326 (twelfth), 424 (eleventh), 614 (thirteenth), 629 (fourteenth), 945 (eleventh).

Catholic letters: 69 (fifteenth), 322 (fifteenth), 623 (1037), 945 (eleventh), 1243 (eleventh), 1505 (1084), 1846 (eleventh), 1852 (thirteenth), 1881 (fourteenth), 2298 (eleventh), 2464 (tenth).

In order to provide the reader with more information and to increase familiarity with manuscripts, the minuscules listed here have their dates by century shown in parentheses as it was done above for the manuscripts belonging to the second class of "constant witnesses" (cf. pp. 247f.; for dated manuscripts the year is shown). The manuscript list in Nestle-Aland[26] (Appendix I, pp. 702-710) enumerates more than two hundred manuscripts as cited in the apparatus. This number corresponds rather closely to the percentage of minuscules whose textual significance has been demonstrated by studies at the Institute for New Testament Textual Research: from 10 to 15 percent have independent and valuable texts, while the rest contain either a purely Byzantine text (the list on pp. 711f. of Appendix I is merely a sampling; cf. pp. 138ff.) or a text so permeated by its influence that their value as textual witnesses is severely limited. Naturally the criteria for citing from this group of more than two hundred manuscripts include not only their textual value for a given variant, but also the critical significance of the variant under consideration itself. For such instances as the ending of Mark, or the passage known as the Comma Johanneum (1 John 5:7-8), etc., the documentation in the apparatus is practically complete, comparable to expectations for a large critical edition.

This should be a sufficient introduction to the Greek manuscript evidence cited in *GNT*[3] and in Nestle-Aland[26]. The **early versions** of the New

18. For the special circumstances in Revelation, where 𝔐 frequently divides into 𝔐ᴬ and 𝔐ᴷ, cf. p. 247.

Testament are discussed in chapter IV (pp. 185-221), so that only a review of the symbols used for them is necessary here.

The Old Latin witnesses are indicated by the traditional lowercase roman letters (in the list of manuscripts in Appendix I on pp. 712-16 the Beuron numbers have been added beside them solely for clarity). The support of all or
it   of a majority for a particular reading is indicated by the sign it (Itala); manuscripts which differ are normally indicated with the other variants. Agreement
vg   of the Old Latin with the Vulgate (vg) to form a united Latin witness is indicated
latt by the sign latt. If a part of the tradition apparently presupposes the same Greek translation base, but a certain freedom of translation makes absolute certainty
lat(t) impossible, the sign lat(t) is used. Agreement of only a part of the Old Latin
lat with the Vulgate is indicated by the sign lat (the manuscripts which differ are then recorded with the other variants where possible; cf. the examples cited on pp. 298ff.). Only rarely is one reading supported by it and another by lat. A consistently detailed enumeration of the versional variations in such instances would overload the apparatus, while the use of comprehensive signs simplifies the presentation of evidence without becoming simplistic.

The various editions of the Vulgate are indicated by the following ab-
vg^s breviations when information about their text is necessary or informative: vg^s
vg^{cl} for the Sixtine edition (Rome: 1590); vg^{cl} for the Clementine edition (Rome: 1592) (vg^s is not indicated independently when its text agrees with vg^{cl}). The modern editions of John Wordsworth, H. J. White, and H. F. D. Sparks (Ox-
vg^{ww} ford: 1889-1954) (vg^{ww}), and the "Stuttgart Vulgate" edited by Robert Weber in association with Bonifatius Fischer, Hermann Josef Frede, Jean Gribomont,
vgst H. F. D. Sparks, and Walter Thiele (Stuttgart: ^{3}1984) (vgst), are also cited, especially when the texts of the editions differ. The citation of important
vg^{ms} Vulgate manuscripts is limited to the indication of vg^{ms} for a single manuscript
vg^{mss} and vg^{mss} for more than one manuscript.

The evidence of the Latin version comes in the apparatus immediately following that of the Greek witnesses, and is itself followed by the evidence of the Syriac versions. For these the following signs are used.
sy^s The Sinaitic Syriac preserves the text of the Gospels with considerable lacunae: Matt. 6:10–8:3; 16:15–17:11; 20:25–21:20; 28:7–end; Mark 1:1-12; 1:44–2:21; 4:18-41; 5:26–6:5; Luke 1:16-38; 5:28–6:11; John 1:1-25; 1:47–2:15; 4:38–
sy^c 5:6; 5:25-46; 14:10-11; 18:31–19:40. The Curetonian Syriac similarly lacks Matt. 8:23–10:31; 23:25–end; Mark 1:1–16:17; Luke 1:1–2:48; 3:16–7:33; 24:44-51;
sy^p John 1:42–3:5; 8:19–14:10; 14:12-15, 19-21, 24-26; 14:29–21:25. The Peshitta comprises the Gospels, Acts, the Pauline letters, and the longer Catholic letters;
sy^{ph} the Philoxenian version is cited for the shorter Catholic letters (2 Peter, 2-3 John, Jude) and for Revelation, which are lacking in the Peshitta. The edition of the Harklean by Joseph White ends at Heb. 11:27; the remainder of Hebrews
sy^h is therefore cited from Robert Lubbock Bensly, *The Harklean Version of the Epistle to the Hebrews, Chapter XI.28–XIII.25* (Cambridge: 1889). For the text of Revelation we must rely on Brian Walton's *Polyglot*, vol. 5 (London: 1657). In citing the Harklean version the marginal notes, which are of particular in-
sy^{hmg} terest, are indicated by sy^{hmg}, and the readings marked with an asterisk by the

Harklean translator (additions to his exemplar derived from one or more manuscripts) are indicated by sy^{h**}. The agreement of all the Syriac witnesses for a reading is shown by the sign sy. The use of the sign sy with parenthetical superscripts needs comment here. For example, sy$^{(p)}$ indicates that a reading is attested by the whole Syriac tradition, and that sy^p alone exhibits a subvariant which does not affect its witness to the same basic text. The same holds for sy$^{(s)}$, sy$^{(s.c)}$, sy$^{(c.p)}$: each indicates that the witness of the Syriac version is essentially united, and although the witnesses indicated in parentheses do exhibit certain variations, these are not of sufficient significance to merit further attention. In order to avoid misunderstanding, the use of the sign sy with parenthetical superscripts must be distinguished from its use described first above, where the sign and its superscript are without parentheses (e.g., sy^p, sy^c, and so forth), indicating respectively that the Peshitta, the Curetonian Syriac, etc., have the reading in question, and again from the sign standing together with its superscript within parentheses (e.g., (sy^p), (sy^c), (sy$^{s.c}$), and so forth), indicating that the reading in question is attested by witness enclosed in the parentheses and by it alone, although in a form exhibiting a negligible variation. Thus the parentheses serve the same function for the Syriac as elsewhere, only their position must be carefully observed.

After the evidence of the Syriac in the apparatus (which always stands after the Latin), and consequently in third position, comes the evidence of the Coptic versions.

These include the following dialects: ac Akhmimic; ac^2 Subakhmimic; bo Bohairic; mae Middle Egyptian; mf Middle Egyptian Fayyumic; pbo Protobohairic; sa Sahidic.

These signs without further qualifications always refer to the whole tradition of a given dialect. The agreement of all the Coptic versions available for a passage is represented by co. Naturally it is frequently necessary to indicate the readings of single important manuscripts: sa^{ms} and bo^{ms} indicate a single witness, while sa^{mss} and bo^{mss} indicate more than one witness in support of a given reading (for the Sahidic the correctors and for the Bohairic the correctors and also the marginalia are counted as witnesses). If five or more witnesses support a particular reading in Bohairic they are represented as bo^{pt} (Bohairic^{partim}). When bo is cited for one reading and bo^{ms} or bo^{mss} for another, this means that one or more Bohairic manuscripts differ from the rest, corresponding to the usage followed for the Latin evidence. The manuscript groups identified in Horner's editions are cited in the apparatus as single witnesses. They are considered and counted individually only when their readings differ. Since Horner's editions no longer satisfy current requirements and standards, we rely for supplementary information upon a number of manuscripts available either in critical editions or on microfilm. These are noted in chapter IV (pp. 200-204) for the various Coptic dialects.

The other early versions have been discussed adequately in chapter IV so that nothing further need be added here. Similarly the **patristic quotations** from the New Testament noted in the critical apparatus have been adequately reviewed for the Greek Church Fathers in chapter III (pp. 171-184) and for the

(margin notes)
sy^{h**}
sy
sy$^{(p)}$
sy$^{(s)}$
sy$^{(s.c)}$
sy$^{(c.p)}$

(sy^p) etc.

ac ac^2
bo mae mf
pbo sa

co
sa^{ms} bo^{ms}
sa^{mss}
bo^{mss}

bo^{pt}

Church Fathers in other languages in chapter IV (pp. 214-221) together with their abbreviations, so that nothing remains to be added here.

We can now turn, therefore, to the supplementary information found in Nestle-Aland[26] in the inner and outer margins of the pages (*GNT*[3] does not have this material, and can accordingly be omitted from consideration here). The information in the **inner margin** is only of historical concern for the student reader, but for the specialist it is both interesting and useful. These notes refer *1 2 3 4* to the *kephalaia,* a chapter division system found in the manuscripts (essentially the pericope system of lectionary units, designated by italic numerals), and in the Gospels also the Eusebian section and canon table references. Eusebius' letter to Carpianus, which explains the system together with the canon tables themselves, is given in a corrected form in Nestle-Aland[26], pp. 73*-78*, based on Nestle-Aland[25]. This ingenious system designed by Eusebius is still of interest III x̄ etc. today. It is quite effective as a provisional synopsis of the Gospels. Thus III is found at Matt. 1:1; $\frac{2}{x}$ at 1:17; and $\frac{3}{v}$ at 1:18; and so forth. These mean that the parallels for Matt. 1:1ff. are to be found in canon III, where beside no. 1 for Matthew is found the no. 14 for Luke (Luke 3:23-38), and nos. 1, 3, and 5 for John (John 1:1-5, 9-10, 14). The sign $\frac{3}{x}$ refers the reader to canon table X: there it is shown that for Matt. 1:17 there are no corresponding passages in the other Gospels (canon X is repeated for each of the Gospels, listing for each in sequence the paragraphs which are peculiar to them). At Matt. 1:18 $\frac{3}{v}$ refers to canon table V, which shows that for Matthew no. 3 the parallel section in Luke is no. 2 (Luke 1:35), and so forth. By dividing the Gospels into appropriate units Eusebius was able to arrange the material systematically: canon I brings together material common to all four Gospels, canons II-IV material common to three Gospels, canons V-IX material common to two Gospels, and canon X registers in four lists the material peculiar to each of the Gospels. As kephalaia numbers and section numbers are (usually) found in New Testament manuscripts, their inclusion in this edition makes it useful when working with manuscripts. It is not an error, incidentally, that kephalaion 1 in Matthew begins at Matt. 2:1; it is the regular usage in manuscripts not to number the first section. Where the beginning of an early division does not coincide with the beginning of a verse it follows the stronger punctuation division, and when this is not sufficiently * clear it is indicated in the text by an asterisk.

While the inner marginalia of Nestle-Aland[26] are essentially of interest to specialists, the information in the **outer margin** is designed especially for the student as a full reference resource. (Students taking New Testament examinations will readily appreciate the advantages this apparatus offers to anyone familiar with its principles.) The earlier editions of Nestle were already quite impressive for the amount of source and reference material they provided. In Nestle-Aland[26] this apparatus has been thoroughly revised with the aim of combining a maximum of information (far more than in the Old Nestle) with a maximum of clarity. This has been generally successful, although at times (e.g., at the beginning of Romans) the text requires a range of references that can be marshaled concisely only with difficulty. But even in such instances the principle

has been consistently observed of placing references beside the line, or at least the verse, to which they are related. If the references extend too far, they are separated from those of the next verse by a solid vertical line | . When two verses share the same line the same divider is used to avoid confusion. References to different parts of a verse are separated by a raised dot · .

Differences in type face are important. References to parallel passages are in larger type, with the verses concerned given in italics. For example, at Matt. 1:2 the margin reads: *2-17:* L 3,23-38. This means that Luke 3:23-38 contains material that is parallel to the whole of Matt. 1:2-17. And so it continues throughout the Gospels, e.g., Matt. 7:1: *1-5:* L 6,37-42; Matt. 8:2: *2-4:* Mc 1,40-45 L 5,12-16; Matt. 9:1: *1-8:* Mc 2,1-12 L 5,17-26. Not only are parallel passages indicated in this way, but similarly reference summaries occur a great number of times, e.g., Matt. 1:3: *3-6a:* Rth 4,12.18-22; Matt. 1:4: *4-6a:* 1 Chr 2,10-12.15; Matt. 1:6: *6b-11:* 1 Chr 3,5, and so forth.

References to passages within the same New Testament book are given by chapter and verse only (or by verse only when they are in the same chapter). Thus at Matt. 1:16: 27,17 refers to Matt. 27:17; at Matt. 1:20 the marginal note 2,13.19 refers to Matt. 2:13,19. Verses within the same chapter are separated by a period, as the example immediately above shows, and a semicolon separates references to different chapters. For example, it should be noted at Matt. 1:1 in the marginal reference 18 Gn 5,1; 22,18 that the reference after the semicolon intends Gn 22,18, while the 18 at the beginning, which stands without any indication of book or chapter, refers to Matt. 1:18. At times a semicolon is placed before a raised dot; cf. the marginal apparatus at Matt. 1:2 where we find: Gn 25,26; · 29,35. The latter reference 29,35 is also to a passage in Genesis and therefore requires the semicolon before it, but it is concerned with a different part of the verse, and therefore requires the raised dot to separate it from the preceding reference. A reference with cf (confer, or compare) placed before it should be understood as provided merely for reference, just as a question mark ? indicates that it is questionable.

In order to offer a maximum of information in the marginal apparatus it has been condensed as much as possible. Consequently the **abbreviations for the books of the Bible** are as brief as possible. The following forms are used:

Old Testament:
Gn (Genesis), Ex (Exodus), Lv (Leviticus), Nu (Numbers), Dt (Deuteronomy), Jos (Joshua), Jdc (Judges), Ru (Ruth), 1 Sm, 2 Sm (1,2 Samuel; 1,2 Kingdoms in the Septuagint), 1 Rg, 2 Rg. (1,2 Kings; 3,4 Kingdoms in the Septuagint), 1 Chr, 2 Chr (1,2 Chronicles; 1,2 Paralipomenon in the Septuagint), Esr (Ezra; 2 Esdras 1–10 in the Septuagint), Neh (Nehemiah; 2 Esdras 11–23 in the Septuagint), Esth (Esther), Job, Ps (Psalms), Prv (Proverbs), Eccl (Ecclesiastes), Ct (Song of Solomon), Is (Isaiah), Jr (Jeremiah), Thr (Lamentations of Jeremiah), Ez (Ezekiel), Dn (Daniel), Hos (Hosea), Joel, Am (Amos), Ob (Obadiah), Jon (Jonah), Mch (Micah), Nah (Nahum), Hab (Habakkuk), Zph (Zephaniah), Hgg (Haggai), Zch (Zechariah), Ml (Malachi).

Apocrypha and Pseudepigrapha of the Old Testament:
3 Esr (3 Ezra; 1 Esdras in the Septuagint), 4 Esr (4 Ezra), 1-4 Mcc (1-4 Maccabees), Tob (Tobit), Jdth (Judith), Sus (Susanna; Part II of the Additions to Daniel), Bel (Bel

and the Dragon), Bar (Baruch), EpistJer (Letter of Jeremiah), Sir (Wisdom of Jesus ben Sirach), Sap (Wisdom of Solomon), Jub (Book of Jubilees), MartIs (Martyrdom of Isaiah), PsSal (Psalms of Solomon), Hen (Enoch), AssMosis (Assumption of Moses), BarAp (Apocalypse of Baruch); the Testaments of the Twelve Patriarchs are cited individually: TestRub (of Reuben), TestLev (of Levi), TestSeb (of Zebulun), TestDan (of Dan), TestNaph (of Naphtali), TestJos (of Joseph), TestBenj (of Benjamin), VitAd (Life of Adam and Eve). One of the lost pseudepigrapha is also cited: ApcEliae (sec Orig), the Apocalypse of Elijah (according to Origen).

New Testament:

Mt (Matthew), Mc (Mark), L (Luke), J (John), Act (Acts of the Apostles), R (Paul's letter to the Romans), 1K, 2K (1,2 Corinthians), G (Galatians), E (Ephesians), Ph (Philippians), Kol (Colossians), 1Th, 2Th (1,2 Thessalonians), 1T, 2T (1,2 Timothy), Tt (Titus), Phm (Philemon), H (Hebrews), the Catholic letters: Jc (James), 1P, 2P (1,2 Peter), 1J, 2J, 3J (1-3 John), Jd (Jude), Ap (Revelation).

References to the Old Testament (both its text and its textual divisions) ⅏ are based on the *Biblia Hebraica* unless expressly qualified by ⅏ to designate the Septuagint as the source used by the author for a particular passage. A note in parentheses after ⅏ indicates that only the manuscript within the parentheses is intended, and not the whole Septuagint tradition. Thus for example ⅏ (A) means that the text represents the reading in Codex Alexandrinus. If the text is based Aqu, on the translation of Aquila, Symmachus, or Theodotion instead of the Septu-Symm, agint, this is indicated by Aqu, Symm, or Theod. Literal quotations are indicated Theod by italics (cf. *Mch 5,1.3* at Matt. 2:6, etc.). Allusions are shown in normal *Mch 5,1.3* (roman) type — admittedly the distinction cannot always be drawn with precision, especially when they occur in clusters as in parts of Hebrews or in Stephen's address in Acts 7.

s ss   It should further be noted only that s (sequens) and ss (sequentes) added to a reference includes the following verse or verses, e.g., Matt. 1:3: Gn 38,29s p means Gen. 38:29-30. When p is added to a reference (in the Gospels) it means that not only the passage indicated is intended but also its synoptic parallels ! (which are indicated there). An exclamation point ! following a reference indicates that further references to parallels are to be found there. Thus at Matt. 4:1 there is the reference: H 4,15! This means that at Heb. 4:15 is found a full list of further references. It would obviously be impractical to repeat the full list for each instance; the sign ! is used to relate each instance to the main reference list. Here again it is important to gain a practical familiarity with the system. Anyone who looks up all the references to parallels for a verse will soon understand not only the system itself, but also what a wealth of material has been summarized in the marginal apparatus.

For a practical example let us look at the **Parable of the Two Sons in Matt. 21:28-32** which we examined above (pp. 233ff.) together with the pericopes immediately preceding and following it. At Matt. 21:23 the inner margin has the italic numeral 48, at 21:28 there follows 49, and at 21:23 the number 50. These numbers mark the kephalaia, an early chapter system which is practically equivalent to the pericopes (cf. p. 252). We find confirmation here that our pericope divisions are identical with the divisions in Greek manuscripts (of the later period), with the difference that in the manuscripts the pericope headings

are not placed before the paragraphs in the text, but gathered in lists preceding the New Testament books (and repeated in the upper margin of the page).

The titles (τίτλοι) of these pericopes appear as follows (in the Byzantine tradition, cf. von Soden, I, 407):

μη̄   περὶ τῶν ἐπερωτησάντων τὸν κύριον ἀρχιερῶν καὶ πρεσβυτέρων (at 21:23)
μθ̄   περὶ τῶν δύο υἱῶν παραβολή (at 21:28)
v̄   περὶ τοῦ ἀμπελῶνος (at 21:33)

μη, μθ, and v are the Greek numbers 48, 49, and 50. In *GNT*, following the paragraph headings proposed for translators by the United Bible Societies, the corresponding titles are:

at 21:23   The Authority of Jesus Questioned
   21:28   The Parable of the Two Sons
   21:33   The Parable of the Vineyard and the Tenants

Not only here, but in the following ch. 22 as well, the correspondence of text divisions continues (not to diverge until ch. 23), suggesting how old the tradition of our pericope divisions is.

There is a second type of information in the inner margin. Below the chapter number at 21:23 is found $^{217}_{II}$, at 21:28 $^{218}_{X}$, and at 21:33 $^{219}_{II}$. The arabic numbers correspond to the divisions adopted by Eusebius as synoptic sense units. In Matthew the total number of these units is 355. For reference purposes we do not begin with the arabic but with the roman number, which identifies the canon (i.e., the table) in which the arabic number is to be found. Note that canon X lists those units in the four Gospels which have no parallels: accordingly at 21:28 the note $^{218}_{X}$ indicates that the Parable of the Two Sons does not have a parallel account in the other Gospels. Canon II is for texts where three Gospels have parallel accounts (in this instance the synoptic Gospels), and here the following correspondences are given:

Matt. 217 = Mark 127 = Luke 240
Matt. 219 = Mark 128 = Luke 241

Turning to these numbers in the inner margins of the respective Gospels we learn that:

Mark 127 = Mark 11:27-33
Mark 128 = Mark 12:1-11
Luke 240 = Luke 20:1-8
Luke 241 = Luke 20:9-18

And we can formulate the parallels:

Matt. 21:23-27 = Mark 11:27-33 = Luke 20:1-8
Matt. 21:33-44 = Mark 12:1-11 = Luke 20:9-18

In the first example these correspond precisely with the modern editions (e.g., the *Synopsis Quattuor Evangeliorum*), though in the second example Eusebius differs somewhat by marking Mark 12:12 as $^{129}_{I}$ and Luke 20:19 as $^{242}_{I}$, analyzing these in smaller units than is commonly accepted today. The Eusebian canons, however, must be viewed as a whole to appreciate the ingenuity of the system, which still commands the respect of biblical scholars today.

As for the outer margin, the lack of any references to parallel passages makes our passage hardly a representative Gospel passage. This is because this

pericope is found only in Matthew. The usual form occurs at verse 33 (33-46: Mc 12,1-12 L 20,9-19) for a pericope found in all three synoptic Gospels. The first parallel passage is indicated at the beginning by the parallel reference to L(uke) 15,11. This reference is to the two sons in the Parable of the Prodigal Son, where the parallel is superficial. Then opposite verse 30 is a reference to 7,21! Since no New Testament book is indicated explicitly, the reference is to a passage within the present book, and the exclamation point further indicates that at the passage indicated is found a group of references related to the present theme, in this instance the fulfillment of the Father's will as a prerequisite for entrance into the kingdom. This is simple to grasp. The next group of references in the margin at verses 31-32 is a little more difficult: four distinct references appear in close sequence, separated by a slight spacing between lines, with the separation between the first two further indicated clearly by a raised dot. The first group of references (all from Luke, and separated by semicolons) is related to the statement about tax collectors; the second refers to the story of the anointing of Jesus in Luke 7:36-50. The third relates to "the way of righteousness" (the fact that Prov. 21:21 is not cited here from the Hebrew text, but from the Septuagint, is indicated by ⑥), and the fourth to the particular statement in 21:32 (there is no explicit reference to a book or chapter for the initial reference "25" because it intends verse 25 of the chapter under discussion, i.e., Matt. 21:25).

And so it continues. Only a few details require mention, and the full potential of the reference apparatus can only be realized through actual use. Yet the reader should not expect too much, because a marginal apparatus can never (nor should it) be a substitute for commentaries.

Relatively little need be said about the appendices. **Appendix I** (pp. 684-716) with the **list of Greek and Latin manuscripts referred to in the critical apparatus** has already been mentioned repeatedly and requires no further discussion here. It may be appropriate, however, to call attention to distinctions in the list with regard to the "constant witnesses."

*

(*) Witnesses which are always cited explicitly are marked by a prefixed asterisk *; those which are cited explicitly only when they differ from 𝔐 have the prefixed asterisk in parentheses (*): e.g., *B, (*)K. The content of these manuscripts has been carefully described (based on examination of the manuscripts themselves, because complete and reliable information cannot be obtained otherwise), whether negatively by indicating the lacunae in otherwise complete manuscripts, or positively by giving the extent of the actual contents, e.g., for fragments. Manuscripts which are cited as "constant witnesses" only in part or in only one group of writings have the pertinent information given in the list of

[*] contents and are distinguished in the list of manuscripts by the sign [*]. Naturally the contents of manuscripts which are not included among the "constant witnesses" are described more summarily (e = Gospels, a = Apostolos, i.e., Acts

e a

p r and the Catholic letters, p = Pauline letters, r = Revelation). For further abbreviations, cf. Kurt Aland, *Kurzgefasste Liste der griechischen Handschriften des Neuen Testaments*. ANTF 1 (Berlin: 1963): 23-26.

Appendix II (pp. 717-738) with a **survey of variants in modern editions** from the text of Nestle-Aland[26] and *GNT*[3] is probably of comparatively

little interest to the beginning student, but of greater interest to exegetes and especially to textual critics. It offers a survey of all the textual differences in the editions of the last hundred years which have enjoyed any considerable circulation. This is where the new text is, in a sense, placed on trial. Anyone can verify here the extent to which it departs from the text of the editions since Tischendorf, and whether it is justified in doing so. Each instance of textual deviation is represented in the critical apparatus. The amount of work represented here can be imagined. It goes far beyond the requirements of a scholarly manual edition. But we felt it important not only to summarize the results of the past century of achievement in textual criticism, but also to present the evidence necessary for their evaluation — and neither goal has been a possibility for textual criticism until now. Appendix II reviews the texts of seven editions, which are identified as follows:

T H   T = Tischendorf, *Editio octava critica maior* (1869-1872); H = Westcott-Hort
S V M   (1881); S = von Soden (1913); V = Vogels (1922; [5]1955); M = Merk (1933;
B N   [10]1984); B = Bover (1943; [5]1968); N = Nestle[25] (1963)

h
(H)
T V
ꟾ *bis*
V B

ꟾ *bis* S V
M B *ut* 𝔐
ꟾ T M N
ut ℵ

○ [H N]

○ T S;
[H N]
ut txt

    The decisions of Westcott-Hort could not be represented here by citing only the readings accepted in their text, but had to include (indicated by the sign h) the marginal readings which they designated as of equal value (although not those which they rated as inferior). When Westcott-Hort not only differs from the text of Nestle-Aland[26], but also offers a marginal reading of equal value, the sign H is given in parentheses (H). This summarizes, then, the range of readings which have either been identified as the text, or considered seriously as possibilities for the text, during the past hundred years. The system of notation is relatively simple, as the following examples show. As each of the variants (apart from orthographical matters and such differences as εἶπον/εἶπαν) is represented in the apparatus of Nestle-Aland[26], only the critical signs used in the text need be repeated here. As an example, for Matt. 1:6 ꟲ V means that Vogels reads ὁ βασιλεύς as indicated in the apparatus by the sign ꟲ . At Matt. 1:7/8 is ꟾ *bis* V B, meaning that Vogels and Bover read ᾿Ασά at both occurrences. Even where there are several variants included under a single critical sign the identification of a particular reading poses no greater problem than the addition of the sign of one of the supporting witnesses. Thus at Matt. 1:5 ꟾ *bis* S V M B *ut* 𝔐 means that von Soden, Vogels, Merk, and Bover read Βοόζ together with 𝔐; at Matt. 4:2 ꟲ T M N *ut* ℵ means that Tischendorf, Merk, and Nestle[25] read the order καὶ τεσσεράκοντα νύκτας together with ℵ. When the signs are given in square brackets it means that the reading is placed within square brackets by the editions indicated. Thus at Matt. 1:25 ○ [H N] means that [οὗ] is found in the text of Westcott-Hort and of Nestle[25]. Frequently there are differences among the texts of the various editions compared, but such situations are also easily accommodated by the system adopted. Thus at Matt. 1:24 ○ T S; [H N] *ut txt* means that Tischendorf and von Soden omit ὁ before ᾿Ιωσήφ, while Westcott-Hort and Nestle[25] read [ὁ] ᾿Ιωσήφ.

Reviewing the Parable of the Two Sons in Matt. 21:28-32 in terms of the data in Appendix II, we find the following results.

Matt. 21:24: δέ is questioned by the brackets in Westcott-Hort, although surely without justification, as the support for it shows.

Matt. 21:25: Von Soden places τό (2) in brackets, probably because of external evidence; internal criteria argue for its integral character in the context.

Matt. 21:25: παρ' is read by Tischendorf, Westcott-Hort's margin, Vogels, and Bover in place of ἐν, which is supported by internal criteria as well as by external evidence of at least equal authority.

Matt. 21:26: Vogels reads ἔχουσιν τὸν Ἰωάννην ὡς προφήτην with the Byzantine text, which is quite characteristic of his edition although not defensible by external evidence.

Matt. 21:28: Westcott-Hort gives the word order δύο τέκνα in the margin, indicating it as of equal value with the reading τέκνα δύο in the text. This is ill advised and typical of how their preference for B (Codex Vaticanus) so frequently distorted their judgment.

Matt. 21:28: καί is omitted by Tischendorf, Merk, and Nestle[25], while Westcott-Hort adjudges its retention or omission as equally defensible. The new text reads καί primarily on the basis of external evidence, but the coincidence of stylistic support (i.e., the fact that the omission of καί produces a smoother text) is decisive for the reading adopted without reservation for the text only by Bover and Vogels, and bracketed by von Soden.

Matt. 21:28: The addition of μου by B C[2] W Z and so forth is accorded marginal status by Westcott-Hort, and accepted in the text only by Vogels. Similarly in verse 32 the transposition of the text to πρὸς ὑμᾶς Ἰωάννης is accepted in the text by Vogels alone (verses 29-31 will be discussed later; cf. pp. 312ff.). In both instances the external evidence is negative, and it is significant that Vogels stands alone.

Matt. 21:32: οὐδέ in the new text is replaced by οὐ in both Tischendorf and Vogels, despite the clear preponderance of external evidence to the contrary.

Matt. 21:38: κατάσχωμεν is read by Vogels in the text.

Matt. 21:43: The omission of ὅτι is given by Westcott-Hort as a marginal reading, due to the influence of Codex Vaticanus.

Matt. 21:44: This is relegated to the apparatus by Tischendorf alone; Westcott-Hort, von Soden, Vogels, and Nestle[25] read it in the text with brackets (as in Nestle-Aland[26]), while only Merk and Bover accept it for the text without qualification. A critical discussion of this passage has already been presented,[19] and need not be repeated here.

Matt. 21:45: The alteration of the text to ἀκούσαντες δέ as preferred by Tischendorf and proposed as a marginal reading by Westcott-Hort is condemned not only by external evidence but also by the same stylistic reasons that apply to the omission of καί in verse 28. Here again the scribe sought a smoother text.

Matt. 21:46: Vogels' adoption of ὡς for εἰς is consistent with the criteria for his distinctive readings elsewhere.

These are all the differences in Matt. 21:20-46 (excepting only vv. 29-31) to be found in the seven editions since Tischendorf reviewed in Appendix II. Only in verses 29-31 do problems appear, with the seven editions differing from the new text and also among themselves. We will discuss this passage in detail in chapter VII when discussing the praxis of New Testament textual criticism. The comments above on the textual differences among the editions in Matt. 21 admittedly assume more background on the part of the reader than this book has provided. Yet we feel that a bare statement with no

19. Cf. p. 236.

evaluation would be inadequate, and that furthermore the factors involved are so transparent that they are not beyond the grasp of the reader. If this assumption is wrong, the reader is requested to omit this section for the present and to return to it after reading chapter VII (just as the comparative treatment of the various editions at the end of chapter I might well have been deferred until after chapter III). The arrangement of this book with recommended alternative reading sequences (here and similarly elsewhere) does not follow from a neglect of pedagogical principles, but from the attempt to present as complete a treatment of subjects as possible, so that the reader may progress step by step. It will be useful for the reader to refer back to earlier chapters and notes while reading on, rereading them for new perspectives made possible by further knowledge, and seeing implications which could not be appreciated at first reading (meanwhile we hope that the detailed table of contents and the indices will also prove useful).

Appendix III provides the fullest **list of Old Testament quotations and allusions** yet available in this edition of the New Testament. All the references in the outer margin of the text are brought together here in the order of the Old Testament books. It should merely be noted that the New Testament references in italics indicate direct quotations, that normal type indicates allusions, and that here again the chapter and verse divisions follow the usage of *Biblia Hebraica*. Quotations from the Septuagint (based on the Alfred Rahlfs edition) are given following the Hebrew usage (excepting only texts transmitted only in Greek, such as in Daniel). Accordingly when the signs ⅏, Aqu, Theod, and Symm are found beside a marginal reference, the comparative charts given at the beginning showing chapter and verse differences for the various Old Testament books should be consulted. These tables, incidentally, which indicate in full detail all the differences in numbering between the Hebrew text and the Greek (based on the Rahlfs edition), are a welcome convenience for even the specialist. The student is probably aware of differences between the numbering of the Psalms in the Hebrew text (and in all the versions based on it) and in the Greek Septuagint (as well as the Latin Vulgate, and their dependent versions). But there are many more differences, extending even to textual traditions, which are reflected in the chapter and verse numbers. Simply identifying these differences can be a tedious chore (even the lists in Rahlfs' edition of the Septuagint are not always adequate). With some effort we have been able to formulate their differences not only completely but also, we trust, conveniently for the reader. Opinions often differ greatly in identifying quotations and allusions, so that many would probably prefer an italic reference in this list to have been in normal type, or a normal type reference to have been in italics. But there should be no question that this appendix is far more extensive than comparable lists. Also listed are **allusions and quotations from Greek non-Christian writers** found in the New Testament, as well as quotations from unknown sources (designated by unde?). unde?

Appendix IV (pp. 776-79) with its brief identification of **signs and abbreviations** should serve the reader as a brief review and survey of the matters discussed in this introduction, and also as a key to the abbreviations which have

not been explained here in detail. A similar "Master List of Symbols and Abbreviations" is found in the introduction of *GNT*[3], pp. xlvii-liii, as we have mentioned above. In this context we should note particularly the inclusion of special **key cards** for each of these editions, listing the signs for the manuscripts and versions, as well as giving the more important signs and abbreviations with their explanations. Keeping these close beside the Greek New Testament and making constant use of them from the beginning will help the reader avoid any serious problems with the critical apparatus. All the obvious questions will be solved in the introductions of the editions and in the present book. And further, it should be repeated in conclusion that everything is much simpler than it may appear at first. Practice develops skill. It is only necessary to proceed systematically, gaining familiarity gradually with all the relevant material (cf. p. vi on the arrangement of this book). Things which appear quite confusing at the beginning will soon become increasingly clear as the reader grows more familiar with the material and gains experience.

4. *THE SYNOPSES*

So much for an introduction to the use of *GNT*[3] and Nestle-Aland[26]. A further word is necessary about the *Synopsis Quattuor Evangeliorum (SQE)* and its diglot editions, and also the synopses that have appeared after it. Among those which appeared before *SQE* we will notice only the synopsis associated with the name of Hans Lietzmann since 1936, which represents an extensive revision of Albert Huck's *Synopsis* prepared by Hans Georg Opitz and which has since been reprinted frequently for German and English readers.[20]

It cannot be denied that these other synopses have their very distinct advantages. For example, the Huck-Lietzmann edition is a slim volume that offers a maximum of clarity (and at a very modest price). *SQE* in comparison, with its 590 pages, is a heavy caliber book both in size and format, confronting the beginning student with more than can be easily assimilated. The larger size is due to its scope, for it comprises in synoptic format not only all four of the Gospels but also the whole apocryphal tradition, including the complete text of the gospel of Thomas (in three translations), supplementary material on the history of the text which is otherwise quite difficult to assemble (pp. 531-548), and extensive indexes which are easy for even beginners to use (pp. 551-590). There is no real question that the most convenient tool for studying a *single* Gospel is an edition of the Greek New Testament, but when addressing the Gospel tradition as a whole for any particular aspect or theme, a synoptic arrangement becomes necessary (preferably a Four Gospels synopsis). It is not enough to have simply the parallel passages from the gospel of John printed beside the synoptic texts (as in Huck-Lietzmann). The entire sequence of the texts in each of the Four Gospels must be available, with all their similarities

---

20. Cf. especially the adapted English edition *A Synopsis of the First Three Gospels*, prepared by Frank Leslie Cross (Tübingen: 1936). For a detailed historical survey of synoptic editions, cf. Greeven's essay referred to in n. 2 above.

and differences visible in such a way that they may be seen comprehensively, whatever the reader's theories or presuppositions may be. The scholar should be confident that the texts are not only presented as closely in parallel as possible, but that for each pericope all the principal and related secondary parallel references are available, each with its full text, and so arranged that the whole range of material is visible at a glance, regardless of which Gospel forms the basis of study. We believe that these conditions are found today only in *SQE*, which further offers in its extensive subject apparatus a wealth of references, allusions, and illustrations (frequently exceeding the information found in the outer margin of Nestle-Aland[26]). Further, although the supplementary material from the New Testament Apocrypha is of interest to only a limited group, it has been added here because (1) nowhere else can it be found in so complete a form, and (2) while the material is easy enough to omit or ignore, it is not otherwise easily accessible.

The era of Huck-Lietzmann's *Synopsis* has now apparently ended, for the new "Huck-Greeven" has just been published.[21] This new synopsis maintains continuity with its predecessor edited by Lietzmann in its appearance, from the typeface used for the text to the pericope divisions and their headings. Only the numbering of the pericopes has been changed, because the introductory and concluding sections which were numbered separately before have now been included in the total sequence, bringing the number of pericopes from 253 in Huck-Lietzmann to 275 in Huck-Greeven (the earlier numbers are shown in the margin in parentheses). And yet on each page the general impression is quite changed. One factor is that the severely limited critical apparatus in Huck-Lietzmann has been considerably augmented, now frequently occupying half a page or more (expanding the book from 213 to 298 pages). Further, Huck-Greeven has taken fully into the text the synoptic parallels from the lower margin, as well as the Johannine parallels given earlier only by chapter and verses references (set in boxes). These are now shown *in extenso,* separated by heavy lines. This is helpful. But largely sacrificed in the process is the clarity (and elegance) which was one of the chief advantages of Huck-Lietzmann. This is inevitable, however, in a modern synopsis that seeks to present all the working material necessary. A full comparison of all the forms of a pericope is presented only once. Cross references to these full comparative presentations of texts from the individual sections of text with their critical apparatus are given by italic numbers in parentheses, and reverse references to the individual sections by boxed boldface numbers.

The extensive critical apparatus to the text is not easy to use, as soon becomes apparent. Greeven's criteria for the selection of variants and their rationale reveal the purpose of the synopsis.

Instead of making a subjective selection I have consistently taken into the apparatus:

(a) variants which have been regarded by other textual critics as original . . .

---

21. So it is called on the cover; the title page reads "Albert Huck, *Synopsis of the First Three Gospels, with the Addition of the Johannine Parallels, 13th edition, fundamentally revised by Heinrich Greeven"* (Tübingen: 1981).

(b) variants which are extant in Greek, where a passage has been assimilated in greater or less degree to a parallel pericope or to another passage related to it in content or in form. The reason for this is that the Synoptic problem is mirrored precisely in the history of the text, namely in an unremitting tendency to harmonisation. We must always keep before our eyes this trend and especially the significant tendency to assimilate to Mt, if we wish appropriately to investigate textual questions in the Synoptic Gospels. So the variants included in (b) are an essential element in an apparatus to a synopsis. They are presented in the apparatus without omission; I know of no other harmonising variants. "Interesting" variants which are not included can easily be found in the apparatus of any Greek NT, I assume to be in the hands of each user of the Synopsis.[22]

In their succinctness these principles appear quite impressive. The second principle in particular is indubitably significant and useful for studying the important problem of textual assimilation. It should naturally be considered that the completeness of the variants selected depends on the manuscripts chosen as a base, and the adequacy of the collations on the witnesses selected. Different or additional collations would have provided different variants.

The editor explicitly refuses to mention any interesting variants which lie beyond the range of those dictated by the two criteria for the selection of variants. He thereby deprives the reader, at least on occasion, of both resources and the opportunity for tracing the history of interpretation as it is reflected in the harmonistic variants of the manuscripts. His criteria for the selection of variants correspond with the vague statement that his selection of minuscule manuscripts "serves merely practical ends" and "is not intended to make any contribution to the determining of manuscript groups" (p. VI, 8).

The editorial theory of the editor as reflected in the selection of variants and the restraints observed involves essentially a careful comparison of variants, but little consideration of the manuscripts which attest the variants or of their value. The new text so constituted is meticulously constructed (a tremendous labor for a single scholar), and a standing challenge to all other editors, especially to those who would give greater consideration than Greeven to the quality and peculiarities of individual manuscripts and manuscript groups in determining the text. His text "departs some nine times in each chapter from . . . Nestle-Aland[26]" (p. X, 1; cf. p. 223). This seems rather slight in view of the editorial differences between Greeven and the editors of the Nestle text. It attests the quality and integrity of the Gospel tradition as a whole, despite its many unsolved questions.

There is one ambiguity in Greeven's otherwise quite clear preface and introduction. On the one hand, he mentions that "for the variants in the apparatus I have given all witnesses known to me; accordingly inferences *e silentio* are permissible" (p. VI, 8). If the reader can accept this significant clause, it must be inferred that all the readings of all the manuscripts listed on pp. XXVIIIf. may be

---

22. *Ibid.*, p. V.

deduced wherever the edition cites textual variants. This is astonishing, for it implies that even the singular readings, etc., of manuscripts can be reconstructed in full for all the passages where the apparatus cites a variant. On the other hand, it is stated in the Introduction that the uncials and minuscules are "noticed in the apparatus as far as they are known" (p. XVII, 2, b and c). This would imply that inferences *e silentio* are not justified. Some clarification would be desirable, especially a clarification of the editor's intention. That is the most important thing. No one is more acutely aware how easily errors can occur than the authors of the present book.

The synopsis edited by John Bernard Orchard, O.S.B., *A Synopsis of the Four Gospels in Greek arranged according to the Two-Gospel Hypothesis*, which appeared in 1983, is quite different in character. The very title indicates the position taken by the editor, whereas *SQE* and Greeven both explicitly claim impartiality with regard to possible solutions of the synoptic problem (*pace* Orchard, p. xii). Orchard explains that "The present Synopsis is the very first in the two-hundred year history of modern synopses to set out the Four Gospels according to the principle that Lk is the Mean between Mt and Mk, a principle that has been logically carried through from beginning to end. In other words this Synopsis provides the first complete illustration of the Two-Gospel Hypothesis, namely, that the actual order of composition was first the Gospel of Matthew; that then Luke, the disciple of Paul, looked to Matthew for the main literary framework of his Gospel, while the sole written sources of the Gospel of Mark were our Matthew and our Luke" (pp. xiii f.).

With regard to the text of his Synopsis he writes: "The text presented here has been constructed by me on the principle that for the source critical purpose of this Synopsis it is preferable to view in the actual Gospel context the words and passages which modern text critics either reject outright or about which they have serious misgivings, rather than to relegate them to the Apparatus at the foot of the page or elsewhere" (p. 307).

For the bare twenty-five page "selective" (p. xv) appendix devoted to matters of textual criticism it is noted that "printed sources have been drawn on for the material in the Apparatus; in the first place, on the standard editions, Tischendorf and von Soden, and on Legg for Mark (1935) and Matthew (1940). In addition the various manual editions have been consulted" (p. 307). The editor further alludes to the *GNT* and Nestle-Aland[26] (with its "select apparatus" which "seems to be the best we have so far"). Nestle-Aland "has gladly been drawn on here, especially for material not otherwise obtainable in print" (p. 308).

From these editorial statements it is evident that this synopsis will be useful only for scholars who either espouse the "Griesbach hypothesis" or are otherwise interested in it. Yet it may also be welcome to a wider circle as an impressive example of the difficulties posed by the "Synoptic problem." However, it is hardly to be recommended for interpretation, as the limitations of Orchard's proposed text and the secondary character of his critical apparatus provide inadequate controls.

The third synopsis we should notice is M.-E. Boismard and A. Lamouille, *Synopsis Graeca Quattuor Evangeliorum* (Louvain: 1986). A French edition appeared earlier.[23] The text of the Greek synopsis (the only aspect which concerns us here) is described as follows: "We have adopted a standard Greek text, thereby setting aside a number of our personal choices, in order not to inconvenience those who do not share our text-critical views. This text is essentially Alexandrian, close to the text attested by the great uncial manuscripts: B, S, C, L. We have, however, tried to eliminate from it the most glaring harmonizing readings, following in this regard the example of the Huck-Greeven Synopsis; but our corrections of the Alexandrian text are less dependent on the *Koinè* text and closer to the Western text than those adopted by Greeven. In the case of John's gospel, certain variants have been adopted because they seemed to us preferable on grounds of internal criteria" (p. XI).

A proper critical apparatus to the text is not provided for reasons of space. It is further regarded as unnecessary because "it is likely that most buyers of this Synopsis will already possess a critical edition of the New Testament, probably the Nestle-Aland edition. . . . The critical apparatus does not intrude except when our text presents variants from the text of Nestle-Aland's manual edition (the twenty-sixth edition), by far the most widely used" (p. XI).

Thus the Four Gospels synopsis offers a clearer, more elegant display than even the Huck-Lietzmann synopsis, further amplified by formatting the text in "the *cola* and *commata* of the ancients" and without pericope titles (though arranged in paragraphs). Each of the four Gospels is printed in its own sequence, with parallel passages shown in the margin with dotted lines (so that they may easily be ignored), with double parallel lines for passages with only literary associations.

The apparatus is divided into three registers, for textual critical notes, for Old Testament quotations, and for other annotations. These include "texts drawn from the four Gospels, from the Acts of the Apostles or from the Johannine letters, which underline certain stylistic characteristics of one or other of the four gospels" (p. XII), as well as parallel texts from the New Testament, the Apocrypha, and the Church Fathers. These apparatus are further so neatly arranged that they only become noticeable when there are quotations from the Apocrypha or the Church Fathers. The dominating principle in the development of this synopsis was a "concern to let the gospel text stand out clearly by itself" (p. XII), and it has been ingeniously and strikingly successful. But is it adequate when the critical apparatus "makes no pretensions to being exhaustive; it only mentions the main witnesses for each variant" (p. XII), especially when textual alterations are at stake? The reader must always have an edition of the Greek New Testament open beside the synopsis to test the validity of the Gospel text. As for the third apparatus, the editor explains that it is essentially the work of Alfred Resch (*Aussercanonische Paralleltexte zu den Evangelien*, 5 vols. TU 10/1-5 [Leipzig: 1893-1897]), "a work by which [they were] largely inspired,

23. *Synopse des Quatre Evangiles en français avec parallèles des apocryphes et des Pères*, 3 vols. (Paris: 1965-1977).

while completing it a bit" (p. XIII). There is no mention of the devastating and widely accepted criticism of Resch and his work. The editors are remarkably cautious and reserved in the Greek synopsis in comparison with their French edition. In their introduction they advance only two examples for their thesis that the Apocrypha and the Church Fathers possibly quote "from a tradition different from the one attested by the canonical text" (p. XIII). Our own practical experience advises an extreme skepticism in this matter as well as in the textual adaptations to the "Western" text, but this requires a more detailed discussion than is possible here. It should be noted incidentally that the way evidence is presented in the third apparatus may occasionally raise questions for the reader. The editors reproduce the gospel of Thomas in the Latin version of Gérard Garritte (from Kurt Aland, *Synopsis Quattuor Evangeliorum*), quite understandably limiting their citations to the Logia "which coincide in some measure with the text of the canonical gospels" (p. XII). But when they note that in drawing on the Sahidic tradition, "whenever there was identity of vocabulary and of grammatical phrasing we have given a Latin translation as close as possible to the Latin Vulgate" (p. XIII), it tends to raise doubts — not just with regard to the gospel of Thomas.

A brief note should be appended on Reuben J. Swanson, *The Horizontal Line Synopsis of the Gospels*, whose first volume on Matthew appeared in 1982. The amount of space required by the format of the work (more than 440 pages for the gospel of Matthew alone) made it necessary to issue the edition in four volumes (Dillsboro, N.C.: 1982 –). All the variants mentioned are written out in full successive lines, making for a constant repetition of the text. This is intended to produce a better perspective on the variants and the texts of the Gospels (agreements with Matthew are underlined both in the parallel Gospel passages and in the variant readings). But in actual practice the horizontal printing of the text cannot fully represent the complications of the Synoptic problem, much less present an adequate apparatus. Swanson does print the texts in parallel, but the whole context is set by Matthew, and this gives the reader a biased perspective. It is predictable that even when all four volumes are published it will still be difficult to achieve the necessary balance of perspective for decisions about the history of the text and composition of the Gospels. In his undoubtedly original work Swanson attempts to achieve a "neutral source" (p. IX): the text used "is The United Bible Societies' third edition of 1975" and the variants are cited "from original collations by the compiler" (p. XI). But unfortunately the basis is narrow, with the papyri represented by only $\mathfrak{p}^{45}$ and the minuscules by only 28, 565, and 1582, apart from f^1 and f^{13}. Clement of Alexandria plays a special role, because Swanson believes that for particular readings there is "even the possibility that Clement alone of all witnesses, manuscript and version, has preserved the original reading" (p. XIV). A full evaluation will not be possible until all four volumes are available.

The Synopses we have mentioned and those now to be introduced supplement each other and together provide the scholar with an excellent starting point for the many questions of research in the Gospels. To return now to the *Synopsis Quattuor Evangeliorum* edited by Kurt Aland (and its diglot editions), little needs to be said about the **arrangement of the critical textual apparatus**.

It follows the Nestle system, so that the explanations on pp. 232-254 apply here as well. Only a few comments are necessary. Neither the selection of passages for which variant readings are shown nor the attestation cited for them is closely coordinated with the new Nestle. In both respects they surpass Nestle-Aland[26]. This is particularly significant for the thirteenth edition, where there is also a change in the citation of uncials with a Byzantine text. For details the reader is referred to the Introduction of the thirteenth edition.

The most important question for the new reader of *SQE* is probably the **quickest way to find any particular pericope**. One very simple way is to consult the index on pp. 576-584, which indicates all the occurrences of every verse of each pericope by page and pericope number (bold type for principal text, normal type for primary parallels, and smaller type for secondary parallels). But reference to this index is made unnecessary by the running heads at the top of each page. To take an example at random, on p. 287 the running head reads: Matth. 18,23-35–Mark. 9,42-50–**Luk. 12,33-34**–Joh. 6,67-71. This means that the principal text on this page is Luke 12:33-34 (with its parallels Matt. 6:19-21 and Mark 10:21). To find where the other references in the running head appear as the principal text (with their parallels) it is necessary to turn back through the pages until they are found in bold type at the top of the page, which occurs for Matt. 18:23-35 on p. 254 (until which the reference is in normal type), and for Mark 9:42-50 on pp. 249-250 (until which the reference at the top of the page is again in normal type). And there is more information easily at hand: immediately below the title of each pericope is printed the reference to any parallel pericope(s), which is no. 64 in this instance. And further, immediately before every text cited in each pericope, even to the least of the secondary parallels, is given the number of the pericope in which it is found as the principal text, along with the number of the page where it is found.

If the reader wishes to follow the text of a single Gospel continuously, this can also be done with no difficulty. Naturally the text of the Gospel should be read from the pericope where it is printed in bold type as the primary text. Immediately following the text in these pericopes the reference to the number and page of the next pericope in sequence is always indicated. For the passage Luke 12:33-34 in pericope 202 which we have selected at random, the text of Luke continues uninterruptedly as the primary text through Luke 18:9-14 in pericope 237 on p. 320. Then at the end of the text there is the note that the continuation with Luke 18:15-17 is found in pericope 253 on p. 337. A corresponding note is found at the beginning of the sequel indicating that it resumes the text from pericope 237 printed on p. 320. The pericopes are consistently cross referenced in this way. The reference at the beginning or end of a pericope is lacking only when the continuation of the text is found in the pericope immediately preceding or following. After using the *Synopsis* a few times the reader will be quite at home with it. It is perhaps as well to note that at the beginning of a pericope all the texts cited in it are listed (however many there may be in the more extensive and complex examples) in order to give a summary of the situation at a glance.

There is no need to describe the *Synopsis of the Four Gospels* in any detail here. In its arrangement it is precisely like the *editio maior,* but without the materials from the Apocrypha and from the early Church Fathers in the pericopes and in the appendix. Even the secondary parallels in smaller type are somewhat abbreviated (though the omitted portions are clearly indicated by references) to make possible the reduction of the number of pages required from 514 in the *editio maior* to 338 in the *editio minor.* Something had to be sacrificed to prevent the volume from becoming too unwieldy in size (due to the additional 338 pages of parallel English text), and the elimination of these elements was indicated because anyone studying the Synoptics with the aid of a translation is not primarily interested in the apocryphal writings or in the witness of the early Church Fathers, or in having the text of every possible synoptic parallel printed out in full. It should also be remarked that the English text (which has been carefully arranged to parallel the Greek text) is designed not simply as an interpretation of the Greek text, but with due regard to its own scholarly significance. It is furnished with a detailed apparatus which records all the variants found in the tradition of the official English versions, beginning with the Authorized (King James) Version, providing the reader with a glimpse of the history of English Bible translating from the vantage of the second edition of the Revised Standard Version New Testament, which is printed as the text.

A Greek-English edition of Nestle-Aland[26] appeared in 1981, extending the principles represented here in the Gospels to the whole of the New Testament. A Greek-Latin edition of Nestle-Aland[26] appeared in 1984 with the text of the Neo-Vulgate and an apparatus noting the differences of the Latin Vulgate of Jerome as well as those of the Sixto-Clementine Vulgate which was the official text until 1979. In 1986 a Greek-German edition of Nestle-Aland[26] was published with two German versions paralleling the Greek text: the 1984 Luther revision and the Roman Catholic Einheitsübersetzung of 1979. New printings of each have since appeared. In 1982 the English portion of *SFG* was published separately under the title *Synopsis of the Four Gospels, English Edition,* and a Greek-German edition appeared in 1989, with two German versions as in the 1986 Greek-German edition of Nestle-Aland[26].

VI

RESOURCES

This chapter can be relatively brief. Among the six categories of working tools for textual criticism not all require equally detailed consideration here. For some a general discussion will be sufficient. In their order of importance for text-critical work these categories are (1) concordances, (2) dictionaries, (3) grammars, (4) synoptic editions for use with editions of the Greek New Testament for work in the Gospels, (5) special literature, and (6) commentaries.

1. *CONCORDANCES*

Constant reference to a concordance is imperative not only for work in textual criticism, but for exegetical work as well. It is unfortunate that this has not always been recognized. Yet our generation is the first to have a genuinely complete concordance to the New Testament. Until the present there have been only two major concordances available.

Karl Hermann Bruder, *Tamieion* τῶν τῆς καινῆς διαθήκης λέξεων: *sive Concordantiae omnium vocum Novi Testamenti Graeci. Editio stereotypa septima e quarta auctiore et emendatiore, lectionibus Tregellesii atque Westcottii et Hortii locupletata repetita* (Göttingen: 1913; final edition, repr. 1975)

William Fiddian Moulton and Alfred Shenington Geden, *A Concordance to the Greek New Testament According to the Texts of Westcott and Hort, Tischendorf, and the English Revisers* (Edinburgh: 1897)

The latter by Moulton-Geden has been reprinted frequently (most recently in 1963), but two facts should be noted. First, it is incomplete: many of the entries are supplied only with references instead of with full context lines (which renders them useless — no one will ever look up all the references, and it is precisely the function of a concordance to present a comparison of a word's uses by reproducing its various contexts). Second, the text it is based on is a venerable century old, differing from the text in use today in hundreds of instances (many of which are quite significant). The Moulton-Geden concordance appeared in 1963 in a new smaller format edited by Harold K. Moulton. In an appendix the entries for ἀπό, εἰς, ἐκ, ἐν, ὅτι, οὖν, and σύν, which had hitherto

been listed only with references, are given in full with context lines based on
GNT[3](!). But even in this fifth edition entries for δέ and καί are completely
lacking, and the entries for ἀλλά, γάρ, ἤ, οὐ, and τέ are given only with
references, while the entry for αὐτός is given in full only for the nominative
case (distinguishing ὁ αὐτός and αὐτὸς ὁ) in both singular and plural, but with
only references for all other cases. The entry for ἐγώ is given in full only for
ἐγώ itself and ἡμεῖς, again with references only for the other cases. In the entry
for εἰμί the form ἐστίν has references only, while the article ὁ, ἡ, τό is given
in full only for particular idioms and limited to references elsewhere. It is the
same for the entry for οὗτος, and σύ is treated precisely like ἐγώ, as though
the nominative case were more important than the other cases. Even in its new
1978 edition the Moulton-Geden concordance remains incomplete, and the criticism of its century-old text is still valid (if we ignore the embarrassing shift of
its textual base in the new appendix, which only succeeds in making the book a
hybrid — it appears that a completely revised edition is being planned).

The concordance by Bruder has the great advantage of giving variant
readings of manuscripts, but it is just as incomplete as Moulton-Geden (though
in a different way). And furthermore, the text it follows is practically the Textus
Receptus of the past generations, not to say centuries. This makes it practically
incredible that both editions continue to be reprinted (and sold), except for their
prices. In comparison with the *Vollständige Konkordanz zum griechischen Neuen
Testament* both are cheap beyond competition.

The same is true also of Alfred Schmoller's *Manual Concordance to
the Greek New Testament* (Stuttgart: German Bible Society), printed repeatedly
in numerous editions since 1869. It was based on the fifteenth and sixteenth
editions of Nestle until 1989, when it was issued in a new, inexpensive, and
more convenient smaller format, based on the text of Nestle-Aland[26] and *GNT*[3a].
This "Schmoller" offers far more than would be suspected at first glance.

Not only is the *Vollständige Konkordanz* based on the new text, but
the context lines also show (by means of a keyed system) all the differences
found in the texts of the major editions of the Greek New Testament since
Constantin von Tischendorf (as well as in the Textus Receptus), so that the
reader can observe the various textual possibilities and select independently the
basis for further research from among the readings of the different editions. For
each entry (including καί and ὁ, ἡ, τό) every instance of a word's occurrence
is shown with its context, edited in such a way (again by means of a keyed
system) that its relationships are clear, and that the entry can be read and studied
without constant reference to an edition of the New Testament (as is necessary
with other concordances). Finally, a well-developed index system makes it possible to establish groupings by particular uses or collocations within an entry.

The full title of the work is *Vollständige Konkordanz zum griechischen
Neuen Testament: unter Zugrundelegung aller modernen kritischen Textausgaben
und des Textus receptus, in Verbindung mit H. Riesenfeld, H.-U. Rosenbaum, Chr.
Hannick, B. Bonsack neu zusammengestellt unter der Leitung von K. Aland* (Berlin
and New York: de Gruyter). Its two volumes appeared in 1975-1983. The

first volume (Part I: A-Λ, Part II: M-Ω) has been adequately noted, but the second volume requires some comment. The first section of volume II contains vocabulary statistics, the first thoroughly reliable count (because it was computer generated) of the occurrences of each word in each book and for the whole of the New Testament (pp. 1-305). This supersedes Robert Morgenthaler, *Statistik des neutestamentlichen Wortschatzes* (Frankfort: 1958, [2]1972), in this respect because the latter is based on the twenty-first edition of Nestle. Then follows an "alphabetical arrangement of the words of the New Testament and their grammatical forms," with data on their frequency (pp. 307-404), supplementing Walter Bauer's lexicon extensively. While Bauer's first five editions were careful to provide information on accidence, e.g., the forms in which verbs occur in the New Testament (which is important not only for grammarians but for exegetes as well), the sixth edition is the first to report such information fully with frequency statistics for the vocabulary of the New Testament. But even the sixth edition does not give any detailed statistics on the incidence of individual word forms, which is an aspect of critical significance when weighing word frequencies. The same is true of the third part of the volume, which presents a "survey of New Testament vocabulary frequencies arranged in descending order" (pp. 405-446). This section may appear to be of less significance to the exegete (though not to the textual critic), but a careful review of it yields some interesting conclusions. The word which occurs most frequently in the New Testament (as might be expected) is the article ὁ, ἡ, τό (19,904 times). This is followed by καί (9,164 times). And so it continues, with only nineteen words (of which γάρ is the last) exceeding the one thousand mark. Ἰησοῦς occurs only 919 times, the 81st word (ἰδού) reaches the two hundred mark, and the 172nd (ἀλλήλων) the one hundred mark. The 975th word brings the frequency to only 11, with a full 4,500 words to follow. Almost seven pages of the index are of words occurring only twice, and hapax legomena occupy more than 14 pages! These are arranged alphabetically here, and also in the next section (pp. 447-460), where they are grouped by New Testament writings. It is here finally that exegetical and theological attention is aroused, for it is most interesting to observe in each of the New Testament books just where its peculiar usages are found, and what factors they may reflect.

The final section of the volume (pp. 461-557) is a "reverse index of inflected forms." This may hold little appeal for exegetes, or perhaps even for textual critics, but for scholars who work with manuscripts it is of the greatest importance, quite apart from the fact (which is itself not without some significance) that here for the first time New Testament scholarship has gained a tool which classical philologists have had for decades, and which they regard as a regular part of their equipment. This compilation of data as well as the other parts mentioned above was made possible only by close cooperation between the Institute for New Testament Textual Research and the Computer Center of the University of Münster/Westphalia. Once the new text was recorded on magnetic tape by the Institute, the groundwork was laid for a variety of applications.

The second volume of the *Vollständige Konkordanz* as well as the *Concordance to the Novum Testamentum Graece of Nestle-Aland, 26th edition, and to the Greek New Testament, 3rd edition* (Berlin-New York: ³1987; formerly *Computer-Konkordanz*) are only the first examples of possible applications.

This concordance is designed for those who consider the *Vollständige Konkordanz* too expensive (understandably) and also as providing more information than they require, because they are not interested in the textual variants of the past century but only in the new text which is given in it exclusively. The limitation should be noted that while this *Concordance* has the advantage of a smaller size (and a much lower price), yet (1) it lacks completeness in its lemmata; twenty-eight words (including those occurring most frequently) are given in an appendix (cols. 1-66) with references only and without their contexts; (2) it lacks the index system of the *Vollständige Konkordanz* which is of substantial help in studying the entries; and (3) although the context lines are defined here more selectively than in other computer-generated concordances, they reflect the standards of mass production and lack the finer individual tailoring characteristic of the *Vollständige Konkordanz*. The fact that accents are added in the text only when they are significant for meaning is due to the fact that the *Concordance* was produced with the aid of a computer (and therefore formerly called the *Computer-Kondordanz*). Further information on its use may be found in its foreword.

2. DICTIONARIES

The second most important tool for textual criticism after the concordance is the dictionary. For decades the undisputed leader here has been the *Griechisch-Deutsche Wörterbuch zu den Schriften des Neuen Testaments und den übrigen urchristlichen Literatur* by Walter Bauer. A completely revised sixth edition has appeared (Berlin/New York: 1988), edited by Kurt and Barbara Aland. It has not only been expanded by the addition of 250 new articles and conformed to the new text, but now includes references to all occurrences of words in the New Testament, and for all significant terms in the Apostolic Fathers and the early New Testament Apocrypha (hitherto ignored). The list of the Christian, pagan, and Jewish literature represented has been expanded by more than a hundred names. But equally important, it has been redesigned for greater efficiency and usefulness.

This work appeared in an English edition in 1957 under the names of William F. Arndt and Felix Wilbur Gingrich.[1] Only later did Bauer's name

---

1. The names of Arndt and Gingrich were too prominent on the title page of the 1957 publication, which was based on the fourth revised and augmented edition of Bauer's work. The second edition of this English translation appeared in 1979, "revised and augmented by F. Wilbur Gingrich and Frederick W. Danker from Walter Bauer's Fifth Edition, 1958." Meanwhile an abridgment appeared in 1965, edited by Gingrich and limited to the vocabulary of the New Testament (excluding the Apostolic Fathers and other early Christian literature), giving only the essential meanings of the words, without bibliography, and including a greater number of more or less difficult inflectional forms.

receive due recognition in the book, which was essentially no more than a translation of his work with the bibliographical references expanded to include more English literature and with the format of the entries better organized. If "Bauer" is to be criticized, it is because the forest is often obscured by the trees, e.g., the biblical references did not stand out sufficiently in the entries. This is achieved now in the sixth edition by a new typography which not only contributes to greater clarity, but also makes it possible to increase the information by a third within the limits of the same space.[2]

With regard to bibliographical information a most useful tool is volume X, part 2, of the *Theologisches Wörterbuch zum Neuen Testament,* initiated by Gerhard Kittel and edited by Gerhard Friedrich in collaboration with numerous specialists,[3] which appeared in 1979 with a 350-page supplementary section of bibliographical addenda. The entries of this theological dictionary are arranged in word groups, and as suggested by its title the work is in no sense comprehensive, yet the index of Greek words in volume X, part 1, pp. 109-153 (English trans. 10:61-84), goes far toward compensating this lack. The beginner interested in a particular word will find listed not only the word group where it receives primary treatment, but also references to other articles where it receives only incidental treatment in passing. This monumental *Theologisches Wörterbuch* with its nine volumes and two index volumes is not popularly priced for students. The *Exegetische Wörterbuch zum Neuen Testament,* edited by Horst R. Balz and Gerhard Schneider and published by the same press as the *Theologisches Wörterbuch,* appeared in three volumes (Stuttgart: 1978-1983). It is a successor to Kittel (i.e., the *Theologisches Wörterbuch*) and not to Bauer, and it aims primarily to serve readers "whose knowledge of Greek and Hebrew is weak" (foreword to the first fascicle). An English translation is forthcoming.

The same is true to an even greater degree of the *Theologische Begriffslexikon zum Neuen Testament,* edited by Lother Coenen, Erich Beyreuther, and Hans Bietenhard in two volumes (Wuppertal: 1967-1971, [4]1986).[4] This also takes Kittel as its model. These three works belong to the class of dictionaries which deal only with the more important vocabulary items. A supplement to them is the important work by Ceslas Spicq, *Notes de lexicographie néotestamentaire,* 3 vols. Orbis Biblicus et Orientalis 22/1-2 (Fribourg-Göttin-

---

2. For early Christian literature the following are useful as supplementary aids (although all the essentials, even for the Apologists, may be found in Bauer):
in the forthcoming ninth edition):
Heinrich Kraft, *Clavis Patrum Apostolicorum* (Darmstadt: 1963)
Edgar Johnson Goodspeed, *Index patristicus sive Clavis Patrum Apostolicorum operum* (Leipzig: 1907; repr. 1970)
————, *Index Apologeticus sive Clavis Iustini Martyris operum aliorumque apologetarum pristinorum* (Leipzig: 1912)
3. English translation, *Theological Dictionary of the New Testament,* ed. Geoffrey W. Bromiley, 9 vols. (Grand Rapids: 1964-1974); vol. 10: Index, comp. Ronald E. Pitkin (Grand Rapids: 1976).
4. English translation, *The New International Dictionary of New Testament Theology . . . translated, with additions and revisions, from the German,* ed. Colin Brown, 3 vols. (Grand Rapids: 1975).

gen: 1978-1982), and also the compilation of special literature on New Testament and patristic concepts by Hermann J. Sieben, *Voces*. Bibliographia Patristica, supp. 1 (Berlin: 1980). These works are all especially useful in gaining a deeper understanding of particular concepts. They presuppose the knowledge and use of such dictionaries as Bauer, which are always basic to New Testament studies.

Bauer is indispensable both for textual criticism and exegesis, and will remain so for some time.[5] But besides Bauer two classical dictionaries should be mentioned:

Henry G. Liddell and Robert Scott, *A Greek-English Lexicon*. A new edition by H. S. Jones, 2 vols. (Oxford: [9]1940, and subsequent reprints), *Supplement* by E. A. Barber (Oxford: 1968) and Robert Renehan, *Greek Lexicographical Notes: Hypomnemata 45 and 74* (Göttingen: 1975, 1982)
G. W. H. Lampe, *A Patristic Greek Lexicon* (Oxford: 1961)

The former is basic for secular Greek, and the latter for the usage of the Greek Church Fathers. Both lexicons, however, are useful primarily for advanced students. For most purposes in these areas the requirements of the textual critic and of the exegete (and not just beginning students) are adequately met by Bauer without consulting Liddell-Scott's 2,200 pages (quarto size) and Lampe's 1,600 pages (quarto size) for their additional evidence. In any event, it can be said that for the early Christian literature through the Apologists, Bauer is more detailed and succinct than Lampe.

A new kind of lexicon is the *Greek-English Lexicon of the New Testamant Based on Semantic Domains*, 2 vols. (New York: 1988), edited by Johannes Louw and Eugene A. Nida. The vocabulary of the New Testament is analyzed in ninety-three semantic domains which are divided into subdomains. Thus Domain 3 for plants is subdivided into the following subdomains: Plants (general meaning), Trees, Plants that are not trees, Fruit parts of plants, Nonfruit parts of plants, Wood and wood products. The dictionary provides insight to the complexity and ranges of these domains, especially noting the precise distinctions between synonyms. It was originally designed as an aid for Bible translators, but it will undoubtedly be useful for exegetes as well.

---

5. A manual traditionally used by beginning English students is Samuel Bagster, *Analytical Greek Lexicon to the New Testament* (recently revised by H. K. Moulton [Grand Rapids: 1978]). This has been supplemented recently by a variety of publications, e.g., Max Zerwick and Mary Grosvenor, *A Grammatical Analysis of the Greek New Testament* (Rome: 1974-1979), based on Zerwick, *Analysis philologica Novi Testamenti* (Rome: [3]1966); Cleon Rogers, *Linguistic Key to the Greek New Testament* (Grand Rapids: 1976-1980); a translation of Fritz Rienecker, *Sprachliche Schlüssel zum Griechischen Neuen Testament* (Giessen: 1970); Barbara and Timothy Friberg, *Analytical Greek New Testament* (Grand Rapids: 1981), the *GNT*[3] text with an interlinear analytical key identifying the form and function of each word; John R. Alsop, *An Index to the Revised Bauer-Arndt-Gingrich Greek Lexicon* (Grand Rapids: 1981), with the words in the New Testament order indexed to the lexicon; J. D. Douglas, P. W. Comfort, and R. K. Brown, *The Greek-English Interlinear New Testament* (Wheaton: 1989), based on *GNT*[3]/Nestle-Aland[26]. These works offer an immediate aid for identifying vocabulary and word forms in every verse of the New Testament, but the use of such tools, and especially an exclusive reliance upon them, does not lead to a knowledge of Greek.

3. *GRAMMARS*

Grammars are tools as indispensable to the textual critic (and to exegetes) as concordances and dictionaries. There is a whole range of school text and reference editions. These will not be discussed here because they are already familiar to students from their Greek studies. Each has its virtues — and its faults. But whatever text is used, the student should master it thoroughly before attempting to proceed further. And yet students *must* go beyond this level because these provide only a groundwork. For anyone wishing to pursue independent studies in textual criticism (or in exegesis), the following works are available:

Friedrich Blass and Albert Debrunner, *A Greek Grammar of the New Testament and other Early Christian Literature: A Translation and Revision of the ninth-tenth German edition incorporating supplementary notes of A. Debrunner by R. W. Funk* (Cambridge and Chicago: 1961)

————, *Grammatik des neutestamentlichen Griechisch* [final 13th ed., with a Supplement by D. Tabachovitz] (Göttingen: 1970); 14 ed., fully revised and expanded (with paragraph numbers unchanged) by Friedrich Rehkopf (Göttingen: 1976), further revised [15]1979, [16]1984.

The detailed indexes, especially the index of passages cited, are most useful in locating necessary information. Not to be neglected is the four-volume work:

James Hope Moulton and Nigel Turner, *A Grammar of New Testament Greek* (Edinburgh: 1906-1976, and reprints)

Recommended for further research are:

Raphael Kühner and Bernhard Gerth, *Ausfürliche Grammatik der griechischen Sprache* [vols. 1 and 2 originally written by Blass], 3rd ed. (Hanover: 1890-1904, and reprints), with the Index locorum by W. M. Calder (Darmstadt: 1965)

Eduard Schwyzer and Albert Debrunner, *Griechische Grammatik, auf der Grundlage von Karl Brugmanns Griechischer Grammatik* (vol. 3 with an exhaustive *Index* by D. J. Georgacas. Handbuch der Altertumswissenschaft 2/1-3 ([2]1953-1958)

Finally, in a class by themselves there should be noted:

Ludwig Radermacher, *Neutestamentliche Grammatik*, 2nd ed. (1925). Hans Lietzmann, ed., *Handbuch zum Neuen Testament* 1

Francis Thomas Gignac, *A Grammar of the Greek Papyri of the Roman and Byzantine Periods*, to date 2 vols. (Milan: 1976-1981)

4. *SYNOPSES*

The value of a synopsis among the tools indispensable for textual criticism as well as for exegesis in the study of the Gospels has been discussed above (pp. 260-67), and needs no further comment here.

5. *SPECIAL LITERATURE*

Among the works devoted to New Testament textual criticism the leading manual is still a work written more than fifty years ago:

Eberhard Nestle, *Einführung in das Griechische Neue Testament,* 4th ed., thoroughly revised by Ernst von Dobschütz (Göttingen: 1923)[6]

This summary of Eberhard Nestle's research still provides in concise form a range of materials not easily found elsewhere, together with practical suggestions for scholars, although it is surpassed and in many ways superseded both in scope and in range of material by:

Marie-Joseph Lagrange, *Critique textuelle,* 2: *La critique rationnelle* (Paris: 1935)

Next should be mentioned:

Bruce Manning Metzger, *The Text of the New Testament: Its Transmission, Corruption, and Restoration* (New York: [1]1964, [2]1968)
Heinrich Zimmermann, *Neutestamentliche Methodenlehre: Darstellung der historisch-kritischen Methode* (Stuttgart: [6]1978); newly revised by K. Kliesch ([7]1982)
Wilhelm Egger, *Methodenlehre zum Neuen Testament* (Freiburg: 1987)

Although the book by Zimmerman and Kliesch conceives the subject broadly, the work is popular as an introduction (especially among Roman Catholics), as the number of editions attests. Actually, it offers a great number of well-selected examples for the praxis of textual criticism, and it has been considerably modified by the new editor.

Besides these and in a class by itself (not solely because it treats the Greek New Testament along with the Septuagint) should also be noted:

Frederic George Kenyon, *The Text of the Greek Bible,* revised by A. W. Adams (London: 1975)

Other introductions to New Testament textual criticism are less useful, whether Heinrich Joseph Vogels, *Handbuch der Textkritik des Neuen Testaments* ([2]1955), or the various introductions from Léon Vaganay to Harold J. Greenlee, among others. The following collections of essays, however, are important.

Ernest Cadman Colwell, *Studies in Methodology in Textual Criticism of the New Testament* (Leiden: 1969)
Bruce Manning Metzger, *Chapters in the History of New Testament Textual Criticism* (Leiden: 1963)
─────── , *The Early Versions of the New Testament: Their Origin, Transmission, and Limitations* (Oxford: 1977)
─────── , *New Testament Studies: Philological, Versional, and Patristic* (Leiden: 1980)
Kurt Aland, *Studien zur überlieferung des Neuen Testaments und seines Textes* (Berlin: 1967)
─────── , *Neutestamentliche Entwürfe* (Munich: 1979)

The major positions taken in textual criticism today are clearly sketched in these volumes, each of which makes significant contributions with reference to a variety of particular problems.

6. English translation, *Introduction to the Textual Criticism of the Greek New Testament. Translated from the Second Edition (with Corrections and Additions by the Author) by William Edie, B.D. . . . and Edited with a Preface by Allan Menzies, D.D.* (London and New York: 1901).

Special attention should be given to: *A Textual Commentary on the Greek New Testament, A Companion Volume to the United Bible Societies' Greek New Testament (third edition) by Bruce M. Metzger on behalf of and in cooperation with the Editorial Committee of the United Bible Societies' Greek New Testament, Kurt Aland, Matthew Black, Carlo M. Martini, Bruce M. Metzger, and Allen Wikgren* (London and New York: 1971; corrected ed. 1975). This volume gives assistance, particularly for beginners, in making critical judgments on textual questions. For each passage where GNT^3 provides a critical apparatus to the text (and for many other passages as well, e.g., in Acts) it explains how and why the Editorial Committee of the new text came to their decision. Not all the arguments given by Metzger (who was more responsible for the book than the broad attribution of the title would suggest) should be taken too literally. Thus, for example, reference is made frequently to the "variety of text-types" whose support justifies the choice of a particular reading. This kind of argument is not universally convincing, especially as it is spelled out in some instances. As for terminology, "Proto-Alexandrian" and "Later Alexandrian" correspond to "Alexandrian" and "Egyptian" in the present book, while for the terms "Caesarean" and "Proto-Caesarean" as well as "Western witnesses" the reader is referred to the various discussions of them above. It is especially in the dissenting notes signed by Metzger (who registered by far the greatest number) that his conservatism as a textual critic is apparent: it is no mere coincidence that the decision for a particular reading is so often attributed to "a majority of the Committee." This commentary is a veritable monument to the most painstaking and detailed kind of work that we have come to expect from Metzger. It is based on the minutes of the deliberations and decisions of the Editorial Committee, but both in their quality and in their degree of detail these minutes were so uneven overall, due to the constant rotation of the Committee's secretarial office through the years, that in many of its aspects Metzger had to rework the material completely.

For **Greek manuscripts of the New Testament** the standard reference work today is Kurt Aland, *Kurzgefasste Liste der griechischen Handschriften des Neuen Testaments* 1: *Gesamtübersicht.* ANTF 1 (Berlin: 1963). This must be supplemented by addenda which have appeared in ANTF 3: *Materialien zur neutestamentlichen Handschriftenkunde* 1 (Berlin: 1969): 1-53 (Suppl. List VII), and in the successive *Reports* of the Hermann Kunst Foundation for New Testament Textual Research for 1970-1971, pp. 14-19; 1972-1974, pp. 11-13; 1975-1976, pp. 11-16; and 1985-1987, pp. 59-60. *Kurzgefasste Liste* registers New Testament witnesses through $\mathfrak{p}^{76}$, 0250, 2646, ℓ 1997, and the supplements provide addenda through $\mathfrak{p}^{96}$, 0274, 2795, and ℓ 2209. A new edition of *Kurzgefasste Liste* is in preparation. The concordant lists of manuscript symbols at the conclusion of *Kurzgefasste Liste* are particularly useful for practical purposes, making it simple for the reader to match the symbols used by Constantin von Tischendorf and his predecessors (Concordance I, pp. 321-333) and Hermann Freiherr von Soden (Concordance II, pp. 334-349) with the Gregory symbols in use today. The difficulties posed by von Soden's symbols are notorious. It is only too easy to forget that practically none of Tischendorf's symbols for the minuscules

from Acts on is still in use: they must all be transposed (cf. pp. 72f. above). Many of his symbols for New Testament uncials have also been changed. These two concordant lists of symbols are designed for the practical needs of scholars who use Tischendorf's *Editio octava critica maior* or von Soden's edition (unless other tools are preferred such as Kraft's volume [cf. p. 40], although it should be noted that the concordant lists in *Kurzgefasste Liste* are far more complete). Concordance III (pp. 350-371) follows the order of the current symbols and shows their parallels in von Soden's system. This is designed to facilitate access to the wealth of information in his introductory volumes of textual studies, where not only are the most detailed modern descriptions of individual manuscripts to be found, but also notes on manuscript groups and families that have not yet been fully explored.

For New Testament **papyri** the most detailed source of information available today is found in Kurt Aland, ed., *Repertorium der griechischen christlichen Papyri* 1: *Biblische Papyri: Altes Testament, Neues Testament, Varia, Apokrypha*. Patristische Texte und Studien 18 (Berlin: 1976). *Kurzgefasste Liste* gives only the barest of the essential data, and the various articles on New Testament papyri by Kurt Aland which have appeared in *New Testament Studies* deal only with certain select groups. A new series of publications has been started for the study of individual papyri: *Das Neue Testament auf Papyrus*. Volume I with the Catholic letters appeared in 1986 (ANTF 6), and volume II with Romans and the Corinthian letters is in press. These exhibit the text of all the papyri, with a full critical apparatus of all the uncials.

And finally, for **patristic citations** from the New Testament there has now been made available in our generation an invaluable tool:

Biblia patristica: Index des citations et allusions dans la littérature Patristique. 1:*Des origines à Clément d' Alexandrie et Tertullien* (Paris: 1975, repr. 1986); 2: *Le troisième siècle (Origène excepté)* (Paris: 1977, repr. 1986); 3: *Origène* (Paris: 1980); 4: *Eusèbe de Césarée, Cyrille de Jérusalem, Epiphane de Salamine* (Paris: 1987)

This work is being published under the supervision of A. Benoît and P. Prigent at the Center for Patristic Analysis and Documentation at Strasbourg. While its primary interest is hermeneutical, it also provides the basic materials necessary for reconstructing the New Testament text read by the Fathers. The data is based essentially on evidence from the editions of the respective Church Fathers. When the volumes for the Church Fathers of the fourth and fifth centuries appear in the near future, New Testament textual criticism will not be the only field to benefit.

6. *COMMENTARIES*

Commentaries have been reserved for treatment last in this section for the good reason that there are so few that discuss the problems of textual criticism in any detail. We cannot give any evaluations or recommendations here, beyond mentioning briefly some commentary series which give particular attention to textual criticism. Among German commentaries the leading example is the *Handbuch zum Neuen*

Testament series founded by Hans Lietzmann (cf. Lietzmann's discussion of the textual history of the Pauline letters in vol. 8: *Kommentar zum Römerbrief*, 5th ed. [Tübingen: 1971]). Along with the "Handbuch" series should be mentioned "Meyer," the *Kritisch-exegetische Kommentar über das Neue Testament*, founded by H. A. W. Meyer more than a century ago. These volumes, which have been revised repeatedly by many scholars over several generations, are always well worth comparing with those of our own generation. In 1970 reprints were published of Johannes Weiss' 1910 commentary on 1 Corinthians and Hans Windisch's 1924 commentary on 2 Corinthians, and in 1974 Ernst von Dobschütz' 1909 commentary on the Thessalonian letters was reprinted, clearly demonstrating that they still have much to offer us even today, especially with reference to textual criticism and history — areas allotted far less discussion in modern commentaries than earlier. For the same reason Theodor Zahn's multivolume *Kommentar zum Neuen Testament* deserves mention, especially the volumes which he himself authored.

Of course there is much in the commentaries of an earlier generation that will appear dated to many, even embarrassingly antiquated. But in any event they frequently have critical discussions of textual problems not to be found elsewhere, and offer stimulating suggestions. This is true not only of early German commentaries, but of English ones as well. The commentaries by Brooke Foss Westcott, F. J. A. Hort, and Joseph Barber Lightfoot (several of which are available in reprints) are as valuable today for textual criticism as when they were first published. Commentaries in this tradition are still being produced, e.g., by Edward Gordon Selwyn, *The First Epistle of Peter* (London: [2]1947, and many reprints [recently Grand Rapids: 1981]). The extensive *International Critical Commentary* (ICC) series is also a mine of information, and should always be consulted.

Anyone consulting the old (and mostly forgotten) commentaries will be surprised by how much they have to offer. Other commentaries will of course be found useful — there are too many available for us even to venture any selective recommendations here. But the work of textual criticism begins with external evidence, and only after its contribution has been duly analyzed should internal criteria be considered. This is why using the concordance, the dictionary, and the grammar comes *before* turning to the commentaries, for these find their usefulness essentially in establishing whether and in what sense the reading already marked as preferred corresponds with the theological expressions of the particular writing or the theological position of the author of the corpus. At the beginning of the next chapter we will attempt to give twelve basic rules for critical textual work. It is important to state here emphatically that decisions in textual criticism cannot be based on internal criteria alone, especially in opposition to external evidence. And yet, "only the reading which best satisfies the requirements of both external and internal criteria can be original" (Rule 2). While this is the position of textual criticism when pursuing textual criticism, it is no less valid for exegesis, where an equal tendency may be observed

for judgments to be made primarily in the light of internal criteria, with very little if any concern for external evidence. The parallel and mutual character of these two types of criteria reflects the parallel and mutual relationship of textual criticism and exegesis. The closer their cooperation, the more profitably each can function, and the more reliable their results.

Among the many scholarly periodicals available, *Ephemerides Theologicae Lovaniensis*, edited by the Catholic University of Louvain, deserves special notice for regularly publishing articles on the text and textual criticism of the New Testament (including many by Frans Neirynck).

VII

INTRODUCTION TO THE PRAXIS OF NEW TESTAMENT TEXTUAL CRITICISM (SELECTED PASSAGES)

Despite any possible methodological misgivings, we have decided to preface this chapter with a statement of basic principles which we will proceed to demonstrate and explicate by means of practical applications, rather than to derive the principles inductively from practical examples. Meanwhile examples have not been lacking in the preceding text, and besides, this approach is more space-saving and instructive.

1. *TWELVE BASIC RULES FOR TEXTUAL CRITICISM*

1. Only *one* reading can be original, however many variant readings there may be. Only in very rare instances does the tenacity of the New Testament tradition present an insoluble tie between two or more alternative readings. Textual difficulties should not be solved by conjecture, or by positing glosses or interpolations, etc., where the textual tradition itself shows no break; such attempts amount to capitulation before the difficulties and are themselves violations of the text.

2. Only the reading which best satisfies the requirements of both external and internal criteria can be original.

3. Criticism of the text must always begin from the evidence of the manuscript tradition and only afterward turn to a consideration of internal criteria.

4. Internal criteria (the context of the passage, its style and vocabulary, the theological environment of the author, etc.) can never be the sole basis for a critical decision, especially in opposition to external evidence.

5. The primary authority for a critical textual decision lies with the Greek manuscript tradition, with the versions and Fathers serving no more than a supplementary and corroborative function, particularly in passages where their underlying Greek text cannot be reconstructed with absolute certainty.

6. Furthermore, manuscripts should be weighed, not counted, and the

peculiar traits of each manuscript should be duly considered. However important the early papyri, or a particular uncial, or a minuscule may be, there is no single manuscript or group of manuscripts that can be followed mechanically, even though certain combinations of witnesses may deserve a greater degree of confidence than others. Rather, decisions in textual criticism must be worked out afresh, passage by passage (the local principle).

7. The principle that the original reading may be found in any single manuscript or version when it stands alone or nearly alone is only a theoretical possibility. Any form of eclecticism which accepts this principle will hardly succeed in establishing the original text of the New Testament; it will only confirm the view of the text which it presupposes.

8. The reconstruction of a stemma of readings for each variant (the genealogical principle) is an extremely important device, because the reading which can most easily explain the derivation of the other forms is itself most likely the original.

9. Variants must never be treated in isolation, but always considered in the context of the tradition. Otherwise there is too great a danger of reconstructing a "test tube text" which never existed at any time or place.

10. There is truth in the maxim: lectio difficilior lectio potior ("the more difficult reading is the more probable reading"). But this principle must not be taken too mechanically, with the most difficult reading (lectio difficilima) adopted as original simply because of its degree of difficulty.

11. The venerable maxim lectio brevior lectio potior ("the shorter reading is the more probable reading") is certainly right in many instances. But here again the principle cannot be applied mechanically. It is not valid for witnesses whose texts otherwise vary significantly from the characteristic patterns of the textual tradition, with frequent omissions or expansions reflecting editorial tendencies (e.g., D). Neither should the commonly accepted rule of thumb that variants agreeing with parallel passages or with the Septuagint in Old Testament quotations are secondary be applied in a purely mechanical way. A blind consistency can be just as dangerous here as in Rule 10 (lectio difficilior).

12. A constantly maintained familiarity with New Testament manuscripts themselves is the best training for textual criticism. Anyone interested in contributing seriously to textual criticism should have the experience of making a complete collation of at least one of the great early papyri, a major uncial, and one of the significant minuscule manuscripts. In textual criticism the pure theoretician has often done more harm than good.

While the first statement in Rule 12 applies universally, no one would make equal claims for the second statement. The latter applies only to those who are interested in productive studies, i.e., in making a positive contribution to the reconstruction of the text. Of course, students whose interest in critical studies of the text is more passive would also profit from some familiarity in this area, e.g., for exercising a degree of independent judgment in accepting or

rejecting solutions encountered in their own research or in their reading of commentaries.

2. *SELECTED PASSAGES: CAUSES OF VARIANTS AND THEIR EVALUATION*

As the plates in this volume show (e.g., pp. 88-92), the earliest manuscripts were written in **scriptio continua**, i.e., the uncial letters were written continuously, word after word and sentence after sentence, without a break and with extremely few reading aids. In **Mark 10:40,** at the conclusion of the pericope about the request made by James and John the sons of Zebedee for positions at the right and left of Jesus in his kingdom, the text of Jesus' refusal reads in the uncial manuscripts: ΤΟΔΕΚΑΘΙCΑΙΕΚΔΕΞΙΩΝΜΟΥΗΕΞΕΥΩΝΥ ΜΩΝΟΥΚΕCΤΙΝΕΜΟΝΔΟΥΝΑΙΑΛΛΟΙCΗΤΟΙΜΑCΤΑΙ. Without changing the letters but by dividing them into words differently the text is susceptible of two completely different meanings. The letters ΑΛΛΟΙC can be divided as ἀλλ᾽ οἷς, or they can be taken as the single word ἄλλοις. The seats beside Jesus, then, are reserved either for certain ones who have already been designated (and these might well be the sons of Zebedee themselves), or for others (excluding the sons of Zebedee).

    The apparatus of Nestle-Aland[26] reads: 40 ⸋·ἄλλοις 225 it sa[ms] ¦ ἄλλοις δε sy[s] ¦ *txt* B[2] Θ Ψ f[1.13] 𝔐 lat sy[p.h] bo (*cet. incert.*). This indicates that the scribes interpreted the text correctly as ἀλλ᾽ οἷς — when they observed a distinction; *cet. incert.* (ceteri incerti, the rest are uncertain) refers to the uncials, where the letters are written continuously and without punctuation (characteristically B[2], a later hand in Codex Vaticanus, clarifies the interpretation by a mark that was not available to the first scribe). The minuscule 225 (together with a few others), however, along with a part of the Old Latin tradition (it as distinct from lat, which supports the text), and a single Sahidic manuscript, agree in reading ἄλλοις, which the Sinaitic Syriac further reinforces with the addition of δέ. We may note in passing (anticipating a later discussion) that the second variant noted in the apparatus (the addition at the end of the verse) ⸆ *p)* υπο του πατρος μου ℵ[*.2] (Θ) f[1] 1241 *pc* a r[1 vid] sy[hmg] bo[ms] represents the influence of a parallel passage (this addition is derived from Matt. 20:23), and the category of devotional supplements. Both these factors occur repeatedly as a source of variants in manuscripts.

    Mark 10:40 is the best-known example of variants developing in a text where there is no variation of the letters, but there are several more similar examples, e.g., in **Matt. 9:18,** should ΕΙCΕΛΘΩΝ be read εἷς ἐλθών as in the new text, or εἰσελθών as in a group of manuscripts followed by the Majority text (not to mention the related variations with προσελθών)? Both forms make sense in their contexts, and the variants which developed in the tradition show how scribes dealt with such problems.

    However neat the uncial hand may appear (cf. the plates), the very similarity of many uncial letters to each other could be the source of variants.

Some were so similar that a **confusion of letters** was almost inevitable, especially when carelessly written by one scribe and then misread in haste by another, e.g.:

C Є Θ O

Γ Π Τ

ΛΛ Μ

Δ Λ

In **Rom. 6:5** the text reads ἀλλά and in the apparatus the variant ἅμα is supported by F G (and the Latin versions); this is easily explained as a misreading of uncial letters ΑΛΛΑ / ΑΜΑ. In **Jude 12** the apparatus has ἀπάταις for ἀγάπαις in the text. The cause here is again the same: ΑΓΑΠΑΙΣ / ΑΠΑΤΑΙΣ. In **Heb. 4:11** the text and apparatus read ἀπειθείας and ἀληθείας (ΑΠΕΙΘΕΙΑΣ / ΑΛΗΘΕΙΑΣ), and in **1 Cor. 5:8** πονηρίας and πορνείας (ΠΟΝΗΡΙΑΣ / ΠΟΡΝΕΙΑΣ).

Many further examples could be cited. It was bad enough when the word resulting from such a confusion made some sense in its context, but it was even worse when it made nonsense. The next copyist would then attempt to repair the damage by altering the word or its phrase further to produce a new sense. A good number of variants can be explained as resulting from just such a mechanical sequence of stages. A completely different text may frequently be traced to a single stroke.

At the beginning of **Acts 1:3**, for example, are the words οἷς καὶ παρέστησεν. Some manuscripts read here ὁ Ἰησοῦς καὶ παρέστησεν . . . The words fit the context, but it is puzzling to us why the variant should have occurred until we remember that in the uncials the text could have been OIC, and that the nomina sacra were written in abbreviated form, with ΘC for θεός, KC for κύριος, IC for Ἰησοῦς, so that OIC represented ὁ Ἰησοῦς. Then it becomes clear that the scribe who wrote ὁ Ἰησοῦς at Acts 1:3 was copying from an uncial exemplar in which a bar had inadvertently been placed over IC (as it actually happens in Codex Ephraemi Syri Rescriptus [C]). The error is obvious (and the variant is not noted in the apparatus of Nestle-Aland[26]). The reverse process may also occur, as in the hymn to Christ in 1 Tim. 3:16. The original reading here was ὃς ἐφανερώθη (as in ℵ* A* C* F G 33. 365 *pc*), i.e., in the uncial script ΟCΕΦΑΝΕΡΩΘΗ. Only a stroke needed to be added above OC, and the misreading of O̅C̅ as Θ̅C̅ (θεος) was almost inevitable (perhaps in a single step), with an enhancement of devotional overtones. The correction was made accordingly by later hands in ℵ, A, and C: θεος is read by ℵ^c A^c C^c D² Ψ 𝔐 vg^ms, and in a further stage (in 88 *pc*) the article ὁ was added.

While the confusion of letters can account for many variants, there are also other causes which should be mentioned, such as the tendency for a scribe to repeat one or more letters or a syllable by accident (**dittography**) or inadvertently omit one of a pair of letters or sequence of letters (**haplography**). This happens all too frequently and there are many examples. Among the more con-

troversial examples of this kind is the passage in **1 Thess. 2:7**, which may be taken as typical. Here we read ΑΛΛΑΕΓΕΝΗΘΗΜΕΝΝΗΠΙΟΙΕΝ ΜΕCΩΥΜΩΝ. The question is whether Paul originally wrote ἤπιοι here, so that the ν of νήπιοι is the result of dittography from the final ν of the preceding ἐγενήθημεν, or whether the ἤπιοι resulted from the disappearance of a ν by haplography. The new text reads νήπιοι, and the apparatus of Nestle-Aland[26] presents the following evidence: ⌐¹ † ηπιοι ℵ^c A C² D² Ψ^c 𝔐 vg^st (sy) sa^mss ¦ *txt* p^65 ℵ* B C* D* F G I Ψ* 104*.326^c.2495 *pc* it vg^ww sa^ms bo; C1. The dagger indicates that Nestle formerly read ἤπιοι, and in Nestle-Aland[26], Appendix II, we find that this is also the reading of Tischendorf, von Soden, Vogels, and Merk, which leaves only Westcott-Hort and Bover reading νήπιοι in the text.

An examination of the manuscript tradition makes it clear that the earlier stratum reads νήπιοι (p^65 is from the third century!), and that the change was made from νήπιοι to ἤπιοι: Codex Sinaiticus (ℵ), Codex Ephraemi Syri Rescriptus (C), Codex Bezae Claromontanus (D^p), as well as Ψ and the minuscule 104 all have νήπιοι in the original hand corrected to ἤπιοι by a later hand. Only Codex Alexandrinus (A) (with the Majority text) reads ἤπιοι in the original hand from the beginning, while the codices Vaticanus (B), F, G, and I, and the minuscule 2495 read νήπιοι unaltered from the beginning in company with Clement of Alexandria (and a great number of the Church Fathers, according to the apparatus of *GNT*). The reverse movement from ἤπιοι to νήπιοι is found only in minuscule 326. Thus the external evidence seems unequivocal. Of course, it may be objected that the corrections in the great uncials mark the restoration of texts marred by an original dittography. But such an objection has little weight against the evidence: could the identical dittography have occurred accidentally in ℵ, C, D, Ψ, and 104? This would be extremely unlikely.

The tendency we can observe here is related to embarrassment caused by the word νήπιοι, to which modern exegetes are also sensitive. But in preferring the term ἤπιοι such critics ignore the fact that this word is not a part of the Pauline vocabulary. νήπιος is far more typically a Pauline word. A glance at the word's statistics as found in the *Vollständige Konkordanz zum griechischen Neuen Testament,* volume 2 (demonstrating the importance of constant reference to concordances, as we have stressed above) shows that νήπιος occurs fifteen times in the New Testament, eleven of which are in the Pauline letters (twice in Matthew, and once each in Luke and Hebrews). In addition, νηπιάζω is used only by Paul (once in 1 Corinthians). In contrast, ἤπιος is found only once in the New Testament, in 2 Timothy.

The situation is therefore rather clear. The argument that νήπιος is a scribal correction to the usual term is weak, however often repeated. The decisive fact is that it is precisely contrary to the trend among the manuscripts (cf. the uncials). νήπιοι is actually the harder reading (lectio difficilior; cf. Rule 10), and the exegetes should accept it.

Unfortunately it seems likely that here as elsewhere the exegetes confuse their own interpretation with what Paul should have said. It is hard to avoid

this impression when we see the way the Pauline letters are analyzed into such a variety of new units. Ernst Käsemann's commentary on Romans, for example, enumerates a whole group of passages where texts long regarded as spurious are shown to be not only genuinely Pauline, but the only appropriate Pauline formulation. We are not concerned with exegesis here, but it should be remarked that νήπιοι in 1 Thess. 2:7 is no more offensive than the allusion in Gal. 4:19 to the birth pangs which he is suffering with his "children" in Galatia. ἤπιοι is just one example of the tendency we find so often in New Testament manuscripts to make the text more polished and acceptable. In all such instances the judgment of textual criticism can only be that the more polished and acceptable form of the text is secondary.

It is certainly no secret that a scribe engaged in copying a manuscript is susceptible to **fatigue**, especially when copying continuous script. When word divisions are observed as in minuscule manuscripts the strain is somewhat relieved, but it cannot be entirely avoided. Fatigue can explain such errors as are found in F and G at **Rom. 3:20**, where the manuscripts read διὰ γὰρ νόμου ἐπιγνώσεως ἁμαρτίας instead of ἐπίγνωσις (i.e., the nominative is attracted by inadvertence to the genitive case of the neighboring words), and many other slips (a tired scribe is particularly liable to confuse similar letters; cf. pp. 282f.), minor omissions, and the like.

When words or phrases begin with similar groups of letters, it is easy for the eye of a tired scribe to move directly from one group to the other. One of the most frequent causes of omissions is found in such similarities, known as **homoioteleuton** and **homoioarcton** when occurring at the end or at the beginning of a word, phrase, or sentence respectively. In the Sermon on the Mount, for example, the first sentence of **Matt. 5:19** and the verse itself both end with the words ἐν τῇ βασιλείᾳ τῶν οὐρανῶν, and the following verse 20 ends similarly with εἰς τὴν βασιλείαν τῶν οὐρανῶν. We notice that consequently the text goes from the first ἐν τῇ βασιλείᾳ τῶν οὐρανῶν directly to the beginning of verse 20 in ℵ* (Codex Sinaiticus, first hand), and in W (Codex Freerianus). In each instance the scribe confused the first with the second occurrence of the phrase. The scribe of Codex Bezae Cantabrigiensis was even more unfortunate. From the end of the first sentence in verse 19 he passed directly to ἠκούσατε ὅτι in verse 21, confusing the first with the third occurrence of the repeated phrase.

In the same chapter there are at least two more parallel examples; looking further through the critical apparatus will reveal a good number more, especially where there are parallel expressions or forms in the text. When an omission did not disturb the sense of a passage it often remained unnoticed by correctors (as attested by occurrences in the critical apparatus). If an omission disturbed the sense or had any disruptive effect, however, things were different. Thus in **Matt. 18:18** Codex Bezae Cantabrigiensis (D) at first reads: ὅσα ἐὰν δήσητε ἐπὶ τῆς γῆς ἔσται λελυμένα ἐν τοῖς οὐρανοῖς (D ends the verse with a plural form in place of the singular in the new text); the second occurrence of ἐπὶ τῆς γῆς had been confused with the first, resulting in the

omission at first of the intervening text: ἔσται δεδεμένα ἐν οὐρανῷ, καὶ ὅσα ἐὰν λύσητε ἐπὶ τῆς γῆς. This absolute nonsense was detected by the corrector and emended.

If the scribe read the words aloud, or when copying was done from dictation (a technique undoubtedly used to facilitate mass production in many a scriptorium), there was the risk of homonyms being misinterpreted. The ita-cisms of the period (which anticipated modern Greek pronunciation) made ἡμεῖς and ὑμεῖς sound alike, i.e., both initial vowels sounded like ι. Similarly αι and ε were homphones, making the infinitive and the second person plural forms indistinguishable, e.g., ἔρχεσθαι and ἔρχεσθε. The sounds ει and ι were also identical: in 1 Cor. 15:54-55 p[46] B D* 088 twice read νεῖκος for νῖκος, so that death is swallowed up by controversy instead of by victory, and the question is asked where the controversy of death is. But νεῖκος (which occurs nowhere else in the New Testament) was pronounced like νῖκος (in the apparatus of Nestle-Aland[26] the warning note ex itac. [ex itacismo, "by itacism"] is added to forestall the suggestion of any strange construction). It is popular in some places today to speak of Clement of Alexandreia and of Eirenaios, although in their age these names were pronounced precisely like the less exotic forms following the common Latin usage: Alexandria and Ireneos (or Latinized: Irenaeus).

Also, ω and ο were pronounced alike, but this has a considerable range of implications because it can make the difference between the indicative and the subjunctive mood, as in that much debated text in **Rom. 5:1**. Should it be read εἰρήνην ἔχομεν πρὸς τὸν θεόν, i.e., "we have peace with God," or as an exhortation (ἔχωμεν)? A long series of earlier editions preferred the latter interpretation: Tischendorf, Westcott-Hort, von Soden, Vogels, Merk, Bover. Only the earlier Nestle had ἔχομεν as does the "new Nestle"). The earlier Nestle read this despite its ground rules: this is one of the few instances where Erwin Nestle, on the advice of German biblical scholars (and rightly, we believe), altered the text he inherited from his father. With regard to ἔχομεν and ἔχωμεν the evidence of the Greek manuscripts (and therefore also of the versions based on them) remains ambiguous: ω can stand for ο, as well as ο for ω. Many scholars believe that in the original dictation of the letter Tertius may well have written ἔχωμεν for Paul's dictated ἔχομεν. We can be certain only that the correctors of ℵ and B intended ἔχομεν when they emended the ἔχωμεν of their exemplars.

The external criteria yield no certainty here, so that internal criteria become determinative. From the context of Rom. 5, as well as from Pauline theology generally, we believe that only the indicative ἔχομεν is possible for Rom. 5:1. An interesting parallel occurs in **1 Cor. 15:49**: καὶ καθὼς ἐφορέσαμεν τὴν εἰκόνα τοῦ χοϊκοῦ, φορέσομεν καὶ τὴν εἰκόνα τοῦ ἐπου-ρανίου. The evidence for φορέσωμεν here is far stronger than for ἔχωμεν in Rom. 5:1 (from 𝔓[46] through nearly all the great uncials and the whole manu-script tradition apart from only B I and a few minuscules together with the Sahidic tradition), and yet the new text reads the indicative (correctly, we believe, and in agreement with Merk, Bover, and Nestle[25]).

Finally, in concluding our remarks on itacisms and their influence in the textual transmission of the New Testament, a warning is necessary not to throw out the baby with the bath water, which is a strong temptation for beginners. It is quite possible for itacisms to be significant, reflecting the role of the oral element in textual transmission, whether by the dictation of texts in scriptoria or by the solitary scribe's audible pronunciation of the text in transcribing it. If the scribe simply copies an exemplar, the result should be a faithful copy. Of course even then ὑμεῖς may be copied as ἡμεῖς if the scribe feels involved in the text, or again ἡμεῖς may become ὑμεῖς if it appears inappropriate to associate the apostle with some particular expression. But such adaptations approach the category of intentional changes, which will be discussed as soon as some details of importance for textual criticism have been dealt with.

The scriptio continua of the original texts not only ignored the division of words, but naturally also lacked any **punctuation**. Occasionally this can be critical for the interpretation of a sentence. There is a German nursery saying which can be taken to assert (by misplaced punctuation), "I have ten digits on each hand, five and twenty on my hands and feet." The correct punctuation is obviously, "I have ten digits: on each hand five, and twenty on my hands and feet." Similar examples can be found in any language to show how radically the punctuation of a sentence can affect its meaning.[1] In the apparatus of Nestle-Aland[26] are noted most of the important (though by no means all) of the instances where punctuation variants are critical. At **Mark 2:15-16** it depends on whether the period is placed (wrongly) after πολλοί or (correctly) after αὐτῷ whether or not the γραμματεῖς τῶν φαρισαίων also followed Jesus. At **Matt. 25:15** the position of the period before εὐθέως (correctly) or after it (wrongly) determines its construction. At **Matt. 11:7-8** in the question about John the whole construction depends on the place of the question mark. The difference can be quite significant exegetically and theologically, e.g., in **John 1:3-4** whether we read χωρὶς αὐτοῦ ἐγένετο οὐδὲ ἕν. ὃ γέγονεν ἐν αὐτῷ ζωὴ ἦν (correctly), or χωρὶς αὐτοῦ ἐγένετο οὐδὲ ἕν ὃ γέγονεν. ἐν αὐτῷ ζωὴ ἦν (as traditionally).

The difficulty of tracing such problems through the manuscripts, versions, and Church Fathers is evident in the number of pages devoted to their investigation by Kurt Aland and other scholars (cf. Aland, "Über die Bedeutung eines Punktes: Eine Untersuchung zu Joh 1,3/4," *Neutestamentliche Entwürfe* [Munich: 1979], pp. 351-391).

There is nothing apparently more "minor" or "trivial" than a mere dot, and yet matters of significance can depend on one. Controversy over the length of a vowel may not seem very important, but we have seen how much can be involved. And this is always true: the smallest of details may well have an important bearing on not only the text, but also its exegesis. Textual criticism must therefore claim for "trivialities" and "unessentials" a significance differing from that accorded them by some other New Testament scholars. In all matters

---

1. Cf. Peter Quince's reading of the prologue in Shakespeare's *Midsummer Night's Dream*, V, 1; a more popular example is the legendary antiphonal arrangement of Ps. 50:3, "Our God shall come, and He shall not / Keep silence, but shout out!"

of basic research (and thus in textual criticism), it is essential to proceed without glancing at the possible implications of the results. As the natural sciences have demonstrated repeatedly, this is necessary for success. And further, nothing which contributes to establishing the text of the New Testament should be regarded as trivial or unimportant, especially for the New Testament scholar who is interested in the theology of the New Testament. The scholar who accepts uncritically the readings in the text of a Greek New Testament without considering the critical apparatus should also refrain from bold theories challenging positions established by textual criticism, and not assert readings to be genuine when they are derived solely from exegetical considerations without justification in the manuscript tradition, or pronounce parts of the text to be spurious, interpolated, or in any way suspect when they are firmly established in the textual tradition. Uncritical procedures make for uncritical results: garbage in, garbage out. To avoid the latter, the student must avoid the former and engage the task of textual criticism seriously. With deeper study, arbitrary theories and assertions will dissipate quite naturally.

New Testament textual criticism has genuine theological relevance even when it appears to be purely philological and confined to trivialities. Only two examples will be offered of the difference made by the **change of a single letter** in a statement. The "typographical gremlin" is familiar enough through its activities in the daily press. To take an example from the religious press, in the *Lutherische Monatschrift*[2] recently there was a reference to the "verhassten Kirche" ("the detested Church"; in an article by S. Markert on "Kein Neuland für Aussenmissionen?" ["No New Lands for Foreign Missions?"]). The author immediately made the correction:[3] what he had intended was "verfassten Kirche" (the "organized Church").

But illustrations of this may also be found in the text of the New Testament. As recently as in the Revised Luther version of 1956 the message of the angel in **Luke 2:14** concluded (as in the English Authorized Version, following a centuries-old tradition) with the words:

und Friede auf Erden	On earth Peace,
und den Menschen ein Wohlgefallen.	good will to men.

In the revisions of 1975 and 1984 it reads (with the English Revised Standard Version):

und Friede auf Erden	On earth Peace
bei den Menschen seines Wohlgefallens	among men with whom he is pleased.

This new translation with a significant difference in meaning is due to a single Greek letter, a sigma, depending on whether it reads ἐν ἀνθρώποις εὐδοκία or ἐν ἀνθρώποις εὐδοκίας, in the uncial form ΕΥΔΟΚΙΑ or ΕΥΔΟΚΙΑC. If the word were at the end of a line (or even elsewhere) it could very well have been written ΕΥΔΟΚΙΑᶜ. It is possible that the letter was omitted uninten-

2. Vol. 5 (1977), p. 289.
3. *Idem*, p. 491; cf. the familiar "Untied Church" for "United Church."

tionally by a copyist (whether in the uncial or in the minuscule script). But it is certain that εὐδοκία is the secondary form, and εὐδοκίας the more difficult reading. The latter is attested only by ℵ* A B* D W and a few others. Development could only have been from εὐδοκίας to εὐδοκία, as the change in ℵ and B demonstrates: in these a later hand has shown a preference for εὐδοκία by deleting the sigma. The external evidence for εὐδοκία is indubitably far more extensive, but the force of internal criteria favoring εὐδοκίας is irrefutable.

In this instance it is not certain the change from the one form of text to the other was accidental or intentional. To a certain degree the same is true of the change from καυχήσωμαι to καυθήσομαι in **1 Cor. 13:3.** Here again the 1956 Revised Luther text still retained the traditional reading καυθήσομαι (in agreement with all the editions since Tischendorf except Vogels), which was not changed until the 1975 Luther revision: "and if I deliver my body that I may glory" (RSV mg.).

The external evidence for καυχήσωμαι is distinctly stronger. The combination of 𝔭⁴⁶ ℵ A B 048.33.1739* pc co (for καυχήσωμαι) is distinctly superior to C D F G L 6.81.104.630.945.1175.1881* al latt (for καυθήσομαι). The reading κανθήσωμαι supported by Ψ 𝔐 is literally a grammatical impossibility (cf. Blass-Debrunner-Funk, par. 28), and can only be understood as a variant of καυθήσομαι (cf. Rom. 5:1), but even this would not strengthen the attestation for καυθήσομαι significantly. From vocabulary statistics we learn that καυχάομαι is typically Pauline (only two of its thirty-seven occurrences in the New Testament are non-Pauline), while καίω (twelve times in the New Testament) occurs nowhere else in the Paulines. But this is indecisive, because an unusual context could well have required the use of an uncharacteristic word. The most that can be said is that whereas the first future form καυθήσομαι occurs nowhere else in the New Testament although καίω is found in ten other forms, it would appear to be a back-formation in view of καυχήσωμαι, or more simply an example of a transcriptional error: Θ for X.

In such exegetically difficult passages as this it becomes quite evident that all may depend on a single letter. It is not clear whether we have here, as in Luke 2:14, an instance of intentional alteration of the text or merely a variant due to a possible misreading of the scriptio continua in the uncial tradition, and consequently both passages have been mentioned before proceeding to discuss intentional variants. We have not discussed the relevant factors here in any great detail, reserving this for fuller treatment in the following pages with more than fifty examples arranged by categories (an exhaustive enumeration of the factors either here or elsewhere would be impossible in any event).

The most obvious type of intentional change is the **explanatory supplement**, e.g., οἱ μαθηταί in the text is expanded to οἱ μαθηταὶ αὐτοῦ; such words as λέγει, εἶπεν, ἔφη, or ἔλεγεν suggest the addition of ὁ Ἰησοῦς or αὐτοῖς. Among such innumerable minor expansions may be counted the frequent insertion of the article, and the particles γάρ, δέ, οὖν, and so forth (especially of following a solitary μέν). These expansions quite frequently go

beyond the purely stylistic level to add a devotional touch: Ἰησοῦς may first become Ἰησοῦς Χριστός or κύριος Ἰησοῦς, then κύριος Ἰησοῦς Χριστός, and grow further to become κύριος ἡμῶν Ἰησοῦς Χριστός. Such devotional elements are not confined to single words, but may comprise whole phrases, sentences, or even verses. From the very beginning the text had a tendency to expand. This is why the shorter reading is generally the better, the original reading (cf. p. 281. Rule 11). This rule applies to textual traditions in the framework of their normal transmission. It does not apply when a manuscript (or a tradition it represents) has a new and thoroughly revised form of the text, replete with additions, omissions, and transpositions reflecting a particular theological position. The argument that Codex Bezae Cantabrigiensis (D), which represents essentially just such a revision, has a shorter text and can therefore claim originality is patently false despite its constant reappearance among some New Testament scholars.

Not only does the text tend to grow, it also becomes more **stylistically polished**, conformed to the rules of Greek grammar. In **Mark 1:37**, for example, there is a typically Marcan construction: καὶ εὗρον αὐτὸν καὶ λέγουσιν. The overwhelming majority of Greek manuscripts replace this with the better Greek expression: εὑρόντες αὐτὸν λέγουσιν. Only a few manuscripts such as Codex Sinaiticus (ℵ), Codex Vaticanus (B), L, and a small number of other manuscripts withstand the temptation and preserve the stylistically embarrassing text. Apparent errors in the text invite correction. In **Mark 1:2** the source of the Old Testament text is identified by γέγραπται ἐν τῷ Ἡσαΐᾳ τῷ προφήτῃ. The quotation is actually a composite from multiple sources, so that in the manuscripts we find the correction: τοῖς προφήταις (cf. Nestle-Aland[26] *in loc.*). In **Matt. 27:9** the quotation in the text is ascribed to the prophet Jeremiah, although it is actually from Zech. 11:13; correspondingly in the manuscripts we find the information either omitted or corrected (cf. Nestle-Aland[26] apparatus *in loc.*). Quotations from the Old Testament which differ from the text of the Septuagint popular in the Church were often corrected to agree with it.

Particularly frequent are **harmonizations** between parallel texts with slight differences. In the Synoptic Gospels this could be quite unintentional. The scribe knew the text of the Gospels by heart, and when copying a pericope the details from a parallel passage would be suggested automatically. But again it could also be intentional, because it was impossible that sacred texts should not be in agreement. The text of the gospel of Mark (which was the "weakest," i.e., used least extensively among the churches) was particularly susceptible to influence from parallel texts in the course of manuscript transmission. In the apparatus of Nestle-Aland[26] these readings are identified by the sign *p)*; on p. 94 (showing Mark 2:16-24), to take a sample page at random, there are eight occurrences of the sign *p)*. It is very instructive to scan the whole edition for this and other particular factors. In this way insight can be gained on the value of manuscripts and the reason why textual critics regard one manuscript as specially authoritative while recognizing another as moderately important and yet another as worthless. Such judgments reflect a familiarity that comes from studying the manuscripts con-

stantly (cf. p. 281, Rule 12), distinguishing which ones satisfy the criteria for originality of readings most frequently and deserve a preference of credibility when decisions are very close.

From the foregoing discussion it will be appreciated that manuscripts sometimes replace words found in their exemplars with **synonyms**, or alter their order, and so forth. The Greeks did not share the view of the orientals, for whom the very letter had a sanctity of its own. The Hebrew text of the Old Testament, like the text of the Quran, is alike in all manuscripts (except for unintentional errors). For Greeks it was the message contained that was sacred. Characteristic of the Greek attitude toward the transmission of a textual tradition is the statement of the neoplatonist Porphyry about his anthology of oracles (Eusebius, *Praeparatio evangelica* iv.7; *GCS* 43/1: 177): he appeals to the gods to attest that he has neither added nor deleted anything. He has only corrected readings which were faulty, improving their clarity, supplying minor omissions, and omitting irrelevant accretions: "but the meaning of the words I have preserved faithfully." This is not a comment made incidentally in passing, but a formal statement of basic principles.

When we compare the variations found in the New Testament manuscripts they appear to be quite innocuous, especially since an extensive manuscript tradition provides a means of control and correction. If a scribe introduced a change into a text in the process of copying it, the influence of this change would be limited to the scribes using his unique manuscript as an exemplar. But from the earliest beginnings there were numerous, not to say innumerable manuscripts of the same text, each leading its own independent and individual life, quite beyond the range of any single scribe's influence. Naturally they all exhibit differences from the original form of the text, but from the moment it becomes possible to compare all the manuscripts of the New Testament together at one time (and at the Institute for New Testament Textual Research in Münster this can now be done for the first time in the history of New Testament textual studies), it also becomes possible to distinguish which of the readings are later adaptations and which are the originals. In each passage the variants, however many or few, can be arranged in a stemma (the local-genealogical method; cf. Rules 6, 8) reflecting the lines of development among the readings, demonstrating which reading must be original because it best explains the rise of the other readings.

An impression of the variations found in the manuscripts may be gained from the wealth of evidence presented by von Soden in the introductory volumes to his edition of the New Testament, e.g., for the Catholic letters 1:1842-1894, for Rom. 1–5 1:1899-1902, or for individual manuscripts, e.g., for B 1:906-917, for ℵ 1:917-935, and so forth.

The transmission of the New Testament textual tradition is characterized by an extremely impressive degree of **tenacity**. Once a reading occurs it will persist with obstinacy. It is precisely the overwhelming mass of the New Testament textual tradition, assuming the ὑγιαίνουσα διδασκαλία of New Testament textual criticism (we trust the reader will not be offended by this application

of 1 Tim. 1:10), which provides an assurance of certainty in establishing the original text. Even apart from the lectionaries (cf. p. 163), there is still the evidence of approximately 3,200 manuscripts of the New Testament text, not to mention the early versions and the patristic quotations — we can be certain that among these there is still a group of witnesses which preserves the original form of the text, despite the pervasive authority of ecclesiastical tradition and the prestige of the later text.

Let us take for example the **ending of the gospel of Mark**, Mark 16:9-20. This passage, which is known as the "longer Marcan ending," reads an absolutely convincing text, and yet among the editions of the Greek New Testament since Tischendorf only Merk and Bover admit it to their text without some form of qualification. All the others place it within either single or double brackets. In Nestle-Aland[26] Mark 16:9-20 is given in double brackets and preceded by a shorter paragraph called the "shorter Marcan ending," which is also within double brackets. This is the result of a careful evaluation of the manuscript tradition.

It is true that the longer ending of Mark 16:9-20 is found in 99 percent of the Greek manuscripts as well as the rest of the tradition, enjoying over a period of centuries practically an official ecclesiastical sanction as a genuine part of the gospel of Mark. But in Codex Vaticanus (B) as well as in Codex Sinaiticus ($\aleph$) the gospel of Mark ends at Mark 16:8, as it did in numerous other manuscripts according to the statements of Eusebius of Caesarea and Jerome. The same is true for the Sinaitic Syriac sy^s, the Old Latin manuscript k of the fourth/fifth century, and at least one Sahidic manuscript of the fifth century, the earliest Georgian, and a great number of Armenian manuscripts, while k (a manuscript representing a tradition which derives from a quite early period) has the shorter ending in place of the longer ending. The widespread practice in the early Church of concluding the gospel of Mark at 16:8 was suppressed by Church tradition, but it could not be eradicated. It persisted stubbornly. As late as the twelfth century in the minuscule 304 the gospel ends at 16:8. A considerable number of manuscripts add Mark 16:9-20 either with critical notations, or with a marginal comment questioning its originality, even as late as the sixteenth century! This is a striking example of what is called tenacity in the New Testament textual tradition (cf. p. 291). The text of Mark 16:9-20 contains not only a summary account of the appearances of the resurrected Jesus, but also the command to evangelize in a form more radical than that in Matthew, and also an account of the ascension of Jesus. Despite the great, not to say fundamental, importance of these statements in the theological and practical life of the Church, a significant number of Greek manuscripts, including among them the two important uncials B and $\aleph$, remained faithful to the transmitted text and preserved it through the centuries, at least calling attention to the doubts surrounding 16:9-20 — a witness shared also among the versions and the Church Fathers.

This tenacity is even more strikingly demonstrated by the persistence of what is called the shorter ending in k and elsewhere. The shorter ending is

preserved as the sole ending, as we have noted above, only in the Old Latin manuscript k. But there is a whole group of uncials (0112 from the sixth/seventh century, 099 from the seventh century, L from the eighth century, and Ψ from the eighth/ninth century) which preserve it along with 16:9-20, even placing it first, i.e., resulting in the order 16:1-8, shorter ending, 9-20. In addition there is 𝓵 |1602, an uncial lectionary of the eighth century and the minuscule 579 from the thirteenth century which support this order. Outside the Greek tradition it is found also in the versions, in the Coptic and in the Syriac, as well as in the Ethiopic with its generally quite late manuscripts. This is almost inconceivable because these two endings are rival and mutually exclusive forms. And yet they have been preserved side by side in manuscripts and versions for centuries, simply because scribes found them in their exemplars (however independently in each instance). The situation can be explained only by assuming that the ending of the gospel at 16:8 was felt to be unsatisfactory as its use spread through all the provinces of the early Church in its early decades. In this form it tells of the empty tomb, but appearances to the disciples are only foretold and not recounted. Therefore the gospel was provided with an ending, certainly by the second century. The shorter ending was an ineffective solution, either because it was a very early stage of development or represented an outlying and relatively undeveloped community, while the longer ending was far more effective because it was formulated later and/or it represents a far more competent author. Both endings probably originated quite independently and in different provinces of the Church. There can be no doubt that the longer ending was superior to the shorter ending and would displace it in any competition. And yet the shorter ending did exist at one time, and it continued to be copied not only so long as the longer ending was unknown but even afterward, and it was generally placed before the longer ending. Furthermore, even the original tradition of ending the gospel at 16:8 could not be effaced completely by the longer ending, however inadequately it was felt to serve the needs of the Church: it also survived through the centuries.

The transmission of the ending of the gospel of Mark is the most striking example of tenacity in the New Testament textual tradition. Any reading that occurred once would continue to be preserved faithfully. **Mixed or conflate readings** attest that what is true of the larger units is true also of the smaller units. To give only two examples: **Matt. 13:57** reads ἐν τῇ πατρίδι in the text. Following the pattern of John 4:44 a group of manuscripts (ℵ Z f¹³ etc.) reads ἐν τῇ ἰδίᾳ πατρίδι. Another group of manuscripts (L W 0119 etc.) is influenced by Mark 6:4 and Luke 4:24 to read ἐν τῇ πατρίδι αὐτοῦ. Taken together these produced in C and some other manuscripts the reading ἐν τῇ ἰδίᾳ πατρίδι αὐτοῦ. This is typical: a scribe familiar with both readings will combine them, reasoning that by preserving both texts the right text will certainly be preserved.

In **Mark 1:16** the new text today has τὸν ἀδελφὸν Σίμωνος. A group of manuscripts (A Δ 0135 etc.) reads instead τὸν ἀδελφὸν τοῦ Σίμωνος, while others (D W Γ Θ etc.) have τὸν ἀδελφὸν αὐτοῦ, both of which (as also at Matt. 13:57) are likely variants within the scope of the general rules stated

above (pp. 282f.). There is also, of course, a **mixed reading** found in the manuscript tradition (K 074 etc.): τὸν ἀδελφὸν αὐτοῦ τοῦ Σίμωνος. Similar examples are found repeatedly in the critical apparatus. In each instance it is (or at least it should be) obvious that the reading which conflates two separate readings is itself secondary, and that it remains only to be determined which of the two (or more) component readings is the original. In every instance this should be the one which can best explain the origin of the others. At both Matt. 13:57 and Mark 1:16 the sequence is obvious.

Matt. 13:57   (a) ἐν τῇ πατρίδι
                (b) ἐν τῇ πατρίδι αὐτοῦ (Mark 6:4; Luke 4:24)
                (c) ἐν τῇ ἰδίᾳ πατρίδι (John 4:44)
                (d) ἐν τῇ ἰδίᾳ πατρίδι αὐτοῦ

Only (a) explains all the others. It may be questioned whether (b) is older than (c) or about the same age; the connection between (b) and the two other Synoptic Gospels is an argument for its priority. But it is obvious that (d) is the latest of the readings.

The situation is quite similar in Mark 1:16. According to local-genealogical principles the only possible sequence seems to be:

                (a) τὸν ἀδελφὸν Σίμωνος
                (b) τὸν ἀδελφὸν τοῦ Σίμωνος
                (c) τὸν ἀδελφὸν αὐτοῦ (Matt. 4:18)
                (d) τὸν ἀδελφὸν αὐτοῦ τοῦ Σίμωνος

The order of (b) and (c) could possibly be reversed, for they could well have arisen quite independently of each other. In any event, it is certain that (d) is the latest form, and consequently that (a) is the original text, the source of the other readings. Evidence justifying the above construction by the local-genealogical method (cf. pp. 280f., Rules 8 and 6) is amply available in the critical apparatus of Nestle-Aland[26] (*GNT*[3] does not provide an apparatus for these readings).

The consideration of these mixed or conflate readings at this point is only an apparent interruption of our train of thought. Neither example is in any way significant theologically or textually, and they are therefore the more instructive. For when theological or pastoral interests affect a reading they can break through the normal laws of textual transmission and exert their influence in distinctive ways. When such matters are in no way a consideration the operation of the laws of textual criticism can be seen more clearly (we trust this may appear self-evident). It is probably quite clear that the element of tenacity in the New Testament textual tradition not only permits but demands that we proceed on the premise that in every instance of textual variation it is possible to determine the form of the original text, i.e., the form in which each individual document passed into the realm of published literature by means of copying and formal distribution — assuming a proper understanding of the textual tradition. The vast number of witnesses to the text is not simply a burden — it is also a positive aid.

There are certainly instances of **major disturbances in the New Testament text** caused by theological as well as by pastoral motives, because many

expressions in the original text were not easily adapted to later needs. But even when these theological or pastoral needs were as urgent as for the ending of the gospel of Mark (cf. pp. 292f.) they could not abrogate the laws of New Testament textual transmission. When an alteration was made in the text of the New Testament — however strategically important the text, however extensively it was adopted for theological or pastoral reasons, and even if it became the accepted text of the Church — there always continued to be a stream of the tradition (sometimes broad, sometimes narrow) which remained unaffected, and this for purely technical reasons. From the very beginning the tradition of the New Testament books was as broad as the spectrum of Christian churches and theologians. Even in the first, and especially in the second century, their numbers were remarkably large. This tradition could not be closely controlled because there was no center which could provide such a control (church centers were not developed until the third/fourth century, and even then their influence was limited to their respective provinces). Furthermore, not only every church but each individual Christian felt "a direct relationship to God." Well into the second century Christians still regarded themselves as possessing inspiration equal to that of the New Testament writings which they read in their worship services. It is not by chance that in extracanonical literature the earliest traces of the text of the Gospels cannot be distinguished with confidence until the writings of Justin in the mid-second century, and that the period following is still characterized by a sense of freedom. Practically all the substantive variants in the text of the New Testament are from the second century (except for the "paraphrastic" text; cf. p. 95), although the general principles outlined on pp. 282f. continued to be valid.

Major disturbances in the transmission of the New Testament text can always be identified with confidence, even if they occurred during the second century or at its beginning. For example, about A.D. 140 Marcion dealt radically with the **ending of Romans**, breaking it off with chapter 14. This bold stroke, together with the two different endings (Rom. 16:24 and 16:25-27) which were then added, despite the presence of the solemn epistolary conclusion at 16:20 (because its function was obscured by the greetings appended at 16:21-23), all resulted in a proliferation of readings in the tradition.

Kurt Aland has enumerated no fewer than fifteen different forms here in his *Neutestamentliche Entwürfe* (Munich: 1979), without counting the further varieties represented by the subgroups of the fifteen forms. (Considerations of space preclude more than a reference here to this essay or to the chapter in the same volume on the ending of Mark; the facts can only be mentioned in their broadest outlines. The discussion of the endings of Mark on pp. 292f. deals only with the external evidence; for the internal criteria the reader is referred to this essay.)

This confirms the tenacity of the tradition, but it also shows something else (which is new for the beginner, although it is a familiar fact for the experienced textual critic — or at least it should be): the limitless variety and complexity of the New Testament textual tradition serves the function of a seismograph,

because the higher it registers the greater the earthquake, or in the present context the greater the disruption of the New Testament textual tradition. The textual tradition for the conclusion of Romans is so complicated that it can be dealt with only by analyzing the text into four units: 1:1–14:23 = A, 15:1–16:23 = B, 16:24 = C, 16:25-27 = D. The earliest surviving form of the tradition appears as follows:

1. ℵ B C 048, important minuscules,   1:1–16:23 + 16:25-27
   the Coptic tradition, and important   (A + B + D)
   Vulgate manuscripts
2. D (in Paul this is no longer Codex   1:1–16:23 + 16:24
   Bezae Cantabrigiensis 05, but Codex   (A + B + C)
   Claromontanus 06), F (010), G (012),
   and others

Evidently 16:25-27 (D) represents the ending of Romans found commonly in the East and 16:24 (C) the dominant form in the West. Each was added to Romans quite independently (as were also the Marcan endings). The result was utter chaos: C was added to manuscripts with the D ending, and D to those with the C ending, either after chapter 14 (as in manuscripts with chs. 14-15 deleted following Marcion, whose influence also survived in the manuscript tradition) or after chapter 16. Not only did the sequence A-B-C-D and A-B-D-C occur, but also A-D-B, A-D-B-C, and even A-D-B-D (i.e., with 16:25-27 repeated), A-D-B-C-D, and A-D-B-D-C, in splendid profusion! In our view this demonstrates two reliable principles: (1) when the text of the New Testament has been tampered with in its transmission, the readings scatter like a flock of chickens attacked by a hawk, or even by a dog; and (2) every reading ever occurring in the New Testament textual tradition is stubbornly preserved, even if the result is nonsense. The scribe who already has the (secondary) ending 16:24 adds to it the (equally secondary) ending 16:25-27, sometimes even twice, with less concern for the possibility of repetition than for the danger of losing a part of the text. What we observed in the conflate reading is repeated here on a larger scale. This confirms the conclusion that any reading ever occurring in the New Testament textual tradition, from the original reading onward, has been preserved in the tradition and needs only to be identified. Any interference with the regular process of transmission (according to the rules described above on pp. 282f.) is signaled by a profusion of variants. This leads to a further conclusion which we believe to be both logical and compelling, that where such a profusion of readings does *not* exist the text has not been disturbed but has developed *according to the normal rules*. None of the composition theories advanced today in various forms with regard to the Pauline letters, for example, has any support in the manuscript tradition, whether in Greek, in the early versions, or in the patristic quotations from the New Testament. At no place where a break has been posited in the Pauline letters does the critical apparatus show even a suspicion of any interference with the inevitable deposit of telltale variants. In other words, from the beginning of their history as a manuscript tradition the Pauline letters have always had the same form that they have today.

This is not, however, the final word, because the **competence of New Testament textual criticism is restricted** to the state of the New Testament text from the moment it began its literary history through transcription for distribution. All events prior to this are beyond its scope. To illustrate this from the gospel of John: for purposes of textual criticism the gospel comprises twenty-one chapters in their present sequence of 1 through 21. It is only in this form, with the final chapter appended and in the present order of chapters, that the book is found throughout the manuscript tradition. Any editing, rearrangement, revision, and so forth it may have undergone must have occurred earlier, if at all (with the exception of the Pericope Adulterae, which is lacking in a considerable part of the tradition). Similarly, any imagined recomposition of the Pauline correspondence to form the present corpus of Pauline letters must have occurred before copies of it began to circulate as a unit, if at all. The question of such a possibility cannot be discussed here, yet it should be observed that the way in which **chapter 21 has been attached to the gospel of John** argues against any such complex theories as Rudolf Bultmann's, for example. A redactor needed only to delete 20:30-31, and the sequence would have been quite smooth — but this is precisely what was *not* done. Also very dubious is the theory that somewhere an original collection of Paul's letters was compiled which contained all the essential texts but in a revision made by the collector on the basis of the autographs. It is far more probable that the tradition began with several small groups of letters collected under quite different circumstances, and that any theory of an overall revision is gratuitous (cf. Aland, *Neutestamentliche Entwürfe*, pp. 302-350).

3. VERSES RELEGATED TO THE APPARATUS OF NESTLE-ALAND[26] AND GNT[3]

To pursue such matters further at this point would lead too far afield. Instead, let us return to the discussion of specific passages which have a special importance, either for their content or for pedagogical reasons, especially since the appearance of Arthur L. Farstad and Zane C. Hodges, eds., *The Greek New Testament According to the Majority Text* (Nashville: 1982). Advocates of the Majority text may be asked to consider the following examples without prejudice. To begin with, the reader of the Greek New Testament or of its modern versions is probably owed an explanation by textual criticism of why a large number of verses have been included in practically all the editions and versions for centuries. The new text has relegated nearly a score of verses apparatus, which is a sizable number — and as the new text becomes more widely adopted an increasing number of versions in modern national languages are doing the same. For clarity of presentation these passages will first be enumerated together with their full attestation (both for and against) as found in Nestle-Aland[26] (the apparatus of *GNT*[3] meets its limits here, and is added for only the first five examples). Notes on these passages then follow (pp. 301-4) to provide the reader an opportunity of forming an independent judgment of them as well as of the newly proclaimed return to the Textus Receptus (cf. p. 19) on the basis of the knowledge and practical experience gained thus far.

1) Matt. 17:21

Τp) [21] τουτο δε το γενος ουκ εκπορευεται (εκ-βαλλ- ℵ²; εξερχ- al) ει μη εν προσευχη και νηστεια ℵ² C D L W f¹·¹³ 𝔐 lat (syp.h) (mae) bopt; Or ¦ txt ℵ* B Θ 33. 892* pc e ff¹ sys.c sa bopt

⁴ 20 {B} omit verse 21 ℵ* B Θ 33 892txt ite,ff¹ syrc,s,pal copsa,bomss ethro,ms geo Eusebius // add verse 21 τοῦτο δὲ τὸ γένος οὐκ ἐκπορεύεται εἰ μὴ ἐν προσευχῇ καὶ νηστείᾳ. (see Mk 9.29) (ℵᵇ οὐκ ἐκβάλλεται εἰ) C D K L W X Δ Π f¹ f¹³ 28 565 700 892mg 1009 1010 1071 1079 (1195 omit δέ) 1216 1230 1241 1242 1253 1344 1365 1546 1646 2148 2174 Byz Lect it(a),aur,(b),(c),d,f,ff², g¹,l,(n),q,r¹ vg (syrp,h) copbomss arm ethpp geoBmg Diatessaron Origen Hilary Basil Ambrose Chrysostom Augustine

2) Matt. 18:11

Τ (L 19,10) [11] ηλθεν γαρ ο υιος του ανθρωπου (+ ζητησαι και (Lmg) 892c. 1010 al c syh bopt) σωσαι το απολωλος D Lc W Θc 078vid 𝔐 lat syc.p.h bopt ¦ txt ℵ B I.* Θ* f¹.¹³ 33. 892* pc e ff¹ sys sa mae bopt; Or

² 10 {B} omit verse 11 ℵ B L* Θ f¹ f¹³ 33 892txt ite,ff¹ syrs,pal copsa,bo geoᴬ Origen Apostolic Canons Juvencus Eusebius Hilary Jerome // add verse 11 ἦλθεν γὰρ ὁ υἱὸς τοῦ ἀνθρώπου σῶσαι τὸ ἀπολωλός. (see 9.13; Lk 19.10) D K W X Δ Π 078vid 28 565 700 1071 1079 1230 1241 1242 1253 1344 1365 1546 1646 2148 2174 Byz Lect l185pt ita,aur,b,d,f,ff²,g¹,l,n,q,r¹ vg syrc,p arm geol,B Diatessaron Hilary Chrysostom Augustine // 11 ἦλθεν γὰρ ὁ υἱὸς τοῦ ἀνθρώπου ζητῆσαι καὶ σῶσαι τὸ ἀπολωλός. (see 9.13; Lk 19.10) (Lcmg omit καί) 892mg 1009 1010 1195 1216 (l10,12,69,70,80,185pt,211,299,303,374,1642 καί for γάρ) l950 itc syrh copbomss eth

3) Matt. 23:14

Τ [14] Ουαι δε υμιν, γραμματεις και Φαρισαιοι υποκριται, οτι κατεσθιετε τας οικιας των χηρων και προφασει μακρα προσευχομενοι · δια τουτο ληψεσθε περισσοτερον κριμα. f¹³ pc it vgcl syc bopt ¦ idem, sed pon. p. vs 12 W 0104. 0107. 0133. 0138 𝔐 f syp.h bomss ¦ txt ℵ B D L Z Θ f¹ 33. 892* pc a aur e ff¹ g¹ vg sys sa mae bopt

² 13 {B} Οὐαὶ δὲ ὑμῖν...εἰσελθεῖν. (omit verse 14) ℵ B D L Θ f¹ 33 892txt 1344 ita,aur,d,e,ff¹,g¹ vgww syrs,palms copsa,bomss arm geo Origengr,lat Eusebius Jerome Druthmarus // 14, 13 Οὐαὶ δὲ ὑμῖν, γραμματεῖς καὶ Φαρισαῖοι ὑποκριταί, ὅτι κατεσθίετε τὰς οἰκίας τῶν χηρῶν καὶ προφάσει μακρὰ προσευχόμενοι· διὰ τοῦτο λήμψεσθε περισσότερον κρίμα. 13 Οὐαὶ ὑμῖν...εἰσελθεῖν. (see Mk 12.40; Lk 20.47) K W Δgr Π 0107 0138 28 565 700 892mg (1009 μικρά) 1010 1071 1079 1195 1216 1230 1241 1242 (1253 λήψονται) 1365 1546 1646 2148 2174 Byz Lect (l76 μικρά) itf syrp,h copbomss eth Chrysostom Ps-Chrysostom John-Damascus // 13, 14 Οὐαὶ δὲ ὑμῖν... εἰσελθεῖν. 14 Οὐαὶ δὲ ὑμῖν...κρίμα. (see Mk 12.40; Lk 20.47) f¹³ l547 itb,c,ff². h,l,r¹ vgcl syrc,palmss copbomss Diatessaronn.t Origen Hilary Chrysostom

4) Mark 7:16

T[16] ει τις εχει ωτα ακουειν ακουετω A D W Θ Θ f¹·¹³ 𝔐 latt sy sa^mss bo^pt ¦
txt א B L Δ* 0274. 28 sa^mss bo^pt

⁸ **15** {B} *omit verse 16* א B L Δ* 28 *Lect* l^{333pt,950pt,1127pt} cop^bomss geo¹ //
include verse 16 εἴ τις ἔχει ὦτα ἀκούειν, ἀκουέτω. (*see* 4.9, 23) A D K
W X Δᶜ Θ Π f¹ f¹³ 33 565 700 892 1009 1010 (1071 ὁ ἔχων ὦτα) 1079 1195
1216 1230 1241 1242 1253 1344 1365 1546 1646 2148 2174 *Byz* l^{76,185,313,333pt,}
^{950pt,1127pt} it^{a,aur,b,c,d,f,ff²,i,l,n,q,r¹} vg syr^{(s,p),h} cop^{sa,bomss} goth arm eth geo²
Diatessaron^{a,p} Augustine

5) Mark 9:44 and 46

T[44] (48)
οπου ο σκωληξ αυτων ου τελευτα και το πυρ ου σβεννυται A D Θ f¹³ 𝔐 lat sy^{p,h};
Bas ¦ txt א B C L W Δ Ψ 0274 f¹ 28. 565. 892 pc k sy^s co ● **45** T (48) εις το πυρ το
ασβεστον A D Θ f¹³ (700) 𝔐 f q (sy^h) ¦ txt א B C L W Δ Ψ 0274 f¹ (28). 892 pc b k sy^{a,p}
co ¦ ⊤[46] *ut vs* 44

⁹ **43** {A} *omit verse 44* א B C L W Δ Ψ f¹ 28 565 892 1365 l²⁶⁰ it^k syr^s
cop^{sa,bo,fay} arm geo // *include verse 44* ὅπου ὁ σκώληξ αὐτῶν οὐ τελευτᾷ
καὶ τὸ πῦρ οὐ σβέννυται. (*see* Is 66.24) A D K X Θ Π f¹³ 700 1009 1010 1071
1079 (1195 τὸ πῦρ αὐτῶν) (1216 *omit* ὁ) 1230 1241 1242 1253 1344 (1546 σκόλυξ
ὁ ἀκύμητος καί) 1646 2148 2174 *Byz Lect* it^{a,aur,b,c,d,ff²,i,l,q,r¹} vg syr^{p,h} goth
(eth) Diatessaron^{a,p} Irenaeus^{lat} Basil Augustine // ὅπου ὁ σκώληξ
αὐτῶν οὐ τελευτᾷ. it^f

¹¹ **45** {A} *omit verse 46* א B C L W Δ Ψ f¹ 28 565 892 1365 l¹⁹ it^k syr^s
cop^{sa,bo,fay} arm Diatessaron^a // *include verse 46* ὅπου ὁ σκώληξ αὐτῶν οὐ
τελευτᾷ καὶ τὸ πῦρ οὐ σβέννυται. (*see* Is 66.24) A D K X Θ Π f¹³ 700 1010
1071 1079 1195 1216 1230 (1241 πῦρ αὐτῶν) 1242 (1253 *omit* αὐτῶν) 1344 1546
1646 2148 2174 *Byz Lect* it^{a,aur,b,c,d,f,ff²,i,l,q,r¹} vg syr^{p,h} goth (eth) geo
Diatessaron^p Basil Augustine

6) Mark 11:26

[26] ει δε υμεις ουκ αφιετε ουδε ο πατηρ υμων ο εν τοις ουρανοις αφησει τα παρα-
πτωματα υμων A (C, D) Θ (f¹·¹³) 𝔐 lat sy^{p,h} bo^pt; Cyp ¦ txt א B L W Δ Ψ 565. 700. 892
pc k l sy^s sa bo^pt

7) Mark 15:28

T¹[28] (Lc 22,37; Is 53,12) και επληρωθη η γραφη η λεγου-
σα· και μετα ανομων ελογισθη L Θ 0112. 0250 f¹·¹³ 𝔐 lat sy^{p,h} (bo^pt) ¦ txt א A B C
D Ψ pc k sy^s sa bo^pt

8) Luke 17:36

T[36] p) δυο εσονται (- D pc) εν τω (- D) αγρω· εις παραλη(μ)φθησεται και
ο ετερος (η δε ετερα f¹³) αφεθησεται D f¹³ 700 al lat sy

9) Luke 23:17

16 T*p)* [17] αναγκην δε
ειχεν απολυειν αυτοις κατα εορτην ενα ℵ (D sy^s.c *add. p.* 19) W (Θ Ψ) 063 *f*^1.13 (892^mg)
𝔐 lat sy^p.h (bo^pt) ¦ *txt* 𝔓^75 A B K L T 0124. 892^txt. 1241 *pc* a sa bo^pt

10) John 5:3b-4

3 T (, παραλυτικων D it), εκδεχομενων την του υδατος κινησιν A^c C^3 D (W^s) Θ Ψ 063.
078 *f*^1.13 𝔐 lat sy^p.h bo^pt ¦ *txt* 𝔓^66.75 ℵ A* B C* L 0125 *pc* q sy^c co ¦ T^1[4] αγγελος γαρ (δε
L; + κυριου A K L Δ 063 *f*^13 (1241) *al* it vg^cl) κατα καιρον (- a b ff^2) κατεβαινεν (ελου-
ετο A K Ψ 1241 r^1 vg^mss) εν τη κολυμβηθρα (- a b ff^2) και εταρασσε (-σσετο C^3 078
al c r^1 vg^cl) το υδωρ · ο ουν πρωτος εμβας μετα την ταραχην του υδατος (*om.* μετα ...
υδ. a b ff^2) υγιης εγινετο ω (οιω A L 1010 *pc*) δηποτε (δ' αν K *pc*; + ουν A) κατειχετο
νοσηματι A C^3 L Θ Ψ 063. 078^vid *f*^1.13 𝔐 it vg^cl sy^p.h** bo^pt; Tert ¦ *txt* 𝔓^66.75 ℵ B C* D
W^s 0125. 33 *pc* f l q vg^st sy^c co

11) Acts 8:37

36 T [37] ειπεν δε αυτω (+ ο Φιλιππος E) · ει (εαν E) πιστευεις εξ ολης της καρδιας
σου (- 323 *pc*) εξεστιν (σωθηση E). αποκριθεις δε ειπεν · πιστευω τον υιον του θεου
ειναι τον Ιησουν Χριστον (εις τον Χριστον τον υιον του θεου E) E 36. 323. 453. 945.
1739. 1891 *pc* (it vg^cl sy^h** mae; Ir Cyp)

12) Acts 15:34

33 T [34] εδοξε δε τω Σιλα επιμειναι αυτου (C)
33. 36. 323. 453. 614 (945). 1175. 1739. 1891 *al* sy^h** sa bo^mss ¦ εδ. δε τω Σ. (-λεα D*) επιμ.
προς (- D*) αυτους, μονος δε Ιουδας επορευθη (+ εις Ιερουσαλημ w vg^cl) D gig l w
vg^cl ¦ *txt* 𝔓^74 ℵ A B E Ψ 𝔐 vg^st sy^p bo

13) Acts 24:6b-8a

● 6 Tκαι κατα τον ημετερον νομον ηθελησαμεν κριναι (-νειν 614. 2495 *pc*). [7] παρ-
ελθων δε Λυσιας ο χιλιαρχος μετα πολλης βιας εκ των χειρων ημων απηγαγεν [8] κελευ-
σας τους κατηγορους αυτου ερχεσθαι επι (προς E 2464 *pc*) σε E Ψ 33. (323. 614.) 945.
1739. (2495) *pm* gig vg^cl sy^(p) ¦ *txt* 𝔓^74 ℵ A B H L P 049. 81. 1175. 1241 *pm* p* s vg^st co

14) Acts 28:29

T 29 και ταυτα αυτου
ειποντος απηλθον οι Ιουδαιοι πολλην εχοντες εν εαυτοις συζητησιν (ζητ- 104 *pc*)
𝔐 it vg^cl sy^h** ¦ *txt* 𝔓^74 ℵ A B E Ψ 048. 33. 81. 1175. 1739. 2464 *pc* s vg^st sy^p co

15) Rom. 16:24

24 η χαρις του
κυριου ημων Ιησου Χριστου μετα παντων υμων. αμην (*sed pon.* [25-27] *p.* 14,23) Ψ 𝔐
sy^h ¦ *id.* (*sed* - Ιησ. Χρ.) *et om.* [25-27] *totaliter* F G (629) ¦ *id. et add.* [25-27] *hic* D (630)
al a vg^cl ¦ *id., sed p.* [25-27] *add.* P 33. 104. 365 *pc* sy^p bo^ms; Ambst ¦ *txt* (*sed add.* 25-27
hic) (𝔓^46, *sed add.* [25-27] *p.* 15,33) 𝔓^61 ℵ (A) B C 81. 1739. 2464 *pc* b vg^st co

For **Rom. 16:24**, to begin with the last example, the essentials have already been given on pp. 295f. There we saw that Rom. 16:25-27, which is printed in the text although in single brackets, is also secondary and belongs strictly with 16:24 in the apparatus rather than in the text. For the examples from the Gospels (it is no coincidence that in the above list they are in the majority) the apparatus should be read in conjunction with a synopsis (preferably *SQE*[13]). The synopsis will frequently make the source of the deleted verse obvious. In these instances we can observe the tangible influence of the general rules of textual development described above (cf. pp. 282f.), and our comments will be correspondingly brief.

1) With **Matt. 17:20** the story of the pericope comes to its proper conclusion, and 17:21 constitutes a duplicate ending taken from the parallel text in Mark 9:29. Even there it is a secondary form because the original text ends with εἰ μὴ ἐν προσευχῇ. The addition of καὶ νηστείᾳ is secondary.

The relative lack of support here for the lectio brevior is not surprising in view of the significance of fasting and the respect for it characteristic not only of the early Church but also of monasticism throughout the medieval period. Yet ℵ* B 0274 k and Clement of Alexandria are quite adequate support for the shorter form of Mark 9:29. It is significant that in Matt. 17:21 the phrase ἐν οὐδενὶ δύναται ἐξελθεῖν taken from Mark is changed in the majority of the witnesses to the smoother ἐκπορεύεται. It is also significant that besides ἐκπορεύεται the tradition also has the readings ἐκβάλλεται and ἐξέρχεται. It is a further indication of the secondary character of Matt. 17:21 that the influence of the Marcan text occurred at various times and in various forms. ℵ* (the verse is added typically by the second hand) B Θ 33.892* *pc* e ff[1] sy[s] and sy[c] as well as the preponderance of the Coptic tradition are more than adequate evidence for the originality of the omission of verse 21 from Matthew's text. On the other hand, no one would have deleted a text of such popular appeal, and the relatively great number of witnesses for the omission (particularly astonishing is the presence of the Old Syriac and the Coptic traditions, representing cultures where monasticism and fasting were especially esteemed) offers further confirmation of the hardy tenacity characteristic of the New Testament textual tradition.

2) The external evidence for the insertion of **Matt. 18:11** is not very impressive: the manuscripts here, with the exception of D and W, are all of secondary rank (in L and Θ and also in 892 it is an addition by a later hand), some even representing the Byzantine text. Further, the insertion itself has a divided tradition, with one strand reproducing Luke 19:10 verbatim and the other abbreviating it. The evidence for omission is far stronger. The "mission of Jesus" so impressively formulated in this verse is found inserted elsewhere as well; cf. the discussion of Luke 9:54-56 below (p. 309). It echoes statements found elsewhere in the Gospels, e.g., Mark 2:17; Matt. 9:13; Luke 5:32. The Parable of the Lost Sheep and the saying about the Little Ones provided an occasion for the insertion here.

3) Here again the evidence against the insertion of **Matt. 23:14** is unusually strong, and very weak for it (the fact that W 0104 and others place

it after verse 12 is a clear indication of its secondary character). The text is doubtless derived from parallel traditions in Mark 12:40 and Luke 20:45-47, and it was introduced here to satisfy the same tendency toward completeness that is observed also in the scribal tendency to conflate readings (cf. pp. 293f.).

4) **Mark 7:16.** This saying is found repeatedly in the original text of the Gospels (cf. Matt. 11:15; 13:9; 13:43; Mark 4:9; 4:23; Luke 8:8; 14:35), and it is only too easy to understand how a part of the manuscript tradition would add it in contexts where it seemed appropriate, as in the present passage (the evidence for the insertion is clearly inferior to that for the omission when internal criteria are considered).

The absence of a corresponding insertion at the parallel passage in Matt. 15:11 is no valid counterargument, quite apart from the fact that the gospel of Mark is usually on the receiving rather than the giving end of parallel influences. While it is true that in no. 3 above the manuscript tradition of Matthew shows the insertion of a reading that occurs in Mark, it should also be noted that the same reading also occurs verbatim in Luke, which is the more probable source.

5) This is an example of the tradition inserting Mark 9:48 as almost a liturgical refrain at **Mark 9:44** and again **9:46** (perhaps suggested by the repeated εἰς τὴν γέενναν in each instance), with stronger attestation the first time than the second, though without as strong support in either instance as for the omission. Because the apparatus in Nestle-Aland[26] for verse 46 says simply "*ut vs* 44," the apparatus of *GNT*[3] is reproduced in full to enable the interested reader to examine the details. Naturally the tradition of any verse is not precisely identical with that of any other. Yet a careful comparison will show that the evidence for the addition and omission of these two verses is amazingly parallel. It is evidently a closely knit tradition: the differences are so slight, such as the omission of verse 44 in *l* 260 (according to the apparatus of *GNT*) and of verse 46 in *l* 19, or the addition of verse 44 but not of verse 46 in the minuscule 1009, and so forth, that as differences they are scarcely worth noting in view of the overall agreement between the lists of witnesses otherwise.

6) Hereafter, for reasons already mentioned, only the apparatus of Nestle-Aland[26] will be cited. It offers enough for forming a judgment. If more information is desired the apparatus of *GNT*[3] or *SQE*[13] may be consulted. In the present example, in any event, the verdict is clear. **Mark 11:26** represents an adaptation of Matt. 6:15 typical of the way parallel texts have influenced the gospel of Mark. The evidence for omission is excellent, and in view of internal criteria it is convincing.

7) **Mark 15:28.** Here the verse is derived from Luke 22:37, converting the prediction Jesus made there into a theological comment by recounting its fulfillment.

The external attestation for omission is clearly superior. The presence of the verse in the Byzantine text explains why it (like the others) is in the text printed by Erasmus and in subsequent editions of the Greek text, and consequently in the versions made in the centuries following.

8) **Luke 17:36.** Here the external evidence is so weak, as well as being divided, that there seemed to be no necessity for the Nestle apparatus to cite the evidence for the text (i.e., all the witnesses not cited for the insertion). Luke 17:36 is derived from the parallel tradition at Matt. 24:40.

9) **Luke 23:17.** In contrast to the parallel accounts, Luke has neither referred to Pilate's releasing of a prisoner at the festival nor yet mentioned Barabbas, so that the insertion is understandable. For one part of the tradition this was felt to be inadequate, and introductory phrases from the narratives in Matt. 27:15 and Mark 15:6 were added in different places and in a slightly adapted form. Even though ℵ reads the insertion, the evidence for the originality of the omission is the stronger by far.

10) The insertions considered thus far have all been derived from parallel texts, whether in other Gospels or in the same Gospel. But in **John 5:3b-4** we meet another category: expansions of the original text by various later legendary supplements developed from the account itself. From the attestation for the "shorter text" it should be clear that the expansion of the ending of verse 3 and the whole of verse 4 represents a later insertion. Note that D adds only the ending of verse 3 without adding verse 4, and that $\mathfrak{p}^{66}$, which frequently has a freer tendency (cf. p. 59), agrees with $\mathfrak{p}^{75}$, which follows its exemplar strictly. The ending of verse 3 represents more or less an explanatory editorial comment, but verse 4 is a skillfully related supplement based on a suggestion in verse 7, where the sick man complains that he has no one to assist him to the pool when the water is stirred, and that when he finally gets there he finds someone else has entered before him. From this it is inferred that (1) the water in the pool is stirred, for which verse 4 identifies the cause, and (2) the first person to enter is healed, as verse 4 states explicitly. The secondary character of this is obvious. But Rule 3 should be remembered (cf. p. 280): these are all later considerations, because in this instance the decision has already been determined by the external evidence. When internal criteria confirm the decision (cf. Rule 2), it becomes certain. If the internal criteria oppose the external evidence, both should be reviewed. If the external evidence retains its validity, then the possibility should be considered that the internal criteria have not been examined in all their aspects. Vestigia terrent ("loose ends are disturbing"): exegetes are tempted only too often to offer an interpretation for a passage based on inner criteria without considering thoroughly all relevant perspectives.

11) Now we leave the Gospels and come to the book of Acts. The first addition in **Acts 8:37** is somewhat akin to John 5:3b-4. Here also a later age supplied an element which the original account simply assumed and did not make explicit. The external evidence is so weak that the Nestle apparatus cites only the support for the insertion and not for the original omission. The uncial E (cf. p. 110) together with a limited number of minuscules which are not without a certain weight in their own right does not give the insertion sufficient support to qualify it for a claim to originality. These witnesses may be identified by reference to *GNT*³: Acts 8:37 is omitted by $\mathfrak{p}^{45}$ $\mathfrak{p}^{74}$ ℵ A B C P Ψ 049.056.0142, a long sequence of minuscules, including even the Majority text, and so forth,

while the addition is variously divided in the tradition. The voice which speaks in Acts 8:37 is from a later age, with an interest in the detailed justification of the treasurer's desire for baptism.

12) The insertion of **Acts 15:34** appears in a variety of forms. The form in C and others represents what we may call the first stage. It states only that Silas remained in Antioch (this seemed necessary because in 15:40 it says that Paul chose Silas to accompany him, and according to 15:33 he had already departed); D and others attempt to deal with the inconsistency more directly by explaining that Silas remained (in Antioch), and only Judas had departed. The origin of this text (and accordingly its secondary character) is therefore clear. Only the omission of Acts 15:34 (attested by even the Majority text!) can qualify as the original form of the text, quite apart from the unambiguous voice of the external attestation (cf. p. 281, Rule 8; only the omission can explain the alternative readings).

13) The omission of **Acts 24:6b-8** in the indictment by Tertullus is supported by evidence that is absolutely conclusive. It leaves no grounds for questioning the secondary character of the text. The insertion was prompted by the conclusion of the speech in verse 8, which states that when Felix examined Paul he would learn directly from him all the Jewish charges against him. There seemed to be a hiatus between verse 6, which tells of Paul's arrest by the Jews, and verse 8. Verses 6b-8a fill in the details (cf. Acts 21:31ff.) by telling how the chiliarch Lysias had taken Paul from them and ordered the case to be tried before the governor (Acts 23:23ff.). This is no more than stylistic polishing, contributing no new information despite the claims of many exegetes in the past.

14) Here again the external evidence is unequivocal: **Acts 28:29** cannot have been a part of the original text of Acts. The transition from verse 28 to verse 30 was felt by the Majority text to be too abrupt. A concluding sentence was lacking, and it was supplied by repeating the content of verses 24-25.

15) **Rom. 16:24** needs no further discussion here (cf. the beginning of this section; pp. 295f., 301). Instead, we recommend a practical exercise for the reader who has persevered to this point. From the descriptions of manuscripts on pp. 96-102, 107-128, and 129-138, some idea (or at least some preliminary impression) of their textual quality has been formed. But this has been on the theoretical level, and practical experience is far better. Only by a constant use of manuscripts can one learn to recognize their textual quality (cf. p. 281, Rule 12). The passages discussed above may provide an opportunity to form a perspective and gain some impressions.

Of the fifteen examples listed above, in only three (nos. 8, 11, and 15) does the Nestle apparatus omit the listing of support for the text. This leaves twelve instances where it is possible to distinguish quite clearly between the original text and the later insertion. Accordingly, the witness of the manuscripts which retain the original readings in these instances should be the more highly valued for having withstood the authority of church tradition despite the seductive artistry, stylistic smoothness, and other attractions of the additions. How do the

manuscripts acquit themselves here? Reviewing the data on pp. 298ff. we find these results: in the nine passages considered from the Gospels (the three passages from Acts are best considered separately), the incidence of agreement with the original text against the later additions is:

ℵ	8	L	6	f^1	3	892	6
A	2	W	2	f^{13}	1	1241	1
B	9	Δ	3	28	2	1344	1
C	3	Θ	3	33	3	1365	1
D	2	Ψ	3	565	2		
K	1			700	1		

Omitted from this count are the "number uncials" 0124, 0125, 0274 (because of their fragmentary character), as well as the "letter uncials" T and Z (represented in only two and one of the passages, respectively), and the papyri $\mathfrak{p}^{75}$ (containing only Luke and John) and $\mathfrak{p}^{66}$ (containing only John). We are quite aware that a survey of this kind is subject to many qualifications. But it has some usefulness for the beginner: it shows that the textual value of a minuscule may well rival or be superior to that of a prestigious uncial, and that the textual value of the uncials is very uneven. The three examples from Acts yield the following picture. The incidence of preservation of the original text is:

$\mathfrak{P}^{74}$	3	E	2	Ψ	2	1175	2
ℵ	3	H	1	$\mathfrak{M}$	1(!)	1241	2
A	3	L	1	33	1	1739	1
B	3	P	1	81	3	2464	2
						2495	1

$\mathfrak{p}^{74}$ is counted (because it contains all the relevant passages) but C, D, and 048 are not (because they do not contain all the passages). Here again the minuscules show up well. The change in A is remarkable, from little more than 20 percent in the Gospels to 100 percent! This is a good example of how greatly the textual quality of manuscripts can vary (cf. p. 50): in the Gospels A transmits an exemplar with a rather poor text, but in the rest of the New Testament it is different (in Revelation it represents one of the best witnesses).

4. SMALLER OMISSIONS IN THE NEW TEXT

The foregoing tables may have their problems, but they are also effective in pointing to some useful insights. The reader may find it interesting to apply the method to the apparatus of Nestle-Aland[26] in other passages. This is the best way to gain familiarity with the textual value of manuscripts and versions, especially if variant readings are always approached with the question of how they can best be explained. The solutions are not always as apparent as in the examples discussed above. It may be best to begin with the New Testament passages we will discuss next. In the new text, and increasingly in modern versions, not only are there complete verses omitted which we have discussed above, but

frequently there are also shorter units, less than a verse in length, which are familiar to the reader and noticeable by their absence. The modern versions are only adopting in these passages a practice long followed in editions of the Greek text, eliminating readings which originated in the same way as the verses discussed above. They were not a part of the original text but were inserted in it later, usually under the influence of the Koine or Byzantine Imperial text. They were usually found in the editions of Desiderius Erasmus, in the later editions of the Textus Receptus, and in translations made from the sixteenth to the late nineteenth century. Consequently they have achieved a popular acceptance which continues into the twentieth century. In practically all the modern national languages there is a well-established versional tradition which is only now in our generation beginning to give way, as Bible readers realize they should not insist on keeping as part of their New Testaments the readings which have long been recognized by scholars as later additions to the text. We will give only a few examples taken exclusively from the major versions of today, where they are usually explained by a footnote.

In the **gospel of Matthew** the text of **5:44** used to read (with some variation): "Bless them that curse you, do good to them that hate you, and pray for them which despitefully use you, and persecute you." This is nothing more than an adaptation from the parallel text of Luke 6:27-28. The variety of forms in which this occurs in the manuscript tradition only underscores the secondary character of the expansion. It undoubtedly made for a more edifying text, but it was not in the original gospel of Matthew.

Admittedly the selection of Greek manuscripts preserving the original text is not very large ($\aleph$ B f^1 and a few others), but they are supported by representatives of all the early versions. As in the ending of Mark and frequently elsewhere as well, the expanded text is more impressive and "better" than the original form, and few manuscripts have been able to withstand its momentum. Furthermore, the conclusive argument here (as in so many similar instances) is that if the expanded form were actually the original text, what would have been the motive for altering it? Accidental omission is hardly a plausible cause (although a scribe could certainly have omitted a phrase by sheer chance as described above, and his manuscript could then have been copied by other scribes; cf. pp. 285f.), because the shorter text is found in all parts of the early Church. Further, an important point for all similar examples is the variety of forms assumed by the expansion, which is an irrefutable argument for its secondary character.

At **Matt. 6:13** the doxology of the Lord's Prayer ("thine is the kingdom . . .") appears in the apparatus of the Greek text, and for good reasons modern versions are increasingly tending to bracket the passage. Here again the question is pertinent, if the doxology originally stood in the gospel of Matthew, who would have deleted it? Its supplemental character is obvious from the variety of forms it has taken, and the witness for its original absence is far stronger than for Matt. 5:44. The reason for the addition is quite clear. Whether the Lord's Prayer is used in public worship or for private devotions, the text needs an

ending. The expansion must have been supplied quite early because it is found in the Didache, a writing composed shortly after A.D. 100.

The saying in **Matt. 16:2b-3** represents a very early tradition, as does the Pericope Adulterae in **John 7:53 – 8:11.** In view of the support for their omission in the Greek manuscript tradition, the versions, and the Church Fathers, there can hardly be any doubt that both these passages were lacking in the original text of the Gospels. Matt. 16:2b-3 may possibly have been suggested by Luke 12:54-56, but it is not a parallel in the strict sense. In any event both texts must have been admitted in parts of the Greek Gospel tradition at some time in the second century — a period when there was greater freedom with the text (cf. p. 64). Only then were such extensive insertions possible, and considering the amount of opposition apparently encountered by the Pericope Adulterae, it must have been quite strongly rooted in the evangelical tradition.

At **Matt. 20:16** the popular saying that "the last shall be first and the first last" (cf. p. 237 above) is followed by another equally popular saying that "many are called but few are chosen." The argument for the secondary character of the addition, which is derived from Matt. 22:14, is the same as in all these examples: the attestation for the omission (which is relatively strong in this instance), together with the objection that no reason can be found for deleting such a prudent statement if it had originally been a part of the Gospel of Matthew.

Matt. 20:22 and 23 are obvious examples of influence from parallel texts. In both places the words of Jesus to the sons of Zebedee have been expanded to the fuller form found in Mark 10:38 and 39. The impressive manuscript evidence against it needs no comment.

In **Matt. 25:13** the insertion ("in which the Son of Man comes") belongs to the category of the interpretive or explanatory addition so dear to the Byzantine Imperial text (in the score or more examples thus far 𝔐 has been prominent among the witnesses supporting such expansions, and this trait will remain characteristic of it!). The attestation for the addition is weak, and the source is Matt. 24:44.

In **Matt. 27:35** the supplementary quotation from the Psalms is derived from John 19:24. Besides the obvious presence of a devotional motive, the support in the manuscript tradition is so weak that no discussion is necessary (in the Nestle-Aland[26] apparatus the evidence for omission is not even given).

In the **gospel of Mark** the text of **9:49** presents exegetical difficulties which have given rise to a variety of improvements in the tradition. Cf. the apparatus in *GNT*[3] where the variety is presented in full detail, although the more concise form in Nestle-Aland[26] is also quite clear. The most radical change is found in the D tradition (as usual), which simply replaces the text with Lev. 2:13. This new text and the reading of the earlier exemplar were then variously combined to form conflate readings in the Majority text and in numerous other manuscripts. Not only does the manuscript evidence require πᾶς γὰρ πυρὶ ἁλισθήσεται as the original text, but so do the internal criteria. It is the lectio difficilior which alone can account for the development of the other

forms of the text (including the misconstructions) in a genealogical pattern.

In **Mark 10:7** the decision is difficult, and the reading has been retained in single brackets. The manuscripts supporting the omission are of considerable authority. Furthermore, the addition makes very good sense: by omitting the familiar words from Gen. 2:24 the text of Mark seems incomplete and possibly misleading (cf. the sequel). Besides, as we have seen in a number of instances, it is the gospel of Mark that tends to borrow from the gospel of Matthew rather than the reverse. All this would argue for the omission. Against this the possibility of homoioarcton should be considered (from καὶ at the beginning of the omission to καὶ at the beginning of verse 8). And yet is it credible that the identical omission could occur accidentally in all the manuscripts (ℵ B Ψ 892* 2427 and others) attesting the omission?

In the Parable of the Rich Young Man (a pericope which must have been of particular interest to later scribes, most of whom were monks) there are two places where a part of a verse differs from the traditional text in modern versions: "and take up your cross" in **Mark 10:21**, and "for those who trust in riches" in **10:24**. An accommodative interest is clear in the addition to Mark 10:24: it is only those who *put their trust* in riches that find the kingdom of God difficult to enter. This softens the statement in 10:23, making its secondary character obvious (cf. the severity of verse 25), especially in view of its variations in the manuscript tradition. At Mark 10:21 the addition was probably suggested by Mark 8:34. Although the sequence of words there is reversed (ἀράτω τὸν σταυρὸν αὐτοῦ καὶ ἀκολουθείτω μοι), the phrase δεῦρο ἀκολούθει μοι prompted the association of 8:34 and led to the insertion of ἄρας τὸν σταυρόν σου at the end of the sentence in a number of manuscripts. The evidence for omission is incomparably stronger.

In **Mark 14:68** the final words of the verse (καὶ ἀλέκτωρ ἐφώνησεν) are placed in single brackets because the evidence for their omission is of considerable strength, and for their inclusion it is distinctly superior. The internal criteria, however, are ambivalent. It can be argued that the omission occurred because the accounts in the other Gospels mention only a single cockcrow, and the texts directly parallel to Mark 14:68 do not refer to it. Yet on the other hand it can be argued that at the end of the pericope, where Matt. 26:74 and Luke 22:60 mention a cock's crow, Mark 14:72 has the cock crow ἐκ δευτέρου and concludes with a reference to φωνῆσαι δίς. Of course there are manuscripts which omit both δίς and ἐκ δευτέρου, but their authority has little weight. Both are evidently a part of the original text of the gospel of Mark. The parenthetical phrase seems accordingly to belong to the structure of the account here.

In the **gospel of Luke** the answer Jesus gave to the devil in **Luke 4:4** in the traditional version was: "Man shall not live by bread alone, but by every word of God." Modern versions omit the last phrase. This conforms to the external evidence and to the internal requirements as well. The expanded text is derived from Matt. 4:4, where Deut. 8:3 is cited in full. The lectio brevior is preferable here to the expanded text for the same reason we have advanced

so often elsewhere: if the phrase had been in the original text, what reason could there have been for its removal?

In **Luke 8:43** the detail that the woman with a hemorrhage "had spent all her living (in vain) on physicians" is single bracketed in the Greek text (and correspondingly in modern versions). The witnesses for the omission — B (and D, with a slight variation) sy[s] and sa — are now joined by p[75], which makes their combined weight definitely stronger. And yet the motif of wasting money on doctors is already a part of the Marcan account, where it is stated even more emphatically in 5:26. But Luke 8:43 can hardly be explained (as so frequently) by the influence of parallel texts, especially when the phrase is so freely and freshly expressed, even including a hapax legomenon. It has a genuinely Lucan ring about it, so that it is an open question whether in the second century, to borrow a modern analogy, the medical profession had the phrase deleted or, to echo another modern complaint, the phrase was inserted as a protest against the rising costs of ineffective medical services (is this the reason for the hapax legomenon προσαναλώσασα?). The single brackets reflect the indecision of the editors of the new text at this point.

In **Luke 9:54-56** there are two similar textual variants found in modern versions. In 9:54 the phrase "as Elijah did" is omitted, and 9:55-56 lacks the saying "and he said, You do not know what manner of spirit you are of. The Son of man came not to destroy men's lives but to save them." This pericope does not have a parallel, but is a part of Luke's special material. Yet it is easy to understand how the manuscript tradition would (1) add an allusion to the biblical story of Elijah in 2 Kgs. 1:10ff., and (2) describe Jesus as rejecting such an attitude by supplying a saying on saving the lost in terms reminiscent of so many other scribal insertions elsewhere (cf. the comments on Matt. 18:11; p. 301). Both insertions serve to temper the offensiveness of the disciples' attitude. The external evidence for both insertions requires no special comment: the first is opposed by p[45] p[75] ℵ B L and so forth, while the attestation for the second is so weak that Nestle-Aland[26] does not list the support for the text, i.e., the omission (which again includes p[45] p[75] ℵ A B C L and so forth; cf. the apparatus of GNT[3] in loc.).

The text of the Lord's Prayer in **Luke 11:2-4** with the various major and minor differences of its manuscript tradition in the Lucan Sermon on the Plain naturally invited comparison with the fuller form of the prayer in Matt. 6:9-13. It would be amazing if it had not. A full discussion is not necessary here, especially as the Greek manuscript tradition contains a far greater number of additions than are familiar to readers of the traditional translations of Luke (and would therefore be noticed today). The essential information is found in the apparatus of Nestle-Aland[26], and only a selection in GNT[3] (p[75] and B should be noticed as the only manuscripts to preserve the original text in *all* its details; even ℵ and the other great uncials succumb here and there to the temptation to add something from Matthew, although interestingly enough none is tempted to add the doxology from Matt. 6:13 in the Lucan text).

In **Luke 11:11** the Byzantine Imperial text expands the text on the model of the parallel traditions. Traditional versions correspondingly read ". . . a stone to his son who asks for bread, or a serpent when he asks for fish?" This is a typical instance of parallel influence. The Lucan text originally spoke only of serpents and fish: the bread and stone are derived from Matt. 7:9. Naturally the expanded text was found more edifying and impressive, and its acceptance was correspondingly extensive. But it was opposed by $\mathfrak{p}^{45}$ $\mathfrak{p}^{75}$ B 1241, and a group of the early versions.

Luke 22:43-44 is placed in double brackets in the Greek text. This expresses the editors' conviction that these verses were not a part of the original text of the gospel of Luke. The fact that they were not removed and relegated to the apparatus, but retained in the text within double brackets (cf. the Pericope Adulterae), indicates that this is recognized as a very early tradition coming at least from the second century if not even earlier (attested by patristic quotations and allusions; cf. *GNT*[3cor]). The external evidence leaves no doubt that these verses were added to the original text of Luke — not just because the witness for their omission is so strong ($\mathfrak{p}^{75}$ $\aleph^1$ A B and so forth; there is a further group of manuscripts which have the verses but with critical marks added to indicate their doubtful authenticity, as also at Mark 16:9-20). These verses also exhibit a conclusive clue to their secondary nature (like the Pericope Adulterae) in the alternative locations for its insertion. While the majority of the (now known) manuscripts place them at Luke 22:43-44, they are found after Matt. 26:39 in the minuscule family 13 and in several lectionaries. This kind of fluctuation in the New Testament manuscript tradition is one of the surest evidences for the secondary character of a text.

The insertion at **Luke 24:42** of καὶ ἀπὸ μελισσίου κηρίου ("and of a honeycomb"), which is the last passage in the gospel of Luke to be discussed here, does not require special treatment. But because it is a part of the Majority text it is found also in traditional versions. This insertion is significant as an allusion to early popular customs of eating (and liturgical usage), but in view of the opposing witness of $\mathfrak{p}^{75}$ $\aleph$ A B D L W and so forth it could not have been a part of the original Lucan text.

As for the **gospel of John**, all the important passages have already been discussed under the preceding rubric of whole verses now removed from the Greek text and from modern translations. The same is true for Acts, except for **Acts 28:16**, where the Majority text and the traditional translations have added the clause: "the centurion delivered the prisoners to the captain of the guard (but Paul was permitted . . .)." This addition fills out the narrative smoothly, but its attestation in the tradition is too weak to merit serious consideration.

As for **Romans**, the conclusion of the letter has been discussed in some detail (cf. pp. 295f.), with the conclusion that not only **16:24** (which has been transferred from the text to the apparatus), but also **16:25-27** (which is retained single-bracketed in the text) are not a part of the letter in its original form. Other passages have already been discussed (e.g., Rom. 5:1), leaving nothing further to be added here.

As for **1 Corinthians**, one passage requires comment. The textual variants in **1 Cor. 11:24** bear on only a detail of Paul's account of the Last Supper. Here the Majority text together with the traditional versions add at the beginning the words of institution λάβετε φάγετε. These words are taken from Matt. 26:26, and they represent nothing more than parallel assimilation, clearly opposed by the evidence of the textual tradition. More important in this connection is an observation on the account of the Last Supper in Luke 22. Under the influence of Westcott-Hort's theory of "Western non-interpolations," the whole of verses 19b-20, from τὸ ὑπὲρ ὑμῶν διδόμενον to τὸ ὑπὲρ ὑμῶν ἐκχυννόμενον, was printed earlier in double brackets, even as recently as *GNT*[2]. But no longer. Most (though not yet all) of the exegetes under the influence of nineteenth-century theories have yielded to the overwhelming evidence attesting the originality of **Luke 22:19b-20** in the Gospel text, recognizing that for the presentation and perspective of the gospel of Luke it is not the "shorter," but the "longer" account of the Last Supper that is authentic.

Many other passages could be mentioned, such as the famous "Comma Johanneum" of **1 John 5:7-8**. But for anyone who has read this far, a glance at the data in the critical apparatus of Nestle-Aland[26] (which is exhaustive for this passage) should make any further comment unnecessary to demonstrate the secondary nature of this addition and the impossibility of its being at all related to the original form of the text of 1 John. There is an abundance of still further instances of textual variation which are noted in modern versions and which would well be worth further investigation. Many are mentioned, for example, in the Revised Standard Version. It is most unfortunate that the latest editions have standardized the introductory formula for textual footnotes to the form "Other ancient authorities read." Granted that strictly speaking this formula may be quite accurate, because even the latest manuscript of the Majority text, i.e., the Byzantine Imperial text, written as recently as the sixteenth century, may qualify as an "ancient authority" from the perspective of the twentieth century. Yet such an egalitarian representation of the manuscript tradition (although certainly contrary to the intention of those responsible for the new edition of the Revised Standard Version) must give the impression to readers of the version who are not specialists in textual criticism that the variant readings in the notes are of equal value with those in the text — and nothing could be more false and insidious!

The examples discussed above have shown how the alternative readings compare with the new text as a rule, and these were selected especially for their representative character. For the mass of other variants such as are found in the footnotes of the Revised Standard Version the situation is much simpler. The present formula introducing them is unfortunate, tending to encourage readers of the Revised Standard Version in a misunderstanding. The editors of the new text certainly do not claim infallibility. They do, however, recognize that to the best of their knowledge and abilities, and with resources unmatched for any manual edition of the New Testament in modern times, they have edited a text which comes as close as possible to the original

form of the New Testament writings. In comparison with their predecessors they have enjoyed the incomparable advantages of the papyrus discoveries of the last generations, and also access to nearly all the known Greek manuscripts of the New Testament at the Institute for New Testament Textual Research at Münster. This may reflect no special credit to the editors, but the results have been achieved. It is now for translators to transmit these results to those who are unable to read the original texts of the New Testament, and to share with them an appreciation of the variant readings found in this Greek text.

5. THE PARABLE OF THE TWO SONS

This concludes the "introduction to the praxis of New Testament textual criticism" in selected examples. The last words here should be underscored, for the authors can only hope that the "selected examples," not only in this chapter but in the other sections of the book as well, will serve to make the reader not only familiar with the critical apparatus in the editions, but also capable of forming independent (and sound) judgments. In conclusion we return once more to the pericope of the Two Sons in Matt. 21:28-32, which we have chosen to use several times as a demonstration model because of its peculiar difficulties (cf. pp. 233f., 254f., 258), but avoiding the discussion of verses 29-31 thus far because of the special difficulty of the problem they pose. Some idea of the difficulties involved may be gained from the variety of treatment given this passage in the editions of the last century (cf. Nestle-Aland[26], Appendix II, p. 719).

The new text of Matt. 21:29-31 in Nestle-Aland[26] reads as follows:

29 ὁ δὲ ἀποκριθεὶς εἶπεν ⸆οὐ θέλω, ὕστερον °δὲ μεταμεληθεὶς ἀπῆλθεν⸃. 30 ⸂προσελθὼν δὲ⸃ τῷ ⸀ἑτέρῳ εἶπεν ὡσαύτως. ὁ δὲ ἀποκριθεὶς εἶπεν· ⸆ ⸂ἐγώ, κύριε, καὶ οὐκ ἀπῆλθεν⸃. 31 τίς ἐκ τῶν δύο ἐποίησεν τὸ θέλημα τοῦ πατρός; λέγουσιν ⸆· ⸂ὁ πρῶτος⸃. λέγει αὐτοῖς ὁ Ἰησοῦς· ἀμὴν λέγω ὑμῖν ὅτι οἱ τελῶναι καὶ αἱ πόρναι προάγουσιν ὑμᾶς εἰς τὴν βασιλείαν τοῦ θεοῦ.

The critical apparatus reads:

29-31 ⸋⸆ εγω (υπαγω Θ f¹³ 700 pc), κυριε (– Θ)· και ουκ απηλθεν et ⸌⸆ ου θελω, υστερον (+ δε Θ f¹³ 700 pc) μεταμεληθεις απηλθεν et ⸌⸆ ο υστερος (εσχατος Θ f¹³ 700 pc) B Θ f¹³ 700 al saᵐˢˢ bo; Hierᵐˢˢ ¦ txt (ℵ) C (L) W (Z) 0138 (f¹) 𝔐 f q vgʷʷ syᵖ·ʰ saᵐˢˢ mae; Hierᵐˢˢ ¦ txt, sed + εις τον αμπελωνα p. απηλθεν¹ et εσχατος loco πρωτος D it syˢ·⁽ᶜ⁾ ¦ O ℵ* (B) 1010 pc it saᵐˢˢ ¦ ⸋και προσελθων C W 0138 𝔐 h q syᵖ·ʰ (– syˢ·ᶜ) ¦ txt ℵ B D L Z Θ f¹·¹³ 33. 700. 892 pc lat mae bo ¦ ⸂τ δευτερω ℵ² B C² L Z f¹ 28. 33. 700. 892. 1424 pm mae bo ¦ Ταυτω C W 0138 f¹ 𝔐 it vgᶜˡ sy sa mae boᵐˢ ¦ txt ℵ B D L Θ f¹³ 33. 892 pc lat bo

Earlier the text circulated in basically three different forms:

I. Constantin von Tischendorf, *Editio octava critica maior* (1869-1872)

29 ὁ δὲ ἀποκριθεὶσ εἶπεν· οὐ θέλω,
ὕστερον μεταμεληθεὶσ ἀπῆλθεν. 30 προσελθὼν δὲ τῷ ἑτέρῳ εἶπεν
ὡσαύτωσ. ὁ δὲ ἀποκριθεὶσ εἶπεν· ἐγὼ κύριε, καὶ οὐκ ἀπῆλθεν.
31 τίσ ἐκ τῶν δύο ἐποίησεν τὸ θέλημα τοῦ πατρόσ; λέγουσιν· ὁ
πρῶτοσ. λέγει αὐτοῖσ ὁ Ἰησοῦσ· ἀμὴν λέγω ὑμῖν ὅτι οἱ τελῶναι
καὶ αἱ πόρναι προάγουσιν ὑμᾶσ εἰσ τὴν βασιλείαν τοῦ θεοῦ.

II, 1. B. F. Westcott-F. J. A. Hort (1881)

ὁ δὲ ἀποκριθεὶς εἶπεν Ἐγώ, κύριε· καὶ 29
οὐκ ἀπῆλθεν. προσελθὼν δὲ τῷ δευτέρῳ εἶπεν ὡσαύτως· ὁ 30
δὲ ἀποκριθεὶς εἶπεν Οὐ θέλω· ὕστερον μεταμεληθεὶς ἀπῆλθεν. τίς ἐκ τῶν δύο ἐποίησεν τὸ θέλημα τοῦ πατρός; 31
⸀λέγουσιν Ὁ ὕστερος.⸀ λέγει αὐτοῖς ὁ Ἰησοῦς Ἀμὴν λέγω
ὑμῖν ὅτι οἱ τελῶναι καὶ αἱ πόρναι προάγουσιν ὑμᾶς εἰς τὴν
βασιλείαν τοῦ θεοῦ.

II, 2. Hermann Freiherr von Soden (1913)

29 30 ²⁹ ὁ δὲ ἀποκοριθεὶς εἶπεν· ὑπάγω κύριε, καὶ οὐκ ἀπῆλθεν. ³⁰ προσελθὼν δὲ τῷ
δευτέρῳ εἶπεν ὡσαύτως. ὁ δὲ ἀποκριθεὶς εἶπεν· οὐ θέλω, ὕστερον δὲ μεταμεληθεὶς
31 ἀπῆλθεν. ³¹ τίς ἐκ τῶν δύο ἐποίησεν τὸ θέλημα τοῦ πατρός; λέγουσιν· ὁ ἔσχατος.
λέγει αὐτοῖς ὁ Ἰησοῦς· ἀμὴν λέγω ὑμῖν, ὅτι οἱ τελῶναι καὶ αἱ πόρναι προάγουσιν
32 ὑμᾶς εἰς τὴν βασιλείαν τοῦ θεοῦ.

All other forms are variations of these. The earlier Nestle editions closely followed Westcott-Hort, just as Augustinus Merk adhered to the text of von Soden. Tischendorf provided a model for the others, though with minor variations: ὕστερον δὲ μεταμεληθείς is read in verse 29 by Heinrich Joseph Vogels (⁴1955), José Maria Bover (⁵1968), and Nestle-Aland²⁶. In verse 30 Vogels begins with καὶ προσελθών, and in the same verse Bover reads τῷ δευτέρῳ for τῷ ἑτέρῳ. In the Nestle apparatus the variations observed here are brought together by the sign ⸀ :

a) 29⸀ οὐ θέλω, ὕστερον δὲ μεταμεληθεὶς ἀπῆλθεν⸀
b) 30⸀ ἐγώ, κύριε, καὶ οὐκ ἀπῆλθεν⸀
c) 31⸀ ὁ πρῶτος⸀

The reading of an edition in these three places defines its position; other variants are of secondary importance (cf. below, p. 315). In Tischendorf (type I) the first son to be asked refuses at first, but then obeys the request to work in the vineyard. The second son agrees to go, but then does not. The answer to the question of who did the father's will is therefore ὁ πρῶτος. In Westcott-Hort and von Soden the sequence is precisely reversed (type II, 1 and 2; the differences in details may be ignored here). Here the first son asked makes a positive response but does nothing, while the second son declines at first but then carries

out his father's orders. Correspondingly the answer to the question of which did the father's will now becomes ὁ ὕστερος or ὁ ἔσχατος. In spite of the different sequences the answer is the same, and Jesus' words of condemnation are an apt rejoinder to the challenge of the "chief priests and elders of the people" (in 21:23). But there is still a third type, beginning with the same sequence as in a) and b), but instead of the answer c) it reads ὁ ἔσχατος. This third type is found in D, a group of the Old Latins, and the Sinaitic Syriac; although it has not been accepted in any modern edition, it has been favored by several exegetes (e.g., Julius Wellhausen, Emanuel Hirsch).

A review of the manuscript tradition shows the following picture:

[2] **29–31** {C} *οὐ θέλω, ὕστερον δὲ μεταμεληθεὶς ἀπῆλθεν...ἑτέρῳ...ἐγώ, κύριε, καὶ οὐκ ἀπῆλθεν...πρῶτος* (ℵ* 1010 *omit δέ*) C* K W X Δ Π 0138 565 1071 1079 1195 (1216 *ὑπάγω κύριε*) 1230 1241 1253 1546 *Byz*^{pt} *l*^{63,76,185,211,1642,1761} (*l*^{80} *τίς οὖν*) it^{f,q} vg syr$^{(c),p,h}$ cop$^{sa\,mss}$ eth$^{ro?pp?}$ Diatessaron^{a,i,n} Irenaeus Origen Eusebius Hilary Cyril // *οὐ θέλω, ὕστερον δὲ μεταμεληθεὶς ἀπῆλθεν...δευτέρῳ...ἐγώ, κύριε. καὶ οὐκ ἀπῆλθεν... πρῶτος* ℵ^{c} C^{2} L *f*^{1} 28 33 892 1009 1242 1344 1365 1646 2148 2174 *Byz*^{pt} *Lect* (*l*^{1127} *τίς οὖν*) syr$^{pal\,ms}$ eth$^{ro?pp?}$ Chrysostom // *οὐ θέλω, ὕστερον δὲ μεταμεληθεὶς ἀπῆλθεν εἰς τὸν ἀμπελῶνα...ἑτέρῳ...ἐγώ, κύριε, καὶ οὐκ ἀπῆλθεν ...ἔσχατος* D it$^{(a,aur,b),d,(e,ff1,2,g1,h,l)}$ syr^{s} // *ἐγώ, κύριε, καὶ οὐκ ἀπῆλθεν... δευτέρῳ...οὐ θέλω· ὕστερον μεταμεληθεὶς ἀπῆλθεν...ὕστερος* B (700 *ὑπάγω κύριε...ὕστερον δὲ...ἔσχατος*) syr$^{pal\,mss}$ (cop^{bo}...*ἔσχατος*) eth^{ms} (geo^{2} *ὑπάγω for ἐγώ and insert "I will not go" before ὕστερον*, geo^{A} *πρῶτος for ὕστερος*) Diatessaron Ephraem Isidore Ps-Athanasius // *ὑπάγω καὶ οὐκ ἀπῆλθεν... ἑτέρῳ...οὐ θέλω· ὕστερον δὲ μεταμεληθεὶς ἀπῆλθεν...ἔσχατος* Θ (*f*^{13} 4 273 geo^{1} *ὑπάγω κύριε καί*) (4 273 *δεύτερος for ἔσχατος*) (*l*^{547}) cop$^{sa?}$ // *ἔρχομαι, κύριε, καὶ οὐκ ἀπῆλθεν...ἀλλῷ...οὐ θέλω, ἀλλὰ ὕστερον μεταμεληθεὶς ἀπῆλθεν ἐν τῷ ἀμπελῶνι...ἔσχατος* arm

The above is taken from *GNT*[3], which is far more detailed in its apparatus where it provides one than the Nestle edition with its concise summaries of data. Yet as we noticed earlier, a detailed presentation of evidence is not without its handicaps. In order to review the situation effectively the variant readings need to be arranged in some perspective that will permit their evaluation, i.e., they must be digested as they have been for the Nestle apparatus.

It may be most useful to begin by examining both apparatuses, and clear away the minor textual differences in order to gain a freer view of the primary problem and its evaluation. On the basis of the external evidence none of the readings can claim originality (the arguments from internal criteria are added in parentheses): e.g., the addition of εἰς τὸν ἀμπελῶνα at the end of verse 29 by D, Old Latin manuscripts, and the Old Syriac (an unnecessary detail of clarification); of καί before προσελθών; the substitution of δευτέρῳ for ἑτέρῳ (paralleling πρώτῳ more precisely, and thus demonstrably secondary); the addition of αὐτῷ in verse 31 (λέγουσιν αὐτῷ, a typically late addition; cf.

pp. 289f.); the transposition in verse 32 to πρὸς ὑμᾶς Ἰωάννης (stylistic polishing); finally, οὐ instead of οὐδέ in the same verse.

Now the external evidence for the three types is not such as to command a spontaneous decision. With a little simplification the evidence appears roughly as follows:

I 　　 ℵ C* K L W Z Δ Π 0138 f^1 𝔐 f q sy$^{p.h}$ sa^{mss} mae (some with slight variation)

II (1,2) B Θ (with some major deviations), f^{13} and 700 (also with deviations), *al* sa^{mss} bo

III 　　 D it sy$^{s.(c)}$

The witness of B naturally weighs heavily for type II, while the support of 𝔐 for type I may arouse misgivings (it should not, however, be overlooked that the support here includes not only the Byzantine text, but also a whole group of important manuscripts such as N P Q Γ 28.33.565.700.892.1010.1241). Besides, the Koine itself can very well attest correct readings, because in its origins it also goes back to the text of the early times (cf. pp. 50ff.). Nevertheless, the attestation for type II is somewhat weakened by the variations of Θ f^{13} 700 (as well as by further variations in the other minuscules): ὑπάγω for ἐγώ and ὁ ἔσχατος for ὁ ὕστερος in all three, not to mention lesser variants. These variations have very much the appearance of later forms that have developed in a variety of ways.

From the standpoint of internal criteria type I must be original. Basically, if the father spoke to the first son and then made the same request of the second son, the first son must have refused the request. Type II is intrinsically illogical, because after the first son has promised to do what his father asked, why should the father turn to the second son? A shrewd person today could answer that it was because the father saw that the son was doing nothing despite his promise. But this is a modern perspective, and if the evangelist had intended it he would have written it in the text. Consequently type I must represent the original text. Type III belongs to the category of the lectio difficilima: "it is nonsensical" is Bruce Manning Metzger's verdict in his commentary on the passage. It represents the people as answering Jesus with a provocative absurdity: that the one who promises but does not obey his father's request is the one who satisfies his father's will. Jesus' words in 21:31-32 then become a sheer tirade in response to this provocative answer (unless the D text of the pericope is an example of the anti-Jewish tendency in D, and was intentionally framed to incriminate the questioners beyond any doubt as damnable; they are identified in 21:23 as ἀρχιερεῖς καὶ πρεσβύτεροι). While this might be conceivable by modern standards, it does not accord with the style and narrative methods of the gospel of Matthew. We should not forget that the vineyard, the father, the son who does his father's will after an initial refusal — these are all deeply symbolic.

It is difficult to see how type II could be derived from type I. A possible suggestion for type II has been considered above. But types I and II are prac-

tically identical in content with only the sequence changed. The reason for the change remains an open question; the narrative could have been designed as a graded sequence: first the promise without obedience, then the rash refusal followed by obedience, and finally the recognition of the latter as doing the father's will. The exegetes should discuss this and come to a decision (they might adopt the new text; Nestle[25] follows type II, the text usually found in commentaries). According to the local-genealogical method, however, only type I could have been the first stage in the developing sequence, with the first son refusing his father's request at first (because it seemed too difficult for him: remember the symbolism of the vineyard), but then obeying.

The pericope of the Two Sons is unquestionably among the most difficult problems of New Testament textual criticism, and it cannot be denied that here also certain questions remain open (which do not affect the substance of the text as a whole). But an introduction to the praxis of New Testament textual criticism would be incomplete without a consideration of some particularly difficult problems.

VIII

CATEGORIES AND TEXT TYPES, AND THE TEXTUAL ANALYSIS OF MANUSCRIPTS

1. *THE TEXT AND TEXTUAL VALUE OF NEW TESTAMENT MANUSCRIPTS*

A new methodological tool for analyzing the New Testament manuscript tradition[1]

All critical work on the text of the New Testament has labored throughout the history of our discipline under a difficulty that has yet to be resolved: the haphazard selection of manuscripts for editions of the text. From Desiderius Erasmus and Francisco Ximénes de Cisneros, the first editors, to Constantin von Tischendorf, Brooke Foss Westcott and F. J. A. Hort, and Herman Freiherr von Soden, the giants of our discipline, the resources used were what was immediately available. Of course the special characteristics of individual manuscripts were noted, and they were given preference in accordance with the particular textual theories adopted. Families of manuscripts were identified and so forth, but it has been true of all editors down to the present that the selection of manuscripts, especially of minuscule manuscripts, has been determined by the limitations of their knowledge of these manuscripts, and therefore by chance. Methods developed for selecting individual manuscripts from the greater mass of manuscripts have not altered the general situation. None of the methods, however well suited for particular purposes, has offered a reliable and verifiable way of examining the *total* range of known manuscripts and identifying *all* the ones pertinent to a given investigation.

For example, we consider 1739 and 33 to be outstanding manuscripts, and we think of 565 and 700 as codices significant for the history of the text. But we cannot possibly tell whether other comparable codices may not be among the 5,400 known manuscripts which would contribute to a better understanding of these minuscules. In other words, the duty "to establish what *must* or *may* be regarded as transmitted" (*recensio*), which is the first and foremost duty for the

---

1. A paper read by Barbara Aland at a conference on textual criticism in Birmingham, September 1987, reporting on Kurt Aland, *Text und Textwert der griechischen Handschriften des Neuen Testaments*. I: *Die Katholischen Briefe*, vols. 1-3. ANTF 9-11 (Berlin/New York: 1987).

editor of any text,[2] cannot be accomplished in the New Testament field. Consequently, the second step of reviewing the tradition (*examinatio*) is impossible. At least it cannot be done in a way normal for the editor of any other text, that is, by examining the *whole* of the manuscript tradition.

In order to deal with this common and fundamental crux, we should like to propose a tool that, in brief, makes three things possible.

1. A clear determination and exclusion of all *eliminandi*, that is, discovering which among the great wealth of manuscripts have simply been copied from others with practically no significant differences, and are therefore of no value for reconstructing the original text and its early history. This is relevant particularly for the mass of manuscripts of the Byzantine text.

2. The identification in a reliable and verifiable manner, by the process of excluding the *eliminandi*, of those New Testament manuscripts whose texts deserve closer examination, or rather, which should properly constitute the basis for an *editio critica maior* of the New Testament.

   These remaining manuscripts, it should be noted, are not chosen on the basis of any textual theory, since only duplicates and copies fully reproducing the Byzantine text type are excluded. Depending on the criteria employed, the remainder will represent between 10 to 20 percent of the total number of known manuscripts, which is a manageable number for the textual critic to work with, whatever textual theory is followed.

3. The examination of the remaining manuscripts for their interrelationships, establishing families and groups among them where possible. The purpose here is to achieve as clear a view as possible of the history of the New Testament text in order to retrace the stages of its development back to the original text. The tool we offer promises significant aid for this most difficult of tasks as well.

This new tool has been developed on the corpus of the Catholic letters, but in principle it is equally useful for each of the New Testament scriptures. In the present application all existing manuscripts of the Catholic letters were considered. There were 540, more than could possibly be examined by any of the traditional methods of textual criticism. This tool, or rather this method for evaluating all the manuscripts of a New Testament corpus, is based on a series of test passages. These short units have been carefully selected and are spread over the complete range of a book (or a corpus) of scripture like a net. These passages make it possible to evaluate the quality of a manuscript and determine whether it belongs to a certain type of text, that is, to the Byzantine or to another text type. These test passages for the Catholic letters are found in volume 1, pp. 15-229, along with a collation of the readings found in all 540 manuscripts of the Catholic letters. Let us look, for example, at test passage no. 2[3] in table 9.

2. Paul Maas, *Textual Criticism*, trans. Barbara Flower (Oxford: 1958), p. 1.
3. Aland, *Texte und Textwert*, p. 17.

Table 9. Test passage no. 2, James 1:12[4]

■■   2 JAK. 1,12

στεφανον... ον επηγγειλατο ADD.

1   ADD. ο κυριος

018	020	025	049	056	0142	0246	1	2	3
5	6	18	35	36	38	42	43	51	57
62	69	76	82	88	90	93	94	97	103
104	105	122	131	133	141	142	149	172	175
177	180	181	189	197	201	203	204	205	206C
209	216	218	221	223	226	234	250	254	256
296	302	307	308	309	312	314	319	321	326
327	328	330	337	363	365	367	378	383	384
385	386	390	393	394	400	404	421	424	425
429	431	432	436	440	442	444	450	451	452
453	454	456	457	458	460	462	464	465	466
467	468	469	479	483	489	491	496	522	567
582	592	601	603	604	605	606	607	608	610
614	615	617	618	619	620	622	623	624	625
626	627	628	629	630	632	634	635	636	637
638	639	640	641	642	643	644	664	665	676
680	699	720	757	796	801	808	824	832	876
901	910	911	912	913	914	915	917	918	919
920	921	922	927	928	935	941	959	986	997
999	1003	1022	1040	1058	1067	1069	1070	1072	1075
1094	1099	1100	1101	1102	1103	1104	1105	1106	1107
1115	1127	1149	1161	1162	1240	1242	1244	1245	1247
1248	1249	1250	1251	1270	1277	1292	1297	1311	1315
1319	1352	1354	1359	1360	1367	1390	1398	1400	1404
1405	1409	1424	1448	1456	1482	1490	1495	1501	1503
1505	1508	1509	1521	1524	1548	1563	1573	1594	1595
1597	1598	1599	1610	1611	1617	1618	1619	1622	1626
1628	1636	1637	1643	1646	1649	1652	1656	1668	1678
1702	1704	1718	1719	1721	1722	1723	1725	1726	1727
1728	1730	1731	1732	1733	1734	1736	1737	1738	1740
1741	1742	1743	1744	1745	1746	1747	1748	1749	1750
1752	1753	1754	1757	1758	1761	1763	1765	1767	1768
1769	1780	1827	1828	1830	1831	1832	1835	1837	1838
1839	1841	1845	1847	1848	1849	1850	1851	1853	1854
1855	1856	1858	1859	1860	1861	1862S	1863	1864	1865
1867	1868	1869	1870	1871	1872	1874	1875	1876	1877
1880	1882	1885	1888	1889	1890	1891	1892	1893	1894
1895	1896	1897	1902	1903C	1904	2080	2085	2086	2125
2127	2130	2131	2138	2143	2147	2180	2186	2191	2194
2197	2200	2201	2218	2221	2242	2243	2255	2261	2279
2289	2303	2310	2318	2352	2356	2378	2400	2401	2404
2412	2423	2431	2466	2473	2475	2483	2484	2494	2495
2502	2508	2511	2516	2523	2541	2544	2554	2558	2587
2625	2626	2627	2652	2674	2675	2691	2696	2704	2705
2712	2718	2723	2736	2746	2774	2776	2777	2799	

4. It may be useful to list in alphabetical order the terms used in this and the following tables: Add = addition; Anzahl der Zeugen = total number of witnesses; bezeugte Variante = the attested reading; Filmfehler = filming error; Luecke = lacuna in manuscript; mit Mehrheitstext = with the Majority text; mit Singulaerlesart = with a singular reading; sine add = without addition; Testst(elle/n) = Test passage(s); Uebereinstim(mende) Zeugen = supporting witnesses; Unleserlich = illegible; zu bearbeitende Teststelle = passages to be considered.

ANZAHL DER ZEUGEN: 449

1B   ADD. κυριος

04	61	263	398	459	616	621	631	633	656
794	1642	1720	1729	1759	1829	1842	1843	1873	1899
1903*	2288	2501	2653						

ANZAHL DER ZEUGEN: 24

2   SINE ADD.

P23	01	02	03	044	81	206*	996	1661	2344

ANZAHL DER ZEUGEN: 10

3   ADD. ο θεος

4	33	322	323	547	945	1175	1241	1243	1609
1735	1739	1852	1857	1886	2298	2464	2492		

ANZAHL DER ZEUGEN: 18

4   ADD. ο αψευδης θεος

1751   2374   2805

ANZAHL DER ZEUGEN: 3

X   UNLESERLICH

1384

ANZAHL DER ZEUGEN: 1

Y   FILMFEHLER

102   110   325   1717

ANZAHL DER ZEUGEN: 4

Z   LUECKE

P9	P20	P54	P72	P74	P78	P81	048	093	0116
0156	0173	0206	0209	0232	0245	0247	0251	0285	0296
356	368	498	506	517	602	612	712	743	1066
1523	1526	1673	1724	1762	1836	1840	1844	1846	1862
1881	2441	2527	2716	2731	2741				

ANZAHL DER ZEUGEN: 46

A first glance reveals what the Majority text reads: it adds the implicit subject ὁ κύριος. A clear subvariant of this reading (κύριος only) is found in a number of other manuscripts. This is followed by the reading we consider the original one, with no addition (= the Nestle reading). Finally, some manuscripts replace the added ὁ κύριος with ὁ θεός or expand it to ὁ ἀψευδὴς θεός. After listing the supporting witnesses for each reading, their total number is also shown.

The picture we gain from this randomly selected test passage recurs elsewhere almost consistently: the overwhelming majority of manuscripts support *one* reading, the reading of the *majority text*. This is the reading of the Byzantine text, to which some stray witnesses of different text types may also conform. On the whole the manuscripts listed are always the same. This shows how pointless it would be to list them all in an edition of the New Testament. These manuscripts are essentially mere copies, repeating the same text with only minor variation, irrelevant to the reconstruction of the original text, and properly to be eliminated.

Glancing through the list of test passages and collations also makes it obvious that the profusion of data represented cannot be managed or effectively arranged for evaluation without the aid of data processing. Taking any one manuscript through all the test passages could require a great amount of time. Therefore various rearrangements are offered in the last half of the volume (pp. 232-430) and in the remaining volumes for textual critics to use as they wish. For convenience in data processing and for elegance of presentation, each of the readings in a variant is given a number. In table 9 these identifying numbers are found immediately preceding each variant reading. The readings are arranged in the following sequence:[5]

1	The Majority text	(which includes the Byzantine text).
2	The ancient text	= the reading of Nestle-Aland[26], assumed to be the original text. If a critic prefers to identify a different reading as the original, there is no problem. The important thing here is for each reading to have an identifying number.
3, 4, 5, etc.		Readings other than those in 1 or 2 and hence special readings (*Sonderlesarten*), some of which can be highly important for identifying groups. Subvariants are marked by adding B, C, etc. to the numbers. When the Majority text and the ancient text coincide, this is indicated by 1/2, sometimes abbreviated to 1/ (cf. table 13).

By substituting these numbers for the full variants a maximum of information can be given in very limited space. The precise wording of a variant may always be found by reference to the full listing of test passages.

Of greatest importance are the evaluations which follow next. But before we proceed to these a crucial question must be posed: Can we actually evaluate the textual quality of manuscripts on the basis of these test passages? Are they actually significant, and is their number sufficient? In brief, the answer is: yes. This answer is based on our practical experience with them in the Institute at Münster. These test passages have consistently produced remarkably accurate evaluations when used in a variety of different projects, and they amply suffice

for the three main tasks outlined above. Special investigations, of course, will still need to make use of full collations. But even such special investigations may now be based on all the manuscripts whose relevance has been demonstrated by this test.

Essential for the evaluations are the lists in the second volume: the Supplementary List (*Ergänzungsliste*), and the crucial Main List (*Hauptliste*).

The **Supplementary List** (a separate insert in the pocket of vol. II, part 1) takes each manuscript successively as the basis for a comparison with every other manuscript in the total number of test passages. For each manuscript in turn all the other manuscripts are listed in descending order according to their percentage of agreement with it.

Take, for example, the familiar 614 in table 10:

Table 10. Relational statistics for 614 as control manuscript

```
••614      (89 TESTST., DAVON 44 MIT MEHRHEITSTEXT,  1 MIT SINGULAERLESART)
• 100.00% 2/2 0246 • 96.62% 86/89 2412 • 85.37% 76/89 1292 • 82.93% 73/88
1611 • 81.37% 70/86 2138 • 79.75% 71/89 2200 • 79.50% 70/88 2495 • 77.50%
69/89 1505 • 77.31% 58/75 206 • 76.12% 67/88 2652 • 75.25% 67/89 630
• 75.00% 3/4 0209 • 73.00% 65/89 429 • 72.18% 26/36 1523 • 71.87% 64/89
2147 • 70.25% 26/37 1844 • 69.31% 61/88 522 • 68.31% 41/60 1758 • 68.12%
60/88 1890 • 68.00% 17/25 1836 • 66.25% 59/89 1524 • 64.00% 57/89 1490
• 62.50% 55/88 876 1448 1765 2374 • 61.75% 55/89 254 • 60.62% 54/89 36 378
2494 • 60.18% 53/88 1831 1832 • 59.06% 52/88 453 • 57.93% 51/88 2243
• 57.87% 11/19 197 • 57.43% 50/87 621 ¶ 27/47 517 • 57.25% 51/89 436 918
2080 2197 • 57.12% 4/7 1526 • 56.81% 50/88 720 • 56.43% 48/85 1678
• 56.12% 50/89 296 307 • 56.00% 14/25 743 • 55.87% 19/34 368 • 55.62%
49/88 1067 2541 • 55.50% 5/9 612 • 55.00% 49/89 94 321 1409 1501 1885 2508
44/80 1856 • 54.50% 48/88 808 1852 • 53.87% 48/89 442 1643 2298 • 53.43%
46/86 643 • 53.37% 47/88 464 1127
```

Note that 614 and 2412 (in second position)[5] agree in 96.62% of all the instances, that is, in 86 of the 89 mutually extant passages (in the remaining passages 614 has lacunae). Next comes 1292 with 85.37 percent agreement, and so forth.

In this list each variant reading is simply counted like any other; the significance of individual readings is not weighed. And yet the information gained is significant. If any manuscript agrees with another in 86 out of 89 instances (as do 614 and 2412), the incidence is so high that a direct relationship between them must be inferred: these are "sister manuscripts." But this does not occur very frequently, and the next closest manuscript recorded (1292) agrees in 76 of 89 instances, differing in 13 readings. The reasons for such a difference should be considered in detail, with reference to the complete collations of both manuscripts.

An important clue for the evaluation of agreement ratios is found in the parenthetical summary on the first line for each manuscript in the Supplementary List. It shows the total number of extant test passages (*Testst[ellen]*) in the

---

5. The 100 percent agreement between 0246 and 614 may be ignored. It is irrelevant because the figure is based on only two test passages: 0246 is a fragment.

control manuscript used as the base for comparison, the number of its agreements with the Majority text (*mit Mehrheitstext*) and of its singular readings (*mit Singulaerlesart*). When the number of agreements with the Majority text is high, there is also a relatively high number of manuscripts showing an agreement ratio of more than 90 percent. Manuscript 618 is an example in table 11.

Table 11. Relational statistics for 618 as control manuscript

```
••618     (98 TESTST., DAVON 85 MIT MEHRHEITSTEXT,  0 MIT SINGULAERLESART)
• 100.00% 7/7 1526 ¶ 5/5 640 ¶ 2/2 0246 2731 ¶ 1/1 P54 • 97.93% 96/98 177
337 • 96.93% 95/98 460 • 96.50% 28/29 644 • 96.00% 24/25 1652 2303
• 95.68% 45/47 624 • 94.81% 92/97 1738 • 92.81% 91/98 625 • 92.25% 12/13
2441 • 91.25% 63/69 122 • 90.87% 30/33 2799 • 90.00% 63/70 1277 ¶ 18/20
356 • 89.75% 88/98 638 1149 2423 • 89.68% 87/97 607 • 89.43% 85/95 941
1730 ¶ 17/19 197 • 89.31% 84/94 1859 • 89.25% 75/84 639 • 89.06% 49/55 602
• 88.87% 80/90 2356 ¶ 48/54 567 ¶ 8/9 612 • 88.75% 87/98 82 466 605 699
920 1668 1894 2484 • 88.62% 86/97 622 1244 2625 ¶ 78/88 2777 • 88.50%
85/96 627 • 88.37% 61/69 110 • 87.87% 80/91 314 997 • 87.75% 86/98 1 221
250 452 547 1103 1107 1161 1352 1841 1847 1851 • 87.68% 50/57 2310
• 87.62% 85/97 226 458 986 ¶ 78/89 2511 • 87.50% 84/96 457
```

This illustrates what we noticed above (p. 321) in our first example of test passage collations: the greatest number of manuscripts, comprising the bloc of Majority text witnesses in most instances, are always the same — they are manuscripts with a Byzantine text. The representatives of this text type are extremely homogeneous, exhibiting a high ratio of agreement among themselves.

For manuscripts with the fewest Majority readings, that is, most of the early manuscripts, exactly the opposite is true. Even the most closely related among them generally show agreement ratios of between 60 and 70 percent. This is clearly illustrated by the great uncials from 01 (ℵ) to 04 (C) in table 12. One of the reasons for this is that very few witnesses have survived from the early period of these manuscripts (their immediate relatives have all been lost). The early manuscripts also show a greater degree of independence than the later copies prepared so meticulously in Byzantium. In view of this fact, it is surprising to find as high an agreement ratio as 76.81 percent (73 of 95 instances) between 02 (A) and 2344 (eleventh century!), with the more familiar manuscripts 33, 1735, 81, 01, and 1739 trailing below.

The summaries are equally useful in evaluating manuscripts with a moderate proportion of majority readings, such as 614 (cf. table 10). There the 96 percent agreement with 2412 is extraordinary, but the manuscripts with 80 percent or more agreement also deserve to be examined carefully for their relationship to 614.

Thus the supplementary list with its parenthetical summaries contribute significantly toward accomplishing the first two tasks mentioned:

1. By distinguishing manuscripts of the majority text. These are all the manuscripts which read the Majority text in 60 to 70 percent *or more* of the test passages (including subgroups of the Byzantine text).

Table 12. Relational statistics for ℵ, A, B, C

••01 (98 TESTST., DAVON 19 MIT MEHRHEITSTEXT, 9 MIT SINGULAERLESART)
● 100.00% 2/2 P81 0156 0173 ¶ 1/1 0251 ● 75.00% 3/4 0209 ● 64.25% 63/98 02
● 62.06% 59/95 2344 ● 61.43% 51/83 33 ● 57.68% 56/97 044 ● 55.50% 10/18
048 ● 55.06% 54/98 03 ● 54.50% 36/66 04 ● 54.06% 53/98 2805 ● 53.00% 52/98
1739 ● 52.62% 50/95 1852 ● 52.43% 43/82 2464 ● 51.00% 50/98 1735 ● 50.00%
18/36 1846 ¶ 5/10 P74 ¶ 1/2 P23 0296 ● 49.43% 48/97 1243 ● 48.93% 48/98 81
● 46.93% 46/98 436 ● 45.81% 44/96 623 ● 44.87% 44/98 5 ● 44.31% 43/97 1067
● 43.87% 43/98 322 323 442 ● 43.81% 32/73 1881 ● 42.81% 42/98 1409
● 42.25% 41/97 2541 ● 42.18% 38/90 025 ● 41.75% 38/91 1241 ● 40.81% 40/98
945 ● 40.62% 39/96 621 ● 39.12% 38/97 1611 ● 38.87% 35/90 2138 ● 38.75%
38/98 1505 ● 38.18% 13/34 1836 ● 37.75% 37/98 630 2298 ● 37.06% 36/97 2495
● 36.68% 36/98 1292 2200 ● 35.68% 35/98 1845 ● 35.50% 16/45 1523 ● 35.00%
34/97 1448 ● 34.75% 16/46 1844 ● 34.68% 34/98 6 ● 34.62% 26/75 206
● 34.00% 33/97 61 808 2374 ● 33.68% 31/92 629 ● 33.31% 1/3 0232 ● 32.93%
32/97 1718 ● 32.62% 32/98 642 ● 32.56% 29/89 614 ● 32.25% 30/93 2492
● 31.93% 31/97 218 1359 1837 ● 31.62% 31/98 676 1842 2412

••02 (98 TESTST., DAVON 17 MIT MEHRHEITSTEXT, O MIT SINGULAERLESART)
● 100.00% 3/3 0232 ¶ 2/2 0173 ¶ 1/1 0251 ● 83.31% 15/18 048 ● 76.81% 73/95
2344 ● 73.43% 61/83 33 ● 69.37% 68/98 1735 ● 68.31% 67/98 81 ● 64.25%
63/98 01 ● 63.25% 62/98 1739 ● 61.18% 60/98 436 ● 60.93% 50/82 2464
● 60.56% 40/66 04 ● 60.00% 6/10 P74 ● 59.37% 57/96 623 ● 59.12% 58/98 2805
● 58.31% 21/36 1846 ● 56.68% 55/97 1067 ● 56.06% 55/98 03 ● 55.62% 54/97
1243 ● 55.06% 54/98 5 ● 54.62% 53/97 044 ● 54.06% 53/98 322 323 442 1409
● 53.62% 51/95 1852 ● 53.56% 52/97 2541 ● 52.00% 38/73 1881 ● 50.00% 49/98
2298 ¶ 2/4 0209 ¶ 1/2 P23 P81 0156 0296 2731 2741 ● 48.31% 44/91 1241
● 46.93% 46/98 945 ● 46.87% 45/96 621 ● 44.87% 44/98 1292 ● 44.43% 4/9 612
● 43.25% 42/97 2374 ● 42.81% 42/98 1505 1845 ● 42.25% 41/97 1611 ● 42.18%
38/90 2138 ● 41.18% 40/97 2495 ● 40.43% 36/89 614 ● 40.18% 39/97 1359 1718
● 40.00% 36/90 025 ¶ 2/5 640 ● 39.75% 39/98 2200 2412 ● 39.12% 38/97 808 ¶
36/92 629 ● 38.87% 35/90 720 ● 38.75% 38/98 36 642 ● 38.12% 37/97 218 453
1563 ● 37.75% 37/98 6 93 2197

••03 (98 TESTST., DAVON 1 MIT MEHRHEITSTEXT, 4 MIT SINGULAERLESART)
● 100.00% 3/3 0232 ¶ 2/2 0156 0173 ¶ 1/1 0251 0285 ● 62.18% 61/98 1739
● 61.00% 58/95 1852 ● 59.06% 39/66 04 ● 57.68% 56/97 044 ● 56.06% 55/98 02
● 55.06% 54/98 01 ● 54.62% 53/97 1243 ● 53.37% 39/73 1881 ● 52.75% 19/36
1846 ● 50.00% 49/98 322 323 ¶ 19/38 P72 ¶ 5/10 P74 ¶ 1/2 P23 P81 0296
● 49.43% 47/95 2344 ¶ 45/91 1241 ● 48.18% 40/83 33 ● 44.43% 8/18 048
● 41.81% 41/98 81 1735 ● 40.81% 40/98 436 945 1505 2805 ● 40.18% 39/97
1067 ● 40.00% 36/90 2138 ● 39.75% 39/98 2298 ● 38.18% 13/34 1836 ● 38.12%
37/97 2495 ● 37.75% 31/82 2464 ● 37.06% 36/97 1611 ● 36.43% 35/96 623
● 35.68% 35/98 442 1409 ● 33.62% 33/98 2200 ● 33.31% 30/90 025 ¶ 15/45
1523 ● 32.93% 32/97 2541 ● 32.62% 32/98 630 ● 32.56% 29/89 614 ● 31.62%
31/98 5 ● 30.62% 23/75 206 ● 30.56% 30/98 1175 2412 ● 30.18% 29/96 621
● 29.56% 29/98 1292 1845 ● 28.81% 28/97 1448 ● 28.25% 13/46 1844 ● 27.81%
27/97 522 ● 26.75% 26/97 808 1718 2374 ● 26.06% 24/92 629 ● 25.75% 25/97
1359 ¶ 24/93 2492 ● 25.50% 25/98 6 429 ● 24.68% 24/97 1563

••04 (66 TESTST., DAVON 11 MIT MEHRHEITSTEXT, 4 MIT SINGULAERLESART)
● 100.00% 2/2 0173 ¶ 1/1 P81 0251 0285 ● 65.43% 36/55 33 ● 65.12% 43/66
1739 ● 61.50% 40/65 1243 ● 60.56% 40/66 02 ● 60.00% 3/5 640 ● 59.37% 38/64
2344 ● 59.06% 39/66 03 81 ● 57.12% 28/49 1881 ¶ 4/7 P74 ● 56.87% 37/65 044
● 56.00% 37/66 323 945 ● 54.50% 36/66 01 322 ● 53.31% 8/15 1846 ● 53.00%
35/66 436 1735 2805 ● 51.87% 27/52 2464 ● 51.56% 33/64 1852 ● 50.00% 33/66
2298 ¶ 5/10 048 ¶ 1/2 0246 ● 49.18% 32/65 1067 ● 48.43% 32/66 5 ● 46.93%
31/66 442 1409 ● 46.87% 30/64 1241 ● 45.43% 30/66 621 1505 ● 44.56% 29/65
623 2495 ● 44.43% 12/27 1844 ● 43.75% 7/16 1836 ● 43.06% 28/65 1611 2541 ¶
25/58 2138 ● 41.87% 13/31 P72 ● 40.87% 27/66 2200 ● 39.37% 26/66 630
● 39.06% 25/64 1678 ● 38.43% 25/65 2374 ¶ 20/52 206 ¶ 10/26 1523 ● 37.87%
25/66 36 307 453 918 1292 2197 2412 ● 37.50% 6/16 197 ● 37.06% 23/62 025
● 36.87% 24/65 1359 1563 1718 ● 36.81% 21/57 614 ● 36.31% 24/66 218
● 35.87% 14/39 2718 ● 35.37% 23/65 808 1448 2652

2. By identifying, although only roughly at this stage, all the manuscripts that must be considered for a major critical edition and deserve more careful examination. These are the codices which read the Majority text in *no more than* 60 percent of the test passages (or, perhaps better: 50 percent).

The **Main List** (*Haupliste*) can yield considerably more detailed inferences. The Supplementary List is based on counting variants without weighing their significance, but the Main List considers such distinctions thanks to a principle of New Testament textual transmission that has long been familiar. It is known that the Byzantine text is not preserved solely in purely Koine manuscripts. In medieval Byzantium it had become so dominant (so subtly pervasive and firmly lodged in the scribes' minds) that to varying degrees it found its way into copies of non-Byzantine origin as well, with or without the copyists' awareness. This means that an agreement in a Koine reading between any two manuscripts tells very little about their mutual relationships. There is always the possibility that later copyists would inadvertently introduce Byzantine readings when copying from a manuscript of a different text type.

In the Main List, therefore, both majority readings and singular readings are disregarded for each control manuscript, and only the remaining passages have been considered. As in the Supplementary List, each control manuscript has been compared in turn with every other manuscript in the total number of test passages where the control manuscript has neither the Byzantine text nor a singular reading. The instances of agreement have been counted and tabulated in descending order in volume 2, parts 1 (p^{23}-999) and 2 (1003-2805).

The two lists, the Supplementary List and the Main List, are complementary. As a **general rule**, if the same manuscripts rank high on both lists for a given control manuscript, it may be assumed that the two are related to each other. A high percentage of agreement on only one of the two lists means very little.

For practical reasons it was decided to print in the Main List only the 66 manuscripts most closely related to each control manuscript. These will prove sufficient for nearly any investigation. If required, however, a complete printout is always available in Münster.

For 614 (cf. table 13), this rule means that the seven manuscripts at the top of the Main List (omitting the first two with 100 percent agreement for obvious reasons) are most probably related to 614. They definitely deserve to be more closely examined in any study of manuscript 614 and its kin. The same applies to 206 and 630, the manuscripts that follow on the list. On the other hand, it applies to 1852 only to a very limited extent if at all, and it does not apply at all to the next manuscripts, 1739, p^{74}, and 03. The reason for this can easily be recognized. The parenthetical summaries for these manuscripts as well as the descriptive list of manuscripts in volume 3 clearly show that these manuscripts have a very high proportion of readings in class 2 and in the higher classes, but not of class 1 readings. This means that in the Main List they *must* show a

Table 13. Agreements with control manuscript 614

614 : 44 ZU BEARBEITENDE TESTSTELLEN + 1 MIT SINGULAERLESART + 44 MIT MEHRHEITSTEXT   427

TESTSTELLE			1	3	5	7	8	9	11	12	14	19	20	22	23	24	25	30	32	34	35	36	37	39	43	45	46
UEBEREINSTIM. ZEUGEN			149	3	22	46	17	139	56	20	59	467	76	36	56	48	5	115	25	56	33	17	6	29	27	29	73
BEZEUGTE VARIANTE			2	11B	3	2	3	2	2	4	2	2/	2	2	2	2	3	2	2	2	5B	5	4	2	2	3	4
0173	100.00%	(1/ 1)	2	2																							
0232	100.00%	(1/ 1)	2	2																							
2412	97.68%	(43/44)			12																						
2138	90.43%	(38/42)																									
1505	88.62%	(39/44)		1/										2C			1		1				1			1F	
2495	88.31%	(38/43)		1/		1		4	1								1	U								2C	
1611	86.31%	(38/44)		1/													1		1	1B			1			2C	
1292	84.06%	(37/44)		1/													1		1	1B	1		2			1F	
2200	79.50%	(35/44)		1/													1						1		1	1	
1852	76.68%	(33/43)		1/						2	3		2	2B			1					1	1			3D	2
206	73.62%	(28/38)		1/		1	6								1		1		2	2	2	1	2			1	2
630	72.68%	(32/44)		1/		1											1		1		4	1	1		2	1D	
1523	70.56%	(12/17)	2	2	2	2	2	2	2	2	2	2	2	2	2	2	2			2	4	2	2		2	1	
1739	70.43%	(31/44)	2	2	2	2	6	2	2	2	2	2	2	2	2	2	2		1	2	2	1	2		1	1D	
P74	66.62%	(4/ 6)		1/			W	4		2					2B		2				4	2	2			1B	
03	65.87%	(29/44)	2	2			5		1		3						2			1B	N	2	1	6B		1B	2
429	63.62%	(28/44)		11	2	1	2	2	2	2	3	6	2	2C	2	2	1		1	1B	4	1	2	5	1D	2	2
522	63.62%	(28/44)		1/	2	1	5	4	2					1	1		2	38	1	2	4	1	2	5		2	1/
02	59.06%	(26/44)		1/			2	2	2	2	2	2	2	2	2	2	1		1B		2	2	1	2		1	
1243	59.06%	(26/44)	N	1/	2	1	5	2	2	3	3					1		1		N	1	2	5	2	1	Z
1844	58.81%	(10/17)	N	1/	2	1	2	2	2	2	2	2	2	2	2	2	2		1		4	2	2	5	2	2	1/
1881	58.56%	(17/29)		1/			2	2	2	2	2	2		2		1	2		1	1	N	2	2	5	2	3C	Z
2652	58.12%	(25/43)		1/		1	4	1	1	1	1					1	2				1/	1	1	1		2	
04	57.68%	(15/26)		1/			1	2B		6B				2C			2B				4	5	2	5	1	3E	
2344	57.12%	(24/42)		1/			1	1	1	1	1	2C	2C	2C	2	1	1		1		1/	1	5	6C	5	2	
044	56.81%	(25/44)		7				2B			3			2C			2B				6C	1	5	6C	1		
436	56.81%	(25/44)		1/	2	1	1	1	1	1					1	1	1	38	1	1	1/	1	1				
2147	56.81%	(25/44)		1/			5	1	1	2B				2C	1	1	2B	38	1B		4	1	2	5		3E	
2298	56.81%	(25/44)	N	1/	2		8		1	3	1			2C			2		1B	1	4	2	1	5	1	2	2
33	56.75%	(21/37)	N	1/	2	1B	8	3	1	1				1	1	1	1		1		4	1	1	6			Z
322	54.50%	(24/44)	N	1/	2	1	8	3	1	2B	1			1	1	1	2		1	x	4	2	2	6		3E	Z
323	54.50%	(24/44)	N	1/	2	1	8	3	1	1	1	1	1	1	1	1	2		1		4	2	2	6	1		5B
945	54.50%	(24/44)	N	1/	2	1	6	3	1	2B	1	1	1	1	1	1	1		1B		4	1	2	5	5		

Table 13. (Continued)

614 : 44 ZU BEARBEITENDE TESTSTELLEN + 1 MIT SINGULAERLESART + 44 MIT MEHRHEITSTEXT 428

TESTSTELLE	1	3	5	7	8	9	11	12	14	19	20	22	23	24	25	30	32	34	35	36	37	39	43	45	46
	149	3	22	46	17	139	56	20	59	467	76	36	56	48	5	115	25	56	33	17	6	29	27	29	73
UEBEREINSTIM. ZEUGEN / BEZEUGTE VARIANTE	2	3	3	2	3	2	2	4	2	1/	2	2	2	2	3	2	2	2	5	5	4	2	2	3	4
1735 54.50% (24/44)	Z	Z	1/	Z	1	Z	Z	Z	Z	Z	Z	2C	2C		3	Z	Z	Z	Z	Z	1	6B	Z	Z	Z
1846 53.81% (7/13)	Z	Z	Z		Z	Z		Z	Z	Z	Z	Z	Z		1	Z	Z		Z	Z	Z		Z	Z	X
1067 53.43% (23/43)		Z	1/		1							2C	1		2C		Z		Z	Z	1		1	3C	4C
1241 52.37% (22/42)	9	9	1/		5			2B					1	1	2	Z	1		4	1	2	6C		3C	
2541 52.25% (23/44)	1/	Z	Z	Z	1	Z	Z	1	Z	Z	Z	2C	1		2	Z	Z	Z	Z	1	1	Z	Z	1	Z
048 50.00% (5/10)	Z	Z	Z	Z	Z	Z	Z	Z	Z	Z	Z	X	X		Z	Z	Z	Z	Z	Z	Z	Z	Z	Z	Z
0296 50.00% (1/ 2)	Z	Z	Z	Z	Z	Z	Z	Z	Z	Z	Z	Z	Z		Z	Z	Z	Z	Z	Z	2C	6B	Z	Z	
442 50.00% (22/44)	Z	1/	1/		8		Z	2	Z	1	1		1	1	1	3B	1	1B	4C	1	2C		5C		
1524 50.00% (22/44)	1	1/		1	1	1	1		1			1	1	1	1B		1	Y	Y	1	1		Y	3D	Z
1758 50.00% (15/30)	1/	1/		1	1		1						1		1		1		1	1	1	5	Y	Y	Y
1890 50.00% (22/44)		12B			1		1	1	1					7	1		7	1	1/	1	1		1	1	1/
1448 48.81% (21/43)		1/	1/		8	1	1	1	1			2C	1		1		1	1	1/	1	1	5	1	5	
2374 48.81% (21/43)		1/	1/	1	2	1		3	1			2C	1		1		1B	1B	4	1	2	5	1	1G	Z
81 47.68% (21/44)		1/	1/		8	1	1	2	1	6			3	1	2B		1	1	4	1	2B	5	5B	3C	X
621 47.68% (21/44)		1/	1/	1	1	1	1	1	1			2C	1		2		1	1B	4	1	1	5	1	3C	4C
1409 47.68% (21/44)		1/	1/	1	1	1	V1	1	1			1B	1		2		1	1	6B	1	1	1	Z	6	1/
623 47.56% (20/42)		11	1/		1	1	1	2	1				1		2		1B	1	2	2	2	5	1	2	
01 45.43% (20/44)	1/	1/	1/	1	1	1	1	2	Z	Z	Z	Z	1	Z	Z	Z	Z	1B	Z	Z	1	1	1	Z	Z
5 45.43% (20/44)	11	1/	1/	1	1	1	1	3	1	1	Z	Z	1	1	1	Z	1	1B	Z	2	2	5	1	3C	5
1836 45.43% (5/11)	Z	Z	Z	Z	2	Z	Z	2	Z	2	Z	Z	Z	Z	Z	Z	Z	Z	Z	Z	1	1	1	3D	
2805 45.43% (20/44)		Z	1/		8	1	1	3	Z	4	Z	Z	1	1	2	1	1B	1	4	1	2	6	1	3C	1
025 43.87% (18/41)		1/	1/	1	8	1	1	2	Z		1	2C	1		2		1	1B	4	1	2	5	1	3C	
2464 43.87% (18/41)		12	1/		1	1	1	1	Z		1	3	1		1		1	1	3B	1	1	5	1	1	
1490 43.12% (19/44)	1	1/	1/	1	8	1	1	1	Z		Z	Z	1	1	1	3B	1B	1B	1/	1	2B	2C	5C	2B	
P72 42.81% (6/14)	Z	Z	1/	1	1	1	1	1	Z	Z	Z	Z	1	Z	1		1	1	1	1	1	1	1	3D	Z
254 40.87% (18/44)	1	1/	1/	1	8	1	1	1B	Z	1	1	2C	1	1	1	3B	1	1B	1/	1	1	1	1	1D	5
808 37.18% (16/43)	1	1/	1/		1	1	Z	1	Z	1	1	3	1		2	U1	U1	Z	1/	1	1	1	1	W	
1765 37.18% (16/43)	1	1/	1/	1	6	1	1	1B	1	8	1	1B	1	1	1	3B	1D	1B	4	1	2D	2D	1	1	1/
378 36.31% (16/44)	1	12	1/	1	5	1	Z	3	1		1	3	1		1		5	1	1/	1	1	5	1	2D	
876 36.31% (16/44)	1	8	1/		8	1	1	1	1		1	2C	1	1	1	5	1B	1B	4	2	1	8		1	1/
1175 36.31% (16/44)	1	1/	1/	1		1					1	1	1					1	1/		1				
2492 36.31% (16/44)	1	1/	1/	1								2C								1					
1127 34.87% (15/43)	1	1/	1/	1	8	1	1	1	1	1	1	2C	1		1	5	1B	1B		2		1	1	1	4B

Table 13. (Continued)

614 : 44 ZU BEARBEITENDE TESTSTELLEN + 1 MIT SINGULAERLESART + 44 MIT MEHRHEITSTEXT 429

TESTSTELLE	47	50	54	56	57	58	60	63	65	68	70	71	72	77	78	81	86	88	89
UEBEREINSTIM. ZEUGEN	23	23	76	475	93	26	108	67	139	38	286	74	445	45	85	56	75	24	54
BEZEUGTE VARIANTE	5	2	2/	2	2	2	2	3	3	2	1/	4	1/	2	2	2	2	8	2
0173 100.00% (1/ 1)	N	N	N	N	N	N	N	N	N	N	N	N	N	N	N	N	N	N	N
0232 100.00% (1/ 1)	N	N	N	N	N	N	N	N	N	N	N	N	N	N	N	N	N	N	N
2412 97.68% (43/44)																			
2138 90.43% (38/42)																			
1505 88.62% (39/44)								2D									1		3
2495 88.31% (38/43)								2C									1		3B
1611 86.31% (38/44)																	1		3B
1292 84.06% (37/44)																	3		3
2200 79.50% (35/44)	4	5		1/B													1	1/	N
1852 76.68% (33/43)			1									5	1/B	2B				N	N
206 73.62% (28/38)	N							2D			3	5		1B			N	N	
630 72.68% (32/44)	N											5					1	1/	
1523 70.56% (12/17)	N																1	1/	
1739 70.43% (31/44)	N	N	N	N		1										2B			N
P74 66.62% (4/ 6)	N					N	N												
03 65.87% (29/44)	2	5	N			1	N	N	N		N	1/	1/B	Z	Z	Z	1	N	N
429 63.62% (28/44)	6	5	1			1	N	N	1/		1/		1/B	1	1	1	1	1/	1
522 63.62% (28/44)	3B	5	1											1	1	1	1	1/	1
02 59.06% (26/44)	2	1								2C				1B	1	1	1	1/	1
1243 59.06% (26/44)	N	5	4	1/B					3B			5	1/K	2D	2C		1	1/	1
1844 58.81% (10/17)	2	2				1						5			1		1	1/	2C
1881 58.56% (17/29)	5B																		2C
2652 58.12% (25/43)	2	4B	4						U	1	Z	1/	Z						
04 57.68% (15/26)	6	3								1	N								
2344 57.12% (24/42)	6	1				1			X	1	N		Z		Z			Z	W
044 56.81% (25/44)	1	1				1				1		1/	1/F					X	4
436 56.81% (25/44)	5B	1																	
2147 56.81% (25/44)	2	4B				1							1/I	2B				1/	2C
2298 56.81% (25/44)	6	1				1			1/B							1	X	1/	X
33 56.75% (21/37)	2					1				7		1/						1/	
322 54.50% (24/44)	2					1						W	X		2E			X	
323 54.50% (24/44)	2					1						1/						X	
945 54.50% (24/44)	2					1	1					3					1		1

Table 13. (Continued)

614 : 44 ZU BEARBEITENDE TESTSTELLEN + 1 MIT SINGULAERLESART + 44 MIT MEHRHEITSTEXT 430

TESTSTELLE			47	50	54	56	57	58	60	63	65	68	70	71	72	77	78	81	86	88	89
UEBEREINSTIM.	ZEUGEN		23	23	76	475	93	26	108	67	139	38	286	74	445	45	85	56	75	24	54
	BEZEUGTE VARIANTE		5	2	2	1/	2	2	2	2	2	2	1/	4	1/	2	2	2	2	2	2
1735	54.50%	(24/44)	6	1	1	1/B		1			1/					1				1/	U
1846	53.81%	(7/13)	2	2	Z	Z	Z	Z	Z	Z	1/	1	3	5	1/I			1		1/	1
1067	53.43%	(23/43)	1	1	1				1					3				1C		1/	1
1241	52.37%	(22/42)	2					1B		2B	3B	5	3	3	2B	2B		Z		1/	Z
2541	52.25%	(23/44)	1	1	1			1							1/I	X	Z	Z		Z	Z
048	50.00%	(5/10)	6	1	1			1	Z	Z	Z	Z	3	5		X	Z	1C	Z	Z	Z
0296	50.00%	(1/ 2)	1	1				Z					M	5			Z	Z		Z	1
442	50.00%	(22/44)	2	2	Z	Z	Z	1	Z	Z	Z	Z	3	5		1	Z	Z	Z	1/	1
1524	50.00%	(22/44)	5B													1B	1		1	Z	1
1758	50.00%	(15/30)	Y	5B	1		Y		1	1	3B	1	1/	5		1	1	1	1	Z	1
1890	50.00%	(22/44)	Y	1	1	1	1		1		1				1/H	1	1	1	2	1/	1
1448	48.81%	(21/43)	X	1	1											1			3	1/	1
2374	48.81%	(21/43)	4	1	1		U3	1		2E		1							1	1	1
81	47.68%	(21/44)	6	6	1		1		Z				3	5	2B	2B	1B			1/	
621	47.68%	(21/44)	1	6	1	1/B		1B						5			1	1	1	1/	4
1409	47.68%	(21/44)	7	1					1											1/	1
623	47.56%	(20/42)	6	4B		1/B		1			3B	2C		5	1/I	2B	1	1	1	1/	2C
01	45.45%	(20/44)	6	1		1/B		1	1	Z	Z	Z	4B	1		1			1	Z	1
5	45.43%	(20/44)	6	4B	Z	1/B	Z	1	Z	Z	Z	Z		5		2B	Z	2B	Z	Z	Z
1836	45.45%	(5/11)	4	2			Z	1	1	Z		1		X		2C	1	1	1	1/	1
2805	45.45%	(20/44)	1	1	Z	Z	Z	1	3	2E	1/	2C		5	1/E	2C	1	2B	Z	1/	2C
025	43.87%	(18/41)	2	3B				1		Z	Z	Z	2	5	1/B	1	1	1	1	Z	1
2464	43.87%	(18/41)	6	4B	1			1	Z	3B	3B		1	5	1/I	2B	Z	Z	1	1/	Z
1490	43.12%	(19/44)	1	5B	1	1/B	Z		1	Z	Z	1	Z	5	1B	1	2	N	1	Z	1
P72	42.81%	(6/14)	2	2B	2	Z		1	Z	Z	Z	Z	2	5	1/I	1B	1	1	1	1/	2C
254	40.87%	(18/44)	5B					1		Z	Z		Z	1/	1/	Z	Z	Z	Z	1/	1
808	37.18%	(16/43)	1	1	1	1/B	1	1	1	Z	1	1	3	1	2B	1		1	1	1/	1
1765	37.18%	(16/43)		3B	1		1	1	1		1/	1	3	1/		2B		1		1	1
378	36.31%	(16/44)	5B	4B	4		1	1	1			1	3		1	1	1	1	1	1/	1
876	36.31%	(16/44)		3B	1		1	1	1	1		1	3	1		1		1	1	1/	1
1175	36.31%	(16/44)	2	3C	1	1/B	1	1	1	1	1/	1	1	1/	1	1		1	1	1/	1
2492	36.31%	(16/44)	1	1	1		1	1	1	1	1/	1	1	5		1		1	1		1
1127	34.87%	(15/43)	1	5	1		1	1	1		1/	4			2B			2B		1/	1

considerable number of agreements with 614 (which contains 44 passages for comparison). In the test passages excluded from the Main List, where 614 has class 1 readings, the other manuscripts (1739, p[74], 03) nearly always have a different reading than 614. Thus the apparently high number of agreements in the Main List does not reflect any close relationship. Accordingly we do not find 1739, p[74], or 03 associated at all with 614 in the Supplementary List, where *all* the test passages are considered. Actually they rank so low that they have been omitted from the list, where only the top 60 to 70 manuscripts are shown. For this reason the general rule mentioned earlier (cf. p. 325) must be strictly observed: only when a manuscript ranks high in *both* lists may a close relationship be inferred.

There is, however, another reason why the Main List can be so extremely helpful a tool. The first line of the table headings lists across the page all the extant test passages (*Teststelle*) for each manuscript taken in turn as a control manuscript, identifying each test passage by its number in the collations found in volume 1. Taking 614 again as an example (cf. table 13), the third line of the headings identifies the reading of the control manuscript (*Bezeugte Variante*) by its number in the collation (cf. table 9; by the principle on p. 325 it can never be "1"). The second line is particularly important for indicating the total number of witnesses that share this reading (*Übereinstimmende Zeugen*). The table itself shows the number of the reading in each test passage for each of the manuscripts listed in the left margin, with blank spaces indicating agreement with the control manuscript.[6] Thus 2412 agrees with 614 in all the text passages, differing only in passage no. 25.[7]

This table provides a basis for evaluating the agreement ratios shown in the left margin. This can be demonstrated easily, for example, in test passage 19 where manuscript 614 has reading 1/2 along with 467 other witnesses. It is obvious that this reading tells us nothing in particular about the relationship between these witnesses. Each manuscript may have adopted this reading from any of the others. It says nothing about the exemplar of any manuscript.

Test passage 37 is quite different. Here 614 has reading 4, an obvious error shared by only 6 other manuscripts. These may be identified by the blank spaces below as minuscules 2412, 2138, 1505, 2495, 1292, and also 1890 (cf. p. 428 just above center page). As this reading is derived from the Byzantine text, it may be assumed that in this instance the manuscripts have copied the error from a common source. The error consequently serves to link together the manuscripts that share it and may serve as a supplementary argument for their being related if other evidence is present. A single such apparent "linking error" is insufficient

---

6. Z = lacuna in the manuscript; see vol. 1, pp. xiv f. for the other sigla used in these tables.

7. 2412 has here a rather interesting misreading which is not discussed in palaeographic manuals. The reading of the manuscript at Jas. 5:20 is γινωσκέτω ὅτι ὁ ἐπιστρέψας ἁμαρτωλὸν ἐκ πλάνης ὁδοῦ αὐτοῦ καὶ καλύψει (sic) ἐκ θανάτου καὶ καλύψει πλῆθος ἁμαρτιῶν. Ἀμήν. Evidently the exemplar of 2412 agreed with the text of 614, but the copyist misread it and then made only a partial correction of the error (for what psychological reason?). The difference in reading no. 25 is consequently no argument against a close relationship between 614 and 2412.

proof in a tradition as radically contaminated as the New Testament text.

The fact that this reading also occurs in 1890, a seemingly unrelated manuscript (only 50 percent agreement with 614), is no real argument to the contrary. The data in the Main List for 1890 as a control manuscript show that its highest agreements are with manuscripts 2138, 1505, 1611, 614, and 2495. The apparent contradiction between the data for 614 and 1890 in the Main List results from 1890 having a significantly higher number of Majority text readings than 614 (i.e., 65 as compared with 44). Thus 1890 was essentially derived from the same source as the other manuscripts, but in the course of transmission it was infiltrated by more Byzantine readings than were 614, 2412, etc. The same also occurred at test passage 37 with manuscripts 1611 and 2200. As these Byzantine readings could have infiltrated at any time quite independently of the exemplar being copied, differences among otherwise related manuscripts in readings of class 1 cannot be considered very significant. This applies conversely to test passages 2, 4, 6, 10, and so forth in 614. These do not appear in the Main List for 614 because in these instances 614 reads 1. Those interested will find the readings of the related manuscripts for these test passages in the manuscript profiles in volume 1. In any event, these passages show 614 as subject to the pervasive Byzantine influence.

A second general rule is therefore needed: manuscripts may be considered as possibly related to each other and deserving further study on the basis of full collations if agreements are found among a *small* group of manuscripts in a fair number of test passages, and preferably with agreements in obvious errors. This makes possible a gradual progress toward the third aim mentioned above, the discovery of families and groups of manuscripts, that is, the members of the same redactions and recensions. In other words, it will be possible to find some order and structure in the hitherto amorphous mass of the total New Testament manuscript tradition. This will be no small achievement.

We conclude with two observations. First, these volumes on the Catholic letters are a working tool. They can prove their worth only as they are used by textual critics: the more use made of them the better, especially from independent critical perspectives. They can help contribute to resolving many questions beyond the ones we have discussed briefly here; for example, it has been invaluable in tracing the Greek sources and the influences of the Syriac Harclensis.

Second, this tool is also able to provide significant information about the Byzantine text, which should not be totally eliminated from editorial consideration, but only to the extent that its manuscripts are merely reproductions of an identical text. To a large extent its subgroups can be distinguished. At Münster, there is a complete computer-generated printout in which each manuscript is compared with every other manuscript in full detail. Considering the high degree of uniformity which characterizes the Byzantine text (with frequently 100 percent agreement among manuscripts!), the limitation of citing only the 66 most closely related manuscripts as in the present volumes would be inadequate. The com-

prehensive twenty-four volume set is naturally available for use by anyone. This tool awaits discovery by textual critics.

2. *CATEGORIES AND TEXT TYPES*
(cf. pp. 106f., 159)

The new concept of categories introduced in this book has need of some further explantion with regard to the distinctions it draws and its relationship to recognized text types, groups, and families. Text types and their subgroups are the traditional means of New Testament textual criticism for describing the history of the New Testament text. Tracing the history from its latest expressions to its earliest beginnings sheds light on the earliest forms of the New Testament text. This principle is as relevant to the variant readings of a single passage (cf. p. 281, Rule 8) as it is to the broader history of whole groups or text types. These traditional procedures of textual criticism are in no way supplanted or challenged by the introduction of categories. On the contrary, the use of categories facilitates and confirms the analysis of manuscripts in text types and their subdivisions.

New Testament text types have always suffered from two weaknesses. Their definitions have been inadequate; that is, with two exceptions there has been no clear identification of what readings constitute a text type for all the New Testament writings. Only the Byzantine text and the D-text (formerly called the "Western text") have been defined precisely enough (i.e., with a sufficient number of characteristic readings) to be useful for classifying manuscripts. All the other text types used by textual critics need to be defined more precisely.

The second serious weakness of the traditional text types is that they are based on too few witnesses in proportion to the great mass of known manuscripts today. Only a minimal number of these manuscripts has yet been classified in the traditional text types and their subgroupings. On the one hand, this is inevitable because any scholar working alone becomes lost in the forest of hundreds if not thousands of unexamined manuscripts of the New Testament writings, finding it impossible to establish a vantage from which to begin. On the other hand, there has been no method for plotting the characteristics of the text types and subgroups which may be represented in these unexamined manuscripts. Possible intermediate stages in the development of the recognized text types remain unknown, and what is more serious, new text types, groups, and families which could clarify the history of the New Testament text remain undiscovered.

In short, an efficient, reliable, and verifiable preliminary sorting process for *all* manuscripts of the New Testament is needed. Such a process should be able to achieve three goals: the elimination of Byzantine clones, the isolation of manuscripts which merit close examination with full collations, and finally a preliminary assignment of manuscripts to text types, groups, and families, whether already known or newly defined.

This preliminary sorting of the whole manuscript tradition has been undertaken at the Institute for New Testament Textual Research. It has been

described in detail above. The *categories* represent essentially a résumé of the results of this process. They are based on collations of the test passages (cf. pp. 318ff.), each one contributing to the totals which determine the assigments in the categories I-V. Consideration is also given to some further aspects which should be mentioned.

First, let us review the series of somewhat simplified symbols in recording the results of the test passage collations mentioned above (cf. p. 321). These simplified terms are significant as part of the system of categories used for the evaluation of manuscripts in the manuscripts lists above (cf. pp. 107-128 and 129-138).

1 The Majority text (includes the Byzantine text).

2 The ancient text, presumably the original text. As a working hypothesis this is the text of Nestle-Aland[26].

S Special readings, i.e., readings 3, 4, 5, etc., the variant readings which do not fall under 1 or 2.

1/2 (1/) Readings in which the ancient text and the Majority text are in agreement (sometimes abbreviated as 1/).

Readings designated by 1 are determined objectively. These are the readings in each of the test passages which are attested by the great mass of manuscripts, the Byzantine text. Readings designated by 2 are determined by careful critical consideration. They correspond to the text of Nestle-Aland[26] (*GNT*[3]). This provides a clear, easily understood foundation. In the text passages the original text can generally be inferred with the greatest probability. When a reader's judgment differs in particular passages, the effect of these instances on the total figures in each of the classes should be taken into consideration.[8]

The important statistics for a manuscript are its total number of readings in each of the respective classes of readings: 1, 1/2, 2, and S. These totals are the basis for assigning its category. Some specific examples of the evaluation of manuscripts in the *Synoptic Gospels* will illustrate this.[9] Percentages have been added beside the numbers given here in order to allow for comparisons with manuscripts which are mutilated.

The difference between the totals in 1-readings and 2-readings is striking,[10] permitting an initial assessment of the manuscripts. ℵ and B both belong to category I ("manuscripts of a very special quality"), yet the various statistical relationships reflected within the same category permit some refinement of

8. In general this should be unnecessary, in spite of occasional differences in judgment about the original readings, because the high number of test passages makes it unlikely that a few differences with regard to class 2 readings will be of any great significance. Readings removed from class 2 reappear as S-readings, and a high number of S-readings will always assure a manuscript of close attention.

9. It would be more significant to cite the data for each of the three Synoptic Gospels individually, as they have been recorded in our files at the Institute in Münster. But the total figures for the three Gospels are given here for consistentcy with the descriptive manuscript lists in this book.

10. These figures are simply totals without any evaluation of the individual instances, but it makes no critical difference at this preliminary sorting level because they are based on significant selected test passages.

Table 14. Manuscript statistics: readings by category

Manuscript	1	1/2	2	S	Total Test Passages
ℵ (01)	23 = 6%	80 = 22%	170 = 46%	95 = 26%	368 [11]
A (02)	151 = 56%	84 = 31%	18 = 7%	15 = 6%	268
B (03)	9 = 3%	54 = 16%	196 = 59%	72 = 22%	331
D (05)	65 = 20%	48 = 15%	77 = 24%	134 = 41%	324
L (019)	52 = 16%	75 = 24%	125 = 40%	64 = 20%	316
S (028)	206 = 63%	105 = 32%	4 = 1%	12 = 4%	327
W (032)	118 = 36%	70 = 21%	54 = 16%	88 = 27%	330
θ (038)	89 = 28%	59 = 19%	75 = 24%	95 = 30%	318

characterization for each. Both witnesses are well known. The cast of their "Alexandrian" character is apparent in the evidence of the test passages: a minimal presence of 1-readings, a high percentage of 2-readings (both manuscripts serve as a kind of standard for comparing other manuscripts; cf. L), and finally, an astonishing amount of S-readings (which demonstrates the individual character of the early manuscripts, in contrast to the homogeneity of later manuscripts).[12]

A (02) has hitherto been assigned in the Gospels to the catchall category III because of its early date (fifth century) and its share of interesting S-readings. But the statistics show the presence of strong influence from the Byzantine text (56 percent 1-readings and only 7 percent 2-readings), and that the manuscript is very close to the Byzantine witnesses (category V). L (019) is a characteristic representative of category II. Manuscript S (028) is obviously to be assigned to category V (with only 1 percent 2-readings and 4 percent S-readings, this is a consistently Byzantine text).

From the foregoing it follows that the system of categories functions as a coding device for manuscripts based on their performance in the test passages. By taking into consideration the incidence of each manuscript in each class of readings it is possible to distinguish certain relationships among them.

Before proceeding to define the categories there are some additional aspects we should notice. To take the example of D (05) shown above, no one who has any familiarity with the manuscript will be surprised by the high incidence of special readings (134 = 41%). Since the D-text (the "Western text") is recognized as having highly characteristic readings which place it in stark con-

11. For ℵ these statistics include its correctors (duly distinguished). Therefore the total number of readings is increased.

12. The 1/2-readings are ambivalent in this context. These are passages where the original text and the Byzantine text are identical, and a spectrum of variants has developed independently of the ancient form and failed of adoption by the Byzantines. These readings are important as special readings because their deviations from the 1/2-readings, usually with relatively little support, affords a clue to manuscript relationships. A manuscript without a special reading in such a passage is classified as a 1/2-reading; it may equally represent the ancient or the Byzantine tradition. Thus nothing significant can be inferred from the number of 1/2-readings in a manuscript. In B, for example, the 1/2-readings are derived from the ancient text, while in S, a purely Byzantine manuscript, they represent the Byzantine tradition. The same holds for the rest of the manuscripts. The maximum number of 1/2-readings found in a manuscript is 107 — which provides a point of reference.

trast to all other textual traditions (represented in the high number of S-readings), a separate category has been designated for its text type (category IV). In this instance the basis is not simply the statistics derived from the test passages, but these statistics still have a relevance for evaluating the manuscripts of this category. For D (05) the relatively high proportion of 2-readings (77 = 24%) indicates that the D-tradition resulted from the revision of a good early manuscript, retaining a substantial element of the early text. Category V also largely represents a particular text type, the Byzantine type.

It is different with categories I through III, which cannot be directly identified with a particular text type (cf. the definitions below). These have to do with some rather neutral results of the preliminary sorting which aid in achieving a better historical perspective on the text, but without anticipating it in detail. Yet a certain qualification may be detected in the fact that these categories represent a decreasing proportion of 2-readings. Specifically:

Category I

> Manuscripts of a very special quality, i.e., manuscripts with a very high proportion of the early text (2-readings), presumably the original text, which has not been preserved in its purity in any one manuscript. To this category have also been assigned all manuscripts to the beginning of the fourth century, regardless of further distinctions which should also be observed, in order to include the witnesses of the period before the tradition was channeled into types (the text of the early times), such as $\mathfrak{p}^{75}$ and $\mathfrak{p}^{45}$.[13]

Category II

> Manuscripts of a special quality, i.e., manuscripts with a considerable proportion of the early text (2-readings), but which are marked by alien influences. These influences are usually of smoother, improved readings, and in later periods of infiltration by the Byzantine text.

> Here we would place the Egyptian text, a form of text which developed from the Alexandrian tradition, clearly preserving its original core, but with an admixture of Byzantine influence. Here as elsewhere the basic rule of New Testament textual transmission is apparent, that the Byzantine text exerted a constantly increasing influence on all the other text types. An example is L (019) of the eighth century (cf. p. 113), and also Θ (038) of the ninth century (cf. p. 118) where other alien influences besides Koine infiltration have modified an early tradition.

Category III

> Manuscripts with a small but not a negligible proportion of early readings, with a considerable encroachment of polished readings (a relatively strong Byzantine influence), and significant readings from other sources as yet unidentified.

---

13. Actually most of the manuscripts of this category belong to the "Alexandrian" text type, but this also requires further definition.

The deliberately open definition of this category indicates that it is intended as a catchall for manuscripts which should be examined more closely. It includes manuscripts of a unique character with independent texts, such as W (032) of the fifth century (cf. p. 113). Members of this category naturally reveal in part a strong, but not overpowering, influence from the Byzantine text. They deserve further investigation.

In a certain sense the categories I–III are all catchalls calling for closer attention. Categories II and III cover manuscripts which have hitherto been assigned to hypothetical text types (Caesarean) or belong to groups not yet identified. This has the advantage of placing these manuscripts in specific categories, and by defining the limits, prescribing the tasks to be engaged.

Category IV
Manuscripts of the "Western text," or the D-text.

Category V
Manuscripts with a purely or predeominantly Byzantine text.

The apparently subjective element in the criteria for assigning manuscripts to these categories ("with a considerable proportion of early readings," etc.) is offset by the statistical data from the test passages on which they are based: compare the differences between ℵ and B (both category I), L and Θ (both of category II), and so forth. In the descriptive manuscript lists (pp. 107-128, 129-138) these statistics are given for each manuscript. The category assignments for the papyri (pp. 96-102), however, are based on full collations, since their fragmentary nature precludes the possibility of any system of test passages.

By using the categories, together with the statistical data they are based on, the user of a critical apparatus can now get (for the first time) a quick summary of the textual character of any manuscript, based on precisely defined data and calibrated numerically.

With these categories the student is now finally in a position to gain some idea of the textual character of minuscules which (with such probable exceptions as 33 and 1739) have always been merely numbers. These minuscules will accordingly be able to assume a more significant role in textual decisions based on their (probable) reliability. They need no longer be simply counted.

New Testament scholars will be able to use them with greater discrimination in conjunction with all the considerations of internal criticism. Those interested particularly in textual criticism will concern themselves with the manuscripts of categories II and III, because in these will be found any of the potential text types beyond the Alexandrian (included in category I), the "Western" (category IV), and the Byzantine (category V). The manuscripts of these two categories, which comprise some 10 percent of the total number, simply must be investigated for their relationships, their value, and their origins — these more than any others. The analytical method proposed here promises better assistance for the specialist.

It should not be forgotten that the categories only summarize the results

of preliminary sorting procedures based on test passages. The advantage of this system of analysis is that it can be applied to *all* manuscripts;[14] it is verifiable, discriminating, and supports as full an analysis of manuscripts as the state of textual research will permit, with no prejudice to the direction that further more sophisticated analysis may take. With these categories there is ample room for specific exploration of matters yet to be explored without being overwhelmed by the sheer mass of materials, and yet making full use of the unique abundance of the New Testament manuscript tradition.

The categories are essentially useful for manuscripts from the fifth century and later. The earlier tradition requires special research. But with their help the strands of tradition which derive from the early period may be traced in their later stages of transmission. It would be decidedly harmful if the limitations of the categories were not observed. They are *not* a final system of evaluation intended to supplant all the traditional rules of textual criticism. But they do provide a hint of the average reliability of manuscripts, and lay the groundwork for canons of external criteria in textual criticism.

---

14. The text types recognized hitherto are by no means adapted to all manuscripts. Using them for reviewing and analyzing manuscripts yields meaningless descriptions (e.g., "mixed text") in so many instances, not to mention the vagueness of hypothetical text types (e.g., the Caesarean text).

INDEX OF
BIBLICAL CITATIONS

Italic figures indicate pages on which plates appear.

OLD TESTAMENT

Genesis
  1-4:2 204
  2:24 308
  5:1 253
  22:18 253
  25:26 253
  29:35 253
  38:29-30 254
  46:28 109

Leviticus
  2:13 307

Deuteronomy
  8:3 308

Ruth
  4:12,18-22 253

2 Kings
  1:10ff. 309

1 Chronicles
  2:10-12,15 253
  3:5 253

Nehemiah
  5-7 212

Psalms
  33,34 100
  50:3 287
  105:27-137:6 109

Proverbs
  21:21 256

Isaiah
  7:14 243

Jeremiah
  38:15 243

Micah
  5:1,3 254

Zechariah
  11:13 290

NEW TESTAMENT

Matthew
  beginning *208*
  1 122
  1:1 252, 253
  1:1-14 127
  1:1-9,12,14-20 96
  1:2-17 253
  1:2 253
  1:3 253, 254
  1:4 253
  1:5 257
  1:6 253, 257
  1:7,8 257
  1:10 241
  1:16 253
  1:17 252

  1:18 252, 253
  1:20 253
  1:21-24,25-2:2 119
  1:23-2:2 120
  1:23 243
  1:24 243, 257
  1:25 243, 257
  2:1 252
  2:4 243
  2:6 254
  2:12 243
  2:13,19 253
  2:13-16 100
  2:13 243
  2:18 243
  2:22-3:1 100
  2:23 241
  3:9,15 100
  3:10-12 102
  3:10 243
  3:13-15 102
  4:1 254
  4:2 257
  4:4 243, 308
  4:13 241
  4:18 294
  5-26 127
  5 122
  5:1-11 124
  5:3-19 127
  5:6 243
  5:13-16,22-25 101
  5:19 285
  5:20-22,25-28 100

5:20 285
5:25-26,29-30 127
5:44 241, 306
6:5-6,8-10,13-15,17 123
6:9-13 309
6:10-8:3 250
6:13 306, 309
6:15 302
6:19-21 266
7:1 253
7:9 310
7:21 256
8:2 253
8:23-10:31 250
8:25-9:2 126
9:1 253
9:13 301
9:18 282
10:17-23,25-32 104
10:32-11:5 97
11:7-8 287
11:15 302
11:20-21 124
11:25-30 100
11:26-27 100
11:27-28 121
12-15 121
12:4-5 100
12:24-26,32-33 97
12:27-39 127
13-15 121
13:9 302
13:20-21 123
13:32-38,40-46 126
13:43 302
13:46-52 122
13:57 293, 294
14-28 201
14 119
14:6-13 122
14:19-15:8 120
14:22,28-29 127
14:28-31 120
15:11 302
15:12-15,17-19 126
16:1-11 5
16:2b-3 307
16:15-17:11 250
• 17-18 120
17:1-3,6-7 98
17:20 301
17:21 298, 301
18:11 298, 301, 309

18:15-17,19 98
18:18-29 119
18:18 285
18:23-35 266
18:32-34 97
19-21 121
19 120
19:1-3,5-7,9-10 97
19:3-8 120
19:10-11,17-18 100
20:3-32 120
20:16 307
20:22-23,25-27 124
20:22-23 307
20:23-25,30-31 101
20:23 282
20:24-32 98
20:25-21:20 250
21 239, 258
21:11 238
21:13-19 98
21:19-24 120
21:20-46 258
21:23-27 255
21:23 254
21:24-24:15 121
21:24 258
21:25 256, 258
21:26 258
21:28-32 233, 254, 258, 312
21:28 258
21:29-31 312
21:32 258
21:33-35 233
21:33-44 255
21:38 258
21:39 238
21:43 258
21:44 236, 258
21:45 258
21:46 258
22-23 121
22:3-16 120
22:7-46 123
22:14 307
22:30-32,34-37 124
23-27 122
23 121
23:14 298, 301
23:25-end 250
23:30-39 101
23:39-24:1,6 101
24-26 119

24:3-6,12-15 100
24:9-21 120
24:39-42,44-48 125
24:40 303
24:44 307
25-27 122
25 119, 239
25:1-9 126
25:6 109
25:8-10 98
25:9-16,41-26:1 122
25:12-15,20-23 98
25:13 307
25:15 287
25:32-45 122
25:33 239
25:41-26:39 98, 99
25:41-26:18 *94*
25:43 101
26 119, 239
26:2-9 127
26:2-4,7-9 120
26:2-3 101
26:4-7,10-12 120
26:7-8,10,14-15,22-23,31-33 100
26:17-21 127
26:19-52 98
26:24-29 127
26:25-26,34-36 123
26:26 311
26:29-40 99
26:39 310
26:52-27:1 121
26:53 239
26:59-70 119
26:74 308
26:75-27:1,3-4 126
27:2,3-5 *116*
27:7-30 119
27:9-16 127
27:9 290
27:15 303
27:17 253
27:35 307
27:44-56 119
27:56 *58*
28 119
28:5-19 123
28:7-20 250
28:11-15 126

Mark
  beginning *147*

1:1-16:17 250
1-6 122
1-3 122
1 119, 121
1:1-12 250
1:2 290
1:16 293, 294
1:31-2:16 122
1:34-2:12 119
1:37 290
1:40-45 253
1:44-2:21 250
2 119
2:1-26 102
2:1-12 253
2:2-5,8-9 101
2:15-16 287
2:16-24 290
2:17 301
2:23-3:5 120
3:2-3,5 125
3:15-32 122
4-5 121
4:9 302
4:18-41 250
4:23 302
4:24-29,37-41 123
4:36-9:31 98
5 119
5:16-40 122
5:16-31 122
5:26-6:5 250
5:26-27,31 127
5:26 309
5:34-6:2 122
6-16 127
6-10 127
6:4 293, 294
6:9-11,13-14,37-39,
   41,45 123
6:14-20 127
6:30-41 124
6:30-31,33-34,36-37,
   39-41 101
6:47-7:14 122
7:3,6-8,30-8:16 122
7:16 237, 299, 302
8:15-18 226
8:17-18,27-28 122
8:33-37 125
8:34 308
9-10 120
9 119

9:2,7-9 122
9:29 301
9:42-50 266
9:44,46 299
9:44 302
9:46 302
9:48 302
9:49 307
10-11 122
10:7 308
10:21 266, 308
10:23 308
10:24 308
10:35-46 123
10:37-45 123
10:38-39 307
10:40 282
10:50-51 119
11:11-17 124
11:11-12 119
11:17-28 123
11:26 299, 302
11:27-12:28 98
11:27-33 255
12:1-12 256
12:1-11 255
12:12 255
12:32-37 120
12:40 302
13-14 121
13 120
13:21-14:67 121
13:34-14:25 121
14 119
14:29-45 120
14:65-67,68-71;14:72-
   15:2,4-7 127
14:68 308
14:72 308
15:6 303
15:20-21,26-27 119
15:27-16:8 120
15:28 299, 302
15:29-38 119
15:36-37,40-41 124
16:1-8 293
16:2-6 203
16:6-8 121
16:8-14 213
16:8 69, 188, 292
16:9-20 69, 232,
   292, 293, 310
16:9-18 121
16:9-10 120

16:14 113
16:19-20 203
ending 112, 114,
   130, 131, 150,
   158, 188, 202,
   206, 211, 232,
   249, 295, 306

Luke
beginning 112, 206
1-11 118
1-2 122
1:1-2:48 250
1:1-2:40 118
1:16-38 250
1:20-31,64-79 122
1:35 252
1:46-51 98
1:54-55 98
1:58-59 96
1:62-2:1,6-7 96
1:73-2:7 124
2:7 243
2:14 288, 289
2:24-48 122
2:27-30,34 126
2:29-32 98
3-24 101
3:1-4:20 121
3:1-2,5,7-11 123
3:8-4:2,29-32,34-35
   96
3:10-24:52 57
3:16-7:33 250
3:18-4:2 101
3:19-30 119
3:23-4:2 121
3:23-38 252, 253
4 122
4:1-2 96
4:3-29 121
4:4 308
4:24 293, 294
4:30-43 121
4:34-5:10 101
5:3-8 96
5:12-16 253
5:17-26 253
5:28-6:11 250
5:30-6:16 96
5:32 301
5:37-18:18 101
6 122
6:23-35 123

6:24-31 123
6:27-28 306
6:28 241
6:31-7:7 98
6:37-42 253
7:20-21,34-35 127
7:21 256
7:22-26,50 96
7:32-34,37-38 101
7:36-50 256
7:36-45 96
7:39-49 120
8 122
8:8 302
8:13-19 119
8:25-27 127
8:43 309
8:55-9:9 119
9 122
9:9-17 119
9:26-14:33 98
9:35-47 121
9:54-56 301, 309
9:59-10:14 124
10:12-22 121
10:19-22 126
10:21-30 119
10:30-39 119
10:38-42 96
10:40-11:6 119
11:2-4 309
11:11 310
11:24-42 119
11:37-45 121
12:5-14 119
12:15-13:32 119
12:33-34 266
12:54-56 307
14:35 302
15:11 256
16-John 6 119
16-17 127
16:4-12 119
17 122
17:36 299, 303
18 122
18:9-14 266
18:14-25 120
18:15-17 266
19 127
19:10 301
19:18-20,22-24 124
20 119
20:1-8 255

20:9-18 255
20:18 237
20:19-25,30-39 127
20:19 255
20:45-47 302
21:4-18 121
21:30-22:2 119
22-24 122
22 311
22:4-24:53 101
22:17-18 194
22:19b-20 311
22:37 302
22:41,45-48,58-61 100
22:43-44 310
22:44-56,61-64 104
22:44-50 *63*
22:54-65 119
22:60 308
22:66-23:6 *196*
23:1-8 *195*
23:4-24,26 119
23:17 300, 303
23:56b 45
24 28, 37
24:1-16 *16*
24:1 45
24:9 45
24:10-19 120
24:13 45
24:26-33 124
24:27 41
24:28 45
24:31-37 *80*
24:33 45
24:36 45
24:42 310
24:44-51 250
24:44 45
24:50 45
24:52 45
ending *7, 8, 10, 12, 13, 15, 91, 115, 152*

John
  beginning *2, 8, 15, 21, 89, 91, 115, 117, 148, 153*
  1-15 101
  1:1-15:8 57
  1-14 100
  1:1-14:30 57
  1:1-11:45,48-57 101

1:1-6:11 100
1 120
1:1-25 250
1:1-5,9-10,14 252
1:3-4 287
1:4-8,20-24 126
1:23-31,33-40 96
1:25-41 120
1:26,28,48,51 99
1:29-32 121
1:30-33 127
1:30-32 127
1:31-33,35-38 99
1:42-3:5 250
1:47-2:15 250
2:2-11 122
2:9-4:14,34-49 120
2:11-22 104
2:15-16 99
2:17-3:5 127
3 120
3:14-18,31-32,34-35 98
3:14-18 100
3:23-32 119
3:34 101
4 120
4:9,12 101
4:9-10 100
4:23-37 127
4:38-5:6 250
4:44 293, 294
4:52-5:8 120
5:3-4 303
5:3b-4 300, 303
5:5 101
5:7 303
5:22-31 119
5:25-46 250
5:26-29,36-38 102
5:31-42 119
5:35-6:2 127
5:44 125
6 119
6:1-2,41-42 125
6:8-12,17-22 97
6:13-14,22-24 120
6:26-31 123
6:32-33,35-37 127
6:35-14:26,29-30 100
6:50-8:52 109
6:67-71 266
6:71-7:46 121

7:3-12 119
7:10-12 126
7:53-8:11 194, 232, 307
8:13-22 119
8:14-22 98
8:19-14:10 250
8:19-20,23-24 127
8:33-42 119
8:42-9:39 119
8:51-53 125
9:3-4 98
9:5-8 125
10:1-12,20 96
10:1-2,4-7,9-10 96
10:7-25 98
10:8-14 98
10:25-26 127
10:30-11:10,18-36,42-57 98
11-12 119
11:1-8,45-52 96
11:40-52 99
11:48-56 119
11:57-12:7 125
12:2-6,9-11,14-16 125
12:3-13:1,8-9 101
12:12-15 96
12:16-18 98
12:25,29,31,35 99
12:27-36 119
12:46-13:4 119
13:1-2,11-12 96
13:15-17 102
13:16-27 119
14-21 100
14 119
14:8-30 101
14:10-11 250
14:12-15,19-21,24-26 250
14:29-21:25 250
15-16 119
15:2-26 100
15:7-8 101
15:25-16:2,21-32 97
16:2-4,6-7 100
16:3-19:41 118
16:7-19 119
16:10-20:20,22-23 100
16:14-30 96
16:29-19:26 100

16:30-17:9 121
17:3,7-8 101
17:24-26 99
18 85
18:1-2,16-17,22 99
18:29-35 120
18:31-19:40 250
18:31-40 121
18:31-33,37-38 *84,* 99
18:36-19:7 102
19 119
19:24 307
20:1-7 128
20:4-10 121
20:11-17,19-20,22-25 96
20:17-26 120
20:25-21:9 100
20:26-27,30-31 121
20:30-31 297
21 297
21:7,12-13,15,17-20, 23 100
21:23-25 128

Acts
1:1,4-5,7,10-11 99
1:2-28:31 101
1:3 283
2:6-17 121
2:11-22 120
2:22,26-28,45-3:2 121
2:30-37 102
2:45-3:8 120
2:46-3:2 102
3:5-6,10-12 119
3:12-13,15-16 126
3:24-4:13,17-20 123
4:27-17:17 98
4:31-37 96
4:36-5:2,8-10 99
5:2-9 96
5:3-21 104
5:12-21 *105*
5:34-38 122
6:1-6,8-15 96
6:7-15 124
7 254
7:6-10,13-18 98
8:24-29 *207*
8:26-39 209
8:26-32 99

8:37 300, 303
9:33-10:1 99
10:26-31 99
11:29-12:5 126
13:18-29 120
13:39-46 121
15:21-24,26-32 98
15:23-28 *86*
15:33 304
15:34 300, 304
15:40 304
16:30-17:17,27-29,31-34 122
17:17 57
17:28-18:2,17-18,22-25,27 98
17:30-18:2,25,27-28 98
18:8-26 122
18:24-19:2 *149*
18:27-19:6,12-16 98
19:1-4,6-8,13-16,18-19 98
19:2-8,15,17-19 98
19:4-16 *198*
20:9-13,15-16,22-24, 26-38 98
20:11-16,26-28 98
20:36-21:3 98
21:3,4,26-27 98
21:31ff. 304
22:11-14,16-17 98
22:12-14,16-17 98
23:11-17,23-29 99
23:11-17 *62*
23:23ff. 304
24:6b-8 304
24:6b-8a 300
24:22-25:5 120
26:7-18 121
26:7-8,20 97
28:8-17 119
28:16 310
28:24-25 304
28:28 304
28:29 300, 304
28:30-31 123
28:30 304

Romans
1:1-16:23 296
1:1-14:23 296
1-5 291
1:1-2:3 204

1 201
1:1-16 97
1:1-7 96, 110
1:24-27 98
1:27-30,32-2:2 124
1:27-30 110
1:31-2:3 98
2:21-23 125
3:8-9,23-25,27-30
    125
3:20 285
3:21-4:8 98
4:23-5:3,8-13 104
4:23-5:3 *60*
5:1 286, 289, 310
5:16-17,19,21-6:3
    125
5:17-6:14 99
6:4-5,16 98
6:5 283
6:10-13,19-22 102
8:12-22,24-27 97
8:15-15:9 99
8:33-9:3,5-9 97
9:16-17,27 98
12:3-8 97
14-15 296
14 296
14:9-23 125
15:1-16:23 296
15:1-2 125
15:11-16:27 99
15:29-33 *88*
16 296
16:20 295
16:23-27 100
16:24 295, 296, 300,
    301, 304, 310
16:25-27,1-3 88
16:25-27 125, 295,
    296, 301, 310
ending *17*, 69, *111,
    143, 145, 146, 151,
    155, 157, 191*, 295,
    296

1 Corinthians
  beginning *111*
  1:1-16:22 99
  1:1-2,4-6 100
  1:17-22 96
  1:25-27 97
  2:5-6,9,13 124
  2:6-8 97

2:9-12,14 96
3:1-3,5-6 96
3:2-3 124
3:8-10,20 97
4:3-5:5,7-8 96
4:12-17 100
4:19-5:3 100
5:1-3,5-6,9-13 100
5:8 283
6:5-9,11-18 96
7:3-6,10-14 96
7:18-8:4 97
9:5-7,10,12-13 125
11:17-19,22-24 124
11:24 311
12:2-3,6-13 124
13:3 289
13:4-2 Cor. 13:13
    126
14:13-22 110
14:20-29 124
15:10-15,19-25 127
15:49 286
15:52-2 Cor. 1:15
    122
15:53-16:9 120
15:54,55 286
16:4-7,10 98

2 Corinthians
  1:1-13:13 99
  1:1-15 125
  1:17-2:2 125
  1:20-2:12 120
  4:4-13 125
  4:5,12-13 124
  4:5-8,10,13 124
  4:13-12:6 109
  5:1-2,8-9,14-16,19-
      6:1,3-5 125
  5:18-21 98
  6:11-7:2 125
  8:16-24 125
  9:2-10:17 125
  10:13-12:5 122
  10:13-14 98
  11:2,4,6-7 98
  11:9-19 121

Galatians
  1:1-6:18 99
  1:1-13 123
  1:2-10,13,16-20 99
  1:9-12,19-22 127

2:5-6 124
3:16-25 124
4:15-5:14 119
4:19 285
4:25-31 127
5:12-6:4 122
5:13-17 127

Ephesians
  1:1-6:24 99
  1:11-13,19-21 102
  4:2-18 120
  4:16-29 99
  4:21-24 123
  4:31-5:13 99
  5:1-3 123
  6:11-12 126

Philippians
  1:1-4:23 99
  3:5-9,12-16 100
  3:10-17 97
  4:2-8 97

Colossians
  1:1-4:18 99
  1:3-7,9-13 100
  1:29-2:10,13-14 125
  3:15-16,20-21 124
  4:15 100
  4:16 48

1 Thessalonians
  1:1 99
  1:2-3 100
  1:3-2:1,6-13 100
  1:9-2:3 99
  2:4-7,12-17 125
  2:7 284, 285
  3:6-9 124
  4:1-5 124
  4:12-5:18.25-28 97
  4:16-5:5 125
  5:5-9,23-28 99

2 Thessalonians
  1:1-2:2 121
  1:1-2 97
  1:4-5,11-12 102

1 Timothy
  1:4-7 127
  1:10 292
  1:15-16 127

3:15-16 119
3:16-4:3,8-11 126
3:16 283
4:1-3 119
6:2-8 119

Titus
1:1-13 120
1:4-8 126
1:11-15 98
2:3-8 98
2:15-3:7 125
3:1-5,8-11,14-15 100

Philemon
4-7 100
13-15,24-25 101

Hebrews
1:1-13:25 99
1:1-4:3 122
1:1 97
2:14-5:5 97
4:11 283
4:15 254
5:8-6:10 122
6:2-4,6-7 126
6:4ff. 49
6:7-9,15-17 102
9:12-19 97
9:14 73, 109
10:8-22 97
10:10-12,28-30 101
10:29-11:13 97
11:18-19,29 125
11:27 250
11:28-13:25 199, 250
11:28-12:17 97
12:19-21,23-25 125
12:20-13:25 122

James
1:1-5:20 101
1:10-12,15-18 97
1:11 123
1:12-14,19-21 126
1:12 319
1:13-5:20 96
1:25-27 124
2:16-18,22-26 99
2:19-3:9 97
3:2-4 99

5:20 330

1 Peter
1:1-5:14 100
1:1-2,7-8,13,19-20,25
   101
2:6-7,11-12,18,24
   101
2:20-3:1,4-12 101
2:22-3:7 120
2:24-3:4 *164*
3:4-5 101
5:1-5 *164*
5:5-13 125
5:13-14 126

2 Peter
1:1-3:18 100
1:1-2:3 125
1:1-2 *144*
1:5-8,14-16 126
2:1 126
2:21 101
3:2-10 123
3:4,11,16 101
ending *92*

1 John
1:1,6 101
2:1-2,7,13-14,18-19,
   25-26 101
2:7-13 123
3:1-2,8,14,19-20 101
3:23-4:1,3-6 126
4:1,6-7,12,18-19 101
4:11-12,14-17 96
5:3-4,9-10,17 101
5:7-8 249, 311

2 John
1-9 126
1,6-7,13 101

3 John
6,12 101
12-15 126
ending *154*

Jude
beginning *154*
1-25 100
3-5 126
3,7,11-12,16,24 101

4-5,7-8 101
12 283

Revelation
1:4-7 97
2:12-13 98
3:19-4:3 123
5:5-8 97
6:5-8 97
7:16-8:12 118
9:2-15 125
9:10-17:2 57, 99
9:19-10:2,5-9 101
11-22 118
13:16-14:4 *90*
15:8-16:2 98
16:17-20 123
18:16-17 125
19:4-6 125
22:16-21 4
ending *156*

INDEX OF MANUSCRIPTS

Italic figures indicate plates. References to sample pages (e.g., plate 12, pp. 226f., 234, 298ff.), and tables 6, 7, and 9-13 are not included.

Papyri

$\mathfrak{p}^1$ 57, 73, 95, 96, 159, 244
$\mathfrak{p}^2$ 73, 85, 96, 160, 244
$\mathfrak{p}^3$ 85, 96, 160, 244
$\mathfrak{p}^4$ 57, 95, 96, 159, 244
$\mathfrak{p}^5$ 57, 95, 96, 159, 244
$\mathfrak{p}^6$ 96, 159, 244
$\mathfrak{p}^7$ 96
$\mathfrak{p}^8$ 96, 159, 245
$\mathfrak{p}^9$ 57, 95, 96, 159, 246
$\mathfrak{p}^{10}$ 85, 96, 159, 245
$\mathfrak{p}^{11}$ 84, 96, 160, 245
$\mathfrak{p}^{12}$ 57, 85, 95, 97, 102, 159, 246
$\mathfrak{p}^{13}$ 57, 95, 97, 102, 159, 246
$\mathfrak{p}^{14}$ 74, 97, 160, 245
$\mathfrak{p}^{15}$ 57, 87, 97, 159, 245
$\mathfrak{p}^{16}$ 57, 95, 97, 159, 245
$\mathfrak{p}^{17}$ 97, 159, 246
$\mathfrak{p}^{18}$ 57, 95, 97, 102, 159, 247
$\mathfrak{p}^{19}$ 74, 97, 159, 244
$\mathfrak{p}^{20}$ 57, 95, 97, 159, 246
$\mathfrak{p}^{21}$ 97, 159, 244
$\mathfrak{p}^{22}$ 57, 97, 102, 159, 244
$\mathfrak{p}^{23}$ 57, 95, 97, 159, 246, 325
$\mathfrak{p}^{24}$ 97, 159, 247
$\mathfrak{p}^{25}$ 97, 244
$\mathfrak{p}^{26}$ 97, 160, 245
$\mathfrak{p}^{27}$ 57, 95, 97, 159, 245
$\mathfrak{p}^{28}$ 57, 95, 97, 159, 244
$\mathfrak{p}^{29}$ 57, 95, 97, 109, 159, 245
$\mathfrak{p}^{30}$ 57, 85, 97, 159, 245, 246
$\mathfrak{p}^{31}$ 97, 160, 245
$\mathfrak{p}^{32}$ 57, 59, 97, 159, 246
$\mathfrak{p}^{33}$ 97, 99, 160, 245
$\mathfrak{p}^{33+58}$ 97, 160
$\mathfrak{p}^{34}$ 85, 97, 160, 245
$\mathfrak{p}^{35}$ 95, 97, 159, 244
$\mathfrak{p}^{36}$ 97, 160, 244
$\mathfrak{p}^{37}$ 57, 95, 97, 159, 244

$\mathfrak{p}^{38}$ 57, 93, 95, 98, 109, 159, 245
$\mathfrak{p}^{39}$ 57, 95, 98, 159, 244
$\mathfrak{p}^{40}$ 57, 95, 98, 159, 245
$\mathfrak{p}^{41}$ 98, 160, 245
$\mathfrak{p}^{42}$ 85, 98, 160, 244
$\mathfrak{p}^{43}$ 85, 98, 160, 247
$\mathfrak{p}^{44}$ 85, 98, 160, 244
$\mathfrak{p}^{45}$ 48, 51, 57, 59, 68, 69, 84, 85, 87, 93, *94*, 98, 102, 159, 244, 245, 265, 303, 309, 310, 335
$\mathfrak{p}^{46}$ 49-51, 57, 59, 69, 75, 79, 84, 85, 87, *88*, 93, 95, 97, 99, 159, 245, 246, 286, 289
$\mathfrak{p}^{47}$ 50, 57, 59, 84, 87, *90*, 95, 99, 109, 159, 247
$\mathfrak{p}^{48}$ 57, *62*, 74, 93, 95, 99, 109, 159, 245
$\mathfrak{p}^{49}$ 57, 99, 159, 245
$\mathfrak{p}^{50}$ 85, 99, 159, 245
$\mathfrak{p}^{51}$ 99, 159, 245
$\mathfrak{p}^{52}$ 57, 69, 76, *84*, 85, 95, 99, 159, 200, 244
$\mathfrak{p}^{53}$ 57, 85, 99, 159, 244, 245
$\mathfrak{p}^{54}$ 99, 160, 246
$\mathfrak{p}^{55}$ 85, 99, 160, 244
$\mathfrak{p}^{56}$ 99, 160, 245
$\mathfrak{p}^{57}$ 99, 159, 245
$\mathfrak{p}^{58}$ 99
$\mathfrak{p}^{59}$ 85, 99, 160, 244
$\mathfrak{p}^{60}$ 85, 100, 160, 244
$\mathfrak{p}^{61}$ 85, 100, 160, 245, 246
$\mathfrak{p}^{62}$ 85, 100, 159, 244
$\mathfrak{p}^{63}$ 85, 100, 160, 244
$\mathfrak{p}^{64}$ 57, 95, 100, 159, 244
$\mathfrak{p}^{64+67}$ 95, 100, 159
$\mathfrak{p}^{65}$ 57, 95, 100, 159, 245, 284
$\mathfrak{p}^{66}$ 51, 57, 59, 69, 75, 76, 84, 87, *89*, 93, 95, 100, 159, 244, 303, 305
$\mathfrak{p}^{67}$ 100

𝔭⁶⁸ 100, 160, 245

𝔭⁶⁹ 57, 93, 95, 100, 159, 244

𝔭⁷⁰ 57, 95, 100, 159, 244

𝔭⁷¹ 100, 159, 244

𝔭⁷² 50, 57, 84, 85, 87, *92*, 93, 95, 100, 159, 246

𝔭⁷³ 101

𝔭⁷⁴ 84, 85, *86*, 95, 101, 160, 245, 246, 303, 305, 325, 330

𝔭⁷⁵ 14, 37, 38, 42, 44, 51, 57, 64, 65, 69, 75, 76, 85, 87, *91*, 93, 95, 101, 107, 159, 244, 303, 305, 309, 310, 335

𝔭⁷⁶ 101, 160, 244, 276

𝔭⁷⁷ 57, 101, 159, 244

𝔭⁷⁸ 57, 85, 95, 101, 159, 246

𝔭⁷⁹ 101, 160, 246

𝔭⁸⁰ 57, 85, 95, 101, 159, 244

𝔭⁸¹ 101, 159, 246

𝔭⁸² 101, 159, 244

𝔭⁸³ 101, 160

𝔭⁸⁴ 85, 101, 160

𝔭⁸⁵ 101, 159, 247

𝔭⁸⁶ 101, 159, 244

𝔭⁸⁷ 57, 95, 101, 159, 246

𝔭⁸⁸ 102, 159, 244

𝔭⁸⁹ 102

𝔭⁹⁰ 57, 85, 102, 159

𝔭⁹¹ 57, 102, 245

𝔭⁹² 57, 102, 245, 246

𝔭⁹³ 102, 244

𝔭⁹⁴ 102, 245

𝔭⁹⁵ 57, 102, 244

𝔭⁹⁶ 74, 102, 244, 276

Uncials

ℵ 01 11, *13*, 18, 20, 39, 41, 42, 59, 73, 78, 79, 103, 104, 107, 108, 159, 192, 233, 234, 236, 239-241, 244-247, 257, 264, 282-285, 289-293, 296, 301, 303, 305, 306, 308-310, 315, 323, 324, 336

A 02 7, 50, 59, 72, 73, 78, 79, 104, 107, 136, 137, 160, 209, 239, 240, 244-247, 254, 283, 289, 293, 303, 305, 309, 310, 323, 324, 334

B 03 14, *15*, 18, 20, 38, 42, 44, 50, 57, 65, 72, 73, 79, 87, 103, 104, 108, 109, 159, 192, 233, 234, 236, 238, 240, 241, 243-246, 256, 258, 264, 282, 284, 286, 289-292, 296, 301, 303, 305, 306, 308-310, 315, 324, 325, 330, 334, 336

C 04 11, *12*, 39, 59, 72, 73, 78-80, 104, 108, 109, 136, 137, 160, 209, 234-236, 239, 241, 243-247, 258, 264, 283, 284, 289, 293, 296, 303-305, 309, 315, 323, 324

Dᵉᵃ 05 15, *16*, 18, 19, 29, 44, 50-52, 55, 69, 72, 73, 98-100, 103, 104, 108-110, 123, 128, 149, 160, 186, 190, 234, 236, 237, 239, 241, 242, 243-245, 283-286, 289, 290, 293, 296, 303-305, 307, 309, 310, 314, 315, 334, 335

Dᵖ 06 *17*, 73, 104, 108, 110, 113, 128, 160, 245, 246, 296

Dᵃᵇˢ ¹ 110

Dᵃᵇˢ ² 110

Eᵉ 07 103, 110, 128, 160

Eᵃ 08 104, 110, 160, 245, 303, 305

Fᵉ 09 103, 104, 110, 160

Fᵖ 010 59, 110, 160, 245, 246, 283-285, 289, 296

Gᵉ 011 103, 110, 160

Gᵖ 012 59, 110, *111*, 118, 160, 245, 246, 283-285, 289, 296

Hᵉ 013 103, 110, 160

Hᵃ 014 103, 110, 160, 305

Hᵖ 015 104, 110, 160, 245, 246

I 016 104, 110, 160, 245, 246, 284, 286

Kᵉ 017 103, 113, 160, 241, 243, 247, 248, 256, 294, 305, 315

Kᵃᵖ 018 103, 113, 160, 247-249, 256, 293

Lᵉ 019 38, 41, 42, 110, *112*, 113, 160, 192, 233, 234, 236, 239, 241, 243, 244, 264, 290, 293, 305, 309, 310, 315, 334-336

Lᵃᵖ 020 103, 113, 160, 247-249, 289, 305

M 021 38, 103, 113, 135, 160

N 022 103, 104, 113, 160, 247, 248, 315

O 023 103, 104, 113, 160

Pᵉ 024 38, *80*, 104, 113, 160, 247, 248, 315

Pᵃᵖʳ 025 113, 160, 246, 247, 249, 303, 305

Q 026 104, 113, 160, 247, 248, 315

R 027 104, 113, 160, 244

S 028 14, 113, 161, 334

T 029 104, 113, 121, 122, 160, 244, 305

U 030 113, 160

V 031 113, 160

W 032 104, 113, *114*, 160, 234-236, 238, 239, 241-244, 258, 285, 289, 293, 305, 310, 315, 334, 336

X 033 113 161

Υ 034 118, 160
Ζ 035 104, 118, 160, 233, 234, 236,
    244, 258, 293, 305, 315
Γ 036 118, 161, 247, 248, 293, 315
Δ 037 118, 160, 235, 241, 247, 248,
    293, 305, 315
Θ 038 38, 41, 42, 113, *115*, 118,
    148, 160, 234-236, 238, 239, 244,
    282, 293, 301, 305, 315, 334-336
Λ 039 118, 129, 160
Ξ 040 104, 118, 160, 244
Π 041 118, 160, 315
Σ 042 104, 113, *116*, 118, 160
Φ 043 104, 118, 160
Ψ 044 38, 42, 118, 160, 244-246,
    282-284, 289, 293, 303, 305, 308
Ω 045 73, 118, 160
046 73, 103, 104, 118, 161, 247
047 103, 113, *117*, 118, 160
048 104, 118, 160, 245, 246, 289,
    296, 305
049 103, 118, 160, 303
050 41, 118, 160, 244
051 103, 118, 161, 247
052 118, 161, 247
053 118, 160, 244
054 118, 160, 244
055 103, 106, 119
056 103, 104, 119, 161, 303
057 60, *61*, 104, 119, 159, 245
058 104, 119, 159, 244
059 104, 119, 125, 159, 244
060 74, 104, 119, 160, 244
061 104, 119, 160, 246
062 104, 119, 160, 245
063 119, 121, 160, 244
064 104, 119, 120, 160, 244
065 104, 119, 160, 244
066 104, 119, 160, 245
067 104, 119, 160, 244
068 104, 119, 160, 244
069 104, 119, 160, 244
070 103, 104, 119, 121, 122, 124,
    160, 244
071 104, 119, 160, 244
072 104, 120, 160, 244
073 104, 120, 160, 244
074 104, 119, 120, 244, 294
075 103, 120, 161
076 104, 120, 160, 245
077 104, 120, 160, 245
078 104, 120, 160, 244
079 104, 120, 160, 244
080 120
081 104, 120, 160, 245

082 104, 120, 160, 245
083 120, 121, 126, 160, 244
084 104, 120, 244
085 104, 120. 160, 244
086 104, 120, 160, 244
087 104, 120, 160, 244
088 104, 120, 160, 245, 246, 286
089 104, 120, 160, 244
090 104, 119, 120, 244
091 104, 120, 160, 244
092 104
093 104, 120, 160, 245, 246
094 104, 120, 160, 244
095 120, 122, 160, 245
096 121, 160, 245
097 121, 160, 245
098 121, 160, 245
099 121, 160, 244, 293
0100 106, 121, 124, 244
0101 121, 160, 244
0102 121, 122, 160, 244
0103 121, 160, 244
0104 121, 160, 244, 301
0105 121, 161, 244
0106 121, 122, 160, 244
0107 121, 160, 244
0108 121, 160, 244
0109 121, 160, 244
0110 104, 119, 121, 244
0111 121, 160, 246
0112 104, 120, 121, 244, 293
0113 104, 113, 121, 244
0114 121, 160, 244
0115 121, 161, 244
0116 121, 160
0117 104, 119, 121, 244
0118 121, 244
0119 106, 121, 122, 244, 293
0120 121, 160, 245
0121 104
0122 122, 160, 245, 246
0123 106, 121, 122, 245
0124 106, 119, 122, 244, 305
0125 106, 113, 122, 244, 305
0126 122, 160, 244
0127 122, 160, 244
0128 122, 160, 244
0129 106, 122, 125, 164, 166
0130 122, 160, 244
0131 122, 160, 244
0132 122, 160, 244
0133 122, 127, 160, 239
0134 122, 160, 244
0135 122, 161, 244, 293
0136 122, 161, 244

0137 106, 122, 244
0138 106, 121, 122, 234-236, 238,
      244, 315
0139 42, 106, 113, 122, 244
0140 122, 161, 245
0141 103, 122, 161
0142 103, 122, 161, 303
0143 104, 122, 160, 244
0144 122
0145 123, 160, 244
0146 123, 160, 244
0147 104, 123, 160, 244
0148 123, 160, 244
0149 106, 123
0150 103, 123, 160
0151 103, 123, 161
0152 106, 123
0153 106, 123
0154 123
0155 123, 160
0156 123, 160, 246
0157 123
0158 104, 123
0159 104, 123, 160
0160 104, 123, 159, 244
0161 74, 123, 160, 244
0162 57, 76, 95, 104, 123, 159, 244
0163 104, 123, 160, 247
0164 123, 160, 244
0165 123, 160, 245
0166 104, 123, 160, 245, 246
0167 123, 160, 244
0168 123
0169 74, 104, 123, 159, 247
0170 104, 123, 160, 244
0171 57, 62, 63, 76, 95, 104, 109,
      123, 159, 244
0172 104, 124, 160, 245
0173 104, 124, 160, 246
0174 104, 124, 245
0175 104, 124, 160, 245
0176 104, 124, 159, 245
0177 124, 161, 244
0178 106, 119, 124, 244
0179 106, 119, 124, 244
0180 106, 119, 124, 244
0181 104, 124, 159, 244
0182 104, 124, 160, 244
0183 124, 160, 245
0184 104, 124, 160, 244
0185 104, 124, 159, 245
0186 104, 124, 125, 160, 245
0187 104, 123, 124, 160, 244
0188 104, 124, 159, 244

0189 57, 76, 95, 104, 105, 124, 159,
      244, 245
0190 106, 119, 124, 244
0191 106, 119, 124, 244
0192 106, 124
0193 106, 119, 124, 244
0194 106, 119, 124
0195 106, 121, 124
0196 124
0197 124, 161, 244
0198 104, 124, 160, 245
0199 124, 160, 245
0200 124, 160, 244
0201 104, 124, 160, 245
0202 106, 119, 124, 244
0203 106, 122, 125, 164, 166
0204 125, 160, 244
0205 125, 160
0206 104, 125, 159, 246
0207 104, 125, 159, 247
0208 74, 104, 125, 160, 245
0209 125, 160, 245, 246
0210 125, 160, 244
0211 103, 125, 160
0212 56, 57, 58, 59, 76, 95, 104,
      125, 159
0213 104, 125, 160, 244
0214 104, 125, 159, 244
0215 106, 119, 125, 244
0216 104, 125, 160, 244
0217 104, 125, 160, 244
0218 104, 125, 160, 244
0219 104, 125, 159, 245
0220 57, 60, 76, 95, 104, 125, 159,
      244, 245
0221 104, 125, 159, 245
0222 104, 125, 160, 245
0223 104, 125, 160, 245
0224 106, 124, 125, 245
0225 104, 125, 160, 245
0226 104, 125, 160, 245
0227 104, 125, 160, 246
0228 104, 125, 159, 246
0229 125, 160, 247
0230 104, 126, 245
0231 104, 126, 159, 244
0232 104, 126, 160, 246
0233 103, 126, 160, 243
0234 126, 160, 244
0235 106, 120, 126, 244
0236 104, 126, 160, 245
0237 104, 126, 160, 244
0238 126, 160, 244
0239 126, 160, 244

0240 104, 126, 160, 246
0241 104, 126, 160, 246
0242 104, 126, 159, 244
0243 126, 161, 245
0244 104, 126, 160, 245
0245 104, 126, 160, 246
0246 104, 126, 160, 246, 322
0247 104, 126, 160, 246
0248 103, 126, 161
0249 126, 161, 244
0250 103, 106, 126, 160, 276
0251 104, 126, 160, 246
0252 104, 126, 160, 246
0253 104, 126, 160, 244
0254 104, 127, 160, 245
0255 127, 161, 244
0256 127, 160, 244
0257 103, 127, 161
0258 104, 127
0259 127, 160, 246
0260 104, 127, 160, 244
0261 104, 127, 160, 245
0262 127, 160, 246
0263 104, 127, 244
0264 104, 127, 244
0265 104, 127, 160, 244
0266 104, 127, 160, 244
0267 104, 127, 244
0268 127, 244
0269 127, 160, 244
0270 104, 127, 159, 245
0271 127, 160, 244
0272 127, 161, 244
0273 127, 161, 244
0274 104, 127, 160, 244, 276, 301, 305
0275 127, 244
0276 127, 244
0277 127
0278-0296 127
0278 103
0281 103
0285 106
0293 106, 120
0296 104
0297 127
0298 127
0299 74; 106, 128

Minuscules
family 1 38, 42, 68, 106, 129, 130, 159, 234-236, 239, 240, 244, 248, 265, 282, 305, 306, 315
family 13 38, 68, 106, 129, 130, 159, 234-236, 238, 240, 243, 244, 248, 265, 282, 293, 305, 310, 315
family 1424 135
1 41, 42, 129, *130*, 161, 244
2ᵉ *5*
5 129, 162
6 129, 162, 249, 289
7 135
13 129, 130, *131*, 162, 244
20 129
21 42
22 42
27 135
28 129, 161, 234, 247, 248, 265, 305, 315
33 41, 42, 128, 129, *143*, 160, 234-236, 243, 247-249, 289, 301, 305, 315, 317, 323, 336
36 129, *144*, 161, 249
61 129, 162
69 38, 73, 129, 162, 244, 249
71 135
81 129, 161, 247-249, 289, 305, 323
88 129, 161, 283
94 129, 161, 162
103 129, 161
104 129, 161, 247, 249, 284, 289
115 135
118 129, 244
124 42, 129, 244
131 129, 244
157 129, 161
160 135
164 129
174 129, 244
179 135
180 129, 161, 162
181 129, 161, 162
185 135
189 132, 161, 162, 249
205 132, 162
205ᵃᵇˢ 78
206 132, 162, 325
209 129, 132, 162, 244
215 129
218 132, 162
225 282
230 129, 244
254 132, 162
256 132, 161
262 129, 138, 140
263 132, 162
267 135, 138, 141
300 129, 138, 140
304 292

307 132, 161
322 132, *145*, 162, 249
323 132, 145, 161, 247-249
326 132, 161, 249, 284
330 132, 161
346 129, 132, 161, 244
348 42
349 135
365 132, 162, 247, 249
376 129
378 132, 161
398 132, 161
424 132, *146*, 249
424* 132
424ᶜ 132
428 129
429 132, 162
431 133, 161
436 133, 161
441 133, 162
442 133, 162
451 133, 161
453 133, 162, 249
459 133, 161
461 133, *147*, 161
467 133, 162
517 135
522 133, 162
543 129, 133, 161, 244
565 118, 129, 133, *148*, 160, 247,
     248, 265, 305, 315, 317
579 133, 162, 293
597 133, 139, 141, 162
610 133, 161
614 133, 137, *149*, 162, 247-249, 322,
     323, 325, 330, 331
618 323
621 133, 162
623 133, 161, 249
629 133, 162, 249
630 133, 162, 247-249, 289, 325
642 133, 162
659 135
686 129
692 135, 139, 141
700 118, 133, 161, 234, 238, 243,
     247, 248, 305, 315, 317
718 129, 139, 141
720 133, 162
788 129, 133, 161, 244
826 129, 134, 161, 244
827 135
828 129, 134, 161, 244
849 134, 162
886 134, 162

892 42, 134, *150*, 160, 234, 236,
     243, 247, 248, 301, 305, 308, 315
892ᶜ 235
911 134, 161
915 134, 162
917 134, 161
918 134, 162
945 134, 135, 161, 247-249, 289
954 135
983 129, 134, 161, 244
990 135
999 325
1003 325
1006 134, 161, 247
1010 134, 135, 161, 234, 247, 248,
     315
1067 134, 162
1071 129, 134, 161, 242
1082 135
1175 134, *151*, 161, 247-249, 289, 305
1188 135
1194 135
1207 135
1223 135
1230 242
1241 38, 134, *152*, 161, 235, 239,
     247-249, 282, 305, 310, 315
1242* 242
1243 134, 161, 249
1251 134, 162
1292 134, 162, 322, 330
1293 135
1319 134, 161
1342 134, 162
1344 305
1359 134, 161
1365 305
1391 135
1398 134, 162
1402 135
1409 134, 162
1419 123
1424 135, 161, 234, 235, 237, 238,
     247, 248
1448 135, 161
1505 135, 161, 249, 330, 331
1506 135, 162, 247, 249
1523 135, 162
1524 135, 162
1542b 135, 161
1563 135, 162
1573 135, 161
1579 42
1582 41, 42, 129, 135, *153*, 161,
     244, 265

1606 135
1611 135, 161, 247, 331
1642 135, 162
1675 135
1678 135, 162
1689 129, 244
1704 135, 162, 249
1709 129, 244
1718 135, 161
1735 135, 161, 323
1739 135, *154*, 161, 247-249, 289,
   305, 317, 323, 325, 330, 336
1751 135, 162
1836 135, 161
1838 135, 161
1841 135, 161, 247
1842 136, 162
1844 136, 162
1845 136, 161
1846 136, 161, 249
1852 136, 162, 249, 325
1854 136, 161, 247
1874 136, 161
1875 136, 161
1877 136, 162
1881 136, *155*, 162, 247, 249, 289
1884 136, 162, 249
1890 330, 331
1891 136, 161, 249
1908 136, 161
1910 136, 161
1912 136, 161
1942 136, 161
1959 136, 162
1962 136, 161
2005 136, 162
2030 136, 161, 247
2050 136, 161, 247
2053 136, *156*, 162, 247
2062 136, 162, 247
2110 136, 161
2127 136, 161
2138 137, 161, 330, 331
2147 137, 161
2191 135, 139, 141
2193 41, 42, 137, 161
2197 137, 162
2200 137, 162, 331
2298 137, 161, 249
2304 74
2329 137, 161, 247
2344 137, *157*, 161, 247, 323
2351 137, 161, 247
2374 137, 162
2377 137, 162, 247

2400 137, 162
2401 74
2412 137, 161, 322, 323, 330, 331
2427 137, *158*, 162, 308
2464 137, 161, 247, 249, 305
2492 137, 162
2495 137, 162, 247-249, 284, 305,
   330, 331
2516 137, 162
2523 137, 162
2541 137, 161
2542 137, 162
2544 137, 162
2596 137, 161
2646 276
2652 138, 162
2718 138, 162
2744 138, 161
2786 138
2787 138
2788 138
2789 138
2790 138
2791 138
2792 138
2793 138
2794 138
2795 138, 276
2796 138
2797-2801 138
2802 138
2803 138
2804 138
2805 138, 325
2806 138
2807 138
2808 138
2809 138
2810 138
2811 138
2812 74, 138

Lectionaries
ℓ 1 73
ℓ 2 73
ℓ 3 73
ℓ 12 229
ℓ 19 302
ℓ 76-s 229
ℓ 76-m 229
ℓ 135-m 229
ℓ 135-pt 229
ℓ 260 302
ℓ 299 118
ℓ 974 *165*

ℓ 1043   76
ℓ 1547   74
ℓ 1575   122, *164*
ℓ 1602   *203*
ℓ 1604   76, 293
ℓ 1609   74
ℓ 1684   126
ℓ 1997   276
ℓ 2094   127
ℓ 2198   138
ℓ 2209   276
ℓ 2210   170
ℓ 2211   170
ℓ 2212-*ℓ* 2259   170
ℓ 2260   170
ℓ 2261   170
ℓ 2262   170
ℓ 2263   170
ℓ 2264   170
ℓ 2265   170
ℓ 2266   170
ℓ 2267   170
ℓ 2268   170
ℓ 2269   170
ℓ 2270   170
ℓ 2271   170
ℓ 2272   170
ℓ 2273   170
ℓ 2274   170
ℓ 2275   170
ℓ 2276   170
ℓ 2277   170
ℓ 2278   170
ℓ 2279   170
ℓ 2280   170
ℓ 2281   74, 170

Early Versions

Old Latin
a (Vercellensis) 189, 227, 239, 282
aur (Aureus) 187, 227, 239
b (Veronensis) 189, 227
c (Colbertinus) 42, 44, 187, 189, 227,
    234, 235
d (Cantabrigiensis) 189, 227
e (Palatinus) 44, 189, 233-235, 301
f (Brixianus) 187, 227, 315
ff¹ (Corbeiensis I) 187, 233-235, 301
ff² (Corbeiensis II) 189, 227
g¹ (Sangermanensis) 187
gig (Gigas) 187
i (Vindobonensis) 189, 227, 228
k (Bobiensis) 187, *188*, 189, 227, 228,
    292, 293, 301
l (Rehdigeranus) 42, 187, 227

q (Monacensis) 187, 227, 315
r¹ (Usserianus) 227, 282

Vulgate
A 192
F *191*, 192
G 192
M 192
N 192
R 192
S 192
Z 192

Syriac
sy^c 42, 44, 193, 194, *196*, 233, 235
    237, 243, 250, 251, 301, 315
sy^s 193, 194, *195*, 228, 233, 234, 236,
    243, 250, 251, 282, 292, 301, 309,
    314, 315
sy^h *198*

Coptic
Berlin P. 15926   204
Chester Beatty Codex A   201, 204
Chester Beatty Codex B   201, 204
Glazier Collection G 67   201
Hamuli H   201
Mississippi Codex   201
P. Michigan 3521   201
P. Palau Rib. 181   204
P. Palau Rib. 182   *202*, 204
P. Palau Rib. 183   204
Papyrus Bodmer III   204
Papyrus Bodmer XIX   201, 204
Pierpont Morgan Libr. M. 569   201
Pierpont Morgan Libr. M. 570   201
Pierpont Morgan Libr. M. 571   201
Pierpont Morgan Libr. M. 572   201

Armenian
Etchmiadzin 229   205, *206*

Georgian
Codex A   *207*

Ethiopic
Codex Aeth. 42   *208*

Gothic
Codex Argenteus   *211*, 212

Old Church Slavonic
Codex Christinopolitanus   214
Codex Marianus glagoliticus   214
Codex Petropolitanus   214
Codex Vaticanus 3   214
Evangelium Dobromiri   *213*

INDEX OF
NAMES AND SUBJECTS

Abgar V, of Edessa 209, 220
Acacius of Caesarea 174
Acts 4, 18, 26, 29, 30, 39, 41, 48-50, 57,
    62, 65, 68, 69, 72, 73, 78, 85, 95,
    107, 109, 128, 187, 194, 197, 199,
    201, 204, 209, 212, 245, 247, 248,
    250, 256, 264, 276, 277, 303-305, 310
Adamantius 174
Adams, A. W. 275
Addai 220
Aedesius 209
Aethiops Petrus 210
Africanus, Sextus Julius 175
Aland, Barbara vi, 33, 34, 197, 199,
    215, 271, 317
Aland, Kurt vi, 20, 21, 30-33, 39, 74,
    93, 96, 100, 101, 106, 128, 167, 186,
    189, 190, 222, 223, 256, 265, 269,
    271, 275-277, 287, 295, 297, 317
Alcuin 192
Alexander of Alexandria 175, 176
Alexander Severus, Caesar 175
Alexandria 50, 53, 59, 65, 66, 70, 71,
    76, 109, 120, 129, 175-178, 180, 182,
    197, 209, 286
Alsop, John R. 273
Altaner, Berthold 173
Ambrose 215, 216, 218
Ambrose, Pseudo- 215
Ambrosiaster 215
Amfilochij, Archimandrite 214
Ammonius of Alexandria 175
Ammonius of Thmuis 175
Amphilochius 175
Amundsen, Leiv 100
Anastasius I, of Antioch 175

Anastasius, Abbot 175
Anasyan, H. S. 205
Andreas of Caesarea 9, 41, 132, 175,
    176, 247
Andreas, Presbyter 41
Andrew of Crete 175
Ansbert 215
Anthony 175, 200
Antioch 41, 51, 53, 54, 64-66, 71, 167,
    175, 176, 178, 179, 181, 183, 304
Antiochus 175
Antiochus Strategius 175
Antoninus Pius 176
Apocrypha 253, 260, 261, 264, 267, 271
    Acts of Thomas 221
    Teaching of Addai 220
Apollos 200
Apologists 54, 68, 176, 180, 272, 273
Apostolic Canons 175
Apostolic Constitution (1979) 190
Apostolic Constitutions 175, 176
Apostolic Fathers 54, 109, 175, 271
Apostolic Preaching 180
Apostolos 4, 41, 50, 72, 78, 79, 163,
    166, 178, 256
Apringius 215
Aquila 254
Arabic 119, 120, 123, 127, 193, 209,
    214, 227
Aramaic 52, 199
Archelaus 176
Archetype 22
Arethas 41, 176
Arians 65
Aristides 176
Arius 176

Arndt, William F. 271, 273
Arnobius 218
Arnobius the Younger 215
Asia Minor 53, 54, 67, 68, 76, 174, 176, 177, 179, 180, 217
Assfalg, Julius 173
Asterisk 102, 233, 250, 252, 256
Asterius 176
Athanasius 65
Athanasius of Alexandria 176, 200, 209
Athanasius, Pseudo- 176
Athenagoras 176
Athens 79, 81, 113, 118, 120, 123, 132, 133, 135-138, 170, 176, 177
Athos 79, 81, 110, 118, 119, 121, 123, 134-138, 170, 209
Augustine 187, 190, 215-219
Augustine, Pseudo- 216, 219
Ausonius 219

Bagster, Samuel 273
Balz, Horst R. 272
Barber, E. A. 273
Bardenhewer, Otto 173
Barnabas 107
Barns, J. W. B. 100
Barsalibi, Dionysius 220
Bartoletti, Vittorio 97, 100
Basel 2-5, 110, 128
Basil 175, 176, 179
Baudrillart, Alfred 179
Bauer, Walter 270-273
Baumstark, Anton 173
Beatus of Liébana 216, 220
Beck, Hans-Georg 173
Bede 216
Bell, Harold Idris 98
Belsheim, Johannes 190, 228
Benešević, Vladmirus 209
Bengel, Johann Albrecht 8, 9, 11
Benoît, A. 277
Bensly, Robert Lubbock 199, 250
Bentley, Richard 9
Bernhardt, Ernst 210, 212
Bernstein, Georg Heinrich 199
Beuron 124, 215, 250
Beyreuther, Erich 272
Beza, Theodore 4, 110, 128
Bible Societies 26
    American Bible Society vii, 31, 32
    British and Foreign Bible Society 19, 25, 32, 118, 197
    German Bible Society 32, 269
    National Bible Society of Scotland 32
    Netherlands Bible Society 32
    United Bible Societies 30, 35, 46, 222, 255, 265, 276
    Württemberg Bible Society 19, 20, 32, 33
Biblia Hebraica 254, 259
Bietenhard, Hans 272
Bilabel, Friedrich 98
Birdsall, J. Neville 209
Black, Matthew 31, 33, 276
Blake, Robert Pierpont 209
Blass, Friedrich 274
Bodmer papyri 44, 57, 84, 86, 87, 89, 91, 92, 100, 101, 201, 204
Bodmer, Martin 57
Boismard, M.-E. 25, 35, 223, 264
Bonsack, B. 269
Bover, José Maria 25, 26, 28, 29, 222, 230, 257, 258, 284, 286, 292, 313
Brackets 37, 38, 42, 44, 45, 232, 236, 237, 243, 257, 258, 292, 301, 308, 309
    Double 232, 236, 237, 292, 310, 311
Brière, Maurice 209
Bromiley, Geoffrey W. 272
Brown, Colin 272
Brown, R. K. 273
Bruder, Karl Hermann 268, 269
Bulgaria 183, 212
Bultmann, Rudolf 297
Burgon, John William 19
Burkitt, F. C. 194

Caelestinus I, Pope 216
Caesarea 49, 66, 67, 172, 174-176, 178, 181
Caesarius 216
Caesarius of Nazianzus 176
Calder, W. M. 274
Callistus, Pope 54
Calvin, John 4
Cambridge 14, 22, 79, 97, 109, 110, 118, 120, 122, 125, 126, 132
Cambridge (Mass.) 96, 119
Candace 209
Canon 49-51, 69, 167
    Definition 54, 68
    Gospel 64, 192, 265
    History 67, 93, 166
    Lists 79
    Muratorian 48, 49, 54, 79
    Pauline 64
Carlini, A. 98
Carpianus 252

Carpocrates 176
Carthage 52, 216-220
Casey, Robert P. 99
Cassian 216
Cassiodorus 177, 216
Casson, Lionel 95, 100
Catechetical School of Alexandria 59,
    178, 181, 182, 200, 221
Catena 144, 175, 182
Catholic letters 4, 24, 26, 30, 41, 49, 50,
    64, 68, 72, 78, 85, 93, 95, 107, 128,
    167, 181, 190, 194, 197, 199, 201,
    209, 212, 246, 247, 249, 250, 256,
    277, 291
Cayré, Fulbert 174
Center for Patristic Analysis and
    Documentation 277
Chalcedon 183, 199
Charlemagne 192
Chemical reagents 11, 40, 109
Chester Beatty papyri 57, 84, 87, 88, 90,
    93, 94, 99, 100
Chicago 31, 119, 123, 135, 137, 168,
    169, 274
Chinese 77
Christian of Stablo 216
Chromatius 216
Chrysostom, John 41, 168, 176, 177,
    179-181, 214, 216
Chrysostom, Pseudo- 176, 177
Church 19, 25, 35
    Byzantine 56, 69, 168
    Carthaginian 52
    Catholic 6, 30, 35
    Centers 65, 71, 173, 295
    Coptic 200
    Corinthian 48, 52, 177
    Early 49, 54, 59, 66, 68, 181, 292,
        293, 301, 306
    Eastern 49, 50, 67, 68, 194, 215, 220
    Egyptian 56, 59, 65, 70, 167, 173,
        200, 221
    History 49, 52, 54, 65-67, 166, 178,
        179, 183, 192
    Laodicean 48
    Latin 53, 68, 190, 215, 216
    Orthodox 167, 177, 212
    Roman 48, 52, 54, 68, 177, 180
    Syriac 18, 50, 194, 220
    Western 49, 52, 67, 69, 215
Church Fathers 18, 20, 34, 36-38, 171-
    174, 194, 214, 215, 220, 227, 228,
    240, 243, 251, 252, 264, 265, 267,
    273, 277, 280, 284, 287, 292, 307

Church Year 163, 168
Churches, Younger 31, 43, 230
Cicero 215
Claudius of Turin 216
1 Clement 48, 52, 54, 109
2 Clement 109
Clement of Alexandria 177, 184, 200,
    243, 265, 284, 286, 301
Clement of Rome 177
Clement VII, Pope 190
Clement VIII, Pope 235
Clement, Pseudo- 177
Clothar 215
Codex 76, 102
Coenen, Lothar 272
Colinaeus 6
Cologny 57, 100, 101, 126
Colossians 29, 30, 49, 85, 245
Colwell, Ernest Cadman 24, 275
Comfort, Philip W. 273
Comma Johanneum 249, 311
Commodus 176
Computer 24, 142, 270, 271, 331
Computer Center, Münster 270
Computer-Konkordanz 271
Conjecture 228, 243, 280
"Constant witnesses" 36, 138,
    243-249, 256
Constantine 212
Constantine, Emperor 64-66, 70, 166,
    178, 218
Context lines 268, 269, 271
Coptic 9, 52, 56, 68, 96, 98, 119, 185,
    186, 200, 201, 204, 209, 228, 232,
    233, 235, 237, 240, 251, 293, 296,
    301
    Akhmimic 200, 201, 251
    Bohairic 41, 200, 201, 204, 234-236,
        238, 251
    Fayyumic 127, 200, 201, 251
    Middle Egyptian 200, 201, 234, 235,
        251
    Proto-Bohairic 200, 204, 251
    Sahidic 38, 113, 200, 201, 203, 204,
        221, 234, 235, 238, 251, 265, 282,
        286, 292
    Subakhmimic 200, 201
1 Corinthians 29, 30, 49, 79, 85, 111,
    191, 245, 284, 311
2 Corinthians 29, 30, 85, 245
Cornelius 54, 218
Corrector 235, 241, 251, 285, 286
Cosmas Indicopleustes 177
Crete 53, 175

Criteria 50, 280, 291, 318, 336
Critical apparatus 9, 18, 20, 74, 84, 171, 186, 210, 214, 223, 288, 336
  Bengel 9
  Boismard-Lamouille 264
  GNT[3] 44, 45, 163, 173, 174
  Greeven 223
  Huck-Greeven 261-263
  Huck-Lietzmann 261
  International Project 24
  Merk 222
  Nestle 22, 31
  Nestle-Aland[26] 35-38, 42, 44, 142, 163, 173, 174, 186, 264
  Nestle[1] 19
  Nestle[13] 20
  SFG 267
  SFG[3] 223
  Soden 23, 40-42
  Souter 25
  SQE[13] 223
  Swanson 265
  Tischendorf 37-39
  Wettstein 9
Cross, Frank Leslie 174, 260
Crum, Walter Ewing 98
Cureton, William 193
Cyprian 171, 187, 216, 241
Cyprian, Pseudo- 216
Cyrenaica 53
Cyril and Methodius 182, 212
Cyril Lucar 109
Cyril of Alexandria 171, 177, 180
Cyril of Jerusalem 177

Damasus, Pope 215, 217
Daniel 175, 259
Daniela, K. 209
Danker, Frederick W. 271
Daris, S. 101, 102
Dearing, Vinton A. 24
Debrunner, Albert 274
Decius, Emperor 51, 64
Dekkers, Eligius 174
Demetrius of Alexandria 59, 200
Diatessaron 18, 56, 58, 95, 97, 104, 183, 192-194, 215, 221, 227
Didache 177, 307
Didascalia 177
Didymus of Alexandria 178
Diglots 47, 260, 265
  Greek-Arabic 122, 170
  Greek-Armenian 132
  Greek-Coptic 119-126, 164, 170

Greek-English 25, 30, 32, 223, 267
Greek-Fayyumic 127
Greek-German 20, 30, 267
Greek-Latin 20, 25, 30, 51, 109-111, 118, 126, 133, 189, 190, 267
Greek-Sahidic 113
Diocletian, Emperor 64, 65, 70, 218
Diodore of Tarsus 178
Diognetus 178
Dionysius Exiguus 175
Dionysius of Alexandria 178
Dionysius the Areopagite, Pseudo- 178
Dittography 283, 284
Divisions 232, 252, 254
  chapters (kephalaia) 43, 112, 115, 189, 191, 252
  Eusebian canons 178, 252, 255
  paragraphs 33, 45
  pericopes 40, 45, 252, 254, 261, 266
  verses 6, 231, 259
Dobschütz, Ernst von 74, 275, 278
Douglas, J. D. 273
Druthmarus 216
Dublin 57, 98-100, 118, 127, 129, 193, 197, 245
Dura Europus 58, 59, 104
Dzocenidze, K'. 209

Eclecticism 34, 281
Edessa 53, 68, 192, 193, 197, 209, 220, 221
Edie, William 275
Editio critica maior 24, 318
Editio octava critica maior 11, 19, 46, 257, 277, 313
Editio princeps 3
Editio Regia 6
Editorial Committee 31-35, 44, 276
Egger, Wilhelm 275
Ehrhard, Albert 168, 174
Elliott, J. K. vi, 47
Elzevir 6, 39
English versions
  American Standard Version 230
  Authorized Version 230, 267, 288
  English Revised Version 25, 230
  New English Bible 25, 230
  Old English 214
  Revised Standard Version 223, 267, 288
Ephesians 29, 30, 49, 79, 85, 245
Epiphanius 178, 182
Epp, Eldon J. 95

Erasmus, Desiderius 2-7, 72, 128, 302, 306, 317
Erevan 205
Estienne, Robert 6
Estrangelo 199
Etchmiadzin 205, 206
Eugippius 216
Eulogius 178
Eumenes 76
Eusebian canons 255
Eusebius of Caesarea 49, 66, 172, 174-176, 178, 183, 194, 220, 236, 241, 252, 255, 291, 292
Eusebius of Nicomedia 65, 212
Eustathius 178
Euthalius 113, 178
Eutherius 178
Euthymius of Athos 209
Euthymius Zigabenus 178
Evagrius Ponticus 181
External criteria 237, 286

Facundus 217
Farstad, Arthur L. 25, 223, 297
Fastidius 217
Fatigue 285
Faustinus 217
Faustus of Mileve 217
Faustus of Riez 217
Fee, Gordon D. 95
Fell, John 7
Ferrandus 217
Firmicus Maternus 217
Fischer, Bonifatius 174, 187, 189-191, 250
Fleck, Ferdinand Florian 109
Florence 79, 96-100, 104, 124-126, 132, 133, 192
Francke, August Hermann 9
Frede, Hermann Josef 190, 191, 250
Freer Logion 113, 114
French versions 3
    Jerusalem Bible 230
    Louis Segond Version 230
Friberg, Barbara 273
Friberg, Timothy 273
Friedrich, Gerhard 272
Friedrichsen, G. W.S. 212
Froben, Johann 3, 4
Frumentius 209
Fulgentius of Ruspe 217
Funk, Robert W. 274

Galatians 29, 30, 49, 79, 85, 245

Galicia-Wolhynia 212
Garitte, Gérard 209
Gaudentius 217
Gaul 52-54, 192, 217, 220
Gebhardt, Oscar von 19
Geden, Alfred Shenington 268, 269
Geerard, Mauritius 174
Geerlings, Jacob 245
Geiserich 219
Gelasius 179
Genealogical method 281, 308
Geneva 4, 100, 101, 132
Gennadius I, of Constantinople 179, 183
Gennadius of Marseilles 217, 218
Georgacas 274
German versions 3
    Einheitsübersetzung 267
    Luther 1912 revision 20
    Luther 1956 revision 230, 288, 289
    Luther 1975 revision 289
    Luther 1984 revision 267
    Old High German 193, 214, 227
    Zürich Bible 230
Germanics 210, 212
Gerstinger, Hans 99
Gerth, Bernhard 274
Gibson, Margaret Dunlop 193, 199
Gignac, F. Th. 274
Gildas 217
Gingrich, Felix Wilbur 271, 273
Giobertini tincture 11
Gnosticism 59
Goodspeed, Edgar Johnson 272
Gospels 4, 14, 22, 26-30, 32, 38, 39, 48-52, 64, 66, 67, 69, 73, 79, 109, 128, 163, 166, 169, 180, 190-192, 194, 197, 205, 209, 212, 223, 243-248, 250, 252, 253, 254-256, 260, 263, 265, 267, 268, 274, 290, 295, 301-303, 305, 307, 308
    Manuscripts 14, 40, 67, 78, 80, 116, 117, 128, 193, 201
    Order of 79, 189
    Synoptic 107, 128, 262, 290, 294, 333
Graef, Hilda C. 173
Greek New Testament 3, 25, 29, 30, 35, 43, 48, 68, 163, 210, 222, 230, 260, 262, 264, 268, 269, 275, 288, 292, 297
    Beza 4
    Erasmus 2-4, 72
    Farstad/Hodges 25, 223, 297
    Fell 7
    International Project 24

Tasker 25
UBS GNT 31-33, 36, 38, 43-45, 47,
  163, 173, 174, 187, 223, 224, 226,
  228, 230, 232, 240, 248, 255, 263,
  276, 284
UBS GNT[1] 32, 33
UBS GNT[2] 33, 311
UBS GNT[3] v, 30, 33, 36, 37, 43-45,
  87, 129, 163, 173, 215, 222, 223,
  226-229, 231, 232, 243, 249, 252,
  256, 260, 269, 273, 294, 297, 302,
  303, 307, 309, 314, 333
UBS GNT[3cor] 45-47, 222, 231, 310
UBS GNT[4] 34, 36, 45, 169, 173, 215,
  226-228, 231
Greenlee, J. Harold 118, 275
Greeven, Heinrich 25, 35, 223, 260-264
Gregory of Elvira 217
Gregory of Nazianzus 176, 179
Gregory of Nyssa 176, 179
Gregory Thaumaturgus 179
Gregory the Illuminator 205
Gregory, Caspar René 9, 39, 40, 72-75,
  84, 96, 166, 167, 187, 229, 276
Grenfell, Bernard Pyne 96-98
Gribomont, Jean 191, 250
Griesbach, Johann Jakob 3, 9, 18, 39,
  263
Grosvenor, Mary 273
Grottaferrata 53, 79, 121, 134, 135
Guidelines 30, 35, 222
Guiding Principles 30, 35, 222
Gutenberg, Johann 3
Gwilliam, George Henry 194, 197
Gwynn, J. 197

Hadrian 176
Haenchen, Ernst 51
Halkin, François 174
Halleux, André de 197
Hannick, Christian 269
Haplography 283, 284
Harnack, Adolf 53, 172
Harris, James Rendell 97
Hatch, William Henry Paine 99
Haymo of Auxerre 217
Hebrews 29, 30, 49, 52, 54, 64, 79, 85,
  107, 215, 245, 246, 250, 254, 284
Hegemonius 176, 179
Hegesippus 179
Helmstedt 9
Heracleon 179
Heraclius 180
Hermann Kunst Foundation 276

Hesychius 65, 66
Hesychius of Jerusalem 179
Hesychius Salonitan 179
Hettich, Ernest Leopold 95
Hexapla 181, 191
Hieracas 179
Hilary of Poitiers 217
Hintze, Fritz 201, 204
Hippolytus 52, 54, 68, 179, 184
Hippolytus, Pseudo- 179
Hirsch, Emanuel 314
Hodges, Zane C. 25, 223, 297
Hofmann, Josef 210
Homoioarcton 285, 308
Homoioteleuton 237, 242, 285
Horner, George 201, 228, 232, 251
Hort, Fenton John Anthony 11, 14, 15,
  18-20, 24, 37, 46, 55, 103, 109, 186,
  224, 236, 278, 317
Huck, Albert 260
Hunger, Herbert 101, 174
Hunt, Arthur Surridge 96
Husselman, Elinor M. 201

Idacius Clarus 220
Ignatius 54, 179
Ignatius, Pseudo- 180
Il'inskij, Grigorij Andreevich 214
Iliad 121
Imnaišvili, Ilia V. 209
Ingrams, L. 101
Inspiration 6, 212, 295
Institute for New Testament Textual
  Research vi, vii, 24, 47, 64, 74, 75,
  83, 104, 107, 140, 168, 204, 224,
  249, 270, 291, 312, 332
Internal criteria 237, 258, 264, 278-280,
  286, 289, 295, 302, 303, 307, 308,
  314, 315
Irenaeus 48, 52, 54, 55, 68, 172, 180,
  182, 286
Isidore of Pelusium 180
Isidore of Seville 80, 113
Itacism 242, 286
Itala 186, 190, 235, 250
Izmailova, T. A. 205

Jacob of Nisibis 221
Jagić, Vatroslav 214
James 29, 30, 49, 68, 85, 201, 246
  of Nisibis 221
  Son of Zebedee 282
Jeremiah 290

Jerome 65, 66, 187, 190-192, 217-219, 267, 292
Jerome, Pseudo- 217
Jerusalem 66, 67, 79, 134, 136, 167, 175, 177, 179, 180, 205, 219
Jerusalem colophon 129
Jewish Greek 52
Jewish literature 75, 102, 271
Jewish Palestinian Aramaic 199
Jewish scribes 51
Jewish war 66
Johannes Climacus 126
Johannes Grammaticus 113
John 2, 8, 14, 15, 21, 24, 29, 30, 32, 79, 85, 87, 89, 91, 107, 115, 117, 148, 153, 166, 190, 201, 209, 212, 215, 232, 244, 252, 260, 264, 297, 305, 310
1 John 29, 30, 49, 85, 246, 311
1-2 John 177
2 John 29, 30, 85, 246
2-3 John 49, 68, 194, 250
3 John 29, 30, 85, 154, 246
John of Damascus 175, 180
John, Presbyter 182
John, Son of Zebedee 282
John Paul II, Pope 190
Jones, Henry Stuart 273
Jude 29, 30, 49, 50, 57, 68, 85, 87, 93, 154, 177, 194, 246, 250
Julian of Eclanum 217
Julian, Emperor 218
Jülicher, Hans 189, 190, 228
Julius I, Pope 218
Junack, Klaus 168
Jurgens, W. A. 174
Justin Martyr 54, 55, 64, 167, 172, 180, 183, 295
Justin, Pseudo- 180
Juvencus 218

Kaluzniacki, Aemilianus 214
Karavidopoulos, Johannes 34
Kase, Edward Harris 99
Käsemann, Ernst 285
Kasser, Rudolf 101, 201, 204
Kenyon, Frederic George 99, 109, 275
Key cards 260
Kilpatrick, George Dunbar 25, 32
Kingston, P. 101
Kittel, Gerhard 272
Kliesch, K. 275
König, Elise 22
Kraeling, Carl H. 99

Kraft, Benedikt 40, 277
Kraft, Heinrich 272
Krüger, Friedrich 40
Krüger, Paul 173
Krumbacher, Karl 174
Kühner, Raphael 274
Kurz, Josef 214

Lachmann, Karl 11, 39
Lactantius 218
Lacunae 57, 72, 74, 109, 128, 201, 243, 248, 250, 256, 322
Lagrange, Marie-Joseph 275
Lake, Agnes Kirsopp 99
Lake, Kirsopp 22, 99, 107, 244
Lake, Silva 99, 245
Lamouille, A. 264
Lampe, G. W. H. 273
Laodicea 175
Laodicean letter 48, 49, 110
Latin versions 2-4, 6, 25, 39, 52, 53, 68, 172, 185-187, 189, 190, 193, 204, 210, 228, 242, 250, 251, 283
  Clementine Vulgate 235, 250
  Neo-Vulgate 25, 190, 222, 267
  Old Latin 14, 15, 37, 44, 186, 187, 189-191, 227, 232-236, 238, 250, 282, 314
  Sixtine Vulgate 250
  Sixto-Clementine Vulgate 20, 25, 192, 267
  Stuttgart Vulgate 191, 192, 250
  Vulgate 3, 6, 65, 110, 122, 187, 190-192, 217, 219, 235-238, 250, 259, 265, 267, 296
Laud, William, Archbishop 110
Leather 75, 76, 102
Lectionaries 36, 72-74, 77, 81, 82, 85, 121, 122, 163, 166-170, 212, 229, 240, 242, 292, 310
Legg, S. C. E. 23, 24, 263
Leloir, Louis 193
Lemma 38, 171
Leningrad 79, 81, 96, 100, 110, 113, 118-122, 128, 132, 133, 136, 137
Leo I, Pope 218, 219
Leonidas, martyr 181
Leontius of Byzantium 180
Leontopolis 179
Lewis, Agnes Smith 193, 194, 199
Libanius 175, 176, 183
Liber Graduum 221
Liberatus 218
Liddell, Henry G. 273

Lietzmann, Hans 35, 223, 260, 261,
    264, 274, 278
Lightfoot, Joseph Barber 278
Literal translation 25, 172, 210
Livingstone, Elizabeth A. 174
Lobel, Edgar 99, 100
Local-genealogical method 34, 291,
    294, 316
London 6, 7, 15, 34, 53, 79, 96-102,
    104, 107, 109, 110, 113, 118-120,
    122, 124-127, 129, 132-134, 192,
    194, 197, 199, 201, 210, 245, 250,
    275, 276, 278
Longstaff, T. R. W. 223
Lort'k'ip'anidze, K'. I. 209
Louw, Johannes 273
Lucian of Antioch 64-66, 176
Lucifer of Calaris 218, 238
Luke 7, 8, 10, 12-16, 23, 24, 28-30, 32,
    57, 85, 87, 91, 95, 109, 112, 115,
    152, 165, 166, 180, 189, 190, 201,
    206, 209, 212, 215, 244, 252, 256,
    266, 284, 302, 303, 305, 308-311
    Evangelist 263
Lyon, Robert W. 109
Lyons 48, 180

Macarius Magnes 180
Maccabees 191, 253
Mace, Daniel 9
Macler, Frédéric 205
Macrobius 218
Maestricht, Gerhard von 11
Mai, Angelo, Cardinal 14
Mani 176, 221
Manichaeans 179, 184, 217
Manichaeism 215, 221
Manitius, Maximilianus 174
Manuel Moschopoulos 122
Manuscripts
    Categories 95, 106, 159, 163, 332
    Classification 40, 59, 72, 73
    Distribution by age 57, 78, 81, 82
    Distribution by category 159
    Distribution by content 78, 79, 83, 85
    Distribution by location 79, 81
    Illuminated 77
    Inherently significant 56, 84, 93, 102,
        104
    Lists 74, 96, 107, 129, 192
    Purple parchment 77, 104, 113, 116,
        118, 120, 133, 148
    Symbols 9, 38, 40, 41, 72-74, 187,
        190, 240, 260, 277

Marcion 22, 49, 54, 68, 79, 172, 180,
    186, 295, 296
Marcus Aurelius 180
Marcus Eremita 180
Marius Mercator 218
Marius Victorinus 218
Mark 23, 29, 30, 32, 85, 165, 166, 189,
    190, 201, 209, 212, 244, 263, 290,
    301, 302, 308
    Ending 69, 112-114, 120, 130, 150,
        158, 188, 189, 202, 203, 206, 211,
        213, 232, 249, 292, 293, 295, 296,
        306, 310
    Evangelist 200
Markert, S. 288
Martin, Victor 100, 101
Martini, Carlo Maria 33, 100, 109, 276
Matenadaran 205, 206
Matthew 23, 29, 30, 32, 79, 85, 166,
    190, 208, 209, 212, 215, 216, 241,
    244, 252, 255, 256, 263, 265, 284,
    292, 301, 302, 306-309, 315
Matzkow, W. 190, 228
Maximus (Eclogues) 175
Maximus Confessor 180
Maximus of Turin 218
Maximus, Bishop of Goths 218
Melchites 199
Melitene 53
Melitius 181
Menaeon 120, 122, 127
Menologion 126, 166, 168, 229
Menzies, Allen 275
Merell, J. 96
Merk, Augustin 25, 26, 28, 29, 99, 222,
    223, 257, 258, 284, 286, 292, 313
Mesrop 205
Methodius see Cyril and Methodius
Methodius of Olympus 181
Metzger, Bruce M. 18, 31, 33, 34, 59,
    95, 166, 168, 186, 189, 275, 276, 315
Meyer, Heinrich August Wilhelm 51,
    278
Migne, Jacques-Paul 171
Mill, John 9
Minuscules 9, 13, 24, 36, 38, 41, 42,
    72-74, 77-79, 81, 103, 128-130, 135,
    138, 140, 142, 143, 159, 163,
    234-236, 238, 240, 244, 247, 249,
    263, 265, 276, 286, 296, 303, 305,
    315, 317, 330, 336
Moesia 210, 212
Moffatt, James 53
Molitor, Joseph 205, 209

Monarchians 54
Monica 215
Monophysites 197
Morgenthaler, Robert 270
Moscow 79, 81, 110, 113, 118-120,
   126, 129, 136, 137, 214
Moses bar Kepha 194
Moulton, Harold K. 268, 273
Moulton, James Hope 274
Moulton, William Fiddian 268
Moulton-Geden 268, 269
Münster vi, vii, 24, 31, 32, 74, 83, 126,
   138, 170, 204, 215, 224, 270, 291,
   312, 321, 325, 331, 333
Muratori, Lodovico Antonio 48

Naldini, M. 100
Neirynck, F. 279
Nerses of Lampron 205
Nestle 11, 20, 22, 25, 26, 28, 31, 36, 48,
   103, 173, 223, 228, 231, 248, 252,
   262, 284, 286, 303, 304, 313, 314
   Nestle[1] 19-21
   Nestle[4] 19
   Nestle[5] 19
   Nestle[13] 20
   Nestle[15] 223, 269
   Nestle[16] 269
   Nestle[21] 20, 22, 31, 270
   Nestle[22] 20
   Nestle[23] 22
   Nestle-Aland[25] 20, 26, 28, 29, 32, 33,
      35, 233, 243, 252, 257, 258, 286, 316
   Nestle-Aland[26] v, 30, 33, 35-38,
      42-47, 87, 109, 110, 129, 138, 142,
      163, 169, 173, 174, 186, 187, 190,
      215, 222-224, 226, 228, 229, 231,
      232, 236, 239, 240, 242, 243, 246,
      248, 249, 252, 256-258, 260, 262,
      264, 266, 267, 271, 273, 282-284,
      286, 287, 290, 292, 294, 297, 302,
      305, 307, 309, 311-313, 333
Nestle, Eberhard 19, 21, 275
Nestle, Erwin 20-22, 26, 31, 248, 286
Nestorians 197
Nestorius 181
Netherlands 6, 9, 32
New York 32, 34, 97, 98, 100, 104, 113,
   120, 173, 189, 201, 269, 271, 273,
   275, 276, 317
Nicetas of Remesiana 218
Nicholas I, Czar 11
Nida, Eugene A. vii, 31, 33, 44, 273
Nile 53, 75, 180

Nilus of Ancyra 181
Nolli, G. 25, 223
Nomina sacra 76, 102, 283
Nonnus 181
Norsi, M. 97
Novatian 54, 68, 218
Numidia 53, 215, 219

O'Callaghan Martinez, José 25
Obeli 198, 199
Oecumenius 181
Oecumenius, Pseudo- 181
Old Testament 49, 55, 64, 107, 109,
   168, 175, 182, 191, 200, 224, 253,
   254, 259
   Greek 3
   Hebrew 3, 51, 69, 93, 291
   Quotations 47, 52, 231, 259, 264,
      281, 290
Opitz, Hans Georg 35, 260
Optatus of Mileve 218
Orchard, John Bernard 25, 35, 223, 263
Order of books 49, 79, 189, 212
Origen 22, 65, 66, 172, 174, 175, 178,
   179, 181, 191, 200, 254
Orosius 218
Orsisius 181
Orthography 33, 231
Ortiz de Urbina, Ignacio 174, 193
Ortiz Valdivieso, Pedro 193
Ostracon 123
Overbeck, J. Joseph 197
Oxford 7, 23, 32, 66, 79, 95, 97,
   99-102, 107, 110, 118, 119, 122, 126,
   129, 132, 133, 136, 169, 174, 186,
   189, 191, 197, 199, 212, 250, 273,
   275, 318

Pachomius 181, 200
Pacian 219
Pagan literature 102, 271
Palaeography 51
Palestinian lectionary 42
Palestinian manuscripts 66
Palimpsest 11, 39, 80, 113, 118-128,
   192, 194, 195
Palladius 181
Pamphilus 66, 178, 181
Paper 77, 128
Papias 182
Papyri vi, vii, 22-24, 36, 56-59, 64, 67,
   69, 73, 74, 76, 78, 81, 83-85, 87, 93,
   95-103, 106, 129, 159, 162, 163, 167,
   168, 172, 176, 178, 200, 236, 237,

240, 242, 244-246, 265, 274, 277, 281, 305, 336
Papyrus 13, 24, 44, 48, 51, 56, 57, 64, 74-76, 84, 85, 87, 93, 96, 98-102, 162, 201, 204, 277, 312
Parchment 56, 76, 77, 85, 104-106, 113, 116, 118, 120, 128, 148, 182, 189
  Purple parchment 77, 104, 113, 116, 118, 120, 133, 148, 189
Paris 6, 79, 96, 109, 110, 113, 119, 121, 122, 126-129, 132-134, 136, 137, 174, 192, 205, 209, 275, 277
Parsons, Peter 101
Paschal Chronicle 182
Pastoral letters 49, 57, 67
Patmos 79, 113, 123, 134, 137
Patristic editions 20, 21
Patristic fragments 96, 118
Patristic quotations 13, 24, 36, 38, 171, 172, 175, 186, 194, 214, 228, 251, 277, 292, 296, 310
Paul of Samosata 184
Paul VI, Pope 190
Pauline letters 4, 14, 22, 24, 30, 41, 49-51, 64, 67, 68, 72, 73, 78, 79, 87, 107, 128, 167, 179-184, 190, 194, 197, 201, 204, 212, 215, 217-219, 228, 245-247, 249, 250, 254, 256, 278, 284, 285, 289, 296, 297
Pauline letters, Deutero- 79
Paulinus of Nola 218, 219
Peeters, Paul 174
Pehlevi 125
Pelagius 192, 219
Pergamum 76
Perrot, Charles 200
Persecution 51, 64, 65, 70, 78, 177, 181, 216, 218
Persia 205, 214, 220
1-2 Peter 57, 87, 100
1 Peter 29, 30, 49, 85, 177, 246
2 Peter 29, 30, 49, 68, 85, 92, 93, 194, 246, 250
Peter of Alexandria 182
Peter of Laodicea 182
Petilian 219
Philemon 29, 30, 49, 85, 246
Philippians 29, 30, 49, 85, 182, 245
Philo of Carpasia 182
Philology 11, 34, 50, 51, 275, 288
Philoxenus of Mabbug 197
Phoebadius 219
Photius 182
Pierius 182

Pietism 9, 11
Pilate, Acts of 182
Pistelli, E. 96, 98
Pistis Sophia 182
Pitkin, Ronald E. 272
Plato 183
Platt, Thomas Pell 210
Pliny the Elder 76
Polycarp 64, 182
Polycarp, Chorepiscopus 197
Polyglots
  Antwerp 6
  Complutensian 3, 4, 6
  London 6, 7, 250
  Madrid 193
  Paris 6
Pontifical Biblical Institute 33
Porphyry 180, 182, 291
Possidius of Calama 219
Prigent, P. 277
Primasius 219
Princeton 31, 95, 97, 99, 118, 123
Priscillian 219
Proclus 182
Procopius of Gaza 182
Prosper of Aquitaine 125, 216, 219
Psalms 200, 259, 307
Psalms of Solomon 109
Psalter 3, 191
Pseudepigrapha 253, 254
Ptolemy 182
Punctuation 33, 44, 45, 47, 228, 230, 231, 243, 252, 282, 287
Punctuation apparatus 31, 43, 44, 230
Pusey, Philip Edward 194, 197
Puteoli 54

Quasten, Johannes 174
Quecke, Hans 201, 204
Quodvultdeus 216, 219
Quran 93, 291

Rabbula of Edessa 197
Radermacher, Ludwig 274
Rahlfs, Alfred 259
Ravenna 53, 192
Rea, John 101
Readings
  Alternative 18, 37, 172, 226, 241, 248, 304, 311
  Classification 9, 11, 44, 45, 128
  Conflate/mixed 293, 294, 296, 302, 307
  Distinctive 107, 123, 135, 258

Harmonizing 264
Lectio brevior 281, 301, 308
Lectio difficilima 281, 315
Lectio difficilior 281, 284, 307
Marginal 19, 37, 231, 241, 257, 258
Original 9, 15, 45, 51, 281, 283, 290,
291, 296, 304, 320, 321
Singular 95, 107, 119, 124, 232, 263,
323, 325, 330
Varia lectio 190, 228
Recensions 22, 50, 87, 176, 182, 192,
331
Reference apparatus
GNT 224
GNT³ 43, 231
Nestle-Aland²⁶ 43, 224, 231, 243,
252, 254, 256, 259
Rehkopf, Friedrich 274
Renehan, R. 273
Reuchlin, Johann 4
Revelation 4, 9, 26, 29, 30, 40, 48-50,
52, 57, 64, 72, 73, 78, 79, 85, 99,
107, 109, 156, 157, 163, 167, 187,
194, 205, 209, 212, 246-248, 250, 305
Rhodes, Erroll F. 205
Rienecker, Fritz 273
Riesenfeld, Harald 269
Roberts, Colin Henderson 84, 99
Roca-Puig, R. 100-102
Rogers, Cleon 273
Romans 29, 30, 49, 54, 79, 85, 245,
252, 277, 310
Ending 17, 69, 111, 143, 145, 146,
151, 155, 191, 295, 296
Rome 25, 48, 49, 52-54, 68, 79, 81,
109, 113, 118, 122, 129, 133, 134,
136, 175, 177, 179, 180, 183, 184,
191, 205, 215-220, 250
Rösch, Friedrich 96, 201
Rosenbaum, H. U. 269
Rotterdam 2, 3
Rufinus 174, 181, 219
Runes 212
Rupert of Deutz 219

Sahak, Patriarch 205
Salama, Abba 209
Salonika 34
Salonius, A. H. 96
Salvian 219
San Girolamo monastery 190
Sanders, Henry A. 98, 99
Sanz, Peter 96, 98, 99
Saubert, Johann 9

Scanlin, Harold P. vii
Ščepkin, Viačeslav Nicolaević 214
Scheil, Vincent 96
Schenke, Hans Martin 201, 204
Schmid, Josef 107, 247
Schmoller, Alfred 269
Schneider, Gerhard 272
Schofield, Elwood M. 96-99
Scholz, Johannes Martin Augustinus 39
Schüssler, K. 204
Schwartz, J. 101
Schwyzer, Eduard 274
Scott, Robert 273
Scriptio continua 282, 287, 289
Scriptoria 55, 65, 66, 69-71, 172, 241,
286, 287
Scrivener, Frederick Henry Ambrose 38
Scrolls 75, 102, 125
Section headings 47, 224
Sedulius Scotus 219
Selwyn, Edward Gordon 278
Semler, Johann Salomo 9
Sense lines 109, 110, 178
Septimius Severus 177
Septuagint 52, 55, 65, 74, 76, 231, 243,
253, 254, 256, 259, 275, 281, 290
Serapion of Thmuis 182
Severian of Gabala 182
Severin 216
Severus of Antioch 113, 181, 183
Shakespeare, William 287
Shenute of Atripe 221
Shepherd of Hermas 52, 54, 107, 175
Sieben, H. J. 273
Sinai 11, 68, 75, 79, 97, 106, 119-122,
127, 134, 136-138, 167, 169, 170,
175, 181, 193, 194, 199, 209
Sirach 191, 210, 254
Sixtus V, Pope 190
Socrates 183
Soden, Hermann von 11, 20, 22-24,
26-29, 35-37, 40-42, 46, 50, 66, 73,
74, 210, 223, 248, 255, 257, 258,
263, 276, 277, 284, 286, 291, 313,
317
Souter, Alexander 25
Sozomen 183
Sparks, H. F. D. 191, 250
Speculum 219
Spicq, Ceslaus 174, 272
St. Catherine's Monastery 11, 68, 75,
79, 97, 107, 120, 134, 136, 137
Stegmüller, Friedrich 174
Stegmüller, Otto 97, 100

Stemma 34, 281, 291
Strasbourg 96, 101, 133, 178, 277
Streitberg, Wilhelm 210, 212
Stutz, Elfriede 212
Stylus 76
Suchanov, Archimandrite 81
Sulpicius Severus 219
Swanson, Reuben J. 265
Symmachus 254
Synaxarion 166, 229
Synesius of Cyrene 183
Synopses 260, 274
  Ammonius 175
  Boismard 25, 35, 223, 264
  Eusebius 252, 255
  Greeven 25, 35, 223, 263
  Huck-Greeven 261, 264
  Huck-Lietzmann 35, 223, 260, 261,
    264
  Opitz 260
  Orchard 25, 35, 223, 263
  Swanson 265
  Synopsis of the Four Gospels (SFG)
    v, 30, 223, 267
  *Synopsis of the Four Gospels, English
    Edition (SFGE)* 267
  *Synopsis Quattuor Evangeliorum
    (SQE)* v, 30, 260, 265, 266
  *Synopsis Quattuor Evangeliorum13
    (SQE13)* 163, 222, 301
Syriac versions 6, 52, 68, 185, 192-194,
    197, 199, 204, 205, 210, 215, 235,
    240, 250, 251, 293
  Harklensis 193, 197
  Old Syriac 14, 15, 44, 186, 190, 193,
    194, 197, 199, 233, 236, 301, 314
  Palestinian Syriac 193, 199
  Peshitta 42, 193, 194, 197, 199, 220,
    235, 237, 250, 251
  Philoxeniana 193, 197, 199, 250

Tabachovitz, D. 274
Talisman 97, 123
Targum 3
Tasker, R. V. G. 25
Tatian 18, 22, 41, 58, 183, 192, 193,
    215, 227
Tenacity 56, 69, 71, 280, 291-295, 301
Tertullian 52, 172, 186, 216, 220
Test passages 37, 95, 107, 128, 318,
    321-323, 325, 330, 331, 333, 334,
    336, 337
Testuz, Michael 100
Text

א-B 18, 103
Alexandrian 9, 56, 59, 66, 67, 70,
    106, 107, 159, 204, 264, 276, 335
Alexandrian Egyptian 28, 248
Byzantine (Imperial) 4, 9, 18, 28, 36,
    56, 64, 66, 70, 71, 77, 95, 103, 104,
    106, 107, 110, 113, 117-119,
    122-126, 128, 138, 142, 147, 159,
    163, 166, 169, 210, 212, 229, 248,
    249, 258, 266, 301, 306, 307, 310,
    311, 315, 318, 321, 323, 325, 330-336
Caesarean 66, 67, 118, 148, 172, 199,
    276, 336
Committee 34
D 4, 18, 62, 64, 65, 67, 93, 95, 106,
    109, 110, 133, 159, 163, 248, 315,
    332, 334, 336
Early 51, 54, 55, 57, 64, 69, 75, 93,
    95, 106, 109, 128, 132, 159, 166,
    172, 187, 190, 315, 335
Egyptian 22, 41, 56, 71, 101, 106,
    110, 113, 159, 186, 204, 230, 248,
    276, 335
Free 59, 64, 93, 95-101
Hesychian 22, 41, 65
History of 49, 56, 65, 68, 70, 87, 106,
    142, 151, 152, 159, 169, 173, 186,
    214, 247, 260, 262, 265, 332
Jerusalem 22, 23, 41, 66, 67
Koine 4, 22, 23, 38, 41, 51, 64, 65,
    67, 70, 71, 128, 178, 197, 210, 229,
    248
Later Alexandrian 276
Lectionary 166-169, 229
"Living" 14, 69, 169
Local 55, 66, 69
Majority 4, 20, 25, 38, 50, 103, 106,
    128, 142, 147, 163, 205, 223, 229,
    234-236, 240, 243, 248, 282, 284,
    297, 302-304, 306, 307, 310, 311,
    320, 321, 323, 325, 331, 333
Neutral 14
New 20, 24, 25, 30, 31, 34-36,
    222-224, 243, 257, 258, 262,
    269-271, 282, 284-286, 293, 297,
    305, 307, 309, 311, 312, 316
Normal 64, 69, 87, 93, 95-101, 123,
    124
Original 14, 22-25, 31, 34, 36, 45, 51,
    59, 64, 70, 71, 93, 95, 106, 107, 142,
    159, 169, 185, 190, 228, 229, 232,
    237, 287, 291, 292, 294, 295, 301,
    302, 303-310, 312, 315, 318, 321,
    333, 335

Paraphrastic 64, 95, 123, 295
Pre-Caesarean 59, 67
Proto-Caesarean 276
Revealed 6
Strict 60, 64, 69, 93, 95-98, 100, 101, 125
Syrian 18
"Test tube" 281
"Western" 9, 14, 51, 54, 55, 59, 67, 68, 109, 149, 172, 264, 265, 276, 332, 334, 336
Text types 55, 56, 59, 64, 65, 67, 69, 70, 84, 93, 95, 104, 142, 192, 194, 244, 276, 318, 332, 335, 336
Textus Receptus 4, 6, 7, 9, 11, 19, 20, 24, 25, 39, 169, 223, 230, 269, 297, 306
Textus Receptus, new 36
Theodore of Heraclea 183
Theodore of Mopsuestia 183
Theodore the Studite 183
Theodoret 41, 180
Theodoret of Cyrrhus 181, 183
Theodoric the Great 216
Theodosius I 217
Theodotion 254
Theodotus 183
Theodotus of Ancyra 183
Theodulus 183
Theodulus, Ps(eudo)- 183
Theophilus 183
Theophylact 41, 183
Theotecnus 184
1 Thessalonians 29, 30, 49, 85, 245
2 Thessalonians 29, 30, 49, 85, 246
Thiele, Walter 190, 191, 250
Thomas of Harkel 197, 199
Thomas, Acts of 221
Thomas, Gospel of 260, 265
Thompson, E. Maunde 109
Thompson, Herbert 201, 204
Thracia 53
1 Timothy 29, 30, 85, 246
2 Timothy 29, 30, 85, 246, 284
Tiridates 205
Tischendorf, Constantin von 11-14, 18-21, 23, 24, 26, 35-39, 40, 46, 73, 74, 84, 103, 107, 109, 224, 276, 277, 284, 286, 289, 292, 313, 317
Titus 29, 30, 85, 246
Titus, Pseudo- 220
Titus of Bostra 41, 184, 194
Transliteration 199
Tregelles, Samuel Prideaux 19

Treu, K. 101
Trithemius 216
Tura papyri 178
Turner, E. G. 100, 274
Tyconius 220
Typicon 121, 124

Ultraviolet photography 11, 40, 109
Uncials vi, 7, 9, 51, 56, 58, 62, 72-74, 78, 81, 95, 102-104, 106, 107, 109, 121, 122, 128, 138, 142, 162, 163, 233, 235, 236, 240, 241, 244-247, 263, 266, 277, 282, 283, 284, 286, 292, 293, 305, 309, 323

Vaganay, Léon 275
Vajs, Josef 212, 214
Valentinus 179, 182-184
Valerian, Emperor 51, 64, 216
Valerian of Cemenelum 220
Varimadum 220
Vatican 4, 30, 35, 57, 81, 109, 113, 118, 122, 129, 133, 134, 136, 192, 222
Versions 6, 7, 9, 13, 18, 20, 24, 31, 34, 36-39, 69, 185, 186, 193, 210, 214, 280, 286, 287, 292, 293, 296, 297, 302, 305-307, 310
  Arabic 6, 123, 193, 209, 214, 227
  Armenian 185, 193, 204, 205, 221, 227, 292
  English see English versions
  Ethiopic 6, 185, 204, 209, 210, 293
  French see French versions
  Georgian 185, 204, 205, 292
  German see German versions
  Gothic 9, 185, 210, 212, 214
  Italian 3, 227
  Latin see Latin versions
  Modern 297, 305, 306, 308, 309, 311
  Nubian 214
  Old Church Slavonic 185, 212, 214
  Old Dutch 193, 227
  Old Georgian 205, 209
  Persian 6, 193, 214, 227
  Soghdian 214
  Spanish 25, 222
  Syriac see Syriac versions
Victor of Antioch 41, 184
Victor of Capua 192
Victor of Tunnuna 220
Victor of Vita 220
Victorinus of Pettau 220
Vigilius of Thapsus 220
Vigilius, Pseudo- 220

Vogels, Heinrich Joseph 25-29, 257,
    258, 275, 284, 286, 289, 313
Vööbus, Arthur 33, 194

Walton, Brian 6, 250
Weber, Robert 191, 250
Wegener, E. P. 99
Weiss, Bernhard 19, 20, 26, 103
Weiss, Johannes 278
Welles, C. Bradford 99
Wellhausen, Julius 243, 314
Wells, Edward 9
Welte, Michael vi
Wessely, Karl 96, 98
Westcott, Brooke Foss 11, 14, 15,
    18-20, 24, 37, 46, 55, 103, 109, 186,
    224, 236, 278, 317
Westcott-Hort 19, 22, 26, 29, 33, 37, 38,
    103, 190, 230, 236, 257, 258, 284,
    286, 311, 313
Western non-interpolations 15, 33, 37,
    236, 311
Wettstein, Johann Jakob 9-11, 39, 72, 73
Weymouth, Richard Francis 19
White, H. G. Evelyn 98
White, H. J. 66, 191, 250
White, Joseph 199, 250
Wikgren, Allen Paul 31, 33, 34, 276
Wilson, R. McLeish 51
Windisch, Hans 278
Winter, J. G. 98
Wordsworth, John 66, 191, 250
Wulfilas 210, 212
Würthwein, Ernst v

Ximénes de Cisneros, Francisco 3, 317

Zahn, Theodor 278
Zeno of Verona 220
Zerwick, Max 273
Zimmermann, Heinrich 275
Zohrapean, Yovhannes 205
Zuntz, Günther 99